Philosophy
Through the Ages

Joan A. Price

Professor Emeritus
Mesa Community College, Mesa, AZ

Wadsworth
Thomson Learning

Australia • Canada • Denmark • Japan • Mexico • New Zealand • Philippines • Puerto Rico
Singapore • South Africa • Spain • United Kingdom • United States

Philosophy Editor: Peter Adams
Assistant Editor: Kerri Abdinoor
Editorial Assistant: Mindy Newfarmer
Marketing Manager: Dave Garrison
Print Buyer: Stacey Weinberger
Permissions Editor: Joohee Lee

Production Service: Ruth Cottrell Books
Copy Editor: Steven Summerlight
Cover Designer: Cuttriss & Hambleton
Cover Image: © 1999 PhotoDisc
Compositor: Ruth Cottrell Books
Printer/Binder: Webcom Ltd.

Printed in Canada
   4 5 6 03

**Library of Congress
Cataloging-in-Publication Data**

Price, Joan A.
   Philosophy through the ages / Joan A. Price
     p.   cm.
   Includes index.
   ISBN 0-534-56700-2
   1. Philosophy—History, I. Title.
B72.P75 1999
190—dc21   99-16079

**For more information, contact
Wadsworth/Thomson Learning
10 Davis Drive
Belmont, California 94002-3098
USA
www.wadsworth.com**

International Headquarters
Thomson Learning
290 Harbor Drive, 2nd Floor
Stamford, CT 06902-7477
USA

UK/Europe/Middle East
Thomson Learning
Berkshire House
168-173 High Holborn
London, WC1V 7AA,
United Kingdom

Asia
Thomson Learning
60 Albert Street #15-01
Albert Complex
Singapore 189969

Canada
Nelson/Thomson Learning
1120 Birchmount Road
Scarborough, Ontario M1K 5G4
Canada

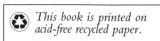
*This book is printed on
acid-free recycled paper.*

Contents

CHAPTER FIFTEEN

CHAPTER SIXTEEN

CHAPTER SEVENTEEN

Existentialism: Sartre, de Beauvoir, Camus   465

Preface

My Story

I shall never forget the experience of my first philosophy course in college. Unskilled in the sophisticated world of philosophical analysis, I was totally overwhelmed trying to read original sources that had little meaning for me. There were complex arguments and concepts that spoke a language foreign to my ears. Had it not been for a friend's encouragement, I may never have taken another philosophy course. In the next course, I caught the philosophy "bug" and it has stayed with me throughout my life. The enduring questions—Who am I? How should I live? What happens when I die? How much can I know? How do I know? Why is there evil? Is there a God? How did the universe come to be?—fascinated me beyond anything else.

I have never forgotten the frustration of that first introduction to philosophy. When I finally became a philosophy professor, I searched for an introductory textbook that would avoid technical jargon as much as possible without being overly simplistic. However, at the end of each semester, my students invariably gave the text we used poor evaluations. Several years and several textbooks later, I decided to write an introductory text that students could comprehend and enjoy. *Philosophy Through the Ages* is that book.

What This Text Is About

Philosophy Through the Ages is a history of philosophy in our Western civilization. The word *philosophy* means the love or pursuit of wisdom. The first philosophers of Greece also pioneered scientific investigation. They asked, What is real? What is the fundamental nature of the universe? Later, Socrates asked, What is the good life? What makes life worth living? To these and similar questions many answers were offered, and this variety of theories led philosophers to ask how they could test the validity of their ideas. Was there a true knowledge that they could distinguish from mere opinion?

Some of the answers given by the great philosophers throughout history can help us understand human nature and the various periods of civilization. Our understanding of Greek culture deepens when we read Plato's *Dialogues*. The decline and fall of Rome gain meaning as we view them from the perspective of St. Augustine's *City of God*. By studying the Renaissance, we get a sense of the emerging modern world, which opens the window to the mind of contemporary thought. Based on the insight and genius of the great philosophical thinkers, civilizations have changed and progressed. How we respond to individual philosophers and their ideas can make a difference in how we lead our own lives.

What's Special About This Text?

In presenting this history of Western philosophy from the early Greek period to today, I have chosen *not* to include my own ideas and evaluations. I have placed short "Pause for Thought" questions throughout the book to capture your important ideas and stimulate your curiosity about issues discussed in the main selections and that pertain to your everyday life. *Philosophy Through the Ages* includes significant original excerpts with clear and readable explanations and commentary. It is my theory that you are curious human beings with a desire to know more than you know now, and that you will enjoy philosophy if you comprehend it. Twentieth-century philosophy often emphasized language analysis. As we move into the twenty-first century, we find more emphasis on the enduring questions mentioned above. The philosophers in this textbook address these important questions.

At the beginning of the major works of each philosopher is a short discussion of their lives and the culture in which they lived. Following the works of each philosopher, you will find a section "On Women." My students often ask why there have been so few women philosophers through history. To answer that question, I have included this short section to detail each philosopher's view of women. These views give some insight into the position of women throughout the history of the Western world. The sections are not intended to be "politically correct" and I have not commented on them. They are for your information and to discuss if you wish.

The end of each chapter has a short summary to help you refresh your memory. Following the summary is a section titled "Connections." This section explains the influence that philosophers in the chapter had on the thinkers who followed them. At the very end of the chapters are several "Study Questions" for your consideration, as well as a list of sources for the items used throughout the chapter.

Enjoy!

Acknowledgments

I want to thank my students, colleagues, and friends. Their support and enthusiasm have played a major role in my writing of this book. Special thanks to Ann Mahoney, Fara Darland, Robert Smith, Pati Nango, Don Geischen, the late Robert Rein'l, Lisa Gopalan, the late Robert Nesby, Barry Brunsman, Judy Christenson, Doroethy Leonard, Karin and Jack Henderson, and my sister, Judy Price. Your loyalty is a gift.

For their helpful suggestions and comments on the manuscript, I would like to thank the reviewers: Ruth C. Beardsley, Pikes Peak Community College; Thomas Carroll, Saddleback Community College; Sidney Chapman, Richland College; Michael Coste, Front Range Community College; Timothy Davis, Essex Community College; W. Laird Durley, Kings River Community College; CA; Greg Holden, Danville Area Community College; Isabel Luengo, Mira Costa College; Edward W. Maine, California State University, Fullerton; Marcia A. McKelligan, De Pauw University; Myron Miller, St. Petersburg Junior College; John Modschiedler, College of DuPage; Jon S. Moran, Southwest Missouri State University; Rich Ownbey, Sacramento City College; Yvette Pearson, Florida International University; Michael Reed, Eastern Michigan University; Jeanne Saint-Amour, Glendale Community College; Pete Self, Arizona Western College; Robert Sessions, Kirkwood Community College; Dan Silber, Florida Southern College; David A. Spieler, University of South Florida; and Robert Trundle, Northern Kentucky University.

My deepest gratitude to Wadsworth's editor, Peter Adams, for staying with the manuscript during the publisher's complex corporate merger, as well as for his insightful ideas and sense of humor. A very special thanks to Steven Summerlight for his brilliant copy editing, and to Ruth Cottrell for handing the production of this text. Finally, thank you to Wadsworth's assistant editors, Mindy Newfarmer and Jake Ward, and permissions editor Joohee Lee for their ongoing help.

CHAPTER ONE

The Pre-Socratics:
Early Greek Philosophers

We begin by studying the earliest rational thinkers in the Western world—the pre-Socratic philosophers (that is, philosophers before Socrates). Through them we will gain insight into the first philosophical questions asked and the first answers given about the nature of the world and those of us who live in it.

It has been approximately 2,500 years since these pioneering philosophers asked such questions as "How did the world come into being?" What is the world made of?" and "How can we explain the process of change?" Even today, scientists and philosophers continue to return to the pre-Socratics for insight into complex philosophical questions—even though those early philosophers lacked today's sophisticated techniques.

The Birth of Philosophy

Western philosophy was born in approximately 600 B.C.E.* in the western Ionian seaport town of Miletus across the Aegean Sea from Athens, Greece. Because Ionia was a meeting place between East and West, Greek philosophy may have Oriental as well as Egyptian and Babylonian influences. In both East and West, philosophers were asking questions about the universe we live in and

---

*Before the common era.

our place in it. Eastern sages probed nature's depths intuitively through the eyes of spiritual sages, while Greek thinkers viewed nature through cognitive and scientific eyes.

Early *Milesian* philosophers were the original scientists of the Western world. Ninety-nine percent of them were males. Because of the suppression of female thinkers (except by the Pythagoreans), few pre-Socratic women left their mark on the history of philosophy.

In approximately 585 B.C.E. the Greek philosophers in Miletus attempted to come to terms with the mythological stories of the gods through scientific reasoning. Until that time, people had found answers to their questions in various religious myths handed down from generation to generation. They thought the gods were responsible for rain or the lack of it, for the success or failure of their crops, and for health and illness in their families.

The Greek philosophers departed from the mythological and poetic accounts of *Homer,* who accepted the gods as superhuman beings who held power over nature and humans. They also questioned *Heisod's* worldview that Heaven and Earth were anthropomorphic figures lying locked in an embrace until their son forced them apart.

The Milesian philosophers are known as *natural* philosophers because their aim was to find natural rather than supernatural explanations for the world and its processes. They asked such questions as "What is the world made of?" and "How can we explain the process of change in nature?" They assumed there was some basic **substance** that was the hidden source of everything in nature. There had to be something from which all things came and to which all things returned. Could such a thing as a baby change from being substance to being a living entity? If so, how can such changes occur? The Milesians wanted to understand the laws of nature.

Their study of change led them to the idea of *permanence.*

Pause for Thought   Consider your own evolution as a human being. You develop from a baby to a child and teenager, then to an adult and eventually old age. As an adult, you are the same person you were as a baby, but there is no direct resemblance. When you look in the mirror, you see no physical likeness to your baby pictures. Also, your emotions have changed, your thinking has changed, your interests have changed, and your needs have changed. Everything about you has changed, yet you are the same person. Is there something that is permanent?

The early Greek philosophers discovered that change is possible only if there is an underlying permanence—a permanent substance. Without this permanence, each change would completely replace another. *Diogenes of Apollonia,* a student of Milesian philosopher Anaximenes, expressed the idea clearly:

> My view is, to sum it all up, that all things are differentiations of the same thing. And this is obvious; for, if the things which are now in this world—earth and water, and air and fire, and the other things which we see existing in this world—if any one of these things, I say, were different from any other, different, that is, by having a substance peculiar to itself; and if it were not the same thing that is often changed and differentiated, then things could not in any way mix with one another, nor could they do one another good or harm. Neither could a plant grow out of the earth, nor any animal nor anything else come into being unless things were composed in such a way as to be the same. But all these things arise from the same thing; they are differentiated and take different forms at different times, and return again to the same thing.[1]

Thus, the speculations of the pre-Socratic philosophers represent a *paradigm shift*—that is, a change from the mythical explanation of the origins of the cosmos to a more rational explanation. These philosophers were looking for the underlying laws of nature. They wanted to understand the processes by studying nature itself, not by listening to stories about the gods. Though the theories developed by the pre-Socratic philosophers may appear unscientific to us in the twenty-first century, they do represent the first intellectual and scientific attempt to understand the origins of the universe.

Only fragments have survived of what these natural philosophers said and wrote. Most of our information comes from the writings of *Aristotle,* who lived two centuries later. He referred only to the conclusions these earlier philosophers reached and not the methods they used to reach them. What we do know is that they were interested in the question of a basic substance and the changes involved in nature.

Monastic Materialism

Thales

A Milesian, *Thales* (circa 585 B.C.E.) is often called the "Father of Western philosophy." He was the first to shift the basis of thought from a mythological to a scientific-philosophical base. According to Aristotle, Thales reasoned that, in spite of differences among the various physical objects we experience (such as earth, lakes, and trees), they all have a basic similarity. There must be one substance that goes into the composition of everything in the universe. And the *many* objects in the world must in some way relate to this *one* substance.

Water   Thales pondered two basic questions: "Out of what substance is the world made?" "Is there something permanent and constant?" His answer to both questions was *water*. This, he said, is the basic substance of all physical reality. All things have moisture. Water also is the permanent substance that holds everything together. As the one substance, water contains its own principle of change. Thales may have meant that all life originated from water and all life returns to water again when it dissolves—as water turns to ice or vapor and then turns back into water again.

Thales left no record that tells how he concluded that water is the underlying substance and the cause of all things. Aristotle wrote that Thales could have seen that moisture nourishes all things, generates heat, and keeps everything alive. Even the seeds of all things have moisture.

Pause for Thought   Could Thales be correct that moisture (water) is the substance that holds all things together? How much moisture does a human body have? Could anything survive without moisture?

The Sun and the Pyramids   A scientist and mathematician as well as a philosopher, Thales was the first Greek to predict the eclipse of the sun; his prediction for such an eclipse came to pass on May 28, 585 B.C.E. He also introduced Egyptian geometry to Greece. Before Thales, the height of the Egyptian pyramids was unknown. Considering Thales' reputation in mathematics, the Egyptian pharoah asked Thales if he could figure a way to measure the height of the pyramids. After a period of contemplation, Thales simply measured a pyramid's shadow at the precise time of day when the length of his own shadow was equal to his height and thus he derived an accurate measurement of the pyramid.

Olive Presses   Aristotle also related a story about Thales that concerned a scheme for making money. Perhaps because Thales was recognized as one of the seven wisest men in Greece, people admonished him for living in poverty: "If you're so smart, why aren't you rich?" Or "If wise men have no money, then philosophy must be useless." Tired of hearing them criticize philosophy, Thales finally accepted their challenge.

Using his knowledge of meteorology, he observed that there would be a heavy crop of olives during the next fall, so he rented all of the olive presses in Miletus and Chios for a small sum of money. When fall came and the olive growers needed presses to make oil for their bumper crop, Thales rented the presses out to them for a huge profit. People grumbled, but he made a fortune, proving that philosophers can become rich if they so desire. However, he reminded them, wealth is not the business that philosophers are really about.

Pause for Thought   Thales also said, "All things are full of gods." As a scientist, he was definitely not talking about Homer's gods. What do you think he meant?

Anaximander

In approximately 565 B.C.E, Thales' student Anaximander, also from Miletus, proposed an alternative solution to the question "Out of what substance is the world made?" Anaximander agreed with Thales that some basic substance is permanent and underlies all change, but he disagreed with the idea that the substance was something as specific as water. Although water is in all things, it is only one among many other elements and therefore limited. All limited elements must have a source. Anaximander concluded that the source of water and all other elements was something indeterminate and boundless.

The Boundless   The *boundless*, said Anaximander, is the *unlimited* source of all elements and the permanent substance that underlies all change. It is indestructible, immortal, and uncreated. Because he described the boundless as the unlimited source of all things, Anaximander could not describe it in terms of sensible qualities such as water, even though he believed it is connected to them. The boundless has eternal motion, and because of this motion, elements come into being by separating from the original substance. First *hot* and *cold* separated and became *moisture*. From moisture came *air* and then *earth*. The boundless, then, produces everything, but it cannot contain any of these qualities, because there is no quality that is common to all objects.

Evolution   Anaximander was the first Western philosopher to propose the idea of *evolution*. He reasoned that humans evolved from fish.

> Living creatures arose from the moist element as it was evaporated by the sun. Man was like another animal, namely, a fish in the beginning.
>   The first animals were produced in the moisture, each enclosed in a prickly bark. As they advanced in age, they came out upon the drier part. When the bark broke off, they survived for a short time.
>   . . . At first human beings arose in the inside of fishes, and after having been reared like sharks, and become capable of protecting themselves, they were finally cast ashore and took to land.[2]

Anaximander argued that human beings after birth require a long suckling period and cannot take care of themselves. Therefore, in the early days, humans, as they are now, could not have survived.

Creation and Destruction   For Anaximander, many worlds exist simultaneously, and all of them go through a continual series of creation and destruction. He said this cyclical process was a rigid necessity based on the conflict of opposite forces in nature. These opposite forces caused an "injustice" or imbalance that necessitated their ultimate destruction. According to Anaximander, "From what source things arise, to that they return of necessity when they are destroyed."

Pause for Thought   Is it possible that humans evolved from fish? Run your tongue over the roof of your mouth. Do you find any resemblance to the mouth of a fish? Isn't there a fish stage in our embryonic development? Are these similarities mere coincidence?

Anaximenes

Another Milesian philosopher, *Anaximenes* (circa 545 B.C.E.), thought the primary substance that holds everything together was *air*.

> Just as our soul, being air, holds us together, so do breath and air encompass the whole world.
>
> And the form of the air is as follows. Where it is most even, it is invisible to our sight; but cold and heat, moisture and motion, make it visible. It is always in motion; for, if it were not, it would not change so much as it does.
>
> When it is dilated so as to be rarer, it becomes fire; while winds, on the other hand, are condensed Air. Cloud is formed from Air by felting; and this, still further condensed, becomes water. Water, condensed still more, turns to earth; and when condensed as much as it can be, to stones.[3]

Like Anaximander's boundless, air is everywhere, but unlike the boundless, air is a specific and tangible material substance. Thales' water, said Anaximenes, is actually condensed air. Air is not merely the gaseous state, but breath, wind, mind, and soul. Bodies originate from air by *condensation* and become air again by *rarefaction*. Air is the force that transforms a body from one state to another. For example, water is condensed air, earth is condensed water, and fire is rarefied air. Air, then, is the origin of earth, water, and fire.

Pause for Thought	Could we compare Anaximenes' notion that air is the primary stuff that holds everything together to the statement in the biblical chapter of Genesis that God formed humankind and breathed into its nostrils the breath of life?

A Mathematical Universe

The key to the Milesian philosophers' thought lay in their belief that a single basic substance is the source of all things. By identifying this single substance as water, the boundless, and air, we call their philosophy *monistic materialism* (one substance).

As materialists, the Milesians disregarded traditional religious beliefs and kept their sights on philosophy and science. Now, however, a philosopher named *Pythagoras* entered the scene. Though he did not follow traditional Greek religious rituals, he did create a spiritual community based on mathematics and mysticism.

Pythagoras

Pythagoras (ca. 570–490 B.C.E.) emphasized the *structure* of the universe rather than its substance. Born on the island of Samos in the Aegean Sea just off the coast of Miletus, he later moved to Crotona in southern Italy. There Pythagoras founded a society that combined mysticism, mathematics, science, religion, and music into a philosophy that added a dimension beyond the rational and materialistic outlook of the Milesians. In so doing, Pythagoras founded a brotherhood dedicated to *philos* (love of) *sophia* (wisdom). As far as we know, he was the first to call himself a *philosopher*—that is, a lover of wisdom.

Rebirth   In addition to their involvement with mathematics and science, Pythagoras and his followers were deeply concerned with the mystical view of immortality. Like the Eastern philosophers, Pythagoras believed in reincarnation. The soul, he said, is immortal and passes through many cycles of birth, death, and rebirth. Each human life depends on the kind of life the soul led in its previous existence. For example, what happens to us in this life is the result of our thoughts and actions in a previous life. Our future life will depend on our attitudes and deeds in this life. The goal for all human beings is to reach liberation from the birth and rebirth cycle by attaining wisdom.

Rules of Purification   To live a spiritual life, said Pythagoras, we must purify the mind and body. Among the rules of purification in his community were the following:

1. Abstain from eating beans.

2. Do not pick up what has fallen.

3. Do not touch a white cock.

4. Do not break bread.

5. Do not step over a crossbar.

6. Do not stir the fire with iron.

7. Do not eat from a whole loaf.

8. Do not pluck a garland.

9. Do not sit on a quart measure.

10. Do not eat the heart.

11. Do not walk on highways.

12. Do not let swallows share one's roof.

13. When the pot is taken off the fire, do not leave the mark of it in the ashes; stir them together.

14. Do not look into a mirror beside a light.

15. When you rise from the bedclothes, roll them together and smooth out the impress of the body.[4]

Pause for Thought   Many of the above rules are metaphors. Can you extract the meaning of the twelfth rule "Do not let swallows share one's roof"? Could "roof" be one's mind?

Three Classes of People   As an astute observer, Pythagoras noticed that people fall into three classes: *lovers of pleasure (or gain)*, *lovers of honor*, and *lovers of knowledge* (wisdom). These three classes, he said, correspond to the three types of people who attend the Olympic games.

1. The "lovers of gain" are those who set up booths and sell souvenirs.

2. The "lovers of honor" are the athletes who compete.

3. The "lovers of knowledge" are those spectators who contemplate reality and show little interest in money or fame (recall Thales?). This class includes philosophers who seek knowledge through music and mathematics to help purify the soul. The correct use of music and mathematics develops harmony in the human soul.

The Harmonic Mean Through his studies in mathematics and music, Pythagoras discovered the *harmonic mean*. He found that the musical intervals (consonants) between the notes could be expressed in numerical terms of ratios of the numbers 1 through 4. The lengths of the strings of a musical instrument are in direct proportion to the interval of sounds they produce. He demonstrated that a string making a sound one octave lower than another string was twice as long as the other string. Because all intervals could be expressed in numerical ratios, music was a good example of numbers in all things. Pythagoras even used music as a medicine to cure internal nervous disorders. As food for the soul, he reasoned, music could help the diseased person regain harmony.

Pause for Thought Pythagoras said this is a harmonic universe. He observed that the heavenly bodies are at exactly proportionate intervals of distance. Have you heard of the *music of the spheres*? Could there be a correlation?

Number: The Key to Nature As musical harmony depends on number, so the harmony of the universe depends on number. According to Pythagoras, the universe is one glorious *harmonia,* or mathematical structure. Number, he said, is the key to nature. Using pebbles to count, number *one* was a single pebble and all other numbers were additional pebbles. A single pebble, as a point, is *one*. *Two* is made up of two pebbles or two points, and these two points make a line. Three points can make a triangle and four points represent a solid. The following figure represents the number 10 as the triangle of four. It shows that $1 + 2 + 3 + 4 = 10$.

.

. .

. . .

. . . .

Pythagoras differentiated triangular numbers, square numbers, rectangular numbers, and spherical numbers as *odd* and *even*. The sums of the series of successive odd numbers are "square numbers," and those of successive even numbers are "oblong."

He discovered the basic mathematical property that the *square of the hypotenuse is equal to the squares of the other two sides of a right-angled triangle.* By saying all things have odd or even numbers, the Pythagoreans, like Anaximander, could explain opposites as one and many, straight and curved, rest and motion—even light and dark.

Form By using number, Pythagoras formulated his concept of *form*. Form meant *limit* or *structure:* the harmony or proper ratio of certain opposites, such as hot and cold or wet and dry. To illustrate that all things are number, he compared the human body to a musical instrument. When the body is "in tune," it is healthy. Disease is the result of tension, the "improper tuning of the strings." Number represents the use of limit (form) to the *unlimited* (matter). As a result, Pythagoras and the Pythagoreans regarded the universe made up of figures, relationships, and forms. Form (structure), not matter (substance), is most important, because substance is broken into pieces, each having a mathematical propensity.

Theano of Crotona

Like most ancient Western civilizations, Greece was male-dominated. But *Theano,* the daughter of a Crotonic orphic* and aristocrat, was able to become a philosopher. She was Pythagoras's first pupil and later became his wife. In the following excerpt, she corrected the misunderstanding of some thinkers about Pythagoras's analogy between things and numbers.

> I have learned that many of the Greeks believe Pythagoras said all things are generated from number. The very assertion poses a difficulty: How can things which do not exist even be conceived to generate? But he did not say that all things come to be from number; rather, in accordance with number—on the grounds that order in the primary sense is in number and it is by participation in order that a first and a second and the rest sequentially are assigned to things which are counted.[5]

The Pythagoreans

The *Pythagoreans* (that is, those who followed Pythagoras's philosophy) made another important contribution to understanding the origin of the universe. Unlike the Milesians, the Pythagoreans argued that the earth rotated—not around the sun, but around a central fire. We do not see this fire, they claimed, because the other half of the universe blocks it out. Their point of view that the universe is an ordered structure that can be known through mathematics laid the groundwork for future speculation.

To move from the premise that mathematics can explain the universe and everything in it by symbols and into mysticism is quite possible. Mystics hold that all things in the universe are interrelated.

Aesara of Lucania

Aesara of Lucania, a female Pythagorean philosopher wrote *On Human Nature.* As a forerunner of Socrates, Aesara thought that by understanding the soul we

---

*An orphic was a disciple of the mythical poet and musician Orpheus.

could understand morality and justice, because the orderly soul is just and moral. With this knowledge, we can create a better society. Note the similarity between Aesara's tripartite arrangement of the soul and Plato's arrangement (see Chapter 3).

> Being threefold, [the soul] is organized in accordance with triple functions: that which effects judgment and thoughtfulness is [the mind] . . . that which effects strength and ability is [spirited] . . . and that which effects love and kindliness is desire. These are all so disposed relatively to one another that the best part is in command, the most inferior part is governed, and the one in between holds a middle place, it both governs and is governed.[6]

In the next century, Plato would turn to Pythagoras and the Pythagoreans for insight into the soul, mathematics, harmony, and form as he probed into the meaning of human nature and the universe.

Explanations of Change

Heraclitus

Another pre-Socratic philosopher who proposed an answer to the questions "Out of what substance is the world made?" and "Is there something permanent underlying this world of change?" was *Heraclitus* (ca. 540–480 B.C.E.) from Ephesus in Asia Minor (or what is now modern-day Turkey).

The Ever-Living Fire   Giving a different kind of answer to Thales' question, Heraclitus argued the substance that holds everything together is *fire*.

> This world, which is the same for all, no one of gods or men has made; but it was ever, is now, and ever shall be an ever-living Fire, with measures of it kindling, and measures going out.[7]

Fire is in a constant process of transformation, and therefore it's in a continuous state of change. Fire *is* the constant process of change. In opposition to the Milesians, Heraclitus's "fire" is not a material thing: It is a unity—not the unity of substance underlying change, but the unity of pattern.

In his "fragments" Heraclitus used fire as an analogy to universal reason or "logos." Fire, he said, consumes what it is fed by giving off heat or smoke or ashes. Thus, fire is a process of change: that which "is fed" into it becomes something else. Heraclitus concluded that although *everything* constantly changes, *nothing* is ever lost in nature. "Nothing is permanent except change."

Pause for Thought   Do you see a connection between Heraclitus's conclusion that every-thing constantly changes yet nothing is ever lost in nature and Einstein's theorem $E = Mc^2$?

Flux   Heraclitus held that constant change, or flow, is the most basic charac-teristic of nature. "Everything flows." *All things are in a state of flux.* Everything is in constant motion; nothing is abiding. Therefore, we "cannot step twice into the same river." When I step into the river for the second time, neither I nor the river is the same.

For Heraclitus, *flux* meant that the world is an "ever-living fire . . . mea-sures of it kindling and measures going out." Measures, he said, are the bal-ance between what kindles and what goes out. The orderly process of flux brings balance to the universe. Harking back to Anaximander, Heraclitus said the world is made up of opposites. If we were never sad, we would not know joy. If we never knew hunger, we would take no pleasure in being full. If there were no winter, we wouldn't experience summer. Without this constant interplay of opposites, imbalance would rule and the world would cease to exist.

> Fire lives the death of earth, and air the death of fire; water lives the death of air, earth that of water.
> Mortals are immortal and immortals are mortal, the one living the other's death and dying the other's life.[8]

God   Heraclitus concluded that fire is not a random movement, but God's uni-versal reason (logos). Reason is the order and structure of the universe. This uni-versal reason guides everything that happens in nature. "God [universal reason] is day and night, winter and summer, war and peace, hunger and satiety," he said. God is the Fire, and the rational human soul is also fire. As a pantheist, he saw the human soul as a part of God, for God is in everything. It is God, the uni-versal reason, the Fire, that is the unity holding everything together. Because God is reason, human beings possess the capacity for thought.

Even as nature obeys universal laws, so must human beings live according to rational rules, such as ethical principles. Only through such conduct can we find happiness. However, Heraclitus thought the masses failed to use this faculty. "The opinions of most people," he said, "are like the playthings of infants." Ordinary people are misled by their senses. He expressed his contempt for the unthinking masses in such aphorisms as "Asses would rather have straw than gold" and "Fools when they do hear are like the deaf: of them does the saying bear witness that they are absent when present."

Pause for Thought   What do you think Heraclitus meant by his aphorism "Asses would rather have straw than gold?" Could this aphorism apply to society today?

Parmenides

A contemporary of Heraclitus and the founder of the *Eleatic School* of philosophy, *Parmenides* (ca. 540–480 B.C.E.) had a totally new concept of change. He not only rejected Heraclitus's idea of change as a unity in diversity, but also disagreed with the Milesian philosophers about the origin of things. Both Heraclitus and the Milesian philosophers believed that one basic substance is the source of everything in the world and that it underlies the process of change.

What Is Is, What Is Not Is Not   Parmenides realized, of course, that nature is in a constant state of flux. He perceived with his senses that things changed, but he could not equate this with what his reason told him. He believed that our senses give us an incorrect picture of the world, a picture that does not tally with our reason. Our reason tells us nothing can come from nothing, and nothing that exists can become nothing. He argued there is no such thing as actual change. To say that something can arise out of nothing, we must assume that nothing is something. But to say that nothing is something is a contradiction because every something is not nothing. He saw the universe much as did Pythagoras—as numbers or points.

Parmenides compared these numbers or points to the stars in the sky. For him, the points that compose the universe represented *Being*. The space separating the points was *Non-Being*. Opposing Pythagoras, who assumed that space exists, Parmenides argued that only the points exist. Space does not exist, and it is not possible to have a void. Because there is no space, it is impossible to distinguish between objects. Also, because points tend to blend, motion is impossible.

Whatever exists, argued Parmenides, "must be absolutely or not at all." "What is" cannot change into "what is not," and "what is not" cannot become "what is." *What is is, what is not is not*. Reality is uncreated, indestructible, eternal, and motionless. The universe of our senses (change) is nothing but appearance, mere opinion, and unreal.

> Come now, I will tell thee—and do thou hearken to my saying and carry it away—the only two ways of search that can be thought of. The first, namely, that *It is,* and that it is impossible for it not to be, is the way of belief, for truth is its companion. The other, namely that *It is not,* and that

it must needs not be,—that, I tell thee, is a path that none can learn of at all. For thou canst not know what is not—that is impossible—nor utter it; for it is the same thing that can be thought and that can be.[9]

Change is the confusion of appearance (motion) with reality (permanence), and therefore change is simply an illusion. Reality is the basis of truth (knowledge), whereas change produces only opinion (lack of knowledge). Although the senses tell us that things appear to change and therefore things *do* change, our reason can distinguish the truth from that which appears to be true. When reason says reality must be a single permanent substance, then there can be no change.

Pause for Thought

Do you agree with Parmenides' assertion that "what is" cannot change without changing into "what is not," and thus there is no change? Can you think of other possibilities?

At age sixty-five, Parmenides and his student, Zeno, visited Athens. There Parmenides conversed with the young Socrates. Years later, with Socrates as the protagonist, Plato wrote a dialogue called *Parmenides*. Parmenides' argument "Nothing can come from what is not" challenged all Greek philosophers who were attempting to explain the nature of change. When this conclusion brought forth criticism and ridicule among his colleagues, Zeno took it upon himself to defend Parmenides' position.

Zeno

Zeno (b. approximately 489 B.C.E.) as a member of the Eleatic School, supported the concept there is no change. He pointed out that paradox results if we accept the assumption that division is possible. One of his arguments is that of Achilles and the tortoise. Achilles is about to race with a tortoise. Being a good sport, Achilles gives the tortoise a head start. But now, said Zeno, Achilles can never overtake the tortoise because he must always reach the point the tortoise has passed. And because the distance between Achilles and the tortoise will always be divisible, no point on the racecourse can be reached before the previous point has been reached.

> You cannot cross a race-course. You cannot traverse an infinite number of points in a finite time. You must traverse the half of any given distance before you traverse the whole, and the half of that again before you can traverse it. This goes on *ad infinitum*, so that there are an infinite number of points in any given space, and you cannot touch an infinite number one by one in a finite time.[10]

Zeno's conclusion was that there could be no motion at all. Because there is no motion, Achilles could never overtake the tortoise. Therefore, Being is the one true reality, and change and motion are only illusions.

> Achilles will never overtake the tortoise. He must first reach the place from which the tortoise started. By that time the tortoise will have got some way ahead. Achilles must then make up that, and again the tortoise will be ahead. He is always coming nearer, but he never makes up to it.[11]

Zeno wanted us to give up the belief that division is possible, which also forces us to give up the belief that our senses provide us with knowledge. His argument remains one of the most famous and difficult paradoxes in philosophy.

Empedocles

A physician and poet as well as philosopher, *Empedocles* (490–430 B.C.E.) agreed with Parmenides that Being *is,* and Being is material. He also agreed with Heraclitus that change is a fact. But, said Empedocles, both philosophers were wrong in assuming the presence of only one element. If this were true, then there could be no bridge between what we see with our senses and what our reason dictates. Though Being does not change, there is not only one Being, there is a *plurality* of Beings or elements—*earth, air, fire,* and *water.* The four elements are "the roots of all." All natural processes result from the coming together and the separating of these four elements. Everything is a mixture of earth, air, fire, and water, but in varying proportions.

Unlike Anaximenes, who argued that air becomes fire, water, and earth, Empedocles reasoned that earth cannot become water, and water cannot become earth. The four kinds of matter are unchangeable, yet by intermingling they form the concrete objects of the world. Flowers and animals come into being through the intermingling of the elements, and when the elements separate, the flowers and animals die. We can see these changes with the naked eye, but earth and air, fire and water remain everlasting, "untouched" by the compounds of which they are part. The four permanent elements continually combine and separate in different proportions.

Love and Strife   Empedocles struggled with the question "What force causes the four elements to combine and to separate in the first place?" He concluded there were two different forces at work in nature—*Love* and *Strife*. Love binds things together, and strife separates them.

> I shall tell thee a twofold tale. At one time it grew to be one only out of many; at another, it divided up to be many instead of one. There is a double becoming of perishable things and a double passing away. The coming together of all things brings one generation into being and destroys it; the

other grows up and is scattered as things become divided. And these things never cease continually changing places, at one time all uniting in one through Love, at another each borne in different directions by the repulsion of strife. Thus, as far as it is their nature to grow into one out of many, and to become many once more when the one is parted asunder, so far they come into being and their life abides not. But, inasmuch as they never cease changing their places continually, so far they are ever immovable as they go round the circle of existence.[12]

Pause for Thought   Do you think the saying "Love makes the world go round" is true? According to Empedocles, what would happen to the world without love?

Anaxagoras

Anaxagoras (500–428 B.C.E.) was the first philosopher to distinguish *mind* (Nous) from *matter*. He agreed with Empedocles that all coming into and going out of being consists in the mixture and separation of preexisting matter, but he rejected love and strife as the responsible forces. Nor did he agree with the Milesians that one particular substance, such as water or air, might be transformed to everything we see in the natural world.

Seeds   There are, said Anaxagoras, an infinite number of minute invisible particles that are the building blocks of nature. We can divide everything into smaller parts, but even in the minutest parts are fragments of all other things. These minuscule particles that carry the blueprint of everything else he called *seeds*.

We can find an example of Anaxagoras's idea today in hologram-producing laser technology (or with just one of my cells, which holds within it a blueprint of my entire body). If we cut a piece of holographic film containing the image of an apple in half, then illuminate it with a laser, each half will contain the whole image of the apple. Even if we divide the halves again and again, we can reconstruct the entire apple from each small portion of the film. Each fragment contains all the information recorded in the whole.

Mind (Nous)   To Anaxagoras, the world appeared an orderly structure produced by the principle of *mind* or *intelligence* (Nous). The power of Nous brings things together and separates them in an orderly fashion. Nous animates everything in nature, including the Earth, life in plants, and sense perception in humans.

And Nous had power over the whole revolution, so that it began to revolve in the beginning. And it began to revolve first from a small beginning; but the revolution now extends over a larger space, and will extend over a larger still. And all the things that are mingled together and separated off and distinguished are all known by Nous. And Nous set in order all things that were to be, and all things that were and are not now and that are, and this revolution in which now revolve not now and that are, and this revolution in which now revolve the stars and the sun and the moon, and the air and the aether that are separated off. And this revolution caused the separating off, and the rare is separated off from the dense, the warm from the cold, the light from the dark, and the dry from the moist. And there are many portions in many things.[13]

Nous is present in all living things—the sun, stars, earth, plants, and human beings. Though Nous is everywhere, it does not create matter, which is eternal. Anaxagoras did not say Nous is immaterial, but that mind, unlike matter, "is mixed with nothing, but is alone, itself by itself." Mind is the "finest of all things and the purest," for mind has all knowledge about everything. For Anaxagoras, mind is a substance even though "mixed with nothing" that is distinguishable from matter. Mind is the principle that gives matter its order. It is the controlling force of everything in the cosmos.

Pause for Thought   Did Anaxagoras mean that the mind is the blueprint of the universe? Could the universe be a hologram?

The Sun and the Moon   Anaxagoras argued that the sun is not a god, but a red-hot stone, bigger than the entire Peloponnesian peninsula where he lived. Shocked, the Athenians accused him of atheism and forced him to leave the city. That didn't stop Anaxagoras's interest in astronomy. After studying a meteorite, he concluded that all heavenly bodies are made of the same substance as Earth. He also announced that the moon produces no light of its own, that its light comes from Earth. However, his greatest contribution to philosophy was his concept of mind as distinguished from matter. This idea was to influence philosophers for generations to come.

The Atomists

Theories of the early Greek Atomists *Leucippus* and *Democritus* bear surprising resemblance to some current postmodern scientific views. The Atomists' philosophy was the final answer the pre-Socratics proposed to Thales' question "Out of what substance is everything made?" After the Atomists, philosophy took a new turn in the minds of Socrates, Plato, and Aristotle.

Atoms

Democritus and Leucippus agreed with their predecessors that transformations in nature could not be the result of anything that actually changed. They believed everything in nature was made of tiny invisible particles or units called *atoms*. The word *atom* means "uncuttable." These philosophers thought you could not divide atoms indefinitely into smaller parts. If atoms could be broken down into smaller parts, then nature would eventually dissolve. Democritus described atoms as hard and indivisible, differing from each other in shape and size, and as invisible to the naked eye. Some are round and smooth, others irregular and jagged. Because they have different shapes, he said, they are able to join together into all kinds of distinctive bodies. When a human body, or a tree, or an animal dies, the atoms disperse and then come together again in new bodies.

Pythagoras posited that *all things are numbers*. The Atomists believed *everything is a combination of atoms,* formed by the motion of atoms moving about in the void. Parmenides had argued that to have a void in space was impossible. Space would then be nothing (nonbeing) and therefore would not exist. Democritus argued there is empty space, but it is infinite—that is, without boundary. The universe is made up of

> atoms and empty space; everything else is merely thought to exist. The worlds are unlimited; they come into being and perish. Nothing can come into being from that which is not nor pass away into that which is not. Further the atoms are unlimited in size and number, and they are borne along in the whole universe in a vortex, and thereby generate all composite things—it is because of their solidity that these atoms are impassive and unalterable. The sun and the moon have been composed of such smooth and spherical masses, and so also the soul, which is identical with reason. We see by virtue of the impact of images upon our eyes. All things happen by virtue of necessity, the vortex being the cause of the creation of all things.[14]

For the Atomists, everything in nature is the product of the collision of atoms moving about in space. As materialists, they did not think there was a conscious design in the movement of atoms. In nature, everything happens mechanically, obeying the inevitable laws of necessity. Everything that happens has a natural cause that is inherent in the object itself.

Pause for Thought   Democritus once said he would rather discover a new cause of nature than be the King of Persia. Would you?

Although the Atomist theory was more or less ignored during the Medieval period, scientists later revived it as their working model. Sir Isaac Newton (1642–1727) referred to the early Atomist theory when he said he wished we could devise the phenomena of Nature by reasoning from mechanical principles. Like the Atomists, he thought the phenomena of nature depended on forces that impelled toward or repelled from each other.

Scientists considered the Atomist theory valid until the twentieth century, when physicists introduced a conception of matter that proved atoms can be split or broken into smaller "elemental particles" such as protons, neutrons, and electrons.

Pause for Thought

Do you think it possible that someday scientists will split "elemental particles" into even lesser particles?

Soul Atoms   As a metaphysical materialist, Democritus reasoned that our *thoughts* also result from atoms. When we see something, it is the result of the movement of atoms in space. When I see a tree, it is because "tree atoms" penetrate my eyes. These atoms make an impact on my *soul atoms,* and a thought is born. The soul, said Democritus, is made up of special round, smooth "soul atoms." At death, the soul atoms will disperse and may become part of a new soul formation. Therefore, there is no individual immortal soul.

Pause for Thought

Do you believe with the Atomists that the soul is connected with the brain, and once the brain disintegrates, we can't have any form of consciousness? Are there other possibilities?

Moral Philosophy   Though everything that happens has a natural cause, Democritus believed we have some control over our thoughts. With natural reason we can understand the "diviner" law. Thus, we can make choices. In his ethics (that is, his moral philosophy), Democritus moved away from a completely mechanistic view by urging people to choose a good and noble life.

If one choose the good of the soul, he chooses the diviner; if the goods of the body, the merely mortal.

Thus [it is] not in strength of body nor in gold that men find happiness, but in uprightness and in fullness of understanding.

Not from fear but from a sense of duty refrain from your sins.

He who does wrong is more unhappy than he who suffers wrong.

Strength of body is nobility in beasts of burden, strength of character is nobility in men.

Those who have a well-ordered character lead also a well-ordered life.[15]

Summary

The *pre-Socratic* philosophers offered alternate theories to their basic questions: "What is the *substance* out of which the world is made?" and "How can we explain the process of change in matter?" As materialists, the Milesians sought to discover the basic substance that held the universe together. For *Thales,* this basic substance was *water,* for *Anaximander* it was the *boundless pool of opposites,* and for *Anaximenes* it was *air.*

As thinkers probed deeper into the structure of the universe, *Pythagoras* found *number* the basic principle on which all else depends. The Pythagoreans were the first to conceive of *form* as well as *matter. Heraclitus* concluded that the universe is in a constant state of flux (change) and that the underlying substance and unity is *fire.*

Parmenides disagreed that motion existed at all. For him, reality is permanent, unchanging, indivisible, and *undifferentiated Being. Zeno* developed clever *paradoxes* to show that motion is impossible in principle. *Empedocles* agreed that Being is the permanent and true reality. But he argued for a plurality of Beings that change only in position. *Love* and *Strife* are the two forces that cause the change of positions.

Anaxagoras argued that *Nous* (mind) puts the universe in motion by acting on matter. The *Atomists* maintained that uncreated, imperceptible, indestructible, indivisible, and *eternal atoms* in motion compose the universe. All of the pre-Socratic philosophers engaged primarily in *natural philosophy,* the study of material substance and the problem of change.

Connections

The Atomists marked the end of Greek natural philosophy. After the Atomists, philosophers turned their concentration from the physical world to questions about how people should behave. The next great development in philosophy started with the Sophists and Socrates, who turned from natural philosophy to concentrate on the nature of human beings, their ethical problems, and philosophy of life. They struggled with the problems that confront every thinking human being: *Who am I? What do I want out of life?*

Study Questions

1. What were the *major questions* posed by the Milesian philosophers?

2. The Pythagoreans believed *all things are number.* What did they mean? Do you find this concept plausible?

3. What is Pythagoras's theory of the *harmony of the universe?* How does this theory relate to mathematics?

4. Explain Parmenides' argument *What is is, what is not is not.*

5. Explain what Heraclitus meant by his statement "*Mortals are immortals and immortals are mortals, the one living the others' death and dying the others' life.*"

6. Compare and contrast the theories of Heraclitus and Parmenides on the notion of *change.*

7. We know hares are faster than turtles, but Zeno concludes that Achilles the hare *cannot overtake* the tortoise. Why?

8. Explain Empedocles' theory of *plurality.*

9. Compare and contrast Empedocles' concept of *Being* with Parmenides' concept of *Being.*

10. According to Empedocles, what role do *Love* and *Strife* play in the universe?

11. How, for Anaxagoras, does *mind* structure the universe?

12. What is the importance of *seeds* for Anaxagoras?

13. What does the word *atom* mean? Has its meaning changed today?

14. According to the Atomists, what is the relationship between *atoms* and the *void?*

15. Why does Democritus think that *thoughts* result from atoms?

16. Compare Anaxagoras's *view of the universe* with that held by the Atomists.

Notes

1. John Burnet, *Early Greek Philosophy,* 4th ed., pp. 353–354. New York: World Publishing Co., 1967.

2. Ibid., pp. 70–71.

3. Ibid., p. 73.

4. Ibid., p. 96.

5. Holger Thesleff, "Pythagorean Texts of the Hellenistic Period, 'Acta Academiae Aboensis—Humaniora'" (trans. by Vicki Lynn Harper), pp. 12–13 in *A History of Women Philosophers,* Vol. 1, 600 B.V.–500 A.D., edited by Mary Ellen Waithe. Dordrecht, Netherlands: Martinus Nijhoff Publishers, 1987.

6. Mary Ellen Waithe, *A History of Women Philosophers,* op. cit., p. 32.

7. John Burnet, *Early Greek Philosophy,* op. cit., p. 134.

8. Ibid., pp. 135, 138.

9. Ibid., p. 173.

10. Ibid., p. 318 (note 1).

11. Ibid., p. 318 (note 2).

12. Ibid., pp. 207–208 (note 17).

13. Ibid., p. 260.

14. Diogenes Laertius, *Lives and Opinions of Eminent Philosophers,* Vol. II, pp. 453, 455 (trans. by R. D. Hicks). Cambridge, Mass.: Loeb Classical Library, Harvard University Press, 1925.

15. C. M. Bakewell (Trans.), "Fragments" 35, 37, 40, 41, 45, 57, 61, 191 (pp. 63–64) in *Source Book in Ancient Philosophy.* New York: Scribner, 1907.

CHAPTER TWO

Socrates and the Sophists

In the last chapter, we saw how the pre-Socratic philosophers sought to understand the nature of the physical world and to know the substance out of which everything is made. This gave them an important position in the history of science and philosophy. But few of these philosophers directed their full attention to the problems of human beings as part of the universe. Only Heraclitus and Pythagoras had seriously delved into questions of ethics and spiritual philosophy.

In this chapter, we find philosophers moving away from the study of the universe to a study of human beings. With the coming of the Sophists, a skepticism arose about how much knowledge an individual could have of universal truths, and a new interest arose in the place of humankind in civilization and ethics. For a short time, Socrates was a student of the Sophists, but he came to disagree with their skepticism. Indeed, Socrates believed in a universal "good" and regarded the search of humankind to know that good as the most important goal in the world.

The Sophists

After approximately 450 B.C.E., philosophy began to focus on the individual and the individual's place in society. Athens, the cultural center of Greece, was in the early stages of developing a democratic government. In a democracy, people require an education to take part in the process of government. It was essential for a good politician or lawyer to master the art of rhetoric—to speak in a convincing manner. Seeing the need for educators, a group of itinerant teachers and philosophers from neighboring colonies flocked to Athens. They called themselves **Sophists** (a Greek word meaning wise or learned), and they made their living by collecting fees for their teaching.

Like the pre-Socratic philosophers, the Sophists were critical of traditional mythology, but they also rejected the validity of the pre-Socratic's speculations. Even if ultimate truths exist, they questioned the human ability to know them. To prove their point, the Sophists illustrated how each of the pre-Socratic philosophers disagreed with the others' answers about the universe. Thales said the ultimate was water, Anaximander the unlimited, and Anaximenes air. The Sophists concluded that we humans could not know the truth about nature's riddles. This view is known as **skepticism.**

Rather than speculating about alternate theories of nature, the Sophists turned their attention to practical day-to-day problems of people and their place in society. Through this fresh method of inquiry, philosophy took a new direction. The most outstanding Sophists in Athens were Protagoras, Gorgias, and Thrasymachus.

"What is the good life?" That's the question the Sophists faced. Could there be a universal good even if no one could know ultimate principles? Or is goodness relative, decided by individual cultures and situations? Most of the Sophists were well traveled and had seen different forms of government. From their experiences, they decided that perceptions of good or bad vary from one city-state to another and from one generation to the next. In this world, they argued, eternal and absolute rules do not exist. Because right and wrong are relative to a culture, the good life depends on each specific situation.

Before the Sophists arrived in Athens, only males from powerful aristocratic families had the advantage of education. But after the Persian Wars, democracy replaced the aristocracy, and this escalated citizen involvement in political life. As newcomers flocked into Athens, energetic businessmen and politicians challenged the privileges of the aristocracy. In this changing climate, anyone who was bright enough and could afford to pay for it had the opportunity to take an education. Free citizens could discuss politics and become political leaders. The Sophists took advantage of the citizens' need to learn public speaking and soon became fashionable teachers. Especially popular were their courses in the art of *rhetoric,* or persuasive speaking.

Anyone who had political ambitions profited by learning how to use the power of rhetoric effectively. The Sophists taught young lawyers how to argue either side of a case whether or not a client was guilty. Young politicians learned the art of using fallacies and emotional language to benefit their cause. The Sophists taught them to present clear and forceful arguments and to attack the logical fallacies in their opponents' arguments.

A story about *Protagoras* (not Pythagoras) and one of his students well illustrates the art of persuasion. A young man who did not have enough money to pay asked Protagoras to accept him as a law student anyway. Protagoras agreed, with the stipulation that the student would pay when he won his first case. For a long time after he completed the course, the student took no cases. Annoyed, Protagoras took the student to court for payment. The student argued, "If I win this case I won't have to pay Protagoras according to the judgment of the court. If I lose this case then I have yet to win my first case, so I won't have to pay according to our agreement. Win or lose, I do not have to pay him." At that point, Protagoras stepped forward to argue his case. "If he loses this case, then by the judgment of the court, he will have to pay. If he wins this case, he will have won his first case and therefore will have to pay me. So, in either case he must pay."

Fictitious or true, the story demonstrates the art of rhetoric on both sides of an argument. Because the Sophists considered "truth" relative to the situation at hand, the intrinsic goodness of many of their arguments was questionable.

At first, the Sophists' reputation as professional teachers of philosophy was highly favorable. Presenting their ideas with strength and conviction was essential for those who wanted to speak before the Athenian Assembly. Education also was necessary for anyone who wanted to sue for personal or business reasons. Soon, however, the Sophists developed the reputation of charging exorbitant fees and of teaching young men to think critically about their traditional religious and ethical views. Even worse, the students learned how to make dishonest arguments appear honest and just cases appear unjust.

Because Socrates had studied under the Sophists, some Athenians considered him just another Sophist, but he and Plato condemned the Sophists for collecting money to teach philosophy. Socrates called the Sophists "prostitutes of wisdom."

Pause for Thought   Do you agree or disagree with the Sophists' view of morality? Should each society make its own rules? Or is there an absolute good that all people in all societies should follow?

Protagoras

Protagoras (481–411 B.C.E.) was possibly the most famous and influential Sophist to enter Athens. He is well known for this statement: "Man is the measure of all things, of the things that are, that they are, and of the things that they are not, that they are not."

"Man is the measure of all things" is an example of the differences between the early Milesian philosophers and the Sophists. Protagoras rejected everything the early philosophers thought was true by denying any ultimate principle that we can know. The idea that "man is the measure" rejects Parmenides' and Zeno's theoretical conclusions for practical judgments. Anything good or bad is in relation to individuals, and all we can know is what we learn from our culture, conditioning, and experience. Truth is relative: Nothing is one thing rather than another. Thus, if you and I disagree, we may both be right depending on our capacity. In his dialogue *Theaetetus*, Plato had Socrates characterize what Protagoras meant:

> *Socrates*: [Protagoras] says . . . that "man is the measure of all things"—alike of the being of things that are and of the not-being of things that are not. . . . He puts it in this sort of way . . . that any given thing "is to me such as it appears to me, and is to you such as it appears to you, you and I being men?"
> *Theaetetus*: Yes, that is how he puts it.
> *Socrates*: Well, what a wise man says is not likely to be nonsense. So let us follow up his meaning. Sometimes, when the same wind is blowing, one of us feels chilly, the other does not, or one may feel slightly chilly, the other quite cold.
> *Theaetetus*: Certainly.
> *Socrates*: Well, in that case are we to say that the wind in itself is cold or not cold? Or shall we agree with Protagoras that it is cold to the one who feels chilly, and not to the other?[1]

To say "man is the measure of all things" suggests that our knowledge depends on our sensations and feelings—perceptions that each of us has but which can be different for each individual.

Pause for Thought   Do you agree with Protagoras that "man is the measure of all things"? Does this mean that we can never discover the true or ultimate nature of anything?

Protagoras's doctrine of **relativism** asserts that knowledge is meaningful, not in some ultimate sense, but in how it *affects* us. For example, the wind is as it appears to each of us. Although it may feel cold to one person and warm to another, we cannot say the wind is cold or warm in itself. Protagoras concluded that one person could not be more or less correct than any other person. Each of us is the judge of how the wind seems.

Religion and Morals   Protagoras extended his view of relativism to religion and ethics. What is true or good is not our speculation on some ultimate principle of truth, but a truth or good that works for us. Religion and morals have value when they produce practical results in our life (see Chapter 13,

"Pragmatism"). As the basis for morality, each society has its own moral rules and laws, for there is no absolute moral standard.

Protagoras did not carry moral relativism to the extreme by saying that because moral judgments are relative anyone can decide what is moral. He took a more conservative position: The state or society makes the laws that everyone should accept because they are as good as they can be. Other states and communities may have different laws; this does not mean their laws are better, only that they suit their needs. In the interest of a community's well-being, citizens should respect and uphold its customs, laws, and moral rules.

The Gods   When asked if he believed in the Greek gods, Protagoras answered, "The question is complex and life is short." Another time he said he didn't know if the gods exist or not. Protagoras's attitude was that of an **agnostic**—that is, one who cannot say if one or more gods do or do not exist. However, he believed that lack of knowledge about the gods should not prevent anyone from worshiping them if they so desired. In fact, if the people in a community worship a certain way, then it would be wise to participate in their rituals. The following of tradition reinforces a society's stability.

Pause for Thought   Do you believe with Protagoras that if you want to succeed, it is wise to follow your community's morals and religion?

Gorgias

Gorgias (483–375 B.C.E.) came to Athens as the ambassador of his native city of Leontini. Although we could consider Protagoras as saying "Anything could be true," Gorgias took exactly the opposite view: Nothing can be true. Gorgias based his philosophy on three premises: (1) Nothing exists; (2) if anything did exist, we could never know it; and (3) if, by chance, we should come to know it, we could not communicate it to others. We do communicate, he said, but our words are only symbols or signs, and we cannot prove they correspond with the object they are meant to identify. Therefore, no one could ever communicate knowledge of universal principles.

Because of his extreme skepticism, Gorgias gave up the philosophical search for truth and turned to rhetoric. Through drama and poetry, he mastered the art of persuasion. In his dialogue titled *Gorgias*, Plato has him say:

> [Rhetoric gives you the power] to convince by your words the judges in
> court, the senators in Council, the people in the Assembly, or in any other

gathering of a citizen body. And yet possessed of such power you will make the doctor, you will make the trainer your slave, and your businessman will prove to be making money, not for himself, but for another, for you who can speak and persuade multitudes.

I have often, along with my brother and with other physicians, visited one of their patients who refused to drink his medicine or submit to the surgeon's knife or cautery, and when the doctor was unable to persuade them, I did so, by no other art but rhetoric.[2]

Gorgias regarded the art of rhetoric as the greatest of all art forms:

The rhetorician is competent to speak against anybody on any subject, and to prove himself more convincing before a crowd on practically every topic he wishes. . . .[3]

Gorgias taught the art of persuasion as a means of political success, and he has entered history as one who was remarkably successful in that pursuit.

Pause for Thought   Do you think that today's courts exhibit Gorgias's viewpoint? Are our court's contests about who can best persuade a jury, or are lawyers truly searching for a defendant's guilt or lack of guilt?

Thrasymachus

Protagoras had advised people to follow the moral rules of their state or society. Gorgias and the next generation of Sophists questioned that advice. They asked, "If laws and moral rules are merely convention, then *why* should they rule us? Why should we obey local laws and morals if it is not to our advantage to do so?" Thrasymachus and others decided there is no real justice or right. These are only words applied by the powerful to keep societies under control.

Thrasymachus (ca. 450 B.C.E.) was one of the first individuals to advocate force by arguing that *might makes right*. Right and wrong, he said, have no meaning at all. We first meet Thrasymachus in Plato's dialogue *The Republic*. In this passage, Socrates and his friends are trying to define justice. Thrasymachus bursts on the scene and aggressively gives his own definition of "right" and "wrong."

> *Thrasymachus*: What I say is that "just" or "right" means nothing but what is to the interest of the stronger party.
> *Socrates*: What makes you say that?
> *Thrasymachus*: . . . "right" actually means what is good for someone else, and to be "just" means serving the interest of the stronger who rules, at the cost of the subject who obeys; whereas injustice is just the reverse, asserting

its authority over those innocents who are called just, so that they minister solely to their master's advantage and happiness, and not in the least degree to their own. Innocent as you are yourself, Socrates, you must see that a just man always has the worst of it. Take a private business: When a partnership is wound up, you will never find that the more honest of two partners comes off with the larger share; and in their relations to the state, when there are taxes to be paid, the honest man will pay more than the other on the same amount of property; or if there is money to be distributed, the dishonest will get it all. . . . "Right," as I said at first, means simply what serves the interest of the stronger party; "wrong" means what is for the interest and profit of oneself.[4]

Instead of seeing injustice as a character defect, Thrasymachus considered the unjust person superior in character and intelligence because he or she is more successful. The ruling party makes laws in their own interest. "Right" becomes "right" when it is to the advantage of the party in power. "*Might makes right.*" As a Sophist who believed that actions are relative, Thrasymachus reduced morality to power.

Pause for Thought   Today we see communities torn between developers who seek to build on land for profit and residents who want to maintain a particular lifestyle. Who usually wins? Do we see this same battle over natural resources? Environmentalists want to protect the planet for future generations. Business and industry justify production for the benefit of technology and jobs. Is there a right and wrong?

After Thrasymachus's argument that might makes right, Socrates presents several objections. The thirst for *power,* he argues, results in competition and dissension. True justice produces harmony. The just soul surrenders the lust for power to rational principles of conduct. The just person, Socrates says, is the moral person, the reasonable and balanced person, who, in turn, is the happy person.

In opposition to the relativistic philosophy of the Sophists, Socrates carefully uncovers their inconsistencies. Then, continuing his dialectic or question-and-answer method, he establishes a foundation for universal truth.

Socrates

Socrates (470–399 B.C.E.) is possibly the most interesting figure in the history of philosophy. Like Jesus and the Buddha, he wrote nothing, yet he has influenced philosophers and civilizations for two thousand years. Much of his influence comes because he fully lived his famous statement "The unexamined life is not worth living," and from his courage in facing death. He was an intense genius with the ability to draw knowledge out of individuals who didn't know they had knowledge.

Socrates combined down-to-earth common sense with high ideas, and he taught those who would listen to cut through each falsehood with swift logical analysis. He was also known and loved for his warmth and hearty sense of humor.

Socrates devoted his life to serving "the god" but was charged with impiety. He taught the young to examine their lives and live morally, yet the second charge at his trial was "corrupting the youth of Athens." A jury condemned him to death.

Because Socrates wrote nothing, most of what we know about him comes from the writings of Aristophanes and Xenophon and especially Plato. In his comedy, *The Clouds*, Aristophanes depicted Socrates as a strutting waterfowl who rolled his eyes and swung around in a basket "sputtering . . . about matters of which I understand nothing at all."

Xenophon portrayed Socrates as a loyal soldier who had a passion for discussing morality. In military campaigns, Socrates could go without food longer than anyone else. During winter months, while others wrapped themselves in coats and wore fleece-lined boots, Socrates wore only a light tunic and sandals. Before sunrise each morning, he meditated; and when the sun rose, he gave thanks to the gods and went about his daily duties. One time, he stood twenty-four hours in a trance-like meditation. During these hours he discovered his mission in life: to seek the highest knowledge and get others to seek with him. He was to question people unrelentingly, expose every hiding place, and get them in touch with their souls.

Plato characterized Socrates as a man with a deep sense of mission and absolute moral purity. His actual teachings come to us through the dialogues of Plato, who used Socrates as his principle character and mouthpiece. Because Plato put his own philosophy in Socrates' mouth, however, it is difficult to distinguish between the philosophies of the two men. Most scholars think that Plato's early dialogues characterize Socrates' philosophy, the middle dialogues combine both of their ideas, and the later dialogues reveal Plato's own mature thought.

Socrates' Life   In 469 B.C.E., Socrates was born in Athens. He died in the same city seventy years later (399 B.C.E.). His mother was a midwife, and his father may have been a stone mason. Little is known of Socrates' life before his service in the military.

We know that, from a physical point of view, Socrates was genuinely ugly. He had a potbelly, bulging eyes, a snub nose, and a squat build. But inside he was "perfectly delightful." Socrates used to laugh at his own appearance, and more than once announced plans to "dance off" his stomach. But his concerns had little to do with physical characteristics. The true self, he said, is not the body but the soul. Virtue is inner goodness, and real beauty is that of the soul.

In his dialogue *Symposium*, Plato gave a celebrated account of Socrates' character. The dialogue describes a dinner party and its aftermath when each guest gives an oration in praise of love. When it was his turn to speak, Alcibiades decided to give his account by praising Socrates instead of the god of love (in Athenian culture, many older men had romantic ties to younger men):

> Were it not that I might appear to be absolutely tipsy, I would have affirmed on oath all the strange effects I personally have felt from his words, and still feel even now. For when I hear him I am worse than any wild fanatic; I find my heart leaping and my tears gushing forth at the sound of his speech, and I see great numbers of other people having the same experience. When I listened to Pericles and other skilled orators I thought them eloquent, but I never felt anything like this; my spirit was not left in a tumult and had not to complain of my being in the condition of a common slave: whereas the influence of [Socrates] has often thrown me into such a state that I thought my life not worth living on these terms. . . . For he compels me to admit that, sorely deficient as I am, I neglect myself while I attend to the affairs of Athens. . . . For he brings home to me that I cannot disown the duty of doing what he bids me, but that as soon as I turn from his company I fall a victim to the favours of the crowd. So I take a runaway's leave of him and flee away; when I see him again I think of those former admissions, and am ashamed. . . .
>
> Such then is the effect that our satyr can work upon me and many another with his piping . . . observe how Socrates is amorously inclined to handsome persons; with these he is always busy and enraptured. . . . And believing he had a serious affection for my youthful bloom, I supposed I have here a godsend and a rare stroke of luck, thinking myself free at any time by gratifying his desires to hear all that our Socrates knew; for I was enormously proud of my youthful charms. . . . Yes, gentlemen, I went and met him, and the two of us would be alone; and I thought he would seize the chance of talking to me as a lover does to his dear one in private, and I was glad. But nothing of the sort occurred at all: he would merely converse with me in his usual manner, and when he had spent the day with me he would leave me and go his way. After that I proposed he should go with me to the trainer's, so I trained with him, expecting to gain my point there. The same story! I got no further with the affair. . . .
>
> Now all this, you know, had already happened to me when we later went on a campaign together to Poridaea; and there we were messmates. Well, first of all, he surpassed not me only but everyone else in bearing hardships; whenever we were cut off in some place and were compelled, as often in campaigns, to go without food, the rest of us were nowhere in point of endurance. Then again, when we had plenty of good cheer, he

alone could enjoy it to the full, and though unwilling to drink, when once overruled he used to beat us all; and, most surprising of all, no man has ever yet seen Socrates drunk. Of this power I expect we shall have a good test in a moment. But it was in his endurance of winter—in those parts the winters are awful—that I remember . . . : we all preferred not to stir abroad, or if any of us did, we wrapped ourselves up with prodigious care, and after putting on our shoes we muffled up our feet with felt and little fleeces. But he walked out in that weather, clad in just such a coat as he was always wont to wear, and he made his way more easily over the ice unshod than the rest of us did in our shoes. . . .

One day . . . immersed in some problem at dawn, he stood in the same spot considering it; and when he found it a tough one, he would not give it up but stood there trying. The time drew on to midday, and the men began to notice him, and said to one another in wonder: "Socrates has been standing there in a study ever since dawn!" The end of it was that in the evening some of the Ionians after they had supped—this time it was summer—brought out their mattresses and rugs and took their sleep in the cool; thus they waited to see if he would go on standing all night too. He stood till dawn came and the sun rose; then walked away, after offering a prayer to the Sun.

Then, if you care to hear of him in battle—for there also he must have his due— . . . let me tell you, gentlemen, what a notable figure he made when the army was retiring in flight from Delium: I happened to be there on horseback, while he marched under arms. The troops were in utter disorder, and he was retreating along with Laches, when I chanced to come up with them. . . . I noticed, first, how far he outdid Laches in collectedness, and next I felt—to use a phrase of yours, Aristophanes—how there he stepped along, as his wont is in our streets, "strutting like a proud marshgoose, with ever a sidelong glance," turning a calm sidelong look on friend and foe alike, and convincing anyone even from afar that whoever cares to touch this person will find he can put up a stout enough defence. . . .

[After Alcibiades ended his speech] a great crowd of revellers arrived at the door. . . . [Soon] the whole place was in an uproar and . . . [everyone] drank a vast amount of wine . . . Aristodemus . . . awoke towards dawn, as the cocks were crowing; and immediately he saw that all the company [except Socrates] were either sleeping or gone. . . . When Socrates had seen them comfortable, he rose and went away . . . ; on arriving at the Lyceum, he washed himself, and then spent the rest of the day in his ordinary fashion; and so, when the day was done, he went home for the evening and reposed.[5]

Pause for Thought   Why can some people withstand extremes of cold and hunger and trance? Do the actions of Socrates remind you of the stories of Hindu yogis who control their heart rates and pain thresholds?

Socrates' Inner Voice   Since childhood, Socrates listened to an inner voice, or what he called his *daimon*. The voice, he said, "always forbids but never commands me to do anything I am going to do." Whenever he thought of going into political life, the voice said, "*No.*" The voice neither brought him knowledge nor suggested a definite action. It merely said "No." All of his life the voice forbade him to say or do anything that would have evil consequences. Socrates always obeyed the voice whether or not he understood why it said "No." He waited for the daimon to say no to his mission as a gadfly★ sent by "the god" to rouse sleepy Athenians and keep them alert to the importance of tending their souls. The voice was silent.

Pause for Thought

Do you have an inner voice that guides you in important matters? Is it your conscience, or is it something else?

The Oracle at Delphi   The ancient Greeks used to consult the famous oracle at Delphi about important problems. Apollo, the god of the oracle, spoke through the priestess Pythia, who sat over a fissure in the earth. Hypnotic vapors put her in a trance that empowered her to become Apollo's mouthpiece. Over the entrance to the temple at Delphi was a famous inscription: *Know Thyself!*

Socrates' friend Chaerophon asked the oracle at Delphi, "Who is the wisest of men?" The oracle answered that Socrates was the wisest. When Socrates heard this, he was shocked. He immediately went to people in Athens who had reputations for being knowledgeable. He conversed with priests, poets, politicians, statesmen, and craftsmen, hoping to discover the answer.

Gradually the true meaning of the oracle dawned on him. People were ignorant of what it is most crucial to know: how to conduct their lives right, and how to make their souls "as good as possible." Socrates knew the importance of this knowledge, but he was also aware of his own ignorance of it. Most people thought they knew when they really didn't. Socrates' said he was at least the "one-eyed" in a "kingdom of the blind." He was the wisest because *he was the only one who knew he didn't know.*

Pause for Thought

There is a saying: "The opinionated person is usually without knowledge." Does the saying fit with Socrates' findings?

★A biting insect such as a horsefly that annoys livestock.

The Dialectic Method   The essential nature of Socrates' art was that he did not teach anyone but instead acted as a "kind of midwife." As a midwife does not herself give birth, but aids the mother, Socrates helped pregnant souls give birth to the wisdom hidden within them. Instead of lecturing, he asked questions and discussed. He would begin a conversation as if he knew nothing, but during the discussion he would get his opponents to clarify their ideas and resolve logical contradictions. With this procedure, he invented the **dialectic method.**

The dialogue *Euthyphro* is an example of the method used by Socrates to clarify one's thoughts. On the steps of the courthouse, Socrates meets the young man Euthyphro, who asks why Socrates is there. When Socrates tells him he has been charged with "impiety," Euthyphro explains that he is suing his own father for impiety. Socrates suggests that Euthyphro can help him. "Tell me," says Socrates, "what is impiety?" Through a series of questions and answers, Socrates hopes to arrive at a clear definition of impiety. However, during his cross-examination, Euthyphro begins to realize that he doesn't have a clear idea of the meaning of either piety or impiety.

> *Socrates*: Well then, Euthyphro, what do we say about piety? Is it not loved by all the gods, according to your definition?
> *Euthyphro*: Yes.
> *Socrates*: Because it is pious, or for some other reason?
> *Euthyphro*: No, because it is pious.
> *Socrates*: Then it is loved by the gods because it is pious; it is not pious because it is loved by them?
> *Euthyphro*: It seems so.
> *Socrates*: But, then, what is pleasing to the gods is pleasing to them, and is in a state of being loved by them, because they love it?
> *Euthyphro*: Of course.
> *Socrates*: Then piety is not what is pleasing to the gods, and what is pleasing to the gods is not pious, as you say, Euthyphro. They are different things.
> *Euthyphro*: And why, Socrates?
> *Socrates*: Because we are agreed that the gods love piety because it is pious, and that it is not pious because they love it. Is not this so?
> *Euthyphro*: Yes.
> *Socrates*: And that what is pleasing to the gods because they love it, is pleasing to them by reason of this same love, and that they do not love it because it is pleasing to them.
> *Euthyphro*: True.
> *Socrates*: Then, my dear Euthyphro, piety and what is pleasing to the gods are different things. If the gods had loved piety because it is pious, they would also have loved what is pleasing to them because it is pleasing to them; but if what is pleasing to them had been pleasing to them because they loved it, then piety, too, would have been piety because they loved it. But now you see that they are opposite things, and wholly different from

each other. For the one is of a sort to be loved because it is loved, while the other is loved because it is of a sort to be loved. My question, Euthyphro, was, What is piety? But it turns out that you have not explained to me the essential character of piety; you have not been content to mention an effect which belongs to it—namely, that all the gods love it. You have not yet told me what its essential character is. Do not, if you please, keep me from what piety is; begin again and tell me that. Never mind whether the gods love it, or whether it has other effects: we shall not differ on that point. Do your best to make clear to me what is piety and what is impiety.

Euthyphro: But, Socrates, I really don't know how to explain to you what is in my mind. Whatever statement we put forward always somehow moves round in a circle, and will not stay where we put it.[6]

As a dialectical midwife, Socrates helped people "give birth" to the correct insight. In some cases, though, the insight might not have been so welcome. Before Socrates had completed the conversation, Euthyphro said "Another time, then, Socrates. I am in a hurry now, and it is time for me to be off."

Real understanding, Socrates said, comes from within. No one else can give it to us. Instead of "filling an empty vessel," he forced the people he met to use their innate reason by reaching down inside themselves to their deeper nature. Sometimes the conversations did not lead to answers, but they always made the participants wiser than before.

Socrates feigned ignorance to help him expose the weaknesses in people's thinking. Today we call such pretended ignorance "Socratic irony." He urged people to discover the difficulties in what appeared self-evident. He confused them, and forced them to think, to search, to inquire again and again, and to never sidestep the answer. When Socrates exposed their ignorance, some people grew angry and frustrated. In fact, two infuriated politicians, Meletus and Anytus, brought him to trial on false charges.

Knowledge   Freedom grows with knowledge. For Socrates, true knowledge was more than a simple inspection of facts. Knowledge is the power of the mind to understand the enduring elements that remain after the facts disappear. *Eternal beauty* remains after the flower fades away. No two flowers are the same; they differ in color, shape, and height. The enduring element remains, however: They are all flowers. Individual people have factual differences in the color of their hair, eyes, and skin, but the enduring element remains: They are all human. They all have a soul.

Behind the world of facts, Socrates believed the mind could discover the essential nature of things. Because human beings have the faculty of rational intuition, acting rationally is the behavior that is appropriate to humankind. Facts can give important information, but an understanding of enduring elements common to all categories is true knowledge. The examined life awakens individuals to the truth of human nature.

Moral Philosophy   For Socrates, the highest concern for human beings should be "to make the soul as good as possible." He believed individuals who attain knowledge of the soul and what makes it good will behave morally. None of us, he said, ever consciously chooses to harm ourselves. Even if we choose pain, we think somehow we will benefit from it. Human nature seeks its own well-being. The problem lies in our ignorance.

To begin his moral philosophy, Socrates posited three special tenets:

1. Virtue (moral excellence) is identical with knowledge.

2. Vice (moral evil) is identical with ignorance (lack of moral knowledge).

3. No one ever commits an evil act knowingly. Doing wrong arises out of ignorance.

These tenets oppose the Sophists' teachings that we purposely choose evil over good. Socrates would agree that most of us commit evil acts, but he would deny that anyone does an evil act simply for the sake of evil. When we commit evil acts, we do it thinking our actions will bring us good in some way. We falsely expect to benefit by them.

We live in a complex society of unbridled materialism and competition. In such a society, some people do evil acts to gain power, recognition, and financial success. They think the results of these acts will make them happy. But, warns Socrates, the guilt of the soul outweighs these supposed gains.

Equating ignorance with vice explains why ignorance cannot produce happiness. We would not do evil acts if we knew what it takes to "make the soul good." Vice results from the hope that our acts will create happiness. But evil acts cannot make us happy. Ignorance is the condition of not knowing what behavior will produce happiness. We think we have knowledge. We think revenge will make us happy. But it doesn't. Only knowledge of the soul can tell us what we require to be happy.

Pause for Thought   Can you remember wanting to "get even" with someone, or making a promise you had no intention of keeping? Do we do these acts with knowledge of the good, or do we do them because they give us selfish satisfaction? Would Socrates consider selfishness to be ignorance?

For Socrates, the so-called goods of wealth, property, and fame are trifling compared to the good of the soul. If we truly knew what the good soul is, nothing could tempt us to do evil. None of us wants to harm our self, yet we harm others by our thoughts, words, and deeds. Socrates believed it is better for our soul if we suffer harm than if we cause harm to another. Plato had Socrates make this point in his dialogue *Crito*.

> *Socrates*: Then we ought never to act unjustly?
> *Crito*: Certainly not.
> *Socrates*: If we ought never to act unjustly at all, ought we to repay injustice with injustice, as the multitude thinks we may?
> *Crito*: Clearly not.
> *Socrates*: Well, then, Crito, ought we to do evil to anyone?
> *Crito*: Certainly I think not, Socrates.
> *Socrates*: And is it just to repay evil with evil, as the multitude thinks, or unjust?
> *Crito*: Certainly it is unjust.
> *Socrates*: For there is no difference, is there, between doing evil to a man and acting unjustly?
> *Crito*: True.
> *Socrates*: Then we ought not to repay injustice with injustice or to do harm to any man, no matter what we may have suffered from him. . . .[7]

Pause for Thought   Do you agree with Socrates' statement "We ought not to repay injustice or to do harm to any man?" Or do you think "An eye for an eye" is a more reasonable way to attain justice?

Socrates said, "The unexamined life is not worth living." He fully understood that only the examined life could produce goodness and that the unexamined life produces vice. Each of us has the desire for happiness and the well-being of our soul. Such happiness comes only with knowledge. In Plato's dialogue *Gorgias*, Socrates reasoned that happiness is a matter of inner qualities: "A good and honorable man or woman, I say, is happy, and an unjust and wicked one is wretched."

Socrates' Trial and Death   Convinced that the care of the soul is the highest human concern, Socrates spent his adult years examining his own life and the lives and thoughts of his fellow Athenians. As the hero to many throughout history who faced death, we cannot separate Socrates' philosophy from his life or his death. He had the courage not only to live his philosophy, but also to die for it.

Many Athenians considered Socrates a dangerous free thinker who raised questions and called into doubt their conventional beliefs. To make matters worse, young men from leading Athenian families learned the dialectic skill of questioning established customs in morality, religion, and politics.

Among Socrates' antagonists was Anytus, a politician who instigated Meletus to bring Socrates to trial. The charges were "not worshiping the gods of the state" and "corrupting the youth." Socrates' prosecutor, Meletus, demanded the death penalty. It was customary for individuals charged with such crimes to accept voluntary exile. Instead, Socrates remained in Athens and defended himself in front of a court with a jury of 501 citizens.

Plato recorded Socrates' brilliant defense in his dialogue *Apology*. Socrates refused to throw himself on the court's mercy, and, ironically, he lectured the jury members on their ignorance.

> And now, Athenians, I am not arguing in my own defense at all, as you might expect me to do, but rather in yours in order you may not make a mistake about the gift of the god to you by condemning me. For if you put me to death, you will not easily find another who, if I may use a ludicrous comparison, clings to the state as a sort of gadfly to a horse that is large and well-bred but rather sluggish because of its size, so that it needs to be aroused. It seems to me that the god has attached me like that to the state, for I am constantly alighting upon you at every point to arouse, persuade, and reproach each of you all day long. You will not easily find anyone else, my friends, to fill my place; and if you are persuaded by me, you will spare my life. You are indignant, as drowsy persons are when they are awakened, and, of course, if you are persuaded by Anytus, you could easily kill me with a single blow, and then sleep on undisturbed for the rest of your lives, unless the god in his care for you sends another to arouse you.[8]

Indignant, the jury found him guilty. Meletus and Anytus asked for the death penalty. But first, as was the custom, Socrates had the opportunity to submit an alternative sentence. If he had suggested exile or promised to stop philosophizing in the streets of Athens, he may have been set free. Instead, Socrates said:

> So he proposes death as the penalty. Be it so. And what alternative penalty shall I propose to you, Athenians? What I deserve, of course, must I not? What then do I deserve to pay or to suffer for having determined not to spend my life in ease? I neglected the things which most men value, such as wealth, and family interest, and military commands, and public oratory, and all the civic appointments, and social clubs, and political factions, that there are in Athens; for I thought that I was really too honest a man to preserve my life if I engaged in these affairs. So I did not go where I should have done no good either to you or to myself.
>
> I went, instead, to each one of you privately to do him, as I say, the greatest of benefits, and tried to persuade him not to think of these affairs

until he had thought of himself and tried to make himself as good and wise as possible, not to think of the affairs of Athens until he had thought of Athens herself; and to care for other things in the same manner. Then what do I deserve for such a life?

Something good, Athenians. . . . There is no reward, Athenians, so suitable . . . as receiving free meals in the prytaneum. It is a much more suitable reward . . . than for any of you who has won a victory at the Olympic games, with his horse or his chariots. Such a man only makes you seem happy, but I make you really happy; he is not in want, and I am. So if I am to propose the penalty which I really deserve, I propose this—free meals in the prytaneum.[9]

The jury sentenced him to death. Undaunted, Socrates said that his death will do those who accuse him unjustly more harm than it will him, for "no harm can come to a good man."

And now I wish to prophesy to you, Athenians, who have condemned me. For I am going to die, and that is the time when men have most prophetic power. And I prophesy to you who have sentenced me to death that a far more severe punishment than you have inflicted on me will surely overtake you as soon as I am dead. You have done this thing, thinking that you will be relieved from having to give an account of your lives. But I say that the result will be very different. There will be more men who will call you to account, whom I have held back, though you did not recognize it And they will be harsher toward you than I have been, for they will be younger, and you will be more indignant with them. For if you think that you will restrain men from reproaching you for not living as you should, by putting them to death, you are very much mistaken. That way of escape is neither possible nor honorable. It is much more honorable and much easier not to suppress others, but to make yourselves as good as you can. This is my parting prophecy to you who have condemned me.

And you too, judges, must face death hopefully, and believe this one truth, that no evil can happen to a good man, either in life or after death.[10]

While in prison waiting execution, Socrates' friends offered to help him escape. Socrates would have none of it. Escape would mean defying his beloved Athens and her laws. The laws, insisted Socrates, were not responsible for his trial and sentence, his accusers were.

Pause for Thought

Because Socrates could have proposed an alternative sentence that would have saved his life, some people believe he committed suicide. What do you think suicide is?

In prison, Socrates and his friends talked about the nature of the soul. During the discussion, Socrates told a mythical story about the soul's immortality. Afterward, his friend Crito asked how they should bury him. Socrates jokingly replied, "In any way you like, but you must get hold of *me*, and take care that I do not run away from you."

Socrates spent the day of his execution conversing with his family and friends. At sunset, the jailer came in and told him it was time. After Socrates sent his family away, the jailer, with tears in his eyes, thanked Socrates for treating him as a friend. Then he handed him a cup of hemlock. Plato recounts the death scene in his dialogue *Phaedo*:

> Then, he put the cup to his lips, and drank the poison quite calmly and cheerfully. Till then most of us had been able to control our grief fairly well; but when we saw him . . . finish drinking, we could do so no longer: my tears came fast in spite of myself, and I covered my face and wept for myself; it was not for him, but at my own misfortune in losing such a friend. Even before that Crito had been unable to restrain his tears, and had turned away; and Apollodorus, who had never once ceased weeping the whole time, burst into a loud wail and made us one and all break down by his sobbing, except Socrates himself. "What are you doing, my friends?" he exclaimed. "I sent away the women chiefly in order that they might not behave in this way; for I have heard that a man should die peacefully. So calm yourselves and bear up." When we heard that, we were ashamed, and we stopped weeping. But he walked about, until he said that his legs were getting heavy, and then he lay down on his back, as he was told. And the man who had given the poison after a while began to examine his feet and legs. Then he pressed his foot hard, and asked if there were any feeling in it, and Socrates said, "No"; and then his legs, and in this way moved upwards, showing us that he was cold and stiff. And again he felt him, and said that when it reached his heart, he would be gone. He was already growing cold about the groin, when he uncovered his face, which had been covered, and spoke for the last time. "Crito," he said, "I owe a cock to Asclepius★; do not forget." "It shall be done," replied Crito. "Is there anything else that you wish?" He made no reply to this question; but after a moment he stirred, and the man uncovered him. His eyes were fixed. Then Crito closed his mouth and his eyes.
>
> Such was the end . . . of our friend, who was, I think, of all the men of our time, the best, the wisest, and the most just.[11]

On Women   In the *Republic*, Plato had Socrates discuss the nature of women and their suitability as leaders. During this period in Athens, women were uned-

---

★When recovering from illness, a Greek customarily offered a cock to Asclepius, the god of healing.

ucated, denied citizenship, and treated as domestics. But Socrates and Plato saw women through revolutionary eyes. Socrates argued that there is nothing inherent in woman's nature to prevent her from seeking the same goals as man. Women, if so inclined, ought join the military or even help rule the state.

> *Socrates*: . . . I said, there is no special faculty of administration in a state which a woman has because she is a woman, or which a man has by virtue of his sex, but the gifts of nature are alike diffused in both; all the pursuits of men are the pursuits of women also. . . .
>
> And those women who have such qualities are to be selected as the companions and colleagues of men who have similar qualities and whom they resemble in capacity and in character?
>
> *Glaucon*: Very true.
>
> *Socrates*: And ought not the same natures to have the same pursuits?
>
> *Glaucon*: They ought.
>
> *Socrates*: . . . You will admit that the same education which makes a man a good guardian [ruler] will make a woman a good guardian; for their original nature is the same?
>
> *Glaucon*: Yes.[12]

Pause for Thought   Do you agree with Socrates and Plato that the original nature of men and women is the same?

Summary

The age of the Sophists began when a group of traveling intellectuals protested the differing conclusions among the pre-Socratics. No two philosophers agreed in their answers to the question "Of what is everything made?" Thales said water, Anaximander the unlimited, Anaximenes air, Heraclitus fire, and Empedocles a plurality of elements. The Sophists, however, argued that even if ultimate truths existed, the human mind is incapable of knowing them. They concluded that knowledge depends on the individual. What each person thinks is true *is* true for that person. Protagoras's notion that "Man is the measure of all things" is the exact opposite of Parmenides and Zeno.

The Sophists taught people to argue both sides of a statement. If opinions conflicted, Protagoras claimed that *all* views are true, though some views are better than others. Gorgias, however, took the position that *no* view is—and even if it was, we couldn't know it or communicate it to others. Among the later Sophists, Thrasymachus looked to *power* as the answer to morality. The powerful individual has the advantage of imposing laws on others: "Might makes right."

Socrates, a student of the Sophists for a short time, opposed what he thought was their failure to recognize the universal good in humankind. Socrates lived by his principle that a person's highest concern was to care for the improvement of the soul. Ironically, he was condemned by his own people on false charges of atheism and corrupting the youth of Athens. For him, knowledge was not only possible but also the cure of all our ills. Knowledge is the highest good. Knowledge is virtue—and without knowledge, virtue is impossible. With virtue comes happiness. Socrates committed his life to seeking this truth.

Connections

As we have seen, Socrates disagreed with the Sophists' views of the world and humankind. Socrates had an anti-*Sophistic* conviction of the reality of goodness, a reality we could know through the depth of the soul. He was an intensely realistic and down-to-earth philosopher who held a passionate mysticism and a steadfast skepticism about ordinary religious beliefs. Socrates' method of teaching (what we now call the Socratic dialogue), his wisdom in living, and his courage in dying deeply affected Plato. Although Plato knew Socrates only during the last few years of Socrates' life, it was the latter's influence that inspired Plato to become a philosopher. We know that Plato set out to defend Socrates' memory, then continued to use him as the protagonist of more than twenty dialogues. Based on Socrates' ideas, Plato's own brilliant philosophy has become the foundation of all Western thought.

Study Questions

1. Explain the *teachings* of the Sophists.

2. What do the Sophists mean by their claim that knowledge and morals are *relative*?

3. Explain the meaning of Protagoras's statement "Man is the measure of all things."

4. Do you agree with Gorgias's doctrine that even if there were universal truths, we could never know them or communicate them?

5. How important is *rhetoric* in today's society?

6. Why did Thrasymachus argue that a life of *injustice* is superior to a life of justice?

7. Explain your agreement or disagreement with Thrasymachus's statement "Might makes right."

8. Give examples of *Sophistic practices* in our society.

9. What were some of the main *differences* between Socrates and the Sophists?

10. Do you agree with Socrates that "Knowledge is virtue"? Why or why not?

11. According to Socrates, what is the true meaning of *ignorance*?

12. Why were *wealth, fame,* and *success* unimportant to Socrates? How important are they in your life?

13. What is the *dialectic method*? What connection does this method have with Socrates' view of himself as a *philosophical midwife*?

14. Do you think *the unexamined life* is worth living?

15. What *goal* did Socrates pursue throughout his life?

Notes

1. Plato, *Theaetetus* (trans. by F. M. Cornford), pp. 856–857 in *Plato: The Collected Dialogues,* edited by Edith Hamilton and Huntington Cairns. New York: Bollingen Foundation, Random House, 1966.

2. Plato, *Gorgias* (trans. by W. D. Woodhead), sections 452e and 456b, pp. 236, 239 in *Plato,* edited by Hamilton and Cairns.

3. Ibid., section 457b, p. 240.

4. F. M. Cornford (trans.), *The Republic of Plato* (London: Oxford University Press, 1974), part I. 338 (p. 18), 343–344 (pp. 25–26).

5. Plato, *Symposium*, pp. 212, 215–217, 219–221, 223 (trans. by W.R.M. Lamb). Cambridge, Mass.: Loeb Classical Library, Harvard University Press, 1925.

6. Plato, *Euthyphro*, XII.10, XIII.11, pp. 12–13 in *Euthyphro, Apology, Crito* (trans. by F. J. Church). New York: Bobbs-Merrill, Library of Liberal Arts, 1956.

7. Plato, *Crito*, X.49, pp. 58–59 in Ibid.

8. Plato, *Apology,* XVIII.31, p. 37 in Ibid.

9. Ibid., XXVI.36, pp. 43–44.

10. Ibid., XXX–XXXI, pp. 46–47; XXXIII, pp. 48–49.

11. Plato, *Phaedo,* p. 70 in Ibid.

12. Plato, *The Republic,* p. B.5 in *The Dialogues of Plato,* Vol. 3, 3rd ed. (trans. by Benjamin Jowett), 3rd. ed. Oxford, UK: Clarendon Press, 1892.

CHAPTER THREE

Plato

So exceptional was Plato's genius that his philosophy of human nature and the world has influenced Western thought for more than two thousand years. Some philosophers estimate him to have been the most brilliant thinker who ever lived. Before him, the pre-Socratics had asked questions about the universe: What caused the world? Out of what substance is everything made? Is there anything permanent in our changing world? The Sophists who followed them were concerned with rhetoric, and Socrates had cared for the soul. In this chapter, we will see how Plato brought together all of the major issues of human thought into a complete system of philosophy.

Succeeding Socrates and followed himself by Aristotle, Plato literally shaped the mind of Western civilization. Perhaps the ultimate in praise came from Alfred North Whitehead, a twentieth-century philosopher, who said the entire European philosophical tradition consists of "a series of footnotes to Plato."

Plato's Mother, Perictione

An important figure in Plato's life was his mother, Perictione. From a prominent Athenian family, she was influential in aristocratic Athenian circles. A vigorous and loving woman, Perictione deeply influenced Plato's thinking on the character of men and women. Her philosophy on the "harmonious woman" demonstrates her thoughts on the role of women in Athenian society.

On Women

One must deem the harmonious woman to be full of wisdom and self-control; a soul must be exceedingly conscious of goodness to be just and courageous and wise, embellished with self-sufficiency and hating empty opinion. Worthwhile things come to a woman from these—for herself, her husband, her children, her household, perhaps even for a city. . . .

Having mastery over appetite and high feeling she will be righteous and harmonious; no lawless desires will impel her. She will preserve a loving disposition toward her husband and children and her entire household. . . .

But one must also train the body to natural measures concerning nourishment and clothing, baths and anointings, the arrangement of the hair, and ornaments of gold and precious stone. Women who eat and drink every costly thing, who dress extravagantly and wear the things that women wear, are ready for the sin of every vice both with respect to the marriage bed and the rest of wrongdoing. . . .

But let her not think that nobility of birth, and wealth, and coming from a great city altogether are necessities, nor the good opinion and friendship of eminent and kingly men. If these should be the case, it does not hurt. But, if not, wishing does not make them so. Even if these should be allotted to her, let her soul not pursue the grand and wonderful. Let her walk also apart from them. They harm more than they help, dragging one into misfortune. Treachery and envy and malice abide with them; such a woman would not be serene.

One must revere the gods in the confident hope of happiness, obeying both ancestral laws and institutions. After these, I say to honor and to revere one's parents, for they are and effect everything equally to the gods for their offspring.

. . . I think a woman is harmonious . . . if she becomes full of wisdom and self-control.[1]

Plato

Plato's Life

Plato (428 or 427 to 348 B.C.E.) was born in Athens when Socrates was approximately forty-two years old. Plato's family was one of the most aristocratic families in Greece. Through his mother's lineage, he was related to Solon, Athen's most famous lawgiver. His father traced his genealogy to the kings of Athens and before them to the god Poseidon. Plato's given name was Aristocles, but in his youth he earned the nickname *Plato,* meaning "broad" or "wide." Some stories refer to his wide forehead and wide shoulders, others to his overall build.

As a young man, Plato excelled in poetry, mathematics, music, and wrestling. When he was a child, his father died. His mother married Pyrilampes, who helped design Athenian democracy. When Plato was born, Athens was fighting Sparta in the Peloponnesian Wars, which lasted twenty years. In 404 B.C.E., when Athens surrendered to Sparta, a group of oligarchs known as the Thirty overthrew democracy and ruled Athens for three years. Some members of Plato's family were part of this group. However, the Thirty were unable to restore aristocratic rule, and Athens reinstated democracy in 403 B.C.E. Although the Thirty had themselves threatened Socrates' life but not carried out their threat, politicians in the new democracy were the ones who actually condemned Socrates to death. Plato was twenty-eight.

Plato followed Socrates' entire trial. That Athens could sentence its most noble citizen to death made such a deep impression on him that it shaped the entire course of his philosophic career. For Plato, the death of his mentor and friend was an example of the conflict that can exist between the *ideal* society and society as it actually is. Having experienced the leadership of both aristocracy and democracy, Plato was well aware of the shortcomings of both forms of government: The former, based on bloodlines, gave too much power to selfish individuals; the latter, rule by "the many," collapsed into mediocrity and corruption. Plato himself had once toyed with entering political life, but he had decided against it.

After Socrates' death, Plato left Athens. For twelve years, he studied Pythagorean mathematics and the esoteric (secret) mysteries of human nature. He may have studied geometry with Euclides. He also went to the island of Sicily as advisor to the ruler of Syracuse. During his stay in that kingdom, enemies kidnapped Plato. His friends offered to pay for his freedom, but his captors eventually freed him without ransom. Returning to Athens, Plato set up a school of philosophy, mathematics, and gymnastics in a grove near the city. He named it after the legendary Greek hero Academus, and the school became known as the Academy. We still speak of "academic subjects" such as philosophy, science, and mathematics. Plato's university lasted for nine hundred years until Justinian closed it in 529 C.E.★

Socrates' life and teaching strongly influenced Plato's philosophy. For both men, philosophy was not only analysis and theory, but also a way of life. Both believed that philosophy could help us understand how we fit into the scheme of the universe.

The Socratic Method

In Plato's hands, Socrates' dialectic method became an important tool for discovering knowledge. Like Socrates, he believed that knowledge lies hidden within the soul. By using the dialectic, he could draw the truth out of a person rather than "fill an empty vessel." Through a series of questions, the conversa-

---

★Of the common era; equivalent to A.D. (*anno Domini*, "in the year of the Lord").

tion climbs closer to the truth. The conversation leads the mind beyond the mutable changing physical world to immutable universal principles. Plato argued that we could not find the truth about human nature or the world by studying the world. True knowledge of the world and humankind can only be found in the eternal world of timeless Ideas, or what he called *Forms*.

Forms are "reality" because they are eternal and immutable. All things in the physical world are symbols of these perfect Forms, but because they are symbols and mutable, the world is not the true reality. Through the dialectic, Plato wanted to draw our attention to what is eternally "true," eternally "beautiful," and eternally "good."

Pause for Thought   Most of education today focuses on the view that knowledge is not within the mind, as Socrates and Plato held, but placed there by external sources such as your parents, teachers, and peers. What do you think?

The Dialogues

Socrates wrote nothing, but Plato wrote more than twenty dialogues with Socrates as protagonist. In his early writings—*The Apology, Crito, Charmides, Laches, Euthyphro, Euthydemus, Cratylus, Protagoras,* and *Gorgias*—Plato concentrated on Socrates' view of ethics. In his middle dialogues—*The Meno, The Symposium, The Phaedo, The Republic,* and *The Phaedrus*—Plato presented a combination of his own and Socrates' theory of knowledge, metaphysics, and political philosophy. Plato's later dialogues—*Theaetetus, Parmenides, The Sophist, The Statesman, Philebus, Timaeus,* and *The Laws*—reveal his reflections on earlier ideas, the structure of the cosmos, and his deepening spiritual convictions.

Though Plato had probably written many of the dialogues before he founded the Academy at age forty, he continued to write and rewrite them and direct the Academy until he died at eighty.

The Forms

Plato believed that to make sense out of human nature and the physical world, we must discover the world of Forms. We usually think of a "form" as the shape of something—the "form" of a sculpture, for example. We fill out application forms. Psychologically, we may say, "an opinion formed in my mind." But for Plato, the word *Form* (note the capitalization) meant something entirely different.

For Plato, Forms are universal principles or eternal and perfect Ideas. Because they exist beyond time and space, we cannot see them with our five senses or even think of them as things that have content. Existing in the realm of the timeless and eternal, Forms have no size, color, or weight. Here in the physical world, we can measure, weigh, and touch things. Because objects in the physical world are material, they will erode over time. But the Forms are immaterial and beyond time and space. That is why Plato said the unchanging Forms are ultimate *reality* and the ever-changing physical world is only *appearance*.

Take, for example, the Form horse. Horses look different. Some are Thoroughbreds, others Arabians, and still others Quarter Horses. They may be black, bay, chestnut, or gray, with a Roman nose or a dished face, but despite their many differences, horses share some universal quality that enables us to recognize them as horses. They have the eternal and immutable *Form Horseness* in common. Also, all humans also have something in common—our humanness. Plato called it the *Form Humankind*. The same is true of trees and beds and tables. And we don't know how many Forms there are in all.

Unlike the pre-Socratics, especially the Atomists, the underlying universal principle or Form is not a basic material substance. For Plato, eternal and immutable Forms are spiritual and abstract in their nature. Plato's point was that Democritus's atoms did not fashion themselves into a horse or a dog or a rabbit by themselves. Without the Forms as patterns, atoms might randomly fashion themselves into hordogs, rabihors, or dogbits. For Plato, there is no random chance. All things in the world are patterned after *unchanging*, eternal models—Forms.

Because the rational part of the human soul knows the Forms, we can have true knowledge of what is eternal. Of sense appearances, however, we can only have opinions. Opinions change, but knowledge is changeless. Thus, for Plato, when we grasp the difference between appearance and reality, we can begin to realize the relationship of human nature to the universe. We can glimpse the meaning of our existence. However, when we see a horse, a dog, or a tree, we too often rest satisfied with our sensory experience and do not shift our sights to their origin.

Pause for Thought   Do you agree with Plato that Forms are the patterns behind the various species we come across in nature? If not, what makes all horses horses, all trees trees, and all humans human?

Creation

To understand Plato's worldview, we begin with his idea of creation. In his dialogue *Timaeus*, Plato compared human nature to the order of the universe. In mythical form, he referred to human beings as microcosms of the universal macrocosm. Everything within the universe is within each of us—Earth, air, fire, water, psyche, mind, and spirit.

The supreme reality is the *Source of the world* (also called the *Godhead*)—which also transcends the world. The source is absolute perfection and impersonal (nonbeing). As nonbeing, the source of the world does not create the world. The being who creates is the *Demiurge* (also called the *Divine Craftsman*). The Demiurge creates the world by emulating the source:

> [Timaeus] . . . Now everything that becomes or is created must of necessity be created by some cause, for without a cause nothing can be created. The work of the creator, whenever he looks to the unchangeable and fashions the form and nature of his work after an unchangeable pattern, must necessarily be made fair and perfect, but when he looks to the created only and uses a created pattern, it is not fair or perfect. . . .
>
> Let me tell you then why the creator made this world of generation. He was good, and the good can never have any jealousy of anything. And being free from jealousy, he desired that all things should be as like himself as they could be. This is in the truest sense the origin of creation and of the world, as we shall do well in believing on the testimony of wise men. God desired that all things should be good and nothing bad, so far as this was attainable. Wherefore also finding the whole visible sphere not at rest, but moving in an irregular and disorderly fashion, out of disorder he brought order, considering that this was in every way better than the other. Now the deeds of the best could never be or has been other than the fairest, and the creator, reflecting on the things which are by nature visible, found that no unintelligent creature taken as a whole could ever be fairer than the intelligent taken as a whole, and again that intelligence could not be present in anything which was devoid of soul. For which reason, when he was framing the universe, he put intelligence in soul, and soul in body, that he might be the creator of a work which was by nature fairest and best. On this wise, using the language of probability, we may say that the world came into being—a living creature truly endowed with soul and intelligence by the providence of God.[2]

The Demiurge formed the world in the image of the perfect patterns—the Forms. Celestial (or lesser) gods, humans, animals, plants, mountains, and seas all reflect the infinite perfection in various degrees.

Unlike most Judeo-Christian theologians, who posit a God who creates the universe from nothing, the Demiurge creates by giving the existing chaos structure and order. Thus, Plato called the creator the *Divine Craftsman*. The goal of the Demiurge is to fashion the unformed materials as closely as possible to their perfection. However, some materials, depending on their degree of imperfection, are more receptive to the divine intelligence than others. Inherent in this imperfection is ignorance, which is evil; thus, evil exists in a world created by a good god. Like the Judeo-Christian god, Plato's Demiurge is good. Unlike the Judeo-Christian god, the Demiurge is not all-powerful, because the Divine Craftsman must work with existing materials.

Materials of the heavenly, unchanging, and therefore more real realm can receive more intelligence than materials in the changing and less real physical realm. With the heavenly materials, the Demiurge fashions the celestial gods, the stars, and the planets, and it structures the orderly movements of the world soul. Then the Demiurge constructs the immortal (rational) part of the human soul with the same ingredients that make up the world soul, though they are somewhat diluted. Next, the celestial gods design the mortal (irrational) parts of the human soul and the body they inhabit.

Though the materials of the human body and the physical world are imperfect, we also have the immortal rational soul fashioned in the image of Divine Perfection:

> . . . he who has been earnest in the love of knowledge of true wisdom, and has exercised his intellect more than any other part of him, must have thoughts immortal and divine, if he attain truth, and in so far as human nature is capable of sharing in immortality, he must altogether be immortal, and since he is ever cherishing the divine power and has the divinity within him in perfect order, he will be singularly happy.[3]

Pause for Thought   Is Plato saying that we humans, having both spiritual and material qualities, are a bridge between the ever-changing physical world and the *never*-changing spiritual world—between animal and god? If so, would this explain some of our moral conflicts?

The Soul

Like the world soul, the rational part of the human soul has divine intelligence and can know the Forms. In his dialogue *The Republic*, Plato described the soul as having three parts: the *reason* (rational), the *spirited* (nonrational), and the *appetites* (irrational). He came to this conclusion from analyzing the three kinds of activity going on in human beings. First is the motivation for goodness and truth: the *reason*. Second is the drive toward action: the *spirited* (will). Third is the desire for pleasures of the body: the *appetites*. The will is neutral and inclined to follow reason, but it can be pulled in either direction.

In *The Phaedrus*, Plato compared the human condition to the plight of a charioteer (*reason*) driving two horses. The good horse (*spirited*) has no need of the whip but is guided by word and admonition. The other horse is headstrong (*appetites*) and so full of insolence and pride that it pays little attention to the

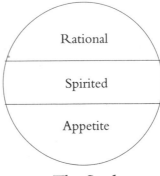

The Soul

whip. Even if the charioteer has a clear vision of where to go and the good horse is on course, the other horse—the unruly horse—often "plunges and runs away," causing all kinds of trouble to the good horse and the charioteer.

The image of horses moving in different directions, one of them disobeying the charioteer, shows the breakdown of the soul's harmony. The charioteer (*reason*) holds the reins and has the job of controlling the horses (*spirited* and *appetite*). The charioteer needs the two horses to get anywhere, so these three must work together. The reason seeks the true goal of human life by seeing things according to their true nature (Forms). But the appetites and the spirited relish worldly pleasures and can fool the reason into believing sensuous pleasures will bring happiness.

Pause for Thought

Imagine you are studying for an exam. A friend calls to ask you to join the group for pizza and beer. The desire part of your soul says, "Yes!" The rational part of your soul says, "I really should study." What do you do?

Plato said the reason must learn to cut through fleeting desires and remember the real truth it knew in its preexistence. It needs to remember that everything in the sensory world is imperfect and there is no lasting truth or happiness in it. Once it remembers the beauty of the eternal Forms, it will direct the spirited and the appetites to the realm of truth, beauty, and goodness. Then the person will "know thyself" and be happy. Unhappiness results when we get caught believing the sensuous world is real.

Pause for Thought

Sensuous pleasures are short-lived. We can eat only so much ice cream without getting a stomachache. Worldly success is also short-lived.

The rich and famous can't take their money and fame with them when they die. Do you think Plato has a point—that knowing the Forms is all that can bring us lasting happiness?

Immortality of the Soul

In *Phaedo*, Plato had Socrates give arguments for the immortality of the soul. First is the argument from opposites. With Anaximander, Socrates argued that opposites generate opposites: Life generates death, and death proceeds to another life.

> *Socrates:* To return then to my distinction of natures which are not opposed, and yet do not admit opposites—as, in the instance . . . three, although not opposed to the even, does not any the more admit of the even, but always brings the opposite into play on the other side; or as two does not receive the odd, or fire the cold—from these examples . . . perhaps you may be able to arrive at the general conclusion, that not only opposites will not receive opposites, but also that nothing which brings the opposite will admit the opposite of that which it brings, in that to which it is brought. . . . Tell me, then, what is that of which the inherence will render the body alive?
> *Cebes:* The soul.
> *Socrates:* And is this always the case?
> *Cebes:* Yes, he said, of course.
> *Socrates:* Then whatever the soul possesses, to that she comes bearing life?
> *Cebes:* Yes, certainly.
> *Socrates:* And is there any opposite to life?
> *Cebes:* There is, he said.
> *Socrates:* And what is that?
> *Cebes:* Death.
> *Socrates:* Then the soul, as has been acknowledged, will never receive the opposite of what she brings.
> *Cebes:* Impossible.
> *Socrates:* And now, what did we just now call that principle which repels the even?
> *Cebes:* The odd.
> *Socrates:* And that principle which repels the musical or the just?
> *Cebes:* The unmusical and the unjust.
> *Socrates:* And what do we call that principle which admit of death?
> *Cebes:* The immortal.
> *Socrates:* And does the soul admit of death?
> *Cebes:* No.
> *Socrates:* Then the soul is immortal?
> *Cebes:* Yes.
> *Socrates:* And may we say that this has been proven?
> *Cebes:* Yes, abundantly proven, Socrates.[4]

Later in *Phaedo*, Plato argued that the soul exists before it enters the body and will continue to exist after the body dies. The body is bound to the physical world and subject to the same fate as everything else in the world—birth and death. It is like an outfit of clothes. Just as we change clothes, we change bodies and continue learning our lessons. But the soul is immortal. Because the rational soul is not physical, it can survey the world of Forms. Each soul will pass through many lifetimes. While in a body, the soul may seek truth or it may succumb to sensuous pleasure. Divine intelligence governs the cycle of rebirths, and each soul is reborn according to what it deserves.

In Book X of his dialogue *The Republic*, Plato wrote, "It was indeed . . . a sight worth seeing, how the souls severally chose their lives—a sight to move pity and laughter and astonishment; for the choice was mostly governed by the habits of their former life." Based on its past thoughts and actions, each soul chooses its future character and destiny. Therefore, counsels Plato, we should always follow the "heavenly way" and live just and virtuous lives.

Pause for Thought   If Plato is correct and we must return to earth to learn lessons, then what lessons do *you* need to learn? What type of life would you choose next if you could choose right now?

Evil

According to Plato, humans are dual creatures, and the cause of evil is in the soul's relationship to the body. In its preexistence, the rational part of the soul has a clear vision of the Forms. It has knowledge of the eternal good, which the sense organs cannot experience. The imperfect, irrational part of the soul is ignorant, and both Plato and Socrates equate ignorance with evil. Therefore, when the celestial gods create the spirited and appetite parts of the soul out of imperfect materials, the possibility of evil comes into existence.

While in its preexistent state, the soul will begin to waver between seeing the truth and the desire of the appetites to acquire a physical body. When this occurs, the spirited part obeys the appetites beckoned by the "downward pull" of matter; the reason follows. The soul then begins its descent into a physical body. However, as soon as the soul wakes up in a human body, it forgets the perfect Forms. Ignorance (evil) is the product of this forgetfulness.

Pause for Thought   Do television advertisers have a vested interest in keeping us chained to the desire soul? Examine their ads. Can you find any that encourage you to concentrate on the goals of the rational soul?

Eventually, said Plato, in some lifetime along the soul's pilgrimage, something starts to happen. As we discover the various objects in the natural world, a vague recollection stirs in the soul. Then, after several lifetimes, the sight of horses (dogs, rabbits, humans, etc.) awakens in us a faint recollection of the perfect "horseness" that the soul once saw in the world of Forms. This awakening stirs the soul with a yearning to return to its true realm. Plato called this yearning—*eros* (love). The soul experiences a "longing to return to its true origin." From now on, we experience the body and the sensuous world as imperfect—even insignificant.

As the rational soul gains its rightful status, the spirited and the appetites aspire to follow. The rational soul yearns to fly home on the wings of love to the world of ideas. And now the whole soul is willing to free itself from the chains of the body.

Moral Philosophy

Plato argued that people are intrinsically good. But when we make judgments with the irrational part of the soul, we land in moral conflict. He agreed with Socrates that we never purposefully choose an evil act, for we don't want to harm ourselves. We may tell a "white lie" or gossip, and even admit these acts are wrong, but we always believe we will somehow benefit from them. However, before we can become moral, we must recognize that we are acting in ignorance (evil).

Morality means waking the reason to its true purpose. In the virtuous soul, reason controls the appetites and directs the will away from sensuous pleasures and toward eternal Ideas. When the appetites and the will dominate, we act irrationally out of ignorance, and sometimes we do evil acts.

Theory of Knowledge

Moral progress begins with the knowledge we gain as we climb beyond the world of ignorance and toward eternal Forms. When the reason begins to "recollect" these perfect Ideas, it experiences an "internal source of awakening," according to Plato. The first way to wake up is through our own insights into ourselves and the Forms. The second way of waking from ignorance is with the help of an external agent. In his Allegory of the Cave (Book VII of *The Republic*), Plato told a dramatic story that illustrates the climb the soul makes from ignorance to knowledge. He had Socrates relate the parable in a conversation with Glaucon.

Allegory of the Cave

Imagine the condition of men living in a [cavernous underground chamber] with an entrance open to the light and a long passage all down the cave. Here they have been from childhood, chained by the leg and also by the neck, so that they cannot move and can see only what is in front of them, because the chains will not let them turn their heads. At some distance higher up is the light of a fire burning behind them; and between the prisoners and the fire is a track with a parapet built along it, like the screen at a puppet-show, which hides the performers while they show their puppets over the top.

I see, said he.

Now behind this parapet imagine persons carrying along various artificial objects, including figures of men and animals in wood or stone or other materials, which project above the parapet. Naturally, some of these persons will be talking, others silent.

It is a strange picture, he said, and a strange sort of prisoners.

Like ourselves, I replied; for in the first place prisoners so confined would have seen nothing of themselves or of one another, except the shadows thrown by the fire-light on the wall of the Cave facing them, would they?

Not if all their lives they had been prevented from moving their heads.

And they would have seen as little of the objects carried past.

Of course.

Now, if they could talk to one another, would they not suppose that their words referred only to those passing shadows which they saw?

Necessarily.

And suppose their prison had an echo from the wall facing them? When one of the people crossing behind them spoke, they could only suppose that the sound came from the shadow passing before their eyes.

No doubt.

In every way, then, such prisoners would recognize as reality nothing but the shadows of those artificial objects.

Inevitably.

Now consider what would happen if their release from the chains and the healing of their unwisdom would come about in this way. *Suppose one of them is set free and forced* suddenly to stand up, turn his head, and walk with eyes lifted to the light; all these movements would be painful, and he would be too dazzled to make out the objects whose shadows he had been used to see. What do you think he would say, *if someone told him* that what he had formerly seen was meaningless illusion, but now, being somewhat nearer to reality and turned towards more real objects, he was getting a truer view? Suppose further that he were shown the various objects being carried by and were made to say, in reply to questions, what each of them was. Would he not be perplexed and believe the objects now shown him to be not so real as what he formerly saw?

Yes, not nearly so real.

And *if he were forced* to look at the fire-light itself, would not his eyes ache, so that he would try to escape and turn back to the things which he could see distinctly, convinced that they really were clearer than these other objects now being shown to him?

Yes.

And *suppose someone were to drag him away forcibly* up the steep and rugged ascent and *not let him go until he had hauled him out into the sunlight*, would he not suffer pain and vexation at such treatment, and, when he had come out into the light, find his eyes so full of its radiance that he could not see a single one of the things that he was now told were real?

Certainly he would not see them all at once.

He would need, then, to grow accustomed before he could see things in that upper world. At first it would be easiest to make out shadows, and then the images of men and things reflected in water, and later on the things themselves. After that, it would be easier to watch the heavenly bodies and the sky itself by night, looking at the light of the moon and stars rather than the Sun and the Sun's light in the day-time.

Yes, surely.

Last of all, he would be able to look at the Sun and contemplate its nature, not as it appears when reflected in water or any alien medium, but as it is in itself in its own domain.

No doubt.

And now he would begin to draw the conclusion that it is the Sun that produces the seasons and the course of the year and controls everything in the visible world, and moreover is in a way the cause of all that he and his companions used to see.

Clearly he would come at last to that conclusion.

Then if he called to mind his fellow prisoners and what passed for wisdom in his former dwelling-place, he would surely think himself happy in the change and be sorry for them. They may have had a practice of honouring and commending one another, with prizes for the man who had the keenest eye for the passing shadows and the best memory for the order in which they followed or accompanied one another, so that he could make a good guess as to which was going to come next. Would our released prisoner be likely to covet those prizes or to envy the men exalted to honour and power in the Cave? Would he not feel like Homer's Achilles, that he would far sooner "be on earth as a hired servant in the house of a landless man" [Here Plato is comparing the Cave to the land of the dead under the earth] or endure anything rather than go back to his old beliefs and the outside world "on earth" and live in the old way?

Yes, he would prefer any fate to such a life.

Now imagine what would happen if he went down again to take his former seat in the Cave. Coming suddenly out of the sunlight, his eyes would be filled with darkness. He might be required once more to deliver his opinion on those shadows, in competition with the prisoners who had never been released, while his eyesight was still dim and unsteady; and it might take some time to become used to the darkness. They would laugh at him and say that he had gone up only to come back with his sight ruined; it was worth no one's while even to attempt the ascent. If they could lay hands on the man who was trying to set them free and lead them up, they would kill him.

Yes, they would.[5]

The Allegory of the Cave illustrates the road we must take from shadowy images to the true Ideas (Forms) behind all natural phenomena. All things in the physical world are merely shadows of the eternal Forms or Ideas. Through ignorance, people inside the cave are content to live among the shadows. They give little or no thought to what is casting the shadows. Plato did not mean the phenomenal world is nothing but dark, drab shadows. He meant that it is dark and drab *in comparison* with the clarity of Ideas. As the prisoner in the cave had to turn completely around to see the light, the entire soul must turn away from believing the phenomenal world of appearance is real. Once outside the cave, the former prisoner delights in his newfound freedom. But instead of basking in his joy, he thinks of all the others who are still down in the cave. He goes back. Inside the cave again, he tries to convince the prisoners that the "shadows on the wall" are mere flickerings of reality, but they don't believe him. In fact, said Plato, if he tries to set them free, they will kill him.

Even the "noblest natures," said Plato, don't always want to look away from their conventional ideas. Therefore, the liberated person may have to "bring [external] compulsion to bear" on the prisoners to ascend from darkness.Pause for Thought

---

Pause for Thought   Plato thought the prisoners in the cave would try to kill the person who dares to show them the ignorance of their ways. Can you think of leaders throughout history who have lost their lives for that reason?

The Divided Line

In The Allegory of the Cave, Plato related the soul's journey from ignorance to knowledge in story form. In his simile *The Divided Line* (Book VI of *The Republic*), he used a more systematic method to explain the stages of the mind's journey.

To reach knowledge the mind moves through four stages of development: *imaging, belief, thinking,* and *rational intuition.* At each stage, there is a parallel between the kind of object the mind sees and the kind of thought that this object stimulates as shown in the table on the next page.

The continuous vertical line from x to y implies that some degree of awareness exists at every stage, from the lowest to the highest. The horizontal dividing line separates the *physical world* from the *world of Ideas.* Each realm has four parts. We can think of the vertical line as beginning in the "cave" (ignorance) at x and moving up to the "sun" (Form of the Good) at y. Each stage represents a different way of looking at the world, and each corresponds to one of the three parts of our soul. Starting at the lowest level of knowledge, at x, we experience the most limited view of the world.

	Objects	*y*	States of Mind	
Reality Intelligible World	The Good [Forms]		Intelligence (Reason and Intuition)	(Speculative, Nonlinear) **Knowledge**
	Mathematical Objects		Thinking	(Discursive, Linear)
Appearance Physical World	Physical Objects		Belief	**Opinion**
	Images		Imaging	

x

The Divided Line

Imaging Stage   At the *imaging* stage, *x*—the mind—meets impressions that contain the least amount of reality. As the prisoners in the cave believe the shadows are real, those who are at the imaging stage believe most of what they hear and see on television is true. They have not learned to think for themselves. Reality for them is the "shadow" world of persuasion, and so they believe that whatever other people tell them is true.

Say, for example, an artist paints a portrait of Socrates. The portrait is three times removed from true reality: (1) the *Form* Humankind, (2) Socrates as a living part of the *Form* Humankind, and (3) the *image* of Socrates painted on canvas. Although the portrait may resemble Socrates, it cannot tell us much about his interests, his character, or his intelligence. The portrait is only a likely resemblance of his physical person; and it is not the real Socrates. People who think of Socrates exactly as they see him in the painting are on the imaging stage.

Today, television advertisers address the public at the imaging stage. They want to convince "unthinking" people that a particular product will change their lives: Use Forever Young lotion for smooth, wrinkle-free skin. Join the action crowd—drink Sporting Life Beer. Increase your popularity by brushing with Bright and & White toothpaste. Eat Sugar Crunch cereal for a happy, healthy life. At the imaging stage, we stimulate the appetite and spirited parts of the soul to silence the rational.

Pause for Thought   Using the power of image persuasion, the news media widely influence public sentiment. Have you ever formed an opinion for or against a foreign leader without ever hearing him or her speak?

Like the painting, the media *do* present some degree of surface truth about the foreign leader—but not the whole truth. However, those people in the imagining stage accept what they hear as absolute truth. At this stage, any knowledge takes a distorted, shadowy form. A shadow is no more the truth than seeing a picture postcard of the Grand Canyon is equal to seeing it in person. The picture postcard will give you some information, but viewing the Grand Canyon for yourself raises you to the next level of knowledge.

Belief Stage   *Belief* is the stage beyond imaging. Plato used the word *believing* instead of *knowing with certainty* to describe the physical world. Common sense tells us the physical world is real. We can see it and touch it. We feel a strong sense of certainty when we actually see a physical object. Also, experiencing objects directly with the eye gives us more information than seeing pictures of them from a second source. Seeing is believing, we say, but for Plato it is only believing and not true knowledge.

Pause for Thought   What would Plato say about the state of knowledge of people who demand concrete proof: "Show me." "Prove it." Can you show the truth? Can you prove you have a soul?

Seeing physical objects firsthand tells us only what the object looks like on the outside. Meeting a person face-to-face reveals to us the person's physical appearance but relates little about character. Seeing the Grand Canyon gives us an inspired sense of its physical grandeur but no information about its age, its rock formations, or the river that runs through it. Belief, as imaging, is a matter of opinion, and not actual knowledge. If we explore the scientific evidence that explains the cause of the rock formations in the Grand Canyon, then we are moving from the *belief stage* to the *thinking stage*.

Thinking Stage   In advancing from *believing* to *thinking*, we proceed from the visible world of the senses to the invisible world of ideas. By *thinking*, we leave the world of opinion and enter the world of knowledge. Plato called scientists the bridge builders between the two worlds, because they view physical objects as symbols of reality (reality can be thought but not seen). Science forces us to think about principles and laws that tell us more than our senses do about physical objects.

Pause for Thought   Most of us believe we think all the time, but Plato would have said that what we call thinking is often imaging. Close your eyes and think of your mind as a giant computer. What crosses the screen—images or ideas?

When scientists look at a particular object such as a brain, they go beyond a particular specific brain and think about the brain *in general*. Science requires that we "let go" of our senses and rely instead on our minds. Plato also referred to the mathematician to illustrate this kind of activity. When mathematicians see the diagram of a triangle, they think about *the Triangle,* the principle common to all triangles. They distinguish between a particular visible triangle and the idea common to all triangles. When the geologist and the physicist look at the Grand Canyon, they will think in general terms about canyon formations, not about picture postcards of the Grand Canyon.

Thinking, said Plato, represents the power of the mind to extract from physical objects the common factor in all those objects. We think the Idea "human" whether we see short, tall, dark, light, young, or old people. Thinking gives us more knowledge than belief or imaging, but it too has limitations. Thinking deals with *that, how,* and *what,* but it still leaves the mind to ask *why* a certain truth is true. Thinking knows *that* 2 + 2 always = 4, but it doesn't know *why,* because thinking is linear: It proceeds through a step-by-step process. To view the world as it truly is, says Plato, we must go beyond thinking to the level of *reason* and *intuition*. At this stage we can discover the interconnectedness of everything.

Intelligence (Reason and Intuition)   At its highest level, the mind deals directly with the Forms, the highest and truest reality. Recall that Forms are changeless, eternal essences or patterns of which our world and everything in it are copies. For example, we make judgments such as "That flower is beautiful" and "That child is good." Such judgments suggest that a standard of beauty and a standard of goodness exist somewhere on which we base our judgments. The beautiful flower lives and dies: It's finite. The Form *Beauty* is eternal because it never dies. We cannot visualize the Forms, and they do not have content: The idea "good" is the principle behind a good action, but not the action itself. The good action is a copy of the Form *Good*. The world of Forms, then, is the true and undying source of knowledge.

Knowing the Forms

Plato presented three different ways to know the Forms. The first is *recollection*. Before uniting with the body, the rational soul knew the Forms. By disciplining ourselves through contemplation, we can recollect what our soul knew in its pre-existence. The second is Socrates' *dialectic method*. Through the power of internal or external conversation, we can awaken to the interconnectedness of everything. The third way to know the Forms is through *love*. Love can lead us from the beautiful object to the beautiful thought to the essence of Beauty itself.

Developing love, like cultivating intelligence, requires that the soul must climb step by step before soaring to the Form Beauty. In his dialogue *The Symposium*, Plato described the objects of love the soul meets on its journey to immortality.

Ladder of Love

The Symposium consists of a group of friends who are giving after-dinner speeches in praise of love. Each speaker reveals his personal stage of love starting at the lowest level of sensuous love and reaching to the highest realm of spiritual love. Whatever level it is on, the soul seeks to recognize its immortality through the objects of its affections.

Many of our myths about love have their origin in this dialogue. For example, Eryximachus the physician suggests that love is a chemical attraction. Aristophanes the playwright suggests the original human state was one of wholeness, but humans became so arrogant the gods cut them in half. Love, said Aristophanes, is our desire to find our missing half.

When Socrates' turn comes to speak of the highest type of love, he alludes to his teacher, Diotima. It was this woman, he said, who taught him about the philosophy of love. Diotima's teaching is an example of nonlinear discursive reasoning and intuition.

> [Diotima] Starting from individual beauties, the quest for the universal beauty must find him ever mounting the heavenly ladder, stepping from rung to rung—that is, from one to two, and from two to *every* lovely body, from bodily beauty to the beauty of institutions, from institutions to learning, and from learning in general to the special lore that pertains to nothing but the beautiful itself—until at last he comes to know what beauty is.
>
> And now Socrates, there bursts upon him that wondrous vision which is the very soul of the beauty he has toiled so long for. It is an everlasting loveliness which neither comes nor goes, which neither flowers nor fades, for such beauty is the same on every hand, the same then as now, here as there, this way as that way, the same to every worshiper as it is to every other.
>
> Nor will his vision of the beautiful take the form of a face, or of hands, or of anything that is of the flesh. It will be neither words, nor knowledge, nor a something that exists in something else, such as a living creature, or the earth, or the heavens, or anything that is—but subsisting of itself and by itself in an eternal oneness, while every lovely thing partakes of it in such sort that, however much the parts may wax and wane, it will be neither more nor less, but still the same inviolable whole.
>
> And if, my dear Socrates, Diotima went on, man's life is ever worth the living, it is when he has attained this vision of the very soul of beauty.

[Socrates] This, Phaedrus—this, gentlemen—was the doctrine of Diotima. I was convinced, and in that conviction I try to bring others to the same creed, and to convince them that, if we are to make this gift our own, Love will help our mortal nature more than all the world. . . .[6]

Pause for Thought   Do you agree with Socrates that love will help our mortal nature more than anything else will? Why or why not?

Political Philosophy

The Ideal State   In Plato's *The Republic*, we find the first examples of systematic political philosophy and utopian literature in Western history. Like many of his dialogues, *The Republic* begins with a group of friends gathering for conversation. During the discussion, a question arises about the meaning of "justice." They try to define the term but fail to capture its true meaning.

Undaunted, Socrates and his friends decide to find the meaning of justice by constructing the *Ideal State*. The Ideal State must be just. They decide to design the Ideal State after the three largest sections of the human body: the head, the chest, and the abdomen. Each part has a corresponding faculty of the soul. *Reason* belongs to the head, *spirited* belongs to the chest, and *desire* belongs to the abdomen. Each soul faculty also has an ideal or a "virtue." Reason aspires to *wisdom*, the spirited aspires to *courage,* and desire, when under control, exercises *temperance.* Only when the three parts of the body function in unity do we get a harmonious or virtuous individual.

As the tripartite human body has head, chest, and abdomen, the State has *rulers, auxiliaries,* and *laborers.* And as the *"just"* person is healthy mentally, emotionally, and physically, a *"just"* state has a similar health—that is, everyone knows his or her place in the larger overall picture.

Plato and Socrates suggested that a state comes into existence because none of us is self-sufficient and we all share many needs. Our many needs require many talents. No one person is capable of specializing in material needs, defense, and leadership. There must be a division of labor:

> More things will be produced and the work more easily and better done, when every man is set free from all other occupations to do, at the right time, the one thing for which he is naturally fitted.[7]

First, a society must have a group of people such as farmers, builders, and weavers who can produce food, shelter, and clothing. Plato called these people the "craftsmen." They belong to the *Artisan Class* and will supply the material needs of the state. This class is the largest class in the Ideal State. This class would be the only one needed if people were ever really satisfied with the bare necessities in life. However, people usually want more possessions, so they will want what others have.

> *Socrates*: Then we shall have to cut out a cantle of our neighbor's land if we are to have enough for pasture and plowing, and they in turn of ours if they too abandon themselves to the unlimited acquisition of wealth, disregarding the limit set by our necessary wants.
> *Glaucon*: Inevitably, Socrates.
> *Socrates*: We shall go to war as the next step, Glaucon. . . .[8]

To control the internal state of affairs, and if outside attacks should occur, an *Auxiliary* or *Warrior Class* is necessary. Plato chose both men and women to defend the state, and he called the members of this class "lower guardians."

Finally, the state needs rulers. Plato suggested a third class that he called the *Philosopher King* (and *Queen*) *Class*. These individuals will make laws and govern the state wisely.

Plato argued that individuals in the Ideal State have a particular function for their own happiness and for the good of the whole. Though all people have the opportunity to reach the philosopher king or queen level, they prefer the level of their natural aptitudes. Both men and women are included in each class.

> If we are to set women to the same tasks as men, we must teach them the same things. . . . There is no occupation concerned with the management of social affairs which belongs either to woman or to man, as such. Natural gifts are to be found here and there in both creatures alike; and every occupation is open to both, so far as their natures are concerned, though woman is for all purposes the weaker.[9]

The craftsmen, who supply the material goods of the state, are lovers of pleasure. For them, the appetite part of the soul predominates. The warriors are ruled by the spirited aspect of the soul, and they love honor and courage. The philosopher kings and queens, led by the rational part of the soul, strive for truth, beauty, and goodness. They want what is good for the State.

Pause for Thought   From what you have read of the Ideal State so far, which class would most people in our democracy choose?

Because each class corresponds to an aspect of the soul, each class has particular duties and limitations. The craftsmen, seeking worldly pleasures, are the only class to have money. They also marry, have family units, and own private property. However, they have no say about the laws of the land or its defense.

The warriors or lower guardians, who live in communities, but do not marry one person for life, handle money, or own individual private property. Plato argued that the guardians of the State should be free from the bonds of material possessions. The warriors would hold property and families in common. If the whole class became a single family, then its members would have fewer temptations to get money or possessions. Sexual relations would occur at special marriage festivals. To ensure that the most courageous and honorable warriors mate with each other at these festivals, the philosopher kings would have them draw lots. The gods, said Plato, will decide on the fairness of these drawings as distributed by the philosopher kings.

At birth, the warrior's children are given into the care of nurses so that all guardians will treat all children with respect and love. The children will regard all warriors as parents. Like the craftsmen, the warriors must obey the policies established by the philosopher kings and queens.

At the highest level of the Ideal State reign the philosopher kings (and queens). As wise rulers, they will exhibit kindness and justice to all. These leaders cannot own private property, and they will live a simple life supported by the state. Through a breeding program, philosopher kings and queens will bear children who hopefully will be the future rulers of the state.

Those who reach the philosopher king or queen level will have had at least thirty years of education. By age eighteen, they will have been trained in mathematics and the humanities.

Plato believed in stiff censorship, especially in literature, art, and music.

Our first business will be to supervise the making of fables and legends, rejecting all which are unsatisfactory; and we shall induce nurses and mothers to tell their children only those which we have approved, and to think more of molding their souls.[10]

There remains the question of . . . music. We [do] not want dirges and laments . . . that express sorrow.[11]

We must compel our poets, on pain of expulsion, to make their poetry the express image of noble character . . . and forbid [the craftsmen] to leave the stamp of baseness, license, meanness, unseemliness, on painting and sculpture, or building, or any other work of their hands. . . .[12]

Literature must promote the noble and good, and music must be wholesome rather than seductive. From ages eighteen to twenty, the students must have extensive physical and military training. From twenty to thirty, the most capable of them would take courses in advanced mathematics. At age thirty, a five-year course in dialectic and moral philosophy would begin. The next fifteen years these budding philosopher kings and queens gather practical experience through public service. Finally, at age fifty, the most able would reach the highest level of knowledge and be ready to govern the state.

Pause for Thought   Do you consider Plato's Ideal State *ideal*? If you had to live in the Ideal State, which class would you prefer?

The nature of those who live in each class relates to the goal and the virtue each person can naturally attain. The craftsmen, who represent the appetite part of the soul, are lovers of pleasure. Their virtue is temperance. The warriors, spirited individuals who defend the state, fulfill the virtue of courage. The philosopher kings and queens love truth and the Good, and thus they manifest wisdom.

Philosopher King and Queen Class (Rulers)

Duty	Rule
Soul	Rational
Goal	Knowledge
Virtue	Wisdom

Auxiliary Class (Warriors)

Duty	Defend the State
Soul	Spirited
Goal	Honor and glory
Virtue	Courage

Artisan Class (Craftsmen)

Duty	Supply material needs of state
Soul	Appetites
Goal	Pleasure
Virtue	Temperance

Pause for Thought   Though the craftsmen may drive the latest cars and wear designer clothes, Plato would say they are ignorant and the least free. Do you agree?

In a democracy, we have certain rights that are ours by virtue of living in the state. In Plato's aristocracy, it is a privilege to live in the state. Those who cannot follow the laws or contribute to the good of the state, lose that privilege.

Plato looks warily at democracy. He thought only philosophers should rule. In a democracy, people vote for the most popular candidate who promises the most to the desires of the appetites. And this, for Plato, is to enslave the higher parts of the soul to the baser. It was a democracy, after all, whose members put Socrates to death. Justice in the state reflects the just individual in whom the reason rules the spirited and the appetites.

On Women

During the time of Socrates and Plato, women in Athens were not considered citizens, and they could not participate in community affairs. Women had to marry to give their husbands legitimate heirs, but they could not choose *who* they would marry. Fathers arranged their daughters' marriages. Women remained uneducated so that they could better serve their husbands and raise families. Most women died at an early age, frequently during childbirth.

In this atmosphere, Plato was a true revolutionary. In *The Republic*, he had Socrates express the unconventional belief that a woman is inherently equal to and should engage in the same social functions as a male citizen—including those of the Philosopher King. However, if women carry the burden of domestic affairs, they cannot participate fully as a philosophers or warriors. This may partly explain why Plato called for the elimination of the nuclear family among the warrior and philosopher king groups and promoted family only in the artisan class alone. He also believed that to be born a woman was inferior to being born a man.

In the following excerpt, Socrates and Glaucon discuss the equality of women.

Socrates: . . . Are dogs divided into hes and shes, or do they both share equally in hunting and in keeping watch and in the other duties of gods? Or do we entrust to the males the entire and exclusive care of the flocks, while we leave the females at homes, under the idea that bearing and suckling their puppies is labour enough for them?

Glaucon: No, they share alike; the only difference between them is that the males are stronger and the females weaker.

Socrates: But can you use different animals for the same purpose, unless they are bred and fed in the same way?

Glaucon: You cannot.

Socrates: Then, if women are to have the same duties as men, they must have the same nurture and education?

Glaucon: Yes.

Socrates: . . . And if the male and female sex appear to differ in their fitness for any art or pursuit, we should say that such pursuit or art ought to be assigned to one or the other of them; but if the difference consists only in women bearing and men begetting children, this does not amount to a proof that a woman differs from a man in respect of the sort of education she should receive; and we shall therefore continue to maintain that our guardians and their wives ought to have the same pursuits.

Glaucon: Very true.

Socrates: . . . You agree then that men and women are to have a common way of life such as we have described—common education, common children; and they are to watch over the citizens in common whether abiding in the city or going out to war; they are to keep watch together, and to hunt together like dogs; and always and in all things, as far as they are able, women are to share with the men? And in so doing they will do what is best, and will not violate, but preserve the natural relation of the sexes.[13]

Summary

Like Socrates, Plato concentrated his philosophy on the well-being of the soul. Unlike the Sophists, Plato believed in the soul and its pre-existence, its survival beyond the death of the body, and its rebirth. When the soul is in a body, it may pursue universal truths in the philosophical life—or it may yield to the temptations of sense. Plato assured us that the rational soul has knowledge of eternal *Forms (Ideas)*. We can regain this knowledge, not with our senses, but through recollection of the rational mind that existed before birth and will exist after death.

In his Ideal State, as in his theory of the soul, Plato insisted that the highest and most developed part rule. Plato inferred that through the process of rebirth, we could all eventually reach the level of the Philosopher King. To do this we must come to know the Forms and the Form of the Good. We can achieve this goal using our intellect and the process of *recollection* as described in the Allegory of the Cave and The Divided Line. We also can achieve knowledge through love as described in *The Symposium*. Finally, Plato advocated a divine creation based on love and the hope there would be as many good things as possible.

Connections

As we shall see in the next chapter, Plato deeply influenced Aristotle, who was a student at the Academy during Plato's later period. Aristotle praised Plato as a great thinker and moral man, yet eventually he departed from some of Plato's theories. For example, Plato said true reality abided in the Forms (Ideas) that are in the intelligible realm beyond time and space. Aristotle, on the other hand, while accepting the Forms, said they exist *in objects in time and space*. Aristotle oriented his thoughts in the realm of *becoming* (change), whereas Plato concentrated on the realm of *Being* (permanence). We will see Plato's influence on Aristotle and all of Western philosophy as we continue to study the great masters of Western thought.

Study Questions

1. What is the goal of the Demiurge in Plato's theory of creation?

2. How can evil exist in a world created by a good God?

3. What are Forms? How do they differ from the physical world?

4. What are the three parts of the soul? What are their functions? How are they related?

5. Give one of Plato's arguments for the Soul's immortality.

6. What is the soul's true purpose?

7. In your own words, explain the Allegory of the Cave and give its meaning.

8. Explain which aspect of the soul relates to each stage of the Allegory of the Cave.

9. What four stages of development does the mind go through to reach knowledge?

10. What is the difference between opinion and knowledge?

11. What are the objects of opinion and the objects of knowledge?

12. What part of the soul corresponds to each level on the Divided Line?

13. Why is a portrait of Socrates three times removed from reality?

14. How do we know the Forms?

15. Explain the Ladder of Love.

16. Compare the stages in the Ladder of Love to the stages in the Divided Line.

17. What is the relationship of each part of the soul to each step on the Ladder of Love?

18. What is happiness in the Ideal State?

19. Why do philosopher kings rule? What knowledge do they have that the craftsmen and the warriors lack?

20. Is Plato's concept of individual happiness different from the idea of happiness in today's world? Discuss.

21. Do you think Plato's views on women are radical even today?

Notes

1. Perictione, *On the Harmony of Women, Fragment 1* (trans. by Vicki Lynn Harper), pp. 32–34 in *A History of Women Philosophers,* Vol. 1, 600 B.C.–500 A.D., ed. by Mary Ellen Waithe. Dordrecht, Netherlands: Kluwer Academic Publishers, 1992.

2. Plato, "Timaeus," 28b, 29e, 30 b–c (trans. by Benjamin Gad), pp. 1161–1162 in *The Collected Dialogues of Plato,* ed. by Edith Hamilton and Huntington Cairns. New York: Bollinger Foundation, Random House, 1963. Copyright © 1989 by Princeton University Press. Reprinted by permission of Princeton University Press.

3. Ibid., 90 c, p. 1209.

4. The form of the dialogue, but not the content, has been modified from Plato, "Phaedo" (trans. by Benjamin Gad), pp. 173–174 in *The Works of Plato,* ed. by Irwin Edman. New York: Random House, 1928.

5. Plato, *The Republic,* Bk VII. 514a–517 (trans. by F. M. Cornford), pp. 227–231 in *The Republic of Plato.* New York: Oxford University Press, 1974.

6. Plato, *The Symposium,* 210e– 212c (trans. by Michael Joyce), pp. 556–563 in *The Collected Dialogues of Plato,* op cit.

7. Plato, *The Republic,* Bk II, 373 (trans. by F. M. Cornford), p. 57 in *The Republic of Plato.*

8. Plato, *The Republic* (trans. by Paul Shorey), in *Plato: The Republic,* Bk II, 373, ed. by Edith Hamilton and Huntington Cairns.

9. Plato, *The Republic,* Bk V, 455 (trans. by F. M. Cornford), *The Republic of Plato,* p. 153.

10. Ibid., Bk II, 377, p. 69.

11. Ibid., Bk III, 399, p. 86.

12. Ibid., Bk III, 401, p. 90.

13. Plato, *The Republic,* in *The Dialogues of Plato* (trans. by Benjamin Jowett), in *The Dialogues of Plato,* Vol. 3, B.5, 3rd. ed. Oxford, UK: Clarendon Press, 1892.

CHAPTER FOUR

Aristotle

So monumental was Aristotle's influence that for hundreds of years he was known simply as *The Philosopher*. Today's philosophers consider him the most gifted of Plato's students, and some regard him as the greatest philosopher who ever lived. To this day we detect his influence in scientific and philosophical systems throughout the West. As a naturalist, Aristotle emphasized the importance of nature, believing that we must understand natural facts before we can begin to theorize.

Aristotle's works appear under seven headings: *The Organum*, six treatises on logic; *Rhetoric and Poetics*; *Physics*, his work on natural science; *De Anima* (on the soul); *Metaphysics*; *Nicomachean Ethics* and *Eudemian Ethics*; and *Politics*.

In this chapter we will see that Aristotle's aim was identical to Plato's. He wanted to discover what is real. Many of the pre-Socratics had tried to find reality in the material universe: water, air, the boundless, seeds, and atoms. Both Plato and Aristotle thought the materialists had given inadequate accounts of nature and of human beings as moral and spiritual creatures. Neither morals, they said, nor the spirit are material. Plato found reality in an immaterial world of Forms and considered the world of our sense perception as an "appearance" of reality, not reality itself. Aristotle was bothered by this explanation. He wanted to develop a theory of reality in which both values and sense objects could be understood as real. Studying Aristotle will open our minds to one of the greatest geniuses of the Western world.

Aristotle's Life

Aristotle (384–322 B.C.E.) was born in Stagira in Thrace. His mother was from a family of physicians, and his father was attending physician to the king of Macedonia. From his father, Aristotle probably developed his strong interest in biology and science. His parents sent this gifted youth to Plato's Academy when he was seventeen. Plato was sixty-one. Aristotle remained at the Academy twenty years as both student and lecturer. Among Academy members Aristotle earned the reputation of being the "mind" of the school. Plato commented that his Academy consisted of the *body* of his students and the *mind* of Aristotle.

Plato's exemplary character and profound thinking ability deeply influenced Aristotle. Though Aristotle eventually formulated his own philosophical position, his philosophical differences never interfered with his admiration of Plato. At the elder man's death, he praised him as the one "who showed in his life and teachings how to be happy and good at the same time." Plato and Aristotle differed on the theory of Forms and on ethics, but they both sought answers to the same two questions: "What is real?" and "What is the good life?"

After Plato's death, the new head of the Academy emphasized mathematics above all other disciplines. Aristotle considered this too extreme, so he left the Academy to stay with his friend Hermeia near Troy. For the next three years, he wrote, taught, and carried on research. He also married Hermeias's niece, who died giving birth to their daughter. After that, Aristotle met Herpyllis with whom he had a long and happy relationship. Aristotle dedicated his *Nicomachean Ethics* to their son, Nicomachus. In approximately 343 B.C.E., King Philip of Macedonia asked Aristotle to tutor Alexander, Philip's thirteen-year-old son, who was to rule the world as Alexander the Great. Aristotle and Alexander became friends, but they had disagreements about the best forms of government. Aristotle believed the largest government organization should be the city-state, while Alexander envisioned a world empire. Aristotle believed Greeks were superior to other races, which he considered barbarian, whereas Alexander considered all races important and wanted to integrate them. Despite their political differences, the two men remained friends. Over the years Alexander had his soldiers collect and send to Aristotle samples of the rare flora and fauna they discovered in their expeditions.

When Alexander ascended the throne of Macedonia, Aristotle returned to Athens and founded his own school. He called it the *Lyceum*, after the god Lycian Apollo. The school became known as the *Peripatetic School* of philosophers (*peripatetic* means to walk about). Aristotle lectured and discussed philosophical issues with his students as they strolled under the tree-covered walks. The hundreds of maps, manuscripts, and specimens he collected helped form the first significant library in the West. He not only originated logic, but also composed most of his own works on an impressive range of subjects: physics, biology, ethics, meteorology, metaphysics, political science, and poetics.

For twelve years Aristotle directed the Lyceum. But in 323 B.C.E., when Alexander the Great died, a wave of anti-Macedonian feeling arose. Because of Aristotle's close connections with Alexander and Macedonia, Athens openly expressed its hostility toward him. Recalling Socrates' fate, Aristotle left the city and the Lyceum "least the Athenians should sin twice against philosophy." He fled to Chalcis on the island of Euboea, where he died of a stomach ailment the following year at age 62.

In his will, Aristotle provided for his family and friends and generously gave many of his slaves their freedom.

Metaphysics

Aristotle referred to his metaphysical writings as the *First Philosophy*, which deals with principles and analyzes the nature of reality. The term *metaphysics* means "beyond physics." Aristotle's First Philosophy takes us beyond the physical world of science and into the abstract world of theory. It asks such questions as "What is it to be?" Thus, metaphysics takes us into the realm of the transcendental, or the world beyond the senses—that is, the spiritual universe. Describing metaphysics, Aristotle said:

> If there is no other substance apart from those that have come together by nature, natural science will be the first science. But if there is a substance that is immovable, the science that studies it is prior to natural science and is the first philosophy. . . . It is the business of this science to study being qua being, and to find out what it is and what are its attributes qua being.[1]

Form and Matter

Like Plato and the philosophers before him, Aristotle wanted to find out what is real. The Milesians and other pre-Socratic philosophers had searched for reality in the material universe. They defined the substance (essence) of matter variously as water, air, the boundless, fire, and atoms. Like the philosophers before him, Plato wanted to find the eternal and immutable in the midst of all change. He found Forms, the perfect ideas that were more real than the sensory world. For Plato, all human beings are copies of the perfect Form Human. The Form Chicken came before both the physical chicken and the egg.

As a scientist, Aristotle found these answers difficult to accept. He agreed with Plato that humans in the physical world live and die and are therefore mortal. He also agreed that the actual form of the human is eternal and immutable. But the "Form" Human, he said, was simply an idea that we discover after seeing a certain number of people. The idea or Form Human has no independent existence of its own, only those characteristics that are common to all humans. Today we define the concept as the human *species*. For Aristotle, the Form

Human cannot exist independently of the individual person. The Form is in the physical person, because the Form contains human characteristics.

Aristotle would disagree with Plato that the Form Chicken came before the chicken. What Aristotle called its Form is present in every chicken as the chicken's class of characteristics. One characteristic is that the chicken lays eggs. The real chicken and the Form Chicken are as inseparable as body and soul. The chicken appeared when the Form Chicken and matter (that is, *substance*) came together. We cannot have an idea of chicken until we first see the chicken. *Nothing exists in consciousness that we do not first experience with the senses.* For Aristotle, there are no innate ideas. We cannot recollect the Forms in the realm of reality, because "forms" only exist in objects here on Earth.

Pause for Thought   Plato said knowledge of the Forms is innate in reason and that through recollection we can remember them. Aristotle said we only know "forms" by experiencing them in objects here on Earth. Which theory seems more reasonable to you?

For Aristotle, *there is no matter without form and no form without matter.* Matter is the substance out of which something (the human or chicken) is made, and "form" is its essence (characteristics). When the human or chicken dies, its "form" ceases to exist. Its "substance" (matter) remains, but it is no longer a person or a chicken. Substance always contains the potentiality to realize a specific "form." "Form" is knowable only when it *actualizes* in the physical world and we can experience it with our senses. The "form" of the acorn is the *actual* oak tree. The "form" of the building materials is the house. The "form" of a human body is the soul. Matter in its pure state needs "form" to trigger its *potential.*

Why, for instance, are these materials a house? Because of the presence of the essence of house. One might also ask, "Why is this, or the body containing this, a man? So what one is really looking for is the cause—that is, the form—of the matter being whatever it is" and this in fact is the substance.[2]

The Four Causes

Aristotle discovered *four causes* that contribute to changes in nature and changes in the products of human art. In nature, life is in a continuous state of change. The artist sculpts a statue. Of change, said Aristotle, we can ask four questions: (1) What is it? (2) What is it made of? (3) What (or who) made it? and (4) For what end is it made? The four responses to these questions are Aristotle's *four causes.*

Aristotle regarded these causes as first principles found in every realm of reality. They are: (1) the *formal cause* (form), (2) the *material cause* (matter),

(3) the *efficient cause* (motion), and (4) the *final cause* (end). The four causes are the principles that govern all things as they develop from potentiality to actuality.

For example, in making a marble statue, the formal cause is the plan the sculptor has in mind, the material cause is the marble, the efficient cause consists of the sculptor shaping the statue, and the final cause is the purpose for the statue—to decorate a museum. The four causes constitute the principles of change from a potential state of unformed matter to the end for which it is made—actuality.

Why does it rain? Aristotle would again refer us to the four causes. The formal cause is the built-in nature of moisture to fall to earth. The material cause is the moisture contained in the clouds. The efficient cause is the cooling of moisture so it can fall to earth, and the final cause is the purpose of rain—to provide moisture for all life on the planet.

Potentiality and Actuality

Aristotle's *form–matter* hypothesis is his basis for the meaning of all life. Everything in nature seeks to realize itself—to develop its potentialities and finally realize its actualities. All things have this "inner urge" to strive toward their "end." The acorn strives to become an oak tree. The child strives to be an adult. The "end" or purpose within everything is to realize its *essence*. Every change in nature is a transformation of substance from the "potential" to the "actual." Aristotle called this process *entelechy,* which is the Greek word for "to become its essence."

Entelechy means that nothing happens by chance. Nature not only has a built-in pattern, but also different levels of being. Some creatures, such as humans, have more actuality than potentiality; and some, such as bees, have more potentiality than actuality. But for the world of potential things to exist at all, there must first be something actual (form) at a level above potential or perishing things (matter).

Aristotle divided everything in the natural world into two main categories: *nonliving things* and *living things.* Examples of nonliving things are rocks, water, and earth. These things have no potentiality for change. They can change only by some external influence. For instance, water changes into ice only when the external temperature reaches freezing. But living things *do* have the potentiality for change.

Aristotle then divided living things into two different categories: plants and creatures. He also divided creatures into two subcategories: animals and humans. All living things have the ability to absorb nourishment, to grow, and to propagate. In addition, all living creatures have the ability to perceive the world around them and to move about in it. Higher yet, humans can think and order their perceptions into various categories and classes.

In nature, no sharp boundaries can be found. We can see the scale from simple to more complex plants, from simple to more complex animals. At the top of this scale are human beings who experience the whole life of nature. Like plants, we grow and absorb nourishment; like animals, we have senses, feelings, and locomotion. But we also have an added characteristic—the ability to think rationally. Because reason is a divine characteristic, humans also have a spark of the divine (see pages 78–82 on the Soul).

At the top of the scale is the Unmoved Mover (God): pure actuality without any potentiality. All things in the world are potentially in motion and continuously changing. Therefore, said Aristotle, there must be something that is actual motion and which is moved by nothing external. He called this entity the Unmoved Mover.

The Unmoved Mover

For Aristotle, the Unmoved Mover is eternal, immaterial, and complete actuality or perfection. The Unmoved Mover is God.

> The following considerations will make it clear that there must necessarily be some . . . thing, which, while it has the capacity of moving something else, is itself unmoved and exempt from all change. . . . Suppose it possible that some principles that are unmoved but capable of imparting motion at one time are and at another time are not. Even so, this cannot be true of *all* such principles, since there must clearly be something that *causes* things that move themselves at one time to be and at another not to be. For . . . the fact that some things become and others perish, and that this is so continuously, cannot be caused by any one of those things that, though they are unmoved, do not always exist: nor again can it be caused by any of those which move certain particular things, while others move other things. The eternity and continuity of the process cannot be caused either by any one of them singly or by the sum of them, because this causal relation must be eternal and necessary, whereas the sum of these movements is infinite and they do not all exist together. It is clear, then, that though there may be countless instances of the perishing of some principles that are unmoved but impart motion, and though many things that move themselves perish and are succeeded by others that come into being, and though one thing that is unmoved moves one thing while another moves another, nevertheless there is something that comprehends them all, and that as something apart from each one of them, and this it is that is the cause of the fact that some things and others are not and of the continuous process of change: and this causes the motion of the other movements, while there are the causes of the motion of other things. Motion, then, being eternal, the first movement, if there is but one, will be eternal also: if there are more than one, there will be a plurality of such eternal move-

ments. We ought, however, to suppose that there is one rather than many, and a finite rather than an infinite number. When the consequences of either assumption are the same, we should always assume that things are finite rather than infinite in number, since in things constituted by nature that which is finite and that which is better ought, if possible, to be present rather than the reverse: and here it is sufficient to assume only one movement, the first of unmoved things, which being eternal will be the principle of motion to everything else. . . .

But evidently there *is* a first principle, and the causes of things are neither an infinite series nor infinitely various in kind. For neither can one thing proceed from another, as from matter, *ad infinitum* (e.g., flesh from earth, earth from air, air from fire, and so on without stopping), nor can the sources of movement form an endless series (man for instance being acted on by air, air by the sun, the sun by Strife, and so on without limit). Similarly the final causes cannot go on *ad infinitum*,—walking being for the sake of health, this for the sake of happiness, happiness for the sake of something else, and so one thing always for the sake of another. . . . If there is no first there is no cause at all.[3]

Thus, for Aristotle the Unmoved Mover is perfection with pure actuality with *no* potentiality. Being eternal, it is the "reason for" and the "principle of motion to everything else." Because motion is eternal, there never was a time when the world was not. Therefore, the Unmoved Mover is not a creator God. Being pure actuality, it has no physical body. Lacking nothing, it has no emotional desires. The activity of the Unmoved Mover consists of pure thought (*Nous*). As such, it is a mind that is perfect and its object of thought can only be itself.

Pause for Thought   If the Unmoved Mover thinks only on Itself as perfection, then would It know that we exist? Would It care? Is the Unmoved Mover a God to which you could pray?

Striving to realize themselves, objects and human beings move toward their divine origin and perfection. Our highest faculty is the reason, which finds its perfection in contemplating the Unmoved Mover. Aristotle explained how an Unmoved Mover can cause motion of the world and everything in it by comparing it to a beloved who "moves" its lover by the power of attraction:

The . . . [Unmoved Mover] then moves things because it is loved, whereas all other things move because they are themselves moved. . . . But since there is something that moves things, while being itself immovable and existing in actuality, it is not possible in any way for that thing to be in any state other than that in which it is. . . . The first mover, then, must exist; and insofar as he exists of necessity, his existence must be good; and thus he must be a first principle. . . .

It is upon a principle of this kind, then, that the heavens and nature depend.[4]

As the "form" adult is in the child directing it toward its natural end, *the Unmoved Mover is the form of the world* moving it toward its divine end. The highest human activity resembles the activity of the Unmoved Mover. Just as the Unmoved Mover thinks *only* perfection, we can think *about* perfection. But because we are imperfect, we can't think perfection itself. According to Aristotle, the most pleasant activity for any living creature is realizing its nature; therefore, the happiest life for humans is thinking about the Unmoved Mover.

The Soul

Let us now . . . endeavour . . . to give a precise answer to the question, What is soul? i.e. to formulate the most general possible definition of it. . . .

Among substances are by general consent reckoned bodies and especially natural bodies; for they are the principles of all other bodies. Of natural bodies some have life in them, others not; by life we mean self-nutrition and growth (with its correlative decay). It follows that every natural body which has life in it is a substance in the sense of a composite.

But since it is also a *body* of such and such a kind, viz. having life, the *body* cannot be soul; the body is the subject or matter, not what is attributed to. Hence the soul must be a substance in the sense of the form of a natural body having life potentially within it. But substance is actuality, and thus soul is the actuality of a body. . . .[5]

The *soul*, therefore, is the "form" of the body. Plato viewed the body as the prison house of the soul. In contrast, Aristotle said that without the body, the soul could neither exist nor exercise its functions. There could be no soul without the body any more than there could be vision without an eye.

By separating the soul and body, Plato could speak of the soul's pre-existence and its immortality. He described learning and knowledge as the process of recollection of what the soul knew in its previous state. Aristotle looked at the soul differently. For him, the soul needs the body to exist, and the body needs the soul to exist. Thus, with the death of the body, the soul also perishes. The mind has no preexisting knowledge. At birth, the mind is like a blank sheet of paper: devoid of content.

Pause for Thought   If the soul does not exist before birth or after death, but only with the body, does Aristotle need to posit a human soul at all?

Psyche is the Greek term for *soul*. Because psyche always applies to life, anything with psyche is alive. Aristotle agreed with other Greek philosophers that plants and animals, as well as humans, have life, and therefore they have psyche or soul:

> . . . What has soul in it differs from what has not in that the former displays life. Now this word has more than one sense, and provided any one alone of these is found in a thing we say that thing is living. Living, that is, may mean thinking or perception or local movement and rest, or movement in the sense of nutrition, decay and growth. Hence we think of plants also as living, for they are observed to possess in themselves an originative power through which they increase or decrease in all spatial directions; they grow up and down, and everything that grows increases its bulk alike in both directions or indeed in all, and continues to live so long as it can absorb nutriment. This power of self-nutrition can be isolated from the other powers mentioned, but not they from it—in mortal beings at least. The fact is obvious in plants; for it is the only psychic power they possess.
>
> This is the originative power the possession of which leads us to speak of things as *living* at all, but it is the possession of sensation that leads us for the first time to speak of living things as animals; for even those things which possess no power of local movement but do possess the power of sensation we call animals and not merely living things.[6]

Aristotle held that three types of soul organize the human body. He called these the *nutritive* (or *vegetative*), *sensitive* (or *sensation*), and *rational* souls. Found in plants, the nutritive soul experiences life—the act of living. In animals, the sensitive soul experiences both living and sensing (touch, smell, taste, hearing, and sight). Human souls include all three souls: living, sensing, and thinking.

> . . . Of the psychic powers above enumerated some kinds of living things, as we have said, possess all, some less than all, others only one. Those we have mentioned are the nutritive, the appetitive, the sensory [sensitive], the locomotive, and the power of thinking. Plants have none but the first, the nutritive, while another order of living things has this *plus* the sensory. If any order of living things has the sensory, it must also have the appetitive; for appetite is the genus of which desire, passion, and wish are the species; now all animals have one sense at least, vis. touch, and whatever has a sense has the capacity for pleasure and pain and therefore has pleasant and painful

objects present to it, and wherever these are present, there is desire, for desire is just appetition of what is pleasant. . . . Certain kinds of animals possess in addition the power of locomotion, and still another order of animate beings, i.e. man and possibly another order like man or superior to him, the power of thinking, i.e., mind. . . .[7]

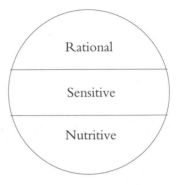

The Soul

Aristotle based the hierarchy of souls on the potentiality of each level of plant, animal, and human. Humans have more potentiality than plants or animals. In plants, the nutritive soul digests "matter" (food and water) and even though it has "form" because it has life, it cannot take in more "form." The nutritive soul keeps the body alive and enables it to grow, because its long-range *good* or *end* is to perpetuate the species.

In animals, the sensitive soul has the power to absorb the forms of things without assimilating their matter. Such action occurs in the same way a piece of wax takes the impression of a signet ring without assimilating its gold. For instance, if an animal sees or smells another animal, it takes in some of its characteristics and its odor without becoming the animal itself. The sense organs are potentially capable of sensing many different forms. What happens in your ear when you hear guitar music? The sense organ listens to the music without assimilating the guitar, and it has the potentiality of hearing certain ranges of music. But we cannot hear music that reaches beyond that range. Through *memory* and *imagination*, the qualities of sense can continue even after an animal or a person perceives an object or hears a sound. From these qualities come the higher form of soul—the rational soul.

Rational human souls include the nutritive and sensitive souls, but they also can think, analyze, and reflect. We have the capacity to think scientifically and philosophically. With reason, we can understand the relationships of objects and ideas to one another. Reason gives us the ability to ask meaningful questions: "Who am I?" "Why am I here?" Through the power of *deliberation*, the mind can discover the scientific truths in nature and how to act morally. Though all people do not exercise the power of deliberation, this knowledge is still potential in the reason.

. . . Mind is in a sense potentially whatever *is* thinkable, though actually it is nothing until it has thought. What it thinks must be in it just as characters may be said to be on a writing-tablet on which as yet nothing actually stands written: this is exactly what happens with mind.[8]

Thought occurs as a result of sense experiences. Aristotle reasoned that no one could learn or understand anything without using the senses. Again, he deviates from Plato, who said the highest thought is free of sense experience. But Aristotle said, "Thinking is both speculative and practical." The mind relates to ideas (intelligible objects) in the same way that sense relates to facts (physical objects). The mind and senses work together.

Potentiality is a characteristic of the rational soul just as it is for the sensitive soul. As the eye can see a purple ball only when it actually sees the purple ball, so the rational soul can actualize its potential to understand the true nature of things. Unlike the pure actuality of the Unmoved Mover, however, our reason cannot sustain a continuous state of actuality. We always have the potential to know other truths, so it is possible for us to attain knowledge, but not perfection. It is also possible for us not to attain knowledge.

The reason is both *active* and *passive*. The passive mind is similar to a blank tablet on which our senses can write. Aristotle argued that because the passive mind depends on our senses to function, this aspect of the soul is not eternal.

The continuity of the world does imply the continuity of truth. And the continuity of truth implies continuous knowledge in some mind. This mind, however, is not human but belongs to the Unmoved Mover—the soul (that is, the Form) of the world. The mind of the Unmoved Mover is in perfect harmony with the truth.

In *De Anima*, his treatise on the soul, Aristotle argued that the *active intellect* (Nous) functions eternally. Because it is eternally active without potentiality, it is the mind of the Unmoved Mover. We can contemplate the active intellect to some degree, but not to its height of eternal perfection. Because the active intellect is eternal, it is neither born nor capable of dying. Because humans are born and do die, we have no personal immortality. When the human body dies, the soul, as the form of the body, also perishes. Anything immortal about a human being after death belongs to the active intellect, which exists eternally whether or not we exist.

Pause for Thought   Plato said the soul could exist without the body. It exists before life on earth, is immortal, and subject to rebirth. Aristotle denied that the soul could exist without the body. It is the form of the body, and there can be no form without matter and no matter without form. Thus, for Aristotle, there can be no individual immortality or any pre-existence of the soul. With whom do you agree? Or do you have another solution?

Moral Philosophy

Aristotle based his ethics on his metaphysics, that everything in nature aims at some *end*. Everything has a "form" that is its purpose and goal. Because the *end* is the fulfillment of each thing's function, and that which satisfies it, Aristotle called it *good*.

> Every art and every inquiry, and similarly every action and choice, is thought to aim at some good; and for this reason the good has rightly been declared to be that at which all things aim.[9]

Aristotle's idea that everything aims at some good is known as *teleology*—that is, the world and everything in it has a design or purpose. Aristotle asked the questions "How should we live?" and "What is the *good* at which humans aim?" Plato thought people aim to know the Form of the Good. To gain such knowledge, we must use reason and intuition to soar beyond the sense world to the intelligible world of ideas. But Aristotle argued that the *good* for anything is to realize its own true nature, which means the good is within a thing. So the only way we can discover the good in human beings is by studying human nature and behavior. However, our study will not bring us specific answers, because morals involve individual judgments:

> Our discussion will be adequate if it has as much clearness as the subject matter admits of; for precision is not to be sought for alike in all discussions, any more than in all the products of the crafts. Now fine and just actions, which political science investigates, exhibit much variety and fluctuation, so that they may be thought to exist only by convention, and not by nature. And goods also exhibit a similar fluctuation because they bring harm to many people; for before now men have been undone by reason of their wealth, and others by reason of their courage. We must be content, then, in speaking of such subjects and with such premises to indicate the truth roughly and in outline, and in speaking about things which are only for the most part true. . . .[10]

Pause for Thought   Mathematics has self-evident principles with which all people agree. Morals, said Aristotle, include individual judgments on which people may or may not agree. Do you agree with Aristotle that moral judgments are *not* like mathematics?

With the Sophists, Aristotle considered opinion the basis for ethics. In opposition to the Sophists, who believed moral judgments are entirely subjective and therefore relative, Aristotle agreed with Plato that a *Form of the Good* exists. His belief in both the Form of the Good and opinion led Aristotle to regard ethics as both *theoretical* and *practical*. Ethics is theoretical when it asks, "What is the good?" It is practical when it asks, "How can I be good?" He thought that *happiness* is the good to which all humans aspire

Ends and Means

According to Aristotle, there are two kinds of ends: *instrumental ends* (acts that are *means* to some end) and *intrinsic ends* (acts that are done for their *own sake*).

1. . . . a certain difference is found among ends. . . . Now, as there are many actions, arts, and sciences, their ends also are many; the end of the medical art is health, that of shipbuilding a vessel, that of strategy victory, that of economics wealth. . . .

2. If then, there is some end of the things we do, which we desire for its own sake (everything else being desired for the sake of this), and if we do not choose everything for the sake of something else (for at that rate the process would go on to infinity, so that our desire would be empty and vain), clearly this must be the good and the chief good. Will not the knowledge of it, then, have a great influence on life? Shall we not, like archers who have a mark to aim at, be more likely to hit upon what we should? . . .

4. . . . In view of the fact that all knowledge and choice aims at some good, what it is that we say political science aims at and what is the highest of all goods achievable by action. Verbally there is very general agreement; for both the general run of men and people of superior refinement say that it is happiness, and identify living well and faring well with being happy; but with regard to what happiness is they differ, and the many do not give the same account as the wise. For the former think it is some plain and obvious thing, like pleasure, wealth, or honour; they differ, however, from one another—and often even the same man identifies it with different things, with health when he is ill, with wealth when he is poor; but, conscious of their ignorance, they admire those who proclaim some great thing that is above their comprehension. Now some thought that apart from these many goods there is another which is good in itself and causes the goodness of all these as well. To examine all the opinions that have been held would no doubt be somewhat fruitless: it is enough to examine those that are most prevalent or that seem to have some reason in their favour.

5. . . . To judge from the lives that men lead, most men, and men of the most vulgar type, seem (not without some reason) to identify the good, or happiness, with pleasure; which is the reason why they love the life of enjoyment. . . . But people of superior refinement and of active disposition identify happiness with honour; for this is, roughly speaking, the end of the

political life. But it seems too superficial to be what we are looking for, since it is thought to depend on those who bestow honour rather than on him who receives it, but the good we divine to be something of one's own and not easily taken from one . . . men of practical wisdom . . . seek to be honoured, and among those who know them, and on the ground of their excellence; clearly, then, according to them, at any rate, excellence is better. . . . But even this appears somewhat incomplete; for possession of excellence seems actually compatible with being asleep, or with lifelong inactivity, and, further, with the greatest sufferings and misfortunes; but a man who was living so no one would call happy, unless he were maintaining a thesis at all costs. Third comes the contemplative lie, which we shall consider later.

The life of money-making is one undertaken under compulsion, and wealth is evidently not the good we are seeking; for it is merely useful and for the sake of something else. . . .

6. We had perhaps better consider the universal good and discuss thoroughly what is meant by it, although such an inquiry is made an uphill one by the fact that the Forms have been introduced by friends of our own. Yet it would perhaps be thought to be better, indeed to be our duty, for the sake of maintaining the truth even to destroy what touches us closely, especially as we are philosophers; for, while both are dear, piety requires us to honour truth above our friends.

. . . And one might ask the question, what in the world they *mean* by "a thing itself," if in man himself and in a particular man the account of man is one and the same.

Let us separate, then, things good in themselves from things useful, and consider whether the former are called good by reference to a single Idea. What sort of goods would one call good in themselves? Is it those that are pursued even when isolated from others, such as intelligence, sight, and certain pleasures and honours? Certainly, if we pursue these also for the sake of something else, yet one would place them among things good in themselves. Or is nothing other than the Idea good in itself? In that case the Form will be empty. But if the things we have named are also things good in themselves, the account of the good will have to appear as something identical in them all, as that of whiteness is identical in snow and in white lead. But of honour, wisdom, and pleasure, just in respect of their goodness, the accounts are distinct and diverse. The good, therefore, is not something common answering to one Idea.

But then in what way are things called good?

7. . . . The good we are seeking . . . [is] surely that for whose sake everything else is done. In medicine this is health, in strategy victory, in architecture a house. . . .

Since there are evidently more than one end, and we choose some of these (e.g. wealth, flutes, and in general instruments) for the sake of something else, clearly not all ends are complete ends: but the chief good is evidently something complete. Therefore, if there is only one complete end, this will be what we are seeking. . . . Now we call that which is in itself worthy of pursuit more complete than that which is worthy of pursuit for the sake of something else, and that which is never desirable for the sake of something else more complete than the things that are desirable both in themselves and for the sake of that other thing, and therefore we call complete without qualification that which is always desirable in itself and never for the sake of something else.

Now such a thing happiness, above all else, is held to be; for this we choose always for itself and never for the sake of something else, but honour, pleasure, reason, and every excellence we choose indeed for themselves (for if nothing resulted from them we should still choose each of them), but we choose them also for the sake of happiness, judging that through them we shall be happy. Happiness, on the other hand, no one chooses for the sake of these, nor, in general, for anything other than itself. . . .

Happiness, then, is something complete and self-sufficient, and is the end of action.[11]

Happiness

For Aristotle, if we are to be happy, we must fulfill our function as a person. Human fulfillment includes the three parts of our soul: nutritive, sensitive, and rational. We are not just nutritive, because even plants share that function. We have sensation (sensitive), but this is common to horses, cats, and every animal, so sensation is not the end we seek. Uniquely, ours is the rational soul, and the rational part of the soul follows or implies a rational principle. Thus, for Aristotle, the function of human beings is to follow the rational principle, which means the human good is an activity of the soul "in accordance with *virtue.*" But we humans also have life and sensation that oppose the rational principle, and *this conflict between the rational and the irrational parts of the soul raises the problem of morality.*

Pause for Thought   Is the same conflict evident in animals? If your dog takes a bone from a neighbor's yard, has the dog committed an immoral act? If you take a camera from your neighbor's house, have you committed an immoral act? What's the difference?

Moral choices always involve action, so human happiness is contingent on our rational and virtuous activity. Our highest function is to live a virtuous life in which reason governs our irrational nature. Happiness, like good, is the soul working by way of excellence or virtue. Virtue is not automatic. There is always the conflict between our animal nature and our reason. None of the moral virtues arises in us by nature, because, said Aristotle, nothing that exists by nature can form habits that conflict with its nature.

According to Aristotle, moral virtue has to do with developing certain habits: (1) right thinking, (2) right choice, and (3) right behavior.

It takes practice to be moral. One swallow, said Aristotle, doesn't make a spring, nor does one day make an individual happy. The happy person is not one who does a good deed now and then, but the person whose whole life is good.

The Golden Mean

Like Homer and other Greek poets before him, Aristotle suggested we take the "middle way" or the *mean between two extremes*. We must have neither too much pride nor poor self-esteem; instead, we must have self-respect. Too little respect results in contempt; too much brings arrogance. We must be neither miserly nor extravagant, but charitable. If we lack charity, we become miserly; but too much charity means extravagance. The same is true of eating. It is dangerous to eat too little and dangerous to eat too much.

Wealth itself cannot give us happiness, but living in poverty makes us miserable. Aristotle rejected all forms of imbalance. If we only develop our body, we are as unbalanced as if we only develop our mind. Both extremes are expressions of a warped way of life.

> First, then, let us consider this, that it is the nature of such things to be destroyed by defect and excess, as we see in the case of strength and of health (for to gain light on things imperceptible we must use the evidence of sensible things); both excessive and defective exercise destroys the strength, and similarly drink or food which is above or below a certain amount destroys the health, while that which is proportionate both produces and increases and preserves it. So too is, then, in the case of temperance and courage and the other excellences. For the man who flies from and fears everything and does not stand his ground against anything becomes a coward, and the man who fears nothing at all but goes to meet every danger becomes rash; and similarly the man who indulges in every pleasure and abstains from none becomes self-indulgent, while the man who shuns every pleasure, as boors do, becomes in a way insensible; temperance and courage, then, are destroyed by excess and defect, and preserved by the mean.[12]

Virtue has to do with our ability to govern excessive or defective feelings. We may feel too much fear or anger, pleasure or pain. Either extreme is a vice. Virtue is the *mean* between these two extremes.

For example, the virtue of *courage* is a mean between two vices or extremes. Imagine two men standing on the end of an ocean pier fifty feet above the water. One man is a good swimmer. The other man cannot swim. Below them a sailboat capsizes and its passenger yells, "Help, I can't swim." For the nonswimmer to jump into the ocean would be foolish (extreme), but for the good swimmer to run down the pier for help is cowardly (defect). It would take courage for the good swimmer to jump in the ocean to save the drowning man and for the non-swimmer to immediately find some way to help (mean).

Reason is the guide to our morality. We want reason to control our emotions and be rational enough to choose a mean. The mean is not the same for each person, and there is no mean for every act.

> Excellence, then, is a state concerned with choice, lying in a mean relative to us, this being determined by reason and in the way in which the man of practical wisdom would determine it. Now it is a mean between two vices, that which depends on excess and that which depends on defect; and again it is a mean because the vices respectively fall short of or exceed what is right in both passions and actions, while excellence both finds and chooses that which is intermediate. Hence in respect of its substance and the account which states its essence virtue is a mean, with regard to what is best and right it is an extreme.[13]

Virtue of the Golden Mean

Excess (Vice)	Mean (Virtue)	Defect (Vice)
Foolhardy	Courage	Cowardice
Gluttony	Moderation	Starvation
Wasteful	Generosity	Stingy
Overly submissive	Friendly	Aloof
Vanity	Pride	Too humble
Promiscuity	Monogamy	Celibacy
Buffoonery	Humor	Boorish
Too shy	Modesty	Showoff

Because character and circumstances will vary from person to person, the mean is relative. The mean of *generosity* will be different for the wealthy corporate owner than for the struggling college student. The mean of *moderation* will differ for the twenty-year-old advanced skier and the eighty-five-year-old advanced skier. There will be a contrast in the mean of *modesty* between the naturally shy introvert and the outgoing extrovert.

Some acts have no mean at all.

> But not every action nor every passion admits of a mean; for some have names that already imply badness, e.g. spite, shamelessness, envy, and in the case of actions adultery, theft, murder, for all of these and suchlike things

imply by their names that they are themselves bad, and not the excesses of deficiencies of them. It is not possible, then, ever to be right with regard to them; one must always be wrong. Nor does goodness or badness with regard to such things depend on committing adultery with the right woman, at the right time, and in the right way, but simply to do any of them is to go wrong. . . .[14]

Two Kinds of Reasoning

Aristotle argued that humans have two kinds of reasoning: *theoretical* and *practical*. Theoretical reasoning gives us knowledge of universal principles. Practical reasoning guides our everyday actions and morals. Theoretical reason alone will not make us moral: We need practical reason. Though we have the ability to act morally, we are not by nature moral creatures. It takes practical reason to actualize the good that lies potentially in us. Socrates and Plato believed *to know the good is to do the good*, but Aristotle thought *we could know the good and do the bad*. Our sensuous desires can overpower responsible choices.

Pause for Thought   Socrates and Plato thought that if we know the good (the Form of the Good) we would never choose to do the bad. Aristotle believed we could know the good and yet choose the bad. What do you think?

Two Kinds of Acts

According to Aristotle, there are two kinds of acts: *voluntary acts* and *involuntary acts*. Moral choices for which we are responsible are voluntary acts. An authentic choice is a voluntary action. Involuntary acts are those times when we are not responsible for our actions. There are three kinds of involuntary acts: (1) acts that result from external compulsion (our body is moved by some external force, for example); (2) acts done out of ignorance of particular circumstances; and (3) acts done to avoid a greater evil. None of these conditions exist in voluntary acts.

Two Kinds of Wisdom

Virtues are the expressions of a balanced life. If we wish to achieve happiness, then we must live a life of reason. Because everything has a purpose, anything that obstructs the purpose will bring sorrow, and anything that fulfills it will bring happiness. By exercising the rational mind to its fullest (*theoretical wisdom*) and acting on responsible choices (*practical wisdom*), we will experience the highest happiness.

Regarding *practical wisdom* we shall get at the truth by considering who are the persons we credit with it. Now it is thought to be a mark of a man of practical wisdom to be able to deliberate well about what is good and expedient for himself, not in some particular respect, e.g. about what sorts of thing conduce to health or to strength, but about what sorts of thing conduce to the good life in general.[15]

Another function of the reason is *intellectual*, which Aristotle divides into two parts: scientific reason and intuitive reason. The intellectual reason seeks to understand the truth about First Principles. A combination of logical scientific reason and the insight into principles through intuitive reason produce philosophical (theoretical) wisdom.

Scientific knowledge is belief about things that are universal and necessary, and there are principles of everything that is demonstrated and of all knowledge (for knowledge involves reasoning). This being so, the first principle of what is scientifically known cannot be an object of scientific knowledge, of art, or of practical wisdom; for that which can be scientifically known can be demonstrated, and art and practical wisdom deal with things that are variable. . . . If, then, the states of mind by which we have truth and are never deceived about things invariable or even variable are scientific knowledge, practical wisdom, philosophic wisdom, and intuitive reason, and it cannot be any of the three (i.e. practical wisdom, scientific knowledge, or philosophic wisdom), the remaining alternative is that it is *intuitive reason* that grasps the first principles. . . .

Therefore wisdom must plainly be the most finished of the forms of knowledge. It follows that the wise man must not only know what follows from the first principles, but must also possess truth about the first principles. Therefore wisdom must be intuitive reason combined with scientific knowledge—scientific knowledge of the highest objects which has received as it were its proper completion.[16]

Pause for Thought   Aristotle said we should not confuse happiness with sensuous pleasures. Do you find a significant difference between sensuous pleasures and happiness?

Sensuous pleasure is short-lived because it soon turns into its opposite. After a single hot fudge sundae, I experience pleasure. After five hot fudge sundaes, I experience pain. Happiness, on the other hand, does not shift from pleasure to pain. Happiness is long-lasting, a result of the highest activity possible: contemplation.

If happiness is activity in accordance with virtue, it is reasonable that it should be in accordance with the highest virtue; and this will be that of the best thing in us. Whether it be reason or something else that is this element which is thought to be our natural ruler and guide and to take thought of things noble and divine, whether it be itself also divine or only the most divine element in us, the activity of this in accordance with its proper virtue will be perfect happiness. . . . This activity is contemplative. . . .

Firstly, this activity is the best (since not only is reason the best thing in us, but the objects of reason are the best of knowable objects); and, secondly it is the most continuous, since we can contemplate truth more continuously than we can *do* anything. And we think happiness has pleasure mingled with it, but the activity of philosophic wisdom is admittedly the pleasantest of virtuous activities. . . .

That which is proper to each thing is by nature best and most pleasant for each thing; for man, therefore, the life according to reason is best and pleasantest, since reason more than anything else *is* man. This life therefore is also the happiest.[17]

The philosopher, said Aristotle, is the happiest of all people. Philosophers can't walk around without the necessities of life, but they know how to spend time alone and don't have to depend on others for entertainment. The philosopher enjoys pleasures but realizes that true pleasure is contemplation. The philosopher has learned to balance the different aspects of the soul and not let emotions rule. The life of a philosopher expresses the divine element in humans, because the highest contemplative act is thinking on perfection, the Unmoved Mover.

Certainly, intelligence is necessary to attain the highest good, but so is the proper environment. Wealth is not a part of happiness, but it frees our mind from worrying about money. Aristotle did not think the poor uneducated person could be happy in the true sense.

. . . it [happiness] needs the external goods as well; for it is impossible, or not easy, to do noble acts without the proper equipment. In many actions we use friends and riches and political power as instruments; and there are some things the lack of which takes the lustre from blessedness, as good birth, satisfactory children, beauty; for the man who is very ugly in appearance or ill-born or solitary and childless is hardly happy, and perhaps a man would be still less so if he had thoroughly bad children or friends or had lost good children or friends by death. As we said, then, happiness seems to need this sort of prosperity in addition; for which reason some identify happiness with good fortune, though others identify it with excellence [virtue].[18]

Pause for Thought   According to Aristotle, there are three forms of happiness. The first form is a life of pleasure and enjoyment. The second is life as a free and responsible citizen. The third form of happiness is life as thinker and philosopher. Which one of these stages appeals to you? Are you happier when you think or when you eat?

Political Philosophy

Aristotle said, "Man is by nature a political animal." By our nature, we need to live in a state. As everything in Aristotle's philosophy aims for its good, the state also exists for a good. The family and the village satisfy our primary needs of food, warmth, marriage, and child rearing. The state offers even a higher form of human need by helping its members achieve moral and intellectual virtues.

Types of States

Aristotle described three good forms of government. The basic difference among them is the number of rulers that each form of government has: *one, few,* or *many.* The first type of government is *monarchy,* or *kingship* with one head of state. For this type of government to be good, it must not degenerate into "tyranny," in which the king becomes selfish and governs to his own advantage. The second type is *aristocracy* with a few rulers. This government must beware of degenerating into an "oligarchy" in which the government is run by a few tyrants. The third good governmental form Aristotle calls *polity,* which includes *many* leaders; this form, however, can degenerate into a democracy or mob rule.

Number of Rulers	Type of Government	Perversion
One	Monarchy	Tyranny
Few	Aristocracy	Oligarchy
Many	Polity	Democracy

We have now to inquire what is the best constitution for most states, and the best life for most men, neither assuming a standard of virtue which is above ordinary persons, nor an education which is exceptionally favoured by nature and circumstances, nor yet an ideal state which is an aspiration only, but having regard to the life in which the majority are able to share, and to the form of government which states in general can attain. . . .

Now in all states there are three elements: one class is very rich, another very poor, and a third is a mean. It is admitted that moderation and the mean are best, and therefore it will clearly be best to possess the gifts of fortune in moderation; for in that condition of life men are most ready to follow rational principle. . . . The middle class is least likely to shrink from rule, or to be over-ambitious for it; both of which are injuries to the state. Again, those who have too much of the goods of fortune, strength, wealth, friends, and the like, are neither willing nor able to submit to authority. The evil begins at home; for when they are boys, by reason of the luxury in which they are brought up, they never learn, even at school, the habit of obedience. On the other hand, the very poor, who are in the opposite extreme, are too degraded. So that the one class cannot obey, and can only rule despotically; the other knows not how to command and must be ruled like slaves. Thus arises a city, not of freemen, but of masters and slaves, the one despising, the other envying; and nothing can be more fatal to friendship and good fellowship in states than this. . . . Wherefore the city which is composed of middle-class citizens is necessarily best constituted in respect of the elements of which we say the fabric of the state naturally consists. . . .[19]

Pause for Thought   Ideally, said Aristotle, kingship is best, aristocracy next best, and democracy the most practical. Do you agree with his evaluation?

On Women

A major difference between Plato and Aristotle is in their views on women. Aristotle maintained that far from being equal to a man, a woman is a mutilated or incomplete man. Women are colder, have less soul, and do not have enough purity. In generation, man gives the form or essence of the embryo while woman merely provides its nutrition. The male creates human life and the rational soul. Women are physically weaker, less capable of rational thought, and should submit to the rule of men.

> Now a boy is like a woman in form, and the woman is as it were an impotent male, for it is through a certain incapacity that the female is female, being incapable of concocting the nutriment in its last stage into semen . . . owing to the coldness of their nature. . . .
>
> [So] no soul will exist in anything except that of which it is soul; it is plain therefore that semen both has soul, and is soul, potentially. . . .
>
> For the female is, as it were, a mutilated male, and the catamenia are semen, only not pure; for there is only one thing they have not in them, the principle of soul. . . .
>
> While the body is from the female, it is the soul that is from the male, for the soul is the reality of a particular body. . . .
>
> The fact is, the nature of man is the most rounded off and complete, and consequently in man the qualities or capacities above referred to are found in their perfection. Hence woman is more compassionate than man, more

easily moved to tears, at the same time is more jealous, more querulous, more apt to scold and to strike. She is, furthermore, more prone to despondency and less hopeful than the man, more void of shame or self respect, more false of speech, more deceptive, and of more retentive memory. . . .

The male is by nature superior, and the female inferior; and the one rules, and the other is ruled; this principle, of necessity extends to all mankind. . . .

The temperance of a man and of a woman, or the courage and justice of a man and of a woman, are not, as Socrates maintained, the same; the courage of a man is shown in commanding, of a woman in obeying.[20]

Pause for Thought   Who do you think came closest to understanding the nature of men and women, Plato and Socrates, or Aristotle?

Summary

In contrast to Plato, Aristotle showed a deep interest in the natural world. For him, there is no intelligible world of Forms that exists independently of this world. Forms are within this world, and everything is a combination of form and matter. There can be no form without matter, and no matter without form.

Like plants and animals, humans have souls. Their three types of soul are the *nutritive* that all life possesses, the *sensitive* that animals also have, and the *rational*, which is uniquely human. Aristotle denied any type of existence for the soul before life on Earth or after death. The soul is the form of the body, and because matter and form cannot exist separately, there is no individual immortality. We also have no innate ideas. Our mind is blank at birth. Only through living life can our mind gain knowledge.

The Unmoved Mover is Aristotle's God. Unlike the Demiurge of Plato, however, the Unmoved Mover does not create the universe. The universe is eternal. The Unmoved Mover is the Form of the world and supports its movement through our attraction to perfection.

Aristotle did not argue for a universal good. The good is moral virtue that we discover through putting our intellectual virtues into practice. Morality is habit. We can know the good and still choose to do the opposite. We must know the good and choose to do the good. Virtue is a search for the mean between two extremes. Evil is not ignorance, as Socrates and Plato claimed, but a failure to act on what we know is good. Aristotle agreed with Plato that the highest human happiness is contemplation of perfection, which for Aristotle is the Unmoved Mover.

Connections

In reviewing this brief survey of Aristotle's philosophy we can better understand his ability to organize and explain every aspect of human experience. He was able to bring together in a unified worldview the physical world, the social world, and our moral life. We have seen the connections between Plato and Aristotle and the departures of Aristotle from his mentor. Since Aristotle's time, the Western world has more or less divided into two camps—the Platonic and the Aristotelian. Because Aristotle was a scientist, most Westerners have followed his route and view the physical world as real and knowable. The writings of Plato and Aristotle were so powerful that over the next six centuries, or until the emergence of Christianity, most philosophy was just modification of their systems.

Study Questions

1. What does it mean to call Aristotle a "natural philosopher"?

2. What is Aristotle's First Principle?

3. Explain the similarities and differences between Plato's view and Aristotle's view of the Forms.

4. What is the association between form and matter?

3. What is the relationship of the soul to the body?

4. Is there more form in some things than in others?

5. For Aristotle, which came first: the chicken or the egg?

6. Why does Aristotle call God the Unmoved Mover?

7. What is the function of the Unmoved Mover?

8. What is our relationship to the Unmoved Mover?

9. Characterize the three aspects of the soul.

10. How does Aristotle's concept of the human soul differ from Plato's?

11. Does Aristotle think there is anything eternal about the human soul?

12. Is there individual salvation after death?

13. What is the highest good according to Aristotle?

14. How does Aristotle's idea of happiness differ from pleasure?

15. Explain Aristotle's doctrine of the Golden Mean. Give three examples of virtues and their excesses and deficiencies.

[handwritten margin notes: "3 humans live/die" "5 form is inverted external)"]

16. Why can't wealth give us the highest happiness?

17. What is the difference between intellectual virtues and practical virtues?

18. Are there any conditions that excuse a person from responsibility?

19. Explain the three types of government in Aristotle's political philosophy.

20. According to Aristotle, what was the woman's contribution in begetting babies?

Notes

1. Aristotle, *Metaphysica* (trans. by W. D. Ross), in *The Basic Works of Aristotle*, edited by Richard McKeon. New York: Random House, 1941.

2. Ibid., Bk 7, 17.

3. Aristotle, *Metaphysics* (trans. by W. D. Ross), in *The Works of Aristotle*, edited by J. A. Smith and W. D. Ross. Oxford: Clarendon Press, 1928.

4. *Metaphysics* (trans. by Ross), op. cit., Bk 12.6, 1072b and 12.7, 1072b 15.

5. Aristotle, *De Anima* (trans. by J. A. Smith), in *Introduction to Aristotle*, edited by Richard McKeon. New York: Random House, 1947.

6. Ibid., Bk 2.2413a–413b.

7. Ibid., Bk 2.3414b.

8. Ibid., Bk 3.4429b–430a.

9. Aristotle, *The Nichomachean Ethics* (trans. by W. D. Ross), revised by J. O. Urmson. Oxford: Oxford University Press, 1980.

10. Ibid., Bk 11094b.

11. Ibid., Bk 1 1094a–1097b.

12. Ibid., Bk II, 1104a.

13. Ibid., Bk 21007a.

14. Ibid., Bk 21107a.

15. Ibid., Bk 6, 1140a.

16. Ibid., Bk 6, 1140b.

17. Ibid., Bk 101177a.

18. Ibid., Bk 11099b.

19. Aristotle, *Politics* (trans. by B. Jowett) in *The Works of Aristotle*. Oxford: Clarendon Press, 1910–52.

20. Aristotle, "De Generatione Animalium" by Arthur Platt, in *The Oxford Translation of Aristotle*, edited by W. D. Ross. Oxford: Clarendon Press, 1912, and *Politics* (trans. by B. Jowett), op cit., Bk 1.

CHAPTER FIVE

Hellenistic Philosophy

The *Hellenistic* period is the next phase we will study in Western philosophical development. The word *Hellenistic* refers to the period in Greek history that began with the conquests of Alexander the Great of Macedonia (d. 323 B.C.E.) and ended with the takeover of his kingdoms by the Romans. Alexander's victory over the Persians and his explorations eastward created a kingdom that stretched from Egypt to India. This marked the beginning of a new epoch in human history.

The period we now call *Hellenism* lasted approximately three hundred years and prevailed in the three Hellenistic kingdoms of Macedonia, Syria, and Egypt. After approximately 50 C.E., however, Rome gradually conquered these kingdoms and became the new superpower. From then on, the Romans, their politics, and their Latin language spread from Spain to Asia. We often refer to this period as late Antiquity.

Religion, Philosophy, and Science

As the borders between countries and cultures disappeared, religion and philosophy began to change. Taking the place of "national religions," new religious ideas trickled into the Hellenic world from around the known world. Oriental beliefs merged with Greek beliefs. With the breakdown of their own cultures and city-states, people experienced doubt and uncertainty about their own religions and philosophies of life. These doubts, when left unresolved, led to cultural dissolution and pessimism.

The new religions often contained teachings about individual salvation after death, the immortality of the soul, and eternal life. Philosophy moved from monumental speculative systems to more pressing concerns of death, salvation, and inner serenity. Philosophical insight was no longer its own reward. People needed practical directions in their lives. Perhaps because no new Socrates, Plato, or Aristotle arrived on the scene, these three giants continued as sources of inspiration for many philosophical trends. With religion and philosophy, science became a blend of knowledge from various cultures. Athens remained the center of philosophy, but Alexandria, a growing city on the mouth of the Nile River delta in Egypt, functioned as a center for mathematics, astronomy, biology, and medicine.

The Hellenistic period is often compared to our world today. The last half of the twentieth century has brought tremendous upheavals in religion, philosophy, and science. A "holistic" view of our relationship to the planet and its creatures may also be the beginning of a new epoch in these fields. And many of today's so-called New Age ideas actually have their roots in Hellenism. The main emphasis in that period, as it is in our own, was finding answers to the enduring questions "What does it mean to be human?" "Why are we here?" "How should we live?" and "What happens after death?"

Hellenistic Philosophy

Five groups of philosophers helped shape the direction of this new ideal for living: the Cynics, the Epicureans, the Stoics, the Skeptics, and the Neoplatonists. Like Plato and Aristotle, these philosophers wanted to propose a rational basis for ethical ideas and relate them to metaphysical theories. They thought the only way to find satisfactory answers to moral questions is through knowing the nature of things. How can we know how we should act in the world unless we know its meaning? Our conduct depends on the kind of universe in which we live. Mystery cults also served a popular need.

Despite its importance, Hellenistic philosophy was not startlingly original. Its practitioners' metaphysical systems reflect their predecessors' influence. The Cynics agreed with Socrates' attitude toward material possessions, and they tell the story of the day he passed a stall that was selling all kinds of wares. As he walked by, Socrates said, "What a lot of things I don't need." Epicurus, the founder of the Epicurean school, relied on Democritus for his atomic theory of nature. The Stoics agreed with Heraclitus that a fiery substance permeates all things. The Skeptics took seriously Socrates' statement that we should define our terms and closely examine our ideas. Plotinus, the major founder of

Neoplatonism, relied strongly on Plato. Each of these schools of philosophy encouraged individuals to find their place in the overall scheme of nature and live contented and meaningful lives.

The Cynics emphasized that we cannot find true happiness in material luxuries, political power, or good health. The Epicureans acquired the label *hedonists* from the Greek root *hedone* (pleasure). Hedonism views anything that is pleasurable as good and anything that is painful as evil. For the Epicurean hedonists, the outcome of living a pleasurable life is serenity. The Stoics, inspired by Socrates' courageous death, sought happiness by controlling their emotional responses to events they could not change. The Skeptics refrained from committing to any philosophy whose truth was doubtful, and Plotinus developed a doctrine that emphasized individual freedom by returning to our source through a mystical union with God.

The Cynics

Antisthenes founded the Cynic school of philosophy in Athens in approximately 400 B.C.E. He had been a pupil of Socrates and was impressed by the wise man's serenity even though he had no money. Based on Antisthenes' ideas, the Cynic school insisted that we could not find happiness in material possessions. If we depend on these things without realizing their fleeting nature, then our so-called happiness soon wanes. Because happiness does not depend on physical luxuries, it is within everyone's reach. Once we attain true happiness, we can never lose it, because happiness, unlike sensuous pleasure, is not subject to change.

Diogenes   Diogenes ("The Dog") was one of Antisthenes's students and the most famous of the Cynics. He reputedly lived in a barrel and owned nothing but a tunic, a stick, and a small leather bag for begging food. Stories about his lifestyle follow him. One day while he was sitting next to his barrel enjoying the sun, Alexander the Great rode up on his magnificent white horse. Impressed with Diogenes' reputation as a philosopher, Alexander asked if there was anything he could do for him. Diogenes nodded. "Stand to one side. You are blocking the sun."

One day Diogenes was seen begging food from a statue. When asked why, he said, "So I'll get used to being refused."

The Cynics believed nothing should disturb us—not our health, our suffering, or even our death. There is nothing after death.

Pause for Thought   The Cynics believed nothing should disturb us, even the thought of dying. If there is nothing after death, then why should we be afraid? Do you think they have a good point?

The Epicureans

Epicurus   Epicurus (341–270 B.C.E.), the founder of the Epicurean school, was born on the island of Samos in the Aegean Sea. When he was eighteen, Epicurus went to Athens to complete his required military service. There he studied under followers of Plato and Aristotle but rejected both of their philosophies. The writings of Democritus, however, had a lasting influence on his life and philosophy. Later, he founded a school in Athens, where he met his students in his own garden; they thus became known as "garden philosophers." Above the entrance to this garden was a sign that read, "Stranger, here you will live well. Here pleasure is the highest good."

Epicurus was a highly popular teacher, and his school became as influential as Plato's Academy, Aristotle's Lyceum, and, as we will see later in this chapter, Zeno's Stoa. He attracted a group of admiring students who looked on him with deep admiration and love. Unspoiled by the adulation, he remained modest and friendly to all, including rich and poor, men and women, adults and children, and slaves.

Ethics   The Cynics had interpreted Socrates' philosophy as meaning that we should free ourselves from material luxuries. But Epicurus believed that pleasure is the highest good. He did not believe in enduring pain, but avoiding it. Though the term *hedonism* has followed his school, Epicurus himself ate plain foods and lived simply. A friend once asked, "My revered teacher, what may I send you?" Epicurus replied, "Send me a cheese that I may fare sumptuously."

Democritus's Atomism influenced Epicurus's physics and his theory of knowledge, but his **ethics**—that is, his body of moral thinking—was altogether different from that of Democritus. The meaning of life, Epicurus held, is to live a life of pleasure. But his notion of living pleasurably is much different from the hedonists, who relish gourmet foods and "life in the fast lane." Epicurus advocated a simple and discerning life marked by a healthy body and a healthy soul. Gourmet foods cause stomach upset, stress results from life in the fast lane, and talk about sensuous pleasures is shallow and unsatisfying:

> We consider that of desires some are natural, others vain, and of the natural some are necessary and others merely natural; and of the necessary some are necessary for happiness, others for the repose of the body, and others for very life. The right understanding of these facts enables us to refer all choice and avoidance to the health of the body and freedom from disturbance, since this is the aim of the life of blessedness. For it is to obtain this end that we always act, namely, to avoid pain and fear. . . . And for this cause we call pleasure the beginning and end of the blessed life. For we recognize pleasure as the first good innate in us, and from pleasure we begin every act of choice and avoidance, and to pleasure we return again, using the feeling as the standard by which we judge every good. . . .

Every pleasure then because of its natural kinship to us is good, yet not every pleasure is to be chosen: even as every pain also is an evil, yet not all are always of a nature to be avoided. . . .

And again independence of desire we think a great good—not that we may at all times enjoy but a few things, but that, if we do not possess many, we may enjoy the few. . . . To grow accustomed therefore to simple and not luxurious diet gives us health to the full, and makes a man alert for the needful employments of life, and when after long intervals we approach luxuries disposes us better towards them, and fits us to be fearless of fortune.

When, therefore, we maintain that pleasure is the end, we do not mean the pleasures of profligates and those that consist in sensuality, as is supposed by some who are either ignorant or disagree with us or do not understand, but freedom from pain in the body and from trouble in the mind. For it is not continuous drinkings and revellings, nor the satisfaction of lusts, nor a pleasant life, but sober reasoning, searching out the motives for all choice and avoidance, and banishing mere opinions, to which are due the greatest disturbance of the spirit.

Of all this the beginning and the greatest good is prudence. Wherefore prudence is a more precious thing even than philosophy: for from prudence are sprung all the other virtues. . . .[1]

Pause for Thought

Do you agree with Epicurus that "Every pleasure is good" or with Plato that pleasure has little to do with the "good"?

Today, the name *epicurean* usually refers to an indulgent and voluptuous life: "Eat, drink, and be merry." But Epicurus considered an indulgent life "vain and idle," and he clearly distinguished between our *natural* and *unnatural* desires. Natural desires include plain food and exclude richly exotic fare. Exercise is natural. Running twenty-five miles a day is unnatural. The difference between natural and unnatural pleasures is the quality of satisfaction. Because natural desires are easy to satisfy, we suffer by discounting them. Unnatural desires are difficult to satisfy: The more chocolate and the more money we have, the more chocolate and money we want.

Epicurus distinguished among four distinct types of pleasure: (1) intense, short-lasting pleasures (e.g., spending all your money on clothes) and pleasures of less intensity, but which are longer lasting (e.g., saving money for future schooling); and (2) pleasures that culminate in pain (eating too much chocolate) and those that give us a sense of peaceful well-being (acting morally).

Epicurus himself lived a simple life and aimed for the pleasure of peace of mind. He avoided politics and involvement in social affairs, and he ate modest amounts of foods. His diet consisted of milk, bread, cheese, and a little wine. "My body," he said, "exalts in living delicately on bread and water, and it rejects the pleasures of luxury, not in themselves, but because of the trouble that follows upon them."[2]

Moderation is the basis of Epicurus' ethics:

> It is not possible to live pleasantly without living prudently and honourably and justly, [nor to live prudently and honorably and justly] without living pleasantly. And the man who does not possess the pleasant life, is not living prudently and honourably and justly, [and he who is not virtuous] cannot possibly live pleasantly."[3]

God and Atoms   Epicurus agreed with the Atomist philosopher Democritus: "Nothing can come from nothing." If there is nothing, there could be no God to create something. There are only eternal material atoms. If a god or gods exist, then they also are made of material atoms and so could not create from nothing. "Nothing," said Epicurus, "can be dissolved into nothing." If everything broke down into nothing, there could be no gods, no world, no humans, no plants, no animals. There are only eternal atoms that have no beginning. Atoms "fall" in space. When they randomly collide with other atoms, they form structures such as rocks, plants, animals, and human beings. Because atoms collide randomly, there is no orderly or created purpose ruled by a god and no reason to fear God's intervention.

If we are going to live a good life, then we must overcome the fear of the gods and the fear of death. According to Epicurus, death should not be a concern, because death isn't with us while we are alive; and when death does come, we no longer exist. With Democritus, Epicurus believed there is no life after death because when we die, the "soul atoms" disperse in all directions. As atoms formed our material body and soul, at death the atoms will separate and we as personalities will cease to be.

> . . . death is nothing to us. For all good and evil consists in sensation, but death is deprivation of sensation. And therefore a right understanding that death is nothing to us makes the mortality of life enjoyable, not because it adds to it an infinite span of time, but because it takes away the craving for immortality. For there is nothing terrible in life for the man who has truly comprehended that there is nothing terrible in not living. [Death] does not then concern either the living or the dead, since for the former it is not, and the latter are no more.[4]

Egocentric Hedonism   Without worrying about a god or afterlife, we can be free to concentrate on controlling our lives here on Earth. Such concentration on our individual selves is *egocentric hedonism*, or self-centeredness. Epicurus not only detached himself from exotic foods, but also abstained from involvement with other people and their problems. For him, happiness was not service to other people, helping suffering animals, or protecting the environment. The good life was the pleasure of pleasant company and studying philosophy. He held that intellectual pleasures, though they may not differ in quality from bodily pleasures, are superior because they last longer and are free from pain. Intellectual pleasures go beyond the pleasures of the moment to pleasures of a lifetime.

> Thus when I say that pleasure is the goal of living I do not mean the pleasures of libertines or the pleasures inherent in positive enjoyment, as is supposed by certain persons who are ignorant of our doctrine or who are not in agreement with it or who interpret it perversely. I mean, on the contrary, the pleasure that consists in freedom from bodily pain and mental agitation. The pleasant life is not the product of one drinking party after another or of sexual intercourse with women and boys or of the seafood and other delicacies afforded by a luxurious table. On the contrary, it is the result of sober thinking—namely, investigation of the reasons for every act of choice and aversion and elimination of those false ideas about the gods and death which are the chief source of mental disturbances.[5]

Intellectual Pleasure   It is our nature to seek pleasure. Instinctively, humans and animals pursue pleasure and avoid pain, thus every pleasure is good and every pain is bad. But we should exercise caution in the choice of our pleasures. If one pleasure lasted as long as another and was equally intense, then one pleasure would be as good as the next. But not every pleasure is worthy of being chosen and not every pain should be avoided. Intellectual pleasures last longer than pleasures of the body and thus are better than physical pleasures. The finest intellectual pleasure is the study of philosophy.

> Let no one when young delay to study philosophy, nor when he is old grow weary of his study. For no one can come too early or too late to secure the health of his soul. And the man who says that the age for philosophy has either not yet come or has gone by is like the man who says that the age for happiness is not yet come to him, or has passed away. Wherefore both when young and old a man must study philosophy, that as he grows old he may be young in blessings through the grateful recollection of what has been, and that in youth he may be old as well, since he will know no fear of what is to come. We must then meditate on the things that make our happiness, seeing that when that is with us we have all, but when it is absent we do all to win it.[6]

Pause for Thought   Epicurus summed up his philosophy with what he called the "four medicinal herbs": We should not fear the gods. Death is nothing to worry about. Good is easy to attain. The fearful is easy to endure. Do you agree: Is good easy to attain? Is fear easy to endure? Should we not fear God or death?

The Stoics

About the same time that Epicurus had his school in the garden, Zeno (not the same-named philosopher of pre-Socratic Athens) founded the Stoic school of philosophy. The Cynics, Epicureans, and Stoics recommended moderation of desires, but their agreement ended at that point. The Cynics emphasized that we cannot find true happiness in external possessions. Epicurus followed Democritus's idea that atoms are the basis for all things and without any ordered purpose in the universe. The Stoics, on the other hand, held that everything happens according to cosmic plan. Stoicism emerged as a reaction against hedonism. Where the hedonists sought pleasure and avoided pain, the Stoics sought a serene and controlled life through self-discipline.

Zeno (334–262 B.C.E.), a Phoenician merchant from Cyprus, came to Athens after being shipwrecked. Shortly after his arrival, he read Plato's *Apology*. Socrates' courage deeply impressed him. Later he met Crates, a Cynic philosopher who reminded him of Socrates, and Zeno became his disciple. In Greek, the word *cynic* means "dog," a label given to the Cynic philosopher Diogenes because he chose to "live like a dog."

Although Zeno admired the Cynics' ability to remain untroubled by the pains and disappointments of life, he thought their attitude toward political and social life was in opposition to Socrates. He also studied the works of other philosophers, especially Aristotle and Heraclitus, and eventually started his own school. He and his followers used to converse and study on a portico (that is, a porch). The name "Stoic" comes from *stoa,* the Greek word for portico.

Stoicism soon spread to Rome and survived as a school until almost the third century of the common era. Among its most famous supporters were Cleanthes (303–333 B.C.E.), Cicero (106–143 C.E.), Epictetus (60–117 C.E.), Seneca (4 B.C.E.–65 C.E.), and the Roman emperor Marcus Aurelius (121–180 C.E.). Stoic philosophy has had a lasting influence in the Western world. We find it throughout Christian theology, in the works of William Shakespeare, and in the philosophy of Benedict de Spinoza. Today we see smatterings of Stoicism in Jungian psychology and in therapy groups. Reinhold Niebuhr's "Serenity Prayer," a form of which is used in Alcoholics Anonymous and many other self-help groups, may also have been influenced by Stoic thought: "God, grant me the serenity to accept the things I cannot change, the courage to change the things I can, and the wisdom to know the difference."

God and Nature   For the Stoics, everything in the world, including God and the human soul, is *matter.* But matter is not a lump of inert carbon—it is dynamic, active, changing, and arranged in an orderly manner. Matter takes different forms. Like Heraclitus, the Stoics believed that the animating principle of all things is fire or reason (logos).

The Stoics defined *logos* (God) as a rational spirit with no shape but as making itself into all things. God permeates the world as the human soul permeates the body. God (divine fire) provides everything with vitality, beauty, and order. Thus, the universe is well organized, good, and a perfect whole. All life and movement have their source in God, so reason governs everything.

Natural Law and Fate   By suggesting that a rational principle permeates the universe, the Stoics took a *Pantheistic* worldview (God is in all, and all is in God). This belief erases the difference between the individual and the universe, and it denies any conflict between "spirit" and "matter." There is only one nature, and it is guided by the principle of reason. The logos is *natural law.* Nothing can exist or act by chance. As Einstein said, "God doesn't play dice. . . . Nothing rattles in the universe." The same rational laws that govern nature also determine human fate. Whatever happens does so for a reason. We can do nothing to alter how the logos determines the course of events.

Human Nature   Humans are a part of the same logos. Each person is like a world in miniature—a *microcosm*—reflecting the *macrocosm*. Each of us has the divine reason and a spark of the divine will. As God is the soul of the world, the human soul is part of God. The soul is the source of speech and the five senses. It is made of subtle matter that comes from God and which is transmitted to children by their parents. The soul has its seat in the heart and circulates through the bloodstream.

The soul gives us the ability to reason, and through reason we can understand the structure and order of nature. All natural processes, such as sickness and death, follow the unbreakable laws of nature. Nothing happens by chance. Therefore, we must learn to accept our destiny. Everything happens through necessity, so it is of little use to complain when fate comes knocking at the door. We also must accept the happy events of life calmly. Like the Cynics, the Stoics claimed that all external events are unimportant.

Ethics   Like the Epicureans, the Stoics considered happiness the highest virtue, but unlike the Epicureans they did not look for virtue in pleasure. They agreed with Socrates in identifying virtue with knowledge. Individuals who understand natural law are wise, and the wise person is happy. Evil is failing to control our emotions and allowing them to cloud the reason. Virtue is the ability to control our emotions.

We can change neither external circumstances such as birth and death nor the family we were born into, the sex of our brothers and sisters, or their characters. Our bodily functions such as digestion, elimination, and the growth rate of our fingernails follow natural law. We can complain about or accept our family, our looks, or even the weather. We have the power to choose our attitude and thus our judgments about events, situations, and others can lead us to happiness or misery. Wisdom consists in our ability to distinguish what is and is not in our power. External things such as wealth, reputation, the lives of our friends, and growing old are not in our power. In our power are our intentions, desires, and choices. Knowledge of human nature (what is and is not in our power) frees us to live life wisely.

Two of the most distinguished Stoic philosophers were the slave Epictetus and the Emperor Marcus Aurelius.

Epictetus   Epictetus (50–130 C.E.) was born a slave in Hierapolis, a small town in Phrygia, Asia Minor (modern Turkey). Though he was a slave to Emperor Nero in Rome, he had a respectable education and studied with a Stoic philosopher of the emperor's court. After Nero's death in 68 C.E., Epictetus gained his freedom and began to teach. However, in 93 C.E. the new Emperor Domitian expelled all philosophers from Rome. Epictetus traveled to northwestern Greece to establish a school of Stoicism; he remained there for the rest of his life. He lived simply with only a mat, a pallet, and a clay lamp (after his iron lamp was stolen). His reputation was that of a kind, humble, and charitable man. In his old age, he married to raise a child whose parents were going to abandon it.

Much of his life, Epictetus was lame from torture. While Epictetus was a slave, Nero had him tied to the rack and tortured. The slave's attitude on the rack showed his stoicism. He told the person in charge, "If you turn the rack one more time both of my legs will break." When the rack turned again and his legs snapped, Epictetus said calmly, "You see."

Pause for Thought   Can you think of examples in your life when you were stoic? Have you ever been so nervous before giving a speech that your fear outran your deodorant, but you managed through it anyway?

The Meaningful Life   In his daily life, Epictetus insisted on rigorous self-examination. He was a moral activist and wanted others to see that they alone were responsible for their actions. Like Socrates, he never wrote anything, but one of his students, Flavius Arrianus, took notes. Based on Epictetus's lectures, Flavius wrote eight *Discourses* and the *Encheiridion* (*Manual*).

The core of Epictetus's philosophy was the Stoic conviction that we cannot change events that happen to us, only our attitude toward those events. To live a meaningful life, we must overcome fear and control our desires. We should perform the role fate has us play, and we must think clearly. Then we will experience serenity. In the *Encheiridion*, he said:

1. Some things are under our control, while others are not under our control. Under our control are conception, choice, desire, aversion, and in a word, everything that is our own doing; not under our control are our body, our property, reputation, office and, in a word, everything that is not our own doing. Furthermore, the things under our control are by nature free, unhindered, and unimpeded; while the things not under our control are weak, servile, subject to hindrance, and not our own. Remember, therefore, that if what is naturally slavish you think to be free, and what is not your own to be your own, you will be hampered, will grieve, will be in turmoil, and will blame both gods and men; while if you think only what is your own to be your own, and what is not your own to be, as it really is, not your own, then no one will ever be able to exert compulsion upon you, no one will hinder you, you will blame no one, will find fault with no one, will do absolutely nothing against your will, you will have no personal enemy, no one will harm you, for neither is there any harm that can touch you. . . .

8. Do not seek to have everything that happens happen as you wish, but wish for everything to happen as it actually does happen, and your life will be serene.

9. Disease is an impediment to the body, but not to the moral purpose, unless that consents. Lameness is an impediment to the leg, but not to the moral purpose. And say this to yourself at each thing that befalls you; for you will find the thing to be an impediment to something else, but not to yourself. . . .

16. When you see someone weeping in sorrow, either because a child has gone on a journey, or because he has lost his property, beware that you be not carried away by the impression that the man is in the midst of external ills, but straightway keep before you this thought: "It is not what has happened that distresses this man (for it does not distress another), but his judgement about it." Do not, however, hesitate to sympathize with him so far as words go, and, if occasion offers, even to groan with him; but be careful not to groan also in the centre of your being.

17. Remember that you are an actor in a play, the character of which is determined by the Playwright: if He wishes the play to be short, it is short; if long, it is long; if He wishes you to play the part of a beggar, remember to act even this role adroitly; and so if your role be that of a cripple, an official, or a layman. For this is your business, to play admirably the role assigned you; but the selection of that role is Another's.

33. . . . Avoid entertainments given by outsiders and by persons ignorant of philosophy; but if an appropriate occasion arises for you to attend, be on the alert to avoid lapsing into the behaviour of such laymen. For you may rest assured, that, if a man's companion be dirty, the person who keeps close company with him must of necessity get a share of his dirt, even though he himself happens to be clean.

If someone brings you word that So-and-so is speaking ill of you, do not defend yourself against what has been said, but answer, "Yes, indeed, for he did not know the rest of the faults that attach to me; if he had, these would not have been the only ones he mentioned.[7]

Epictetus reminded us that we should not demand that events should happen as we wish, only that we should wish them to happen as they *do* happen—and all will be well. There is no need to fear future events or even death, because they will happen in any case. "I cannot escape death," he said, "but cannot I escape the fear of it?"

Epictetus summed up his teachings in two words—*bear* and *forbear:*

If a man will only have these two words at heart, and heed them carefully by ruling and watching over himself, he will for the most part fall into no sin, and his life will be tranquil and serene.[8]

Marcus Aurelius   Marcus Aurelius Antoninus (121–180 C.E.) was an emperor of Rome, one loved by Romans for his kindness and compassion. Although life cast him as emperor and warrior, many of his subjects considered him a saint and a sage. When Marcus was a youngster, Emperor Hadrian convinced Marcus's uncle, Antoninus Pius, to adopt Marcus and make him Pius's heir. Marcus took the name of his new father and became Marcus Aurelius Antoninus, but history remembers him now as simply Marcus Aurelius.

Marcus Aurelius became emperor of Rome at age forty. Against the wishes of the Roman Senate, Marcus generously appointed his adopted brother, Lucius Verus, co-emperor and gave his own daughter to Lucius in marriage. A lover of philosophy and literature, his role as both emperor and general threw him into politics and war.

The subsequent years of this gentle and peace-loving ruler were harassed by long and bloody wars, troubles of state, and domestic unhappiness. Floods, fires, and earthquakes devastate Rome. Verus and his troops, returning from a campaign in Syria, brought back the seeds of plague, which spread over the empire.[9]

Because of vassal kings to the east and the pressure of foreigners migrating into central Europe, this gentle, peace-loving emperor had to wage wars throughout his reign. In 169 C.E., Lucius Verus died; unfortunately, as co-emperor he had been little help to Marcus Aurelius. At that time Aurelius also faced a revolt from one of his generals. On one of his expeditions to the east, his wife died; she had given him five sons, but only one had lived. In spite of exhausting military campaigns and the difficulties in ruling an empire, Marcus Aurelius managed to institute many political and social reforms.

On his return from the east, Marcus Aurelius resumed his exhausting campaign against "barbarians on the Danube." At night in his tent, he wrote his *Meditations.* From these writings, we feel his pain and exhaustion. They were a diary of his private thoughts and not meant for the public. At last, after long and lonely years spent on one military campaign after another, this stoic warrior and saint succumbed to smallpox at age fifty-nine.

His Views on Life   Marcus Aurelius's only work is *Meditations,* and some philosophers consider it one of the greatest ethical writings of ancient times. In these writings we find both his religious view of the universe and his own moral struggles. *Meditations* give us a clear picture of the qualities he admired and the kind of person he was.

> Say to yourself in the morning: I shall meet people who are interfering, ungracious, insolent, full of guile, deceitful and antisocial; they have all become like that because they have no understanding of good and evil. But I who have contemplated the essential beauty of good and the essential ugliness of evil, who know that the nature of the wrongdoer is of one kin with mine—not indeed of the same blood or seed but sharing the same mind, the same portion of the divine—I cannot be harmed by any one of them, and no one can involve me in shame. I cannot feel anger against him who is of my kin, nor hate him. We were born to labor together, like the feet, the hands, the eyes, and the rows of upper and lower teeth. To work against one another is therefore contrary to nature, and to be angry against a man or turn one's back on him is to work against him.[10]

Pause for Thought   Do you view life as did Marcus Aurelius? Do you see everyone as kin—the thief and the saint alike?

> Do not despise death, but find satisfaction in it, since it is one of the things which nature intends. As are youth and age, adolescence and maturity, growing teeth and beard and gray hairs, begetting, gestation, and giving birth, and the other natural activities of the different seasons of life, such too is dissolution. This then is the thoughtful human attitude to death: not exaggerated or violent or arrogant, but to await it as one of nature's activities.[11]

Marcus Aurelius viewed the world much like Heraclitus did: Everything is in a state of flux and "mutually intertwined." The universe is rational, intelligent, and composed of the divine soul. Human beings share in the life and divinity of the universe, and each of us contains the divine spark. Because we have the divine faculty of reason, we can understand the order and workings of the world and our place in it.

> Some things are hurrying to be born, others are hurrying to have been, and some part of that which is in process of being is already extinct. The

streaming changes renew the universe continually, as the unceasing passage of time ever makes new the unending ages. What, among the things which rush past, can a man hold in high honor? It is as if one set out to love one of the sparrows flying past, and behold, it has vanished out of sight. Such indeed is life itself for every man, like an exhalation from the blood or a drawing breath from the air. As is the inhaling of air once and exhaling it again, which we do every moment, so too is the returning of the power of breathing as a whole, which you acquired at birth yesterday or the day before, to the source from which you drew it.[12]

All things are interwoven with one another, and the bond which unites them is sacred; practically nothing is alien to anything else, for all things are combined with one another and contribute to the order of the same universe. The universe embraces all things and is one, and the god who pervades all things is one, the substance is one, the law is one, the Reason common to all thinking beings is one, the truth is one, if indeed there is one perfection for the kindred beings who share in this selfsame Reason.[13]

Universal Brotherhood   The Stoics were distinctly cosmopolitan in their view of society. Unlike the Cynics, they drew attention to human fellowship and involved themselves with politics. Because each person has the divine spark within, everyone is related. People are not just citizens of a state or a nation, they are citizens of the world. All humans are brothers and sisters. The Stoics advanced the idea of universal brotherhood and a universal natural law of justice.

The Skeptics

A group of Skeptics questioned the Stoics claim that we can know God or the way the universe operates. They also questioned the philosophy of Plato, Aristotle, and the Epicureans. What struck the Skeptics as odd was the number of different conceptions of truth the philosophers proposed. They did not deny that truth existed, but they strongly doubted that anyone had found it.

The word *skeptic* comes from the old Greek word *skeptikoi*, meaning "inquirers" or "doubters." It was given to the oral teachings of Pyrrho, the founder of the Skeptic school. The Skeptics took seriously Socrates' philosophy of investigating life and ideas, but they criticized *dogmatic* philosophical doctrines that claimed to contain the truth. Like all other philosophers, their aim was to attain a life of inner peace and calm, but they differed among themselves on how to achieve it.

The Skeptics put *dogmatic* philosophers into two groups: (1) dogmatists who thought they had found the truth, and (2) those who dogmatically said no one could know the truth. As doubters, the Skeptics distrusted the unjustified claims of the dogmatists. They decided to avoid the dogmatic trap by refusing to accept any one belief as the true one.

Sextus Empiricus   Sextus Empiricus argued that the basic principle of skepticism is that for every proposition there is an equally opposed proposition. That is why "we end by ceasing to dogmatize." Anything we experience in the world or outside of it brings with it a variety of explanations. Because each explanation is as strong as the next, the Skeptics chose to suspend judgment. By refraining from denying or affirming anything, they hoped to realize a balanced and calm mental state.

Skepticism moved through many periods of development and different points of view. Many of the original writings by the Skeptics have disappeared. Most of our information comes from Sextus Empiricus, a physician and philosopher who lived in approximately 200 C.E. His treatises, which include this basic definition of Skepticism, are among the finest examples of the philosophy we have.

> Our task at present is to describe in outline the Sceptic doctrine, first premising that none of our future statements do we positively affirm that the fact is exactly as we state it, but we simply record each fact, like a chronicler, as it appears to us at the moment. . . .
>
> Scepticism is an ability, or mental attitude, which opposes appearances to judgements in any way whatsoever, with the result that, owing to the equipollence of the objects and reasons thus opposed, we are brought firstly quietude. Now we call it an "ability" not in any subtle sense, but simply in respect of its "being able." By "appearances" we now mean the objects of sense-perception, when we contrast them with the objects of thought or "judgements." The phrase "in any way whatsoever" can be connected either with the word "ability," to make us take the word "ability," as we said, in its simple sense, or with the phrase "opposing appearances to judgements"; for inasmuch as we oppose these in a variety of ways—appearances to appearances, or judgements to judgements, or *alternando* appearances to judgements,—in order to ensure the inclusion of all these antitheses we employ the phrase "in any way whatsoever" . . . "Equipollence" we use of equality in respect of probability and improbability, to indicate that no one of the conflicting judgements takes precedence of any other as being more probable. "Suspense" is a state of mental rest owing to which we neither deny nor affirm anything. "Quietude" is an untroubled and tranquil condition of soul.[14]

Our senses, said Sextus, give us different impressions about the same object. For instance, imagine you and a friend are walking down a road. You see three people coming your way. "Look," says your friend. "Here come Jack, Tony, and Alice." As they get closer, you both realize the three people are Jake, Manny, and Blanca. That you had the impression is true, but the people looked different to your senses from a distance than they did up close. In other words, we can never be certain that what we perceive with our senses is accurate. Therefore, said the Skeptics, we cannot be sure that our knowledge about the world or anything else is true or not true.

Pause for Thought   Have you ever sat in a circle of people and whispered a sentence one person to another around the circle? What has happened to the sentence by the time it finishes the circle?

Take the word, God. Do all religions agree on its definition? Do the Skeptics have a point?

Morality   Moral ideas are also subject to doubt. Individuals and cultures have different ideas about what is good and what is evil. Though people share the ability to reason, they frequently disagree on moral principles. Skeptics thought one moral argument is probably as good as another. Because we cannot have true knowledge of right and wrong, we should withhold our moral judgments. When we take a stand on morals, passions flare; abortion is a perfect example. By withholding judgment, we can be more serene. Like the Epicureans and the Stoics, the Skeptics wanted peace of mind. According to Sextus Empiricus:

> The Sceptic's end is quietude in respect of matters of opinion. . . . For the Sceptic, having set out to philosophize with the object of passing judgement on the sense-impressions and ascertaining which of them are true and which false, so as to attain quietude thereby, found himself involved in contradictions of equal weight, and being unable to decide between them suspended judgement; and as he was thus in suspense there followed, as it happened, the state of quietude in respect of matters of opinion. For the man who opines that anything is by nature good or bad is forever being disquieted: when he is without the things which he deems good he believes himself to be tormented by things naturally bad and he pursues after the things which are, as he thinks, good; which when he has obtained he keeps falling into still more perturbations because of his irrational and immoderate elation, and in his dread of a change of fortune he uses every endeavour to avoid losing the things which he deems good. On the other hand, the man who determines nothing as to what is naturally good or bad neither shuns nor pursues anything eagerly; and, in consequence, he is unperturbed.[15]

The goal of Sextus Empiricus's arguments was to lead individuals to the Pyrrhonian goal of inner peace. As long as we try to make universal judgments in the dogmatist's sense, we will experience frustration and anxiety. By suspending judgment, we will find peace of mind and be free of "the dogmatist's disease [of] rashness."

Mystery Cults

The transition of the Hellenistic–Roman philosophy from the ethical to the religious standpoint was a result of the needs of the time. After the death of Marcus Aurelius, Rome had a series of weak and incompetent emperors. The Empire was crumbling. In their desire for a more meaningful life, one that had inner significance, people turned to "mystery" cults. One such cult was the Phrygian worship of the Great Mother, which sprang from the myth of the goddess Cybele. According to that myth, when her lover, Attis, died, Cybele brought death to the world with her mourning. When Attis came back to life, Cybele rejoiced and dressed nature in a garment of green. In following this story, Cybele's worshipers prayed for good crops and immortality.

Although the mystery cults began in the third century B.C.E., their popularity flourished with the breakdown of the Roman Empire. During this period, people began to integrate ideas from many sources into new religions. The cult of Isis and Osiris brought together Greek and Egyptian myths. The Romans developed the Imperial cult and worshiped their living and dead emperors. The Mithraic cult worshiped a savior god whose veneration promised eternal life. The festival of Mithra (the sun god or bringer of light) fell on December 25, the day of the sun's nativity, when he was reborn after the winter solstice. These and other mystery cults served a deep popular need that was unfulfilled by the old Greek and Roman gods and corrupt emperors, a need that was also heightened by the political upheavals taking place all around these citizens of Rome.

Because Roman religion limited itself to the worship of local deities, Roman priests and officials did not welcome the mystery cults. Even so, the new cults continued to grow in popularity. Among them was Christianity, which some Romans classified as a cult and the Roman rulers as a sect of Judaism. Christian thinkers endeavored to give their religion a systematic philosophy, but it had no solid foundation until Augustine integrated Christian and Platonic thought.

The Neoplatonists

Cynicism, Epicureanism, and Stoicism all had their roots in the teaching of Socrates. They also looked to the pre-Socratic philosophers Heraclitus and Democritus. The most dominant philosophy in the late Hellenistic period was Neoplatonism, which was inspired by Plato and most clearly postulated by Plotinus.

Plotinus did not mention Christianity anywhere in his writings, but his philosophy had a major influence much later on Augustine. As Neoplatonism's best representative, Plotinus is the bridge between classical and medieval philosophy.

Plotinus   Plotinus (204–270 C.E.) was an Egyptian by birth and a native of Lycopolis. Little is known about his life. One of his students, Porphyry, wrote that Plotinus seemed ashamed of being in the body. For that reason he could not bear to talk about his race, his parents, or his native country. When an artist asked if he could paint his portrait, Plotinus replied:

> Why really, is it not enough to have to carry the image in which nature has encased us, without your requesting me to agree to leave behind me a longer-lasting image of the image, as if it was something genuinely worth looking at?[16]

Pause for Thought   Is there a correlation in the above quote with Plato's imaging stage in the Divided Line? Why would Plotinus be opposed to having his image carved?

We know nothing about Plotinus's early years. We meet him for the first time in Alexandria when he was twenty-eight years old. By then he had devoted himself to the study of philosophy and was seeking a system that would satisfy him. When Plotinus visited Ammonius Saccas, he said, "This is the man I was looking for." He remained Ammonius Saccas's student for eleven years.

When he was thirty-nine, Plotinus left Ammonius Saccas to join Emperor Gordian's army and travel to the Far East to learn from other philosophers, but the expedition proved unsuccessful. Upon his return to Rome, he established a school of philosophy that soon attracted many of the elite, including Emperor Gallenius. Plotinus was a brilliant lecturer with lofty spiritual ideals. One of his goals was to develop a city based on Plato's *Republic* called Platonopolis, but the idea never materialized.

Plotinus wrote fifty-four treatises. However, he put them in no particular order, and his weak eyesight prevented him from rereading them. After his death, Porphyry arranged them into six sets of nines called the *Enneads*.

Plotinus was a *mystic*—that is, one who has experienced merging with God or the "cosmic spirit"—and people revered him for his disciplined spiritual life. Six times in his life he realized a mystical union with God, including four times in Porphyry's presence. According to Porphyry:

> [Plotinus's] end goal was to be united to, to approach the God who is over all things. Four times while I was with him, he attained that goal, in an unspeakable actuality and not in potency only.[17]

At age sixty-four, almost blind and in ill health, Plotinus retired to a friend's estate where he died two years later.

Plotinus's Mysticism   In the *Enneads*, Plotinus described the source of the world, our place in the world, and how we can overcome our moral and spiritual difficulties. His mystical doctrine views the One—that is, God—as the source of everything and the source to which human beings must return. Unlike the Christian God, the One is not a personal creator god. The One, as the source of all, must of necessity overflow; it forms the universe by doing so.

Plotinus based his philosophy on Plato's and rejected the doctrines of the soul put forth by Aristotle, the Epicureans, the Stoics, and the Skeptics. He objected to Aristotle's belief that the soul is the form of the body and cannot exist without a body. According to Aristotle, if the body loses part of its form, such as an arm through amputation, then the loss also would deform the soul. The Epicureans and Stoics understood the soul as a material body, a physical breath. But, Plotinus argued, in agreement with Plato, the soul did not depend on the material body for its existence.

Plotinus also described the universe as a living structure that proceeds eternally from its source in the One. This god overflows or emanates from itself to form Pure Thought (Nous or Divine Mind), which overflows or emanates into heavenly materials that form the world soul. From the world soul emanate various levels of activity to shape matter or the physical world and everything in it.

Plotinus then explained the way humans can ascend upward toward the source by self-purification. The aim of the human soul, the whole meaning of its existence, is to experience union with God, "which alone can satisfy it."

According to Plotinus, the One is beyond human thought or language and present to all things according to their capacity to receive It.

> The One, as transcending intellect, transcends knowing.

> The One is, in truth, beyond all statement; whatever you say would limit It. . . .[18]

> The One is the greatest, not physically but dynamically. Hence it is indivisible, not physically but dynamically. So also the beings that proceed from it; they are, not in mass but in might, indivisible and partless. Also, The One is infinite not as extension or a numerical series is infinite, but in its limitless power. Conceive it as intelligence or divinity; it is more than that. Compress unity within your mind, it is still more than that. Here is unity superior to any your thought lays hold of, unity that exists by itself and in itself and is without attributes.

> As the One does not contain any difference, it is always present and we are present to it when we no longer contain difference. The One does not aspire to us, to move around us; we aspire to it, to move around it. Actually, we always move around it; but we do not always look. We are like a chorus grouped about a conductor who allow their attention to be distracted by the audience. If, however, they were to turn towards their conductor,

they would sing as they should and would really be with him. We are always around The One. If we were not, we would dissolve and cease to exist. Yet our gaze does not remain fixed upon The One. When we look at it, we then attain the end of our desires and find rest. Then it is that, all discord past, we dance an inspired dance around it.

In this dance the soul looks upon the source of life, the source of The Intelligence, the origin of Being, the cause of the Good, the root of The Soul.[19]

Transcending essence, the One also transcends being, because being implies essence. Plotinus may have been the first philosopher to make the distinction between essence and existence. In his view, existence implies essence but is not equivalent to it. That is why he denied both essence and existence to the One. For Plotinus, the One is prior to and the source of essence and existence. The One (God) is Absolute Unity—indivisible, uncreated, and unchangeable. The One transcends the world and all distinctions. It does not create, but it overflows or emanates by necessity.

Emanation   As the Source of all, the One emanates as water flows from a spring that has no source outside itself. Plotinus also used the analogy of the sun. The One emanates in the same way that light flows from the sun. The sun neither exhausts itself nor does anything. Just as the sun generates light rays that are *not* the sun, the One generates all things but is *not* all things:

The One is all things and no one of them; the source of all things is not all things. . . .

It is precisely because there is nothing within the One that all things are from it: in order that Being may be brought about, the source must be no Being but Being's generator, in what is to be thought of as the primal act of generation. Seeking nothing, possessing nothing, lacking nothing, the One is perfect and, in our metaphor, has overflowed, and its exuberance has produced the new: this product has turned again to its begetter and been filled and has become its contemplator and so an Intellectual-Principle [Pure Thought].

That station towards the One (the fact that something exists in presence of the One) establishes Being; that vision directed upon the One establishes the Intellectual-Principle; standing towards the One to the end of vision, it is simultaneously Intellectual-Principle and Being; and, attaining resemblance in virtue of this vision, it repeats the act of the One in pouring forth a vast power.

The second outflow is an image or representation of the Divine Intellect as the Divine Intellect represented its own prior, The One.

This active power sprung from essence (from the Intellectual-Principle Thought considered as Being) is Soul.

Soul arises as the idea and act of the motionless Intellectual-Principle.
—which itself sprang from its own motionless prior—but the Soul's
operation is not similarly motionless; its image is generated from its movement. It takes fullness by looking to its source; but it generates its image by
adopting another, a downward, movement.

The image of Soul is Sense and Nature, the vegetal principle . . . having
moved thus far downwards it produces—by its outgoing and its tendency
towards the less good—another hypostasis or form of being. . . .[20]

Nous (pure thought, divine mind) is the first emanation from the One. Most
like the One, it is universal intelligence or the principle of thought. Nous is the
underlying rationality and order of the world. It has no spatial or temporal
boundaries but contains the ideas or "blueprints" of all things (see Plato's Forms,
pp. 48–49. Nous overflows and generates the world soul. As the light of the sun
becomes less intense the farther away from the sun it gets, so there is a decline
in perfection from Nous to the world soul.

The world soul has two aspects: First, it looks upward to the Divine Mind or
pure rationality to contemplate the eternal ideas (Plato's Forms); second, it
emanates downward, providing the Life Principle to all of nature. Through the
One, Nous and the world soul are eternal together. The world soul bridges spirit
(the timeless and spaceless realm) and matter (the phenomenal world). The world
soul accounts for time, space, and nature, all of them as reflections of eternal ideas.

The human soul is an emanation or overflowing from the world soul. It also
has two aspects. First, gazing up, it shares in the world soul and Nous. Second,
looking down, the human soul connects with the body. Plotinus agreed with
Plato that the soul preexists and is the result of a "fall" when it joins with the
body. The soul provides the body with life, the senses, and rationality.

After death, the soul survives the body and eventually takes birth again in
another body. After many rebirths, when the soul reaches the highest stage of
knowledge and love, it joins all other souls again in the world soul. Unlike
Aristotle, Plotinus believed souls could be immortal.

Pause for Thought

Do you agree with Plotinus that rebirth is necessary for a human soul
to reach the highest stage of knowledge and love? Or do you think we
can reach the highest stage of knowledge and love in one lifetime, or
after death?

The physical world, consisting of matter, is the lowest level of emanation
and the farthest away from the One. In Plotinus's idea of emanation, each level
of being overflows into the realm below it, causing that realm to realize its pos-

sibilities. Using the sun analogy, because matter is the farthest away from the light, it is almost the opposite of spirit (the One). But matter, though dim, is not complete darkness. Like the soul, matter has two aspects: First, the higher aspect follows the laws of cause and effect; second, the lower aspect moves aimlessly and chaotically toward collision and extinction. As light tends to flow downward to the point of darkness, so matter tends to disappear into nothingness.

Evil   As matter faces upward, it follows natural laws of cause and effect, and this accounts for its orderliness. But the natural momentum of matter is to flow downward; as it does, it plunges into darkness away from order. At this point, matter becomes the container of evil, which exists when there is chaos, or an absence of natural laws and order. Though matter is farthest from the One and lacks perfection, it is still necessary. Without it, something would be lacking in the overall scheme of things. The darkness or evil in matter is not a force in itself, but the absence of light. Evil also serves a purpose in the overall scheme of the universe: It is the shadow that enhances the beauty of the light.

The problem of moral evil arises when the soul generates a material body. The rational aspect of the soul (Nous) is moral, but it is the nature of the material body to turn from rationality toward its nonrational aspects of sensation and appetites. Evil occurs when the appetites pull the soul toward disorder and away from the light of reason. For Plotinus, evil is not a powerful force competing with good, it is the absence of good. The body, he said, has a beauty of its own and is therefore not evil. But without rational control by the soul, the body inclines toward evil.

The Ascent of the Soul   By descending into the lower realms, the One shares as much of its perfection as possible with them. Plotinus called the process a double movement of *descent* and *ascent*. All things ascend (evolve), seeking to unite with their source. As a mystic and rebirth philosopher, Plotinus viewed the soul's return to union with the One (God) as a difficult and painful endeavor that includes many lifetimes. The ascent to its source requires the soul to develop moral values, the love of beauty, and disciplined thinking.

According to Plotinus, the good for all humans is to attain likeness to God by "becoming just and holy, and living by wisdom." All lovers of beauty should follow the path laid down in Plato's *Symposium* by Diotima: to contemplate the eternal values and then await the vision of the One. Individuals can accomplish this when they are no longer chained by desire to the world.

In his treatise on beauty, Plotinus described "the way" of the soul's return:

> Withdraw into yourself, and look. And if you do not find yourself beautiful yet, act as does the creator of a statue that is to be made beautiful. He cuts away here, he smoothes there, he makes this line lighter, this other purer, until a lovely face has grown upon his work. So do you also: cut away all

that is excessive, straighten all that is crooked, bring light to all that is over-cast, labour to make all one glow of beauty and never cease chiselling your statue, until there shall shine out on you from it the godlike splendour of virtue, until you shall see the perfect goodness surely established in the stainless shrine.

When you know that you have become this perfect work, . . . when you find yourself wholly true to your essential nature . . . you are now become very vision: now call up all your confidence, strike forward yet a step—you need a guide no longer—strain, and see.[21]

Pause for Thought   What would you have to chisel away to uncover your inner beauty?

Like Plato, Plotinus said the soul must begin with love of physical beauty through appreciation of abstract beauty and rise to the vision of beauty itself. This is the key to immortality. The human intellect belongs on a higher plane that it can regain. Reunion with the One is not an absorption that annihilates individuality:

The intellects there do not cease to be because they are not corporeally divided, but each remains distinct in otherness, having the same essential being.

This is the life of gods and divine and blessed men, deliverance from the things of this world, a flight of the alone to the Alone.[22]

Plotinus's philosophy, especially his idea of liberating the soul to a mysti-cal union with God, strongly influenced Christian mystics. A later mystic known as Pseudo-Dionysius the Areopagite introduced Neoplatonism into the Church where it remained for nine centuries with just a few changes. In this way, Plotinus's philosophy was the wellspring for most future Western mystics.

Hypatia of Alexandria   Hypatia (ca. 370 to 375–415 c.e.) was a female philosopher, mathematician, and astronomer. Although she was a pagan, Rome's Christian government named her to the position of philosopher at the museum of Alexandria. Her appointment was an exceptional honor because women were seldom elected to public office. Hypatia's father, Theon of Alexandria, was the museum's most famous mathematician and astronomer. Hypatia taught the works of Plato, Aristotle, and the neo-Platonists.

One of her students, Synesius, became a Christian and later a church bishop at Ptolemais. According to Synesius, Hypatia was such an outstanding teacher that students came long distances to study philosophy, mathematics, and astronomy under her. In one story, a student tried to court her, but her only interest in him was discussing goodness, wisdom, and virtue of Platonic philosophy. She finally ended his harassment by throwing a handkerchief she had been using as a sanitary napkin in his face: "This is what you love, young fool, and not anything that's beautiful."

Philosophy provided her the basis for her mathematical and astronomical writings. She was a towering intellect and considered the greatest philosopher of her day. But it was a time when a woman—especially one who was a pagan in a Christian world—would pay with her life for her talents. Socrates Scholasticus reported her tragic death as follows:

> [A group of Nitrian monks] pull her out of her chariot: they hail her into the Church called Caesarium: they stripped her stark naked: they rase the skin and rend the flesh of her body with sharp shells, until the breath departed out of her body: they quarter her body: they bring her quarters unto a place called Cinaron and burn them to ashes.[23]

Summary

The Cynics emphasized that we cannot find true happiness in externals such as material luxuries, political power, or good health. If we depend on these things without realizing they are fleeting, our so-called happiness soon dwindles. True happiness occurs when nothing disturbs us.

The Epicureans believed not in enduring pain and fear, but in avoiding them. It is natural, said Epicurus, "to seek pleasure and avoid pain." However, the greatest pleasure is not in the senses, but in philosophy. Like Democritus, Epicurus believed there are only eternal atoms. If there is a god, then god is composed of atoms. There is no life after death, because atoms separate and personalities cease to be.

The Stoics saw God as "a rational spirit having itself no shape but making itself into all things." The universe and everything in it has its source in God. "God is in all, and all is in God." God directs the universe. Humans cannot change events, but we can change our attitudes toward events. In so doing, we can control our emotions and live a life of serenity. "Bear and forbear" is the key to Stoic philosophy.

The Skeptics wanted to eliminate dogmatism from their thinking. Not only are our senses inaccurate, but also our moral ideas are subject to doubt. Individuals and cultures have different ideas about what is good or evil. About this time in the Hellenistic period, the mystery cults grew in importance, even when Romans objected to them, because people yearned for a deep spiritual fulfillment. Among these cults was Christianity.

Plotinus was the major proponent of Neoplatonism, offering the world the doctrine of emanation. The One (the source of all) overflows and, by doing so, forms the universe and everything in it. Plotinus saw evil not as a force in itself, but as the absence of light—or that which is farthest from its source. A result of the descent is the ascent of all things seeking unity with their source.

Another Neoplatonist, Hypatia of Alexandria, was one of just a few women philosophers over the ages, and she also excelled in mathematics and astronomy. Her students came from afar because she was considered the great intellect of her day. Hypatia was appointed to the position of philosopher at the museum of Alexandria; there she taught Plato, Aristotle, and Neoplatonism.

Connections

Hellenistic philosophy, especially Stoicism and Neoplatonism, influenced the next philosophers we shall study. The coming of Christianity brought a rejection of the naturalistic ideal in favor of a transcendent God. One of the turning points was the philosophy of the Stoics, their view of God, their deprecation of worldly life, and their emphasis on divinity and duty. Early Christianity was much like the mystery cults and treated by the Romans as such. Later, when Christianity became socially respectable, its scholars sought answers through philosophical questioning. Augustine looked to Neoplatonism as the answer to his intellectual searching. His study of Plotinus and Plato moved him closer to Christianity. He was confident that among the Platonists he would find what was not opposed to the teachings of Christianity. With this in mind, we now turn to the Medieval world.

Study Questions

1. What is Cynicism?

2. Where do the Cynics look for happiness?

3. What is the relationship of Socrates to Cynicism and Stoicism?

4. Compare and contrast Cynicism and Epicureanism.

5. What is hedonism?

6. Compare and contrast the meaning of Epicurus's hedonism and the meaning of hedonism today.

7. What is Epicurus's view of God?

8. What is Epicurus's view of life after death?

9. Compare and contrast Epicureanism and Stoicism.

10. According to Epicurus, what are natural pleasures and unnatural pleasures?

11. How would Epicurus view religion?

12. Compare and contrast Epicureanism and Stoicism.

13. What is logos?

14. What is the relationship of God to the universe?

15. Describe how God relates to the concept of fate in Stoicism.

16. According to the Stoics, what are some of the things we can and cannot change?

17. What is pantheism?

18. What is Marcus Aurelius's view of human relationships?

19. Can the Stoic philosophy work in today's society?

20. What is a Skeptic?

21. Why do the Skeptics avoid dogmatic philosophy?

22. Why do the Skeptics doubt moral absolutes?

23. What is Plotinus's theory of emanation?

24. How does Plotinus view evil?

25. Compare and contrast your understanding of creation and Plotinus's view of emanation.

26. For Plotinus, what is the goal of human life?

27. Why is Plotinus called a mystic?

28. Do you see a resurgence of mystery cults in our society today?

Notes

1. "Letter to Menoeceus" (trans. by C. Bailey), 127 ff., pp. 87–91 in *Epicurus: The Extant Remains*. Oxford, UK: Clarendon Press, New Oxford University Press, 1926.

2. Stobaeus, "Anthology" (Bk. 3, sec. 17, line 33), p. 170 in Giovanni Reale, *A History of Ancient Philosophy*, Vol. 3. *The Systems of the Hellenistic Age*. Albany: State University of New York Press, 1985.

3. "Principle Doctrines," XVII, p. 99, in *Epicurus: The Extant Remains*. Oxford, UK: Clarendon Press, New Oxford University Press, 1926.

4. "Letter to Menoeceus," ibid., 124–125, p. 85.

5. Ibid., p. 8.

6. Ibid., p. 4.

7. Epictetus, *Encheiridion* (trans. by W. A. Oldfather), Sec. I, 8, 9, 16, 17, 33. Cambridge, MA: Harvard University Press, 1928.

8. H. Crossley (trans.), *The Golden Sayings of Epictetus,* p. 147. New York: Macmillan, 1925.

9. Joseph Maxwell, "Marcus Aurelius Antoninus," p. 156 in *Encyclopedia of Philosophy*, Vol. 5, edited by Paul Edwards et al. New York: Macmillan, 1967.

10. Marcus Aurelius, *The Meditations* (trans. by G.M.A. Grube, Bk. II, 1). New York: Library of Liberal Arts, 1963.

11. Ibid., Bk. IX, 3.

12. Ibid., Bk. VI, 15.

13. Ibid., Bk. VII. 9.

14. "Sextus Empiricus" (trans. by R. G. Bury), Bk. I, 4, 8–10 in *Outlines of Pyrrhonism,* Vol. I. Cambridge, MA: Harvard University Press, Loeb Classical Library, 1933.

15. Ibid., Bk. I, 25–27.

16. Porphyry, "The Life of Plotinus" Vol. I, p. 3 in *Plotinus* (trans. by A. H. Armstrong). Cambridge, MA: Harvard University Press, 1966.

17. Ibid., p. 71.

18. Plotinus, "Enneads" (trans. by G. H. Turnbull), pp. 12–17 in *The Essence of Plotinus,* Vol. III. Oxford, UK: Oxford University Press, 1934.

19. Plotinus, "Enneads" (trans. by Elmer O'Brien) Bk. VI, 6, 8, 9 in *The Essential Plotinus*. New York: New American Library.

20. Plotinus, *The Enneads* (trans. by Stephen MacKenna), Bk. V, 2.1. London: Faber & Faber, 1917–1930.

21. Ibid., Bk. I, 6.9.

22. Plotinus, *Plotinus* (trans. by A. H. Armstrong), op. cit., VI 9.11.

23. The quote is originally from Anne Freemantle, *A Treasurey of Early Christianity,* p. 380 (New York: Viking, 1953), and was cited in Mary Ellen Waithe (Ed.), *A History of Women Philosophers,* Vol. I, *Ancient Women Philosophers 600 B.C.–500 A.D.,* p. 172. Boston: Kluwer Academic Publishers, 1987.

CHAPTER SIX

The Medieval World

By rising and spreading throughout Europe, Christianity came to dominate the period after the Hellenistic–Roman era. Though the Hebrew Bible was written in the Semitic family of languages, the Christian New Testament was written in Greek, so Christian theology and philosophy had close ties with Hellenistic philosophy.

In this chapter, we shall see that Christian philosophers of the Medieval era were also theologians. They were concerned with God, the story of Creation, and the human relationship with both. With Jews and Muslims, Christians share a belief in a single God (monotheism). God is omniscient, omnipotent, and omnipresent. God intervenes during history to manifest His will in the world. One major difference between Christianity and Judaism and Islam, however, is its belief in what is called the "Trinity." According to Christian doctrine, God is threefold: Father, Son, and Holy Spirit. But Judaism and Islam proclaim, "God is one and only one." No Trinity exists for these religions.

The Hellenistic schools had shown a strong interest in discovering the workings of human nature through science as well as philosophy. Some Christians, however, took a dim view of the sciences. In Christian philosophy, God is the ultimate concern. Hellenistic schools thought morality was the means to "know thyself" and achieve happiness. Christian moralists, on the other hand, did not believe self-knowledge and happiness were the ultimate goals of human beings. Relying on the supernatural, Christians looked to God's commands and His judgment of good and evil.

Recall that Plato and the Neoplatonists viewed humans as basically good, and that they fell from the Ideal through ignorance. Christians, however, viewed humans as sinners who willfully rejected a loving God's commands. Gradually, Christianity became such a powerful philosophy that the Church itself closed Plato's Academy in Athens.

Religious Doctrines

During the Middle Ages, many of the religious doctrines known to modern Christians came into existence. Eventually, these doctrines grew into religious dogmas that were binding on all Christians. Perhaps the most significant shift was in how Medieval philosophers viewed humanity. Plato had argued that humans are innately good but ignorant. Medieval philosophers, however, said that humans are born with **original sin** that they inherit from the first man, Adam, and the first woman, Eve. Because sin is inherent, we as humans are wicked, evil, and depraved. Many theologians and philosophers from this era believed that most humans deserved to go to Hell and that only God's mercy and love could save them from such a future.

Early Christianity and Philosophy

Jesus and his disciples, especially Paul, were not systematic philosophers. In fact, Paul warned the faithful to "beware lest any man spoil you through philosophy and vain deceit." Based on revealed truth and Paul's admonition, Christianity held *faith* supreme over reason and logic. The question soon rose, however, whether Christians must simply have faith in the Christian revelation or whether they could approach the Christian truths with the help of reason.

Pause for Thought   Do you believe there is a contradiction between the Bible and reason, or do you believe faith and reason are compatible?

As more and more educated people showed an interest in Christianity, they wanted to understand the relationship between the Greek philosophers and what the Bible said. Most philosophers and Biblical scholars realized the importance of including rational Greek arguments as a doctrinal base for Christianity. But some Christian theologians, such as Tertullian (160–230 C.E.), considered Greek rationality heretical: "What has Jerusalem to do with Athens?" he demanded. He further said that reason is not important: "I believe because it is absurd."

In spite of opposition from Tertullian and others, a rational philosophical system evolved from the gospels and Christian beliefs. The mark of Hellenistic converts to Christianity is evident in John's gospel that opens by using the Greek logos, meaning word, or reason. "In the beginning was the logos, and the logos was with God, and the logos was God."

> The influence of Greek philosophy is apparent throughout this gospel, the most popular of the four★ in Christianity's formative years. The greatest apologist of the third century, Origen, had been a classmate of Plotinus in the Neoplatonic school of Ammonius Saccas in Alexandria. The "Nicene Creed," for example, strives to define the Holy Trinity in terms of the Aristotelian category of substance. Theology, in fact, is not only a Greek word but also an enterprise that is wholly Greek in origin.[1]

Thus, we see the influence of Greek and Hellenistic philosophy in the doctrines of Christianity. But the question of faith and reason continued throughout the Medieval period. Augustine and Aquinas, two of the most prominent Medieval philosophers and among the Church's greatest saints, both dealt with this question. Augustine based his philosophy on the teachings of Plato and Plotinus, and Aquinas looked to Aristotle as the basis of his philosophy.

Saint Augustine

One of the most acclaimed Christian philosophers in history, Augustine accepted that Platonic Ideas were "contained in the divine intelligence." And from Plotinus, he accepted that evil was a lack of good rather than a force in itself. Accordingly, he tried to fuse his own Christian spirituality with the metaphysics of Plato and Plotinus.

Augustine's Life   Aurelius Augustinus was born in Thagaste (now Algeria), North Africa, in 354 C.E. His mother was a Christian and his father a pagan. Augustine did not convert to Christianity until he was an adult. As a youngster, Augustine showed intellectual promise, and at seventeen his parents sent him to Carthage to study rhetoric. While there, he found philosophy, spurned Christianity, and took a mistress who bore their son.

After rejecting Christianity, he studied other religions. What interested him in particular was the problem of moral evil and why it exists in people. His personal moral dilemma was his strong desire for sensual gratification. But he also showed

---

★Matthew, Mark, and Luke are the other gospels.

concern for all the suffering in the world. He asked, "If God is all good, and He created a good world, how then is evil possible?" Christianity's answer did not satisfy him, so Augustine turned to a group called the Manichaeans. Mani, the third-century C.E. prophet of the Manichaeans, developed and extended the ancient Persian teachings of Zoroaster (Zarathustra), who believed in a dualistic universe.

According to the Manichaeans, there are two basic principles: light or goodness on the one hand, and darkness or evil on the other. These two principles are eternally equal and eternally in conflict with one another, both in the world and in human beings. In humans, the conflict exists between the soul (light) and the body (darkness). For Augustine, this dualism was the answer to why he could not overcome his life of sensual indulgence. He attributed his lust to the power of darkness.

So the Manichaean dualism solved one mystery. But Augustine wondered how two eternally equal and conflicting principles could exist in the universe. Finally, he reasoned that there could *not* be conflicting absolute principles. Thus, he broke with the Manichaeans and became a Skeptic. The Skeptics, he said, "were wiser than the rest in thinking that we ought to doubt everything, and that no truth can be comprehended by man."

Shortly after his switch to Skepticism, Augustine left Africa and his mistress for a teaching position in Rome and then Milan. In Milan, he met Bishop Ambrose, who gave him a greater appreciation of Christianity. Also in Milan, he found another mistress. While teaching, he came upon Plotinus's *Enneads*. After reading them, he realized how there could be a unity of the world without two equally dual principles. Soul and body are from a single graduated system, with matter merely on a lower level. Through Neoplatonism, Augustine overcame his skepticism.

From Plotinus, Augustine received a new viewpoint on evil. Before, he believed evil to be a powerful force, but now he realized evil as an absence of good and not a force at all. Listening to Bishop Ambrose's sermons and reading Plotinus made Christianity more reasonable. Still, his sensual desires perplexed him. To God, he mourned, "Grant me chastity . . . but not yet."

Then, one day in 386, he lay aside an apostle's book as he strolled in a friend's garden. While walking, a child's voice came to him: "Pick it up and read it; pick it up and read."

> So I quickly returned to the bench . . . for there I had put down the apostle's book when I had left there. I snatched it up, opened it, and in silence read the paragraph on which my eyes first fell: "Not in rioting and drunkenness, not in chambering and wantonness, not in strife and envying, but put on the Lord Jesus Christ, and make no provision for the flesh to fulfill the lusts thereof." I wanted to read no further, nor did I need to. For instantly, as the sentence ended, there was infused in my heart something like the light of full certainty and all my gloom of doubt vanished away.[2]

Augustine gave up his mistress and became baptized. Returning to Africa, he founded a monastic community and, after two years, answered a call to priesthood. For the rest of his life, he served as a priest and as bishop of Hippo in Africa. His thinking focused on two realms: God as the source of all reality and truth, and the sinfulness of human beings. He died in 430 at age seventy-six.

Thomas Aquinas said that when Augustine found anything in the writings of the Platonists that was consistent with the faith, he adopted it, and what Augustine found inconsistent with the faith, he corrected. Some scholars say that Augustine "baptized" Plato and the Neoplatonists into Christianity.

Augustine called Plato's Forms "ideas in the mind of God." He agreed with Plato and Plotinus that evil was not a separate power in itself, merely the absence of good. "There are two realms, an intelligible realm where truth itself dwells, and this sensible world which we perceive by sight and touch." But Augustine rejected certain of Plato's ideas: (1) a preexisting soul, (2) reincarnation, (3) knowledge as recollection, and (4) evil is ignorance.

God   Completely unlike his years and experience as a skeptic, Augustine discovered through **mystical experience** that we could know certain eternal truths. Compared to his experiences of pleasure and sensations, these revealed truths were long-lasting and gave him profound peace. Still, Augustine wanted to know how such knowledge of the eternal was possible for a finite mind. Because the knowledge of eternal truths was superior to what his own limited mind could know, he concluded that it must come from an outside source—that is, from God. Such knowledge of eternal truths thus meant the existence of one eternal truth—God. Without God as the source of immutable truth, we could never understand eternal truths, so God is in some sense *within* human beings as well as *transcending* them. Because of this relation between humans and God, those who know most about God will come closest to understanding the true nature of the world.

Although Augustine often wrote as a rational philosopher, when he wrote about God, he used the language of mysticism:

> Great art Thou, O Lord, and greatly to be praised; great is Thy power, and Thy wisdom infinite. And Thee would man praise; man, but a particle of Thy creation; man, that bears about him his mortality, the witness of his sin, the witness that Thou resistent the proud: yet would man praise Thee; he, but a particle of Thy creation. Thou awakest us to delight in Thy praise; for Thou madest us for Thyself, and our heart is restless until it repose in Thee. Grant me, Lord, to know and understand which is first to call on Thee or to praise Thee? and, again, to know Thee or to call on Thee? . . . I will seek Thee, Lord, by calling on Thee. . . .
>
> And how shall I call upon my God, my God and Lord, since, when I call for Him, I shall be calling Him to myself? and what room is there

within me, whither my God can come into me? Whither can God come into me, God who made heaven and earth? Is there, indeed, O Lord my God, aught in me that can contain Thee? Do then heaven and earth, which Thou hast made, and wherein Thou hast made me, contain Thee? or, because nothing which exists could exist without Thee doth therefore whatever exists contain Thee? Since, then, I too exist, why do I seek that Thou shouldest enter into me, who were not, wert Thou not in me? . . .

What art Thou then, my God? What, but the Lord God? For who is Lord but the Lord? or who is God save our God? Most highest, most good, most potent, most omnipotent; most merciful, yet most just; most hidden, yet most present; most beautiful, yet most strong; stable, yet incomprehensible; unchangeable, yet all-changing; never new, never old; all-renewing, and bringing age upon the proud, and they know it not; ever working, ever at rest; . . . Thou lovest, without passion; art jealous, without anxiety; repentest, yet grievest not; art angry, yet serene; changest Thy works, Thy purpose unchanged; . . . And what have I now said, my God, my life, my holy joy? or what saith any man when he speaks of Thee? Yet woe to him that speaketh not, since mute are even the most eloquent.[3]

Pause for Thought   Augustine believed Christ is a divine mystery, one that we can only perceive through faith. And if we believe in Christ, then God will "illuminate" the soul so we can experience a supernatural knowledge of God. Do you agree with Augustine's views on Christ and God, or do you have different ideas?

The Creation   Augustine accepted the Old Testament idea that God created the world *ex nihilo*—meaning "out of nothing." This was a new idea to Greek and Roman philosophers, who believed that getting something from nothing is logically impossible. In Plato's *Timaeus*, the Demiurge creates the world from preexisting materials. For Augustine and most Medieval philosophers, this concept was unimaginable. Because Christianity inherited strictly monotheistic worldview from Judaism, it held that there could be no uncreated materials in the beginning because that would be dualism, and dualism was heresy. Thus, we have Augustine's theory that God created the world *ex nihilo*. The world is a product of God's free act, and everything in it depends on God for existence.

Unlike the Neoplatonists, who held that the One overflowed by necessity to create the realm below, Augustine said God creates by a *free act*. His Creation is continuous, because if God did not sustain the world, it would dissolve. We cannot say that creation of the world took place in time, because before God created the world there was no time. God created time when He created the world, but He is timeless. Augustine, in fact, struggled with the notion of time.

"What is time?" he asked. "Where does time exist?" His answer showed his confusion. Time was something he understood until he tried to explain it. Then he was baffled.

Augustine saw three divisions to time: the past, the present, and the future. But the present is the only aspect of time that has any existence. The past is no more, and the future is not yet. He concluded that the past is in our memory, the present is our direct awareness, and the future is our expectation. Where do these times exist? Augustine said the only place these times could possibly exist would be in the mind. Because our minds vacillate and change, they are not eternal, and therefore must be created. God alone is eternal. Thus, time realizes itself only in our minds. Although we are not divine, because we are absolutely dependent on God, our relation to time is part of the image of God within us. Because God is eternal, He sees time in a single moment; because *we* are finite, we see time as past, present, and future. This relation to time, especially our ability to project into the future and remember the past, is the foundation for our free will and our expectation of happiness.

From God's eternal mind came the *seminal principles* or the seeds of everything in the world. The idea of seminal principles helped Augustine interpret the Genesis story that God created the world in six days. Believing that God created all at once, Augustine questioned that the sun was not "created" until the fourth day. He thought the scripture meant that God created everything simultaneously, but some things were created only in potential form that would actualize over time.

Today, some philosophers view Augustine's seminal principle theory as a doctrine of evolution. However, if Augustine were to argue with a biological evolutionist, he would use this argument to deny that the appearance of a new species is a matter of the survival of the fittest. He also would deny that biology is the central explanation behind changes in how humans or animals appear today in contrast to how they appeared in the ancient past.

Moral Philosophy

Good and Evil   God is good, and God created the world out of infinite love. The whole of Creation is an expression of God's goodness. *God created matter, therefore matter cannot be evil.* By extension, this includes our physical bodies. God has willed everything for the betterment of His creatures. With Plotinus, Augustine said evil must be good in its own way. Like the shadows in a picture that give beauty to the light, evil is vital to the goodness of the world. That is not to say evil itself is good, but it is good that evil exists. Evil is not a power in itself, but a defect, an absence of the good. Good is possible without evil, but evil is not possible without good. Evil does not spoil the beauty of Creation, but it is defective because it lacks beauty.

Pause for Thought   If evil is a lack of good, then what happens to the notion of Satan?

Free Will   God could have abolished evil from the scheme of things, but he saw it serving the good. He foresaw that human beings, by their *free will*, would turn away from the good to sin. By permitting it, God predetermined human punishment. Thus, evil neither lies in ignorance as Plato said nor is the principle of darkness as held by the Manichaeans. The cause of evil or sin is an act of (human) free will, so the responsibility for evil lies not in God's Creation, but with human beings.

> For it is He [God] Who in the beginning created the world full of all visible and intelligible beings, among which He created nothing better than those spirits whom He endowed with intelligence, and made capable of contemplating and enjoying Him. . . . It is He who gave to this intellectual nature free will of such a kind, that if he wished to forsake God his blessedness, misery should forthwith result. It is He who, when He foreknew that certain angels would in their pride desire to suffice for their own blessedness, and would forsake their great good, did not deprive them of this power, deeming it to be more befitting His power and goodness to bring good out of evil than to prevent the evil from coming into existence. . . .
>
> It is He who made also man himself upright, with the same freedom of will—an earthly animal, indeed, but fit for heaven if he remained faithful to his Creator, but destined to the misery appropriate to such a nature if he forsook Him. It is He Who, when He foreknew that man would in his turn sin by abandoning God and breaking His law, did not deprive him of the power of free-will, because He at the same time foresaw what good He Himself would bring out of the evil. . . .[4]

Evil then has its origin in the free will. As did other Medieval philosophers, Augustine maintained that every human being inherited original sin from the fall of Adam and Eve. Original sin is the divided will—our capacity to turn either toward or away from God. In moral evil, the will to follow the truth (which we can know in obeying God) has been damaged. Because this will has been damaged by the original act of human rebellion, we incline toward selfishness. From this comes moral evil—turning away from God. By turning away from God, we turn to the world. We also have the power to choose the good, but our salvation and ability to live the good life is not within human power. To achieve moral goodness, we must have the grace of God. Only then are we free to obey Him. Augustine's point was that no one deserves God's redemption. Yet God has chosen to save some from damnation. Salvation is preordained. We are entirely at God's mercy.

Other philosophers and theologians argued in opposition to Augustine: The human will can choose and receive salvation. Augustine's position—that only God's grace can lead a person to salvation—triumphed. For more than a thousand years, Augustine's idea of the sinful predicament of humankind remained the basic Christian attitude. It has left the indelible impression on the Western mind that if something feels good, then it must be bad.

Pause for Thought

Even if you do not *feel* guilty, do you sometimes have a sense of guilt because you think you *should* feel guilty? Is Augustine's philosophy still a living view?

The Role of Love   Augustine agreed with the Greeks that the goal for humans is happiness, but he disagreed with Aristotle who said that people find happiness when they satisfy their natural functions through living a well-balanced life. Augustine thought that because we are creations of God, we have to go beyond the natural to find happiness in the supernatural—in God. God is love, therefore He created humans to love. Our problems lie in the objects we choose to love. We expect the wrong things to give us happiness, and this, said Augustine, is Disordered Love.

We can love physical objects. In fact, many people today believe that they would be happy if they only had a larger house, a bigger car, or a newer computer. However, physical objects do not last, and an excessive love of them leads to the sin of greed. Augustine would frown on the pursuit of money that motivates large segments of the world population today.

We can love other people. Think how often you hear people say, "If only so-and-so loved me, I'd be happy." But, said Augustine, other people cannot provide us with lasting happiness. They die, or they leave us, and they often fail to measure up to our expectations. Worse yet, the excessive love of another person can lead to the sin of jealousy. We need only look at the evening news to see how often jealousy leads to crimes of passion.

We can love ourselves. Because we are products of a society that accepts the importance of self-esteem, we believe that we must love ourselves. In contrast, Augustine thought that self-love could lead to the sin of pride, which, he said, is the root of all sin—including the fall of Adam and Eve.

We can love God. Love is the supreme virtue. Only by loving God can we find real happiness. The love of God is neither temporary like other types of love nor does it lead to sin. Therefore, we must love God first and everything else to a lesser extent. All things are worthy of love, but we must love them properly. If we love God first, then everything else will fall into place.

Another cause of disordered love lies in our confusion of what God wants us to use and what He wants us to enjoy. Food is not for enjoyment. We must eat to survive, but must we have filet or even a McDonald's Big Mac and fries? We must consume liquid to survive, but do we need beer or Coke? Like food and drink, sex is for procreation, not enjoyment. Augustine maintained that God creates everything for a purpose, and the purpose of sex is to procreate within the confines of marriage. Sex for enjoyment is a sin. Engaging in enjoyable sex and preventing reproduction is preventing the fulfillment of God's purpose.

Pause for Thought

Is Augustine right? How would our world change if we stopped expecting happiness from physical objects and other people? Are many of the crimes we see around us the result of seeking happiness in the wrong places? Do Augustine's ideas explain why the Roman Catholic Church opposes birth control and prolife supporters oppose abortion?

Original Sin   God created Adam and Eve in his image. God gave them supernatural gifts of grace, holiness, immortality, justice, and freedom of will. According to Augustine, when Adam and Eve chose to disobey God, they not only lost their gifts but also corrupted the entire human race. For their punishment, God cast them out of Eden. Now every human "will" is corrupt, and it is impossible for people not to sin without the gift of divine grace.

Being sinful, all men and women deserve Hell. Had not God sent his son who was without sin, all of us would spend eternity in its flames. His son inspired people to turn back to their source in God. Baptism in the name of Jesus Christ purged individuals of original sin. To some of the baptized, God would grant the grace of salvation. Those who did not receive grace would go to Hell. "From this [Hell] upon earth there is no escape, save through the grace of the Saviour Christ, our God and Lord." The basis of predetermining that some would experience eternal bliss and others Hell was solely an act of God's will. Why God would choose some for eternal happiness and others for eternal punishment is a mystery, said Augustine, but God is just. Humans, by their original sin, gave up any claim to salvation.

That the whole human race has been condemned in its first origin, this life itself, if life it is to be called, bears witness by the host of cruel ills with which it is filled. Is not this proved by the profound and dreadful ignorance which produces all the errors that enfold the children of Adam, and from which no man can be delivered without toil, pain, and fear? Is it not proved by his love of so many vain and hurtful things, which produces gnawing cares, disquiet, griefs, fears, wild joys, quarrels, law-suits, wars, treasons, angers, hatreds, deceit, flattery, fraud, theft, robbery, perfidy, pride, ambition, envy, murders, parricides, cruelty, ferocity, wickedness, luxury, insolence, impudence, shamelessness, fornications, adulteries, incests, and the numberless uncleannesses and unnatural acts of both sexes. . . . These are indeed the crimes of wicked men, yet they spring from that root of error and misplaced love which is born with every son of Adam. . . .

From this hell upon earth there is no escape, save through the grace of the Saviour Christ, our God and Lord.[5]

Grace   Part of Augustine's theory of salvation was his view of predestination. According to this view, all of humankind is damned, but God in his mercy elects some to be saved. The Church is the mediator of God's grace.

Almighty God, the supreme and supremely good Creator of all natures, . . . was not destitute of a plan by which He might people His city with the fixed number of citizens which His wisdom had foreordained even out of the condemned human race, discriminating them not now by merits, since the whole mass was condemned as if in a vitiated root, but by grace, and showing, not only in the case of the redeemed, but also in those who were not delivered, how much grace He has bestowed upon them. For every one acknowledges that he has been rescued from evil, not by deserved, but by gratuitous goodness, when he is singled out from the company of those with whom he might justly have borne a common punishment, and is allowed to go scathless.[6]

Pause for Thought   Does Augustine's theory of grace involve any problems for you? If his view is correct, then do we really need the Church? Are the acts of avoiding temptation, engaging in prayer, and trying to lead a good life also meaningless because our eternal fate is already decided? Would there even be a need for the incarnation of Christ or for his resurrection?

The Two Cities   One of Augustine's most famous works is *The City of God*. He divided humanity into two groups: those who love God, and those who turn away from God to love themselves and the world. Those who realize that the only eternal good is in God belong to the City of God (or Jerusalem), and those who seek their good in the world live in the Worldly City (or Babylon). These are not political states, but the struggles that take place inside each of us. The difference is that between disordered and ordered love that we explored earlier.

We see then that the two cities were created by two kinds of love: the earthly city was created by self-love reaching the point of contempt for God, the

Heavenly City by the love of God carried as far as contempt of self. In fact, the earthly city glories in itself, the Heavenly City glories in the Lord. The former looks for glory from men, the latter finds its highest glory in God, the witness of a good conscience. The earthly lifts up its head in its own glory, the Heavenly City says to its God: "my glory; you lift up my head." In the former, the lust for domination lords it over its princes as over the nations it subjugates; in the other both those put in authority and those subject to them serve one another in love, the rulers by their counsel, the subjects by obedience. The one city loves its own strength shown in its powerful leaders; the other says to its God, "I will love you, my Lord, my strength."[7]

Saintly individuals who live in the Worldly City are actually citizens of the City of God. They live *in* the world but are not *of* the world. In the Worldly City, Christians obey the laws. They "render unto Caesar the things which are Caesar's," yet they serve and love God above all.

Pause for Thought   Could Augustine's idea of the two cities have developed into the issue between church and state—that is, between temporal and spiritual authority? Could his two cities' belief have influenced the framers of the U.S. Constitution to separate the powers of church and state?

In the next world, the two cities are symbols of Heaven and Hell. Heaven is a state of being in which the soul finds peace and love with God. Hell, for Augustine, is on the one hand quite literal and the other more metaphysical. In his literal view, Augustine suggested that the occupants of Hell have their bodies devoured by fire and gnawed by worms. When he wrote as a metaphysician, he viewed Hell as a separation from God brought about by our failure to love properly.

Science   Like most Medieval thinkers, Augustine showed less interest in science and the world of space–time in which we live than in the spiritual world. His view is a direct consequence of his belief that the physical world is important only as it relates to either man or God. The physical world, which does not share the freedom of human beings, is the expression of the divine rationality at work. The most important world is the next world, especially for those who escape the terrors of Hell. Augustine believed that God designed the natural world to provide lessons about salvation. God even designed temptation as a means to test worthiness of individual souls. The universe is the stage on which humankind plays out its salvation. The obstacles we meet are but props that contribute to the success or failure of each soul who walks onstage.

All causes originate in and with God, therefore scientific causality even ceases to be worth questioning. Augustine viewed any attempt to seek a natural explanation of cause and effect as an attack on God's power and on our total dependence on Him. Like many of his contemporaries, Augustine believed that the Bible contained all the science that human beings needed. If it wasn't in the Bible, then God didn't intend for us to know it. The Church viewed attempts at science as magic, and anyone who sought explanations outside of God and the Church often paid with their lives. In Alexandria, however, some theologians and philosophers held the conviction that nature is God's Creation and thus worthy of study. This idea enhanced an interest in nature and ultimately science.

History   Unlike the Greeks who viewed history as cyclic, with civilizations rising and falling and then replaced by new civilizations, Augustine saw history as linear. The world began with the act of creation and would end with the "Second Coming" and the destruction of the world as we know it. In the meantime, history is the struggle between the City of God and the City of the World. In the end, the City of God will triumph.

The Bible describes all great historic events, and all have occurred except the return of Christ and the final judgment of humankind. History is the unfolding of God's plan for Creation. It is not just a series of human-made events that may or may not be meaningless. History has meaning. Our failure to comprehend some events does not mean they are irrational or meaningless in the overall scheme of God's plan. God needs all of history to realize his Kingdom of God on earth. History is necessary for the enlightenment of humankind and the destruction of evil.

By studying history, we can learn what is necessary for salvation. That is the real point of history. Also in contrast to the Greeks, Augustine viewed history as universal and not just pertinent to a particular civilization or state. He believed that God's foresight directs the history of humankind from Adam to the end of time as if it were a story of one man gradually developing from childhood to old age.

Church and State   Augustine thought that humans are social animals by nature, but he denied that they are political animals. The state provides a place to work out our salvation, but it is not essential for us to reach our ultimate destiny. The Church plays that role. The Church holds ultimate moral authority over humanity. Kings and princes do not. In their original state, Adam and Eve had God as their only authority. After the fall, an external authority was necessary to control the sinful nature of human beings. Although the Church is that authority, God will not save everyone within the Church. However, He will not save anyone outside the Church.

On Women   Unlike Jesus's example of woman's role in society, Augustine saw woman as *temptress, wife,* and *mother.* As temptress, she is evil, a product of Satan's design. As wife, she is subservient to her husband, who is the family authority (God created woman for man). As mother, woman is the instrument of God. In the earthly city where she is the sexual object of temptation, she is damned. When she functions as an instrument of her husband, and the mother of his children, she is blessed.

> God created only one single man. . . . He did not even create the woman that was to be given him as his wife, as he created the man, but created her out of the man, that the whole human race might derive from one man. . . .
>
> God, then, made man in His own image. For He created for him a soul endowed with reason and intelligence, so that he might excel all the creature of earth, air, and sea, which were not so gifted. . . . He made also a wife for him, to aid him in the work of generating his kind, and her He formed of a bone taken out of the man's side, working in a divine manner. . . .
>
> [The fallen angel chose the serpent as his mouthpiece] because, being slippery, and moving in tortuous windings, it was suitable for his purpose. And this animal being subdued to his wicked ends by the presence and superior force of his angelic nature, he abused as his instrument, and first tried his deceit upon the woman, making his assault upon the weaker part of that human alliance, that he might gradually gain the whole, and not supposing that the man would readily give ear to him, or be deceived, but that he might yield to the error of woman. . . . "And Adam was not deceived, but the woman being deceived was in the transgression." . . .[8]

The "Not-So-Dark-Ages"

After the fall of the Roman Empire in 476 C.E., intellectual life in Europe largely moved to within the monasteries. The Church men preserved libraries, copied manuscripts, and wrote books. Charlemagne made a major effort to revive public education and decreed that every bishop set up a school at his cathedral, but with the fall of his Carolingian Empire, education once again declined. Finally, in the eleventh century, an intellectual excitement began that was to change the culture of Europe.

The awakening began with the cathedral schools, but by the latter half of the eleventh century, newly founded universities replaced the cathedral schools as the major centers of learning. Among other controversial subjects, the new Medieval philosophers tackled the following problems: (1) understanding the relationship between faith and reason, (2) incorporating the philosophical works of the Greek philosophers with the teachings of Christianity, and (3) rationally proving the existence of God.

Faith Versus Reason

As we have seen, one of the problematic controversies of the Medieval world was the conflict between the values of reason and faith. Theologians argued that only a few individuals had access to God's revelation. Therefore, people should have faith in the authority of those who had received special communication from God.

But the question arose, what if those to whom God revealed Himself contradicted one another? Thus far in history, philosophers had not always agreed with each other. Could scholars ever depend on reason to answer their questions about God? Most philosophers assumed that faith and reason do not conflict. Because God is the perfection of reality and truth, He must operate in a perfectly rational manner. They argued that God endowed men—but not women—with rational minds and intended them to use those minds to establish communication with His rational order. One of the leading Christian writers on faith and reason was John Scotus Erigena, an Irish theologian.

John Scotus Erigena John Scotus Erigena (ca. 810–877) was born in Ireland, studied Greek in an Irish monastery, and went to France in approximately 847. He taught at the Palace School in Paris, where he became involved in disputes over difficult theological questions about free will and the Eucharist (the celebration of Holy Communion). Erigena asserted that faith and reason do not conflict:

> There is no doubt [that reason and authority] both flow from one fountain, namely divine wisdom. . . . Consequently no authority should frighten you away from these things, which the rational persuasion of right contemplation firmly teaches. For true authority does not oppose right reason, nor right reason true authority. . . . True authority seems to me to be nothing other than truth discovered by virtue of reason and committed by the holy Fathers to words for the use of posterity.[9]

Erigena's notion of free will was contrary to Augustine's belief that individuals needed God's grace to do good. Erigena argued that humans had the capacity to be good in their own free will. The Church did not agree; while it accepted his arguments for reason, it condemned his ideas about free will.

If Erigena was correct, then humans do have the capacity to be good on their own. Which theory do you prefer—Augustine's or Erigena's?

Proving God's Existence

Anselm   Although all Medieval theologians and philosophers believed in God, Anselm of Canterbury (1033–1109 C.E.) set out to *prove* God's existence.

Anselm's Life   Born in Italy, Anselm grew up wanting to be a monk, but his father forbade it. Finally, at age twenty-three, he left home to study for three years at Fleury-sur-Loire and Chartres, in France. Then in 1060 he became a monk in the Benedictine abbey of Bec, where Lanfranc, a countryman, was both prior (subordinate only to an abbot) and master of its school. He succeeded Lanfranc as prior three years later. In 1078 he became abbot.

During this period, William the Conqueror was in the process of reorganizing England's government and church, and he appointed Lanfranc as Archbishop of Canterbury. When Lanfranc died, William Rufus, who had succeeded William the Conqueror as king of England appointed Anselm to the office of archbishop. From the time he arrived in England, Anselm fought William to gain ecclesiastical freedom from royal control. He took his case to Rome and did not return to England until William Rufus died and Henry I took the throne. Although both Anselm and Henry were stubborn in their pursuits, they finally reached a compromise that became the formula for settling church–state disputes in the twelfth century. Anselm held the position of Archbishop of Canterbury until he died and was later canonized, becoming St. Anselm.

Anselm wanted to prove the existence of God in opposition to the intellectuals who felt that theology was little more than Bible commentary and to support those who thought that rational analysis was needed. Anselm believed that we could not hope to reach the truth except through God's revelation and by accepting that revelation in faith. However, once we have faith, we can then develop rational proofs to understand our faith. He said that he desired only a little understanding of the truth that his heart believed and loved. Human reason, he argued, has the ability to create a natural theology or metaphysics based on reason. Anselm's best known works are *Monologium* and *Proslogium*. Both aim to prove the existence and nature of God. *Proslogium* ("Faith Seeking Understanding") contains his *ontological* argument (*ontos* is Greek for "being," and *logos* means "knowledge"). Thus, the ontological argument is based on our knowledge of the existence of God.

Ontological Argument   In *Proslogium*, Anselm said we believe that God is "that than which nothing greater can be thought." The question is whether that really exists? There are people, said Anselm, who disbelieve in God's existence. He then quoted Psalms 14:1: "The fool has said in his heart: There is no God." Yes, said Anselm, and the *fool* by denying God's existence is involved in contradiction. For when the fool hears the words "something than which nothing greater can be thought," he understands intellectually what he hears and whatever is understood is in the understanding. So even the fool knows at least intellectually a being than which nothing greater can be thought.

Anselm reasoned that because God exists in the understanding, He must exist in reality, because reality is greater than existence in the understanding alone. In other words, we can understand and consistently think about the concept of God, but we cannot consistently think of a round square.

Chapter II

That God Truly Exists

Well then, Lord, You who give understanding to faith, grant me that I may understand, as much as You see fit, that You exist as we believe You to exist, and that You are what we believe You to be. Now we believe that You are something than which nothing greater can be thought. Or can it be that a thing of such a nature does not exist, since "the Fool has said in his heart, there is not God' [Ps. xiii. I, lii. I]? But surely, when this same Fool hears what I am speaking about, namely, 'something-than-which-nothing-greater-can-be-thought', he understands what he hears, and what he understands is in his mind, even if he does not understand that it actually exists.

For it is one thing for an object to exist in the mind, and another thing to understand that an object actually exists. Thus, when a painter plans beforehand what he is going to execute, he has [the picture] in his mind and understands that it exists because he has now made it.

Even the Fool, then, is forced to agree that something-than-which-nothing-greater-can-be-thought exists in the mind, since he understands this when he hears it, and whatever is understood is in the mind. And surely that-than-which-nothing-greater-can-be-thought cannot exist in the mind alone. For if it exists solely in the mind even, it can be thought to exist in reality also, which is greater.

If then that-than-which-nothing-greater-can-be-thought exist in the mind alone, this same that-than-which-nothing-greater-*cannot*-be-thought is that-than-which-a-greater-*can*-be-thought. But this is obviously impossible. Therefore there is absolutely no doubt that something-than-which-a-greater-cannot-be-thought exists both in the mind and in reality.[10]

Gaunilo, a contemporary monk of Anselm, wrote an attack on Anselm's argument titled "On behalf of the fool." Gaunilo argued that if we replaced "an island than which none greater can be conceived" for "something than which nothing greater can be conceived," then we would prove the existence of that island. Gaunilo wanted to point out that by using Anselm's argument, we could prove the existence of almost anything. Therefore, he said, Anselm's ontological argument is invalid.

Anselm replied that Gaunilo's reference to an island missed the point. Anselm said we could move from an idea to its necessary existence only in the case of that being whose nonexistence cannot be thought. An island does not have to be, because being finite, it is contingent, and this is true of all finite things. Only one something exists through which everything else has its being and which has its existence only from itself—and this is God.

Pause for Thought   Do you think that Gaunilo's argument of the "island than which nothing greater can be conceived" is a valid rebuttal of Anselm's proof for God's existence?

Islamic Philosophy

Medieval Islamic philosophers wrote influential treatises on metaphysics, human nature, and faith and reason. Avicenna and Averroes, in particular, had access to the works of Aristotle centuries before Western Europe received them. Their interpretations of Aristotle influenced many Christian and Jewish writers. Some Christian philosophers, such as Bonaventura, believed that Aristotle's philosophy conflicted with Christian doctrine and so rejected the Greek's writings. Thomas Aquinas, however, had access to other versions of Aristotle, and, so the story goes, just as Augustine baptized Plato into Christianity, Aquinas Christianized Aristotle's philosophy.

Of the Islamic philosophers, Avicenna was the most important. To express the difficulty of Aristotle's writings, he said, "I have read his metaphysics forty times and I think I am beginning to understand it."

Avicenna

Avicenna's Life   Avicenna★ (980–1037) was born in Persia and grew up studying logic, mathematics, science, philosophy, and medicine, all of which he mastered by age eighteen. After such strenuous learning, he said the rest of his life was spent deepening his knowledge. Although Avicenna was primarily a physician, he wrote more than a hundred works that discussed philosophy, science, religion, and literature. Aristotle and Neoplatonism were pivotal in his

---

★In Arabic, Abu Ali al-Husayn ibn Abd Allah ibn Sina.

philosophical system, and he is especially remembered for his doctrine of Creation.

The Latin translation of his *Canon of Medicine* was one of the main textbooks in the medical faculties of Medieval universities. Some of his philosophical writings were also translated into Latin and were deeply influential in Medieval philosophy.

God   Avicenna envisioned God as a Necessary Being who emanated the temporal world out of himself as a result of his self-knowledge. Avicenna argued that everything must have a cause and that all caused things must be caused by a prior being. Because there cannot be an infinite series of causes, there must be a First Cause, whose being is not simply *possible* but *necessary*. (Thomas Aquinas uses this same reasoning in his own Third Proof.)

Because God is the First Cause and prime mover, God has no beginning and has therefore always been in the act of creating—that is, Creation is eternal. Following the lead of Neoplatonism, Avicenna argues that for a gradation of beings there is a hierarchy of intelligences. First is intelligence itself, and this intelligence creates a subordinate intelligence and so on for Ten Intelligences. The tenth intelligence—the Active Intellect—creates the four elements of the world and the individual souls of human beings. The souls differ from the intellects because they have a secondary substance—material aspect.

The Soul   The human soul "receives" rational knowledge that emanates from the Active Intelligence and the body "receives" the soul. Unlike Plato, the human soul does not preexist before entering the body. The soul is created *with* the body and not, as Aristotle held, "imprinted" on it. At death, the soul separates from the body to exist eternally as an individual. Souls that have led pure lives realize eternal bliss. Contaminated souls continue in eternal torment seeking their bodies.

Avicenna rejected bodily resurrection, but he accepted the soul's immortality. The rational, being immaterial, is incorruptible. Also, the soul is individual. It is the "I" that is permanent throughout all bodily change. The ultimate goal of human activity, said Avicenna, is a prophetic mind that attains an intuitive knowledge of God and His Creation.

Averroes

Averroes's Life   Averroes* (1126–1198 C.E.) was born in Cordova, Spain, most of which was then ruled by Muslims, into a family of prominent lawyers and

---

*In Arabic, Abu al-Walid Muhammad ibn Ahmad ibn Muhammad ibn Rushd.

judges. Like Avicenna, Averroes was a precocious student in philosophy, mathematics, medicine, theology, and jurisprudence. He was appointed a judge in Seville at age forty-four. That year he translated Aristotle's book *De Anima*. Two years later he was transferred to Cordova, where he spent ten years as judge in the town of his birth. During those years, Averroes wrote commentaries on the works of Aristotle including *Metaphysics*. In 1182 he was called to Marrakesh, Morocco, as physician to Caliph Abu Yaqub Yusuf, ruler of both Morocco and Muslim Spain, but was banished from the court by the new Caliph Abu Yusuf Yaqub al-Mansur because he claimed that reason must be put in front of religious belief. Shortly before Averroes died, Mansur restored him to favor. During his life, he wrote a series of detailed commentaries on the works of Aristotle. These commentaries became so famous that Averroes was known as the Commentator. He also wrote a medical encyclopedia and several books on law, religion, and philosophy.

Just as Avicenna, Averroes looked to Aristotle for the foundation of his ideas, but he was strongly influenced by Christian scholasticism and philosophy, as well as by Jewish philosophers. He also incorporated Plato and Neoplatonism in his philosophical works. Although he represents a continuation of Avicenna, he disagreed with Avicenna's notion that Creation is eternal and necessary.

God   Averroes rejected the idea of Creation, arguing that it is a doctrine of religion without philosophical substance. The world, he said, had no beginning. Prime matter is coeternal with God and not the term of the creative act. God is behind everything, for God is the one who makes everything come true—the one who holds everything up. God forms material things from the potency of pure matter and brings into being the Ten Intelligences, each connected with a sphere. There is, he argued, no emanation.

The Soul   Averroes also rejected Avicenna's notion of immortality. The soul, said Averroes, is the material and not the spiritual form of a human being. Because the soul is material, it perishes like the body at death. The active intellect is what makes humans higher than animals, but the Active Intellect is neither personal nor individual.

True Knowledge   Averroes claimed that *true knowledge* is knowledge of God and His Creation. This knowledge includes knowing the various means that lead to worldly satisfaction and the avoidance of misery in the hereafter. This type of practical knowledge covers two branches: (1) jurisprudence, which deals with the tangible part of human life; and (2) the spiritual sciences, which are concerned with such matters as patience, gratitude to God, and morals. Averroes compared spiritual laws to medicine for their effects on human beings: physically on one hand, and morally and spiritually on the other. True knowledge leads to happiness, which includes mental and psychological health. Humans can only enjoy psychological health if they believe in God and His oneness.

Jewish Philosophy

Moses Maimonides

Jewish philosopher Moses Maimonides was introduced to the writing of Aristotle through the Moors. He had an especially strong influence on Christian philosophers because they shared a common belief in the Old Testament. A renowned philosopher of the Medieval period, Maimonides integrated Jewish Biblical thought with Greek philosophy and science. His writing served as a model for Thomas Aquinas on such issues as faith and reason.

Maimonides' Life   Moses ben Maimonides, known as "Rambam" for "Rabbi Moses ben Maimon," was born in 1135 at Cordova, Spain. As a boy, he studied the Bible, the Talmud, and science under the tutelage of his father. When he was thirteen, the Almohad Muslims from North Africa conquered Cordova and closed the synagogues. For awhile, Maimonides and his family stayed in the city as secret Jews, then migrated to Morocco. Eventually, he settled in Cairo, Egypt, where he became a physician. His brilliance as a doctor led to his appointment as physician for the Arab general Saladin who defeated Richard the Lionhearted in the Third Crusade. His deep spirituality led his peers to elect him spiritual head of the Egyptian Jewish community. Following his death in 1204, they took his body to Tiberias on the Sea of Galilee. In reverence to his life and work, people today still visit his tomb.

Faith and Reason   Maimonides' philosophical fame rests squarely on his book *Guide for the Perplexed*. This work draws together both Jewish law and Greek philosophy and is a guide for those who are perplexed about how best to live their lives. Maimonides looked to Aristotle and his ideas on using reason to the search for truth. According to Aristotle, by reason alone we can prove the existence of God. Maimonides addressed his work mainly to those believing Jews who had studied the sciences of the philosophers and had become perplexed by the literal words of scripture. In *Guide for the Perplexed*, Maimonides demonstrated that no basic conflicts exist between theology, philosophy, and science—and between faith and reason. He viewed biblical prophecy as a continuous flow of reason and inspiration from God to the human mind. Here, in fact, Maimonides defends reason as a faculty that can refer to God:

I shall illustrate this by the example of the rational faculty subsisting in man. It is one faculty with regard to which no multiplicity is posited. Through it he acquires the sciences and the arts; through the same faculty he sews, carpenters, weaves, builds, has a knowledge of geometry, and governs the city. Those very different actions, however, proceed from one simple faculty in which no multiplicity is posited. Now these actions are very different, and their number is almost infinite—I mean the number of the arts brought forth by the rational faculty. It accordingly should not be regarded as inadmissible in reference to God, may He be magnified and honored. . . .[11]

The highest human perfection, said Maimonides, is acquiring rational virtues, "which teach true opinions concerning the divine things. That is in true reality the ultimate end. . . ." And he saw the counterpart of rational virtue in faith: "The prophets too have explained the self-same notions—just as the philosophers have interpreted them." Faith and reason are both necessary.

God   Maimonides anticipated three of Thomas Aquinas's proofs for the existence of God, but he rejected the possibility of knowing what God is like. He denied any anthropomorphic ideas of God, who is one, eternal spirit without finite human traits that can be defined. When reading the Bible, people should know that terms used to describe God are allegorical. No language can do justice to God's infinite nature. Only by negating our finite characteristics can we have insight into the Deity.

Pause for Thought   Do you agree with Maimonides that God is one eternal spirit without any finite human traits that can be defined? Do we project on God our human personal terms?

High Point of the Middle Ages

During the thirteenth century, the high point of Medieval intellectual life, most philosophers and theologians considered Augustine the master. But Thomas Aquinas soon made the most successful attempt yet in dealing with faith and reason. By incorporating Greek philosophy into Christianity and giving a rational proof of God's existence, he challenged Augustine's position.

Before the twelfth century, Aristotle's only works known in the Western world were *Categories* and *Interpretation*. However, between 1150 and 1250, all of his other works were introduced to the West with commentaries written by Islamic and Jewish philosophers. The effect of Aristotle on Christian thinking was to change spiritual and intellectual life throughout the West. A contemporary portrayal of Aristotle's effect on the Western mind is in the novel *The Name of the Rose* by Umberto Eco and in the movie of the same title.

Aristotle provided the tools of reasoning and logic that were useful for developing arguments to support Christian teachings. And he introduced scientific ideas new to late Medieval thinking. But his works brought their share of controversy. First, Aristotle had denied a god who creates, and he held that the world is eternal—that is, has no beginning in time. Second, he denied any personal immortality. Third, Aristotle's god has no interest or concern for the world of everyday experience. The way in which Thomas Aquinas dealt with these ideas was one of the highlights of the Medieval period.

Thomas Aquinas

Aquinas's Life   Thomas Aquinas (1225–1274) was born in Aquino, a town between Rome and Naples in southern Italy. He was the youngest son in a large and wealthy family. When Aquinas was five, his father, the Count of Aquino, sent him to the Benedictine monastery of Monte Casino. His family hoped Thomas would get a good education and someday become abbot of Monte Casino. However, when he was fourteen, political conflicts between the Holy Roman Emperor and the papacy made the monastery unsafe, so his family moved Thomas to the Imperial University in Naples.

While at the university, he decided to join the Dominican order in the same year his father died and live in simple poverty. Dismayed by his decision, the rest of his family had him kidnapped and held him captive in the family castle for a year. They tried everything to sway his resolve, even tempting him with a prostitute, but Thomas stood firm. When his family finally realized he would never change his mind, they released him and he became a Dominican friar.

Four years later, in 1245, Aquinas went to Paris, where he studied with Albertus Magnus (Albert the Great), an advocate of Aristotle. Aquinas followed his teacher to Cologne to continue his studies under him. As a student, Aquinas was so methodical and deliberate that, seeing his stout build, his peers dubbed him the "Dumb Ox." But Albertus rebutted them, "You call him a Dumb Ox; I tell you the Dumb Ox will bellow so loud his bellowing will fill the world." In 1252, Thomas returned to the University of Paris. Four years later, he received his doctorate degree in theology, and with the pope's permission, joined the university faculty.

Aquinas was just as enthused with Aristotle's philosophy as Albert the Great, and he now began to weave it into Christian thought. Called from the university, Aquinas spent the next nine years teaching under the auspices of the papal court before returning to Paris. There he became involved in a famous controversy with the Averroists. He took a middle position between those who accepted Aristotle through Averroes's interpretation and those who rejected Aristotelian philosophy as anti-Christian.

A prolific writer, Aquinas wrote twenty-five volumes. But in December 1273, he suddenly stopped writing. As the result of a profound mystical experience, he said to a friend, "All I have written seems like straw to me." The next year, 1274, Pope Gregory X asked Aquinas to attend a general council in Lyons. On his way, Aquinas became ill and died in the Cistercian monastery at Fossanova. He was forty-nine. Forty-nine years later, in 1323, the Church canonized him as Saint Thomas Aquinas. His most famous work is the *Summa Theologica*; in that work he developed a systematic Christian theology that integrated Christian thinking from earlier centuries to his own time.

Faith and Reason   For Aquinas, there need not be a conflict between the reason that philosophy uses and faith based on Christian revelation. We often can reason ourselves to the same truths that we read in the Bible.

Pause for Thought   Can reason tell us that God exists? Must we rely on faith that God created the world in six days or made humankind from dust?

Aquinas did not intend to say we can know God through reason, only that certain "natural theological truths" can be reached through Christian faith and through our innate or natural reason. For example, the truth that there is a God is something we can trust through both faith and reason. Theology, he said, begins with faith in God. Through the authority of revelation, the theologian can understand certain principles. Reason begins with objects of sense experience and proceeds upward to more universal ideas until the mind reaches the highest principle of being or God.

Theological knowledge comes directly through revelation from a higher authority. Philosophy is not direct revelation, but a step-by-step procedure that draws conclusions based on preceding premises. Although different in method, faith and reason do not contradict each other, so there need not be any conflict between a philosopher such as Aristotle and the Christian doctrine.

> As other sciences do not argue in proof of their principles, but argue from their principles to demonstrate other truths in these sciences, so this doctrine does not argue in proof of its principles, which are the articles of faith, but from them it goes on to prove something else. . . .
>
> However, it is to be borne in mind, in regard to the philosophical sciences, that the inferior sciences neither prove their principles nor dispute with those who deny them, but leave this to a higher science. But the highest of them, namely, metaphysics, can dispute with one who denies its principles, only if the opponent will make some concession. But if he con-

cede nothing, it can have no dispute with him, though it can answer his objections. Hence Sacred Scripture, since it has no science above itself, can dispute with one who denies its principles only if the opponent admits some at least of the truths obtained through divine revelation. Thus, we can argue with heretics from texts in Holy Writ, and against those who deny one article of faith, we can argue from another. But if our opponent believes nothing of divine revelation, there is no longer any means of proving the articles of faith by reasoning, but only of answering his objections— if he has any—against faith. Since faith rests upon infallible truth, and since the contrary of a truth can never be demonstrated, it is clear that proofs brought against faith cannot be demonstrations, but are arguments that can be answered.[12]

For Aquinas, Aristotle demonstrated some truths about God by reason alone. For example, Aristotle called the Unmoved Mover that which sets all natural processes going. But through revelation, the Bible, and the teachings of Jesus, Christians can determine more about God than Aristotle had. Faith does not contradict reason, but supplements it, because "faith rests upon infallible truth." There is then a theology of faith and a natural theology.

Five Ways to Prove God's Existence   That God exists is an article of faith. But through the process of reason, Aquinas formulated five proofs to demonstrate the truth of God's existence. His argument is called the *Cosmological Argument* and is considered an argument from cause and effect. Unlike Anselm, who began his proof with the idea of a perfect being "than which no greater can be conceived," Aquinas begins his argument with our experience of sense objects.

Although Aquinas's philosophical and theological writings fill many volumes, he is most famous for his "Five Ways."

The existence of God can be proved in five ways.

1. Proof from Motion

The first and more manifest way is the argument from motion. It is certain, and evident to our senses, that in this world some things are in motion. Now whatever is in motion is put in motion by another, for nothing can be in motion unless it is in potency to that towards which it is in motion. But a thing moves in so far as it is in act. For motion is nothing else than the reduction of something from potentiality to actuality. But nothing can be reduced from potentiality to actuality, except by something in a state of actuality. Thus that which is actually hot, as fire, makes wood, which is potentially hot, to be actually hot, and thereby moves and changes it. Now it is not possible that the same thing should be at once in actuality and potentiality in the same respect, but only in different respect. For what is actually hot cannot simultaneously be potentially hot; but it is simultaneously potentially cold. It is therefore impossible that in the same respect and in the same way a thing should be both mover and moved, i.e., that it should move itself. Therefore whatever is in motion must be put in motion by another. If that by which it is put in motion be itself put in motion, then this also must needs be put in motion by another, and that by another again. But this cannot go on to infinity, because then there would be no first mover, and, consequently, no other mover; seeing that subsequent movers move only inasmuch as they are put in motion by the first mover; as the staff moves only because it is put in motion by the hand. Therefore, it is necessary to arrive at a first mover, put in motion by no other; and this everyone understands to be God.[13]

In his "Proof from Motion," Aquinas observed that all things in the natural world are moving. Imagine a row of dominoes standing one next to another. Although at rest while standing, these dominoes are potentially in motion. When one domino falls over, it is no longer potentially in motion but actually in motion. In turn, the falling domino hits and sets in motion the next domino and so on until all of the standing dominoes fall over. But the first domino cannot move unless someone or something actually moves it. And there had to be something or someone to put that person or something in motion and so forth. This series could go on ad infinitum unless there is a First Mover of all motion. The argument is like Aristotle's argument for the Unmoved Mover, except the Unmoved Mover is not a creator god. Because the Christian God creates, Aquinas substitutes the term "First Mover" for "Unmoved Mover."

Pause for Thought   Do you agree that Aquinas had to call a creator God the First Mover instead of the Unmoved Mover?

---

2. Proof from Efficient Cause

The second way is from the nature of the efficient cause. In the world of sense we find there is an order of efficient causes. There is no case known (neither is it, indeed, possible) in which a thing is found to be the efficient cause of itself; for so it would be prior to itself, which is impossible. Now in efficient causes it is not possible to go on to infinity, because in all efficient causes following in order, the first is the cause of the intermediate cause, and the intermediate is the cause of the ultimate cause, whether the intermediate cause be several, or one only. Now to take away the cause is to take away the effect. Therefore if there be no first cause among efficient causes, there will be no ultimate, nor any intermediate cause. But if in efficient causes it is possible to go on to infinity, there will be no first efficient cause, neither will there be an ultimate effect, nor any intermediate efficient causes; all of which is plainly false. Therefore it is necessary to admit a first efficient cause, to which everyone gives the name of God.[14]

The second way is like the first. Nothing in the sensible world causes itself. For anything to cause itself, it would have to exist before its own existence—and this is impossible. Yet everything is the effect of a previous cause. For instance, you are the effect of your parents, who are the effect of their parents, who are the effect of their parents, and so on—back to Adam and Eve. Adam and Eve, however, were not their own cause. God created them. That is why Aquinas argued that God is the First Cause.

3. Proof from Necessary Versus Possible Being

The third way is taken from possibility and necessity, and runs thus. We find in nature things that are possible to be and not to be, since they are found to be generated, and to corrupt, and consequently, they are possible to be and not to be. But it is impossible for these always to exist, for that which is possible not to be at some time is not. Therefore, if everything is possible not to be, then at one time there could have been nothing in existence. Now if this were true, even now there would be nothing in existence, because that which does not exist only begins to exist by something already existing. Therefore, if at one time nothing was in existence, it would have been impossible for anything to have begun to exist; and thus even now nothing would be in existence—which is absurd. Therefore, not all beings are merely possible, but there must exist something the existence of which is necessary. But every necessary thing either has its necessity caused by another, or not. Now it is impossible to go on to infinity in necessary things which have their necessity caused by another, as has been already proved in regard to efficient causes. Therefore we cannot but postulate the existence of some being having of itself its own necessity, and not receiving it from another, but rather causing in others their necessity. This all men speak of as God.[15]

In nature, it is possible for some things not to exist. For instance, according to Aquinas, it is possible for my dog to either exist or not exist. Because my dog is in existence, it is possible that she will some day go out of existence. The same is true for trees and people. All possible beings at one time did not exist, will exist for awhile, then will go out of existence.

Because everything in the natural world could possibly not exist, there must exist something that not just possibly exists, but necessarily exists. The necessary being would be the cause of all possible beings. Aquinas then asked if there could be more than one necessary being caused by another necessary being. He concluded that it was not possible: One necessary being could not cause another necessary being, because a being to be caused would have to have been out of existence at one time. There must be one necessary being that is its own necessity, and that being is God.

4. Proof from the Degrees of Perfection

The fourth way is taken from the gradation to be found in things. Among beings there are some more and some less good, true, noble, and the like. But "more" and "less" are predicated of different things, according as they resemble in their different ways something which is the maximum, as a thing is said to be hotter according as it more nearly resembles that which is hottest; so that there is something which is truest, something best, something noblest, and, consequently, something which is uttermost being; for those things that are greatest in truth are greatest in being, as it is written in *Metaph.* ii. Now the maximum in any genus is the cause of all in that genus; as fire, which is the maximum of heat, is the cause of all hot things. Therefore there must also be something which is to all beings the cause of their being, goodness, and every other perfection; and this we call God.[16]

We view some things in the world as better than others. Some people are less good, truthful, and noble than others. Because we perceive various grades of beauty from ugly to exquisite, we must have a standard of what is pure good, pure truth, and pure beauty. We also can compare lesser and higher beings. A rock is a lesser being than a monkey, and a monkey is a lesser being than a human. Even in humans, some are closer to perfect goodness and truth than others. From this, Aquinas concluded there must be something perfect to cause all the degrees of perfection, and this is what we call God.

5. Proof from the Order of the Universe

The fifth way is taken from the governance of the world. We see that things which lack intelligence, such as natural bodies, act for an end, and this is evident from their acting always, or nearly always, in the same way, so as to obtain the best result. Hence it is plain that not fortuitously, but designedly, do they achieve their end. Now whatever lacks intelligence cannot move towards an end, unless it be directed by some being endowed with knowledge and intelligence; as the arrow is shot to its mark by the archer. Therefore some intelligent being exists by whom all natural things are directed to their end; and this being we call God.[17]

Aquinas predicated the fifth way by observing that everything in nature has a purpose and behaves in an orderly way. All nature seeks certain ends. Everything functions according to a plan or design: The acorn grows into an oak tree, never a carrot; the girl becomes a woman, never a fish. However, people, creatures, and other things in nature can only carry out their function if they are directed by something intelligent. Where there is order, there is a mind responsible for that order, and this intelligent being is God.

Pause for Thought	The alternative to this argument is to claim that the universe has no order and that what we call order is merely a projection of our mind. How would Aquinas respond to the chaos theory posited by some physicists today?

Aquinas's first three proofs of God's existence are *cosmological arguments*, proving that nothing in this world could exist without its source in God. God is the ultimate cause of the world, and all things in the world are effects.

Aquinas's fourth way that considers the degrees of goodness or perfection is his *moral argument*, and the fifth proof is the *teleological argument*—the argument from design. Based on the observation that this is an orderly universe and everything in it strives to fulfill its function, there must be an orderer or designer—God.

For Aquinas, the five proofs provide a foundation that rational people not only can follow, but also agree upon. Reason is a legitimate faculty for proving God's existence. However, the full truth of God, he said, can only be known through revelation based on grace—a profound mystical experience.

Can We Know God?   With reason and revelation, we know that God exists, but can we know the essence of God? According to Aquinas, "The divine reality surpasses all human conceptions of it." We can know the results of the five proofs: God is First Mover, God is First Cause, God is necessary being or pure actuality, God is the ultimate perfection, and God is the intelligent designer of the universe. Based on revelation, we can know that *God is will* and *God is creator*.

But can we understand God? Aquinas said God exceeds the limitations of our finite minds. Like John Scotus Erigena, he believed we could approach God only by the negative way: *God is not this or that*. God is not corporeal, because reason tells us anything physical has limitations. The best way to consider positive ideas about God is through *analogy*. When we refer to a human being as glorious, wise, good, loving, or merciful, then we can apply these same words, these analogies, also to God. As God is to us, so God's wisdom, power, and goodness are to our wisdom, power, and goodness. We cannot know these in their infinite perfection, but we can appreciate their qualities.

Evil   If God is all good, all-knowing, all-wise, and all-powerful, then how can there be evil in the world? Is God responsible for evil? If so, can God really be all good? Aquinas tackled this problem by saying God created this universe to communicate His love of His own essence. Our world is a reflection of God's unconditional love. Aquinas accepted Augustine's solution that evil is not a force in itself but the absence of good. With Augustine, he believed evil is a product of our free will, but not a product of the "informed" human will. He agreed with Socrates that no one could intentionally will evil knowing it is evil. An adulterer does not consciously will a sin but is willing an act that appears good such as sensual pleasure. However, such pleasure lacks goodness and is therefore evil.

Pause for Thought   Do you agree with Aquinas that no one ever intentionally wills evil knowing it is evil?

The question remains why God allows flaws in moral behavior (e.g., murder) or in nature (e.g., a bird born without wings). Aquinas answers that God did not will suffering, only a natural order that allowed for physical defects and suffering:

> Now it is necessary that God's goodness, which in itself is one and simple, should be manifested in many ways in His creation: because creatures in themselves cannot attain the simplicity of God. Thus it is that for the completion of the universe there are required diverse grades of being, of which some hold a high and some a low place in the universe. That this multiformity of grades may be preserved in things, God allows some evils lest many good things should be hindered.[18]

In his love, God willed human beings the freedom to choose good or evil. If we could choose only good, then we would not be free. A complete universe needs deformity as well as perfection.

Moral Philosophy   For Aquinas, the law of reason is the basis of morality. By understanding how human nature functions, we can reason the way we should behave. To avoid going against God's intentions, we must be honest, keep our promises, and refrain from lust and adultery. The *natural law of reason* tells us what choices we should make. Individual freedom is the power to make choices between alternatives.

Like Aristotle, Aquinas thought that virtue is a mean between the extremes of too much and too little. Making right choices means finding the mean. We attain virtues when our will and reason control the sensuous appetites. Our natural end is knowledge of human nature and the moral law.

According to Aquinas, there are two types of sin: *venial* and *mortal*. Venial sins are pardonable, because we can make amends. Mortal sins, however, harm the soul, so they are unpardonable. Aquinas also described three kinds of virtue: *theological, moral*, and *intellectual*. God gives us theological virtues—faith, hope, and love. Moral virtues consist of temperance, courage, and justice. Intellectual virtues are wisdom, science, and understanding. All virtues eventually lead us to happiness in God.

Divine Law

We know natural law through our reason, but to reach eternal happiness, we must follow the laws of God. *Divine law* is not found in natural life, because it is not the product of reason. It is a gift of God's grace that comes by contemplating the divinity.

> The more our mind is raised to the contemplation of spiritual things, the more is it withdrawn from sensible things. Now the divine substance is the highest term to which contemplation can reach: hence the mind that sees the divine substance must be wholly freed from the senses, either by death or by rapture. Wherefore it is said in God's person (Exod. xxxiii, 20): *Man shall not see me, and live. . . .*[19]

On Women

Aquinas embraced Aristotle's view of women. Aristotle thought a woman was an incomplete man and lacked reason. A child also inherits the father's characteristics, because the man provides them in reproduction. The woman is passive, providing the receptacle and nourishment to the embryo. In this way and for hundreds of years, Aquinas's *Summa Theologica* provided the Roman Catholic Church with its views on women.

First Article

Whether The Woman Should Have Been Made in the First Production of Things?

Objection 1. It seems that the woman should not have been made in the first production of things. For the Philosopher [Aristotle] says . . . that the *female is a begotten male.* But nothing misbegotten or defective should have been in the first production of things. therefore woman should not have been made at that first production.

Obj. 2. Further, subjection and limitation were a result of sin, for to the woman was it said after sin (Gen. iii. 16), *Thou shalt be under the man's power.* . . . *I answer that.* It was necessary, as the Scripture says, for woman to be made as a help to man; not, indeed, as a helpmate in other works, as some say, since man can be more efficiently helped by another man in other works; but as a help in the work of generation. . . . Among perfect animals the active power of generation belongs to the male sex, and the passive power to the female . . . man is yet further ordered to a still nobler vital action, and that is intellectual operation. . . .

Reply Obj. 2. Subjection is twofold. One is servile, by virtue of which a superior makes use of a subject for his own benefit; and this kind of subjection began after sin. There is another kind of subjection, which is called economic or civil, whereby the superior makes use of his subjects for their own benefit and good; and this kind of subjection existed even before sin. For good order would have been wanting in the human family if some were not governed by others wiser than themselves. So by such a kind of subjection woman is naturally subject to man, because in man the discretion of reason predominates. . . .[20]

Summary

During the Medieval period, we saw the development of Christian philosophy and the influence of Greek philosophy in scripture and in the writings of the two most influential philosophers of the Medieval ages, Augustine and Thomas Aquinas. Both men were later canonized for their contributions to the Church and its theology. The major problem facing the Medieval period was the question of *faith* and *reason*.

Augustine viewed Christianity as a divine mystery that we can only perceive through faith. If we believe in Christianity, however, God will illuminate the soul so we can experience a supernatural knowledge of God.

According to Augustine, God created the world *ex nihilo*, not out of the existing materials as Plato proposed or by the emanation perceived by Plotinus. God created everything simultaneously, but some things only in *potential* form that would become *actualized* over time. Because God created out of infinite love, the whole creation is an expression of God's goodness. God created matter, therefore matter cannot be evil.

The origin of evil is in free will. Because of Adam and Eve's disobedience, we are born with original sin, but we have the ability to choose good or evil. However, to achieve moral goodness, we must have God's grace.

History is the unfolding of God's plan for creation. By studying history, we can learn what is necessary for salvation.

During the "Not-So-Dark-Ages," the controversy and tension between faith and reason continued. Philosophers concluded that God endowed men with rational minds and intended them to use those minds to establish communication with the rational order. John Scotus Erigena argued that true authority does not oppose right reason, and right reason does not oppose true authority. Muslim philosopher Avicenna believed that the spiritual journey to God begins with faith, but rational knowledge emanates from God and is one way to understand God's intelligence. Averroes, another Muslim theologian, argued that reason is an aspect of God's intelligence and can, if properly directed, understand the truth of ultimate reality. Jewish philosopher Moses Maimonides argued that the highest human perfection is acquiring rational virtues "which teach true opinions concerning the divine things."

Thomas Aquinas argued that conflict does not have to exist between faith and reason. We can trust the truth that God exists through both our faith and our reason. Theology begins with faith—that is, through revelation. Reason begins with objects of sense and proceeds upward to universal ideas until the mind reaches the highest principle of being: God.

Aquinas is famous for his Five Proofs for the Existence of God: (1) Proof from Motion, (2) Proof from Efficient Cause, (3) Proof from Necessary Versus Possible Being, (4) Proof from Degrees of Perfection, and (5) Proof from the Order of the Universe.

There are, said Aquinas, two types of sin: venial (pardonable) and mortal (unpardonable), and three kinds of virtue: theological, moral, and intellectual.

Connections

In the Middle Ages, philosophy and theology were so closely interwoven that they laid the foundation for the doctrines of Christianity. Their main concentration was on understanding God with a view to human salvation. For hundreds of years, Medieval philosophers took a dim view of science, but gradually they began to separate from theology by viewing religion as a matter of faith rather than as a matter of reason. Though philosophers and scientists did not reject religion out of hand, they developed a keen interest in the natural world. The vertical relationship of human beings to God, which was the most important focus of the Medieval period, was replaced by a more horizontal view of nature and our place in it. We shall now turn to modern philosophy, a time of philosophical and scientific discovery and liberation from the fixed doctrines of the Middle Ages.

Study Questions

1. Explain what is meant by the term Creation ex nihilo.

2. What are the seminal principles?

3. Plato, Aristotle, and Augustine offer different explanations for the origin of the universe. Compare their views and defend the one that you regard as the best explanation.

4. What is original sin?

5. With the introduction of Christianity and its belief in original sin, the Medieval view of human nature differed significantly from the Greek view. Compare them.

6. If God created a good world, then where does evil originate? *131*

7. Socrates and Plato said we do evil acts through ignorance. Augustine disagrees. What is Augustine's argument?

8. How does Augustine reconcile free will with God's foreknowledge?

9. According to Augustine, will God grace all "good" people? What is Augustine's view of salvation?

10. How is virtue related to grace?

11. What is the role of love in Augustine's moral philosophy? *133* What is disordered love?

12. What is the City of God?

13. What is the Worldly City?

14. What is Augustine's view of history?

15. According to John Scotus Erigena, what is the importance of right reason?

16. How did Erigena's notion of free will differ from Augustine's?

17. What did Avicenna call the Tenth Intelligence?

18. According to Averroes, what are the two branches of practical knowledge?

19. For Moses Maimonides, what is the highest human perfection?

20. How did Maimonides view biblical prophecy?

21. According to Maimonides, how much can we know about God?

22. What is the significance of Aristotle to Thomas Aquinas?

23. Compare and contrast Aquinas's *148-9* with Aristotle's *129* view of God.

24. What does Aquinas mean that we know about God through analogy?

25. What are Aquinas's five proofs for the existence of God?

26. Which of the Five Ways is the strongest?

27. What is Aquinas's view of evil? *153*

28. How does Aquinas solve the problem of evil? *154*

29. How does Aquinas solve the problem of faith and reason? *154*

30. Why did Aquinas stop writing philosophy?

31. What was Aquinas's view of women? What effects have St. Augustine's and St. Thomas Aquinas's views on women had on Christianity and the Western world?

Notes

1. Wallace I. Matson, *A New History of Philosophy*, p. 193, Vol. I. San Diego: Harcourt Brace Jovanovich, 1987. The "Nicene Creed" reads as follows:

We believe in one God,
the Father, the Almighty,
maker of heaven and earth,
of all that is, seen and unseen.

We believe in one Lord, Jesus Christ,
the only Son of God,
eternally begotten of the Father,
God from God, Light from Light,
true God from true God,
begotten, not made,
of one Being with the Father.

Through him all things were made.
For us and for our salvation
he came down from heaven;
by the power of the Holy Spirit
he became incarnate from the Virgin Mary,
and was made man.
For our sake he was crucified under Pontius Pilate;
he suffered death and was buried
On the third day he rose again
in accordance with the Scriptures;
he ascended into heaven
and is seated at the right hand of the Father.
He will come again in glory to judge the living and the dead,
and his kingdom will have no end.

We believe in the Holy Spirit, the Lord, the giver of life,
who proceeds from the Father and the Son.
With the Father and the Son he is worshiped and glorified.
He has spoken through the Prophets.

We believe in one holy catholic and apostolic Church.
We acknowledge one baptism for the forgiveness of sins.
We look for the resurrection of the dead,
and the life of the world to come. Amen.

2. Augustine, *Confessions* (trans. by Henry Chadwick), VIII, vols. 10 and 12. Oxford, UK: Oxford University Press, 1991.

3. Augustine, *The Confessions* (trans. by Edward Bouverie Pusey), Vol. I. 1, 2, 4. Chicago: Encyclopedia Britannica, 1952.

4. Augustine, *City of God* (trans. by Marcus Dods), Vol. XXII, 1. Chicago: Encyclopedia Britannica, 1952. Reprint from Great Books of the Western World. © 1925, 1990 Encylopaedia Britannica, Inc.

5. Ibid., Vol. XIV, 14; Vol. XXII, 22.

6. Ibid., Vol. XXII, 22.

7. Augustine, *The City of God* (trans. by Henry Betterison), Vol. XIV, 28. Harmondsworth, UK: Penguin Books, 1972.

8. Augustine, *The City of God* in *Works of Aurelius Augustine* (trans. by Marcus Dods), Vol. I, Bks. XII, XIV. Edinburgh, Scotland: T. & T. Clark, 1871.

9. "Joinvilles' Chronicle of the Crusade of St. Louis," p. 142 in *Memoirs of the Crusades* (trans. by Marzials). New York: E. P. Dutton, 1908.

10. From Anselm, in *Anselm: Proslogium* (trans. by M. J. Charlesworth), Ch. 2. London: Oxford University Press, 1965.

11. Moses Maimonides, *Guide for the Perplexed* (trans. by S. Pines), Ch. 58. Chicago: University of Chicago Press, 1963.

12. Thomas Aquinas, *Summa Theologica* (trans. by the Fathers of the English Dominican Province), Vol. I, Part 1, Ques. 1 & 2, Art. 8. New York: Benziger Brothers, 1947.

13. Ibid., Part 1, Ques. 2, Art. 3.

14. Ibid.

15. Ibid.

16. Ibid.

17. Ibid.

18. Aquinas, *Summa Contra Gentiles* (trans. by the Fathers of the English Dominican Province), op. cit., Vol. II. Part 3, Ques. 25.

19. Ibid., Ques. 27.

20. Aquinas, *Summa Theologica*, op. cit., Vol. XIII, Part 1, Ques. 92.

CHAPTER SEVEN

Modern Philosophy: The Reformation, Science, and Rationalism

The Renaissance

In the late fourteenth century, a cultural enrichment began to develop. With the coming of this *Renaissance,* or "rebirth," we find a new view of humankind emerging. Human beings are no longer considered no more than sinful creatures; they are now thought noble and worthy. One important Renaissance figure, Marsilio Ficino, said, "Know thyself, O divine lineage in mortal guise!" Pico della Mirandola, another figure of note, wrote his *Oration on the Dignity of Man,* something that was unheard of in the Medieval period. We are not only human beings, said the Renaissance philosophers, but also unique individuals. The ideal in this era became the Renaissance man, one of universal genius who embraced all aspects of life, art, and science.

Recall that the Medieval philosophers emphasized the view that God is "other than" nature. An insurmountable barrier exists between God and the Creation. Renaissance humanist Giordano Bruno proclaimed an altogether different view: God is present in His creation. Like the Stoics, Bruno saw God in everything, a view known as **pantheism**. Nature is divine. He also believed that the universe is infinite in scope. The Church, however, saw Bruno as a pagan heretic and insisted that he refute his ideas. When he refused, the Church burned him alive at the stake. This chapter will provide insight into the new thinking of philosophers and scientists about the nature of humankind and the world, thinking that often presented its adherents with similarly dramatic life-and-death choices.

The Reformation

During the fourteenth and fifteenth centuries, the papacy was in disarray, and the Church seemed more interested in politics than in serving the needs of the masses. During one period, there were claimants for pope in both Rome and Avignon, France. Even devout Catholics expressed concern about the excesses and abuses they recognized within their church. One of them, an Augustinian monk named Martin Luther (1483–1546), finally presented a challenge that the Church could not ignore.

Martin Luther

Luther's Life   Born in what is now northern Germany on November 10, 1483, Martin Luther was the son of Hans Luder, who was in the copper mining business. He was a stern man who fought intensely with his son. Martin's early schooling took place in Mansfeld, but when the family moved to Magdeburg, Luther attended the cathedral school. There he came into contact with a spiritual movement called the Brethren of the Common Life. Between 1498 and 1501, he attended school in Eisenach, later graduating from the University of Erfurt. After receiving his Master's degree in 1505, Luther studied law to please his father, but that summer he had a spiritual experience that led him to drop out of law school and become a monk instead.

In July 1505, Luther entered the monastery of the Eremites of Saint Augustine in Erfurt and was ordained to the priesthood two years later. In his recollections, he wrote of his awesome experience in celebrating his first Mass. That year he began graduate studies in theology, first at Erfurt and then at the University of Wittenberg, where he was a philosophical lecturer in the liberal arts department.

In 1509, Luther returned to Erfurt to continue his theological studies, and shortly after the Augustinian order sent him to Rome on monastic business. He had looked forward to Rome as a spiritual center but found it overwhelmingly worldly. After his return, he transferred again to Wittenberg to complete his doctorate in theology. After receiving his degree, he became a professor in Bible as endowed by the Augustinian order.

Throughout these years, he had become increasingly disenchanted with Church authority. His disillusionment grew even more until finally, on October 31, 1517, Luther fastened sheets of paper with ninety-five theses to the chapel door at the University of Wittenberg. In these pages, he challenged certain doctrines and practices of the Church. His protest and urge for reform started the movement that we now know as the Protestant Reformation.

Luther's Reforms   In rejecting the papacy's religious authority, Luther emphasized that the individual was responsible for living a good life. He criticized the Church's practice of selling or awarding *indulgences*—that is, the guarantee of forgiveness of sins without punishment in purgatory—which he considered blasphemous. He argued that indulgences performed by a human being could not earn anyone salvation. That comes only from God's grace. Luther also criticized the pope's control of the treasure of merits out of which he might "draw credits." And he spoke strongly against focusing economics on the Mass.

In his criticism of papal pride, Luther said:

> . . . the Pope is not satisfied with riding on horseback or in a carriage, but though he be hale and strong, is carried by men like an idol in unheard-of pomp. My friend, how does this Lucifer-like pride agree with the example of Christ, who went on foot, as did also all the Apostles?[1]

Pause for Thought

The meaning of the word *Protestant* is "to protest." The first Protestants spoke out against certain practices in the Catholic Church. However, it is not unusual to this day for Protestants to disagree with each other on issues. What are some of the contemporary disagreements among "fundamental," "mainstream," and "liberal" Protestants?

Luther wanted to return to early Christianity as it was in the New Testament: "The Scripture alone," he said. He believed that everyone should read the Bible and communicate with God in his own way without the intercession of a priest. He also rejected the doctrine of purgatory and called monastic life an aberration.

Summoned in 1521 before the Diet of Worms (an advisory council to the Holy Roman Emperor comprising both clerical and secular officials), Luther refused to withdraw his controversial statements. The pope excommunicated him, and the emperor declared him an outlaw. When a friendly and sympathetic duke offered him refuge in his castle at Wartbury, Luther accepted. There he translated the Bible into German, thus putting it within reach of all literate German-speaking people.

Like Augustine, Luther viewed humans on two levels that were always in conflict: the body or "the Flesh" and the soul or "Spirit." He believed that humankind was totally depraved after its fall from grace. Justification for humans could come only through the grace of God.

Luther married an ex-nun, and they had several children. Woman's only secular vocation, he said, was her family. He died in his birthplace February 16, at age sixty-three.

Faith and Reason   Luther considered faith more important than reason because, for him, the heart of the gospel lay in Paul's teaching known as "justification by faith." With Paul, he believed that reason demonstrates that God must exist but not what God is like. For that, we must rely on faith. Luther described three kinds of reason: *natural reason*, which is adequate for dealing with human affairs on earth; *presumptuous reason,* which falsely claims to arbitrate truth in religious matters; and *regenerate reason*, which uses disciplined thought to understand the world of God.

Reason, said Luther, can play a positive role in spiritual life, but only faith makes us right with God.

> It is a quality of faith that it wrings the neck of reason. . . . But how? It holds to God's Word: lets it be right and true, no matter how foolish and impossible it sounds. So did Abraham take his reason captive and slay it, in as much as he believed God's word, wherein was promised him that from his unfruitful and as it were dead wife, Sarah, God would give him seed. . . . There is no doubt faith and reason mightily fell out in Abraham's heart about this matter, yet at last did faith get the better, and overcame and strangled reason, that all-cruelest and most fatal enemy of God. So, too, do all other faithful men who enter with Abraham the gloom and hidden darkness of faith: they strangle reason . . . and thereby offer to God the all-acceptablest sacrifice and service that can ever be brought to Him.[2]

Pause for Thought   Do you agree with Martin Luther that only faith makes us right with God? What role, if any, does reason play in spiritual matters?

The Reformation Spreads   Many Christians were disgusted with corruption among the clergy, so they liked Luther's proposed reforms. His reforms also appealed to princes and kings who were eager to rid themselves of papal authority over their own subjects. When Luther left the church, thousands of his followers fled their monasteries and convents to join the Reformation. Lutherism quickly took root in Germany and Scandinavia.

The Protestant Reformation had a strong influence on philosophy, especially ethics. For instance, as we will see in Chapter 9, in his moral thought, Immanuel Kant believed—with Luther—that moral merit is a function of the inner person, not outward behavior. For Kant, motive alone is the gauge of an action's moral value. Moral practices do not depend on priestly authority. In this way, the Reformation weakened the respect for dogmatic authority by steering people to look within themselves.

The Rise of Science

From their religion's beginnings, Christians had considered science a poor substitute for theology. All views of nature required justification by religious authorities. For instance, because God created humankind in His image, nobody has doubted that the Earth was the center of the universe. This *geocentric* view was widely believed: The Earth remained still while the "heavenly bodies" traveled in their orbits around it. Christians believed that God ruled from high above these bodies.

In 1543, however, *On the Revolutions of the Celestial Spheres* was published by Nicolaus Copernicus (1473–1543), a Polish astronomer, who died the very day his book was released. Copernicus had discovered that it was not the sun that moved round the Earth, but the Earth and other planets that revolved around the sun. With Copernicus, science moved from geocentrism to a *heliocentric* view of the heavens—*everything* circles the sun.

Galileo Galilei (1564–1642), an Italian scientist, discovered moons circling Jupiter and so confirmed Copernicus's hypothesis of a century earlier that the Earth was not the center of the solar system. Church officials, however, insisted on the correctness of Aristotle's theory that the Earth was the center of the solar system. Because of his heretical teaching, the Church summoned Galileo to face a council of inquisition in Rome. In 1633, the council forced him to recant by threatening him with excommunication. Agreeing to its demands, he recanted. But as he left the room, he whispered, "I recant, but nonetheless my findings are true." For the rest of his life, he was under house arrest. After Galileo died, his place among scientific geniuses was soon confirmed, although the Church held firm against him for centuries. In 1992, the Church officially restored his good name and reputation.

This sudden infusion of reason into natural inquiry began to supplant the prevailing reliance on precedence and the Church's steadfastly Aristotelian teachings. A new and profoundly scientific method of investigation began to take place all across Europe. For example, Dutch microscopist and scientist Anton van Leeuwenhoek (1632–1723) discovered spermatozoa, protozoa, and bacteria.

English anatomist William Harvey (1578–1657) postulated a theory of the circulation of blood. Englishman Robert Boyle (1627–1691), a chemist and "father" of chemistry, formulated a famous law on the relation of temperature, volume, and pressure of gases. English physicist Sir Isaac Newton and German philosopher Gottfried von Leibniz, working independently, both invented differential and integral calculus.

The Roman Catholic Church placed Copernicus's treatise about the solar system "Concerning the Revolutions of Heavenly Bodies" on its index of forbidden books. His theory fared no better with Martin Luther and other Protestant leaders who also believed that his findings conflicted with Old Testament statements that Joshua had commanded the sun to stand still.

Pause for Thought   As we look at religious history today, did these theories actually harm Christian doctrine? Do you think modern theories of evolution contradict Christianity? Can you reconcile evolution theories with creation theories?

The New Science

English physicist Isaac Newton (1642–1727) provided the final description of the solar system and the planetary orbits. He not only explained that the planets moved round the sun, but also *how* these bodies in motion behaved. One day, while he sat under an apple tree, an apple fell on his head. Proceeding from this "A-ha!" experience, he formulated his Law of Universal Gravitation: Every object attracts every other object with a force that increases in proportion to the size of the objects and decreases in proportion to the distance between the objects. Thus, there is greater attraction between two horses than between two butterflies. And two horses in the same pasture have stronger attraction to each other than does a horse in Arizona with a horse in Alaska.

Though Newton spoke of God as the creator of the machine of nature, scientists found it increasingly unnecessary to refer to God when explaining nature. They began to view the universe as a system of bodies in motion. Such mechanical behavior, scientists concluded, must be capable of mathematical description.

In this way, observation and the use of mathematics emerged as the motive forces of the new scientific method. This new science immediately affected the development of modern philosophy. Copernicus, Galileo, and German astronomer Johann Kepler (1571–1630) all emphasized the importance of basing scientific conclusions on observation. Instead of looking to Church authority and tradition, scientists and philosophers now would look to nature for truth. They organized the information that they received by observation and discovery into a system of axioms.

Pause for Thought   We can almost feel the excitement of these scientists with their discoveries. Are you enthusiastic about any scientific breakthroughs today?

Through scientific observation, sixteenth- and seventeenth-century philosophers sought to explain the human condition and the nature of society. Thomas Hobbes was an extremely influential philosopher of the seventeenth century. He called the relationship between people and their society a **social contract.**

Thomas Hobbes

Hobbes's Life   Thomas Hobbes (1588–1679) lived for ninety-one years. Born in Westport, England, he was educated at Oxford University, where he found Aristotle's logic dull and so turned toward more exciting adventures in classical literature. Following his education, Hobbes became the tutor for the son of the important Cavendish family. This association allowed him to travel widely and meet many leading contemporary thinkers.

When he was forty, Hobbes discovered Euclid's *Elements,* a work that helped shift Hobbes's interest from classical literature to mathematics and analysis.

> Being in a gentleman's library, Euclid's *Elements* lay open, and 'twas the 47th [theorem of Book 1]. He read the proposition. "By God," said he, "this is impossible . . . " So he reads the demonstration of it which referred him back to such a proposition: which proposition he read. That referred him back to another, which he also read . . . at last he was demonstratively convinced of that truth. This made him in love with geometry.[3]

Caught up in the spirit of his time, Hobbes saw geometry as the key to understanding nature. By applying the methods of science to study human nature, he profoundly altered the course of philosophy.

Metaphysics   The basis of Hobbes's metaphysics is that everything is matter and all that exists are *bodies in motion* that continually move from place to place. Human beings are nothing but material bodies following the laws of motion. For Hobbes, two main types of bodies existed: the physical and the political. He saw his task as working out the social, political, and ethical theories using his ideas of materialism.

The principal parts of philosophy are two. For two chief kinds of bodies, and very different from one another, offer themselves to such a search after their generation and properties; one whereof being the work of nature, is called a *natural body*, the other is called a *commonwealth*, and is made by the wills and agreement of men.[4]

If nothing exists except bodies in motion, then are our thoughts, will power, and emotions also matter in motion? "Yes," said Hobbes. Even hatred and love? "Yes."

Human Nature   Hobbes believed that before humanity's "socialization," our state of nature was a "war of all against all," making life "nasty, brutish, and short." People, he said, are fundamentally egotistical, chiefly concerned about their own survival and identifying goodness as the satisfaction of their own appetites.

Nature hath made men so equal, in the faculties of the body, and mind, as that though there be found one man sometimes manifestly stronger in body, or of quicker mind than another; yet when all is reckoned together, the difference between man, and man, is not so considerable, as that one man can thereupon claim to himself any benefit. . . .

From this equality of ability, ariseth equality of hope in the attaining of our ends. And therefore if any two men desire the same thing, which nevertheless they cannot both enjoy, they become enemies; and in the way to their end, which is principally their own conservation, and sometimes their delectation only, endeavour to destroy, or subdue one another. . . .

So that in the nature of man, we find three principal causes of quarrel. First, competition; secondly, diffidence [shyness]; thirdly, glory.

The first, maketh men invade for gain; the second, for safety; and the third, for reputation. The first use violence, to make themselves masters of other men's persons, wives, children, and cattle; the second, to defend them; the third, for trifles, as a word, a smile, a different opinion, and any other sign of undervalue, either direct in their persons, or by reflection in their kindred, their friends, their nation, their profession, or their name. . . .

[D]uring the time men live without a common power to keep them all in awe, they are in that condition which is called war; and such a war, as is of every man, against every man. For war consisteth not in battle only, or the act of fighting; but . . . in the known disposition thereto, during all the time there is no assurance to the contrary. All other time is peace.

Whatsoever therefore is consequent to a time of war, where every man is enemy to every man; the same is consequent to the time, wherein men live without other security, than what their own strength, and their own invention shall furnish them withal. In such condition, there is no place for industry, because the fruit thereof is uncertain: and consequently no culture of the earth; no navigation, nor use of the commodities that may be imported by sea; no commodious building; no instruments of moving, and removing, such things as require much force; no knowledge of the face of the earth; no account of time; no arts; no letter; no society; and which is worst of all, continual fear, and danger of violent death; and the life of man, solitary, poor, nasty, brutish, and short. . . .[5]

Social Contract   According to Hobbes, people formed a society to harness their selfish and brutish power. As a society, they agreed to surrender authority to a sovereign who would keep them in check. In other words, society is a compromise, a social contract by which we sacrifice individual freedom for security and cooperation. Because the sovereign has the power to judge what is best for the people, religion and the Church also were subordinate to the state. If a Christian thought the sovereign's command violated the law of God, according to Hobbes, he could either obey the sovereign or "go to Christ in martyrdom."

Pause for Thought   Is Hobbes correct? Are we willing to sacrifice our individual freedom for security? What do we expect from our elected government officials? Insurance companies? The military and the police?

Influence on Philosophy   With his materialistic outlook on human nature, Hobbes changed philosophy's direction. During the Medieval period, philosophy had virtually ignored science, instead joining with theology by concentrating on God as the source and director of the world. Hobbes, on the other hand, ignored Medieval views of God so that he could concentrate on the scientific method. This led him to accept a materialistic view of human nature. His conclusions that humans were amoral and secular may have offended the religious community, but their boldness challenged philosophers and scientists to find an optimistic view of the world and human life.

On Women   In *De Cive* (1642), Hobbes argued that being a father does not mean being a lord. By nature, dominion is maternal. First, only the identity of the child's mother is certain. Second, power over the child is in the mother who nourishes and trains it. Physical strength is not the only strength. Just as important are wit and cunning. Therefore, there is no natural patriarchal right in the family, much less in the state.

We must therefore return to the state of nature, in which, by reason of equality of nature, all men of riper years are to be accounted equal. There *by right of nature* the conqueror is lord of the conquered. By the right therefore of *nature*, the dominion over the infant first belongs to him who first hath him in his power. But it is manifest that he who is newly born, is in the *mother's* power before any others; insomuch as she may rightly, and at her own will either breed him up or adventure him to fortune.

If therefore she breed him, because the state of nature is the state of war, she is supposed to bring him up on this condition; that being grown to full age he become not her enemy; which is, that he obey her. . . . And thus in the state of nature, every woman that bears children, becomes both a *mother* and a *lord*. But what some say, that in this case the *father,* by reason of the pre-eminence of sex, and not the *mother* becomes *lord*, signifies nothing. For both reason shows the contrary; because the inequality of their natural forces is not so great, that the man could get the dominion over the woman without war. . . .[6]

Pause for Thought   Which view of women comes closest to your own—the Medieval Christian view or that of Thomas Hobbes? Do you have a view that differs from both?

The Continental Rationalists

The so-called Continental Rationalist philosophers of Europe considered truth a universal concept. Like Socrates and Plato, these philosophers believed that the laws of truth are beyond our control and discoverable only through reason. Such thinking gave intellectuals a new zest for learning. Reason, they said, is superior to and independent of sense experience. It is the only path to knowledge. Because reason supersedes tradition and Church authority, we can conduct our own affairs.

Impressed by the scientific method and mathematics, the Rationalists wanted to give philosophy the exactness of mathematics. Three of the most notable Continental Rationalists were René Descartes, a dualist who described reality as two separate substances, *thought* and *extension;* Benedict de Spinoza, who posited reality as a single substance with *attributes* and *modes;* and Gottfried Leibniz, who saw reality as one kind of substance, the *monad.*

René Descartes

Descartes' Life   Born at La Haye, Tourain, in France, René Descartes (1596–1650) was the son of a noble family and would become known, by the end of his life, as the "father of modern philosophy." His mother died of consumption soon after his birth, and his health was frail. Still, by age eight he was able to begin a nine-year course at the Royal Jesuit College of La Fleche, where he studied ancient literature, theology and philosophy, and mathematics. Because of his health, the Jesuit teachers allowed him to stay in bed mornings and attend classes in the afternoons. Descartes was an excellent student, but he was disillusioned by the uncertainty and differences of opinion he found in his studies. Only in mathematics did he find the certainty he craved. There could be no dispute over mathematical truths. Whether one was a Platonist, an Aristotelian, or a follower of Augustine, two plus two always equaled four.

An inheritance left by his father allowed Descartes to travel Europe in pursuit of the type of life that appealed to worldly young playboys. But he found social life boring and hid from his companions to study in seclusion. Finally, he left Paris to study law at Poitiers. After receiving his law degree, he joined the army of Maurice of Nassau (a region in what is now Germany) as a gentleman volunteer. While in the army, Descartes had time to meditate on his idea of connecting mathematical certainty with philosophy.

After three years, Descartes left the army to retire to Holland and that country's intellectual freedom. The next twenty years he spent writing and publishing his ideas. In 1649, Queen Christina of Sweden invited him to Stockholm to instruct her in philosophy. When he politely refused, she sent a warship to convey him to the "land of bears, ice, and rocks," as he called her kingdom. When he arrived in Sweden, he discovered the only time Queen Christina had for her lessons was at five A.M. in her cold, damp castle. Within a few months, at age fifty-four, Descartes caught pneumonia and died.

Descartes' contribution to mathematics, optics, physiology, and philosophy is remarkable. In mathematics, he introduced what are now known as Cartesian coordinates and curves, and he invented analytic geometry. Descartes would have liked to reconcile the Church teachings (he was Roman Catholic) with the new science. Instead, the Church placed his writings on its index of prohibited books, and Protestant theologians similarly attacked his findings.

The Cartesian Method

The word *Cartesian* comes from the Latin form of Descartes' name, *Cartesius*, which he did not like. Still, the term for his method stuck. The method began when Descartes asked himself, "What, if anything, can I know with certainty?" First, he looked back on his studies. He saw that ancient literature provided him wonderful fables that stimulated his mind, but it couldn't guide his behavior. Poetry may hold knowledge through its "imaginative force," but it is a gift, not a method for perceiving the truth. He looked to the revealed truths of theology, but realized they were beyond most people's comprehension. He turned to the philosophers, but found that although all philosophers looked for truth, they could not agree on any one answer. Finally, Descartes turned to the "book of the world"—that is, the common experiences and wisdom of ordinary people. But once again he found just as many differences of opinion among these people as among philosophers.

> After I had employed several years in thus studying the book of the world
> and trying to acquire some experience, I one day formed the resolution of
> also making myself an object of study and of employing all the strength of
> my mind in choosing the road I should follow. . . .[7]

On the night of November 10, 1619, Descartes had three dreams. They
were so vivid that he was sure God had sent them. The dreams directed him to
construct the system of knowledge using just the powers of human reason.

Pause for Thought   Do you listen to your dreams? Can they guide you in ways that your
conscious mind cannot? Or do you think dreams are the result of
eating a sandwich with too much mustard or riding on a roller coaster
at the amusement park?

Following the instructions of his dreams, Descartes set out to develop an
entirely new system of philosophy. He would not rely on the findings of his previous studies or model his thoughts after those in authority. Using reason as his
guide, Descartes hoped to arrive at a system of thought whose principles were
true and related to each other in a clear and meaningful way.

Role of Mathematics

In his quest to develop a method that would lead to
certainty, Descartes looked to the rules of mathematics and made certain that his
method contained everything that gave certainty to the rules of arithmetic.
Mathematical certainty, he said, is a special way of thinking. By using mathematical thinking, he discovered that the human mind has two powers: (1) **intuition,** which is the ability to apprehend directly certain truths; and (2) **deduction,** which is the power to discover what we do not know by progressing in
an orderly way from what we do know.

As a *rationalist*, Descartes believed reasoning could produce absolute truths
about nature, existence, morality, and God. We can discover these truths
through intuition and deduction without observation or sense experience. Such
truths are *a priori* (meaning, from the reason without referring to sense experience). A priori ideas do not rely on sense experience because they are innate in
the human mind. Convinced that to know with certainty depended on these
powers of reason, Descartes laid down the foundation of his method.

Rules of Method

It took Descartes many years to formulate his twenty-one
"Rules for the Direction of the Mind." Rule III may be the most important.

Rule III

In the subjects we propose to investigate, our inquiries should be directed, not to what others have thought, nor to what we ourselves conjecture, but to what we can clearly and perspicuously behold and with certainty deduce; for knowledge is not won in any other way. . . .

[W]e shall here take note of all those mental operations by which we are able, wholly without fear of illusion, to arrive at the knowledge of things. Now I admit only two, viz. intuition and deduction.

By *intuition* I understand, not the fluctuating testimony of the senses, nor the misleading judgment that proceeds from the blundering constructions of imagination, but the conception which an unclouded and attentive mind gives us so readily and distinctly that we are wholly freed from doubt about that which we understand. Or, what comes to the same thing, *intuition* is the undoubting conception of an unclouded and attentive mind, and springs from the light of reason alone . . . thus each person can mentally have intuition of the fact that he exists. . . .

By *deduction* . . . we understand all necessary inference from other facts that are known with certainty . . . though not by themselves evident, but only deduced from true and known principles by the continuous and uninterrupted action of a mind that has a clear vision of each step in the process. It is in a similar way that we know that the last link in a long chain is connected with the first, even though we do not take in by means of one and the same act of vision all the intermediate links on which that connection depends, but only remember that we have taken them successively under review and that each single one is united to its neighbour, from the first even to the last.

Hence we distinguish this mental intuition from deduction by the fact that into the conception of the latter there enters a certain movement or succession, into that of the former there does not. . . .

These two methods are the most certain routes to knowledge, and the mind should admit no others. All the rest should be rejected as suspect of error and dangerous. . . .[8]

Intuition and Deduction   Descartes decided to accept as true only that which he found as clear and distinct as his own existence. By the power of intuition, the mind can apprehend such basic truths directly and clearly. He defined *intuition* as an intellectual activity or vision of such clarity that it leaves no doubt in the mind. For example, I cannot doubt that *I exist*. Descartes described deduction as "all necessary inferences from facts that are known with certainty." By the power of deduction, the mind arrives at a truth by a step-by-step process. He chose fact over premise, because conclusions drawn syllogistically (that is, deductively) from premises could be untrue or based on authority. Descartes wanted to rely only on knowledge in his own mind. Intuition gives the truth of first principles and deduction shows the relation of these truths to each other.

Descartes believed that philosophy should go from the simple to the complex. Only then would it be possible to construct a new insight and ensure by constant enumeration that nothing was left out. A philosophical conclusion would then be within reach.

Pause for Thought   Many people accept deduction as a valid mental process, but what about intuition? Can you think of examples in your life when you relied on intuition to solve a problem?

Method of Doubt   Wanting to avoid what he considered the faulty rationalism of the Medieval philosophers (he thought their conclusions dubious), Descartes subjected every idea to doubt. Before he would accept any idea as true, it had to meet his test of certainty. He began by trying to doubt everything: (1) the reality of the physical world (the senses), (2) the validity of mathematics (universals), and (3) God (transcendence).

[Surely I] cannot reasonably . . . doubt . . . that I am here, seated by the fire, attired in a dressing gown, having this paper in my hands and other similar matters. And how could I deny that these hands and this body are mine. . . .

At the same time I must remember that I am . . . in the habit of sleeping, and in my dreams representing to myself the same things or sometimes even less probable things. . . . How often has it happened to me that in the night I dreamt that I found myself in this particular place, that I was dressed and seated near the fire, whilst in reality I was lying undressed in bed! At this moment it does indeed seem to me that it is with eyes awake that I am looking at this paper; that this head which I move is not asleep . . . what happens in sleep does not appear so clear nor so distinct as does all this. But in thinking over this I remind myself that on many occasions I have in sleep been deceived by similar illusions, and . . . I see . . . that there are no certain indications by which we may clearly distinguish wakefulness from sleep that . . . it is almost capable of persuading me that I now dream.

Now let us assume that we are asleep and that all these particulars, e.g. that we open our eyes, shake our head, extend our hands, and so on, are but false delusions. . . . At the same time we must at least confess that the things which are represented to us in sleep are like painted representations which can only have been formed as the counterparts of something real and true. . . .

[On the other hand] Arithmetic, Geometry and other sciences of that kind which only treat of things that are very simple and very general, without taking great trouble to ascertain whether they are actually existent or not, contain some measure of certainty and an element of the indubitable.

For whether I am awake or asleep, two and three together always form five, and the square can never have more than four sides, and it does not seem possible that truths so clear and apparent can be suspected of any falsity [or uncertainty].

Nevertheless I have long had fixed in my mind the belief that an all-powerful God existed by whom I have been created such as I am. But how do I know that He has not brought it to pass that there is no earth, no heaven, no extended body, no magnitude, no place, and that nevertheless [I possess the perceptions of all these things that] seem to me to exist just exactly as I now see them? . . . [and] how do I know that I am not deceived every time that I add two and three, or count the sides of a square. . . . But possibly God has not desired that I should be thus deceived, for He is said to be supremely good. If, however, it is contrary to His goodness to have made me such that I constantly deceive myself, it would also appear to be contrary to His goodness to permit me to be sometimes deceived, and nevertheless I cannot doubt that He does permit this. . . .

I shall then suppose, not that God who is supremely good and the fountain of truth, but some evil genius not less powerful than deceitful, has employed his whole energies in deceiving me; I shall consider that the heavens, the earth, colours, figures, sound, and all other external things are nought but the illusions and dreams of which this genius has availed himself in order to lay traps for my credulity. . . .

At the end I feel constrained to confess that there is nothing in all that I formerly believed to be true, of which I cannot in some measure doubt, and that not merely through want of thought or through levity, but for reasons which are very powerful and maturely considered.[9]

Using the *dream argument*, Descartes doubted the reality of the physical world. But he could not use the dream argument to doubt mathematics. Surely, he argued, mathematics contains certainty, because two plus two equals four whether I am asleep or awake. I can trust mathematical certainty, because, I think, God has created an orderly universe. Then Descartes asked himself if it was possible to doubt God and His goodness. "Can God, whom I had thought was all good, actually be an evil genius deceiving me into thinking He is all good and that mathematics is valid?" Descartes confessed that he could doubt God's goodness and the validity of mathematics. Now, he reasoned, there is nothing he formally believed to be true that he could not somehow doubt.

Pause for Thought   Could the physical world be a dream that would no longer exist when you wake up? Or could someone else be dreaming *you*—and when that being wakes up, you will no longer exist?

Could the God you believe to be good actually be an evil genius tricking you into thinking he is all good? Could an evil deceiver be playing a huge joke on everyone?

I Think, Therefore I Am   Though I can doubt that my body exists, or that I am awake, or that I am being deceived, said Descartes, I cannot doubt that I am doing the doubting. I must then surely exist in order to doubt that I exist:

> I suppose, then, that all the things that I see are false; I persuade myself that nothing has ever existed of all that my fallacious memory represents to me. I consider that I possess no senses; I imagine that body, figure, extension, movement and place are but fictions of my mind. What, then, can be esteemed as true? Perhaps nothing at all. . . .
>
> Yet I hesitate, for . . . am I so dependent on body and senses that I cannot exist without these? But I was persuaded that there was nothing in all the world, that there was no heaven, no earth, that there were no minds, nor any bodies: was I not then likewise persuaded that I did not exist? Not at all; of a surety I myself did exist since I persuaded myself of something [or merely because I thought of something]. But there is some deceiver or other, very powerful and very cunning, who ever employs his ingenuity in deceiving me. Then without doubt I exist also if he deceives me, and let him deceive me as much as he will, he can never cause me to be nothing so long as I think that I am something. So that after having reflected well and carefully examined all things, we must come to the definite conclusion that this proposition: I am, I exist, is necessarily true each time that I pronounce it, or that I mentally conceive it.[10]

To doubt is to think. For Descartes, this truth was so certain that he could not reject it, and he judged that he could use it "without scruple" as the first principle of his philosophy. "I think, therefore I am." The concept's Latin expression—*Cogito ergo sum*—is one of Descartes' most enduring legacies.

Reversal of Doubt   Descartes has not proved the existence of his body, the validity of mathematics, or the goodness of God. Descartes *has* proved intuitively that he exists as a thinker. He perceived not only that he was a thinking *I*, but also that this thinking *I* was more real than the material world that we perceive with our senses.

So clear was the truth that he was a thinking *I* that Descartes used it as the basis of his philosophy. Then he asked, "What is a thing that thinks?" Following his own rules, he deduced that a *thinker* "is a thing that doubts, understands, affirms, denies, wills, refuses and that also imagines and feels."

Descartes now wanted to go beyond the certainty of his own existence as a thinker. He needed to prove that God exists as a perfect being and not as an evil genius deceiving us into believing things are true or false.

Proofs of God's Existence   Because Descartes still doubted the existence of the physical world, he could not use Thomas Aquinas's argument for the existence of God (recall that Aquinas based his proofs on what we experience in the physical world). Still doubting the reality of the physical world, Descartes must prove God's existence based only on the light of his reason. He began by looking at the kinds of ideas that passed through his mind. First, he realized that ideas are the effects of different causes.

> Among these ideas, some appear to me to be innate, some adventitious, and others to be formed [or invented] by myself. For, as I have the power of understanding what is called a thing, or a truth, or a thought, it appears to me that I hold this power from no other source than my own nature. But if I now hear some sound, if I see the sun, or feel heat, I have hitherto judged that these sensations proceeded from certain things that exist outside of me; and finally it appears to me that sirens, hippogryphs, and the like, are formed out of my own mind.[11]

Thus, there are three kinds of ideas: (1) innate (those born with me), (2) those invented by me, and (3) those that come from outside of me. Reason tells us that we can neither get something from nothing nor get more from less. Therefore, the idea (the effect) cannot be greater than its cause. "The more perfect . . . cannot be a consequence of . . . the less perfect."

Through intuition, Descartes had a distinct idea of perfection, but he also knew intuitively (and with certainty) that he was imperfect. Based on the notion that you cannot get something more from something less, how could an imperfect being have an idea of perfection? Even if he were *potentially* perfect, the idea of perfection could not come from that potentiality. Descartes concluded that because he is finite and imperfect, the cause of his idea of perfection must come from outside himself, from a perfect being—from God. The idea of God must come from God. He then defined what he meant by the name *God:*

> By the name God I understand a substance that is infinite, independent, all-knowing, all-powerful, and by which I myself and everything else, if anything else does exist, have been created. Now all these characteristics are such that the more diligently I attend to them, the less do they appear capable of proceeding from me alone; hence, from what has been already said, we must conclude that God necessarily exists.
>
> For although the idea of substance is within me owing to the fact that I am substance, nevertheless I should not have the idea of an infinite sub-

stance—since I am finite—if it had not proceeded from some substance which was veritably infinite. . . .

Although it were true that every day my knowledge acquired new degrees of perfection, . . . nevertheless . . . it can never be actually infinite, since it can never reach a point so high that it will be unable to attain to any greater increase. But I understand God to be actually infinite, so that He can add nothing to His supreme perfection. And finally I perceive that the objective being of an idea cannot be produced by a being that exists potentially one, which properly speaking is nothing, but only by a being which is formal or actual. . . .[12]

The proof from cause and effect (Descartes' **cosmological argument**) demonstrates that the idea of God as a perfect being could not come from himself, because he is imperfect. Thus, the idea of perfection must come from outside him—from a perfect being.

Pause for Thought   Is Descartes' argument valid? Do we really have a clear and distinct idea of an absolutely perfect being?

Mathematics and the Physical World   Descartes has argued that God is perfect and that He exists. From this it is evident that He cannot be a deceiver, because intuition (the "natural light of reason") tells us that fraud and deception proceed from some defect. Because mathematical propositions are so clear and distinct that they leave no doubt in the mind, God would not deceive us into thinking they were true if they were not. Therefore, through the light of reason, we can accept such propositions as true.

From his own existence, Descartes proved God's existence and the reliability of mathematics. Now he had to prove the existence of the physical world and his own body.

[Besides my] clear and distinct idea of myself . . . as . . . a thinking and unextended thing, . . . I possess a distinct idea of body . . . as an extended and unthinking thing. . . .

I observe also in me some other faculties such as that of change of position, the assumption of different figures and such like, it is very clear that these faculties, if it be true that they exist, must be attached to some corporeal or extended substance, and not to an intelligent substance, since in the clear and distinct conception of these there is some sort of extension found to be present, but no intellection at all. There is certainly further in me a certain passive faculty of perception, that is, of receiving and recognizing the ideas of sensible things, but this would be useless to me, if there were not

either in me or in some other thing another active faculty capable of forming and producing these ideas. But this active faculty cannot exist in me seeing that it does not presuppose thought, and also that those ideas are often
produced in me without my contributing in any way to the same, and often
even against my will; it is thus necessarily the case that the faculty resides in
some substance different from me in which all the reality which is objectively in the ideas that are produced by this faculty is formally or eminently contained. . . . And this substance is either a body, that is, a corporeal nature
. . . or it is God Himself. . . . But, since God is no deceiver, it is very manifest that He does not communicate to me these ideas immediately and by
Himself. . . . For since He has given me no faculty to recognise that this is
the case, but, on the other hand, a very great inclination to believe that they
are conveyed to me by corporeal objects, I do not see how He could be
defended from the accusation of deceit if these ideas were produced by
causes other than corporeal objects. Hence we must allow that corporeal
things exist.[13]

Mind Substance	Corporeal Substance
Spirit (Ideas)	Matter (Physical)
I think, therefore I am	Size, shape, motion

The Mind–Body Problem   As opposed to Hobbes, who argued that everything
is matter and explainable by physical laws, Descartes demonstrated that the mind
and body are distinct substances. Hoping to reconcile science and the Church,
Descartes suggested that science studies bodies but cannot address minds or souls,
and thus it is no threat to the Church. Also, to know something about the mind we
don't need to refer to the body. Before Descartes, philosophers considered the soul
a sort of "breath of life" that pervaded all living creatures. For Aristotle, the soul was
something that was present everywhere in the organism as its "life principle" and
thus not separate from the body. He could speak of a plant soul or an animal soul.
But Descartes saw the soul (mind) as a substance separate from the body. That conclusion left him with the problem of determining the relationship between mind
and body. He solved the problem by locating the point of interaction in the *pineal
gland*, an organ located between the two hemispheres of the brain.

Nature also teaches me . . . that I am not only lodged in my body as a
pilot in a vessel, but that I am very closely united to it, and to speak so
intermingled with it that I seem to compose with it one whole. For if that
were not the case, when my body is hurt, I, who am merely a thinking
thing, should not feel pain, for I should perceive this wound by the understanding only, just as the sailor perceives by sight when something is damaged in his vessel. . . .

[Yet] there is a great difference between mind and body, inasmuch as body is by nature always divisible, and the mind is entirely indivisible. . . .

[It follows] that the soul is really joined to the whole body [by] a certain very small gland which is situated in the middle of [the brain] and so suspended above the duct whereby the animal spirits in its anterior cavities have communication with those in the posterior, that the slightest movements which take place in it may alter very greatly the course of these spirits; and reciprocally that the smallest changes which occur in the course of the spirits may do much to change the movements of this gland.[14]

Pause for Thought   Do you think Descartes found the right solution to the so-called mind–body problem? Has he really answered the following questions?

1. How can any physical organ (the pineal gland, for example) be the connection of a mind that is nonphysical?

2. Descartes said the mind dwells in the body as a pilot in a ship. How can the nonphysical mind move physical organs that move only on contact?

3. Can the body affect a mind that it cannot contact?

Animals as Machines

Based on his mind–body findings, Descartes believed that all biological processes are purely mechanical. The body, he said, is like "a machine," because it is composed of bones, muscles, blood, and skin with no mind in it. The body moves under the "direction of the will" and with the "aid of the mind."

He also believed that animals have no feelings. They can neither think nor feel pain. He argued that the greatest of all human prejudices is "believing that brutes think." We believe they think when they act like humans. When they perform tricks or acts of obedience, we assume that their minds work as ours do. That is false, he said. Animals do not think. Their actions are mechanical only. Animals are machines. It is merely nature acting in them according to the make-up of their organs, which we can compare to a clock, "which is only composed of wheels and weights."

Descartes held that all animals except humans are mere stimulus–response mechanisms without consciousness. He also said that because animals cannot think, they feel neither pleasure nor pain. Based on Descartes' mind–body dualism, some biologists have defended the painful vivisection of monkeys, dogs, cats, rabbits, mice, and other species. They have compared the howls and cries of mutilated dogs to the squeaks of an unlubricated machine. Vivisectionists operated on live dogs without using an anesthetic. They did not equate the dogs' agonizing cries with pain.

Such cruelty shocked eighteenth-century philosopher Jeremy Bentham. "The question is not can animals reason," he protested, "but can they suffer?"

Pause for Thought

Do you agree with Descartes that animals are machines and feel no pain? Do animals think?

On our walk this morning, one of my dogs ran through an open gate into a fenced field. She ran along the other side of the fence until the fence turned at a right angle. Caught in the corner, she stood as if deciding what to do. Then she whirled around and ran along the fence back to the open gate and soon caught up with us on our side of the fence. Did her actions involve some level of reasoning?

Do animals feel physical and psychological pain?

To address the mind–body problem and Descartes' view of God, we turn next to Jewish philosopher Benedict de Spinoza.

Benedict de Spinoza

Except for Socrates himself it would be difficult to find a philosopher who was a more highly regarded person than Benedict (Baruch) Spinoza. Like Socrates, he was not interested in power or wealth. Like Socrates, he was accused of atheism and was hounded for his unorthodox beliefs. And, like Socrates, he was interested in philosophy as a way of life, not as a professional discipline.[15]

Spinoza's Life   Benedict (Baruch) de Spinoza (1632–1677) was born in Amsterdam, the son of a wealthy Jewish merchant who had fled persecution in Portugal. Because his parents wanted him to train as a rabbi, Baruch received an education in both traditional Hebrew literature and Latin. He was familiar with the writings of the great Jewish philosopher Maimonides, and one of Spinoza's teachers introduced him to Cartesian philosophy.

As a Jew, Spinoza could not be a citizen of Holland. Later, because of his original ideas on God and nature, the Jewish community accused him of heresy. He also expressed doubts about the soul's immortality and the existence of angels. The synagogue of Amsterdam insisted Spinoza repudiate his own philosophy. He refused. In 1656, at age twenty-three, he was officially excommunicated from his own synagogue.

> With the judgment of the angels and the sentence of the saints, we anathe-
> matize, execrate, curse and cast out Baruch Spinoza. . . . Let him be
> accursed by day, and accursed by night; let him be accursed in his lying
> down, and accursed in his rising up; accursed in going out and accursed in
> coming in. May the Lord never more pardon or acknowledge him; may the
> wrath and displeasure of the Lord burn henceforth against this man, load
> him with all the curses written in the Book of the Law, and blot out his
> name from under the sky. . . .[16]

Spinoza's own family tried to disinherit him on the grounds of his heresy. When someone attempted to kill him, he changed his name to Benedict, the Latin equivalent of Baruch, and left Amsterdam. Opposition on all sides led him to The Hague, where he lived a quiet and secluded life devoted entirely to philosophy. He earned a meager living by grinding lenses. His unselfishness, kindness, and simplicity became an example to others as his reputation as a brilliant philosopher spread. When he was forty-one, the University of Heidelberg offered him a professorship in philosophy. He declined the offer for the freedom to write his own philosophy.

Spinoza published only two works during his lifetime. *Principles of Descartes' Philosophy* examined the structure and presuppositions of Descartes' system. Although he disagreed with the French philosopher's dualism, he admired his rationalism and method. His second book, *Theological–Political Treatise,* concluded that the Bible aims not at truth, but at pious and obedient behavior. This and his pantheistic system aroused wide criticism. *Ethics*, Spinoza's posthumous work, is his masterwork. He died at forty-four of lung problems that were probably caused by dust from grinding lenses.

God   As a rationalist and mathematician, Spinoza, like Descartes, set out to develop a philosophy based on the arrangement of principles and axioms. By developing a geometry of philosophy, Spinoza believed that he could demonstrate the nature of reality. In Books I and II of his *Ethics*, Spinoza reasoned that if we are to understand the universe and human nature, then we must first formulate ideas about God.

Agreeing with Plato and Descartes, Spinoza held that God is an "infinite substance" completely independent and necessary. But he believed Descartes was mistaken when he posited the two separate substances of mind and matter. This mistake led Descartes to the mind–body dualism. To Spinoza, God did not create spirit and matter as separate substances. God is in matter. Matter is in God. *God is the one and only substance with infinite attributes*. Two of the attributes we humans can know are thought (mind) and extension (matter). These attributes are not separate substances, but two ways of expressing the activity of one single substance— God. Being infinite, God contains everything.

Prop. XIV. Besides God no substance can be granted or conceived.

Proof.—As God is being absolutely infinite, of whom no attribute that expresses the essence of substance can be denied . . . if any substance besides God were granted it would have to be explained by some attribute of God, and thus two substances with the same attribute would exist, which . . . is absurd; therefore, besides God no substance can be granted, or, consequently, be conceived. . . . Q.E.D.[17]

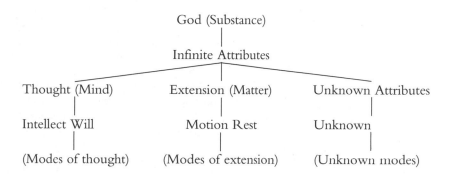

Equating God with nature—God is one **substance,** containing both spirit and matter—makes Spinoza a pantheist. It was this idea that got him in trouble with Jewish and Christian theologians. Augustine, Maimonides, Aquinas, and Descartes held, as does every traditional Jew and Christian, that God created nature and finite beings. Therefore, God's creations are separate and dependent on God, the ultimate reality. Spinoza agreed with Jewish and Christian philosophers that God is ultimate reality and the source of whatever reality the finite parts have. But he denied that God is a person, a creator, or a loving father. God is an infinite substance with an infinite number of attributes, but we humans know only two of them—spirit and matter.

Pause for Thought   With which conclusion do you agree—the Judeo-Christian doctrine or Spinoza's? Is there yet another way of viewing God?

The World   Unlike Christian philosophy, in which the world is something different from God, Spinoza saw the world as **modes** of God's attributes. Thus, the world is not separate from God but *is* God as expressed in various modes of thought and extension. Modes differ from attributes in degree, not in kind. Your individual body is a mode of the one substance, *extension;* and your mind is a mode of the one substance, *thought.* A tree is a mode of the attribute of extension, and a poem about the tree is a mode of the attribute of thought. Both, however, are expressions of substance, God, or nature.

Freedom   All material things are an expression of God or nature. All of our thoughts are also God's thoughts. Everything is One. There is only one God, one nature, or one substance. Everything in the world follows God's laws, even our thoughts and actions. We can only act according to nature.

The belief that we are free arises from our ignorance of the causes and desires that motivate us. When we judge people to be good or bad, we are saying they could have acted differently. We direct love and hate to individuals whom we think caused our joy and our sorrow. But Spinoza pointed out that good and evil are relative to human standards, not to God. We consider things good that we desire. We do not desire them because they are intrinsically good.

> With regard to *good* and *evil*, these themes indicate nothing positive in things considered in themselves, nor are they anything else than modes of thought or notions which we form from the comparison of one thing with another. For one and the same thing may at the same time be both good and evil or indifferent. Music, for example, is good to a melancholy person, bad to one mourning, while to a deaf man it is neither good nor bad.[18]

Pause for Thought   Do you agree with Spinoza's claim that our idea of good and evil as separate forces is true only at the level of confused thought?

According to Spinoza, we will continue to be slaves of confusion until we realize rationally that the causes of what happens to us flow from the nature of God. Only then can we understand. Understanding leads to acceptance, which means we no longer hate or fear.

> *Prop. 28. The highest good of the mind is the knowledge of God, and the highest virtue of the mind is to know God.*
>
> *Demonst.* The highest thing which the mind can understand is God, that is to say. . . . Being absolutely infinite, and without whom nothing can be nor can be conceived, and therefore that which is chiefly profitable to the mind, or which is the highest good of the mind, is the knowledge of God. Again, the mind acts only in so far as it understands, and only in so far can it be absolutely said to act in conformity with virtue. To understand, therefore, is the absolute virtue of the mind. But the highest thing which the mind can understand is God, and therefore the highest virtue of the mind is to understand or know God. Q.E.D.[19]

Free will is only in God. There is, however, a sense in which one person is a slave and another is free. The slave is the servant of confusion and lives in ignorance of the causes of that confusion. The free individual, led by reason and intuition, wills to understand God's law.

> It is therefore most profitable to us in life to make perfect the intellect or reason as far as possible, and in this one thing consists the highest happiness or blessedness of man; for blessedness is nothing but the peace of mind which springs from the intuitive knowledge of God, and to perfect the intellect is nothing but to understand God, together with the attributes and actions of God, which flow from the necessity of His nature. The final aim, therefore, of a man who is guided by reason, that is to say, the chief desire by which he strives to govern all his other desires, is that by which he is led adequately to conceive himself and all things which can be conceived by his intelligence. . . .[20]

> If the way . . . I have shown . . . seems very difficult, it can nevertheless be found. It must indeed be difficult since it is so seldom discovered; for if salvation lay ready to hand and could be discovered without great labour, how could it be possible that it should be neglected almost by everybody? But all noble things are as difficult as they are rare.[21]

Pause for Thought   Recall the Stoics? They would agree with Spinoza that the universe is God and is rational. The Stoics held that we cannot control events, but we can control our attitudes. How does this idea fit with Spinoza's idea of human freedom?

Gottfried Leibniz

Leibniz's Life   Baron Gottfried Wilhelm von Leibniz (1646–1716) was born in Leipzig, a city in the German state of Saxony, and raised in academia. A precocious youth, at age thirteen, he was reading advanced scholastic treatises with ease. When he was only sixteen years old, he entered the University of Leipzig to study the history of philosophy. At seventeen, he enrolled in the University of Jena to study mathematics and law. At eighteen, he published his treatise on law, and at twenty he applied to become a candidate for the doctor of law degree. Although the University of Jena refused him because of his young age, the University of Altdorf accepted him, and there he earned his doctoral degree. The University of Altdorf offered him a professorship, but he refused and entered the civil service, a field in which he had a distinguished career.

Leibniz was a first-rate mathematician. He and Newton independently invented the infinitesimal calculus, although each suspected the other of stealing his ideas. He was a diplomatist and administrator, and later became the librarian, archivist, and historian for the Duke of Hanover. One of the interesting and com-

plex tasks he undertook was reconciling Catholicism and Protestantism and trying to mend the breach that divided the various Protestant denominations.
During all of this activity, he also found time to travel extensively and to correspond with hundreds of people.

With all of his accomplishments, one wonders when Leibniz had time to
write philosophy, yet he is the author of several significant works that have influenced such important philosophers as Immanuel Kant and Bertrand Russell. He
was personally acquainted with Spinoza and impressed with his philosophy,
though he disagreed with some of the Dutch philosopher's ideas, especially his
notion of God as infinite substance.

Despite his accomplishments, Leibniz's public influence and his status with
members of the royalty declined. When he died in 1716, his secretary is said to
have been his only mourner.

Substance   Leibniz rejected Descartes' and Spinoza's concepts of substance.
Descartes claimed that extension is a substance, and Spinoza argued that extension
is an attribute of substance. According to Leibniz, when Descartes said that two
independent substances existed—thought and extension—he had plunged himself
into a dilemma in trying to explain how they interact as mind and body. Spinoza
had tried to solve the problem by arguing that only one infinite substance existed with two attributes that we can know, and these attributes are thought and
extension. But Leibniz did not accept this answer: Extension still remained a
closed system with this reasoning.

Monads   To develop a solution, Leibniz created an entirely new theory on
the existence of substances that he called **monads** (from the Greek *monos,*
meaning one). Leibniz rejected the notion that extension implies actual size
and shape. He observed that things we perceive with our senses are divisible
into smaller parts. If we divide any aggregate or composite, then the components themselves, being physical, will always have the characteristics of being
composite. Because endless division is theoretically if not physically impossible, we must conclude that an aggregate is ultimately composed of indivisible
things that have no parts or extension. Such an infinite division is logically
absurd to Leibniz because it would imply that the universe has no ultimate
explanation. There are, he said, "simple" substances called *monads.* Unlike the
classical physical atoms that were viewed as extended bodies, Leibniz argued
that monads are the "true atoms of nature . . . the elements of things." He
described monads as being the *force* or *energy* that constitutes the essential substance of things.

Leibniz arrived at his conclusion from the Cartesian principle that everything that is not body is mind. Because the monad is not a body, it is a mind. It
is unextended without shape or size. A monad is an indivisible point and inde-

pendent of other monads. As simple substances (lives, souls, spirits), monads are units. Each monad has within itself an internal principle of "appetition" that causes it to change. There is no causal interaction between monads. There is, however a "pre-established harmony" that God created for each monad to "mirror" others.

[Monads] "have no windows through which anything can enter or depart." Leibniz concluded with Spinoza that to bring an infinite number of monads together in unity, the whole universe is in every part and every part is in the whole universe; in terms of monads, the whole universe is in every monad, and every monad is in the whole universe.

1. The object of this discourse, the *monad*, is nothing else than a simple substance, which enters into the composites; *simple* meaning, which has no parts.

2. And there must be simple substances, since there are composites; for the composite is nothing else than an accumulation or aggregate of the simples.

3. But where there are no parts, neither extension, nor figure, nor divisibility is possible. Thus, these monads are the veritable atoms of nature, and, in one word, the elements of all things.

4. Hence no dissolution is to be feared for them, and a simple substance cannot perish naturally in any conceivable manner.

5. For the same reason, no simple substance can come into being naturally, since it cannot be formed by composition.

6. Thus it may be maintained that monads cannot begin or end otherwise than instantaneously, that is, they can begin only by creation, and end only by annihilation; while what is complete begins and ends through and in its parts.

7. It is impossible also to explain how a monad can be altered, that is, internally changed, by any other creature. For there is nothing in it which might be transposed, nor can there be conceived in it any internal movement which could be excited, directed, or diminished. In composites this is possible, since the parts can interchange place. The monads have no windows through which anything could come in or go out.[22]

Every monad, no matter how elementary it is, is a perceiving entity. Because they are "windowless," they cannot be influenced by other monads and their perceptions; they are only open to God, who brings the monads into perfect harmony.

Pause for Thought   If the human soul is a "windowless monad," then does that mean no one can influence you in any way?

Pre-Established Harmony   Each "windowless" monad has its own created purpose and follows its own purpose in carrying out a pre-established harmony. Leibniz saw the world as a harmoniously functioning whole because it is an ordered system created by God. He used the visual analogy of a clock, as did other writers of the period who viewed God as a clockmaker. The universe, he said, "is God's clock," and it keeps perfect time. He compared the monads to many musicians and choirs playing their own notes in such a way that anyone who hears them would find a wonderful harmony "much more surprising than if there had been any connection between them."

The monads "mirror" the world in slightly different ways and with different levels of awareness. For example, rocks are on a lower level of awareness than human beings, although even rocks have an "internal state" by which they represent external things. Human bodies are colonies of lower monads, while the human soul is of a higher degree. The dominant monad in a person is a "spirit" that is capable of knowing the universe and of entering into a relationship with *the* Monad—God.

Pause for Thought   If the world is a pre-established harmony, then how do you account for so much violence in our society?

God and the Problem of Evil   For Leibniz, the universal harmony was proof of God's existence, because a harmony of many windowless substances "can only come from a common cause." Leibniz appreciated the ontological argument offered by Anselm and the argument from Augustine's eternal truths. What puzzled Leibniz was not that God is all-perfect and all-good, but the possibility that evil could exist in a world that the good God made.

Leibniz argued that God created the "best of all possible worlds," yet within this world we find disorder and evil. Probing deeply into the subject he found Augustine's conclusion: Although God was perfect, anything less than God has to be limited, and, depending on the extent of its limitation, we find imperfection or evil. We find the source of evil in an original imperfection in the creature before sin, "because all creatures are limited in their essence." Because evil is to be found in the very nature of created being, it will be found in any world that God might choose to create. Still, as imperfect as our world is, it is the best possible world God could have created. Acting out of absolute power, wisdom, and benevolence, He would always create the "Best World."

Pause for Thought   Do you agree with Leibniz that this is the "best of all possible worlds"?

God could produce a world with the greatest amount of good only by creating one in which there would be evil. Therefore, God permits the evil so that He can produce the good: He does not cause or choose the evil. With an analogy similar to one by Plotinus, Leibniz wrote about how the downstream motion of a river carries the boats along with it; the more heavily laden boats proceed more slowly. The river is the cause of the motion, not its retardation. "God is the cause of perfection" in our nature and our actions, but the limitation of our receptivity, or the receptivity of any creature, is the cause of defects in nature and in actions. Evil, then, is merely the absence of perfection.

We are not puppets of evil, because God pre-establishes an orderly arrangement into each monad and gives it a purpose. Each person is free to overcome confused thoughts and arrive at truth. When our potentialities become actualized, we can see things as they truly are. This is freedom. It is our internal nature that determines our acts, not outside forces. Thus, freedom is built into each person; the free person is the one who follows his or her original purpose as received from God.

Summary

Closing the Middle Ages were the Renaissance, the Protestant Reformation, and the rise of science. The Renaissance brought a revival of humanism. The Reformation began with Martin Luther, who protested the "corrupt" practices of the Roman Catholic Church. Martin Luther promoted faith over reason and rejected the papacy's religious authority.

Before the rise of science, everyone believed the geocentric view of the world. With Copernicus, however, science moved to a heliocentric conception of the heavens. Other scientists confirmed Copernicus's conclusions, and their discoveries expanded science into other fields.

Thomas Hobbes applied scientific methods in his study of human nature. He concluded that everything is matter; all that exists is bodies in motion. He viewed society as a *social contract* in which we sacrifice individual freedom for security and cooperation. The sovereign rules. The people and the Church are subordinate to the state.

The Continental Rationalists saw science as a limitation. They believed that universal truths exist and that we can know them through the reason. René Descartes emphasized intellectual autonomy—our ability to think for ourselves. Reason, he believed, can produce certainty about reality. Through the "natural light of reason," we can know there is a God. Other truths we can know through our innate or a priori ideas. In knowing truth, we never have to rely on authority, sense experience, or experiment.

Descartes used the method of doubt to find one truth that he could not doubt. He found that truth in *Cogito ergo sum*—"I think, therefore I am." Next, through the process of his own mind, he tried to prove to be true all that he previously doubted. Using a cosmological argument, he proved the existence of God to his own satisfaction. Based on his definition of God, he could prove the validity of mathematics and the reality of the physical world.

Before Descartes proved the reality of the physical world, he concluded that the mind and the body were separate substances. This dualistic outlook of human nature presented him with the *mind–body problem*: What is the relationship of the mind to the body? How can a nonmaterial mind affect a material body?

To solve Descartes' mind–body problem, Benedict de Spinoza held that the universe is rational and everything in it is an attribute or mode of God's substance. Nature is an eternal aspect of God. Because nature and God are one, the more we understand of reality, the more we understand God. Our intellectual and intuitive knowledge of God embrace an understanding of the whole universe. When our intellect guides us correctly, we reach happiness and inner peace. We are free.

Gottfried Leibniz rejected Descartes' notion that extension is a substance—or an attribute of substance, as Spinoza claimed. Leibniz called the basic substance a *monad*. Monads are simple and without parts: They have "no windows through which anything may come in or go out." God created only those substances that will harmonize with other entities to the fullest possible extent. Therefore, we exist in "the best of all possible worlds."

Connections

In this chapter, we have seen the bold ventures of the modern mind. Religion, the chief element in the Medieval world, had become a matter of faith rather than reason. The new intellectual mood of modern philosophy stressed scientific observation and mathematics. It was a time of freedom and expression for philosophers to formulate organized systems of truth based on clear rational principles. They accepted, almost without question, the intellectual powers of the rational mind: It was capable of producing certain knowledge about science and human nature.

Following the Rationalists, however, the British Empiricists called into question the ability of the reason. They questioned the assumption that the human mind has the capacity to know and understand the true nature of God, the universe, or humankind. They asked whether knowledge, as something certain, is possible at all. To discover their challenge, we now turn to the British Empiricists.

Study Questions

1. What were two major changes that took place at the close of the Medieval world?

2. In what ways had the Church grown corrupt?

3. Why did Luther object to indulgences?

4. To what authority does Luther appeal?

5. What was the Protestant Reformation?

6. Name three differences between Catholics and Protestants.

7. What were the philosophical consequences of the Copernican revolution?

8. What effects did the changes in science have on the Church?

9. How did Galileo confirm Copernicus' discovery?

10. What was Newton's view of God?

11. What was Thomas Hobbes's view of human nature?

12. Hobbes said society is a social contract. What did he mean?

13. What do intuition and deduction have to do with Descartes' method?

14. What is the Cartesian method of doubt? Give Descartes' arguments for doubting the reality of the physical world, mathematics, and God.

15. What is the meaning of *Cogito ergo sum*? Explain its significance in Descartes' philosophy.

16. Give Descartes' cosmological argument. Is it convincing?

17. What is the mind–body problem? How did Descartes solve it?

18. How did Spinoza solve the mind–body problem?

19. Was Spinoza a pantheist? Explain.

20. How did Spinoza's and Descartes' views of God differ?

21. For Spinoza, what is human freedom?

22. How did Spinoza regard good and evil?

23. What did Spinoza consider the highest good of the mind?

24. Who said, "All noble things are as difficult as they are rare"?

25. Compare Leibniz's theory of substance with those held by Descartes and Spinoza.

26. What did Leibniz mean by "pre-established harmony"?

27. What did Leibniz mean by the term *monad*?

28. How did Leibniz defend God from the charge of being the creator of evil?

Notes

1. Henry Wace and C. A. Buchein, *Luther's Primary Works*, p. 53. Philadelphia: Luther Publishing Society, 1885.

2. J. Gerson, *On the Way to Unite and Reform the Church in a General Council*; quoted in C. Beard, *The Reformation of the Sixteenth Century*, p. 163. London: Williams and Norgate, 1903.

3. Quoted in L. Stephen, Hobbes, pp. 17–18. London: Macmillan, 1904.

4. *Elements of Philosophy*, in *The English Works of Thomas Hobbes*, Vol. I, Ch. I, Sec. 9 (ed. by W. Molesworth). London: John Bohn, 1839.

5. *Leviathan*, in ibid., Part I, Chaps. 11 and 13.

6. From Thomas Hobbes, *Philosophical Rudiments Concerning Government and Society* in ibid., Vol. 2, Chaps. 8, 9. Originally published as *De Cive*.

7. René Descartes, "Discourse on Method" (trans. by E. S. Haldane and G.R.T. Ross), in *The Philosophical Works of Descartes*. London: Cambridge University Press, 1931. Reprinted with the permission of Cambridge University Press.

8. *Rules for the Direction of the Mind*, pp. 5–6.

9. *Meditations on First Philosophy*, pp. 145–48.

10. Ibid., pp. 149–50.

11. Ibid., p. 155.

12. Ibid., pp. 165–67.

13. Meditations, in *Works*, op. cit., Vol. I, pp. 190–91.

14. Ibid., Vol. I., pp. 192 and 196; and from The Passion of the Soul, in *Works*, op. cit., Vol. I, pp. 345–46.

15. Walter Kaufmann and Forrest E. Baird, *From Plato to Nietzsche*. New Jersey: Prentice Hall, 1994.

16. Willis, *Benedict de Spinoza* (London, 1870) pp. 35–36. Quoted Wallace I. Matson, *A New History of Philosophy*, Vol. II. New York: Harcourt Brace Jovanovich.

17. Spinoza, *Ethics* (trans. by R. H. M. Elwes). London, 1919.

18. Spinoza, *Ethics* (trans. by W. H. Whiteby and A. H. Stirling). Oxford: Oxford University Press.

19. Ibid., Part 4, Prop. 28.

20. Ibid., Part 4, 4.

21. Ibid., Prop. 42.

22. Gottfried Wilhelm Leibniz, *Monadology and Other Philosophical Essays* (trans. by Paul Schrecker and Anne Martin Schrecker) New York: Macmillan, 1965.

CHAPTER EIGHT

British Empiricism:
Locke, Berkeley, and Hume

The British Empiricists—John Locke in England, George Berkeley in Ireland, and David Hume in Scotland—indeed challenged the Continental Rationalists, but they also challenged all rationalists including Plato. Ever since Plato, rationalists had proposed that true knowledge is innate (**a priori**) in reason. By using reason properly, we can know the meaning of human existence and the universe. The British Empiricists, however, held that no innate knowledge exists. They agreed with Aristotle that rather than rely on reason and speculation we should place our confidence in experience and in our ability to learn and know about the world through our senses; in other words, knowledge comes **a posteriori.** Table 1 below compares the two schools and their views. In this chapter, we will concentrate on the British Empiricists and trace their arguments as they advance a new way of viewing the world and humankind.

Table 1

Rationalists	*British Empiricists*
1. Knowledge comes from the reason.	1. Knowledge comes from sense experience.
2. Knowledge is a priori.	2. Knowledge is a posteriori.
3. Knowledge is necessarily and universally true—for example, "All triangles have three sides."	3. We can never know anything that is beyond the realm of immediate experience—for example, "The apple is green."

193

John Locke, the founder of the school of empiricism, said the scope of human knowledge is limited to and by our experience. The word *empiricism* comes from the Greek *emperiria* ("experience"). Thomas Hobbes also had suggested that we derive knowledge from observation, but he did not raise the same questions about the powers of the intellect that the British Empiricists later would. Locke questioned the notion of innate ideas and that the mind can understand the nature of the universe. George Berkeley went further by questioning the existence of matter—and David Hume asked whether any knowledge is possible at all!

John Locke

Locke's Life

Born in Wrington, England, John Locke (1632–1704) was the son of a Puritan lawyer and small landowner. His father fought on the side of the Parliament against Charles I, and, like his father, John Locke was a lifetime defender of the parliamentary system.

As a teenager, Locke attended Westminster School. In 1652 he won a scholarship to Christ Church at the University of Oxford, where Oliver Cromwell was chancellor and the Puritans were initially in control. The traditional program of studies consisted of grammar, rhetoric, logic, geometry, and moral philosophy. In fact, Locke later condemned the English educational system for its one-sided emphasis on the past. After receiving his Bachelor's and Master's degrees, he became a lecturer in Greek, a reader in rhetoric, and a censor of moral philosophy. Interested in science, his experiments in chemistry and meteorology led him to enter the school of medicine.

While at Oxford, Locke became interested in political questions, such as the constitution of society, the relation of church and state, and the importance of religious toleration. In 1665, he interrupted his medical studies to assist a diplomatic mission. On his return to England, he entered the political world of London, "the society of great wits and ambitious politicians."

In 1662, Locke met Lord Ashley, later the Earl of Shaftesbury. They became close friends, and Lord Ashley invited Locke to Shaftesbury to serve as his personal physician. He received his medical degree and license in 1674. At Shaftesbury, Locke saved Lord Ashley's life by operating on an "internal abscess." He also helped write a constitution for the New World colony of Carolina, and continued to pursue his scientific and philosophical interests. He traveled extensively with the Earl of Shaftesbury, meeting "the wisest men and the greatest wits" of the day.

When the Earl led Parliament against King James II, the king suspected Locke's involvement, so when the Earl of Shaftesbury died in 1683, Locke fled to Holland and became an advisor to Prince William and Princess Mary of Orange. Following the bloodless revolution of 1688 that overthrew King James,

Locke returned home with William and Mary, the new King and Queen of England. At last Locke could argue for his favorite ideas: freedom of the press, religious toleration, new methods of education, improvement of the poor, and economic management of the kingdom.

When he was fifty-seven, Locke published his most important works, *Two Treatises on Civil Government* and *Essay Concerning Human Understanding*. Although philosophers before him had written about human knowledge, Locke was the first to write a full-length inquiry into the scope and limits of the human mind. This work was instrumental in ushering in a new era of thought that came to be known as the Enlightenment. His treatise on civil government justified the Glorious Revolution of 1688 and some of its concepts: All men are "equal and independent" and possess the natural rights to "life, health, liberty and possessions." These ideas helped shape the American Declaration of Independence and the subsequent U.S. Constitution.

Locke spent the rest of his life writing and serving the new government as Commissioner of Appeals and later as Commissioner of Trade and Plantations. Theologians bitterly attacked his ideas on theology, but Locke took it in stride. He spent his last years in retirement at Oates studying scripture, especially the Epistles of St. Paul. In 1704, he died quietly at the home of a friend.

The Human Mind

One winter evening while Locke and his friends were discussing morality and religion, their discussion reached a stalemate. They became confused, unable to find a single clear and distinct direction to follow. Their inability to reach right or wrong answers on such a subject as "the principles of morality and revealed religion" deeply affected Locke.

> [D]ifficulties . . . rose on every side. After we had awhile puzzled ourselves, without coming any nearer a resolution of those doubts which perplexed us, it came into my thoughts that we took a wrong course; and that before we set ourselves upon inquiries of that nature, it was necessary to examine our own abilities, and see what *objects* our understandings were, or were not, fitted to deal with.[1]

This experience led Locke to ask, what kind of instrument is the human mind? Descartes considered rational thought to be mathematical reasoning. But Locke, the physician, took a more practical look at reasoning. For instance, as a doctor, how was he to treat the "internal abscess" of the Earl of Shaftesbury? If he waited until he had "mathematical certainty about the correct treatment," then the patient would die. So he operated. During the surgery he took detailed notes of the procedure for other doctors to use if the operation were a success. The patient lived.

After twenty years of thinking about it, Locke concluded that knowledge results from *ideas*—not Plato's Ideas and Forms, but ideas produced a posteriori by the objects we experience. Such experience takes two forms: *sensation* and *reflection*. First, we experience objects through our senses and then we reflect upon them. Unlike Descartes and the Rationalists, these ideas are not innate. There are no a priori ideas. Our mind at birth is a blank slate.

Pause for Thought   What do you think? Is our mind a blank slate at birth or are we born with innate ideas? Do we know immediately that "A cannot be both A and not A" at the same time or must we first learn the principle of contradiction?

No Innate Ideas

Locke argued that philosophers and others who believe in innate ideas could not actually prove them to be innate. The axiomatic principles of logic such as the **principle of identity** ("Whatever is is. Whatever is not is not") and the **principle of contradiction** ("The same thing cannot both be and not be") are not known to children or idiots, so they could not be with us or imprinted on our minds at birth. We are sure the principles of identity and contradiction are true because when we reflect on them, our minds will not let us think otherwise. Our ability to reflect on these ideas does not make them innate. And moral principles such as the Golden Rule or justice are also not innate. They require proof. Even the idea of God is not innate. Locke insisted it was possible to prove the existence of God without referring to innate principles. The doctrine of innate ideas contained nothing that experience could not explain better.

Pause for Thought   Do we have some kind of innate idea about a higher intelligence and power that we call "God"? Or do we learn about God from sense experience? What kind of experience might prove there is or is not a God?

Tabula Rasa

Following Aristotle, Locke wrote that the mind at birth is a *tabula rasa*—a blank tablet. And experience makes its imprint on this "blank paper." There are two kinds of experience—*external* and *internal*—and two corresponding paths of knowledge: (1) *sensations* give us ideas based on external objects outside ourselves, and (2) *inner reflection* provides ideas based on our understanding of the sense objects we experience.

Pause for Thought   Locke held that we are born with a tabula rasa. Our mind receives ideas the same way a chalkboard receives marks on it. Plato argued that when the soul (mind) is born into a body, it brings impressions, interests, and abilities from past lives with it. Which theory is most believable to you?

According to Locke, *Nihil in intellectu quod prius non fuerit in sensu*—"Nothing exists in the mind that wasn't first in the senses." Sense experience presents sensible qualities to the mind, such as yellowness, heat, softness, hardness, sweetness, bitterness. While reflecting on these qualities, the mind receives a second set of ideas: thinking, doubting, believing, reasoning, knowing, and willing. But these reflections and ideas can occur only after the mind has had a sense experience.

All ideas come from sensation or reflection—Let us suppose the mind to be, as we say, white paper, void of all characters, without any ideas:—How comes it to be furnished. . . . Whence has it all the *materials* of reason and knowledge? To this I answer, in one word, from EXPERIENCE. In that all our knowledge is founded; and from that it ultimately derives itself. Our observation employed either about external sensible objects, or about the internal operations of our minds perceived and reflected on by ourselves, is that which supplies our understandings with all the materials of thinking. These two are the fountains of knowledge, from whence all the ideas we have, or can naturally have, do spring.

The objects of sensation one source of ideas.—First, our Senses, conversant about particular sensible objects, do convey into the mind several distinct perceptions of things, according to those various ways wherein those objects do affect them. And thus we come by those *ideas* we have of *yellow, white, heat, cold, soft, hard, bitter, sweet,* and all those which we call sensible qualities; which when I say the senses convey into the mind, I mean, they from external objects convey into the mind what produces there those perceptions. This great source of most of the ideas we have, depending wholly upon our senses, and derived by them to the understanding, I call SENSATION.

The operations of our minds, the other source of them. Secondly, the other fountain from which experience furnisheth the understanding with ideas is, —the perception of the operations of our own mind within us, as it is employed about the ideas it has got;—which operations when the soul comes to reflect on and consider, do furnish the understanding with another set of ideas, which could not be had from things without. And such are *perception, thinking, doubting, believing, reasoning, knowing, willing,* and all the different actings of our own minds;—which we being conscious of, and observing in ourselves, do from these receive into our understandings as distinct ideas as we do from bodies affecting our senses. . . . I call this

REFLECTION, the ideas it affords being such only as the mind gets by reflecting on its own operations within itself. . . .

All our ideas are of the one or the other of these.—The understanding seems to me not to have the least glimmering of any ideas which it doth not receive from one of these two. . . .

Let any one examine his own thoughts, and thoroughly search into his understanding; and then let him tell me, whether all the original ideas he has there, are any other than of the objects of his senses, or of the operations of his mind, considered as objects of his reflection. And how great a mass of knowledge soever he imagines to be lodged there, he will, upon taking a strict view, see that he has not any idea in his mind but what one of these two have imprinted;—though perhaps, with infinite variety compounded and enlarged by the understanding, as we shall see hereafter.[2]

Pause for Thought   Is Locke correct? Can you come up with any ideas other than those stemming from the objects of your senses or of reflections on the objects of your senses?

Simple and Complex Ideas

Simple ideas are the major source of the raw materials from which our knowledge comes. Simple ideas can originate from all of the senses: taste, touch, smell, hearing, and sight. These ideas are simple because they cannot be defined. If I do not understand the idea of "red," you cannot simply explain it to me. All you can do is point to a red object and say, "That's red." When I eat an apple, I do not sense the whole apple in one single sensation. Actually, I receive a whole series of simple sensations, such as this something is red, it smells fresh, and it tastes juicy and tart. Our minds receive simple ideas passively either through sensation or by reflection.

Some ideas we receive from one sense only, and some ideas we get from two or more senses combined. The rose, for example, may have many combined qualities, such as redness and sweet smell, but the mind can sort out the differences. The mind receives each idea—red (sight) and sweet (smell)—separately because each idea enters through a different sense. The mind also can separate two or more qualities when they come through the same sense. Although warm water comes through the single sense of touch, the mind can separate the qualities of warm and water.

Though the qualities that affect our senses are, in the things themselves, so united and blended, that there is no separation, no distance between them; yet it is plain, the ideas they produce in the mind enter by the senses simple and unmixed. For, though the sight and touch often take in from the same object, at the same time, different ideas;—as a man sees at once motion and colour; the hand feels softness and warmth in the same piece of wax: yet the simple ideas thus united in the same subject, are as perfectly distinct as those that come in by different senses. The coldness and hardness which a man feels in a piece of ice being as distinct ideas in the mind as the smell of whiteness of a lily; or as the taste of sugar, and smell of a rose. And there is nothing can be plainer to a man than the clear and distinct perception he has of those simple ideas; which, being each in itself uncompounded, contains in it nothing but one uniform appearance, or conception in the mind, and is not distinguishable into different ideas.[3]

All simple ideas come from sensation, but they also arise from reflection. Ideas we get by reflection come from our **power of thinking** (the understanding) and our **power of volition** (the will). Examples of these powers are memory, discerning, reasoning, judging, knowing, and believing. Also, simple ideas can be made of both sensation and reflection such as ideas of pleasure, pain, power, existence, and unity.

When we repeat and compare simple ideas, they become complex ideas. For example, after I have become used to eating apples, I think, "Now, I am eating an 'apple.'" I have formed a *complex idea* of an apple. As an infant, when I tasted an apple for the first time I had no such complex idea. But I saw something red, and I tasted something fresh and juicy and a little sour. Little by little these sensations came together and formed my complex idea of apple.

Thus for Locke, the mind has the power to join ideas and bring ideas together, but it holds them separate and abstracts something. We can bundle ideas of whiteness, coldness, and sweetness to form an idea of vanilla ice cream. So our mind brings ideas together and also holds them apart when we think of relationships and comparisons. By comparison, the ice cream is sweeter than a tart apple. We can also separate ideas "from all other ideas that accompany them in their real existence," such as abstracting the idea of *man* from Socrates.

When the understanding is once stored with these simple ideas, it has the power to repeat, compare, and unite them, even to an almost infinite variety, and so can make at pleasure new complex ideas. But it is not in the power of the most exalted wit, or enlarged understanding, by any quickness or variety of thought, to *invent* or *frame* one new simple idea . . . : nor can any force of the understanding *destroy* those that are there. . . . I would have any one try to fancy any taste which had never affected his palate; or frame the idea of a scent he had never smelt: and when he can do this, I will also conclude that a blind man hath ideas of colours, and a deaf man true distinct notions of sounds.[4]

Pause for Thought

Locke said God is a complex idea resulting from an enlargement on our simple ideas. Two of these simple ideas are *power* and *knowledge*. What other simple ideas would you use to describe God?

Primary and Secondary Qualities

Locke next asked, do our ideas reproduce exactly what we sense in the world out there? This is the same problem Descartes and other philosophers before him faced. Locke distinguished between what he called *primary* and *secondary* qualities. By *primary qualities*, Locke meant extension, weight, motion, number, and so on. We can be certain, said Locke, that the senses reproduce these qualities objectively.

We also sense other qualities in things. We say that something is sweet or sour, green or red, hot or cold, loud or quiet. Locke called these *secondary qualities*. Sensations such as color, taste, and sound do not reproduce the real qualities that are inherent in the objects themselves. They reproduce only the effect of the outer reality on our senses. Secondary qualities are the characteristics we give to external objects, but they actually exist only in our minds. For instance, color and taste vary from person to person and from animal to animal, depending on the nature of the individual's sensation.

An apple has the power to produce in us the ideas of size, shape, and weight. Size is a primary quality of the apple: It exists in the body of the apple itself. Our ideas caused by primary qualities resemble exactly those qualities that belong to the object. The apple looks round—and it *is* round.

Secondary qualities of the apple are red, sweet, hard, tart. They produce ideas in our mind that have no exact correlation in the apple itself. The apple looks red and feels hard to the touch, but there is no redness or hardness *in* the apple. What *is* in the apple is the quality to create an idea of red and hard when we see it and touch it.

Primary qualities such as solidity, extension, size, shape, and motion *do* exist in the object. Secondary qualities such as color, sound, taste, and smell do *not* exist in the object, except as powers to produce these ideas in our mind. Democritus, the pre-Socratic philosopher, influenced not only Locke but also Galileo and Descartes. Democritus said that colors, tastes, and odors are the effect of atoms in motion. Newton also influenced Locke when he explained the appearance of red as the motion of invisible minute particles. Redness is not the primary quality, only the effect of something in motion that causes redness.

> Qualities thus considered in bodies are,
>   *First*, such as are utterly inseparable from the body, in what state soever it be; and such as in all the alterations and changes it suffers, all the force can be used upon it, it constantly keeps; and such as sense constantly finds in every particle of matter which has bulk enough to be perceived; and the mind finds inseparable from every particle of matter, though less than to make itself singly be perceived by our senses: e.g. Take a grain of wheat, divide it into two parts; each part has still solidity, extension, figure, and mobility: divide it again, and it retains still the same qualities; and so divide

it on, till the parts become insensible: they must retain still each of them all those qualities. For division (which is all that a mill, or pestle, or any other body, does upon another, in reducing it to insensible parts) can never take away either solidity, extension, figure, or mobility from any body, but only makes two or more distinct separate masses of matter, of that which was but one before; all which distinct masses, reckoned as so many distinct bodies, after division, make a certain number.

These I call *original* or *primary qualities* of body, which I think we may observe to produce simple ideas in us, viz. Solidity, extension, figure, motion or rest, and number.

Secondly, such qualities which in truth are nothing in the objects them-selves but powers to produce various sensations in us by their primary qual-ities, i.e. by the bulk, figure, texture, and motion of their insensible parts, as colors, sounds, tastes, etc. These I call *secondary qualities*. . . .

From whence I think it easy to draw this observation, —that the ideas of primary qualities of bodies are resemblance's of them, and their patterns do really exist in the bodies themselves, but the ideas produced in us by these secondary qualities have no resemblance of them at all. There is nothing like our ideas, existing in the bodies themselves. They are, in the bodies we denominate from them, only a power to produce those sensations in us: and what is sweet, blue, or warm in idea, is but the certain bulk, figure, and motion of the insensible parts, in the bodies themselves, which we call so.[5]

Locke's view of the mind is known as **Representative Realism:** The mind represents the external world but does not duplicate it. **Naive Realism** is the view that the mind, like a photograph, actually duplicates external reality.

Pause for Thought   How can we know that our senses duplicate reality as it is if these senses are our only means for knowing reality?

Substance

Descartes had said we could not derive the idea of substance from sense experi-ence, because the senses can only produce qualities. As a rationalist, Descartes considered the idea of substance an innate idea. Though Locke rejected innate ideas, he agreed with Descartes that substance or extended reality does have certain qualities that we can understand with our reason.

[However] . . . if any one will examine himself concerning his notion of pure substance in general, he will find he has no other idea of it at all, but only a supposition of he knows not what *support* of such qualities which are capable of producing simple ideas in us; which qualities are commonly called accidents. If any one should be asked, what is the subject wherein colour or weight inheres, he would have nothing to say, but the solid extended parts; and if he were demanded, what is it that solidity and extension adhere in, he would not be in a much better case than the Indian . . . who, saying that the world was supported by a great elephant, was asked what the elephant rested on; to which his answer was—a great tortoise: but being again pressed to know what gave support to the broad-backed tortoise, replied—*something, he knew not what.* . . . The idea . . . to which we give the *general* name substance [is] nothing but the supposed, but unknown, support of those qualities we find existing, which we imagine cannot subsist *sine re substante,* without something to support them. . . .[6]

Locke thought that substances exist as things in themselves, not just as qualities of color, weight, size, and so on. He held that substance is power and is real, but he could not answer the question, What is its nature? He called substance an "I-know-not-what" thing. We can know the qualities associated with a substance, but not the substance itself. Still, he held tight to the ideas that (1) substance causes our sensations, and (2) substance gives consistency to our ideas. For example, if I have a round ball, you can't think it is square. You may think it is blue or green, but you can't think it weighs two hundred pounds if it only weighs two pounds. And you cannot think I have twelve balls if I have only one.

Substance, said Locke, is the object of sensitive knowledge. For instance, if motion exists, there must be something that moves. Qualities cannot float around without something holding them together. The problem, said Locke, is that we can never prove the idea of a substance.

Degrees of Knowledge

When Locke said the idea of substance is "something we know not what," he raised the question of how much knowledge we can have. He decided that knowledge depends on the relations our ideas have to each other. Knowledge is "the perception of the connexion of and agreement, or disagreement" of any of our ideas. Ideas enter single file into our minds, but once they are inside they can relate to each other in many ways. The ways in which ideas relate to each other depend on the object of our perception. There are three kinds of perception: intuitive, demonstrative, and sensitive.

Intuitive knowledge is direct and leaves no doubt in our mind. It is "the clearest and most certain" knowledge that we humans have. We know intuitively that we exist, that a straight line is not a curve, and that the number 2 is not the number 4 because we can perceive the repugnancy of these ideas to each other.

Pause for Thought   Do you think there is any difference between intuitive knowledge and a priori knowledge?

Demonstrative knowledge is a kind of perception that leads the mind to know the agreement and disagreement of ideas by bringing our attention to other ideas. Demonstrative knowledge starts from intuitive certainty. We know intuitively that things begin and end in time; we also know that a "nonentity cannot produce any real being" and that this adequately demonstrates that there has been something from eternity. It is inherent in the human reason to be able to know that God exists.

> *And therefore God.*—thus, from the consideration of ourselves, and what we infallibly find in our own constitutions, our reason leads us to the knowledge of this certain and evident truth, —*That there is an eternal, most powerful, and most knowing Being. . . .*[7]

Sensitive knowledge only "passes under the name of knowledge," because it cannot give us certainty. We sense that we see a tree. We are certain the tree exists. Yet, when we walk away, we are no longer sure the tree exists. George Berkeley, whom you will meet in just a few paragraphs, carried this argument to its extreme conclusion when he said "to be is to be perceived." Sensation, said Locke, never tells us how things are connected. Therefore, sensitive knowledge gives us some degree of knowledge, but not certainty.

Intuition gives us knowledge of our own existence and of relations of ideas. Demonstration shows the truth of mathematics and of God's existence. Sensitive knowledge tells us that other people and objects exist. Our knowledge does not extend to the connections of primary with secondary qualities or of secondary qualities with each other, or with our ideas, or of the powers of substances.

The result of Locke's investigation showed that we are not really fit to deal with the metaphysical inquiries that had been the focus of attention for earlier philosophers. Locke thought metaphysics was useless and even harmful. First, it distracted thinkers from more important matters: second, it resulted in skepticism. Ethics and politics, he said, were more important fields to explore.

Moral Philosophy

Because no innate ideas naturally exist, moral, religious, and political values must come from sense experience. For example, the word *good* refers to pleasure, and the word *evil* alludes to pain.

Things are good or evil only in reference to pleasure or pain. That we call *good*, which is apt to cause or increase pleasure, or diminish pain in us; or else to procure or preserve us the possession of any other good or absence of any evil. And, on the contrary, we name that *evil* which is apt to produce or increase any pain, or diminish any pleasure in us.[8]

Though we cannot analyze or define terms as pleasure and pain, we can know them by experience. Moral acts are those that produce the "greatest and positive good." Unlike Socrates and Plato, who claimed if we know the good then we will do the good, Locke held that we don't always act on our information.

Let a drunkard see that his health decays, his estate wastes; discredit and diseases, and the want of all things, even of his beloved drink, attends him in the course he follows: yet the . . . habitual thirst after his cups . . . drives him to the tavern. . . . It is not want of viewing the greater good: for he sees and acknowledges it.[9]

For Locke, morality has to do with choosing or willing the good. The reason some people choose a lesser instead of a greater good usually has to do with a desire to avoid immediate pain. If I am a philosophy major and put off taking mathematical logic, then it is because the immediate pleasure of avoiding the hard work is greater than the pain of thinking about a future class deficiency. My mistake is not about immediate pleasures and pains, but about future ones. The pain of not receiving my degree in philosophy next semester will be greater than the pain of taking the mathematical logic class this semester.

Moral good and evil, then, is the conformity or nonconformity of our "voluntary actions to some law." Locke alluded to three laws: (1) law of opinion, (2) civil law, and (3) divine law. In the law of opinion, we tend to call actions that we judge praiseworthy *virtuous,* and those that we judge blameworthy *vice.*

If you conform to the community's law, then you are virtuous. Remember, however, that different communities have different ideas of virtue.

Civil law is "set by the commonwealth" and enforced by the courts and the police. The law of opinion and the civil law usually coincide.

Pause for Thought   Does the pressure of public opinion influence your moral actions? Does civil law deter you from committing immoral acts?

Divine law is the law that "God has set to the actions of men."

He [God] has a right to do it; we are his creatures: . . . and he has power to enforce it by rewards and punishments . . . in another life. . . . This is the only true touchstone of moral rectitude; and, by comparing them to this law it is that men judge of the most considerable moral good or evil of their actions. . . .[10]

Locke held that, through reason or revelation, we could discover the moral rules that conform to God's law. The divine law is the true law for human behavior. Both the law of opinion and the civil law should conform to the divine law, which is the "touchstone of moral rectitude." The discrepancies among these three laws lies in our inclination to choose immediate pleasures instead of future pleasures. But the divine law is eternally true and the one law we should always follow.

Political Philosophy

In *Two Treatises on Government*, Locke, like Hobbes, distinguished between "the state of nature" and "the political state." For Hobbes, "the state of nature" is the instinct for survival, but for Locke it is a moral state of natural rights given to us by God: the right to "life, health, liberty and possessions." According to Locke, reason teaches everyone who consults it that all of us are equal and independent, and thus we ought not to harm another "in his life, health, liberty or possessions." For Hobbes, the only natural right was trying to survive in the "war of all against all." No such moral state as the right to liberty and property even existed.

Right to Property   Locke held that people have a natural right to property. They have a right to their bodies' labor and to whatever things they "mix their labor with." They also have a right to these things if they do not already belong to someone else. All people have a right to acquire property, but there should be a limit to the amount of property a person can have. On inheritance, Locke said every man has a right "to inherit with his brethren his father's goods."

Pause for Thought   Can you compare Locke's moral state of natural rights and his natural right for property to the American Declaration of Independence and the U.S. Constitution's Bill of Rights?

Government   The majority must decide what form of government it wants, then delegate its ruling power to an elect few, or they will adopt some other arrangement. The delegated body is the *legislative* or law-making branch of government. Locke, however, thought that the same people making the laws should not be the ones to execute them. The government should have an *executive* branch to administer its laws. Also, a *federative* branch should have the power to make war and peace.

Unlike Hobbes's social contract idea that political power belongs to an executive authority, Locke's social contract allows the people to delegate power to their legislature. Hobbes thought the people should be servants of the author-ity in power, but for Locke it was the reverse: The people entrust power to the government, thus making government the servant of the people.

On Women

Locke rejected the patriarchal idea of the rights of kings. Like Hobbes, he spurned the idea that, by natural right, the father is the ruler of his family. However, he disagreed with Hobbes that, also by nature, the mother has power over children. In *Second Treatise of Civil Government* (1690), Locke said the mother and father should share equally in family power and duties. He based his position on scripture, which reveals that children should be obedient to both father and mother.

> For whatever obligation nature and the right of generation lays on chil-dren, it must certainly bind them equally to both concurrent causes of it. And accordingly we see the positive law of God everywhere joins them together without distinction, when it commands the obedience of chil-dren: "Honour thy father and thy mother, " Exod. xx.12. "Whosoever curseth his father or his mother, " Lev. xx.9. "Ye shall fear every man his mother and his father, " Lev. xix.5. "Children, obey your parents, " etc., Eph. vi. 1, is the style of the Old and New Testament.[11]

George Berkeley

Berkeley's Life

George Berkeley (pronounced "Bark-ley") was born in 1685 in Ireland. Although an Anglican of English ancestry, he considered himself Irish. At the young age of fifteen, he entered Trinity College in Dublin, where he studied Descartes, Newton, and Locke. He became a fellow of the college and an ordained Anglican priest. Over the next six years he wrote some profoundly important philosophical works: *Essay Towards a New Theory of Vision, A Treatise Concerning the Principles of Human Knowledge,* and *Three Dialogues Between Hylas and Philonous*.

For eleven years, Berkeley traveled widely and met many of the thinkers of the day, including Joseph Addison and Jonathan Swift. While in London, he asked Parliament to consider his project of founding a college in Bermuda to teach the Gospel and English manners to the "American savages." With promises of financial support, he and his new wife sailed for America. For three years, he stayed in Rhode Island planning his college, but the promised money never arrived. Finally, he gave up and returned to London. Shortly after, he returned to Ireland and became Bishop of Cloyne.

Berkeley thought that the contemporary philosophies and science were both dangerous to the Christian way of life, and that scientific materialism represented a threat to the Christian faith and God as Creator and the preserver of all nature.

He wrote articles proposing education and public works as remedies to poverty. He strongly promoted the medicinal value of "tar-water," which was made from pine tree pitch, a remedy he learned from the American Indians. In fact, he prescribed tar-water to the members of his diocese as a cure for many ailments.

After losing his oldest son in 1752, Berkeley and his wife and family moved to Oxford where another son attended college. A year later at age sixty-eight, Berkeley died unexpectedly. His will asked that his body not be buried "until it grow offensive by the cadaverous Smell." Whether his family waited that long, we don't know, but he was buried in Christ Church Chapel at Oxford University. One of the world's leading university towns—Berkeley, California—is named for him. His Rhode Island home, White Hall, was designated United States' first national monument in the late nineteenth century.

Berkeley's Idealism

Consistent with empiricism, Berkeley believed we could only know what we perceive through the senses. But he went a step farther when he added that although the world *is* as we perceive it, we do not perceive "material" or "matter." We do not perceive objects as tangible, because we have no perception that is a material thing itself.

Locke had said such primary qualities as density, gravity, and weight exist in material substance independently of our minds. But secondary qualities exist only in our minds. We cannot say an apple *is* red and juicy. We can only say we *perceive* it as red and juicy. With Descartes and Spinoza, Locke reasoned that the material world is a reality.

If Locke is correct, said Berkeley, then we can only experience primary qualities through secondary qualities. For instance, we directly experience our own perceptions of apples and people. We do not experience apples and people directly. Thus, we can only know our own perceptions and ideas and not ever really know whether apples and other people exist. If you eat an apple, you have a sensation of something juicy and tart, but you don't feel the actual matter in the apple.

> They who assert that figure, motion, and the rest of the primary or original qualities do exist without the mind, in unthinking substance, so at the same time acknowledge that colours, sounds, heat, cold, and suchlike secondary qualities, do not; which they tell us are sensations, existing in the mind alone, that depend on and are occasioned by the different size, texture, and motion of the minute particles of matter. . . . Now, if it be

certain that those *original* qualities are inseparably united with the other sensible qualities, and not, even in thought, capable of being abstracted from them, it plainly follows that *they* exist only in the mind. But I desire any one to reflect, and try whether he can, by any abstraction of thought, conceive the extension and motion of a body without all other sensible qualities. For my own part, I see evidently that it is not in my power to frame an idea of a body extended and moving, but I must withal give it some colour or other sensible quality, which is acknowledged to exist only in the mind. In short, extension, figure, and motion, abstracted from all other qualities, are inconceivable. Where therefore the other sensible qualities are, there must these be also, to wit, in the mind and nowhere else.[12]

Pause for Thought   Berkeley said that given Locke's position, we could not really know if such things as apples and people exist. Locke had said that it is not the object we experience, but rather our perceptions or ideas of it. If Locke is correct, then can you even know that *you* exist?

To Be Is to Be Perceived

Berkeley said we do indeed experience sensations or ideas such as color, taste, smell, size, and shape. These, in turn, are sensations or ideas. Because material objects have color, taste, smell, size, and shape, then they are also sensations or ideas. Therefore, objects we think of as having color, taste, smell, size, and shape but which do not have sensations or ideas cannot exist. Finding no matter in these objects, they must be clusters of ideas or sensations. Thus, the objects only exist when a mind perceives them.

Such a formula produces the shocking conclusion, *Esse est percipi*—"To be is to be perceived."

Pause for Thought   Does Berkeley mean if something isn't perceived then it does not exist? We have all heard the question, "If a tree falls in the forest and no one is around to hear it, does it make a sound?" Does Berkeley take this a step farther? If there is no one around to see it, does the tree even exist?

The table I write on I say exists; that is, I see and feel it: and if I were out of my study I should say it existed; meaning thereby that if I was in my study I might perceive it, or that some other spirit actually does perceive it. . . . This is all that I can understand by these and the like expressions.

> For as to what is said of the *absolute* existence of unthinking things
> [matter], without any relation to their being perceived, that is to me per-
> fectly unintelligible. Their *esse* is *percipi*; nor is it possible they should have
> any existence out of the minds of thinking things which perceive them.[13]

When I look at the computer on my desk, I experience the sensation of
seeing a computer. The computer that appears in my perception is immaterial,
an idea consisting of the same ingredients as my sensation. All material things
such as computers, books, tables, apples, horses, dogs, and people exist only if
there is someone, some mind, to perceive them. "To be is to be perceived."

Pause for Thought

When Dr. Samuel Johnson heard that Berkeley denied the existence
of matter (material things), he kicked a stone. "I refute him thus."
Does his action really refute the nonexistence of matter?

Berkeley is not a *solipsist* (one who believes he alone exists and the external
world is merely a projection of his own inner experiences). For Berkeley, the
world is real. If it were not real, he could not experience it. Because material
objects are of the same qualities as our experience, we can sense them. If matter
were only sensitive substance, then we could not experience it. The only
genuine substance is the spirit (that which perceives). The substance of humans
or of God is the true substance. No unthinking substance exists.

However, if to be is to be perceived, then what happens to this computer
and this desk when I leave the room? What happens to sensible objects when
no one is around to perceive them?

Ronald Knox wrote this limerick and tacked it on a tree:

There was a young man who said, "God
Must think it exceedingly odd
If he finds that this tree
Continues to be
When there's no one about in the Quad."

(reply)
Dear Sir: Your astonishment's odd;
I am always about in the Quad.
And that's why this tree
Will continue to be,
Since observed by
Yours faithfully,
God.

Berkeley accepted the existence of sensitive things and the order in nature, but he needed to explain how objects that are external to our minds exist when we don't perceive them, and how they acquire order. He concluded that these objects exist in some other mind during the intervals of my perceiving them. An "omnipresent eternal Mind" (God) exists that knows and comprehends all things, and exhibits them to us according to the rules that He has ordained and which we call the laws of nature.

Thus, the existence of sensitive objects depends on the existence of God, who is also the cause of order in nature. Everything we see and feel is "an effect of God's power," for God is present in our consciousness, causing the existence of ideas and perceptions that we experience. The whole world and our whole life exist in God. He is the one cause of everything that exists. We exist only in the mind of God.

There is no need to posit material substance as Locke did. The ideas that exist in our minds are God's ideas that He communicates to us. God, *not* substance, causes the material objects we perceive. The regularities that we experience in the world depend on the human mind for their existence, but our finite minds cannot account for the infinite regularities that are possible. The only kind of mind that would make such infinite regularities possible would be an infinite mind, which Berkeley called God.

Pause for Thought	Did Berkeley mean that God's ideas are our ideas? If an apple is an idea in God's mind and we perceive the apple, then are we really perceiving God's idea? Are our own perceptions of space and time merely figments of the mind?

David Hume, the last of the British Empiricists, considered Berkeley's philosophy "one of the greatest and most valuable discoveries" made by a philosopher. Also an empiricist, Hume took Locke's and Berkeley's ideas to their logical conclusion.

David Hume

Hume's Life

David Hume (1711–1776) was born in Edinburgh, Scotland. His father, a lawyer, died before Hume was two years old. His mother was a deeply religious woman, and when Hume was a child, he "passed briefly through a period of piety, worrying greatly about his vices and especially about his pride." At the young age of twelve he enrolled in the University of Edinburgh, and shortly after he lost his faith. His family hoped he would follow his father into law, but, as Hume wrote, "I found an unsurmountable aversion to everything but the pursuit of philosophy and general learning."

After three years, he left the university to devote himself to philosophy and literature. After reading Locke and other philosophers, he never again "entertained any belief in religion."

From 1734 to 1737, Hume lived in "rigid frugality" in Le Fleche, France, where Descartes had studied. There Hume completed his first work, *A Treatise of Human Nature,* published in 1739. He hoped this work would bring him fame and fortune but it "fell still-born from the press."

For the next thirteen years, Hume was a tutor to an insane marquis and secretary to a general. He had many friends who saw him as kind and witty with an easy disposition.

Hume wrote and published *Essays Moral and Political* in 1741–42, and it was an immediate success. He then revised and retitled his *Treatise;* the new *An Enquiry Concerning Human Understanding* enjoyed moderate success, but its antireligious nature may have been the reason two universities rejected his applications for positions to teach philosophy. In 1751, he wrote *Enquiry Concerning the Principles of Morals,* and *Political Discourses* followed in 1752.

The same year *Political Discourses* was published, Hume became librarian for the Faculty of Advocates in Edinburgh. While librarian, he wrote a six-volume *History of England.* His tenure as librarian aroused controversy not only for his unorthodox ideas, but also because he refused to remove books that the curators considered obscene. Finally, they asked him to resign.

When he returned to Paris in 1763 as secretary to the British ambassador, French intellectuals lionized him. They admired his writings and sought his company. Among his friends was the philosopher Jean-Jacques Rousseau. Two years later, Hume returned to Edinburgh, and his house became the preferred gathering place for many intellectual celebrities, including Adam Smith.

In the spring of 1775, he developed cancer, and he died the next year. After his death, his nephew carried out an injunction in Hume's will and published *Dialogues Concerning Natural Religion* in 1779.

Hume's Purpose

Hume took it upon himself to clean up the woolly concepts of past philosophers. In doing so, he gave Empiricism its clearest and most rigorous formulation. In the beginning, he was optimistic, believing in the scientific method to analyze human nature and the workings of the human mind. He wanted to do for human nature what Isaac Newton had done for physical nature by providing an explanation of how the mind works.

Hobbes had said mind is matter and only a name for certain ways a human body operates. Descartes, believing mind is spirit, separated mind from the material body. Hume thought both philosophers had drawn unwarranted hypotheses. Following the method set down by Locke and Berkeley before him, Hume wrote:

> For me it seems evident, that the essence of the mind being equally unknown to us with that of external bodies, it must be equally impossible to form any notion of its powers and qualities otherwise than from careful and exact experiments, and the observation of those particular effects, which result from its different circumstances and situations. And tho' we must endeavour to render all our principles as universal as possible, by tracing up our experiments to the utmost, and explaining all effects from the simplest and fewest causes, 'tis still certain we cannot go beyond experience; and any hypothesis, that pretends to discover the ultimate original qualities of human nature, ought at first to be rejected as presumptuous and chimerical.[14]

As he traced the process of how we form ideas and discovered the limitations of human thought, Hume turned from his original optimism to skepticism.

Contents of the Mind

In *An Enquiry Concerning Human Understanding*, Hume set out to analyze the contents of the mind.

> Nothing, at first view, may seem more unbounded than the thought of man, which not only escapes all human power and authority, but is not even restrained within the limits of nature and reality. To form monsters, and join incongruous shapes and appearances, costs the imagination no more trouble than to conceive the most natural and familiar objects. And while the body is confined to one planet . . . the thought can in an instant transport us into the most distant regions of the universe. . . .
> But though our thought seems to possess this unbounded liberty, we shall find, upon a nearer examination, that it is really confined within very narrow limits, and that all this creative power of the mind amounts to no more than the faculty of compounding, transposing, augmenting, or diminishing the materials afforded us by the senses and experience.[15]

Thus, for Hume, we receive the contents in our mind from materials that are given "us by the senses and experience" and which he called *perceptions*. We have two different types of perceptions, namely, impressions and ideas. By "impressions" he meant the immediate sensation of external reality. By "ideas" he meant the recollection of such impressions. These impressions and ideas make up the total content of the mind.

The original impression is much more vivid than the idea it produces. If you burn your hand on a hot stove, you get an immediate impression. Afterward you can recollect that you burned yourself. The recalled impression is an idea. Impressions are stronger and "livelier" than your memory (idea) of the original impression.

> Here therefore we may divide all the perceptions of the mind into two classes or species, which are distinguished by their different degrees of force and vivacity. The less forcible and lively are commonly denominated *Thoughts* or *Ideas*. The other species wants a name in our language, and most others. . . . Let us, therefore, use a little freedom, and call them *Impressions*; employing that word in a sense somewhat different from the usual. By the term *impression*, then, I mean all our more lively perceptions, when we hear, or see, or feel, or love, or hate, or desire, or will. And impressions are distinguished from ideas, which are the less lively perceptions, of which we are conscious, when we reflect on any of those sensations or movements above mentioned.[16]

Without impressions, Hume said, we have no ideas. Because ideas are copies of impressions, for every idea we must first have an impression. However, ideas do not always reflect a corresponding impression.

> When we think of a golden mountain, we only join two consistent ideas, *gold* and *mountain*, with which we were formerly acquainted. A virtuous horse we can conceive; because, from our own feeling, we can conceive virtue; and this we may unite to the figure and shape of a horse, which is an animal familiar to us. In short, all the materials of thinking are derived either from our outward or inward sentiment: the mixture and composition of these belongs alone to the mind and will. Or, to express myself in philosophical language, all our ideas or more feeble perceptions are copies of our impressions or more lively ones.[17]

The imagination, said Hume, has the ability to join two ideas, such as thinking of a flying red horse. He called this a *complex idea* because it consists of two different experiences that are not related in fact, only associated in our imagination. It is that which joins the wings, the horse, and the red that we have perceived through our sense impressions. But a flying red horse is a false idea that we must immediately reject.

We must tidy up our thoughts and ideas. As Hume put it, if we take in our hands any volume, let us first ask if it contains any abstract reasoning concerning quantity or number. Next we should ask if it contains "any experimental reasoning concerning matters of fact and existence." If the answer is no, then we should commit it "to the flames," for it contains only "sophistry and illusion." Hume later subjected even the idea of God to this procedure.

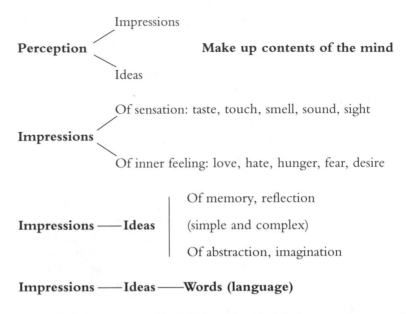

**Words are meaningful if, and only if, they can be traced
to impressions or ideas that copy impressions.**

Pause for Thought　　　Let's turn to the idea of angels. We often picture angels as celestial
human figures with wings. You have seen human figures, and you
have seen wings. Have you ever seen wings on a human figure? Is the
idea of angels a false idea?

Association of Ideas

One question Hume addressed is how our ideas relate to each other. There
must be, he said, "some bond of union, some associating quality, by which one
idea naturally introduces another." When we have a conversation with another
person, reflect on daily events, or daydream, our ideas follow regular patterns.
When Hume examined these patterns of thinking, he formulated three principles by which one idea relates to another: (1) the principle of resemblance (a
picture of a person naturally leads us to think about the original person), (2) the
principle of contiguity (the mention of one room in a building naturally leads
us to think about other rooms), and (3) the principle of cause and effect (when
we think about a wound, we also think about the pain that follows).

　　Of these three principles, Hume thought the cause and effect principle was
most important for a grounding of knowledge. However, when he analyzed the
relation of cause and effect carefully, what he discovered surprised not only him
but also the entire scientific world.

Relations of Ideas and Matters of Fact

Leading to his analysis of the relation of cause and effect, Hume took a look at a fundamental division between demonstrative reasoning or *relations of ideas* ("That three times five is equal to the half of thirty") and *matters of fact* and existence ("The sun will rise tomorrow"). We know relations of ideas by our reason; they do not depend on the existence of objects outside the mind. Although relations of ideas are logical, they give us no information about what exists or about how the things that exist behave. "That three times five is equal to the half of thirty" expresses a relation between numbers and an absolutely certain demonstrable truth. In this respect, Hume agreed with the Rationalists. But, he added, although there are certain demonstrable truths, they are empty— that is, they are devoid of information about matters of fact and existence.

Matters of fact, on the other hand, are not certain or demonstrable. They may or may not happen. "That the sun will not rise tomorrow" is no more a contradiction than our affirmation "The sun will rise tomorrow." It would be impossible to demonstrate the falsehood of the statement that the sun will not rise tomorrow.

Hume said we think we know things far beyond our senses. Using both our ordinary experiences and scientific reasoning, we apply past experiences to the future. We believe that the sun will rise tomorrow because it has always risen in the past. We believe that trees will lose their leaves in the winter and bud out again in the spring. This is a fundamental human habit, but we cannot prove logically that this way of reasoning is correct. It is conceivable that the future may not be like the past. With this finding, Hume approached the idea of causality with an original skepticism.

Cause and Effect

Philosophers before him had taken the principle of causality for granted, but Hume now asked, "What is the origin of the idea of causality?" Is there an impression that gives us the idea of cause and effect? No, he answered, there is no impression that corresponds to the idea of causality. He found no necessary connection between a cause and an effect. So how does the idea of causality arise in the mind?

The idea must arise when we experience certain relations between objects. When we speak of cause and effect, we are saying that A causes B. For instance, while playing golf, you drive your ball off the tee (A), and you search for your ball and find it in the lake (B). Or, if you are watching billiard players, you see the cue ball (A) hit and move the eight ball (B). It's obvious. In each case, A caused B.

Wait, said Hume. If you pay close attention, you will realize that you did not experience the cause producing the effect. You did not see your drive cause the ball to land in the lake. You did not see the cue ball move the eight ball.

You saw a sequence of events: (1) contiguity (A and B are always close together), (2) priority in time (A always precedes B), and (3) constant conjunction (B always follows A). From these events you conclude that a "necessary connexion" exists, although contiguity, priority, or constant conjunction do not imply "necessary" connection between objects. Therefore, "necessity is something in the mind, not in the objects."

Our observation of oxygen cannot tell us that mixing it with hydrogen will give us water. We know this only after we have seen the two together. We do not experience a "necessary connexion." Thus, causality is not in the objects we observe. Rather, we have experiences of constant conjunctions (repetition) that build up "habits of association." We have the habit of thinking that fire (A) gives off heat (B). Because we have experienced fire giving off heat in the past, we think that fire will give off heat in the future. But Hume said what we think does not rely on experience. We have no idea that the future will resemble the past because we have not experienced the future. We can only know our immediate experience and memories of that experience. Causality thus cannot be the basis for knowledge.

The External World

"Does the external world exist?" In answering this question, Hume reminded us that the mind never has anything present to it except perceptions and it cannot possibly reach any experience of the perceptions' "connexion with objects." He did not say the external world does not exist, only that we could not know if it exists, because we are prisoners of our sense impressions.

> That our senses offer not their impressions as the images of something *distinct,* or *independent,* and *external,* is evident; because they convey to us nothing but a single perception, and never give us the least intimation of any thing beyond. . . .[18]

"Let us chase our imagination to the heavens, or to the utmost limits of the universe," but we can never get a step beyond ourselves. And we cannot conceive any kind of existence but those perceptions that have appeared in that "narrow compass."

Pause for Thought   How do you think Hume would answer the question that Berkeley tackled: If our senses don't tell us that anything exists independently of us, then how do we know objects exist when we are not experiencing them?

The Self

Ever since Pythagoras and Plato, philosophers have struggled with the question of human beings and our relationship to the world. Pythagoras and Plato argued that our true nature is in the soul, which is distinct from the body. The soul exists before the body, inhabits it temporarily, and then survives its death. The Atomists held that the soul is made of atoms (matter). Aristotle viewed the soul as the form of the body, born with it but not surviving as an individual entity after death. The Epicurians agreed with the Atomists. The Stoics held that the soul is matter and a spark of God. The Medieval philosophers believed the created soul was a gift from God that held the possibility of individual salvation. The Skeptics argued that even if we had a soul we couldn't know it.

In the modern era, Descartes considered the soul or mind a spiritual substance and immortal. Hobbes, by contrast, held that human beings are strictly material. Hence, there was no unanimous decision on the subject of the soul or mind in human nature.

Hume also probed the science of human nature. What philosophers before him had called *soul*, he called *self*. Supposedly, the self accounts for the thought that I am the same person today as I was at the age of six months. Most of my characteristics have changed over the years—I no longer cry for food, wear diapers, or have the desires of a six-month-old—but "I" am the same person. Is this "I" a permanent self?

Hume came to the conclusion that we do not really have an idea of the self, because ideas rely on sense impressions and we have no sense impressions of a self. When Hume looked for a self, all he could find were bundles of impressions.

> There are some philosophers who imagine we are every moment intimately conscious of what we call our SELF; that we feel its existence and its continuance in existence; and are certain, beyond the evidence of a demonstration, both of its perfect identity and simplicity. . . . Unluckily all these positive assertions are contrary to that very experience, which is pleaded for them, nor have we an idea of *self*, after the manner it is here explained. For from what impression could this idea be derived? . . . It must be some one impression, that gives rise to every idea. But self or person is not any one impression, but that to which our several impressions and ideas are supposed to have a reference. If any impression gives rise to the idea of self, that impression must continue invariably the same, through the whole course of our lives; since self is supposed to exist after that manner. But there is no impression constant and invariable. . . . There is no such idea. . . .
>
> For my part, when I enter most intimately into what I call *myself*, I always stumble on some particular perception or other, of heat or cold, light or shade, love or hatred, pain or pleasure. I never can catch *myself* at

any time without a perception, and never can observe any thing but the perception. . . . The mind is a kind of theatre, where several perceptions successively make their appearance; pass, re-pass, glide away, and mingle in an infinite variety of postures and situations. There is properly no *simplicity* in it at one time, nor *identity* in different. . . . The comparison of the theatre must not mislead us. They are the successive perceptions only that constitute the mind.[19]

For Hume, the idea of self is like the idea of causality. We think self and causality are facts when, in reality, they are fictions. The self we consider our permanent identity is nothing but a "bundle" of perceptions. Because we have no reason to believe in an "external" world independently of our minds, we also have no reason to believe in a permanent, unchanging self. We have no sense impression of a self or causality. Both are actions "of the imagination."

According to Hume, the mind is a "kind of theater" in which many perceptions successively make their appearance, pass by, disappear, and mingle in an infinite variety of positions and situations. He also pointed out that we have no "personal identity" beneath or behind these perceptions and feelings that come and go.

Pause for Thought   Can you conceive of your *self* as the images on a movie screen? They change so rapidly we do not register that the film is made up of single pictures. The pictures are not connected, however, and the film is a collection of instances.

Twenty-five hundred years ago, the Buddha formulated a similar idea of self. What we call the self, he said, is actually a collection of *skandhas* (sensations, thoughts, feelings, consciousness, and perceptions) that are in a continual state of change. There is no permanent "I."

Substance

In denying a permanent *self*, Hume, opposing Locke and Berkeley, denied the existence of substance. According to Locke, substance is "something we know not what" that has shape or color and other qualities. Berkeley rejected the idea that substance has underlying qualities, but he did accept the idea of spiritual substances. Hume claimed that because we have no impression of substance, we could have no meaningful idea of substance distinct from particular qualities such as color and sound.

Pause for Thought   Hume's skepticism is deepening. We have no idea of causality, self (soul), or substance. Can we possibly have an idea of God? Can you think of a convincing argument for the existence of God?

God

Hume could not accept Descartes' idea of God as an idea that comes from outside the mind: "Our ideas reach no further than our experience." Arguments to prove the existence of God usually rely on some argument from causality, which Hume denied. He would not refer to the cosmological arguments of Aquinas or Descartes that God is omniscience and perfect, because we have no sense impression of omniscience or perfection.

As he looked at the world around him, Hume suggested that the argument from design (the teleological argument) is the strongest argument for the existence of God. It claims that we perceive orderly design throughout the universe. Our planet always rotates around the sun. Each year there is summer, fall, winter, and spring. We sense the divine in a beautiful sunrise, a noble horse, and a wildflower. We attribute their beauties to an intelligent designer—God. Hume was unconvinced.

> Look round this universe. What an immense profusion of beings, animated and organized, sensible and active! You admire the prodigious variety and fecundity. But inspect a little more narrowly these living existences, the only beings worth regarding. How hostile and destructive to each other! How insufficient all of them for their own happiness! How contemptible or odious to the spectator! The whole presents nothing but the idea of a blind nature, impregnated by a great vivifying principle, and pouring forth from her lap, without discernment or parental care, her maimed and abortive children.[20]

Was Hume suggesting there might be no divine designer? Was he implying that we could not know whether God exists?

> Right. . . . This is the topic on which I have all along insisted. I have still asserted that we have no *data* to establish any system of cosmogony [the origin of the universe]. Our experience, so imperfect in itself, and so limited both in extent and duration, can afford us no probable conjecture concerning the whole of things.[21]

Just before his death, Hume added this thought to his *Dialogues:* "The cause or causes of order in the universe probably bear some remote analogy to human intelligence." However, he did not suggest that human intelligence infers a creator God. Such a statement does not make Hume an atheist (although he may have been one), it simply tests our ideas of God as he tested our ideas of the self, substance, and cause and effect.

Moral Philosophy

The Greek philosophers had argued that reason should rule the emotions and the sensuous appetites. The Stoics, for example, attempted to control their passions through reason. Descartes argued that reason is the faculty for finding truth, including morality. Hume agreed that reason plays a role in our moral decisions, but reason "is not sufficient alone to produce any moral blame or approbation." Moral judgments are grounded not just in reason, but in sentiment (sympathy or feeling).

> It appears evident that the ultimate ends of human actions can never . . . be accounted for by *reason*, but recommend themselves entirely to the sentiments and affections of mankind, without any dependence on the intellectual faculties. Ask a man *why he uses exercise*; he will answer, *because he desires to keep his health*. If you then enquire, *why he desires health,* he will readily reply *because sickness is painful*. If you push your enquiries farther, and desire a reason *why he hates pain*, it is impossible that he can ever give any. This is an ultimate end, and is never referred to any other object.[22]

Reason makes judgments about matters of fact and relations, but moral judgments go beyond such matters. Consider an act of murder. Can you find anything in the facts of the case that reveals the act is morally wrong? The facts merely show that one person ended the life of another in a certain way at a certain time and place. Our reason reveals how long it took for death to occur, the weapon used, the exact place the crime took place, and other facts about the case. But reason cannot show the moral wrongfulness of the act. Hume challenged us to find the matter of fact or real existence that we call *vice*. You cannot, he said. You can find only certain passions, motives, volitions, and thoughts. The notion of vice arises in your sentiment toward this action. That an act is immoral is a feeling judgment only.

> But can there be any difficulty in proving, that vice and virtue are not matters of fact, whose existence we can infer by reason? Take any action allow'd to be vicious: Willful murder, for instance. Examine it in all lights, and see if you can find the matter of fact, or real existence, which you call *vice*. In whichever way you take it, you find only certain passions, motives, volitions and thoughts. There is no matter of fact in the case. The vice entirely escapes you, as long as you consider the object. You can never find it, till you turn your reflexion into your own breast, and find a sentiment of disapprobation, which arise in you towards this action. Here is a

matter of fact; but 'tis the object of feeling, not of reason. It lies in yourself, not in the object. So that when you pronounce any action or character to be vicious, you mean nothing, but that from the constitution of
your nature you have a feeling or sentiment of blame from the contemplation of it. Vice and virtue, therefore, may be compar'd to sounds, colours,
heat and cold, which according to modern philosophy, are not qualities in
objects, but perceptions in the mind. . . .[23]

Hume concluded that sentiment (feeling) is the basis not only for all moral
judgments, but also for all value judgments. Even the kind of music you like is
not a rational decision; it is the sentiment of sympathy. With reason you can tell
the arrangement of the notes and the instruments playing the piece, but reason
cannot decide whether you like or dislike the music. Reason may help us clarify
experience and identify facts, but it cannot evaluate them.

Is ethics then a matter of taste? If you like something, is it good? And if you
dislike it, is it bad? No, said Hume. Moral judgments do not come from our
individual selfishness—our ego. All people praise and blame the same actions.
We are morally sensitive creatures. What we consider good, just, and noble
pleases our moral sensibilities. Actions that offend our moral sensitivity we
regard as bad, unjust, and despicable. Morality is not a matter of selfish desire,
it is a matter of benevolence.

Where is the difficulty in conceiving, that . . . from the original frame of
our temper, we may feel a desire of another's happiness or good, which by
means of that affection, becomes our own good, and is afterwards pursued,
from the combined motives of benevolence and self-enjoyments? Who
sees not that vengeance, from the force alone of passion, may be so eagerly
pursued, as to make us knowingly neglect every consideration of ease,
interest, or safety; and, like some vindictive animals, infuse our very souls
into the wounds we give an enemy; and what a malignant philosophy it
must be, that will not allow to humanity and friendship the same privileges
which are indisputably granted to the darker passions of enmity and resentment.[24]

Benevolence is the basis of our concern for others. The act that pleases our
moral sensibilities is one that reflects a benevolent character by the person doing
the act. Morality is not a set of rules; it is universal agreement. Even the most
cynical people admit that virtuous qualities are useful and agreeable. Moral qualities are "everything which contributes to the happiness of society," and they
come from our goodwill. Most of us don't like to see others suffer, and we do
like to see people happy. We are sympathetic creatures. Part of our sympathy is
selfish. We help others and praise their actions because it brings us pleasure.
Most of our disagreements over moral judgments result from differences about
whether the conduct we are looking at is useful.

Being thus acquainted with the nature of man, we expect not any impossibilities from him; but confine our view to that narrow circle, in which any person moves, in order to form a judgment of his moral character. When the natural tendency of his passions leads him to be serviceable and useful within his sphere, we approve of his character, and love his person, by a sympathy with the sentiments of those, who have a more particular connexion with him. We are quickly oblig'd to forget our own interest in our judgments of this kind, by reason of the perpetual contradictions, we meet with in society and conversation, from persons that are not place'd in the same situation, and have not the same interest with ourselves.[25]

Sympathy

Hume's moral philosophy developed in opposition to the philosophical trend in his time. He favored a benevolent utilitarianism (see Chapter 11). Hume believed that our moral motivation comes from sympathy, or feelings—especially what he called "fellow feelings," or the ability to experience another person's good or pain as if it were our own. When we have these feelings, reason clarifies and evaluates their situation and their needs in society. He agreed that universal principles of behavior such as benevolence, utility, and agreeableness do exist, giving worth to our human nature; these include friendship, integrity, and justice.

To decide whether an action will be moral or immoral in a given situation, we must detach ourselves from the group to discover its sentiments. As disinterested observers, we can detect the good act from the bad act and then proceed appropriately. This action pertains to societies. But, said Hume, sentiments are different among societies, and so it is the job of reason to judge which practice is the best for each society.

Pause for Thought   Although moral sentiment is universal among human beings, Hume's social ethics depends on the particular society or culture in which you live. Does this mean there can be no absolute ethic—that is, a single morality for all people everywhere, such as provided for by the Ten Commandments?

On Women

In *Treatise of Human Nature* (1740), Hume agreed with Hobbes that it is practically impossible to prove that a child belongs to the man. Without such assurance, said Hume, men may not make the necessary sacrifices to assist their wives in the education and care of their children. A marriage contract does not provide this assurance in itself. The problem is how to instill in women an obligation to bear children and at the same time "impose a due restraint on the female sex."

> We must attach a peculiar degree of shame to their [women's] infidelity, above what arises merely from its injustice, and must bestow proportionable praises on their chastity.
>
> As to the obligations which the male sex lie under, with regard to chastity, we may observe, that according to the general notions of the world, they bear nearly the same proportion to the obligations of women, as the obligations of the law of nations do to those of the law of nature. 'Tis contrary to the interest of civil society, that men shou'd have an *entire* liberty of indulging their appetites in venereal enjoyment. But as this interest is weaker than in the case of the female sex, the moral obligation, arising from it, must be proportionably weaker. And to prove this we need only appeal to the practice and sentiments of all nations and ages.[26]

Summary

The Rationalists held that true knowledge is innate (a priori) in reason. The British Empiricists, however, argued that innate knowledge does not exist and that the mind at birth is a blank tablet. Our knowledge results from ideas produced by objects we experience. Everything we know comes through our senses and thus comes a posteriori. First, we experience objects through our senses, and then we reflect on them.

John Locke argued that the principles of identity and contradiction are not innate; they require proof. Because the mind is a tabula rasa—a blank tablet—nothing exists in it that was not first in the senses. All ideas come from sensation or reflection.

For Locke, there are simple ideas and complex ideas. Simple ideas originate in the five senses. When we bring simple ideas together by comparing and reflection, we form complex ideas. Certain ideas also are caused by primary and secondary qualities. Ideas caused by the former qualities represent exactly the objects we experience. Secondary ideas have no exact correlative in the objects themselves.

Locke did say, however, that the idea of substance, although not innate, does have certain qualities that we can understand with reason.

The way ideas relate to each other depends on our perception and whether it is intuitive, demonstrative, or sensitive.

According to Locke, morals are the result of accepting pleasure and avoiding pain, especially when we look to the future. Assessing moral good and evil is the way we respond to different laws: (1) law of opinion, based on actions; (2) civil law, set by the courts; and (3) divine law, or the law of God. Through reason or revelation we can discover the moral rules that conform to God's law. And, in politics, Locke believed government should be the servant of the people.

Bishop Berkeley agreed with Locke that all we could know we perceive through the senses, but he went a step farther, adding that we do not perceive "matter." We do not perceive objects as tangible objects. All we directly experience is our own perceptions of material objects. Thus, objects exist only when the mind perceives them. His conclusion: To be is to be perceived.

The question then arose, do objects exist when we do not perceive them? Berkeley answered, yes. God perceives the world—everything exists in the mind of God.

David Hume set out to analyze the contents of the mind and traced the process of how we form ideas. He found that we receive the contents in our mind from the materials given us by the senses and by experience (perception), which is of two types: impressions and ideas. *Impressions* are our immediate sensations, and *ideas* are reflections on our impressions.

Hume formulated three principles by which our ideas relate to each other: resemblance, contiguity, and cause and effect. Cause and effect—that is, A always follows B—must have a necessary connection, and no necessary connection is found in the *objects* we experience, only in the mind. Our minds build up habits of association, so causality cannot be the basis for knowledge.

Unlike Berkeley, Hume did not say "To be is to be perceived," but he did find that our minds are limited to the impressions of sense. Therefore, we can never go beyond our "selves" to know whether an external world exists.

Even the self is subject to change. Hume concluded that we do not really have any clear idea of a "self," only bundles of impressions. We have no single impression of a self, and so there is no idea of self. Hume extended this test to God: Because we have no sense impression of God, we can have no idea of God, and so *God* is a meaningless term.

According to Hume, moral judgments are grounded not in reason, but in sentiment. Reason makes judgments concerning matters of fact and relations, but moral judgments go beyond matters of fact to benevolence. All value judgments also have their basis in sentiment.

Connections

Hume's discovery that there is no "necessary connection" among matters of fact is probably the most profound finding to come from the British Empiricists.

This view was so revolutionary that scientists were stunned. Other empiricists' views were also revolutionary, but Hume took them to their logical conclusion, regarding reason as merely an instrument for detecting relations among ideas. Reason tells us nothing, he said, about the real world. Hume's skepticism drove a wedge between reason and nature, a wedge that Immanuel Kant, our next inquirer, said woke him from his "dogmatic slumbers." Recognizing the destructive potential of Hume's critique to philosophy and science, Kant sought to answer Hume by analyzing the capacity of reason. Kant's philosophy was one of the important turning points in Western philosophy.

Study Questions

1. What is Empiricism?

2. Explain the differences between Rationalism and Empiricism.

3. What does Locke mean that the mind at birth is a tabula rasa?

4. How does Locke explain the origin of ideas?

5. What is the difference between simple and complex ideas?

6. What are primary and secondary qualities?

7. Explain Locke's three kinds of perception.

8. For Locke, what do pleasure and pain have to do with morality?

9. Explain Locke's meaning of natural rights.

10. What kind of government does Locke propose?

11. What is the major difference between the empiricism of Locke and the empiricism of Berkeley?

12. What does Berkeley mean by "To be is to be perceived"?

13. Is Berkeley a solipsist?

14. What is the importance of God in Berkeley's philosophy?

15. How does Hume explain the origin of our ideas?

16. Contrast the relations of ideas with matters of fact.

17. What gives us the idea of cause and effect?

18. What part does necessary connection play in our idea of cause and effect?

19. What conclusions does Hume draw about the nature of a self?

20. How is Hume's idea of self like the idea of causality?

21. How do Hume and Descartes differ in their ideas about God?

22. Do moral judgments go beyond matters of fact and relations? Explain.

23. What is the significance of sympathy in Hume's moral philosophy?

Notes

1. John Locke, "Epistle to the Reader, " p. 9 in *An Essay Concerning Human Understanding* (ed. by A. C. Fraser). Oxford, UK: Clarendon Press, 1894.

2. Locke, *Essay*, ibid., Bk. II, Chap. 1, 2–5.

3. Ibid., Bk. II, Chap. 2, 1.

4. Ibid., Bk. II, Chap. 2, 2.

5. Ibid., Bk. II, Chap. 8, 2.

6. Ibid., Bk. II, Chap. 23, 2.

7. Ibid., Bk. IV, Chap. 10, 6.

8. Ibid., Bk. II, Chap. 22, 2.

9. Ibid., Bk. II, Chap. 21, 35.

10. Ibid., Bk. II, Chap. 11, 8.

11. John Locke, *Second Treatise of Civil Government,* Vol. 4, Chap. II in *The Works of John Locke*. London: C. & G. Rivington, 1824.

12. George Berkeley, *A Treatise Concerning the Principles of Human Knowledge* (ed. by A. C. Fraser), in *The Works of George Berkeley,* Vol. I, Part I, Sec. 93. Oxford, UK: Clarendon Press, 1901.

13. Ibid.

14. David Hume, *A Treatise of Human Nature* (ed. by L. A. Selby-Bigge), p. xxi. Oxford, UK: Oxford University Press, 1888.

15. David Hume, *An Enquiry Concerning the Human Understanding* (ed. by L. A. Selby-Bigge), Sec. II, p. 13. Oxford, UK: Clarendon Press, 1894.

16. Ibid., p. 12.

17. Ibid., p. 13.

18. Hume, *Treatise,* op. cit., Vol. I, Part IV, Sec. 2.

19. Ibid., Sec. 6.

20. David Hume, *Dialogues Concerning Human Religion* (ed. by Norman Kemp-Smith), Part 11. Edinburgh: Nelson, 1947.

21. Ibid., Part 7.

22. David Hume, *An Enquiry Concerning the Principles of Morals* (ed. by L. A. Selby-Bigge), Appendix 1. Oxford, UK: Clarendon Press, 1894.

23. Hume, *Treatise,* op. cit., Book 3, Sec I.

24. Hume, *Principles of Morals*, op. cit., Appendix II.

25. Hume, *Treatise,* op. cit., Book 3, Part 3, Sec. 3.

26. Ibid., Sec. 12.

CHAPTER NINE

Immanuel Kant: Critical Philosophy

In this chapter we shall see how the conclusions of the Empiricists, especially Hume, awakened Immanuel Kant "from his dogmatic slumbers." Disagreeing with Hume's skepticism, Kant argued that the mind is not simply passive; it takes an active part in knowing the objects it experiences. The Empiricists had believed that the mind conforms to "impressions," and Hume held that ideas were copies of impressions. The mind, said the Empiricists, takes on the shape of the world it perceives. Kant argued that instead of the mind conforming to the world, the external world conforms to the mind. The world, and not the mind, takes the shape given it by the way the mind operates. Kant also did not agree with the Rationalists, who thought by reason alone we could know God, freedom, and immortality.

By combining experience (a posteriori knowledge) with necessity (a priori knowledge), or British Empiricism with Continental Rationalism, Kant put philosophy back in the saddle. His greatness was in his ability to combine the Empiricist thesis (all we can know we get through sense experience) and the Rationalist thesis (we can attain truth through reason). For Kant, knowledge is a result of human understanding applied to sense experience.

Immanuel Kant

Kant's Life

Immanuel Kant (1724–1804) was born, raised, lived, and died in the town of Königsberg in East Prussia (now part of western Russia). His parents belonged to the Lutheran Pietist movement and raised him with strict moral standards. His mother was a stern Puritan who insisted on a rigorous ritualism, and his father made leather straps—and used them regularly on his eleven children. As an adult, Kant criticized his early training and stayed away from church, but he remained a deeply spiritual man.

At sixteen Kant enrolled in the University of Königsberg, where he studied philosophy and physics. Following his university studies, he worked as a private tutor in a neighboring village. Outside that brief job as tutor, Kant never left his home. Mentally, however, he ranged the universe. His thirst for knowledge led him to study the Asian philosophers, who had a strong influence upon him. However, it was not until he read the writings of French philosopher Jean-Jacques Rousseau that he found the key to his own ideas. For several years he had drifted in a sea of metaphysical doubt. "I have the fortune to be a lover of philosophy," he said, "but my mistress has shown me few favors as yet."

In 1755, Kant joined the faculty of the University of Königsberg where he lectured for the next fifteen years. He preferred to teach students who had only average academic abilities. "The geniuses are in no need of my help, and the dunces are beyond all help." Students described him as a professor who used words "six feet long" to express unimportant thoughts. One of his students remarked, "He carries us over a sea without shores, in a vessel without sails." Nonetheless, his classes were popular and well attended.

Kant was a life-long bachelor, and his biographies describe that he was so precise in his daily habits that his neighbors could set their clocks by his routine. Each afternoon, at exactly 3:30, he left his house for a daily walk. Only once did he fail to appear, and the townspeople thought he was ill. When they arrived to help, Kant sat absorbed in Rousseau's *Emile,* a book that profoundly affected his philosophical life.

Kant must have been a quaint little philosopher. He was approximately five feet tall with a flat chest, protruding stomach, humped shoulders, and head perched quizzically to one side. His usual attire was a gray hat, gray coat, and gray trousers. And he carried a gray cane that he tapped as he walked toward the Avenue of the Lindens. Trudging behind him was his faithful servant, Lampe, an umbrella in hand in case it rained. Probably because of Kant, the people of Königsberg nicknamed the Avenue of the Lindens "The Philosopher's Walk."

Most philosophers wrote their major works early in their lives, but Kant appeared content to teach, not write. He was a popular host and delightful conversationalist with many friends and admirers. No one knew a volcano of ideas was seething within his modest head. Not until Kant was fifty-seven did Hume wake him from his "dogmatic slumbers." And what an awakening. Kant's ideas erupted into the most remarkable philosophical system of modern times.

The founder of German Idealism, Kant wrote three of the most important works in philosophy. He told a friend that he wrote *Critique of Pure Reason*, his first work, "within four or five months, with the utmost attention to the contents, but with less concern for the presentation or for making things easy for the reader." (Kant was not exaggerating. The first reading of *Critique of Pure Reason* is similar to uncovering the design on an Oriental rug by examining the threads on the back of the carpet). His moral views appear in his work *Critique of Practical Reason*, and his *Critique of Judgment* deals with aesthetic theories. Among other of his works, these made him the most well-known, if not the most understood, philosopher in Europe.

Kant's remarkable success in showing the way out of the impasse philosophy had been channeled by Rationalism and Empiricism brought an era in the history of philosophy to an end. Carved on his gravestone in Königsberg is one of his most quoted sayings: "Two things fill my mind with ever-increasing wonder and awe, the more often and the more intensely the reflection dwells on them: the starry heavens above me and the moral law within me."

Kant's Revolution

Kant was familiar with the rationalism of Descartes, Spinoza, and Leibniz, as well as the Empiricism of Locke, Berkeley, and Hume. He thought both general views were partly right and partly wrong. The Empiricists had assumed that our mind is passive, a container for sensations (Locke) or impressions (Hume). Locke had described the mind as a tabula rasa, a blank tablet on which the senses write. Hume had said that because all knowledge relies on impressions, we can only know our own ideas. We can never know "causality" or necessary connections because we do not experience them. What we call "cause and effect" is simply our habit of associating two events because we experience them together. What we call the "self" is actually a "bundle of perceptions," so we have no knowledge of self-identity. As Hume followed his skepticism to its natural conclusion, he discovered that we could not even know the reality of the external world.

Kant answered Hume's skepticism by agreeing that the Empiricists were right in thinking that our knowledge begins with sensations or impressions of the world, but they were wrong in assuming the mind is merely passive. Kant agreed with Hume that all our knowledge begins with experience, but, he added, although our knowledge begins with experience, it does not follow that all of our knowledge arises out of experience. The empirical scientific method impressed Kant, especially the science of Newton.

Kant was aware that rationalism alone could not produce scientific knowledge. Also, the fact that Rationalists from Plato to Spinoza had come to different metaphysical conclusions convinced him that pure "dogmatic" metaphysics could not increase our knowledge about the nature of reality, freedom, and God. But he believed with the Rationalists that in reason are decisive factors that determine *how* we perceive the world. Human reason contributes to our conception of the world.

Kant compared his philosophy to the Copernican revolution in astronomy. Before Copernicus, scholars believed the Earth was the center of the universe and all heavenly bodies revolved around it. When Copernicus challenged this hypothesis scientifically, it broke down. Using a new hypothesis, Copernicus proved that the sun is the center of our solar system, and the Earth and other planets orbit the sun. Similarly, before Kant, Empiricists believed ideas were only copies of objects perceived by the senses. Kant's "revolution" presented the view that we know things as objects, not passively, but because the mind itself contributes organizing principles to the objects. This *active* contribution by the mind makes knowledge possible. Thus, the mind helps shape the world that we can know. But we cannot know, as the Rationalists thought we could, God, freedom, or immortality. How did Kant put philosophy back in the saddle? Like Copernicus, he tried another hypothesis.

The Powers of Human Reason

Kant called his new hypothesis *critical philosophy* because it analyzes the powers of human reason.

> Hitherto it has been assumed that all our knowledge must conform to objects. But all attempts to extend our knowledge of objects by establishing something in regard to them *a priori*, by means of concepts, have, on this assumption, ended in failure. We must therefore make trial whether we may not have more success in the tasks of metaphysics, if we suppose that objects must conform to our knowledge. This would agree better with what is desired, namely, that it should be possible to have knowledge of objects *a priori*, determining something in regard to them prior to their being given. We should then be proceeding precisely on the lines of Copernicus' primary hypothesis. Failing of satisfactory progress in explaining the movements of the heavenly bodies on the supposition that they all revolved round the spectator, he tried whether he might not have better success if he made the spectator to revolve and the stars to remain at rest. A similar experiment can be tried in metaphysics as regards the *intuition* of objects. If intuition must conform to the constitution of the objects, I do not see how we could know anything of the latter *a priori*; but if the object (as object of the senses) must conform to the constitution of our faculty of intuition, I have no difficulty in conceiving such a possibility. . . . As regards objects which are thought solely through reason, and indeed as necessary, but which can never—at least not in the manner in which reason thinks them—be given in experience, the attempts at thinking them (for they must admit of being thought) will furnish an excellent test of what we are adopting as our new method of thought, namely, that we can know *a priori* of things only what we ourselves put into them.[1]

Kant wanted to prove that the mind actively processes something more than sense impressions. His own "Copernican revolution"—his new hypothesis—was that the world conforms to the mind. The mind does not, as Hume had said, conform to the world. By showing that the mind has powers of its own, Kant could prove that laws of science such as cause and effect are valid and demonstrable truths.

A Priori and a Posteriori Knowledge

Kant thought it was important to make a clear distinction between a priori and a posteriori knowledge. As you recall, a priori knowledge is that which reason can know without help from sense experience. Though Kant agreed with the Empiricists that our knowledge begins with experience, he did not think all knowledge arises from it. We can have some knowledge by pure reason completely independent of sense experience.

Hume, we recall, believed that causality was our habit of connecting two events that we call "cause and effect." He claimed that it was only by "habit of association" that we thought we saw a causal link behind all natural processes. Hume said we could not perceive the black billiard ball as the cause of the white ball's movement. Therefore, we cannot prove that the black billiard ball will always set the white one in motion. Because it is only a habit of association in the mind and not a "necessary connection" experienced by the senses, we can have no knowledge of cause and effect.

But Kant disagreed. He said we *do* have knowledge about causality a priori in reason. Our knowledge of cause and effect is inherent in reason—it does not come from sense experience.

Pause for Thought   Do you agree with Hume that our idea of causality is a habit of association, or with Kant, who said we have a priori knowledge of causality in the reason? Is there another way to look at the problem?

Kant agreed with Hume that experience cannot give us knowledge about "necessary connection" or universals (principles that are necessarily true). Still, we do have knowledge about them from both science and mathematics. Though experience cannot show us every change because we have not yet experienced them all, we know that change is universally true. We know that all heavy objects will fall in space and five plus seven always equals twelve. These concepts come from the mind. To say only some objects fall in space, or on Tuesdays seven plus five equals twelve, but on Saturdays and Sundays none of the formulas hold true are false statements. A priori knowledge is always true.

A posteriori (empirical) knowledge comes from our sense experience. Because it applies only to what we observe, it is never universally or necessarily true. From my experience, I can see that a certain building is tall, or the dog has shaggy hair, or the sky is blue. But I cannot correctly conclude that all buildings are tall, all dogs have shaggy hair, or the sky is always blue. The distinction between a priori and a posteriori knowledge is similar to Hume's contrast between matters of fact and relations of ideas. But Kant went a step further, relating a priori knowledge to *analytic judgments* and a posteriori knowledge to *synthetic judgments*.

Analytic and Synthetic Judgments

For Kant, we make a judgment when we connect a subject and a predicate. When I say, "The rose smells sweet, " I make a judgment. The mind can understand a connection between the subject (rose) and the predicate (smells sweet). Because subjects and predicates connect to each other in two different ways, Kant posits two kinds of judgments—analytic and synthetic.

In analytic judgments, the predicate is already contained in the subject. "All triangles have three angles" is an analytic judgment because the predicate is implicit in the subject. The word *triangle* means a three-sided figure. "All bachelors are unmarried men" is another example of an analytic judgment, said Kant. The word *bachelor* means unmarried man. Another example is "All physical bodies take up space."

Analytic: The predicate adds nothing and is contained in the subject.

Analytic judgments are always necessary and universally true. To say an analytic judgment is sometimes true involves a logical contradiction. Because analytic judgments are independent of sense experience, they are a priori.

Pause for Thought   Can you think of some original analytic judgments?

Unlike analytic judgments, synthetic judgments add something new in the predicate that is not contained in the subject. When I say, "The apple is sour," I join two independent concepts, because the concept of apple does not contain the idea of sourness. "All bodies are heavy" also is a synthetic judgment. For Kant, the statement "All bodies take up space" is analytic because the concept of body contains the concept of extension. But the concept of heavy is synthetic, because weight is not an essential attribute of bodies. Still, all of the bodies we experience could, in fact, be heavy.

Synthetic: The predicate adds something not contained in the subject.

Synthetic judgments are a posteriori. We discover by experience that the predicate adds information to the subject.

Pause for Thought   Analytic judgments arise from reason, and synthetic judgments from sense experience. They appear independent of each other. Kant, however, is going to connect them. Before you read on, can you invent an example of a judgment that is both synthetic and a priori?

Synthetic a Priori

Obviously, a judgment cannot be both analytic and synthetic. Analytic judgments are independent of the senses, and synthetic judgments depend on the senses. But Kant finds that one class of judgment remains: judgments that are both synthetic and a priori. We make *synthetic a priori* judgments in mathematics, natural science, and ethics. Synthetic a priori judgments are the one important ingredient the Empiricists left out.

First, Kant wanted to show that mathematics is not only a priori but also synthetic. For example, the judgment that seven plus five equals twelve is a priori because it is necessarily and universally true. Seven plus five has to equal twelve. At the same time, this judgment is synthetic and not analytic because we cannot derive the number twelve merely by analyzing the numbers 5 and 7.

Kant said that *intuition* (sensuous intuition) makes the synthesis of the concepts seven, five, and *plus*.

> *All mathematical judgments, without exception, are synthetic.* This fact, though incontestably certain and in its consequences very important, has hitherto escaped the notice of those who are engaged in the analysis of human reason. . . .
>
> We might, indeed, at first suppose that the proposition $7 + 5 = 12$ is a merely analytic proposition, and follows by the principle of contradiction from the concept of a sum of 7 and 5. But if we look more closely we find that the concept of the sum of 7 and 5 contains nothing save the union of the two numbers into one, and in this no thought is being taken as to what that single number may be which combines both. The concept of 12 is by no means already thought in merely thinking this union of 7 and 5; and I may analyze my concept of such a possible sum as long as I please, still I shall never find the 12 in it. We have to go outside these concepts, and call in the aid of the intuition which corresponds to one of them, our five fingers, for instance, . . . adding to the concept of 7, unit by unit, the five given in intuition. For starting with the number 7, and for the concept of 5

calling in the aid of the fingers of my hand as intuition, I now add one by one to the number 7 the units which I previously took together to form the number 5, and with the aid of that figure see the number 12 come into being. That 5 should be added to 7, I have indeed already thought in the concept of a sum = 7 + 5, but not that this sum is equivalent to the number 12. Arithmetical propositions are therefore always synthetic. This is still more evident if we take larger numbers. For it is then obvious that, however we might turn and twist our concepts, we could never, by the mere analysis of them, and without the aid of intuition, discover what is the sum.

Just as little is any fundamental proposition of pure geometry analytic. That the straight line between two points is the shortest, is a synthetic proposition. For my concept of *straight* contains nothing of quantity, but only of quality. The concept of the shortest is wholly an addition, and cannot be derived, through any process of analysis, from the concept of the straight line. Intuition, therefore, must here be called in; only by its aid is the synthesis possible.[2]

In his argument concerning physics, Kant said the proposition that "in all changes of the material world the quantity of matter remains unchanged" is a priori, because we make this judgment without experiencing every change. This judgment is also synthetic because we cannot find the idea of permanence in the concept of change.

We know there is causality. A world without it would have no order or predictability. We would never know what to expect. Our lives would be in perpetual chaos. We could slowly grow younger, reach old age today, or stop aging at all. If you threw a ball, you would never know if it would bounce, disappear in the sky, or grow green hair.

Without both reason and sensuous intuition, synthetic a priori knowledge is impossible. "Thoughts without content are empty; intuitions without concepts are blind." The understanding can perceive nothing, and the senses can think nothing. Knowledge arises only from the united action of thoughts and sensuous intuition.

The Structure of the Mind

Hume had said the mind is passive when it receives sense impressions. But Kant argued that it is the nature of the mind to organize our experiences. Kant compared the mind to wearing colored glasses. If I wear rose-colored glasses, I am limited to seeing the world in that color. The glasses I am wearing determine everything I see. The mind, too, wears lenses; it brings certain ways of thinking to experience, and this affects our understanding.

"There are," said Kant, "two sources of human knowledge, which spring from a common but to us unknown root, namely *sensibility* and *understanding*.

Through the former objects are *given* to us; through the latter they are *thought*." Together, sensibility and understanding synthesize and unify our experience.

> If the *receptivity* of our mind, its power of receiving representations in so far as it is in any wise affected, is to be entitled sensibility, then the mind's power of producing representations from itself, the *spontaneity* of knowledge, should be called the understanding. . . . Without sensibility no object would be given to us, without understanding no object would be thought. Thoughts without content are empty, intuitions [single representations] without concepts are blind. . . . The understanding can intuit nothing, the senses can think nothing. Only through their union can knowledge arise.[3]

Pause for Thought   Do you agree with Kant that intuition is not a function of our understanding? Would Descartes agree?

Whatever we experience, we will first perceive as phenomena in *time* and *space*. Kant called time and space our two *forms of intuition*. These two forms in our own mind precede every experience. Thus, we know a priori before we experience things that we will perceive them as phenomena in time and space. We cannot take off the "glasses" of reason. For Kant, time and space are the lenses through which we see the world. Time and space do not exist beyond us; they belong to the human condition. Time and space are *modes of perception,* not attributes of the physical world. In other words, time and space are distinct from concepts, and they also are not empirical. They provide an a priori "intuition" that links the subject and predicate of the synthetic a priori judgments, thus making synthetic a priori knowledge possible. For Kant, time and space are innate ordering structures of the mind.

In addition to time and space, the mind has certain categories of thought that help unify or synthesize our experience. Based on Aristotelian logic, Kant developed twelve a priori categories of conception and twelve a priori corresponding categories of judgment.

CATEGORIES OF QUANTITY

1. The category of *unity* corresponds to universal judgments.

2. The category of *plurality* corresponds to particular judgments.

3. The category of *totality* corresponds to singular judgments.

CATEGORIES OF QUALITY

1. The category of *reality* corresponds to affirmative judgments.

2. The category of *negation* corresponds to negative judgments.

3. The category of *limitation* corresponds to limitative judgments.

CATEGORIES OF RELATION

1. The category of *substance-and-accident* corresponds to categorical judgments.

2. The category of *causality and dependence* corresponds to hypothetical judgments.

3. The category of *community* or *interaction* corresponds to disjunctive judgments.

CATEGORIES OF MODALITY

1. The category of *possibility and impossibility* corresponds to problematic judgments.

2. The category of *existence* and *nonexistence* corresponds to assertoric judgments—that is, knowledge of what is actual or occurring, as opposed to knowledge of what might occur or is capable of occurring.

3. The category of *necessity–contingency* corresponds to apodictic judgments—that is, knowledge that is demonstrably or necessarily true.

We use categories such as *quantity* (our ability for measurement), *quality* (value judgment), *relation* (relation of subject to object, cause to effect), and *modality* (judgment that something is either possible or impossible) to integrate all of the differences we experience into a unified world.

> The objective validity of the categories as *a priori* Concepts rests, therefore, on the fact that, so far as the form of thought is concerned, through them alone does experience become possible. They relate of necessity and *a priori* to objects of experience, for the reason that only by means of them can any object whatsoever of experience be thought.[4]

Thus, the mind is not just "passive wax" that simply receives sensations from outside. The mind leaves its imprint on the way we understand the world. Recall that for Kant, it is not only mind that conforms to the world, but also the world that conforms to the mind.

The Self

When Hume searched for his self-identity, he found only bundles of impressions as hot and cold, pleasure and pain. But Kant held that these very experiences imply a unity of the self. Without such a unity among the many operations of the mind, we would have no knowledge of experience. The same self sees an object, remembers its characteristics, and projects the forms of space and time on it. Thus, a single self must exist or there could be no memory or knowledge. Kant called this experience of the self and its unity with objects *transcendental apperception*.

> There can be in us no modes of knowledge, no connection or unity of one mode of knowledge with another, without that unity of consciousness which precedes all data of intuitions, and by relation to which representation of objects is alone possible. This pure original unchangeable consciousness I shall name *transcendental apperception*. . . .
>
> This transcendental unity of apperception forms out of all possible appearances, which can stand alongside one another in one experience, a connection of all these representations according to laws. For this unity of consciousness would be impossible if the mind in knowledge of the manifold could not become conscious of the identity of function whereby it synthetically combines it in one knowledge. The original and necessary consciousness of the identity of the self is thus at the same time a consciousness of an equally necessary unity of the synthesis of all appearances according to concepts, that is, according to rules, which not only make them necessarily reproducible but also in so doing determine an object for their intuition, that is, the concept of something wherein they are necessarily interconnected. . . .
>
> The *a priori* conditions of a possible experience in general are at the same time conditions of the possibility of objects of experience. Now I maintain that the categories, above cited, are nothing but the conditions of thought in a possible experience, just as space and time are the conditions of intuition for that same experience. They are fundamental concepts by which we think objects in general for appearances, and have therefore *a priori* objective validity. This is exactly what we desired to prove. . . .[5]

Kant used the term *transcendental unity of apperception* to signify the self. It is transcendental because we do not experience the self directly, but a priori as a unity. However, because I see the self through the same "lenses" as everything else, I cannot know the self or other things in their essence apart from the way I perceive them.

Pause for Thought   Do you see the self through the colored glasses that you see everything else? Or can you "know thyself" as it truly is—as you truly are?

Kant reasoned we could not know anything except through our "lenses." He concluded that all objects of knowledge, including the self, are phenomenal. The true nature of "things-in-themselves" is altogether unknown and unknowable.

The Two Worlds

Kant answered Hume's skepticism by saying self-identity is a unitary experience—of the self and of other objects. Because of the mind's limitations, we can know the *phenomenal world* (the world of our experience), but not the *noumenal world* (the essence of things-in-themselves). The *noumenal world* (in German, *das Ding an sich*) is purely intelligible, nonsensual reality. It is beyond our comprehension, because the structure of the mind limits our understanding to the phenomenal world. We cannot know with certainty what the world is like "in itself." We can only know how the world appears to us (through our lenses).

Hume had reached the conclusion that we cannot move out of our own sense perceptions. Kant found that the mind uses its categories to organize the data of our sense experience, thus giving us knowledge beyond sense experience. But what we can know has clear limits set by the mind's glasses. When we ask about God or immortality, we are going beyond the ability of our mind, because the material of our knowledge comes to us through the senses. When we ask about God or immortality, reason cannot tell us, because it has no sensory material to process. There is no experience to use, because we have never experienced God or immortality.

The noumenal world of things-in-themselves is a reality beyond the capacity of our reason, and therefore unknowable to us. The noumenal world, however, is the source of the ideas that our minds bring to experience.

Pause for Thought

Kant calls noumena an "object of a non-sensible intuition." It is an intellectual intuition that we do not possess and cannot even comprehend. Compare his statement with Descartes' definition of *intellectual intuition*. Do you agree with Descartes that we can prove God by using the intellectual intuition? Or do you agree with Kant, that we cannot prove God, because we do not possess intellectual intuition?

Transcendental Ideas

Certain ideas—God, freedom, and immortality—lead us beyond sense experience. These ideas are transcendental because they do not correspond to any object of our experience. Kant said they are ideas of pure reason and not of intuition. When pure reason tries to synthesize all of our experience, it awakens such ideas. Although reason has no sense experience of transcendental ideas, it has the irresistible goal of constructing ideas such as God, freedom, and immortality. Unfortunately, these ideas are unattainable goals of pure reason.

Because we cannot locate transcendental ideas in the phenomenal world, they become only possibilities that Kant calls "ideas of reason" without demonstrable proof. Still, they are important ideas because they arise necessarily from the categories we bring to experience. Transcendental ideas are logically possible, not because we can demonstrate them, but because we can think them. Thus, for Kant, it is an attribute of human reason to ask about ideas as God, freedom, and immortality. He believed that thinking individuals need to ask big questions: Did the world have its beginning in time, or is the world eternal? Why am I here? What is our destiny? But reason cannot answer these questions with certainty. We can allege that the world has always existed, but can anything have always existed if there was never any beginning? We can say the world began in time and from nothing, but can something come from nothing? The dilemma arises, said Kant, because without sense experience to work on, reason cannot answer the questions with certainty.

Reason has two functions: theoretical and practical. Theoretical or pure reason is limited to the phenomenal world of our experience—the world of science. Science, as we know, cannot prove God, because God is not an object of our experience. Yet we have an idea of God. Because pure reason lacks the capacity to know this transcendental idea, it must come from another source. The idea of God, like the ideas of freedom and immortality, must arise from practical reason.

> Even the *assumption*—of *God, freedom,* and *immortality* is not permissible unless at the same time speculative reason be deprived of its pretensions to transcendent insight. For in order to arrive at such insight it must make use of principles which, in fact, extend only to objects of possible experience, and which, if also applied to what cannot be an object of experience, always really change this into an appearance, thus rendering all *practical extension* of pure reason impossible. I have therefore found it necessary to deny *knowledge*, in order to make room for *faith*.[6]

Because pure reason is bound to the phenomenal world, we cannot know God objectively. Therefore, Kant cannot use Thomas Aquinas's or Descartes' cosmological argument to prove the objective existence of God. But even if we cannot know transcendental ideas, we still think about God, freedom, and immortality. Because pure reason cannot experience these thoughts, the reason we use must have another aspect. Transcendental ideas must come from our practical reason, not through pure reason and experience, but through faith. Kant called faith in the immortal soul, God's existence, and free will *practical postulates*.

Pause for Thought   When we postulate something, we assume we cannot prove it. By a *practical postulate,* Kant meant something that we have to assume for the sake of *praxis* or practice—for our morality. It is, he said, a moral necessity to assume the existence of God.

Do you agree with Kant, or do you think we have other reasons to act morally?

Moral Philosophy

In *Critique of Pure Reason,* Kant liberated pure reason from the Empiricist's conclusion that mind is passive. In *Critique of Practical Reason,* Kant moved beyond the phenomenal world to the realm of the human will and the "moral law within." The term *practical reason* means that we think about our actions. Morality is not acting on whims or personal pleasures, but acting consciously with a sense of moral of duty and goodwill.

Kant wanted to know if certain moral principles must be followed by all human beings. He said we could not discover these principles by observing people's behavior, because such observation tells us only how people actually behave. He wanted to find out if certain principles tell us how people *should* behave.

Kant had always thought the difference between right and wrong was a matter of reason, not sentiment as Hume had said. In this Kant agreed with the Rationalists, who said the ability to distinguish between right and wrong is inherent in human reason. We know what is right or wrong, not because we have learned the distinction but because it is born in the mind. Kant believed everybody has practical reason—the intelligence that gives us the capacity to discern what is right or wrong. When we make moral judgments such as "We ought to tell the truth," we consider this judgment in principle the same as the scientific judgment "Every change must have a cause." We are all intelligent beings perceiving everything as having a causal relation, so we all have access to the same universal moral law.

When pure reason brings the category of causality to objects, it explains the universal relation of cause and effect. When practical reason brings the concept of "ought" to moral situations, it explains what the principle of our behavior should be. For instance, we know "We ought to tell the truth" always. Thus, the moral law has the same absolute validity as physical laws. It is as basic to our morality as certain statements—everything has a cause, and seven plus five is twelve—are as basic to our intelligence. Moral laws are universally and necessarily true.

The Empiricists had overlooked that all rational beings are aware of having a moral duty to act in certain ways. Moral duty involves an awareness of obligation. When I say it is my *duty* to tell the truth, I am saying all rational people are a priori aware they ought to tell the truth. When I say I ought not envy, covet, lie, steal, cheat, or be disloyal, I am speaking for all rational people. As scientific knowledge is a priori in the pure reason, moral knowledge is a priori in the practical reason. Thus, when I consider what I must do, I am considering what *all* rational people must do.

Goodwill   Because moral rules are similar to the rules of logic and geometry, they are the same for everyone. To act morally, we must be aware that the act is good, and then we must do it with goodwill. Kant did not look at morality as obeying society's rules, but as a duty based on goodwill.

> Nothing can possibly be conceived in the world, or even out of it, which can be called good, without qualification, except a Good Will. Intelligence, wit, judgment, and the other *talents* of the mind, however they may be named, or courage, resolution, perseverance, as qualities of temperament, are undoubtedly good and desirable in many respects; but these gifts of nature may also become extremely bad and mischievous if the will which is to make use of them, and which, therefore, constitutes what is called *character*, is not good. It is the same with the *gifts of fortune*. Power, riches, honour, even health, and the general well-being and contentment with one's condition which is called *happiness*, inspire pride, and often presumption, if there is not a good will to correct the influence of these on the mind, and with this also to rectify the whole principle of acting, and adapt it to its end. The sight of a being who is not adorned with a single feature of a pure and good will, enjoying unbroken prosperity, can never give pleasure to an impartial rational spectator. Thus a good will appears to constitute the indispensable condition even of being worthy of happiness.
> . . .
>
> A good will is good not because of what it performs or effects, not by its aptness for the attainment of some proposed end, but simply by virtue of the volition, that is, it is good in itself, and considered by itself is to be esteemed much higher than all that can be brought about by it in favour of any inclination, nay, even of the sum-total of all inclinations. Even if it should happen that, owing to special disfavour of fortune, or the niggardly provision of a step-motherly nature, this will should wholly lack power to accomplish its purpose, if with its greatest efforts it should yet achieve nothing, and there should remain only the good will (not, to be sure, a mere wish, but the summoning of all means in our power), then, like a jewel, it would still shine by its own light, as a thing which has its whole value in itself. Its usefulness or fruitlessness can neither add to nor take away anything from this value.[7]

Pause for Thought

"The goodwill is good not because of what it causes or accomplishes, not because of its usefulness in the attainment of some set purpose, but alone because of the willing." In other words, morality is a matter of motive or intent. Do you think we should base moral judgments, as Hume held, on sentiment, or, as Kant suggested, on motive?

For Kant, the will is good in the moral sense when it acts out of the proper motive without concern for the results. Our actions have three kinds of motives behind them: (1) inclination, (2) self-interest, and (3) duty.

When we act from inclination or self-interest, we are not acting from a sense of duty. Maybe it is my inclination to be kind to people so they will like me. Such motives differ morally from an act done out of duty to the moral law.

Pause for Thought   Imagine that you and I find billfolds with money inside. You return the billfold to its owner out of a sense of duty. I return the billfold to its owner to collect a reward. We have both performed the same act. Does it matter that our motives are different?

The seat of moral worth is in the will, and goodwill acts out of a sense of duty. For Kant, a moral action done from duty must avoid any influence of inclination.

> *Duty is the necessity of acting from respect for the law.* . . . It is only what is connected with my will as a principle, by no means as an effect—what does not subserve my inclination, but overpowers it, or at least in case of choice excludes it from its calculation—in other words, simply the law of itself, which can be an object of respect, and hence a command. Now an action done from duty must wholly exclude the influence of inclination, and with it every object of the will, so that nothing remains which can determine the will except objectively the *law*, and subjectively *pure respect* for this practical law, and consequently the maxim that I should follow this law even to the thwarting of all my inclinations. . . .
>
> The preeminent good which we call moral can therefore consist in nothing else than *the conception of law* in itself *which certainly is only possible in a rational being*, in so far as this conception, and not the expected effect, determines the will. This is a good which is already present in the person who acts accordingly, and we have not to wait for it to appear first in the result.[8]

Thus, the moral law is a principle that I must obey. I could have an inclination to be kind to people because I want them to like me. Or I might want to renege on a promise to pay a debt. If I follow these inclinations, then am I obeying the moral law? No, Kant would say. Duty implies that I have an obligation to the moral law. It is my duty to be kind to people and to keep my promises. Such actions have their seat in goodwill.

Hypothetical Imperatives   According to Kant, duty comes to us in the form of an *imperative*. It is my duty to keep my promises, therefore I *must* keep my promises. Moral imperatives hold in all situations. But not all imperatives are moral imperatives. We also face *hypothetical imperatives:* If we want to achieve a particular end, then we should act in a certain way. Hypothetical imperatives take a conditional form *if* this, *then* that.

For example, "If you want to be popular, then you must be pleasant to others" is a hypothetical imperative. "If you want to be healthy, then you must exercise!" These hypothetical imperatives are binding only as long as certain conditions apply. "You must exercise" is imperative only on the condition that you want to be healthy.

Among hypothetical imperatives are *technical imperatives* or rules of skill: "If you build a house, you must construct a solid foundation." *Prudential imperatives* or social skills also operate: "If you want your peers to accept you, wear a sweat-shirt and jeans." It is not absolutely necessary that you build a house or that your peers accept you. If conditions change, you could decide not to build a house. Hypothetical imperatives command only if we decide to do certain things. They are relative to the particular situation. Even our goal to be happy is a hypothetical imperative.

> There is *one* end . . . which we may with certainty assume that all actually *have* by a natural necessity, and this is *happiness.* . . . The imperative which refers to the choice of means to one's own happiness, i.e., the precept of prudence, is still always *hypothetical;* the action is not commanded absolutely but only as a means to another purpose. . . .[9]

The Categorical Imperative: First Formulation

For Kant, there are two types of imperatives: (1) hypothetical imperatives, which are conditional; and (2) moral imperatives, which are unconditional or categorical.

> Now all *imperatives* command either *hypothetically* or *categorically.* The former represent the practical necessity of a possible action as means to something else that is willed (or at least which one might possibly will). The categorical imperative would be that which represented an action as necessary of itself without reference to another end, i.e., as objectively necessary.
>
> Since every practical law represents a possible action as good, and on this account, for a subject who is practically determinable by reason as necessary, all imperatives are formulae determining an action which is necessary according to the principle of a will good in some respects. If not the action is good only as a means *to something else*, then the imperative is *hypothetical*; if it is conceived as good *in itself* and consequently as being necessarily the principle of a will which of itself conforms to reason, then it is *categorical.*[10]

A moral imperative is categorical because it includes all rational people and commands "an action as necessary of itself without reference to another end."

Such an action is objectively necessary because it applies to all situations. And it is imperative because it is a principle on which all rational humans should act. It is commanding and therefore authoritative. All people of goodwill should obey the categorical imperative without desiring any particular outcome. We should conform to the moral law simply because it is our duty.

> There remains nothing but the universal conformity of its actions to law in general, which alone is to serve the will as a principle, *i.e.,* I am never to act otherwise than *so that I could also will that my maxim should become a universal law.* Here, now, it is the simple conformity to law in general, without assuming any particular law applicable to certain actions, that serves the will as its principle, and must so serve it, if duty is not to be a vain delusion and a chimerical notion.[11]

Kant considered the categorical imperative a command universally binding on all rational people. It is the foundation of all moral laws. The first formulation of his categorical imperative is:

> *Act as if the maxim of thy action were to become through your will a universal law of nature.*

So, when I do something, I must make sure I want everybody else to do the same if they are in the same situation. Only then will I be acting according to the moral law within. And this applies to all people in all societies always. I should do my moral duty because it *is* my moral duty and for no other reason. If I look for results, such as my own happiness or the betterment of others, then I am acting hypothetically. Because moral laws are categorical, they do not give us any specific rules for a moral formula. We have to figure the laws out for ourselves. But Kant believed that all persons of goodwill arrive at similar conclusions.

Pause for Thought

Based on the categorical imperative, if you are about to tell a lie, you would have to ask yourself, "Would I *will* that lying become a universal law?" As a rational being what would your answer be? What if you said, "I always lie and that's the truth"? Could anyone ever trust anyone else if we will that even little white lies become a universal law?

Kant gave an example of making and breaking promises:

[A man] finds himself forced by necessity to borrow money. He knows that he will not be able to repay it, but sees also that nothing will be lent to him unless he promises stoutly to repay it in a definite time. He desires to make this promise, but he has still so much conscience as to ask himself: "Is it not unlawful and inconsistent with duty to get out of a difficulty in this way?" Suppose however that he resolves to do so: then the maxim of his action would be expressed thus: "When I think myself in want of money, I will borrow money and promise to repay it, although I know that I never can do so." Now this principle of self-love or of one's own advantage may perhaps be consistent with my whole future welfare; but the question now is, "Is it right?" I change then the suggestion of self-love into a universal law, and state the question thus: "How would it be if my maxim were a universal law?" Then I see at once that it could never hold as a universal law of nature, but would necessarily contradict itself. For supposing it to be a universal law that everyone when he thinks himself in a difficulty should be able to promise whatever he pleases, with the purpose of not keeping his promise, the promise itself would become impossible, as well as the end that one might have in view in it, since no one would consider that any-thing was promised to him, but would ridicule all such statements as vain pretenses.[12]

Categorical Imperative: Second Formulation

We want others to treat us as persons rather than objects. This is another reason why we know a priori that we should tell the truth, not break our promises, or steal. What makes us unique as humans is our reason. As rational beings, we wish others to treat us as ends in ourselves. When others treat us as a means to their end, or even tell us a lie, we become objects instead of persons.

That we all want others to treat us as persons led Kant to a second formula-tion of the categorical imperative:

> So act as to treat humanity, whether in thine own person or in that of any other, in every case as an end withal, never as means only.

Man and generally any rational being *exists* as an end in himself, *not merely as a means* to be arbitrarily used by this or that will, but in all his actions, whether they concern himself or other rational beings, must be always regarded at the same time as an end. All objects of the inclinations have only a conditional worth; for if the inclinations and the wants founded on them did not exist, then their object would be without value. But the inclinations themselves being sources of want are so far from having an absolute worth for which they should be desired, that, on the contrary, it must be the universal wish of every rational being to be wholly free from them. Thus the worth of any object which is *to be acquired* by our action is always conditional. . . . Rational beings . . . are called *persons,* because their very nature points them out as ends in themselves. . . . These, therefore, are not merely subjective ends whose existence has a worth *for us* as an effect of our action, but *objective ends,* that is things whose existence is an end in itself: an end moreover for which no other can be substituted, which they should subserve *merely* as means, for otherwise nothing whatever would possess *absolute worth;* but if all worth were conditioned and therefore contingent, then there would be no supreme practical principle of reason whatever.

If then there is a supreme practical principle or, in respect of the human will, a categorical imperative, it must be one which, being drawn from the conception of that which is necessarily an end for everyone because it is *an end in itself,* constitutes an *objective* principle of will, and can therefore serve as a universal practical law. The foundation of this principle is: *rational nature exists as an end in itself.*[13]

Pause for Thought

Do you think human beings have an intrinsic worth that is not contingent on anything else, such as their character, actions, or talent, but only because they are reasoning persons? Should there be additional guidelines, such as how moral we think people are or their actions toward other people?

Because human beings are ends in themselves, we should not exploit other people to our own advantage. And we should not exploit ourselves as a mere means to achieve something. Kant called the "practical imperative" of seeing human beings as intrinsically worthy the *principle of dignity.* If we want to be moral, then we must have a conscience, and we must have conquered ourselves. Only when we are acting out of respect for moral law, are we acting freely.

Pause for Thought

Has anyone ever treated you as a means to his or her own selfish end? Have you ever treated someone as a means to an end you desired? Compare your response to each situation.

Categorical Imperative: Third Formulation

Kant gave a third formulation of the categorical imperative:

> *Always so act that the will could regard itself at the same time as making universal law through its own maxim.*

By this, Kant meant that an autonomous will is free, independent, and the supreme principle of morality. Agreeing with Descartes' notion that humans are dual creatures, Kant divided humans into two parts: body and mind. As material creatures, we are at the mercy of causality's natural law. We do not decide what we perceive; perception comes to us through necessity and influences us whether we like it or not. But we are more than material creatures: We are also creatures of reason.

As material beings, we belong to the natural world and are subject to causal relations. As such, we have no free will. But as rational beings we have a part in what Kant called *das Ding an sich* (the noumenal world of things-in-themselves) independently of our sensory impressions. Only when we follow our practical reason, which enables us to make moral choices, do we exercise free will. When we conform to moral law, we are conforming to the autonomous will.

> The *will* is a kind of causality belonging to living beings in so far as they are rational, and *freedom* would be this property of such causality that it can be efficient, independently of foreign causes *determining* it; just as *physical necessity* is the property that the causality of all irrational beings has of being determined to activity by the influence of foreign causes.[14]

Kant considered the autonomous will so important that even the angels would be inferior to us if they lacked it:

> With all his failings, man is still
> Better than angels void of will.

Pause for Thought   Does something within you tell you not to be cruel to others, or lie, or steal—even if it's against your own desires or interests? When you choose to act morally, do you feel a certain freedom?

Kant's categorical imperatives include the universality of: (1) the moral law (based on duty), (2) the intrinsic worth of all rational persons (as ends in themselves), and (3) the autonomy of the will (freedom to make choices). We know these three not as demonstrative proofs, but a priori through practical reason.

Freedom

> Now I affirm that we must attribute to every rational being which has a will that it has also the idea of freedom and acts entirely under this idea. For in such a being we conceive a reason that is practical, that is, has causality in reference to its objects. Now we cannot possibly conceive a reason consciously receiving a bias from any other quarter with respect to its judgements, for then the subject would ascribe the determination of its judgement not to its own reason, but to an impulse. It must regard itself as the author of its principles independent of foreign influences. Consequently

as practical reason or as the will of a rational being it must regard itself as free. . . . This idea must therefore in a practical point of view be ascribed to every rational being.[15]

We cannot prove we have free will, but Kant said that freedom and morality are so closely connected "that one might define practical freedom as independence of the will of anything but the moral law alone." Therefore, our duty to moral law depends entirely on our freedom to make moral choices.

Immortality   Because we must be free before we make moral choices, we must assume our own immortality. Kant based his belief in immortality on his conception of *summum bonum*—the supreme good (virtue)—and the *perfect good* (virtue and happiness). We strive for the supreme good, but we also look for happiness. By itself, the supreme good does not always bring happiness, because when we follow the moral law, we do what is right. We obey the moral law as a duty, not to make ourselves happy. Yet we also seek happiness. Kant suggested that we think of the supreme good as including both virtue and happiness.

> It has been shown in the Analytic that *virtue* as worthiness to be happy is the *supreme condition* of all that can appear to us desirable, and consequently of all our pursuit of happiness, and is therefore the *supreme* good. But it does not follow that it is the whole and perfect good as the object of the desires of rational finite beings; for this requires happiness also. . . . For to need happiness, to deserve it, and yet at the same time not to participate in it, cannot be consistent with the perfect volition of a rational being. . . . The distribution of happiness in exact proportion to morality (which is the worth of the person, and his worthiness to be happy) constitutes the *summum bonum* of a possible world; hence this *summum bonum* expresses the whole, the perfect good, in which, however, virtue as the condition is always the supreme good. . . .[16]

Kant agreed with Hume that nothing we know about the physical world suggests that virtue is the cause of happiness. Our experience shows no necessary connection between them. But at this point, Kant left Hume. If we limit human experience to the phenomenal world, then we can never achieve the supreme good, so we must reach beyond the limits of sense experience. As reasoning human beings, we have a responsibility to reach the *summum bonum*. Because "ought implies must," we can realize our responsibility.

We must strive for the complete harmony of our will and feeling with the moral law. Kant called this harmonious union with the moral law *holiness*. However, no rational being of the phenomenal world is capable of perfection at any moment of its existence. Even so, our reason impels us to strive for the perfect good—the *union of virtue and happiness*.

Striving for the perfect good implies an "endless progress" of the same rational being. For Kant, this endless progress of each human means the soul is immortal.

> Now, this endless progress is only possible on the supposition of an *endless* duration of the *existence* and personality of the same rational being (which is called the *immortality of the soul*). The *summum bonum*, then, practically is only possible on the supposition of the immortality of the soul; consequently this immortality, being inseparably connected with the moral law, is a postulate of pure practical reason by which I mean a *theoretical* proposition, not demonstrable as such, but which is an inseparable result of an unconditional *a priori practical* law.[17]

In the moral person, the will aspires to become perfect and holy. Perfect happiness results from holiness, "the perfect accordance of the will with moral law." Kant has said that perfection in the present world is impossible, so there must be a future world to perfect ourselves. This means immortality is necessary.

God   Though we try to attain both happiness and virtue, we know we cannot do it by ourselves. None of us is the author of the world, or capable of ordering nature to produce a necessary connection between virtue and happiness. Yet, reasoned Kant, from our idea of the *summum bonum,* we know that in a moral universe, virtue and happiness must go together. Therefore, we must assume the existence of God:

> Therefore, the *summum bonum* is possible in the world only on the supposition of a Supreme Being having a causality corresponding to moral character. Now a being that is capable of acting on the conception of laws is an *intelligence* (a rational being), and the causality of such a being according to this conception of laws is his *will*; therefore the supreme cause of nature, which must be presupposed as a condition of the *summum bonum* is a being which is the cause of nature by *intelligence* and *will,* consequently its author, that is God. . . . Now it was seen to be a duty for us to promote the *summum bonum*; consequently it is not merely allowable, but it is a necessity connected with duty as a requisite, that we should presuppose the possibility of this *summum bonum*; and as this is possible only on condition of the existence of God, it inseparably connects the supposition of this with duty; that is, it is morally necessary to assume the existence of God.[18]

Pause for Thought   Only a Supreme Being can guarantee that we achieve the *summum bonum*. Therefore, "it is morally necessary to assume the Existence of

God." Compare Kant's argument for God's existence with Descartes' cosmological argument. Which argument do you prefer?

Morality and Religion   Kant did not say there could be no morality without religion. He said we can perform our moral duty "for duty's sake" out of respect for moral law. But Kant did believe that moral law leads to religion:

> In this manner, the moral laws lead through the conception of the *summum bonum* as the object and final end of pure practical reason to *religion*, that is, to the *recognition of all duties as divine commands, not as sanctions, that is to say, arbitrary ordinances of a foreign will and contingent in themselves*, but as essential *laws* of every free will in itself, which, nevertheless, must be regarded as commands of the Supreme Being, because it is only from a morally perfect (holy and good) and at the same time all-powerful will, and consequently only through harmony with this will, that we can hope to attain the *summum bonum* which the moral law makes it our duty to take as the object of our endeavours.[19]

Thus, Kant's theology consists of moral laws as divine commands. But the duality of human nature presents a problem in following the divine commands. According to moral law, our duty is to subordinate any sensuous impulses to the moral law. Unfortunately, though our moral nature strives for perfection, our sensuous nature inclines toward evil. We are then conscious of the moral law but sometimes turn away from it. But evil is not necessary. If it were, then we would have no responsibility for it.

Moral law, said Kant, commands us to make ourselves worthy of happiness, but it does not command us to make ourselves happy. We can only arrive at the *summum bonum,* however, through the agency of a God whose holy will desires that His creatures should be worthy of happiness.

> When morality has been completely expounded (which merely imposes duties instead of providing rules for selfish desires), then first, after the moral desire to promote the *summum bonum* (to bring the kingdom of God to us) has been awakened, a desire founded on a law, and which could not previously arise in any selfish mind, and when for the behoof of this desire the step to religion has been taken, then this ethical doctrine may be also called a doctrine of happiness because the *hope* of happiness first begins with religion only.[20]

Because the harmony between virtue and happiness can take place only through divine agency, "morality leads inevitably to religion." Kant was not speaking of organized religion, but of morality. Everything that we do, apart from morality, that we believe we are capable of doing to please God is mere "religious delusion and spurious worship of God." The Kingdom of God is within us. God manifesting in our moral lives is our duty toward perfection. Kant emphasized that we should always see duty as a divine command.

Pause for Thought   Think of your own life. Is your happiness usually proportionate to your moral virtue?

On Women

In *Observations on the Feeling of the Beautiful and the Sublime* (1764), Kant gave his idea of women and their relation to beauty and sublimity. He believed that both men and women in marriage form a "single moral person." The noble male is rational and educated. The beautiful female is sensuous and tasteful. The main criterion of femininity is a charm that Kant saw as "magic" that women exert on men.

> Women have a strong inborn feeling for all that is beautiful, elegant, and decorated. Even in childhood they like to be dressed up, and take pleasure when they are adorned. They are cleanly and very delicate in respect to all that provokes disgust. They love pleasantry and can be entertained by trivialities if only these are merry and laughing. . . .
>
> The fair sex has just as much understanding as the male, but it is a *beautiful understanding*, whereas ours should be a *deep understanding*, an expression that signifies identity with the sublime. . . .
>
> Laborious learning or painful pondering, even if a woman should greatly succeed in it, destroy the merits that are proper to her sex, and because of their rarity they can make of her an object of cold admiration; but at the same time they will weaken the charms with which she exercises her great power over the other sex. A woman who has a head full of Greek, like Mme Dacier, or carries on fundamental controversies about mechanics, like the Marquise de Chatelet, might as well even have a beard. . . . A woman therefore will learn no geometry; of the principle of sufficient reason or the monads she will know only so much as is needed to perceive the salt in a satire which the insipid grubs of our sex have censured. . . . In history they will not fill their heads with battles, nor in geography with fortresses, for it becomes them just as little to reek of gunpowder as it does the males to reek of musk. . . .
>
> Her philosophy is not to reason, but to sense. . . . Similarly, they will need to know nothing more of the cosmos than is necessary to make the appearance of the heavens on a beautiful evening as stimulating sight to them. . . .
>
> I hardly believe that the fair sex is capable of principles, and I hope by that not to offend, for these are also extremely rare in the male. . . .

> A man must never tell his wife if he risks a part of his fortune on behalf of a friend. Why should he fetter her merry talkativeness by burdening her mind with a weighty secret whose keeping lies solely upon him. . . . A man must never weep other than magnanimous tears. . . .[21]

Pause for Thought   Do Kant's ideas on women still linger in our society today? Is this the kind of relationship with the opposite sex you prefer?

Summary

As a result of Continental Rationalism and British Empiricism, philosophy experienced a split down the middle. The Rationalists had said that we could know absolute truth through reason. They thought that, by reason alone, we could know God. The Empiricists claimed that all knowledge comes from sense experience. The mind, said the Empiricists, takes on the shape of the world it experiences.

In his genius, Kant mended these seemingly irreconcilable differences. He argued that the mind does not conform to the world, as the Empiricists claimed; rather, the external world conforms to the mind. He agreed with the Empiricists that our knowledge begins with experience, but he also agreed with the Rationalists that the human reason determines how we perceive the world.

By showing that the mind has powers of its own, Kant proved that the laws of science, such as cause and effect, are valid and demonstrable truths. Our knowledge of cause and effect is inherent in reason. Reason "can perceive nothing, the senses can think nothing. Knowledge arises only from this united action."

We know the reality of the phenomenal world only as our reason organizes it. But we cannot know the noumenal world of things-in-themselves, because our reason has no sense experience to organize. We can never know what the world is like in itself. We can only know how it appears to us. However, the noumenal world is the source of the ideas that our minds bring to experience.

Kant called ideas of the noumenal world *transcendental ideas*. Though we cannot demonstrate them, we can think them. Therefore, it is an attribute of human reason to ask about such ideas as God, freedom, and immortality.

Kant distinguished between theoretical reason (pure reason) and practical reason. Theoretical reason is confined to the phenomenal world; practical reason moves beyond the phenomenal world to the noumenal world—the realm of morality. Practical reason helps us deal with the moral freedom provided by free will.

Because moral rules are similar to the rules of logic and geometry, they are the same for everyone. To act morally, we must be aware that the act is good, and then do it with goodwill. The seat of the moral worth is in the will, and goodwill acts out of a sense of duty rather than look to results.

Moral obligations are not hypothetical and dependent on individual circumstances; they are categorical and universally binding on all rational beings. Kant characterized moral duty in his formulation of the *categorical imperative*. *Act as if the maxim of your action were to become, through your will, a universal law of nature.* Another categorical imperative is to treat ourselves and all others as ends in themselves and never as means only.

Though reason impels us to strive for the perfect good (the union of virtue and happiness), it is incapable of reaching *summum bonum,* the perfect good. We can only arrive at it through the agency of God. Thus, our duty is to act morally and see our moral duty as a divine command.

Connections

Kant's philosophy is one of the most important turning points in the history of Western thought. As we have seen, he made a new analysis of the nature of human knowledge that showed its limitations to the phenomenal world. He argued that metaphysics is impossible; that is, we can think about the noumenal world, but we can have no knowledge of the noumenal world of things-in-themselves. This discovery has placed Kant among the great philosophers of the Western world. Still, some philosophers questioned Kant's conclusions. Georg Wilhelm Friedrich Hegel was one of them.

In the next chapter we will consider Hegel's general proposition that "what is rational is real and what is real is rational." He argued in opposition to Kant that if we can think about the noumenal world, then we can know the noumenal world. The intellect, he said, is not limited to things as they appear, and given that the universe is rational, philosophers could reach agreement about the truth.

Study Questions

1. In general, how did Kant heal the split between Rationalism and Empiricism?

2. Why does Kant say space and time are a priori forms of intuition?

3. Why does Kant think that mathematical propositions are both a priori and synthetic?

4. What does Kant mean: "Thoughts without content are empty, intuitions without concepts are blind"?

5. Explain the differences between the phenomenal world and the noumenal world.

6. Why did Kant feel the necessity to posit the existence of the noumenal world?

7. Compare Kant's answer to self-identity to Hume's bundle of perceptions theory.

8. What is practical reason?

9. What is goodwill?

10. Why does Kant think morality is a matter of motive and not consequence?

11. What is the difference between the hypothetical imperative and the categorical imperative?

12. What is the categorical imperative? Give examples.

13. What does Kant mean by "moral duty"?

14. Explain the relationship between duty and goodwill in Kant's moral philosophy.

15. Why does Kant think the ideas of God, freedom, and immortality are necessary ideas for reasoning beings?

16. Why does Kant claim that the only thing good in itself is goodwill?

17. Why does Kant posit the necessity of faith?

18. What is moral autonomy and what is its relationship to free will?

Notes

1. Immanuel Kant, *Critique of Pure Reason* (trans. by N. Kemp Smith), pp. xii–xviii. London: Macmillan, 1929. Reprinted with permission of Macmillan Press, Ltd.

2. Ibid., pp. 14–16.

3. Ibid., p. 52.

4. Ibid., p. 94.

5. Ibid., p. 164.

6. Ibid., p. xxx.

7. Immanuel Kant, *Fundamental Principles of the Metaphysics of Morals* (trans. by T. K. Abbott), Sec. 1, pp. 9–10. London: Longmans & Green, 1927.

8. Ibid., Sec. 1, pp. 16–17.

9. Ibid., Sec. 2, pp. 32–33.

10. Ibid., Sec 2. p. 31.

11. Ibid., Sec. 1, p. 18.

12. Ibid., Sec. 2, p. 36.

13. Ibid., Sec. 2, pp. 46–47.

14. Ibid., Sec. 3, p. 62.

15. Ibid., Sec. 3 p. 65.

16. Immanuel Kant, *Critique of Practical Reason* (trans. by T. K. Abbott), Bk. II, Ch. 2, Sec. 1, p. 206. London: Longmans & Green, 1927.

17. Ibid., Sec. 4, pp. 218–219.

18. Ibid., Sec. 5, pp. 220–222.

19. Ibid., Sec. 5, p. 226.

20. Ibid., Sec. 5, p. 227.

21. Immanuel Kant, *Observations on the Feeling of the Beautiful and Sublime* (trans. by John T. Goldthwait), Sec. 3. Berkeley: University of California Press, 1960.

CHAPTER TEN

Idealism and Materialism: Hegel and Marx

Throughout the history of philosophy, those who have searched for truth have sought to give an account of the universe and our place in it. Philosophers such as Parmenides, Plato, and Descartes each concluded that truth is absolute, eternal, and unchanging. The universe is orderly and rational. By using our highest faculties—our reason and our intuition—we can know our place in the scheme of things.

The Sophists, Skeptics, and British Empiricists are examples of philosophers who have been skeptical of our ability to know the universe through speculation. They considered our knowledge limited to scientific findings based on empirical observation. British Empiricist David Hume argued that even science could not give us knowledge of the phenomenal world we experience. Immanuel Kant, as we recently observed, reconciled these two opposing epistemologies—Rationalism and Empiricism—but at the expense of metaphysics. He argued for limitations on our ability to know the absolute truth. He believed there are "things-in-themselves," but we cannot know them. Our knowledge is limited to the phenomenal world that we experience. He believed there is eternal truth that is reality, but we cannot know it. The human intellect can know things only as they appear in the phenomenal world. Human nature, however, yearns to know the noumenal world of God, freedom, and immortality, so we must act on these ideals.

Like all philosophers who followed Kant, Georg Wilhelm Friedrich Hegel was deeply influenced by him. Still, he sought to go a step further than Kant by showing the connection between epistemology and metaphysics. In this chapter we shall examine how Hegel took Kant's idea—that the mind imposes ideas on experience—to its ultimate conclusion. Hegel said, if these ideas of the noumenal world exist, then we *can* know them. Whatever exists is knowable. Kant was mistaken when he said the noumenal world exists but that we cannot know it. What makes nature and the noumenal world knowable is that its essence is *Spirit* (which also is translated as *Mind*). Spirit, said Hegel, is the absolute (God)—the total reality.

In this chapter, we also will study the ideas of Karl Marx, who opposed Hegel. Marx believed that no transcendent realm exists beyond the world we experience. Ideas of God and immortality are only by-products of social forces and do not exist as reality. Although Marx rejected the notion of *Absolute Spirit,* he developed Hegel's insights about the different types of consciousness. From Hegel, he accepted the idea of one reality, the connection between consciousness and the culture of a particular epoch, and that history is a process of development and change.

Idealism: G. W. F. Hegel

Hegel's Life

Georg Wilhelm Friedrich Hegel (1770–1831) was born in Stuttgart in southern Germany. His father was a minor government official and his mother a "loving" housewife. Although the family, including his brother and sister, was poor, its members were close and affectionate. Hegel was born in an era of German intellectual giants. He was born the same year as composer Ludwig van Beethoven. Johann Wolfgang Von Goethe, who would write the masterpiece *Faust,* was twenty years old, and Kant was forty-six.

At age eighteen, Hegel received a scholarship to Tübingen University, where he studied theology. While there, he read Plato and Aristotle, considering them the roots of all Western philosophy. He became friends with poet Friedrich Hölderlin and philosopher Friedrich Wilhelm Joseph von Schelling and joined in discussions about issues arising from the French Revolution. As a student, he gave no sign of a budding or brilliant philosophical career. In fact, when he received his diploma from Tübingen, his theology professors rated his work only as adequate, and his philosophy professors as inadequate.

After graduating from the university, Hegel became interested in the relationship between theology and philosophy and began writing essays on his new insights. For the next seven years, he continued to write while tutoring for wealthy families in Frankfurt and Bern, Switzerland. In one of his essays, he compared the ethics of Socrates and Jesus, finding Socrates' moral teachings superior to those of the New Testament.

In 1799, Hegel's father died, leaving him enough money to quit tutoring. He joined his friend Schelling at the University of Jena where he became an unsalaried lecturer and helped Schelling edit a philosophy journal. Schelling and Johann Gottlieb Fichte were influential spokesmen in German idealism when Hegel published his first work, *Difference Between the Philosophical Systems of Fichte and Schelling*. Also at Jena, he wrote his first major work, *The Phenomenology of Mind* (1807). Its critique of Schelling's ideas ended their friendship. The day after Hegel finished *The Phenomenology of Mind*, Napoleon attacked Jena closing the university.

His inheritance gone, Hegel worked for a short time as a newspaper editor and then as rector of a Gymnasium (or high school) in Nuremberg. While there, he met and married Marie von Tucher, with whom he had two sons. His second major work, *Science and Logic* (1812–1816), brought invitations to teach from several universities. In 1816, he joined the faculty at Heidelberg, where he wrote another major book, *Encyclopedia of the Philosophical Sciences in Outline* (1817).

In 1818, Hegel accepted a position at the University of Berlin. There he published his *Philosophy of Right* (1821) and became famous throughout Europe. He remained at the University of Berlin until he died of cholera in 1831. Various essays and lectures—including *Philosophy of History, Aesthetics, Philosophy of Religion,* and *History of Philosophy*—were published posthumously.

Because of the complexity and difficulty of Hegel's writings, there never has been complete agreement on his views. For example, he considered his 750-page work *The Phenomenology of Mind* as a mere introduction to his philosophical system. Here he set out the whole foundation of his system by showing that Absolute Spirit (or Mind) is a rational and dynamic process: *What is real is rational, and what is rational is real.* He viewed absolute knowledge as a mode of spiritual life having its roots in experience.

Reality

Kant had reconciled the epistemologies of Continental Rationalism and British Empiricism, but in doing so, he abandoned metaphysics by denying that humans could have any clear cognition of nature's innermost secrets. For example, Kant said, we experience the existence of the oak tree, but not its essence, the "tree-in-itself." We can never know anything about the thing-in-itself because the categories of the mind apply only to the phenomenal world. To say that we can think about the noumenal world but never know it means we cannot have knowledge about ultimate reality.

Hegel wanted to go farther than Kant by showing the connection between epistemology and metaphysics. For Hegel, the world reaches its ultimate reality in the Absolute Spirit. The human mind, being rational, can know ultimate reality, because all things in existence are related to it. He argued that if we know there is an unknowable world, then it is *not* unknowable; it is "known," hence all of reality is rational. This led Hegel to his most famous statement: "What is real is rational, and what is rational is real."

Plato, Descartes, Spinoza, and other philosophers also saw reality as rational. Unlike Plato, who made a distinction between the physical world as appearance and the world of Forms as reality, Hegel argued that appearance *is* reality. For him, everything is consciousness and thus everything is in relation to everything else. When we view objects as separate from each other, we do not understand the **dialectic process** that will lead us to unity in the Absolute Spirit. He did not mean the Absolute Spirit unifies objects that were once separate. Nor did he believe the ancient philosopher Parmenides and Spinoza much later, who both said that the One is a single substance with attributes. For Hegel, the Absolute Spirit is an intricate process in which all objects are related. The Absolute Spirit is the world.

Hegel was not speaking here of eternal truths or timeless Forms. History, he said, is the only fixed point to which philosophy can hold. History is the Absolute Spirit *in process*. It is much like a running river. Everything that happens in the water depends on eddies and falls in the water upstream. It also depends on our vantage point—from the trees and rocks where we observe it. As reality in process, Absolute Spirit eventually comes to know itself through the human mind. Our thoughts, like the river, are in a constant state of change—correct for a period in history, but not eternally true. Truth is the process.

Absolute Spirit expresses itself objectively in Nature before it becomes conscious of itself in human beings. Through our subjective consciousness, it returns to itself. Because the Absolute Spirit first becomes conscious of itself in the individual, Hegel called this *subjective spirit*. It is *objective spirit* when it reaches a higher consciousness in the family, civil society, and the state. The objective spirit appears in interaction between people.

When Hegel said "The rational is real, and the real is rational, " he was saying Absolute Spirit expresses itself through nature, humans, and everything in the world. The three main parts of Hegel's philosophy give us a clue to the process. In *Logic,* Hegel examines the process by which we deduce the categories that describe the Absolute from our experiences of the actual. In *Philosophy of Nature,* the antithesis to the rational Idea (thesis), he investigates nature as a rational structure and pattern in all of reality. In *Philosophy of Mind,* he argues that the synthesis is Absolute Spirit, and that the Absolute Spirit manifests itself in the minds of individuals, social institutions, civil society, the state, and in art, religion, and philosophy.

Hegel called his triadic method the *dialectic process* of *thesis, antithesis,* and *synthesis*. We can say that Descartes' Rationalism was a thesis, and Hume's

Empiricism the antithesis. Kant resolved the tension between the thesis and antithesis by his synthesis. The synthesis then becomes the point of departure for a new thesis.

Pause for Thought

Have you ever had a discussion with a person of the opposite political party, and a tension developed between your views? You each thought the other person was wrong. Would it have been possible to resolve the tension with a synthesis showing that both of you were partly right and partly wrong?

Logic

For Hegel, logic is a universal concept that forms and precedes the natural world. Absolute Spirit is the ultimate form, the Ideal, or what Hegel would call Absolute Idealism.

The dialectical system in his *Logic* is *being*, *nothing* (or *nonbeing*), and *becoming*. Because being and nothing are empty abstractions, he identified being with nothing. If I reflect on the concept of being, then I also must introduce the opposite concept—nothing. We cannot reflect on our existence without realizing that we will not always exist. Hegel synthesized the tension between being and nothing in his concept of becoming. If something is in the process of becoming, then it is both being and not being.

Hegel agreed with Heraclitus that everything is always in a state of change, therefore becoming is the basis of all existence. All action results from this process of becoming, and the mind is part of this process. If there is no process, then there is nothing or nonbeing. Hegel's equation is *being = nothing* (or *nonbeing*), and *being plus nothing = becoming* (existence).

> PURE BEING makes the beginning: because it is on one hand pure thought, and on the other immediacy itself, simple and indeterminate; and the first beginning cannot be mediated by anything, or be further determined. . . .
>
> When thinking is to begin, we have nothing but thought in its merest indeterminateness: for we cannot determine unless there is both one and another; and in the beginning there is yet no other. The indeterminate, as we here have it, is the blank we begin with, not a featurelessness reached by abstraction, not the elimination of all character, but the original featurelessness which precedes all definite character and is the very first of all. And this we call Being. It is not to be felt, or perceived by sense, or pictured in imagination: it is only and merely thought, and as such it forms the beginning. Essence also is indeterminate, but in another sense: it has traversed the

process of mediation and contains implicit the determination it has absorbed. . . .

But this mere Being, as it is mere abstraction, is therefore the absolutely negative: which, in a similarly immediate aspect, is just NOTHING. . . .

Nothing, if it be thus immediate and equal to itself, is also conversely the same as Being is. The truth of Being and of Nothing is accordingly the unity of the two: and this unity is BECOMING.

The proposition that Being and Nothing is the same seems so paradoxical to the imagination or understanding, that it is perhaps taken for a joke. And indeed it is one of the hardest things thought expects itself to do: for Being and Nothing exhibit the fundamental contrast in all its immediacy, —that is, without the one term being invested with any attribute which would involve its connexion with the other. This attribute however, as the above paragraph points out, is implicit in them—the attribute which is just the same in both. . . . It is as correct however to say that Being and Nothing are altogether different, as to assert their unity. The one is *not* what the other is. But since the distinction has not at this point assumed definite shape (Being and Nothing are still the immediate), it is, in the way that they have it, something unutterable, which we merely *mean*. . . .

It may perhaps be said that nobody can form a notion of the unity of Being and Nought. . . . To say that we have no such conception can only mean, that in none of these images do we recognise the notion in question, and that we are not aware that they exemplify it. The readiest example of it is Becoming. Every one has a mental idea of Becoming, and will even allow that it is *one* idea: he will further allow that, when it is analysed, it involves the attribute of Being, and also what is the very reverse of Being, VIZ nothing: and that these two attributes lie undivided in the one idea: so that Becoming is the unity of Being and Nothing. . . .[1]

Thus, Hegel argued that the concept of being is empty. Therefore, it must be nonbeing or nothing, the antithesis of being. The movement of the mind from being to nothing produces becoming, which is "the unity of Being and Nothing," and therefore its synthesis.

The second part of *Logic* is *essence*. Here, Hegel gave us pairs of related categories such as essence and existence, force and expression, cause and effect, action and reaction. He called these *categories of reflection* because they go beneath the surface of our immediate experience. Essence is not directly present to us, but mediated by what is directly present. Being is immediate, and essence is mediate.

At the essence level, we can relate different categories such as cause and effect. The cause, for example, passes into its opposite—the effect—which we conceive as something different from the cause. Similarly, the effect is an effect by its relation to the cause. At the essence stage, we can distinguish between appearance and reality and ask questions about what is real and what is appearance.

If a thesis is to have any meaning, said Hegel, it must have an antithesis. We understand pain because we can relate to its opposite, pleasure. A thesis always carries its own antithesis. If we assume any idea to be true, then we will meet its opposite—its contradiction. If we relate the idea to its opposite, then we will discover a new truth about them that transcends their previous meanings. Hegel called this discovery *notion,* the third part of his *Logic.*

At the essence stage, Hegel distinguished between cause and effect. When we see that the effect is identical with its cause, and different from it, then essence becomes notion. Notion becomes the synthesis on an even higher plane of subjectivity and objectivity.

Hegel called *subjectivity* a category because we can have a thought about an object, make a judgment about it, and then reason out logical conclusions. Within subjectivity lies its opposite—*objectivity.* Subjectivity contains the idea of objectivity. If I am a subjective self, then there must be an objective "not-self" within the subjective self. Subjectivity consists of psychological thought. Objectivity is what I see in anything external to me. The synthesis of the subjective and the objective is their unity in the Absolute Spirit.

Absolute Spirit

Within the Absolute Spirit, everything is becoming (changing). This leads to conflict and a new thesis, antithesis, and synthesis. Also, all is permanent within the Absolute Spirit; it forms an interrelated, logical whole. Absolute Spirit is "the process of its own becoming, the circle which presupposes its end as its purpose and has its end as its beginning." Hegel's concept of the Absolute Spirit is similar to Plato's highest principle, the Form of the Good, except dynamic in its evolutionary development.

The Absolute Spirit unfolds in the biological, social, and historical evolution of the world. With its aspects of freedom and self-consciousness, the Absolute Spirit develops and expands in its knowledge. Like the river that becomes broader as it nears the sea, history is the story of the Absolute Spirit evolving to greater consciousness of itself.

For Hegel, as much as for Plato, the Absolute Spirit is creative because the rational is the real. As mechanical necessity is the nature of matter, freedom is the essence of reason. Hegel's Absolute Spirit takes three forms: idea, nature, spirit. Each triad contains its own triadic stages.

Philosophy of Nature

For Hegel, Nature is not other than Absolute Spirit, it is Absolute Spirit (idea) in external form. Nature is the world of sense experience. It is the antithesis of the rational idea (logic), but it is also united with it. Nature is the Absolute Spirit in forms, as physical objects, that we experience with our senses.

For Hegel, "Nature is a system of stages, of which one proceeds necessarily from the other." He analyzed nature through the dialectic process, starting with the laws of mechanics, physics, and *organics* to the vegetable and animal world. Internal activity (subjectivity) appears in the animal world, and this is the beginning of synthesis in the spirit.

Through Hegel's dialectic, we have moved from the rational logical idea (thesis) to nonrational nature (antithesis) and finally to spirit (synthesis). Because nature must follow natural laws, the Absolute Spirit cannot fully express itself; therefore, nature is unconscious of its divinity. This means a dialectic opposition between spirit and nature, between freedom and necessity.

Philosophy of Spirit

The spirit is a synthesis of rational idea and nonrational nature. The consciousness that manifested itself in logic and nature now returns to itself. It does this through the triadic dialectic of *subjective spirit* (thesis), *objective spirit* (antithesis), and ab*solute spirit* (synthesis). Hegel divided these triads into a series of subtriads that proceed to his social and political philosophy, as well as his ethics, philosophy of history, art, and religion.

Subjective Spirit (Mind)   The subjective spirit or mind refers to the inner workings of the human mind. It has three characteristics. First, the soul exists in its elementary stage for conscious activity—the relationship of the mind to the body. The soul, said Hegel, is a sensitive, feeling being; as a being, it can express itself to the world through its body. The hand "as the absolute tool," the mouth, and weeping and laughing allow humans to externalize their thoughts and feelings. In addition, the world affects the internal human body. When our organs react to stimuli in the light of our own experience, then the mind has evolved beyond the animal level and reached the stage of consciousness.

Second, the individual is conscious of personal feelings and desires that are like and unlike the feelings and desires of others. Now consciousness can relate, reflect, understand, and perceive. At this stage of personality, consciousness becomes self-conscious by encountering another consciousness from which it seeks recognition. Self-consciousness as desire finds that it cannot simply destroy another consciousness as it could a physical object and satisfy its desires. Thus arises a conflict. Each person can become aware that the other person is exactly that—another person. "They *recognize* themselves as *mutually recognizing* one another." There is simultaneously an antithesis and mutual need between them, and they also recognize that one solution to this conflict is to destroy the other as another person so that "each seeks the death of the other." However, as Hegel pointed out, if the struggle was the literal destruction of the other as a person, then there would be nothing left but a corpse incapable of personal recognition or relationship. At this point, a person "learns that life is as essential to it" as satisfying personal desires, and backs down from the struggle. The person who backs down from the struggle prefers life to independence and becomes subject to the other's will.

The person who does not back down, said Hegel, is the independent consciousness whose "essential nature is to be for itself." The person who backs down depends on the person who does not back down. The result of such a relationship is the "lord and the bondsman" (master and slave). The master prefers independence to life itself and now controls the actions of the dependent slave who has less will. The master now gets the recognition originally desired from the slave who must treat him as lord. The slave gets no recognition at all.

But, said Hegel, such a one-sided relationship is unstable and the dialectic begins to work. The master ironically becomes dependent on the know-how and labor of the bondsman, thus the bondsman becomes other than a slave. The bondsman learns to master the environment by his labors and realizes a kind of recognition and satisfaction. This leads to acquiring a mind of his own, yet he still remains a bondsman subject to an alien will. These extremes of superior and inferior are so frustrating and miserable that they lead to new stages of consciousness—*stoicism, skepticism,* and the *unhappy consciousness.*

In stoicism, the frustrations, limitations, and misery of lord and bondsman drive self-consciousness to an indifference of external events. The aim of stoicism is for people to be free by controlling their attitude, not trying to control events over which they have no control. In the stage of stoicism, the person becomes free through rational thinking. Yet Hegel pointed out that such freedom is empty, exactly because it is cut off from external reality. The highest values are truth and goodness consisting in "reasonableness." Unfortunately, because stoicism has no connection with the world, it becomes alienated from its own ideals.

Emerging from stoicism is the stage of skepticism. Here a person encounters him- or herself as "a real negativity." Hegel compared this stage to the "squabbling of self-willed children" who go back and forth from one idea to another in bewilderment and end by contradicting themselves and each other. A kind of freedom of thought exists at this stage, but it is always negative because there are no stable ideas and values.

From skepticism, said Hegel, arises the stage of unhappy consciousness, which has internalized the struggle for supremacy of master and slave. Because consciousness wars with itself, "agony is inescapable." Unhappiness will always be the outcome in the quest for independence so long as the person assumes a separation between the subject and the external reality. To overcome this assumption, it is imperative for the individual to evolve from personal self-consciousness to universal *reason.*

Third, at maturity, the intelligence organizes ideas, devises language, and understands and interprets its reflections rationally. At this stage, the mind expresses itself through reason, will, and moral choice. When it unites the first two characteristics, the mind reaches the highest truth finding an introspective stage of the subjective spirit. This stage is the free mind, the unity of theory and practice. Human freedom consists of controlling desires with reason.

> This will to freedom is no longer an impulse that demands satisfaction, but the character—the mind's consciousness grown into something non-impulsive.
>
> [Freedom of the subjective mind is] a principle of mind and heart destined to develop into the objective phase, into legal, moral, religious and scientific actuality.[2]

Pause for Thought   Do you feel more freedom when you have control of your impulses no matter how much satisfaction they demand? Wouldn't you be truly free if you threw control to the winds and followed your whims?

Objective Spirit (Mind)   The subjective mind, said Hegel, naturally seeks the objective mind. The subjective mind looks inward, while the objective mind acts in the external world through sociology, ethics, and politics. Through the objective mind, we enter public life where we create rules, institutions, and organizations.

Like the subjective mind, the objective mind develops through three stages of moral experience. The first stage Hegel called *abstract rights*—legal and formal rights through laws and contracts. At this stage, we transform nature by creating property systems, economic organizations, and class distinctions. We interact with the external environment through possessions such as privately owning property. This is a condition of self-awareness that establishes the right of ownership.

Owning property involves contracts. Transferring property involves contracts. We can sell our property, but not our life or another's life. This idea takes us into a higher level of personality than that of abstract rights. At the level of abstract rights, recognition of human dignity has yet to develop.

The second stage concerns *subjective morality*—or conscience. When we own possessions, we may seek some freedom through what we own, but we also must accept responsibility. Inner motives become more important than the outward benefit of our actions. Recall Kant's ethic: We should base moral duty on motives of goodwill alone and not look to the result of our actions. But Hegel believed that people of goodwill also must consider the consequences of their actions.

Conscience, said Hegel, is "the deepest internal solitude" humans have when we make a moral decision. Conscience can check itself and set its own standards. Without conscience, we could still perform virtuous acts but lack inner virtue. As important as it is to have an inner conscience, it is just as important to develop an objective "social conscience."

The third stage is *social morality*—the highest realization of the objective mind. Individuals at this stage find their significance in the life of the family, social institutions, and the state.

> The family, as the immediate substantiality of mind, is specifically characterized by love, which is mind's feeling of its own unity. Hence in a family, one's frame of mind is to have self-consciousness of one's individuality within this unity as the [ab]solute essence of oneself, with the result that one is in it not as an independent person but as a member.
>
> The family reaches completion in three phases:
> (a) *Marriage*, the form assumed by the concept of the family in its immediate phase;
> (b) *Family Property and Capital* (the external embodiment of the concept and attention to these;
> (c) *The Education of Children and the Dissolution of the Family.*[3]

For Hegel, marriage is an ethical union. The husband and wife both give up their individual wills to some degree to blend as one person. The love between partners joins them sexually, emotionally, and spiritually. Their children are the external result of a loving relationship between husband and wife.

> It is only in the children that the unity itself exists externally, objectively, and explicitly as a unity, because the parents love the children as their love, as the embodiment of their own substance.[4]

Children depend on their families, then grow up and leave their parents to start families of their own. In this way, the family contains its own antithesis. Because families are not by themselves self-sufficient, they must depend on civil society—the family's "other." Family members now become citizens of society.

> Civil society contains three moments:
> (A) The mediation of need and one man's satisfaction through his work and the satisfaction of the needs of all others—the *System of Needs*.
> (B) The actuality of the universal principle of freedom therein contained—the protection of property through the *Administration of Justice*.
> (C) Provision against contingencies still lurking in systems (A) and (B), and care for particular interests as a common interest, by means of the *Police* and the *Corporation*.[5]

As the dialectic thesis, the family is "immediate," in contrast to the antithesis or "mediateness" of civil society.

Pause for Thought   Why do you think Hegel called the family "immediate" and civil society "mediate" or the family's antithesis? What will the synthesis be?

The state is the synthesis of the family and civil society, because it includes and transcends both.

The State   Hegel called the family an embodiment of the *universal*. When individuals set their own goals in civil society, he labeled it *particularity*. Universality and particularity are each contained in the other. As their synthesis, the *state* becomes the total culture, the union of objective freedom and subjective passion. Individuals can have freedom and relevance only in a state. Historically, the Absolute Spirit (Hegel also referred to it as the "solute" spirit) manifests itself in individuals as well as particular states. After watching Napoleon ride through Jena, Hegel said that he had seen the Absolute Spirit on horseback.

> The state is the actuality of the ethical Idea. It is ethical mind qua the substantial will manifest and revealed to itself, knowing and thinking itself, accomplishing what it knows and in so far as it knows it. The state exists immediately in custom, mediately in individual self-consciousness, knowledge, and activity, which self-consciousness in virtue of its sentiment towards the state finds in the state, as its essence and the end and product of its activity, its substantive freedom.
>
> The state is [ab]solutely rational inasmuch as it is the actuality of the substantial will which it possesses in the particular self-consciousness once that consciousness has been raised to consciousness of its universality. This substantial unity is an [ab]solute unmoved end in itself, in which freedom comes into its supreme right. On the other hand this final end has supreme right against the individual, whose supreme duty is to be a member of the state.[6]

As a living unity of individuals, the state becomes the true individual. Hegel called it a unity in difference when the ethical idea is actualized. As such, the state represents universal self-consciousness. Some individuals are conscious of themselves as parts of this larger self. Because the state is mind objectified, it is only then that the individual could have objectivity, genuine individuality, and an ethical life.

Human spirituality also is part of the state. Hegel thought that our spiritual reality consists in knowing that our own essence, which is reason, is immediately and objectively present. "The State is the Divine Idea as it exists on earth." It seeks to develop the idea of freedom to its maximum. Thus, the state is the idea of spirit in the external manifestation of our human will in its freedom.

Pause for Thought   How would you interpret the following quotes from Hegel as describing the state's role as the synthesis that includes and transcends the family and society?

"The state is the realization of the ethical idea."

"The true state is the ethical whole and the realization of freedom."

"The state is the march of God through the world."

"The state is an organism."

As the most universal form of humanity, the state is a rational and self-conscious force expressing universal reason. Just as the husband and wife lose their personal identities in their marriage, the citizens of a civil society lose their independence in the unity of the state. Within the state, another dialectic triad takes place: (1) *its constitution*, (2) *international law,* and (3) *world history*.

The Constitution   Hegel preferred a constitutional monarchy to a democracy, because the monarch representing the state fulfills the universal will rationally. The ruler puts the purpose of the Absolute Spirit into action. He does this through the universal will, not through his own personal will. Hegel called it the march of the Absolute Spirit in history. For him, in a well-ordered monarchy the law has objective power to which the monarch has only to "affix the subjective 'I will.'"

Pause for Thought   How do you think Hegel's monarch compares to Plato's Philosopher King? Which of the two forms of government would you prefer?

Like the state, the constitution also is an expression of the Absolute Spirit. But the constitution is not based on the decisions of a group of people as it is in a democracy. The state is a living organism in the process of growth as it actualizes the Absolute Spirit. Thus, the constitution continues to develop; and as it does, the legislators pass laws to fulfill the aims of the Absolute Spirit.

International Law   Although individuals are subordinate to the state, the state itself is not subservient to other states. Each state is a living, independent, and sovereign unity, even when it is at war with another state. No authority is superior to the authority of individual states, therefore there could be no international or world authority. If, by entering into contracts, states cannot settle their conflicts, then they must declare war. Hegel saw an ethical element in war that preserves the health of nations by uprooting their "finite aims." However, because war is a link between states and not between individuals, the state has a responsibility to uphold the rights of its citizens.

Pause for Thought   The Absolute Spirit first becomes conscious of itself in the individual, then in the family, society, and the state. The state, said Hegel, is more than the individual citizen and even more that the sum of its citizens. So, if you want "to find yourself" as an individual—to search for your soul and resign from society—what would Hegel say?

World History   For Hegel, the history of the world is the history of nations. Each state has some stage of the Absolute Spirit, because each state is the Divine Idea (Absolute Spirit) as it exists on earth. The dialectic of the historical process exists in the conflict between states. Each state expresses a "national spirit" of its own collective consciousness. And each national spirit represents a moment in the development of the Absolute Spirit. The conflict between national spirits also is the dialectic in history.

> The history of a single world-historical nation contains (a) the development of its principle from its latent embryonic stage until it blossoms into the self-conscious freedom of ethical life and presses in upon world history; and (b) the period of its decline and fall, since it is its decline and fall that signalizes the emergence in it of a higher principle as the pure negative of its own. When this happens, mind passes over into the new principle and so marks out another nation for world-historical significance.[7]

According to Hegel, a nation cannot choose the time in history in which it will be great: It "is only once that it can make its hour strike." But during the nation's height, special historical figures act as instruments of the Absolute Spirit. These heroes lift nations to new levels of development. So far, world history has shown the unfolding of reason through: (1) the Oriental, (2) the Greek, (3) the Roman, and (4) the Germanic. In an Oriental despotism, only one man was free—the despot. In Greece and Rome, only the citizens were free, not the slaves. Under the influence of Christianity, the Germanic peoples developed the highest rational insight—that humans are free. The highest freedom occurs when we act according to the universal rational will of the Absolute Spirit (God).

Pause for Thought   Do you agree with Hegel that under Christianity's influence the German people developed the highest rational insight—that humans are free? Why do you think he chose the Germanic peoples instead of the French, English, or Italian?

Art, Religion, and Philosophy

Aristotle held that contemplative virtues were higher than practical moral virtues. The rational activity of the mind, he said, is the closest we can get to perfection (the Unmoved Mover). Hegel agreed and took Aristotle's thoughts a step farther. He thought the highest expression of reality was the Absolute Spirit, with subjectivity and objectivity integrated in the spiritual life. Our knowledge of the Absolute Spirit is actually the Absolute Spirit knowing itself through the finite spirit of humankind.

Hegel held that our consciousness of the Absolute Spirit progresses as the mind moves through three stages from art to religion and then finally to philosophy. Beauty, he said, is spirit in sensuous form. We see beauty in plants and animals, but we also can create forms of beauty that are superior to nature. The spiritual beauty of art is obvious in music and poetry, forms that not only imitate nature, but also, as Aristotle said, express moral values and purify the emotions.

Art   Hegel saw art as a triadic development: (1) *symbolic*, (2) *classical*, and (3) *romantic*. Symbolic art is vague in its idea and form of expression. Hegel viewed symbolic art as the art of the Orient, of the East, which suggests a meaning without adequately expressing it. The well-balanced classical art of the Greeks, he said, harmonizes the form and the spirit in equal proportion. In Romantic art, the spirit predominates over form. It is a higher means of expression than either Oriental or Greek art, because its content is of the inner spiritual world.

Art is "the self-unfolding idea of beauty." However, the history of the world will require an "evolution of countless ages" for the developing spirit of beauty to reach the highest realization of the ideal beauty. Hegel looked to poetry as the discipline to lift us from the sensuous to the spiritual, from art to religion.

Pause for Thought   How do you think Hegel would view modern art? Would he consider it a higher spiritual form than Romantic art?

Religion   The Greeks looked on their gods as having bodily forms. They made their gods, said Hegel, in their own image as objects of "naive intuition and sensuous imagination." The god's shapes were "the bodily shape of man." However, the mature Christian intelligence recognizes that God is a spirit. Religion, as in other areas in Hegel's system, has developed through a three-stage unfolding of the Absolute Spirit: (1) religions of nature, (2) religions of spiritual individuality, and (3) [ab] "solute" or what we now call "absolute" religion.

Religions of nature are Oriental religions in which humans use worship to control nature through magic. This level includes those who see the deity as boundless power, but not yet as spirit. Hegel traced these forms of religion to the higher religions that would lead to spiritual individuality. Included in this hierarchy are the Zoroastrian religion of Good combating Evil, the Egyptian religion of world mystery (Osiris dies only to live again), and the Syrian religion of the Phoenix rising from its ashes.

The three religions that represent religions of spiritual individuality are those that provide the cultural background of Christianity: (1) the Jewish religion of sublimity, (2) the Greek religion of beauty, and (3) the Roman religion of utility.

For Hegel, the absolute religion—the highest religion of the Absolute Spirit— is Christianity. He considered it the religion of the freely self-conscious Absolute Spirit. Christianity has the absolute truth for its content. The Christian Trinity has God the Father (Hegel's notion of logic or Absolute Idea), God the Son (the world of nature), and the Holy Spirit (unfolding historical reality in the form of self-conscious Mind or Spirit). The Trinity functions through the Christian Churches as God the Father, the eternal all-embracing universal; God the Son, the infinite, particular self-manifestation; and God the Holy Spirit, individual eternal love.

Christ's death expresses the alienation between the finite (thesis) and the infinite (antithesis), and their ultimate reconciliation (synthesis). Without this doctrine, people would still view God as "other than" and beyond the world.

Pause for Thought   Do some Christian denominations today still view God as beyond the world and not in the world? Do you have a view of God? Does it coincide with Hegel's view?

Although Christianity gives the highest religious expression to the truth of Absolute Spirit, only philosophy can fully clarify its truth.

Philosophy   In philosophy the artist's external sensuous vision (thesis) and the mystic's internal vision (antithesis) unite in thought (synthesis). In philosophy, knowledge of the Absolute Spirit is unique: the idea in and for itself. Thus, the knower and the known are identical. As the synthesis, philosophy is the process of historical development and realization. In philosophy, the Absolute Spirit reflects on its own impact on history. Philosophy is like the mirror of the Absolute Spirit. The history of philosophy is the dialectical unfolding of the Absolute Spirit's self-consciousness in the human mind.

Pause for Thought   Do you agree with Hegel that philosophy is the culmination of art and religion, and therefore the synthesis of both? Or do you view religion as the culmination of art and philosophy? Or is art the culmination of religion and philosophy?

On Women

Hegel treats marriage as a unity that transcends and subordinates the individual personalities of the husband and wife. This does not have the same meaning, however, for the man as for the woman. She should dedicate her entire being to the family unit, which is the reason for her existence. The man enters into involvement with the family, but his life exists also outside the family in his profession, in society, and in the state.

Following the ancient tradition, Hegel thought women could not reason abstractly, so they could never understand rational universal principles or the study of philosophy. Because their minds function at the lowest aesthetic stage, women act only on feeling and opinion. As rational beings, men must take the responsibility of managing affairs of the state and dealing with scientific subjects.

> One sex exhibits power and mastery, while the other is subjective and passive. Hence the husband has his real essential life in the state, the sciences, and the like, in battle and in struggle with the outer world and with himself. . . . In the family the wife has her full substantive place. . . .
>
> Women can, of course, be educated, but their minds are not adapted to the higher sciences, philosophy, or certain of the arts. These demand a universal faculty. Women may have happy inspirations, taste, elegance, but they have not the ideal. The difference between man and woman is the same as that between animal and plant. The animal corresponds more closely to the character of the man, the plant to that of the woman. In woman there is a more peaceful unfolding of nature, a process, whose principle is the less clearly determined unity of feeling. If women were to control the government, the state would be in danger, for they do not act according to the dictates of universality, but are influenced by accidental inclinations and opinions. The education of woman goes on one hardly knows how, in the atmosphere of picture-thinking, as it were, more through life than through the acquisition of knowledge. Man attains his position only through stress of thought and much specialized effort.[8]

Pause for Thought   Does the ancient traditional view on women hold true today to any extent? Do you ever hear derogatory comments about the way women think or about their executive abilities?

Materialism: Karl Marx

Marx's Response to Hegel

The era of the great philosophical systems appear to have ended with Hegel. After him, philosophy took a new direction. Instead of the vast speculative systems, we see more philosophies of action. This is what Karl Marx meant when he said, so far "the philosophers have only interpreted the world differently: the point is to change it." These words were a turning point in philosophy.

As a materialist, Marx agreed with Hegel that the dialectical process takes place in nature and in history. But he rejected Hegel's idealism that the dialectic is the progressive self-unfolding of the rational Absolute Spirit. Hegel's pyramid is upside down, said Marx, and I want to turn it over on its material base. In *Das Capital*, Marx wrote:

> My dialectical method is not only different from the Hegelian but is funda-mentally its direct opposite. For Hegel the thought process . . . is the demi-urge (or creator) of the actual, and actual existence is only the outward manifestation of the Idea. But I, on the contrary, regard the ideal as nothing else than the material reality, transposed and translated in the human head.[9]

According to Marx, what makes us human is that we produce our means of sustenance. We are what we are because of what we *do*. We meet our basic needs in productive activities such as fishing, farming, and building. Unlike animals governed by instinct, we create ourselves by transforming and manipulating nature. Through production we generate a society that in turn shapes us.

> The mode of production of material life conditions the general process of social, political, and intellectual life. It is not the consciousness of men that determines their existence, but their social existence that determines their consciousness.[10]

Karl Marx's Life

Karl Marx (1818–1883), the third of nine children, was born in Trier, Germany, to Heinrich and Henrietta Marx. His parents were of Jewish ancestry, but they changed their name from Levi to Marx and converted to Protestant Christianity to protect Heinrich's job as a government lawyer.

Karl was highly intelligent and deeply influenced by his father's own intelligence and humanitarian concerns. Another influence in his life was a neighbor and distinguished government official, Ludwig von Westphalen, who later became his father-in-law. Von Westphalen introduced Marx to the works of the Greek poets, as well as those of Dante and Shakespeare.

In 1835, at age seventeen, Marx entered the University of Bonn to study law. While there, he spent much of his time partying and writing love letters to his childhood sweetheart, Jenny von Westphalen. The next year, his father insisted that Marx transfer to the University of Berlin and concentrate on his studies. While there, Marx found philosophy and gave up law. At that time, Hegel was the dominant philosopher in every German university. His philosophy impressed Marx so much that he became a member of a group of young radical Hegelians. These college students searched for a new understanding of human nature, the world, and history.

At twenty-three, Marx received his doctoral degree from the University of Jena following his dissertation, *On the Difference Between the Democritean and Epicurean Philosophies of Nature*. After graduation, he had planned to become a philosophy professor. But his involvement with young leftist Hegelians, who had publicly criticized the gospels of Jesus Christ, and his radical leftist politics, made him unemployable. About this time, his father died, leaving only enough money to support Marx's mother and family. Marx was now on his own without a job.

Finally, a Hegelian publisher of a liberal newspaper, the *Rhenish Gazette*, asked Marx to be his editor. Marx agreed, but his editorials caused uproars within the government. After reading his article on the poverty of the Mosel winemakers, the government suppressed the paper and Marx was out of a job. He then went to Paris and found a job as coeditor of the new journal *German–French Annals*. Secure in his new position, Marx was now free to marry Jenny. But his security dissolved when the journal closed soon after his hiring. Happily, Marx received a sizable settlement from the shareholders of the *Rhenish Gazette*, so he and Jenny were financially secure for awhile.

When Marx read an article by Ludwig Feuerbach (1804–1872), he realized a change in his own thinking. Feuerbach was a materialist who challenged Hegel's idea that Absolute Spirit was the absolute reality. Feuerbach argued that reality was not spirit or mind, but matter. History, he said, is not the struggle of Absolute Spirit to realize itself: It is the result of material circumstances that influence people's minds and actions.

The more Marx thought about it, the more he realized that the materialist view was his answer for explaining human thinking and behavior. Humankind is not the product of God's creation. Rather, God is the product of our thoughts. It is humanity that struggles to realize itself, not the Absolute Spirit, not God. Now Marx combined Hegel's dialectic view of history and Feuerbach's notion of the material order.

As well as being a philosopher, Marx was a historian, sociologist, and economist. Having a practical and political aim, he wrote extensively on these subjects. In Paris, he discovered another group of radical thinkers who followed the ideas of Claude Henri de Rouvroy, who is better known as the Comte de Saint-Simon (1760–1825). Their main interest was in the emergence of a new middle class known as the *bourgeoisie*. Like Feuerbach, these thinkers believed that economic conditions determine society. Historical change, they argued, is the result of class conflict. And class conflict arises between those who control production and those who have no control over production.

Marx also met Friedrich Engels (1820–1895) who was to be his friend, collaborator, and financial backer for years to come. Engels came from a wealthy textile family, and he worked as the manager of his family's industry in Manchester, England. Together, Marx and Engels wrote *The Holy Family* (1845). In it they criticized many of their fellow leftists. During his year in Paris, Marx was politically active among the German communists. That same year, his association with communists, his critical writings, and other political activities led to his expulsion from France.

For the next three years, Marx and his family lived in Brussels, Belgium, where he helped organize a German Worker's Union and wrote *The German Ideology* (1846) and *The Poverty of Philosophy* (1847). At a meeting in London, the German Workers Union joined with other European communist groups to form an international organization known as the Communist League. Engels was its first secretary. The league asked Marx to write an easy-to-read pamphlet that outlined the league's doctrines. The result was the famous *Communist Manifesto* (1848). He left Brussels briefly to join revolutionary activities in Paris, but French authorities soon heard of his presence and expelled him again from the country.

For the next twenty years, Marx and his family lived in London, but in hardship and poverty because of financial mismanagement. For the rest of his life, Marx's primary source of income consisted of gifts from Engels. Marx isolated himself in study and writing. He worked long hours with single-minded concentration to produce *Critique of Political Economy* (1859) and his three-volume magnum opus, *Das Kapital*. In this last, he looked forward to a revolution that would crush capitalism.

During his final years, Marx regained some of his financial security, but he was afflicted with boils and then developed a liver disorder. His wife Jenny became ill and his six-year-old son died. In 1881, Jenny died, and Marx's oldest daughter died two years later. In 1883, Marx developed bronchitis and died at age sixty-five.

Dialectical Materialism

Hegel had argued that the world is a history of ideas, and that the force that drives history forward is the Absolute Spirit. Marx took exactly the opposite stance. A popular saying is *Marx stood Hegel on his head*. From Feuerbach, Marx decided that "spiritual relations" do not create material change—it is the other way around. Material change creates new spiritual relations. Economic forces in society create change and drive history forward. Marx's materialism is not the materialism of the Atomists of antiquity, and he did not advocate the mechanical materialism of seventeenth-century science. Instead, Marx thought the material factors in society, as seen in the economy and in production, determine the way we think. The foundation of any social organization, the way it thinks, and its political institutions, laws, morals, art, philosophy, science, and even religion make up its superstructure.

Marx realized that throughout the "five epochs of history" there was an interactive or dialectic relation between foundations and superstructure. Hegel had said ideas develop through a dialectic process that moves from thesis to antithesis and then to synthesis. The synthesis becomes a new thesis and so on. Marx saw this dialectic at work in five epochs in history: (1) the primitive or communal, (2) slavery, (3) feudalism, (4) capitalism, and (5) socialism or communism. The tension between the ruling class (the bourgeoisie) and the oppressed class (the proletariat) create the conflict between rulers and the exploited. The basis for each epoch is its economic structure.

> That in every historical epoch, the prevailing mode of economic production and exchange, and the social organization necessarily following from it, from the basis upon which is built up, and from which alone can be explained, the political and intellectual history of that epoch; that consequently the whole history of mankind . . . has been a history of class struggles, contests between exploiting and exploited, ruling and oppressed classes; that the history of these class struggles forms a series of evolutions in which a stage has been reached where the exploited and oppressed class—the proletariat—cannot attain its emancipation from the sway of the exploiting and ruling class—the bourgeoisie—without at the same time, and once and for all, emancipating society at large from all exploitation, oppression, class distinctions and class struggles.[11]

Pause for Thought   Do you see class distinctions such as the bourgeoisie and the proletariat in society today? If so, what are some examples? If not, how has our society solved the problem?

Production   According to Marx's dialectical materialism, the *condition of production* is the basic level of a society's foundation. Included here are the natural conditions or resources available to society. The natural conditions of the

Arizona desert prohibit downhill skiing, and the Rocky Mountains of Colorado are not suitable for growing cotton. As a result, the way people think in a skiing community is different from the way they think in a farming community.

Pause for Thought   Do you agree with Marx that conditions of production shape our thinking and therefore our society? Can you think of exceptions?

People, said Marx, are social animals with physical needs, and we satisfy those needs by the *means of production*. For instance, the invention of the computer is a means of world communication through e-mail and the Internet. World communication will lead to newer needs for the computer. The production of material goods—such as computers, television, and food products—determines the character of political, social, and religious life of every society in history.

> The mode of production in material life determines the general character of the social, political and spiritual processes of life. It is not the consciousness of men that determines their existence, but on the contrary, their social existence determines their consciousness. . . . With change of the economic foundation the entire immense superstructure is more or less rapidly transformed.[12]

Thus, for Marx, the economic structure controls the outlook of every human being in society. Though we think our ideas control the economy, it is economic production that actually shapes our ideas. He called these social relations *productive relations*, and they depend on the stage of evolution of the means of production.

> It follows from this that a certain mode of production or industrial stage is always combined with a certain mode of co-operation, or social stage, and this mode of co-operation is itself a "productive force."[13]

Based on his idea of the dialectic, these forces of production develop until they conflict with existing social relationships. For example, Marx believed that religion or belief in God is an opiate of the people. Once we straighten out our society by evolving from capitalism to communism, the need for such a projection will simply vanish.

> *Man makes religion*; religion does not make man. Religion is indeed man's self-consciousness and self-awareness so long as he has not found himself or has lost himself again. . . .

> Religion is only the illusory sun out which man revolves so long as he does not revolve out himself. . . .[14]

Marx believed we create religion because we are alienated from (1) nature, (2) ourselves, (3) our *species-being* and *other men*.

Pause for Thought   Do you agree with Marx that religions "are nothing more than stages in the development of the human mind," and that we will no longer need religion or a belief in God when we reach happiness through self-fulfillment?

Alienation   The theory of *alienation* was another Hegelian concept that Marx turned upside down. For Hegel, the Absolute Spirit produced nature out of itself, so an interactive, or dialectic, relationship existed between humans and nature. When we alter nature, we alter ourselves and appear separate from it—like the concept of emanation in Neoplatonism (specifically, in the ideas of Plotinus). But Marx interpreted alienation as the separation of individual workers from the product of their labor. In primitive communities this separation did not exist. Pre-literate people lived in small groups or tribes where everyone helped to produce what the community needed. Some hunted, others grew food, built shelters, and made baskets and pots.

As communities evolved and grew larger, so did production needs; thus began a division of labor. When the basket weaver started exchanging baskets for products made by other people, the basket weaver became alienated from the basket, which had now become an object of trade. As a result, individuals felt separated from their products and cut off from the nature of their own being. They were no longer harmonious individuals in their community sharing all things equally. They became known as specialists in their fields—basket maker, farmer, baker, barber. Workers then became alienated, not from their labor, but from the products of their labor. When workers make products for their market value, oppression is born.

According to Marx, capitalism is the major oppressor. In a capitalist society, the workers slave for another social class. Thus, the workers transfer their own labor—and their life—to the capitalist. In return, they receive only meager wages. By dehumanizing workers into beasts of burden, capitalists have the power to hire and fire their workers at whim. During the early part of the Industrial Revolution, for example, there was no solidarity among workers—no labor union. Workers might endure twelve-hour working days in a freezing cold factory. They competed against each other for jobs. Such competition alienated them not only from their product and their employer, but also from each other.

All these consequences result from the fact that the worker is related to the product of his labor as to an *alien* object. For on this premise it is clear that the more the worker spends himself, the more powerful becomes the alien world of objects which he creates over and against himself, the poorer he himself—his inner world—becomes, the less it belongs to him as his own. It is the same in religion. The more man puts into God, the less he retains himself. The worker puts his life into the object; but now his life no longer belongs to him but to the object. . . . The *alienation* of the worker and his product means not only that his labor becomes an object, an *external* existence, but that it exists *outside him*, independently, as something alien to him. It means that the life which he has conferred on the object confronts him as something hostile and alien. . . .

It is true that labor produces for the rich wonderful things—but for the worker it produces privation. It produces palaces—but for the worker, hovels. It produces beauty—but for the worker, deformity. It replaces labor by machines, but it throws a section of the workers back to a barbarous type of labor, and it turns the other workers into machines. It produces intelligence—but for the worker stupidity, cretinism.[15]

Alienated labor leads to ownership and private property. It leads to human perversion. Rich families lived in large warm houses and ate three-course dinners. Poor families had no heat or warm clothes. Children starved. Such exploitation infuriated Marx. "Man becomes ever poorer as man, his need for *money* becomes ever greater if he wants to overpower hostile being." The rich get richer. The need for money becomes the lust for money, and greed keeps the process alive. Devotion to money becomes a kind of religion.

Pause for Thought   Is greed a motivating factor in capitalism today? Is money a kind of religion? Note the inscription on the penny: "In God we trust." Do we really trust in God or in the penny?

Communism   Marx believed the capitalistic process would continue until the proletariat, the working class, becomes fully aware of itself. Change will come when "all workers of the world unite" and become a revolutionary class. Capitalism cannot survive the socialization of production and thus will fail. Overproduction will result in economic crises. When the working class becomes conscious of itself and its devastating conditions, it will overthrow the current social order and the inequalities of private ownership. Communism will follow in its wake.

The immediate aim of the Communists is the . . . formation of the proletariat into a class, overthrow of bourgeois supremacy, conquest of political power by the proletariat.[16]

Communism is a classless society made up of workers who are guided by this motto: "From each according to his abilities, to each according to his needs!" In the classless society, the economic struggle between the capitalist and proletariat classes will cease as all people merge into one class—the working class.

> The distinguishing feature of Communism is not the abolition of property generally, but the abolition of bourgeois property. But modern bourgeois private property is the final and most complete expression of the system of producing and appropriating products, that is based on class antagonisms, on the exploitation of the many by the few. . . .
>
> Hard-won, self-acquired, self-earned property! Do you mean the property of the petty artisan and of the small peasant, a form of property that preceded the bourgeois form? There is no need to abolish that; the development of industry has to a great extent already destroyed it, and is still destroying it daily. . . .
>
> You are horrified at our intending to do away with private property. But in your existing society, private property is already done away with for nine-tenths of the population; its existence for the few is solely due to its non-existence in the hands of those nine-tenths. You reproach us, therefore, with intending to do away with a form of property, the necessary condition for whose existence is, the non-existence of any property for the immense majority of society.
>
> In one word, you reproach us with intending to do away with your property. Precisely so, that is just what we intend. . . .
>
> Communism deprives no man of the power to appropriate the products of society; all that it does is to deprive him of the power to subjugate the labour of others by means of such appropriation.[17]

A "classless society" replaces the proletariat, and people own the means of production. Labor belongs to the workers themselves, and capitalism's alienation ceases. Marx's and Engels' plan for implementing communism called for the following social reforms:

1. Abolition of property in land and application of all rents from land to public purposes.

2. A heavy progressive or graduated income tax.

3. Abolition of all right of inheritance.

4. Confiscation of property of all emigrants and rebels.

5. Centralization of credit in the hands of the state, by means of a national bank with State capital and an exclusive monopoly.

6. Centralization in State hands of the means of communication and transportation.

7. Expansion of factory systems and increased State ownership of instruments of production. State planning to bring waste lands back into cultivation and improve soils.

8. Equal obligation of all persons to perform useful work. Establishment of industrial armies, especially for agriculture.

9. Establishment of production centers combining agriculture with manufacturing; gradual abolition of the distinction between town and country through a better balanced distribution of the population.

10. Free education for all children in public schools. abolition of child labor. Work-study programs to combine education with industrial production.[18]

Pause for Thought   Although not everything has worked out as Marx proposed, have any of his ideas taken root in our country? Has Marx's vision changed worker exploitation in any way?

On Women

With Friedrich Engels, his friend and coauthor, Marx believed that the economic conditions of the epoch and the society in which they lived explained the relationship between men and women. In *Origin of the Family* (1884), Engels pointed out that the position of women deteriorates outside the communist structure. He based his view on American anthropologist Lewis Morgan's three stages of history: savagery, barbarism, and civilization.

The savagery stage consisted of group marriage and sexual freedom. Economically, the maternal line prevailed and society valued the woman. With barbarism came the "duo" family with its division of labor and private property. Men held women to strict fidelity. Women's property rights were overthrown, and women became economically dependent on men. With civilization we find monogamy and male supremacy. From this emerged the first class struggle, the antagonism between the sexes. *Man is bourgeois and woman is proletarian.*

It is one of the most absurd notions derived from eighteenth century enlightenment, that in the beginning of society woman was the slave of man. Among all savages and barbarians of the lower and middle stages, sometimes even of the higher stage, women not only have freedom, but are held in high esteem. . . .

With the patriarchal family we enter the domain of written history. . . .

The whole severity of this new form of the family confronts us among the Greeks. While, as Marx observes, the position of the female gods in mythology shows an earlier period, when women still occupied a freer and more respected plane, we find woman already degraded by the supremacy of man and the competition of slaves during the time of the heroes. . . . Although the Greek woman of heroic times is more highly respected than she of the civilized period, still she is for her husband only the mother of his legal heirs, his first housekeeper and the superintendent of the female slaves, whom he can and does make his concubines at will.

The modern monogamous family is founded on the open or disguised domestic slavery of women, and modern society is a mass composed of molecules in the form of monogamous families. In the great majority of cases the man has to earn a living and to support his family, at least among the possessing classes. He thereby obtains a superior position that has no need of any legal special privilege. In the family, he is the bourgeois, the woman represents the proletariat. . . .

Only the advance from the pairing family to monogamy must be charged to the account of men. This advance implied historically, a deterioration in the position of women and a greater opportunity for men to be faithless. Remove the economic considerations that now force women to submit to the customary disloyalty of men, and you will place women on an equal footing with men.[19]

Summary

Hegel's center of thought was the notion of Absolute Spirit (Mind). Absolute Spirit is the Absolute Idea (God)—the total reality. Hegel took Kant's concept that the mind imposes its ideas on experience to its ultimate conclusion. If ideas of the noumenal world do indeed exist, he said, then we can know them.

Absolute Spirit is a single, evolving substance and the true reality. It is in a continuous process of relationships unfolding from lower to higher degrees of perfection. The struggle of Absolute Spirit self-actualizing into perfection is what Hegel calls *history*. History itself is a dialectic process that moves in three steps from an original thesis to a contrary antithesis and then, after a struggle between them, to a new idea that combines elements of each—synthesis.

The Absolute Spirit first becomes conscious of itself in the individual, what Hegel called subjective spirit. It reaches higher consciousness in the objective spirit of family, society, and the state. The Absolute Spirit reaches it highest form of self-realization in art, religion, and philosophy. Of these, philosophy is the highest form of knowledge. Through philosophy, the Absolute Spirit reflects on its own impact on history.

Taking Hegel's philosophy as his point of departure, Marx created a philosophy of action. Until now, he said, "philosophers have only interpreted the world in different ways; the point is to change it." Hegel had pointed out that historical development is driven by the tension between opposites—thesis, antithesis, and synthesis. Marx agreed with the dialectical process, but he did not think the force of the process was Absolute Spirit. For Marx, the economic life of the community is the force that creates change.

Marx reasoned that a society's superstructure comprises the way it thinks, as well as its political institutions, laws, morals, science, and philosophy. The three levels that make up the foundation of any society are (1) the condition of production, (2) the means of production, and (3) production relations.

Marx also observed the dialectic at work in five epochs in history: (1) the primitive or communal, (2) slavery, (3) feudalism, (4) capitalistism, and (5) socialism or communism. Economic structure is the basis for each epoch.

Alienation among people occurs with the conflict between the bourgeoisie (the capitalists) and the proletariat (workers). The conflict occurs between those who own the means of production and those who do not. Because the capitalists do not want to relinquish their power, revolution is the only way to better the workers' conditions.

In a capitalistic society, the worker labors for someone else. His labor becomes separated from him: It no longer belongs to him. The worker becomes alien not only to his work, but also to himself. He loses touch with his own inner being. Only when the workers of all countries unite in revolution will such exploitation cease.

The proletariat must rise and take over the means of production. When this occurs, a new "classless society" will begin. In such a society the people themselves own the means of production. Each person gives according to his abilities and receives according to his needs. Capitalism and alienation transform into socialism and communism.

Connections

Like Heraclitus, Parmenides, Plotinus, and Spinoza, Hegel was an integrative philosopher. He saw and influenced others to see the universe as an organic whole and not merely as the sum of its parts.

After Hegel's death, his followers divided into two factions: (1) the Hegelian Right, or religious philosophers who reconciled Hegel's views with Christianity; and (2) the Hegelian Left, a radical movement of young Hegelians, including Karl Marx and Friedrich Engels, who applied Hegel's dialectic to the evolution of materialism.

Marx was especially taken with Hegel's identification of spirit and nature. Hegel had said that spirit is the true reality. Marx thought it was significant that Hegel had rejected the separation of spirit and nature. Standing Hegel on his head, Marx used the same method to argue that matter, not spirit, is the true reality. Marx's philosophy later influenced the Russian revolutionary

Vladimir Ilich Lenin and the Chinese leader Mao Tse-Tung, who both agreed that progress was not possible without physical violence. Although Marx thought his philosophy would change capitalist states, it had less effect on Western capitalism than on underdeveloped countries in Asia, Africa, and Latin America.

Study Questions

1. What was Kant's influence on Hegel?

2. What does Hegel mean by "the real is rational, and the rational is real"?

3. How does Hegel's concept of reality differ from Plato's concept of reality?

4. What is Absolute Spirit?

5. How does Absolute Spirit express itself objectively?

6. How does Absolute Spirit express itself subjectively?

7. What dialectical system does Hegel use?

8. What is the difference between idea in itself and idea *for* itself?

9. What does Hegel mean by the "solute" Spirit?

10. How does Hegel view the family?

11. Why is civil society the antithesis of the family?

12. What part does the state play in Hegel's system?

13. Does Hegel think war is ever necessary?

14. Why does Hegel consider philosophy the synthesis between art and religion?

15. According to Hegel, what is the goal of history?

16. How did Marx stand Hegel on his head?

17. What do the so-called five epochs of history have to do with dialectical materialism?

18. According to Marx, what is the origin of private property?

19. Describe the struggle between the worker and the capitalist.

20. What are some forms of worker alienation?

21. Characterize Marx's concept of the bourgeoisie and the proletariat.

22. Why does Marx think communism is better for society than capitalism?

Notes

1. G.W.F. Hegel, *Encyclopedia of the Philosophical Sciences* (trans. by W. Wallace), Ch. VII, Sec. 85–88. Oxford, UK: Clarendon Press, 1892.

2. G.W.F. Hegel, *The Phenomenology of Mind,* 2nd. ed. (trans. by T. B. Baillie), Sec. 482. London: Sonnenschien, 1931.

3. G.W.F. Hegel, *Philosophy of Right* (trans. by T. M. Knox), Subsec. I, Sec. 158, 160. London: Oxford University Press, 1942.

4. Ibid., Sec. 173.

5. Ibid., Subsec. II, Sec. 188.

6. Ibid., Subsec. III, Sec. 257, 258.

7. Ibid., Sec. 347.

8. Georg Hegel, *The Philosophy of Right* (trans. by S. W. Dyde), Part 3, Sect. 166–173. London: George Bell & Sons, 1896.

9. Karl Marx, *Das Kapital* (ed. by Karl Kaulsky), Vol. I, p. xlvii. Berlin: Dietz, 1928.

10. Richard Schmitt, *Introduction to Marx and Engels,* pp. 7–8. Boulder, CO: Westview Press, 1987.

11. Karl Marx and Friedrich Engels, *Manifesto of the Communist Party* (trans. by Samuel Moore), Preface, p. 416. Chicago: Encyclopedia Britannica, 1952.

12. *A Contribution to the Critique of Political Economy* (trans. by N. I. Stone), p. 11. Chicago: Charles Kerr, 1911.

13. "The German Ideology," p. 121 in *The Marx–Engels Reader* (ed. by Robert C. Tucker). New York: W.W. Norton & Co., 1972.

14. "Contribution to the Critique of Hegel's Philosophy of Right," pp. 43, 52 in *Early Writings* (trans. by T. B. Bottomore). London: C.A. Watts, 1963.

15. *The Economic and Philosophic Manuscripts of 1844* (ed. by Dirk J. Struik), pp. 108–110. New York: International Publishers, 1964.

16. *Manifesto of the Communist Party,* op. cit., p. 425.

17. Ibid., pp. 425–426.

18. Ibid., p. 429.

19. Friedrich Engels, *The Origin of the Family, Private Property and the State* (trans. by Ernest Untermann), Ch. 2, Secs. 3, 4. Chicago: C.H. Kerr & Co., 1902.

CHAPTER ELEVEN

Utilitarianism: Wollstonecraft, Bentham, Mill, Taylor

In this chapter on Utilitarianism, we see the influence of Hume and Kant—some of these philosophers agreeing with Kant, and others with Hume. Hume in particular rejected traditional moral philosophy based on universals and emphasized the individual's capacity for sympathy. For Hume, sympathy is the pleasure we feel when we consider another's happiness. In Utilitarianism, the pleasure principle and happiness for others is a prominent theme.

Though not explicitly a Utilitarian, Mary Wollstonecraft writes in the same spirit and with similar views to Jeremy Bentham, John Stuart Mill, and Harriet Taylor. Wollstonecraft's thesis was that women were to be treated as and to act as autonomous decision makers. Based on Kant's goodwill principle, Wollstonecraft considered women persons instead of the "toy of man, his rattle" when he wanted amusement. Agreeing again with Kant's moral philosophy, she saw women as "ends in themselves" and not as means to someone else's happiness. Wollstonecraft asserted that women have forsaken their freedom and let others make them stunted, although beautiful, bonsai trees. However, through education—the same as provided for men—women can learn to assume responsibility for their own development and growth.

Although Wollstonecraft looked to Kant's ethics as a catalyst for her own philosophy, two Utilitarian philosophers, Jeremy Bentham and John Stuart Mill, largely ignored him. Whereas Kant refuted many of Hume's ideas, these Utilitarian philosophers chose to develop Hume's ideas even further. Hume had denied that we could know universal laws of any kind, whether in physics or in ethics. Morality, he said, has to do with feeling or "sympathy," or the pleasure we experience when we consider the happiness of others.

In opposition to the Empiricist's ethics, Kant placed value not on the effects of our actions, but on the motives from which we act. Expanding Hume's ideas, the Utilitarians defined virtue in terms of utility: The rightness of an action is identical with the happiness it produces as its consequence.

In England, the Utilitarians were influential and responsible for many social reforms during the nineteenth century. As followers of the empirical method, they believed science was the answer to the economic and social problems facing Europe. Through scientific study, they hoped to understand human nature and solve the problems that were resulting from failed conventional structures. Jeremy Bentham and John Stuart Mill were the most famous of the Utilitarians.

Closely connected to Mill and his writings was Harriet Taylor, who later took the name Harriet Taylor Mill. With her husband John Mill, she wrote *Early Essays on Marriage and Divorce* (1832). Harriet Taylor was the primary author of the *Enfranchisement of Women* (1851), and she may have helped write Mill's *The Subjection of Women*.

In a time when women had few civil liberties and lived a life devoted to marriage and motherhood, Harriet Taylor stressed higher education, partnerships in production, and equal rights to form and administer laws. A woman, she said, should have the opportunity to develop her mind and choose a career in the arts, business, or politics. She believed women should have the option to add a career outside the home to their domestic career.

Mary Wollstonecraft

Wollstonecraft's Life

The oldest of six children, Mary Wollstonecraft (1759–1797) was born on a small farm outside London. Her father moved from farm to farm in England and Wales, but always the farm failed and the family moved on. She remembers her father as a man who often broke into violent rages. To defend her mother, Mary would throw herself between them. But she also recalls her mother as too willingly his victim.

Free to play with her brothers in the countryside, Mary escaped the conventions of having to learn the "useless drawing room accomplishments" that most girls endured. Throughout her life, she never forgot the wonders of simple fresh air. Like most educated women of her era, Wollstonecraft was self-taught. Because of her family poverty, she had no library, but she worked on her writing and soon knew it was her talent and strength. While still a young woman, she struck out on her own to London to become a writer. To support herself, she worked as a journalist and as a companion to an elderly widow.

After her mother's death, Wollstonecraft accepted the responsibility for looking after her father. She was not only his sole support, but also financed the education of her younger brothers and sisters. Later, she established a school at Newington Green in London that provided an informal education for novice teachers. She and others struggled to keep the school alive, but they were unsuccessful.

After years of hard work, her writings began to gain acceptance among the intellectuals of London society. By the time she published *A Vindication of the Rights of Woman*, she was already a successful, if not always popular, author. Her personal life was unconventional and turbulent. One of her friends called her a "philosophical sloven" because of her disheveled clothes and hair. Her unconventional lifestyle may have helped convince other women and men of the wickedness of feminism.

During the French Revolution, Wollstonecraft traveled to Paris to see the revolution for herself. While there, she met an American, Gilbert Imlay. Though their three-year relationship was more turbulent than blissful, in 1794 she gave birth to their daughter, Fanny. Soon after Fanny's birth, Imlay left on a business trip. Wollstonecraft followed him from Paris to London and back to Paris. When she found him with another woman, she tried unsuccessfully to commit suicide.

While her daughter Fanny was still very young, Wollstonecraft met William Godwin, a political anarchist. They fell in love, and after Wollstonecraft discovered she was pregnant, they married. She and Godwin had a happy life that ended when Wollstonecraft died after complications during childbirth. She was thirty-eight. Saddened by her death, Godwin wrote a tender book of memoirs about her. The book caused some scandal, because he revealed the illegitimacy of her first child and the fact of her pregnancy when they married.

Their daughter, Mary, married poet Percy Bysshe Shelley and wrote the novel *Frankenstein*. Unlike her mother, she showed little interest in women's rights.

Women in Cages

In *A Vindication of the Rights of Woman*, Mary Wollstonecraft wrote an answer to the traditional philosophers' view of women. Raised in a family that was filled with domestic violence, she saw through the views of the so-called ideal marriage. One belief that had continued through history was that women were more pleasure-seeking, pleasure-giving, emotional, and weak-minded than men. Wollstonecraft argued that if men were confined to the cages in which women find themselves locked, they would develop the same characteristics. If men had no chance to develop their rational powers, become moral persons, or develop commitments beyond personal pleasure, then they, too, would become emotional, narcissistic, and self-indulgent.

Education

Wollstonecraft was especially annoyed by the philosophy and writings of French philosopher Jean-Jacques Rousseau, who once wrote that the educational goal for boys is the development of the rational mind. The only education girls need, he said, is to make them pleasing to men. Rousseau held that "rational man" is the perfect complement for "emotional woman." In *A Vindication of the Rights of Woman*, Wollstonecraft quoted Rousseau at some length to give "a sketch of his character of woman in his own words."

> It being once demonstrated that man and woman are not, nor ought to be, constituted alike in temperament and character, it follows, of course, that they should not be educated in the same manner. . . .
>
> For this reason the education of women should be always relative to the men. To please, to be useful to us, to make us love and esteem them, to educate us when young, and take care of us when grown up, to advise, to console us, to render our lives easy and agreeable—these are the duties of women at all times, and what they should be taught in their infancy. . . .
>
> Boys love sports of noise and activity; to beat the drum, to whip the top, and to drag about their little carts; girls, on the other hand, are fonder of things of show and ornament; such as mirrors, trinkets, and dolls; the doll is the peculiar amusement of the females, from whence we see their taste plainly adapted to their destination. . . . And, in fact, almost all of them learn with reluctance to read and write; but very readily apply themselves to the use of their needles. . . .
>
> The first and most important qualification in a woman is good nature or sweetness of temper: formed to obey a being so imperfect as man, often full of vices, and always full of faults, she ought to learn betimes even to suffer injustice, and to bear the insults of a husband without complaint; it is not for his sake, but her own, that she should be of a mild disposition. . . .
>
> Women . . . ought to have but little liberty. . . .[1]

Pause for Thought

Do Rousseau's thoughts remind you of the children's rhyme "Little girls are made of sugar and spice and everything nice. Little boys are made of snips and snails and puppy dog tails"?

Though times have changed, some of Rousseau's views still hold today. What kinds of toys do boys play with compared to girls? Do some men and women today accept the roles that Rousseau advocates?

Wollstonecraft argued that the subjection of women to men is unjust. Women are taught to be "means" for men's pleasure rather than "ends" in themselves. They are objects and not persons. Wollstonecraft's cure for this inequality is to allow a woman a real education, one that sharpens her mind.

> To render mankind more virtuous, and happier of course, both sexes must act from the same principle; but how can that be expected when only one is allowed to see the reasonableness of it? To render also the social compact truly equitable, and in order to spread those enlightening principles, which alone can ameliorate the fate of man, women must be allowed to found their virtue on knowledge, which is scarcely possible unless they be educated by the same pursuits as men.
>
> I wish to see my sex become more like moral agents, my heart bounds with the anticipation of the general diffusion of that sublime contentment which only morality can diffuse.[2]

Wollstonecraft objected to Rousseau's assumption that man's nature and virtues differ from woman's because women are deficient in reason. Reason, she said, is a human characteristic, and to deny woman reason is to deny her humanity. By using the rational mind, a woman can develop her moral capacities and attain her full human potential—personhood.

> Would men but generously snap our chains, and be content with rational fellowship instead of slavish obedience, they would find us more observant daughters, more affectionate sisters, more faithful wives, more reasonable mothers—in a word, better citizens. We should then love them with true affection, because we should learn to respect ourselves; and the peace of mind of a worthy man would not be interrupted by the idle vanity of his wife, nor the babes sent to nestle in a strange bosom, having never found a home in their mother's.[3]

Jeremy Bentham

Bentham's Life

Born to a wealthy family in London, Jeremy Bentham (1748–1842) was a child prodigy. When only three years old, he read the history of England in eight volumes; at four, he studied Latin grammar; and at eight, he went to Westminster School. When he was twelve, he entered Oxford and received his Bachelor of Arts degree three years later. After graduation, his lawyer father urged him to attend Lincoln's Inn to prepare for the legal profession. That same year, at age fifteen, he heard a lecture series on law by the famous scholar Sir William Blackstone. During the lectures, Bentham "immediately detected Blackstone's fallacy respecting natural rights," calling it "rhetorical nonsense." He thought the way the legal and political professions used their power to oppress those beneath them in the social order was disgusting. He called such actions, including "the inalienable rights" he found in the American Declaration of Independence, "nonsense on stilts."

After receiving his Master of Arts degree, he decided against practicing law in favor of a literary career. In 1776, he published his first book, *Fragment on Government*—a critique on Blackstone.

Bentham showed a deep interest in legal and social reform. He wrote daily commentaries on the need to bring reason, order, empirical evidence, and morality to British law. When Bentham read Hume's *Treatise on Human Nature*, he said it was "as if scales fell" from his eyes about ethics. His own ethical philosophy reflects Hume's profound impact. Bentham advocated prison and educational reform and the extension of voting rights. He wanted to create laws for the best interests of the whole community, not just for the convenience of the elite class. This thinking made him popular with many English citizens, but church authorities, lawyers, members of Parliament, and wealthy businessmen considered him the enemy. Until he died, Bentham was an influential public figure. Today, he continues to remain a public figure. His fully dressed, mummified body, complete with a wax head, still presides over the trustees' meetings at University College in London. He left a large inheritance to the college provided he continued to attend its meetings even after his death.

The Principle of Utility

In his major work, *Introduction to the Principles of Morals and Legislation*, Bentham included both the principles of human nature and a list of twenty-one offenses "to which the condition of a husband stands exposed." The book begins with an explanation of human nature.

> I. Nature has placed mankind under the governance of two sovereign masters, *pain* and *pleasure*. It is for them alone to point out what we ought to do, as well as to determine what we shall do. On the one hand the standard of right and wrong, on the other the chain of causes and effects, are fastened to their throne. They govern us in all we do, in all we say, in all we think: every effort we can make to throw off our subjection, will serve but to demonstrate and confirm it. In words a man may pretend to abjure their empire: but in reality he will remain subject to it all the while. The *principle of utility* recognizes this subjection, and assumes it for the foundation of that system, the object of which is to rear the fabric of felicity by the hands of reason and law. Systems which attempt to question it, deal in sounds instead of sense, in caprice instead of reason, in darkness instead of light.[4]

With this beginning, Bentham viewed *pleasure* and *pain* as the motivating factors of all human beings. That pleasure has value is a philosophy of utility

known as *hedonism*, previously posited by Epicurus and Hobbes. Bentham subscribed to two kinds of Utilitarian hedonism: (1) psychological hedonism (pleasure and pain determine what we do) and (2) ethical hedonism (pleasure is the
only good, and actions are good only if they produce pleasure). The term *utility,*
he said, has two meanings:

> III. By utility is meant that property in any object, whereby it tends to
> produce benefit, advantage, pleasure, good, or happiness, (all this in the
> present case comes to the same thing or (what comes again to the same
> thing) to prevent the happening of mischief, pain, evil, or unhappiness to
> the party whose interest is considered: if that party be the community in
> general, then the happiness of the community: if a particular individual,
> then the happiness of that individual.[5]

Pause for Thought   Is following your own pleasure always better for you and the community? Do you use Bentham's criteria when figuring out a course of
action?

Thus for Bentham, whether we know it or not, we are all hedonists. But he
revolutionized the concept of hedonism by including the happiness for the greatest number.

> VI. An action then may be said to be conformable to the principle of
> utility, or, for shortness sake, to utility (meaning with respect to the com-
> munity at large) when the tendency it has to augment the happiness of the
> community is greater than any it has to diminish it.[6]

Utility is the property in any object that produces benefit, advantage, pleasure, good, or happiness for the individual or the community as a whole. In
Bentham's philosophy, we can exchange the words *good* and *evil* for *pleasure* and
pain. The words *ought, right,* and *good* make sense only when describing pleasure.

All moral standards are pleasure standards in disguise, even our agreement to
obey a "social contract" among members of society, and laws given to us by
God. These standards are reducible to the principle of utility.

For example, Bentham reasoned that if you believe your duty to obey the
law is the result of a "social contract" you have with society, then you have complicated the situation. You obey the law—not for duty's sake—but because your
obedience will bring you more pleasure than your disobedience.

Some people say they obey the law to please God. Well, remarked Bentham,
"What is God's pleasure? God does not . . . either speak or write to us. How

then are we to know that is his pleasure?" We contrive God's pleasure "by observing what is our own pleasure, and pronouncing it to be his."

Pause for Thought   Do you agree with Bentham that you obey social laws and God's laws not as an act of duty, but to avoid the pain of displeasure?

Sources of Pleasure and Pain

Bentham called the sources of pleasure and pain *sanctions*—the forces that influence our conduct. He posited four sanctions: (1) physical, (2) political, (3) moral, and (4) religious.

> A man's goods, or his person, are consumed by fire. If this happened to him by what is called an accident, it was a calamity: if by reason of his own imprudence (for instance, from his neglecting to put his candle out) it may be styled a punishment of the physical sanction: if it happened to him by the sentence of a political magistrate, a punishment belonging to the political sanction; that is, what is commonly called a punishment: if for want of any assistance which his *neighbour* withheld from him out of some dislike to his *moral* character, a punishment of the *moral* sanction: if by an intermediate act of *God's* displeasure, manifested on account of some *sin* committed by him, or through any distraction of mind, occasioned by the dread of such displeasure, a punishment of the *religious* sanction.[7]

Included in a sanction is the threat of pain that follows from ignoring the interests and pleasures of other people. Bentham argued that painful consequences would punish extreme or indiscriminate selfishness.

Pause for Thought   Do you look to possible painful consequences from your acts? Does the fear of AIDS persuade you to forgo sexual pleasure? Would the pain of an IRS audit convince you to file an honest income tax report? Could fear of divine punishment inspire you to give up your excesses? Do you agree with Bentham that the threat of painful consequences influences us to be less selfish?

Bentham wanted to find which sanctions would increase the happiness of society. Unlike Kant, who argued that the morality of an act depends on having the right motive, Bentham and the Utilitarians took the opposite stance. For them, morality depends on the consequences of our acts. Pleasure is the consequence that confers the quality of morality on an act. In society, the law punishes only those who inflict pain on others, no matter what their motive. Bentham did not dismiss motives entirely, but he considered consequences more powerful.

The Hedonistic Calculus

According to Bentham, all people hope to achieve pleasure and avoid pain. Pleasure and pain, however, differ from each other and therefore have independent values. By refining his study to a science, Bentham found seven categories of pleasures:

1. *Intensity.* How strong is the pleasure?

2. *Duration.* How long will the pleasure last?

3. *Certainty.* How sure are we that the pleasure will occur?

4. *Propinquity.* How soon will the pleasure occur?

5. *Fecundity.* How likely is it that this pleasure will produce another pleasure?

6. *Purity.* How free from pain is the pleasure?

7. *Extent.* How many people will experience the pleasure?

Bentham called the seven categories the *calculus of felicity* (pleasure). Through these categories, he believed we could calculate which course of action would produce the greatest amount of happiness, and therefore which one we ought morally to take.

Pause for Thought   Try the calculus for yourself. Pose questions that require certain choices before you can reach a decision. For example, imagine you are studying for a midterm exam in algebra. Some of your friends ask you to join them for pizza and beer. In making your decision, add the number of categories that will be strong in studying compared to those that will be strong for having pizza. Which activity will you choose?

You can attach positive units of pleasure and negative units of pain to each category. If the totals are on the side of pleasure, then your choice is good. If the numbers favor the pain side, then your choice is bad. Bentham said:

Take an account of the *number* of persons whose interests appear to be concerned; and repeat the above process with respect to each. *Sum up* the numbers expressive of the degrees of *good* tendency which the act has, with respect to each individual, in regard to whom the tendency of it is *good* upon the whole: . . . do this again with respect to each individual, in regard to whom the tendency of it is *bad* upon the whole. Take the *balance*; which, if on the side of *pleasure*, will give the general *good tendency* of the act, with respect to the total number or community of individuals concerned; if on the side of pain, the general *evil tendency*, with respect to the same community.[8]

Bentham's desire for social reforms to construct a society that would provide the greatest happiness to the greatest number was the starting point for later Utilitarian philosophy. One of his most famous supporters was John Stuart Mill, who was raised on an "educational experiment" worked out by his father and by Bentham. In his *Autobiography,* John Stuart Mill wrote that his father's opinions gave the "distinguishing character to the Benthamic or Utilitarian propagandism." He also wrote that his father was the earliest Englishman who understood and adopted Bentham's philosophy of ethics, government, and law. Mill called Bentham's *Introduction to the Principles of Morals and Legislation* one of the turning points in his own "mental history." The greatest happiness principle particularly impressed him.

John Stuart Mill

Mill's Life

Born in London to Harriet and James Burrow Mills, John Stuart Mill (1806–1873) was the oldest of nine children. James Mill, his father, was a well known philosopher and champion of Jeremy Bentham. Following his and Bentham's plan, James Mill had son John reading Greek at age three and Latin at eight. By ten, young John had read six of Plato's dialogues. Each morning father and son would go on a walk and James would quiz John on subjects he studied the previous day. His father often lectured on various topics and then had John prepare a summary of his dialogue for the following day. Because of the intensity of this schooling, John Stuart Mill would say later, "Through the training bestowed on me, I started, I may fairly say, with an advantage of a quarter of a century over my contemporaries." Unfortunately, "I was never a boy."

When his father finished writing a history of India, he received a government post as an assistant examiner at the East India House. Five years later, he arranged a position for John, who was then seventeen. John Stuart Mill was to work for the East India House for the next thirty-four years. But at age twenty he fell into "a dull state of nerves." He attributed his breakdown to the fact that his education had overemphasized the analytic and ignored emotional values. Of his nervous state, he wrote:

> I was . . . left stranded at the commencement of my voyage, with a well equipped ship and a rudder, but no sail; without any real desire for the ends which I had been so carefully fitted out to work for; no delight in virtue or the general good, but also just as little in anything else.[9]

> I seemed to have nothing left to live for. At first I hoped that the cloud would pass away of itself; but it did not. A night's sleep, the sovereign remedy for the smaller vexations of life, had no effect upon it. In vain I sought relief from my favourite books, those memorials of past nobleness and greatness from which I had always hitherto drawn strength and animation. I read them now without feeling . . . and I became persuaded that my love of mankind, and of excellence for its own sake, had worn itself out.[10]

He began to read such literary figures as Coleridge, Carlyle, and Wordsworth and was deeply affected by them. Because of their writings, he said, the cultivation of feelings became extremely important in his "ethical and philosophical creed."

At age twenty-five, he met Harriet Taylor, the wife of a successful merchant. They became strong friends and collaborated on several works, including *Principles of Political Economy* (1848) and *On Liberty* (1859). Harriet was his source of many important ideas, including liberal feminism. Next to his father, Mill considered Harriet Taylor his life's chief intellectual influence. She even inspired his work *A System of Logic* (1843). He also could depend on her insight into the feeling aspect of human nature. He wrote about the abstract and scientific, and she wrote about the human element. They finally married in 1851, two years after her husband's death.

In 1858, John and Harriet Mill, both in poor health, moved to Avignon, France. Shortly after their arrival, she died, and her daughter took care of John Mill. Over the next seven years, Mill published *On Liberty* (1859), *Utilitarianism* (1861), *Considerations on Representative Government* (1861), *Auguste Comte and Positivism* (1865), and *The Subjection of Women* (1861). In 1865, Mill returned to England and was elected to Parliament from where he worked for women's suffrage. He was among the founders of the first women's suffrage society, advocated Irish land reform, and spoke out for the rights of blacks in Jamaica. Returning to France, he completed his *Autobiography* just before his death in 1873 at age sixty-seven.

Mill's Utilitarianism

Mill agreed with the British Empiricists that there was no a priori knowledge. Although he respected Bentham's Utilitarianism, he worried about a hedonistic calculus that said pleasures differ "only" in *quantity*. "Prejudice apart," Bentham had said, "the game of push-pin is of equal value with the arts and sciences of music and poetry. If the game of push-pin furnish more pleasure, it is more valuable than either." What concerned Mill was the implication that the only difference between one act and another is the *amount* of pleasure that the act produces.

Bentham was so sure that quantity of pleasure was the key that he had even suggested "there ought to be a moral thermometer" to measure the "degree" of pleasure in a moral act. But Mill, through his own experiences, had discovered that pleasures are not all equal.

> It is quite compatible with the principle of utility to recognise the fact, that some kinds of pleasure are more desirable and more valuable than others. It would be absurd that while, in estimating all other things, quality is considered as well as quantity, the estimation of pleasures should be supposed to depend on quantity alone. . . .
>
> Few human creatures would consent to be changed into any of the lower animals, for a promise of the fullest allowance of a beast's pleasures; no intelligent human being would consent to be a fool, no instructed person would be an ignoramus, no person of feeling and conscience would be selfish and base, even though they should be persuaded that the fool, the dunce, or the rascal is better satisfied with his lot than they are with theirs. . . . A being of higher faculties requires more to make him happy, is capable probably of more acute suffering, and certainly accessible to it at more points, than one of an inferior type; but in spite of these liabilities, he can never really wish to sink into what he feels to be a lower grade of existence. . . . It is better to be a human being dissatisfied than a pig satisfied; better to be Socrates dissatisfied than a fool satisfied. And if the fool, or the pig, are of a different opinion, it is because they only know their own side of the question. The other party to the comparison knows both sides.[11]

Thus, for Mill, there is a *qualitative* pleasure in just being human that is better than any of the pleasures experienced by other creatures.

Pause for Thought   Is Mill really saying that true happiness has less to do with pleasure directly than in fulfilling our higher human faculties? Even if you are an unhappy educated person, would you trade places with a blissfully happy uneducated person?

Kinds of Pleasures

How do we tell which pleasures are better than others? Mill held we could not measure either the quantity or the quality of pleasures. We can express our preference only when we have experienced both their quantity and quality. Setting aside moral considerations, once we have experienced both kinds of pleasures we will see that one exceeds the other in quality and is more desirable.

> On a question which is the best worth having of two pleasures, or which of two modes of existence is the most grateful to the feelings, apart from its moral attributes and from its consequences, the judgment of those who are qualified by knowledge of both, or, if they differ, that of the majority among them, must be admitted as final. . . . What means are there of determining which is the acutest of two pains, or the intensest of two pleasurable sensations, except the general suffrage of those who are familiar with both? Neither pains nor pleasures are homogeneous, and pain is always heterogeneous with pleasure. What is there to decide whether a particular pleasure is worth purchasing at the cost of a particular pain, except the feelings and judgment of the experienced?[12]

Pause for Thought

Do moral acts give you more pleasure than playing computer games or eating ice cream? How do you judge the quality of pleasure in your life?

For Mill, Bentham's pleasure–pain calculus is infeasible. There is no way to measure pleasure and pain. People will express a quality preference based on their experience.

Moral Philosophy

For Bentham, the greatest happiness principle meant that we should choose acts that give us the greatest quantity of pleasure, one of which consisted of helping others. Mill agreed, but he added the quality of *altruism* to Bentham's idea. In contrast to Bentham's egoistic pleasure, Mill's altruism promotes the welfare of others by emphasizing the Golden Rule: Treat others as you would have others treat you.

> The utilitarian morality does recognise in human beings the power of sacrificing their own greatest good for the good of others. . . .
> I must again repeat, what the assailants of utilitarianism seldom have the justice to acknowledge, that the happiness which forms the utilitarian standard of what is right in conduct, is not the agent's own happiness, but that of all concerned. As between his own happiness and that of others, utilitarianism requires him to be as strictly impartial as a disinterested and benevolent spectator. In the golden rule of Jesus of Nazareth, we read the complete spirit of

the ethics of utility. To do as you would be done by, and to love your neighbour as yourself, constitute the ideal perfection of utilitarian morality.[13]

Emphasizing the social nature of human beings, Mill claimed that we could find the foundation of Utilitarian morality in "the social feelings of mankind." The good is our desire to be in unity with our fellow creatures. Without such a desire, civilization would not progress. "The social state is at once so natural . . . to man, that, except in some unusual circumstances . . . he never conceives himself otherwise than as a member of a body." Thus, granting that each individual has a right to his or her own happiness, that act will be right that brings into existence the greatest amount of happiness for the greatest number of people.

Mill's View of Education

Mill thought education should contribute to the common happiness by teaching the skills an individual needs to live well and productively. Using goodwill and reason, people could live healthy and dignified lives. He believed that citizens of goodwill could extinguish poverty, and scientific progress combined with "good physical and moral education" could alleviate the scourge of disease.

As for vicissitudes of fortune, and other disappointments connected with worldly circumstances, these are principally the effect either of gross imprudence, of ill-regulated desires, or of bad or imperfect social institutions.
  All the grand sources, in short, of human suffering are in a great degree, many of them almost entirely, conquerable by human care and effort; and though their removal is grievously slow—though a long succession of generations will perish in the breach before the conquest is completed, and this world becomes all that, if will and knowledge were not wanting, it might easily be made—yet every mind sufficiently intelligent and generous to bear a part, however small and unconspicuous, in the endeavour, will draw a noble enjoyment from the contest itself, which he would not for any bribe in the form of selfish indulgence consent to be without.[14]

When people who are tolerably fortunate in their outward lot do not find in life sufficient enjoyment to make it valuable to them, the cause generally is, caring for nobody but themselves.[15]

Pause for Thought   Do you see any connection between periods of unhappiness and intense self-interest in your own life? According to Mill, what would be the best way out of such a state?

Happiness

For Mill, happiness is the most desirable goal of all human beings. As our most desirable goal, it is our duty to pursue it for ourselves and for others.

Pause for Thought   Do you agree with Mill that happiness is the most desirable end of human life and morality? How can we know if it is or is not the most desirable goal?

When Mill's critics asked him for proof that happiness is our most desirable goal, he answered:

> The only proof capable of being given that an object is visible, is that people actually see it. The only proof that a sound is audible, is that people hear it: and so of the other sources of our experience. In like manner, I apprehend, the sole evidence it is possible to produce that anything is desirable, is that people do actually desire it. If the end which the utilitarian doctrine proposes to itself were not, in theory and in practice, acknowledged to be an end, nothing could ever convince any person that it was so. No reason can be given why the general happiness is desirable, except that each person, so far as he believes it to be attainable, desires his own happiness.[16]

Pause for Thought   Is Mill's argument valid? Is *desirability* related to *happiness* in the same way that *visible* is to *seen*? Does our desire for happiness imply that it is a moral goal?

Duty

In his explanation of our desire for happiness, Mill departed from Bentham's external standard of goodness and turned his sights inward. It is not our desire for happiness alone, he said, but an internal sense of duty arising from conscience that directs moral thought.

> The internal sanction of duty, whatever our standard of duty may be, is one and the same—a feeling in our own mind; a pain, more or less intense, attendant on violation of duty, which in properly cultivated moral natures rises, in the more serious cases, into shrinking from it as an impossibility. This feeling, when disinterested, and connecting itself with the pure idea of duty, and not with some particular form of it, or with any of the merely

accessory circumstances, is the essence of Conscience; though in that complex phenomenon as it actually exists, the simple fact is in general all encrusted over with collateral associations, derived from sympathy, from love, and still more from fear; from all the forms of religious feeling; from the recollections of childhood and of all our past life; from self-esteem, desire of the esteem of others, and occasionally even self-abasement.[17]

Pause for Thought   Does your conscience leave you with a feeling of guilt when you don't do your duty? Does conscience tell us what our duty is?

Agreeing with Hume, Mill concluded that morality is a "powerful natural sentiment—a subjective feeling in our own minds." He concluded that morality is "the conscientious feelings of mankind."

Liberty

In his essay *On Liberty*, Mill advocated unlimited freedom of expression to discover truth. Sticking to the greatest good for the greatest number, Mill thought, citizens should have the freedom to criticize their government, worship as they please, and choose their own lifestyle.

Human liberty. It comprises, first the inward domain of consciousness; demanding liberty of conscience in the most comprehensive sense; liberty of thought and feeling; absolute freedom of opinion and sentiment on all subjects, practical or speculative, scientific, moral, or theological. The liberty of expressing and publishing opinions may seem to fall under a different principle, since it belongs to that part of the conduct of an individual which concerns other people; but, being almost of as much importance as the liberty of thought itself, and resting in great part on the same reasons, is practically inseparable from it.

Secondly, the principle requires liberty of tastes and pursuits; of framing the plan of our life to suit our own character; of doing as we like, subject to such consequences as may follow: without impediment from our fellow creatures, so long as what we do does not harm them, even though they should think our conduct foolish, perverse, or wrong.

Thirdly, from this liberty of each individual, follows the liberty, within the same limits, of combination among individuals; freedom to unite, for any purpose not involving harm to others: the persons combining being supposed to be of full age, and not forced or deceived.[18]

Pause for Thought   Can any of Mill's ideas on liberty be found in the Constitution of the United States?

Mill believed that unlimited freedom of expression was the only means we have to discover truth. People must be free to express their thoughts, because often we can best discover truth by refuting falsehoods. If we never challenge the opinions of others, including governments and religious institutions, then we easily allow ourselves to depend on someone else's authority. When that happens, the public tends toward conformity.

> We can never be sure that the opinion we are endeavouring to stifle is a false opinion; and if we were sure, stifling it would be an evil still.
>
> First: the opinion which it is attempted to suppress by authority may possibly be true. Those who desire to suppress it, of course deny its truth; but they are not infallible. . . . To refuse a hearing to an opinion, because they are sure that it is false, is to assume that *their* certainty is the same as *absolute* certainty. . . . Ages are no more infallible than individuals; every age having held many opinions which subsequent ages have deemed not only false but absure; and it is as certain that many opinions now general will be rejected by future ages, as it is that many, once general, are rejected by the present. . . .
>
> Complete liberty of contradicting and disproving our opinion is the very condition which justifies us in assuming its truth for purposes of action; and on no other terms can a being with human faculties have any rational assurance of being right.
>
> Let us now pass to the second division of the argument, and dismissing the supposition that any of the received opinions may be false, let us assume them to be true, and examine into the worth of the manner in which they are likely to be held, when their truth is not freely and openly canvassed. . . .
>
> Both teachers and learners go to sleep at their post, as soon as there is no enemy in the field. . . . There are many truths of which the full meaning *cannot* be realised until personal experience has brought it home. But much more of the meaning even of these would have been understood, and what was understood would have been far more deeply impressed on the mind, if the man had been accustomed to hear it argued *pro* and *con* by people who did understand it. The fatal tendency of mankind to leave off thinking about a thing when it is no longer doubtful, is the cause of half their errors. A contemporary author [de Tocqueville] has well spoken of "the deep slumber of a decided opinion."[19]

Conformists end up in a stagnant society. Progressive individuals instigate progress. Mill did not advocate performing any kind of action regardless of who it affects. If you get drunk, he might say, you must suffer the consequences of jail, because you are socially harmful to society. But he took a strong stand on what he considered unjustifiable encroachments on personal freedom. He opposed the suppression of the Mormon practice of polygamy, the prohibition of gambling and prostitution, and restrictions other than registration on selling poisons. No one should be subject to the powers of government except to prevent harm to others.

Mill felt that the chief danger of democracy was suppressing individual differences and allowing no real development of minority opinion.

The ideally best form of government is that in which the sovereignty, or supreme controlling power in the last resort, is vested in the entire aggregate of the community; every citizen not only having a voice in the exercise of that ultimate sovereignty, but being, at least occasionally, called on to take an actual part in the government, by the personal discharge of some public function, local or general.[20]

Pause for Thought   Does today's United States government meet Mill's "ideally best form of government"?

Harriet Taylor
(with John Stuart Mill)

Though they wrote nearly one hundred years later, Harriet Taylor (1807–1858) and John Stuart Mill joined Wollstonecraft in celebrating women's rationality. Together Taylor and Mill wrote essays on women's issues, but their writings were always published under John Mill's name. A male author wielded more power.

Taylor and Mill met in 1830 when Harriet Taylor was already married to John Taylor and the mother of two sons. Their daughter was born later. An intellectual and emotional attraction formed between Harriet and John, and they enjoyed a platonic relationship for twenty years. When her husband, John Taylor, died, she married Mill. Before her husband died, however, Harriet Taylor and Mill had spent considerable time together writing and spending weekends along the English coast. So long as Harriet lived "as the wife in his house" for the "external formality, " John Taylor agreed to the arrangement.

On Women

With Wollstonecraft, Taylor and Mill argued that society created the differences between the equality of men and women. They questioned much of the English law of their day. First, everyone expected women to marry and to follow these laws:

1. A married woman can have no property except in her husband; anything she inherits immediately becomes his.
2. There is a way for a woman to secure "her" property from her husband, but even so she is not allowed the use of it; if he by violence takes it from her, he can not be punished or compelled to return it to her.
3. Husband and wife are called "one person in law, " but that means only that whatever is hers is his (not vice versa).
4. Her children are by law *his* children. She can do nothing with them except by his delegation. On his death she does not become their legal guardian, unless he by will makes her so.

5. If she leaves her husband, she can take nothing with her, not even her children. He can—by force, if it comes to that—compel her to return.[21]

Because women were thought to lack intelligence, they could not vote or stand for Parliament. Men considered them best suited for domestic jobs. In fact, Taylor and Mill believed that society thought very much like this:

> [From] the fact that from the very earliest twilight of human society, every woman (owing to the value attached to her by men, combined with her inferiority in muscular strength) was found in a state of bondage to some man.[22]

In close agreement with Mary Wollstonecraft, Taylor and Mill argued that the law of the strongest, which was accepted by both men and women, was the reason why women suffered subordination. The same state of consciousness supported the power of kings over slaves and the power of husbands over wives. Taylor and Mill thought the need for power showed itself in pride, which was common to the "whole male sex."

> It comes home to the person and hearth of every male head of a family, and of everyone who looks forward to being so. The clodhopper exercises, or is to exercise, his share of the power equally with the highest nobleman. And the case is that in which the desire of power is the strongest: for everyone who desires power, desires it most over those who are nearest him, with whom his life is passed, with whom he has most concerns in common, and in whom any independence of his authority is oftenest likely to interfere with his individual preferences. . . . Every one of the subjects lives under the very eye, and almost, it may be said, in the hands, of one of the masters—in closer intimacy with him than with any of her fellow-subjects; with no means of combining against him, and, on the other hand, with the strongest motives for seeking his favour and avoiding to give him offence.[23]

> All men, except the most brutish, desire to have, in the woman most nearly connected with them, not a forced slave but a willing one, not a slave merely, but a favourite. . . . The masters of women wanted more than simple obedience, and they turned the whole force of education to effect their purpose.[24]

Nineteenth-century literature and education that was concerned with the relationships between men and women taught that a woman's place was to please men. She did this through her dress and outer appearance as well as by serving his wants and needs. As Mary Wollstonecraft pointed out, society taught women to exhibit their sensuality, not their intelligence. With all of this, society expected her to be sexually virtuous. When applied to men, however, the idea of virtue had little or nothing to do with sex. Looked on as lesser beings than men, women were taught the "virtue" of submission to their superiors.

All women are brought up from the very earliest years in the belief that their ideal of character is the very opposite to that of men; not self-will, and government by self-control, but submission, and yielding to the control of others. All the moralities tell them that it is the duty of women, and all the current sentimentalities that it is their nature, to live for others; to make complete abnegation of themselves, and to have no life but in their affections. And by their affections are meant the only ones they are allowed to have—those to the men with whom they are connected, or to the children who constitute an additional and indefeasible tie between them and a man. When we put together three things—first, the natural attraction between the sexes; secondly, the wife's entire dependence on the husband, every privilege or pleasure she has being either his gift, or depending entirely on his will; and lastly, that the principal object of human pursuit, consideration, and all objects of social ambition, can in general be sought or obtained by her only through him, it would be a miracle if the object of being attractive to men and not become the polar star of feminine education and formation of character. And, this great means of influence over the minds of women having been acquired, an instinct of selfishness made men avail themselves of it to the utmost as a means of holding women in subjection, by representing to them meekness, submissiveness, and resignation of all individual will into the hands of a man, as an essential part of sexual attractiveness.[25]

Pause for Thought   Has the nineteenth century view of women changed today? Do you men think that a submissive woman is sexually more attractive than a woman who shares equally in intelligence and ability? Are you women taught to be dependent and submissive if you want to be sexually attractive?

Women were taught that their major interest should be in domestic affairs. They were not to live by their independent use of reason. Men said that women, by their very nature, thrived on emotion, not reason.

She neither knows or cares which is the right side in politics, but she knows what will bring in money or invitations, give her husband a title, her son a place, or her daughter a good marriage.[26]

In her essay "Enfranchisement of Women," Taylor argued that women would prove society mistaken about its view of women as pleasure-giving objects when women are given:

1. *Education* in primary and high schools, universities, medical, legal, and theological institutions.

2. *Partnership* in the labors and gains, risks, and remunerations of productive industry.

3. *A coequal share* in the formation and administration of laws—municipal, state, and national—through legislative assemblies, courts, and executive officers.[27]

What Taylor and Mill wanted for women was equality with men before the law, independence, freedom to make their own choices, physical strength, and freedom to get a true education that included philosophy, science, and literature. They wanted society to view women as individuals in their own right, not existing as only relative to men, and for men to stop defining the "nature" of women *to* women. Mill wrote:

> I consider it presumption in anyone to pretend to decide what women are or are not, can or cannot be, by natural constitution. They have always hitherto been kept, as far as regards spontaneous development, in so unnatural a state, that their nature cannot but have been greatly distorted and disguised; and no one can safely pronounce that if women's nature were left to choose its direction as freely as men's, and if no artificial bent were attempted to be given to it except that required by the conditions of human society, and given to both sexes alike, there would be any material difference, or perhaps any difference at all, in the character and capacities which would unfold themselves.[28]

Pause for Thought   Do we have a conflict of views about men and women today? For example, do we see a difference in the portrayal of the roles of men and women in the corporate world as compared to MTV?

Summary

The Utilitarians wanted to reform society by applying the principle of greatest happiness. For Wollstonecraft and Taylor, the greatest happiness would be in the equality of women with men. Bentham and Mill said that a greater happiness for society would be realized by providing decent living conditions and better education for both men and women. All of the Utilitarians wanted to awaken people to the injustices and increasing inequality in society. They hoped to bring more happiness to the poor and working classes by improving their living conditions.

Wollstonecraft's major thesis was to have women treated as persons instead of as the playthings of men. Using Kant's concept of goodwill, she hoped to see women treated as ends in themselves and not as means to the happiness of others.

Wollstonecraft said women deserve the same education as men. She argued that women are neither deficient in reason nor differ in intelligence from men.

By using her rational mind, a woman can develop her moral capacities and attain her full human potential—personhood.

Jeremy Bentham and John Stuart Mill chose to develop Hume's ideas by defining virtue in terms of utility: "The rightness of an action is identical with the happiness it produces as its consequence." Bentham saw the greatest happiness principle as the principle of utility: That action is best which produces the greatest happiness for the greatest number.

Bentham reasoned that pleasure and pain are the motivating factors in all human beings. This thinking resurrected hedonism. He subscribed to two types of hedonism: psychological hedonism, or the belief that pleasure and pain determine what we do; and ethical hedonism, in which pleasure is the only good, and actions are good only if they produce pleasure. If we act selfishly, we will suffer painful consequences. Morality depends on the consequences of our acts. Pleasure is the consequence that confers the quantity of morality on an act. Society punishes those who inflict pain on others.

Based on his "calculus of felicity, " Bentham thought we could calculate which course of action would produce the greatest amount of happiness.

John Stuart Mill coined the term *utilitarianism* and refined Bentham's principle of utility. Mill reasoned that pleasures also differ in quality, not just quantity. Though we cannot measure quality or quantity of pleasure, when we have experienced both, we can express our preference. Mill believed people would express a quality preference based on their experience.

In contrast to Bentham's egoistic pleasure, Mill's altruism promotes the welfare of others by emphasizing the Golden Rule: Treat others as you would have others treat you. Using goodwill and reason, Mill argued that citizens could live healthy and dignified lives and extinguish poverty. Happiness is the most desirable goal of all human beings, and it is our duty to pursue it for ourselves and others. Our internal sense of duty arises from our conscience and directs moral thought. He agreed with Hume that morality is the "conscientious feelings of mankind."

Mill advocated unlimited freedom of expression to discover truth. Without freedom, society falls into a dull conformity. Liberty is the key to a nation's survival.

Harriet Taylor joined Wollstonecraft in celebrating women's rationality. Taylor and Mill both argued that women should not be in subordination to men, because men are not their superiors. Women need equal (1) education, (2) partnership in labor and gains, and (3) an equal share in forming and administrating laws. Society should view women as individuals in their own right, not as existing merely in relation to men.

Connections

For more than one hundred years, the moral and political aspects of Utilitarian philosophy influenced England. English moralists and lawmakers liked its simplicity, and it confirmed what people already thought: Everyone searches for pleasure and happiness. Because of their practicality, the Utilitarians became the spokesmen for the twentieth-century philosophy of Pragmatism. Preceding Pragmatism, however, an anti-Utilitarianism philosophy, **Individualism**, developed. Opposing the social environment, such individualists as Kierkegaard, Nietzsche, and Rand emphasized the inward. In the next chapter we will follow the individualist's argument that a complete autonomous individual is more important than the happiness of the masses. These individualists rejected the traditional concept that sympathy is the proper foundation for moral values.

Study Questions

1. What principles of Kant's ethics did Wollstonecraft consider important for women?

2. According to Rousseau, what kind of education do women need?

3. Give Wollstonecraft's argument for the injustice of women's subjection to men.

4. According to Wollstonecraft, what must women do to attain their full human potential?

5. Explain Jeremy Bentham's principle of utility.

6. For Bentham, what are the motivating factors of all human beings?

7. Explain Bentham's two kinds of Utilitarian hedonism.

8. What is the greatest happiness principle?

9. What is the main difference between the ethics of Kant and Bentham?

10. Explain Bentham's calculus of felicity.

11. Contrast Bentham's notion of self-interest with Mill's.

12. How do Bentham and Mill differ in their methods of calculating happiness?

13. How does Mill propose to determine the quality of pleasures?

14. For Mill, how can education contribute to the common happiness?

15. How does Mill prove that happiness is our most desirable goal?

16. What role does duty play in Mill's ethics?

17. What is Mill's view of liberty?

18. What were some of the English laws regarding women that Harriet Taylor and Mill questioned?

19. According to Taylor, how did men hold women in submission?

20. According to Taylor, how would women be helped by education, partnership, and their participation in law making?

21. In your own words, explain Harriet Taylor's view of women.

Notes

1. Mary Wollstonecraft, *A Vindication of the Rights of Woman* (ed. by Miriam Brody) (6th ed.), pp. 177–181. London: Penguin Books, 1992.

2. Ibid., pp. 300, 306.

3. Ibid., p. 269.

4. Jeremy Bentham, *An Introduction to the Principles of Morals and Legislation*, Ch. I, Sec.1. London: Oxford University Press, 1823.

5. Ibid., Sec. 3.

6. Ibid., Sec. 6.

7. Ibid., Ch. III, Sec. 9.

8. Ibid., Ch. IV, Sec. 5.

9. John Stuart Mill, *Autobiography* (ed. by J. D. Stillinger), pp. 83–84. London: Oxford University Press, 1971.

10. Ibid., pp. 97–98.

11. John Stuart Mill, "What Utilitarianism Is," Chapter 2 in *Utilitarianism* (The Great Books series), pp. 448–449. Chicago: University of Chicago Press.

12. Ibid., p. 450.

13. Ibid., p. 453.

14. Ibid., p. 452.

15. Ibid., p. 451.

16. Ibid., p. 461.

17. Ibid., p. 458.

18. Ibid., pp. 272–273.

19. Mill, *On Liberty* (The Great Books series), op. cit., p. 287.

20. Mill, *Representative Government* (The Great Books series), op. cit., p. 344.

21. Norman Melchert, *The Great Conversation*, 2nd ed., p. 479. Mountain View, CA: Mayfield Publishing Co., 1995.

22. John Stuart Mill, *The Subjection of Women* (ed. by Mary Warnock), p. 223. London: J. M. Dent, Everyman's Library, 1986.

23. Ibid., p. 228.

24. Ibid., p. 232.

25. Ibid., pp. 232–233.

26. Ibid., p. 255.

27. Harriet Taylor (Mill), *Enfranchisement of Women*, in John Stuart Mill and Harriet Taylor Mill, *Essay on Sex Equality* (ed. by Alice S. Rossi), p. 95. Chicago: University of Chicago Press, 1970.

28. Mill, *Subjection of Women*, op. cit., p. 273.

CHAPTER TWELVE

Individualism: Kierkegaard, Nietzsche, Rand

In general, Marx would have disagreed with the Utilitarians, but he shared their belief that we can know human nature through the method of empirical science. The Utilitarians reasoned that by observing the social and psychological processes of people and their societies, we could attain objective knowledge. Both the Utilitarians and Marx looked forward to a social progress that would benefit everyone.

Although the empirical method dominated Europe and America for many years, a countermovement slowly, almost imperceptibly began to take root. As we shall see, Søren Kierkegaard, Friedrich Nietzsche, and Ayn Rand began to ask probing questions. Do the objective inquiries of the Rationalists and Empiricists really affect the conflicts that we as individuals experience in our daily lives? Does an understanding of the synthetic a priori have any bearing on the choices we must make as individuals? Can the cosmological arguments for God provide us with faith? Does an elaborate metaphysical structure of the universe help us make critical decisions in daily life? Is happiness for the masses a fiction?

Kierkegaard, Nietzsche, and Rand said we think of ourselves as individuals, yet we conform to the group. We identify ourselves with a church, a race, a fraternity, a gang, or some type of organization that gives us a sense of belonging. We think we are living the way we choose to, but are we really? Do you know who you are? Do I know who I am? Or do we make choices to please those in our crowd? What does it mean to be an individual person?

Known as the "Father of Existentialism" (see Chapter 17), Kierkegaard was one of the first philosophers to express the importance of shifting from purely rational objectivity to viewing humanity subjectively and as individuals. He said intelligence has to be opposed, and because he had such an "immense intelligence," he was the one for the job.

Søren Kierkegaard

Kierkegaard's Life

Born in Copenhagen, Denmark, Søren Kierkegaard (1813–1855) was the youngest of seven children. His mother had been a servant, and his father grew up in poverty as a peasant. While still a boy, his father had cursed God, blaming him for the conditions of his life. The rest of his life he never forgave himself for his outburst. In his *Journals*, Kierkegaard remarks:

> How terrible about the man who once as a little boy, while herding sheep on the heaths of Jutland, suffering greatly, in hunger and in want, stood upon a hill and cursed God—and the man was unable to forget it even when he was eighty-two years old.[1]

Through hard work and intelligence, his father rose from peasantry to become a successful and influential merchant. But he passed his melancholy disposition to his frail son, Søren. When Søren Kierkegaard was born, his father was already an old man. He raised his children in a strict Christian atmosphere, and as James Mill did with his son, he educated Søren at home, putting him through rigorous intellectual training.

In 1830, the younger Kierkegaard enrolled in the University of Copenhagen to study theology, because his father had wanted him to become a minister. Soon, however, Kierkegaard discovered that his true interests were philosophy and literature. He spent the next ten years living a sensuous life as a rich merchant's son, spending huge sums of money on food, drink, and clothing. He was popular at parties, but his indulgences merely threw him into deep despair:

> I have just returned from a party of which I was the life and soul; wit poured from my lips, everyone laughed and admired me—but I went away————————————————————————
> ————and the dash should be as long as the earth's orbit and wanted to shoot myself.[2]

On his twenty-fifth birthday, May 15, 1838, Kierkegaard's father confessed to him the sexual sins of his own youth and his belief that God had condemned his family. Four days later, Søren Kierkegaard experienced a religious conversion, accompanied by an "indescribable joy." The experience was so powerful he gave up his wild life and returned to studying theology. That same year, his father died.

At age twenty-seven, Kierkegaard fell in love with Regina Olsen, who had just turned fourteen. They became engaged. Within a year, over her protests, he broke off their engagement. His decision haunted him, but as a man with a mission, he believed he must

> live a life wholly dedicated to God, a life in which he was to devote himself to the task of becoming a Christian and . . . of bringing to the attention of others what is involved in becoming a Christian.[3]

Two weeks after ending their relationship, Kierkegaard went to Berlin, where he wrote *Either/Or: A Fragment of Life* and *Repetition: An Essay in Experimental Psychology,* both in 1843. In *Repetition* he hoped to reconcile with Regina, but when he heard of her engagement to a former boyfriend, he destroyed the pages about their possible reconciliation. Kierkegaard compared his sacrifice of his love for Regina with Abraham's offering of Issac to God in the Bible (Genesis 22). He had to make a choice: "*Either* devote my life to God *or* live in comfort with Regina." In Genesis, however, God had saved Issac and Abraham. Why had God not saved his life with Regina? After much pondering, Kierkegaard decided that no universal principle could be applied to such situations. There are only individual predicaments. It was God's will that Kierkegaard lost Regina. But what did God expect him to do? Confused, Kierkegaard wrote:

> What I really lack is to be clear in my mind *what I am to do*, not what I am to know, except in so far as certain understanding must precede every action. The thing is to understand myself, to see what God really wishes *me* to do; the thing is to find a truth which is true *for me*, to find *the idea for which I can live and die*. What would be the use of discovering so-called objective truth, of working through all the systems of philosophy and of being able, if required, to review them all and show up the inconsistencies within each system;—what good would it do me to be able to explain the meaning of Christianity if it had *no* deeper significance *for me and for my life*;—what good would it do me if the truth stood before me, cold and naked, not caring whether I recognised her or not, producing in me a shudder of fear rather than a trusting devotion? I certainly do not deny that I still recognise an *imperative of understanding* and that through it one can work upon men, *but it must be taken up into my life,* and *that is* what I now recognise as the most important thing. That is what my soul longs after, as the African desert thirsts for water. That is what I lack, and that is why I am left standing like a man who has rented a house and gathered all the furniture and household things together, but has not yet found the beloved with whom to share the joys and sorrows of his life.[4]

Finding what God expected of him, Kierkegaard spent the rest of his life in a brilliant literary career. In 1843, he also published *Fear and Trembling*. Following these works were *The Concept of Dread* and *Philosophical Fragments,* both in 1844. The next year he wrote *Stages on Life's Way,* and in 1846 the *Concluding Unscientific Postscript.* In 1848, Kierkegaard experienced another religious revelation that changed his life. He wrote about this joyous event in his *Journal.* In 1848, *Christian Discourses* and *The Point of View* were published. His *Sickness Unto Death* appeared in 1849. He died in 1855 at the early age of forty-two.

Existence

Like Marx, Kierkegaard was a student of but not favorably impressed by Hegel's philosophy. If Hegel had called his own philosophy merely "an experiment in thought," Kierkegaard said, then he would have been one of the greatest thinkers of all time. "As it is, he is merely comic." What did Kierkegaard find so comical in Hegel? The German's attempt to embrace all of reality in a system of thought. But, said Kierkegaard, Hegel had forgotten the most important element: *existence.*

Kierkegaard said Hegel's philosophy shifted people's attention away from the individual to universals. It asked people *to think* instead of *to be.* Where Hegel found truth in the absolute spirit and objectivity, Kierkegaard found truth in the relative and subjective. Life was too precious and mysterious to be molded into a system of abstract logic. Human beings, he said, are not objective spectators, but actors involved in the drama of existence. The truly existing individual must be passionate as well as conscious.

> It is impossible to exist without passion, unless we understand the word "exist" in the loose sense of a so-called existence. Every Greek thinker was therefore essentially a passionate thinker. I have often reflected how one might bring a man into a state of passion. I have thought in this connection that if I could get him seated on a horse and the horse made to take fright and gallop wildly, or better still, for the sake of bringing the passion out, if I could take a man who wanted to arrive at a certain place as quickly as possible, and hence already had some passion, and could set him astride a horse that can scarcely walk—and yet this is what existence is like if one is to become consciously aware of it. Or if a driver were otherwise not especially inclined toward passion, if someone hitched a team of horses to a wagon for him, one of them a Pegasus and the other a worn-out jade, and told him to drive—I think one might succeed. And it is just this that it means to exist, if one is to become conscious of it. Eternity is the winged horse, infinitely fast, and time is a worn-out jade; the existing individual is the driver. That is to say, he is such a driver when his mode of existence is not an existence loosely so called; for then he is no driver, but a drunken peasant who lies asleep in the wagon and lets the horses take care of themselves. To be sure, he also drives and is a driver; and so there are perhaps many who—also exist.[5]

Though Kierkegaard criticized the system of rational knowledge as an answer to life's problems, he said mathematics and science are legitimate methods when used properly. And he rejected the ideas of systematic philosophers that we could use scientific or rational systems to understand human nature. For instance, Plato believed if we know universal "Forms," especially the Form of Good, then we will do the good. Kierkegaard thought such thinking distorted our actual human dilemma. Whether we know the good or not, we stand in the face of having to make individual decisions.

He illustrated his belief that science and mathematics have little to do with daily life by turning again to the biblical story of Abraham in Genesis 22. "God did tempt Abraham and said unto him, Abraham: and he said, here I am. And he said, take now thy son, thine only son, Isaac, whom thou lovest." Kierkegaard asked if science or mathematics can help Abraham decide whether to obey God and sacrifice his son? Like Abraham, we all face situations that compel us to become aware of ourselves.

Truth as Subjectivity

Science and mathematics consider objective principles that are common to all humans, but to exist has little to do with objective principles. To exist means to be subjectively aware of our unique individuality. The important truths are personal. Truth is subjectivity, "the tension of the subjective inwardness." Kierkegaard defined truth as:

> An objective uncertainty held fast in an appropriation-process of the most passionate inwardness. . . . The truth is precisely the venture which chooses an objective uncertainty with the passion of the infinite. I contemplate the order of nature in the hope of finding God, and I see omnipotence and wisdom; but I also see much else that disturbs my mind and excites anxiety. The sum of all this is an objective uncertainty. But it is for this very reason that the inwardness becomes as intense as it is, for it embraces this objective uncertainty with the entire passion of the infinite. In the case of a mathematic proposition the objectivity is given, but for this reason the truth of such a proposition is an indifferent truth.[6]

Kierkegaard agreed with Socrates that ignorance keeps us from the truth.

> The Socratic ignorance, which Socrates held fast with the entire passion of his inwardness, was thus an expression for the principle that the eternal truth is related to an existing individual, and that this truth must therefore be a paradox for him as long as he exists. . . .[7]

Pause for Thought

We can be certain that eight plus four is twelve. That is reasoned truth that every philosopher since Descartes had talked about. But Kierkegaard asked, "Do you include it in your daily prayers? Is it something you will lie awake pondering over?"

Do you agree with Kierkegaard that objective truths are immaterial to your existence? Or do you see the universe through the eyes of Plato or Hegel?

Existence as Alienation

For Kierkegaard, existence means that we humans have fallen away from our essential nature—our immortal relationship to God, the infinite. Our existential condition of mortality and despair is a result of our alienation from God.

Essential Self
(Relationship to God)

The | **Fall**

Existence
(Alienation from God)

According to Kierkegaard, all human beings have the inner drive to find their essential selves. Speculative reason cannot bridge the gap between ourselves and God. The only way we can renew our relationship with God is through the "leap of faith." Through faith alone, we can realize our authentic selves.

The further our actions drive us from God, the greater our sense of alienation and despair. That is why it does no good to lose oneself in the crowd. Christian churches try to immerse people in a crowd, but this is wrong, said Kierkegaard. "A crowd in its very concept is the untruth" because it cultivates personal irresponsibility. It is far higher to relate ourselves to God than to be related to by anything else whether a person, a race, a vocation, or a church.

Pause for Thought

Do you sometimes feel safe in "a crowd" because you don't have to take responsibility for the outcome of an action? For example, do you feel safer in a classroom full of students than you would as the professor's only student?

Kierkegaard argued that until we actualize our essential selves in God, our lives are full of anxiety caused by our alienation. That is why he opposed the mass consciousness of the crowd and advocated individual awareness, commitment, and responsibility. The anxiety of alienation creates in us a dynamic drive to find who we truly are—our essential self. Kierkegaard explained this dynamic drive as the "stages on life's way."

Stages on Life's Way

Based on his own experience, Kierkegaard discovered three stages in life: (1) aesthetic, (2) ethical, and (3) religious. The three stages are three ways to make choices.

The Aesthetic Stage

In the aesthetic stage, choice is taken lightly. The aesthetic individual lives for selfish pleasure and refuses to make commitments. It is a life of whim, immediate satisfaction, and gratification with no concern with the past or the future. For the person in the aesthetic stage, there are no moral principles, no good or evil, only fulfillment and frustration, pleasure and pain, ecstasy and despair.

The aesthetic existence is the life of the romantic such as the legendary Don Juan in his unending quest for "sensual faithless love." Sensual love is only for the moment, and the same thing repeats itself over and over endlessly. Don Juan does not know how to develop a lasting relationship, for "he makes short work of it" and needs always to be the victor. He has no principles. He doesn't see women as individuals, only as objects for his impulsive pleasure.

Whether water skiing, hot air ballooning, eating a gourmet meal, or being the life of the party, the aesthetic wants only the immediate moment. This person lives wholly in the world of the senses and is a slave to personal desires and moods. "The whole secret lies in arbitrariness," because in this stage everything you experience must constantly change. Boredom is the experience the aesthetic wants to avoid. Everything that is boring is bad. Nothing is more horrible!

> People with experience maintain that proceeding from a basic principle is supposed to be very reasonable; I yield to them and proceed from the basic principle that all people are boring. Or is there anyone who would be boring enough to contradict me in this regard? . . . Boredom is the root of all evil.
>
> This can be traced back to the very beginning of the world. The gods were bored; therefore they created human beings. Adam was bored because he was alone; therefore Eve was created. Since that moment, boredom entered the world and grew in quantity in exact proportion to the growth of population. Adam was bored alone; then Adam and Eve were bored together; then Adam and Eve and Cain and Abel were bored *en famille*. After that, the population of the world increased and the nations were bored *en masse*. To amuse themselves, they hit upon the notion of building

a tower so high that it would reach the sky. This notion is just as boring as the tower was high and is a terrible demonstration of how boredom had gained the upper hand.[8]

Once boredom sets in, said Kierkegaard, the aesthetic becomes obsessed with exploring new experiences. In the end, Don Juan lives not for pleasure and gratification, but to escape boredom.

Pause for Thought

Have there been phases in your life when you and your friends lived by the motto: "Eat, drink, and make merry, for tomorrow you may die?" Has boredom ever set in? Have you ever experienced a sense of dread and emptiness? If so, what turned you around?

At this point, the aesthetic, desperately searching for immediate pleasure, falls into despair. No one can live aesthetically without being in despair whether or not the individual knows it. Now the aesthetic dialectic sets in: Either/or (thesis and antithesis). (Notice that both Marx and Kierkegaard retained Hegel's dialectical method.)

Kierkegaard referred to the sensuous life as the cellar of the building that comprises the spirit. An individual, he said, "prefers to dwell in the cellar." But the power of the spirit sets the dialectic in motion, and the antithesis of the sensual life begins. Realizing the prospect of death and the meaninglessness of life, the aesthetic faces the decision *either* to continue the sensuous lifestyle *or* move to the next stage. This, said Kierkegaard, is not a rational choice between good and evil, but a decision made by an act of will, a commitment. It is not a question of choosing the right; it is a question of being earnest.

Pause for Thought

The matter of either/or, said Kierkegaard, is a matter of personal choice. Have you ever decided to quit drinking, smoking, overeating, or doing drugs? Could anybody do it for you?

The Ethical Stage

In the ethical stage, we replace sensuous pleasures by learning to accept moral principles. This is a stage of making decisions and committing to society's laws. Sensuous desires give way to reason and responsibility, and we begin to make authentic choices from within. Instead of yielding to impulses, such as hopping from lover to lover, we accept the responsibility of commitment or marriage as a rational obligation. At this stage, we live according to Kant's imperative to treat all human beings as ends in themselves and never as means only. As Don Juan represented the aesthetic man for Kierkegaard, Socrates, who lived according to the universal moral law, exemplifies the ethical individual.

Pause for Thought   You have accepted the responsibilities that go with being a college student. Do you ever feel the lure of the aesthetic stage? What convinces you to continue with your commitments?

Unlike the immediacy of the aesthetic life, reflection and responsibility characterize the ethical life. We become more serious and show a consistency in our moral choices. This stage is not unlike Kant's ethics of duty. We try to live by moral laws. We develop strong opinions on what is right and what is wrong. What matters is that we choose to have an opinion on what is right or wrong. The aesthetic's only concern is whether something is fun or boring.

Pause for Thought   Do you have strong opinions on the morality of abortion, euthanasia, and capital punishment? What morals are important in your life?

In the ethical stage, we ask the meaning of life and reflect on our principles. Almost everyone takes a stand on moral issues. Most people consider evil actions the product of a weak will or, like Socrates, of ignorance. Kierkegaard pointed to Socrates as an example of a person who took a stand based on universal moral obligation. As you will recall, Socrates' accusers took him to trial and the firm stand he took before his accusers led to his death. In Kierkegaard's eyes Socrates was a "tragic hero" who renounced his life to "express the universal."

But all our responsible choices—even the courage to put one's life on the line to follow a universal moral principle—are not enough, according to Kierkegaard, to escape the despair of sin (alienation from God).

Awareness of guilt, feelings of alienation, emptiness, and sin provide us with the subjective tools to transcend the universal. At this point, the either/or dialectic process begins to work deep within our consciousness. Kierkegaard believed that true insight is subjective: It comes from within.

With fear and trembling, we must either reject our new awareness and continue in the ethical stage, or take the leap of faith. Only through faith can we find ourselves in God, to whom we belong.

The Religious Stage

Kierkegaard's views on the religious stage are complex, and the transition to it is difficult. The religious stage is a higher level than the acceptance of the universal moral law because it is the highest subjective transformation in which the individual can experience complete freedom and self-actualization.

In the religious stage, individuals must see themselves "before God" to see themselves as they really are, with a gulf between themselves and God because of the sins they have committed. This stage is the highest of either/or choices, for it requires the highest commitment the individual can make. No one can know what God demands, thus, based on such uncertainty, Kierkegaard called this the "leap of faith." As an example of this leap, Kierkegaard chose Abraham, the "Father of Faith." Obeying God's command, Abraham reluctantly agreed to sacrifice his son, Isaac. As he lifted the knife to take his son's life, an angel stopped him and offered a sacrificial goat in Isaac's place.

Kierkegaard was telling us that the leap of faith is not rational, but absurd. How was Abraham to make such a decision? He could not rely on the moral codes of his tribe and culture. He knew what his wife and the members of the tribe would answer. No universal moral system could help him. He was alone with his faith in God and could answer to no one but God. And because Abraham could not follow the universal standard of morality, he broke through it. He made the transition from the moral stage into the religious stage.

For Kierkegaard, "The paradox of faith is this, that the individual is higher than the universal." Abraham "exists"—and for the existing individual, truth is that to which he is passionately committed. Thus, for the existing individual, truth and faith are the same. They both involve

the tension of the subjective inwardness. Here is such a definition of truth: *An objective uncertainty held fast in an appropriation-process of the most passionate inwardness is the truth*, the highest truth attainable for an *existing* individual. . . . Thus the subject merely has, objectively, the uncertainty; but it is this which precisely increases the tension of that infinite passion which constitutes his inwardness. The truth is precisely the venture which chooses an objective uncertainty with the passion of the infinite. I contemplate the order of nature in the hope of finding God, and I see omnipotence and wisdom; but I also see much else that disturbs my mind and excites anxiety. The sum of all this is an objective uncertainty. But it is for this very reason that the inwardness becomes as intense as it is, for it embraces this objective uncertainty with the passion of the infinite. In the case of a mathematic proposition the objectivity is given, but for this reason the truth of such a proposition is an indifferent truth [that is, the sort of truth that is contemplated by a thinker].

But the above definition of truth is an equivalent expression for faith. Without risk there is no faith. Faith is precisely the contradiction between the infinite passion of the individual's inwardness and the objective uncertainty. If I am capable of grasping God objectively, I do not believe, but precisely because I cannot do this I must believe. If I wish to preserve myself in faith I must constantly be intent upon holding fast to the objective uncertainty, so as to remain out upon the deep, over seventy thousand fathoms of water, still preserving my faith.[9]

Thus, only in the religious stage can the leap of faith take us into our true essential self in a relationship with God. A passionate commitment to God is all that can free us from meaninglessness and dread. In this stage, said Kierkegaard, we must be willing to give up everything to God, even universal moral laws.

Pause for Thought   Kierkegaard said the leap of faith is taken with fear and trembling, because God is subjectivity, and we don't know what to expect or what may be asked of us. Would you be willing to take such a leap?

As a non–church-going Christian, Kierkegaard saw complete freedom and selfhood as realizable in Christ. By His incarnation, Christ entered the "zone of the existential," thus creating the longed-for bridge between time and eternity. Christ said he would manifest himself to those who love him, and the manifested Christ would transform the lover into the "likeness of the thing beloved." To become what one loves is the only way of understanding.

En Masse

We can exist at any of the three stages on life's way. But despair and guilt will periodically raise their ugly heads to remind us of our alienation from our essential selves. The way we respond to the either/or dialectic that takes place within ourselves will show us the stage of our authenticity.

Unfortunately, said Kierkegaard, most people "flock together" for security.

Mankind *en masse* gives itself up to evil. . . . Nowadays it happens *en masse*. That is why people flock together, in order that natural and animal hysteria should get hold of them, in order to feel themselves stimulated, inflamed and *ausser sich*. . . . only in great masses do they dare to live, and they cluster together *en masse* in order to feel that they amount to something.[10]

Pause for Thought   Is Kierkegaard's statement above as true today as when it was written? Do we gather en masse to feel we amount to something? How strongly do you need the approval of others? Why is it so difficult to be a unique individual?

The key to existence, said Kierkegaard, is having the courage to find our essential self. "The task of the subjective thinker is to transform himself into an instrument that clearly and definitely expresses in existence whatever is essentially human." We can exist in any of the stages, but only through the leap of faith, can we realize our authentic—our essential—self.

On Women

In his work *Stages on Life's Way,* Kierkegaard dramatized a banquet given by Constantine Constantius. The topic of conversation is "Woman." Each speaker represents a different point of view, but none fully understands the nature of woman. As an existentialist, Kierkegaard did not want to limit the nature of woman to only one view. There are, for him, only individuals who are constantly making and remaking themselves. Thus, any attempt to understand all human beings will fail. Ironically, Kierkegaard's banquet speakers claim to know "woman" in a universal sense. They are, however, unaware of women as individuals.

Constantine characterizes woman as a kind of jest. Victor Eremita says woman has no significance whatsoever. The Ladies' Tailor identifies her with social life and fashion. Johannes the Seducer considers her an instrument of the gods and men.

> Constantine spoke as follows: . . .
>
> "And now for woman. . . . She can only be rightly construed under the category of jest. It is man's part to be absolute, to act absolutely, to give expression to the absolute; woman has her being in relationships. Between two such different beings no genuine reciprocal action can take place. This incongruity is precisely what constitutes jest, and it is with woman jest first came into the world. . . . "
>
> Victor Eremita . . . spoke as follows:
>
> ". . . . I will muster all the powers of my soul to express gratitude for the one boon which was accorded me: that I became a man and not a woman. . . .
>
> "The fact that she actually has less significance than man is not what constitutes her misfortune, even if she were to come to know it, for after all this is something that can be endured. No, the misfortune is that, owing to the romantic way in which she is regarded, her life has become meaningless, so that one moment she has the utmost significance and the next moment none whatever, without ever coming to know what her significance really is—yet

this is not the whole of her misfortune, for the worst of it is that she can never come to know it because she is a woman. . . . "

Hardly had Victor finished than the Ladies' Tailor sprang to his feet . . .

" . . . I know woman on her weak side, that is to say, I know her. As in heathen Prussia a marriageable girl wore a bell which served as a signal to the men, so likewise is the existence of a woman of fashion a perpetual bell-ringing, not for debauchees but for lickerish voluptuaries. . . . It is fashion that is a woman, for fashion is changeable in nonsense, is logically consistent only in becoming more and more crazy. . . . "

Thereupon Johannes the Seducer spoke . . . :

" . . . The man who is twenty years old and does not comprehend that there is a categorical imperative: Enjoy thyself—that man is a fool. And he who does not seize the opportunity is a Wesleyan Methodist. . . .

" . . . Oh blissful mode of living! . . . That nothing more marvelous, nothing more delicious, nothing more seductive can be devised than a woman, the gods vouch for, and the necessity which sharpened their invention. . . . "[11]

Pause for Thought   Does your view of woman correspond to any of the above views? How would you characterize woman?

The Unique Individual

Friedrich Nietzsche agreed that we must find our authentic individual self. However, he thought the self is not in God, but in the human being. Nietzsche believed that most human beings are "bungled and botched," and therefore unaware of their true selves. They see the world with a herd mentality. Because the masses or herd have no original thoughts, they pick up the excrement of great minds. So long as we stay in the masses, we remain essentially animals.

While for Hegel the huge cleft is between animal and human, Nietzsche considered the gulf between ordinary people and such extraordinary people as the artist, saint, and philosopher the serious gap. Individuals need to find their individual uniqueness. If we would cease to be "bungled and botched," a member of the herd, we must first feel uncomfortable with ourselves. We must begin, said Nietzsche, by following our conscience, which shouts: "Be yourself! You are not really all that which you do, think, and desire now."

Friedrich Nietzsche

Nietzsche's Life   Friedrich Wilhelm Nietzsche was born in Rocken, Prussia, in 1844 and died on August 25, 1900, at age fifty-five. He was named after

Prussian King Friedrich Wilhelm, whose birthday he shared. Nietzsche's father, Ludwig, was a Lutheran minister; his mother, Franziska Oehler Nietzsche, was the daughter of a Lutheran minister. When Nietzsche was five years old, his father died from "softening of the brain." Young Friedrich grew up in a household of five women—his mother, his grandmother, two aunts, and his sister.

After grade school, he attended a boarding school in Pforta, Germany, where he underwent six years of rigorous intellectual discipline. His work in the classics, German literature, and religion was outstanding. While there, he discovered such classical Greeks as Aeschylus and Plato. Also during these years and for the rest of his life, he suffered migraine headaches, insomnia, upset stomach, and bad eyesight.

In October 1864, Nietzsche enrolled at the University of Bonn to study theology and classical philology (linguistics), but he only stayed a year, following his professor of philology, Friedrich Ritschl, to the University of Leipzig. There Nietzsche discovered the works of Arthur Schopenhauer and gave up religion. While at Leipzig, he became spellbound by Richard Wagner's music. "I could not have stood my youth without Wagner's music," he said. So impressed was Professor Ritschl with Nietzsche's work that he published some of his student's papers and later recommended him for a chair of classical philology at the University of Basel in Switzerland. Nietzsche had yet to finish his doctorate degree, but at the unheard of age of twenty-four, he was given the chair as an associate professor. Leipzig immediately awarded him a doctorate without examination or dissertation, and within a year the University of Basel promoted him to full professor.

In 1872, Nietzsche published his first book, *The Birth of Tragedy,* with a laudatory section on Richard Wagner's music. Over the next four years, he wrote four meditations, *Thoughts Out of Season*. Nietzsche and Wagner became close friends and Nietzsche often visited Wagner at his villa on Lake Lucerne, Switzerland. Later, however, he broke off relations with Wagner because of the composer's nationalism and anti-Semitism.

In 1879, at age thirty-four, Nietzsche's poor health led him to resign his professorship. For the next ten years he traveled through Italy, Switzerland, and Germany searching for a place to regain his health. During this period, he devoted all of his remaining energy to writing. From 1881 to 1887, he wrote *The Dawn of Day, Joyful Wisdom, Gay Science, Thus Spake Zarathustra, Beyond Good and Evil,* and *A Genealogy of Morals.*

In early 1888, before Nietzsche began to show signs of insanity, he wrote five books with amazing speed: *The Twilight of the Idols, Antichrist, Ecce Homo* ("Behold the Man"), and two denunciations of his former friend, *The Case of Wagner,* and *Nietzsche contra Wagner.* The next year his mental illness erupted. One day while walking in Turin, Italy, he saw a man beating his horse. When the horse collapsed in exhaustion in his harness, Nietzsche threw his arms around the animal's neck. His mind snapped. He was taken to a clinic in Basel, then to an asylum in Jena, Germany, and finally to the care of his mother and sister. Nietzsche's insanity lasted for the last eleven years of his life, and he was unable to complete his major work, the *Revaluation of All Values.*

Nietzsche was an unusually creative genius who experienced heights and depths of the human psyche that most of us will never explore. Scholars who have read and studied Nietzsche agree on his remarkable genius and that his works should not be disregarded because of his later insanity.

Truth Above All   Like Kierkegaard, Nietzsche felt a strong distaste for philosophical systems in general, believing that such philosophy ignored the human predicament. The universe is seldom rational, they said, and philosophical systems that try to make everything tidy and orderly are futile attempts to overcome anxiety and despair. In fact, Nietzsche considered systematic philosophers inherently dishonest with "a disease of character."

Nietzsche wrote philosophy to provoke passionate thought, not to give formal answers to questions. He admired Heraclitus's and Socrates' conviction that truth is needed above all else. Though some scholars have proclaimed Nietzsche to be the antichrist, he went so far as to say:

> Even we devotees of knowledge today, we godless ones and anti-metaphysicians, still take *our* fire too from the flame which a faith thousands of years old has kindled: that Christian faith, which was also Plato's faith, that god is truth, that truth is divine. [12]

Pause for Thought   In the above statement, Nietzsche includes himself among the "godless." Does the rest of his statement confirm that remark?

"God Is Dead"   The God that is truth is now dead. Look about you, Nietzsche said to nineteenth-century Europe. You think you are secure with strong military power and material wealth, but I say to you that moral values have collapsed. Nihilism is approaching. What Nietzsche saw was the meaninglessness of life because people had destroyed their faith in God. "Your dignity is gone," he declared. "You have lost your values." You are blind to the fact that "God is dead, and you and I have killed him."

In one of the most famous passages in philosophy, Nietzsche pronounced the death of God. Perhaps it was prophetic insight that had him put the words into the mouth of "the madman."

The Madman.—Have you not heard of that madman who lit a lantern in the bright morning hours, ran to the market place, and cried incessantly: I seek God! I seek God!"—As many of those who did not believe in God were standing around just then, he provoked much laughter. Has he got lost? asked one. Did he lose his way like a child? asked another. Or is he hiding? Is he afraid of us? Has he gone on a voyage? emigrated?—Thus they yelled and laughed.

The madman jumped into their midst and pierced them with his eyes. "Whither is God?" he cried; "I will tell you. *We have killed him*—you and I. All of us are his murderers. But how did we do this? How could we drink up the sea? Who gave us the sponge to wipe away the entire horizon? What were we doing when we unchained this earth from its sun? Whither is it moving now? Whither are we moving? Away from all suns? Are we not plunging continually? Backward, sideward, forward, in all directions? Is there still any up or down? Are we not straying as through an infinite nothing? Do we not feel the breath of empty space? Has it not become colder? Is not night continually closing in on us? Do we not need to light lanterns in the morning? Do we hear nothing as yet of the noise of the grave diggers who are burying God? Do we smell nothing as yet of the divine decomposition? Gods, too, decompose. God is dead. God remains dead. And we have killed him.

"How shall we comfort ourselves, the murderers of all murderers? What was holiest and mightiest of all that the world has yet owned has bled to death under our knives: who will wipe this blood off us? What water is there for us to clean ourselves? What festivals of atonement, what sacred games shall we have to invent? Is not the greatness of this deed too great for us? Must we ourselves not become gods simply to appear worthy of it? There has never been a greater deed; and whoever is born after us—for the sake of this deed he will belong to a higher history than all history hitherto."

Here the madman fell silent and looked again at his listeners; and they, too, were silent and stared at him in astonishment. At last he threw his lantern on the ground, and it broke into pieces and went out. "I have come too early," he said then; "My time is not yet. This tremendous event is still on its way, still wandering; it has not yet reached the ears of men. Lightning and thunder require time; the light of the stars requires time; deeds, though done, still require time to be seen and heard. This deed is still more distant from them than the most distant stars—*and yet they have done it themselves.*"

It has been related further that on the same day the madman forced his way into several churches and there struck up his *requiem aeternam deo.* Led out and called to account, he is said always to have replied nothing but: "What after all are these churches now if they are not the tombs and sepulchers of God?"[13]

Pause for Thought   What do you think Nietzsche meant by saying the churches are the tombs and sepulchers of God? Do you agree with him?

The death of God has not yet reached our ears, and yet we have killed him. Nietzsche said belief in the Christian God, as history shows, destroys individuals, closes in on them, and denies them their freedom. People become part of the herd by looking to the authority of the church for all of their answers to life. For some strong individuals, however, the death of God means freedom:

> Indeed, we philosophers and "free spirits" feel, when we hear the news that "the old god is dead," as if a new dawn shone on us; our heart overflows with gratitude, amazement, premonitions, expectation. At long last the horizon appears free to us again, even if it should not be bright; at long last our ships may venture out again, venture out to face any danger; all the daring of the lover of knowledge is permitted again; the sea, *our* sea, lies open again; perhaps there has never yet been such an "open sea."[14]

Pause for Thought   Is Nietzsche on to something? Do you see the death of the "old God" giving free-spirited individuals more freedom? Or is his madman just that—mad?

The death of God will affect the free spirits and those in the herd in opposite ways. Nietzsche saw in the herd the collapse of religious faith and the mounting belief in the Darwinian notion of a relentless evolution of the species. He could see in this combination the destruction of a basic distinction between humans and animals. Nietzsche prophesied the masses' reactions when he said that "brotherhoods with the aim of robbery and exploitation of the non-brothers" would appear in the world and that people would experience wars such as have never been known before on earth.

Pause for Thought   Have unholy brotherhoods such as the Ku Klux Klan arisen in our century? Have there been wars such as have never happened on earth?

Revaluation of Values   For Nietzsche, the decay of belief in God opens the way for an individual's creative energies to develop fully. The Christian God, with his commands and prohibitions, no longer stands in the way. Human eyes are no longer turned toward an unreal supernatural realm, but now look toward this world. Following the realization of the death of God will be the rejection of absolute values and the idea of a universal moral law. Europeans, he said, will lose faith in Christian moral values, and an age of **nihilism**—the belief that the universe has no purpose or meaning—will begin. In Nietzsche's opinion, nihilism is inevitable. It will mean the final overthrow of the decadent Christian civilization of Europe. It will clear the way for a new dawn, for the transvaluation of values.

Like Socrates, we must apply "the knife vivisectionally to the very virtues of the time. . . . " Nietzsche said it is not necessary to mandate new values, because the old ones have appeared under false names. As "Christianity was a revaluation of all the values of antiquity," today's traditional morality has become a perversion of original natural morality. We must reverse values once again and look to our original and deepest nature. Nietzsche argued that what the masses call "good" is not virtue. What the masses call "truth" is selfishness, and religion is a psychological weapon with which "moral pygmies domesticate natural giants." True values, he said, will emerge only when we remove the disguise from modern morality. The disguise masks the weakness of the masses that readily join the "slave morality."

Walter Kaufmann, Nietzsche's most important translator and interpreter, wrote:

> The revaluation culminates in the claim that the so-called goodness of modern man is not virtuous, that his so-called religion is not religious, and that his so-called truths are not truthful. While those who are truly powerful and rich personalities will be kind and generous, spontaneously and instinctively, the weak who insist on conformity to the old standards . . . find in such conformity a mere screen for what is, according to these very standards, petty wickedness. In the weak the law abets and breeds sin.[15]

Pause for Thought   What do you think of Nietzsche's proclamation that religion is a psychological weapon with which "moral pygmies domesticate natural giants"?

Master and Slave Morality

In *Beyond Good and Evil*, Nietzsche said he has discovered two primary types of morality: *master morality* and *slave morality*. In all higher civilizations, these moralities are mixed with elements of the other even in the same person. Still, we must distinguish them. In the master morality, good and bad are equivalent to noble and despicable, and the characterization applies to people rather than to actions. In the slave morality, the standard is utility, or that which is helpful to the society of the weak and powerless.

> The noble human . . . feels contempt for the cowardly, the anxious, the petty, those intent on narrow utility; also for the suspicious with their unfree

glances, those who humble themselves, the doglike people who allow themselves to be maltreated, the begging flatterers, above all the liars; it is part of
the fundamental faith of all aristocrats that the common people lie.

The noble type of man experiences *itself* as determining values; it does
not need approval; it judges, "what is harmful to me is harmful in itself"; it
knows itself to be that which first accords honor to things; it is *value-creating*.
Everything it knows as part of itself it honors: such a morality is self-glorifi-
cation. In the foreground there is the feeling of fullness, of power that seeks
to overflow, the happiness of high tension, the consciousness of wealth that
would give and bestow: the noble human being, too, helps the unfortunate,
but not, or almost not, from pity, but prompted more by an urge begotten
by excess of power. The noble human being honors himself as one who is
powerful, also as one who has power over himself, who knows how to
speak and be silent, who delights in being severe and hard with himself and
respects all severity and hardness. . . . Noble and courageous human beings
. . . are furthest removed from that morality which finds the distinction of
morality precisely in pity, or in acting for others . . . ; faith in oneself, pride
in oneself, a fundamental hostility and irony against "selflessness" belong just
as definitely to noble morality as does a slight disdain and caution regarding
compassionate feelings and a "warm heart.". . .

A morality of the ruling group, however, is most alien and embarrassing
to the present taste in the severity of its principle that one has duties only to
one's peers; that against beings of a lower rank, against everything alien,
one may behave as one pleases or "as the heart desires, " and in any case
"beyond good and evil.". . .[16]

"The Noble man" creates his own values out of the abundance of his life
and strength. For Nietzsche, he represents the movement of ascending life in
which the consciousness of the slave morality (the masses) represents inferior life,
descending life, degeneracy.

It is different with the second type of morality, *slave morality*. Suppose the
violated, oppressed, suffering, unfree, who are uncertain of themselves and
weary, moralize: what will their moral valuations have in common?
Probably, a pessimistic suspicion about the whole condition of man will
find expression, perhaps a condemnation of man along with his condition.
The slave's eye is not favorable to the virtues of the powerful: he is skeptical and suspicious, *subtly* suspicious, of all the "good" that is honored
there—he would like to persuade himself that even their happiness is not
genuine. Conversely, those qualities are brought out and flooded with light
which serve to ease existence for those who suffer: here pity, the com-
plaisant and obliging hand, the warm heart, patience, industry, humility,
and friendliness are honored—for these are the most useful qualities and
almost the only means for enduring the pressure of existence. Slave morality is essentially a morality of utility.

Here is the place for the origin of that famous opposition of "good" and "evil": into evil one's feelings project power and dangerousness, a certain terribleness, subtlety, and strength that does not permit contempt to develop. According to slave morality, those who are "evil," thus inspire fear; according to master morality it is precisely those who are "good" that inspire, and wish to inspire, fear, while the "bad" are felt to be contemptible. . . .

[The] good human being has to be *undangerous* in the slaves' way of thinking: he is good-natured, easy to deceive, a little stupid. . . . Wherever slave morality becomes preponderant, language tends to bring the words "good" and "stupid" close together.[17]

Members of the slave morality consider sympathy, kindness, and humility virtues. By their standards, strong and independent individuals are dangerous and therefore evil. Slave morality is thus herd morality, its moral values expressing the needs of a herd. Being meek and powerless, those in the slave morality fear the unique and powerful, and they try to curb and tame such individuals by asserting their herd values as absolute values. The revolt of the slaves in morals begins with resentment, but a resentment that is not openly acknowledged by the herd.

Pause for Thought   Are strong, powerful, and unique individuals respected by the masses today, or is everyone expected to follow the moral rules of society?

Nietzsche believed the master and slave morality could coexist if the herd, "incapable of anything higher," was content to keep its values to itself. Unfortunately, it is not content to do this. Instead, it tries to impose its own values universally. Nietzsche saw the resentment characteristic of the herd instinct in Christianity, at least in the West. "I regard Christianity as the most fatal and seductive lie that has ever yet existed. . . ." It seeks to keep life's failures—the defective, the diseased, the degenerating, the infirm, and the suffering—alive. Christianity contradicts nature when it asks us to love our enemies. By routing their thinking toward God, Christianity weakens the vital energies of the strong.

"What must be done!" To become a higher type of individual, the courageous must transcend such herd mediocrity by rising above "good" and "evil." The strong must reverse all values and resist all sentimental weakness.

Will to Power   Nietzsche rejected Kant's notion of a universal ethics based on duty. In fact, he rejected all ethical systems. "People are different, " he said. The only thing all people have in common is the *will to power*. The world is the will to power, and nothing else. All people are the will to power and nothing else. Nietzsche saw the will to power expressing itself everywhere and in every-thing. All the drives that motivate people's acts are just variants of the basic will to power drive. Even at the preconscious level, the will to power expresses itself directly and immediately in the attempt of every organism to use and to over-come those that are not as powerful as itself.

> Suppose, finally, we succeeded in explaining our entire instinctive life as the development and ramification of *one* basic form of the will—namely, of the will to power, as *my* proposition has it; suppose all organic functions could be traced back to this will to power and one could also find in it the solu-tion of the problem of procreation and nourishment—it is *one* problem—then one would have gained the right to determine *all* efficient force uni-vocally as—*will to power.* The world viewed from inside, the world defined and determined according to its "intelligible character"—it would be "will to power" and nothing else.[18]

The human level is more complicated because we try to rationalize our motives and control our instincts, but deeply instilled in human nature is the basic nature of the will to power. All that people want is for the sake of power. According to Nietzsche, power is the only thing good in itself. All other goods such as virtues are expressions of the power held by certain individuals and groups. Both the master morality and the slave morality have their roots in power, but they use power differently. Thus, there is one set of goods and virtues for the strong and another for the weak.

The Overman   Nietzsche understood power in the sense of an intrinsic quality of the individual. He distinguished between two types, the first repre-senting *ascending* life and the second symbolizing *decadence,* decomposition, and weakness. The slave morality, even united together in power, does not represent ascending life.

In *Thus Spake Zarathustra* (1883–85), Nietzsche described his ideal person, the *overman.* He contrasted this superman to ordinary persons in the herd: The overman is as far beyond the ordinary person as the ordinary person is beyond the monkey. Overmen are the few rare individuals who become master of them-selves, of their passions, their powers, and their weaknesses. "Not humanity," said Nietzsche, "but overman is the goal" of human nature. The "bungled and the botched" (slave morality) is something to be surpassed.

> "Man is a rope, tied between beast and overman—a rope over an abyss. A dangerous across, a dangerous on-the-way, a dangerous looking-back, a dangerous shuddering and stopping.
>
> "What is great in man is that he is a bridge and not an end: what can be loved in man is that he is an *overture* and a *going under.*"[19]

In *Thus Spake Zarathustra*, the prophet comes down from the mountain after ten years and enters a village. He has leapt across the abyss without looking back at life. He has bridged the chasm between the mass consciousness and the overman. Now he speaks to the crowd about the overman.

> "Behold, I teach you the overman. The overman is the meaning of the earth. Let your will say: the overman *shall be* the meaning of the earth! I beseech you, my brothers, *remain faithful to the earth,* and do not believe those who speak to you of otherworldly hopes!"[20]

Pause for Thought   Nietzsche expressed his annoyance with Christianity for emphasizing "salvation" over "the meaning of the earth." Which do you consider more important?

The overman represents the highest level of development and the expression of physical, intellectual, and emotional strength. To become the overman, said Nietzsche, you must organize the chaos of your passions, give style to your character, and become creative. You must be conscious of life's terrors, yet affirm life without resentment. One of life's terrors is that it has no meaning—except the meaning you give to your own life. You must raise yourself above the senseless flux. You must cease being "human, all-too-human."

Not everyone can reach such heights. The overman must dive into the muddy darkness of himself as well as love the beauty of his light. His love is inseparable from the contempt he feels for that part of himself that has not yet become perfect. The overman must experience the terrible truth that is in every human.

> But my fervent will to create impels me ever again toward man; thus is the hammer impelled toward the stone, O men, in the stone there sleeps an image, the image of my images. Alas, that it must sleep in the hardest, the ugliest stone! Now my hammer rages cruelly against its prison. Pieces of rock rain from the stone; what is that to me? I want to perfect it; for a shadow came to me—the stillest and lightest of all things once came to me. The beauty of the overman came to me as a shadow. O my brothers, what are the gods to me now?
> Thus spoke Zarathustra.[21]

When God dies, we are left to chisel from ourselves the image of our own beauty. In direct opposition to the slave morality based on resentment, the overman loves himself. Only the most spiritual people can chisel the beauty out of themselves (recall Plotinus), and it is only among these people that we find "graciousness and not weakness."

Who did Nietzsche have in mind as the overman? He referred to literary great Johann von Goethe. Or perhaps "the Roman Caesar with Christ's soul." Nietzsche also cited Alcibiades, Alexander the Great, Cesare Borgia, and Napoleon as men having the kind of spiritual greatness that overman would possess. Their chief characteristics, besides the will to power, were discipline, strength, courage, and creativity. Both Alexander the Great and Napoleon destroyed city-states and republics to create great empires. But Nietzsche most admired the creative and disciplined powers of the artist and philosopher, best embodied by Goethe, the author of *Faust*. There is more power in self-control, art, and philosophy, Nietzsche said, than in the subjugation of others.

Thus, for Nietzsche, the perfectly self-possessed individual who has no fear of others, himself, or death is the acme of power. The personality of the overman is simple, unaided by any props. The lives of those who meet the overman in person or secondhand in literature, philosophy, or art, are changed forever. The overman is the hero, an individual of intelligence, and a passionate person with creative discipline and self-control.

The overman has the courage to say "Yes!" to life.

Pause for Thought   To become the overman, Nietzsche said, we must be hard on ourselves and self-disciplined; we must become creators instead of remaining mere creatures. Are you ready to take the step Nietzsche thought we must take to become an overman?

Eternal Recurrence

Nietzsche asked, what if life eternally recurs? Would the overman have the courage to say "Yes!" to living the same life over and over again? Does anyone have the courage to look at the possibility that life is meaningless, without purpose, and just brute fact? What if everything eternally recurs? What Nietzsche meant by *eternal recurrence* is everything that has ever happened happens again and again and again for an infinite number of times. For example, after the annihilation of our planet, it will eventually reconstruct and once again repeat all the past patterns. Nietzsche will be born again in 1844, repeat the exact same life, and die in 1900. Can even the overman face such a prospect? In *The Gay Science*, Nietzsche considers the problem:

> *The greatest weight.*—What, if some day or night a demon were to steal after you into your loneliest loneliness and say to you: "This life as you now live it and have lived it, you will have to live once more and innumerable times more; and there will be nothing new in it, but every pain and every joy and every thought and sigh and everything unutterably small or great in your life will have to return to you, all in the same moonlight between the trees, and

even this moment and I myself. The eternal hourglass of existence is turned upside down again and again, and you with it, speck of dust!"[22]

If eternal recurrence is a fact and "God is Dead," then we could never look for the meaning of life in a heavenly realm beyond death. Eternal recurrence suggests that this world would exist over and over again. How many of us have the strength to forgo thoughts of personal salvation? But we must do so if God is dead. Nietzsche thought only the strongest could bear this "greatest weight." Only the overman can say "Yes!" to eternal recurrence—to God is dead. Why? Because, said Nietzsche, only the overman can truly love and thereby affirm the earth. Only the overman can give style and meaning to his life to such an extent that he can joyously affirm his existence.

In *Thus Spake Zarathustra,* the prophet meets a few "higher type men" who have risen above the herd. He invites them to his cave where they have a feast, a parody of the Last Supper, and are merry together. Among the group is the "ugliest man," the one who has murdered God. He says:

> My friends, all of you. . . . What do you think? For the sake of this day, I am for the first time satisfied that I have lived my whole life. And that I attest so much is still not enough for me. Living on earth is worth while: one day, one festival with Zarathustra, taught me to love the earth.
>   'Was *that* life?' I want to say to death. 'Well then! Once more!'[23]

Pause for Thought   Can you affirm eternal recurrence for your life and the world? According to Nietzsche, what does your attitude toward eternal recurrence tell you about yourself?

The theory of eternal recurrence avoids the need for a transcendental God, and it avoids pantheism. It does away with the notion of personal immortality and salvation. It voids the idea of the soul reincarnating into a new body to gain new experiences as it progresses from life to life. The universe is shut in on itself. There is no escape from being the person you are now again and again.

Pause for Thought   In eternal recurrence, do we have the freedom to change our character? If we are repeating a former occurrence, can we make no changes? Have I asked these very questions before and before? Will I ever get an answer?

On Women

Nietzsche saw no virtue in women. They are, he said, not yet capable of friendships; they are still cats, or birds, or at best cows. Man shall be trained for war and women for the recreation of the warrior. All else is folly. And he warns the warrior: "Thou goest to woman? Do not forget thy whip."

In his distinction between the master and slave mentalities, woman characterizes the slave. Women, he said, are humble, practical, and sympathetic, and they avoid risk and accept society's values. Because of their limited vision, women yearn for security and stability. Their main goal in life is pregnancy and children. From Nietzsche's "Woman as Dangerous Plaything" in *Thus Spake Zarathustra*, we find again (except for the Utilitarians) traditional negative ideas about women.

> Everything concerning woman is a puzzle, and everything concerning woman has one solution, " it is named pregnancy.
>
> For woman man is a means, the goal is always the child. However, what is a woman for man?
>
> The real man wishes for two things: danger and recreation. Hence man wants woman as the most dangerous plaything. Man should be brought up for the purpose of war and woman for the relaxation of the soldier: everything else is foolish.
>
> The soldier does not enjoy fruit that is too sweet. Hence he enjoys woman; even the sweetest woman is bitter. . . .
>
> And a woman must obey and must find a depth for her superficiality. Superficiality is the character of woman, a moving, tempestuous membrane on shallow water.
>
> But the soul of man is deep; his stream thunders through underground caverns: woman guesses his power but is unable to understand it.[24]

Ayn Rand

Although Ayn Rand's writings occurred nearly fifty years after Nietzsche's death, and she is less of a subjectivist than either Kierkegaard or Nietzsche, she definitely belongs to the individualist category. Like Nietzsche, Rand considered the masses uninspired, weak-willed followers without originality. Her heroes are individuals who rise out of the masses to overcome group hypocrisy and become their true individual selves. Her popularity with youths in the 1960s and 1970s followed from her black-and-white view of individuality and values. Her writings gave college students the incentive to take a firm stand for their principles and not back down in the face of mediocrity.

Known for her novels *The Fountainhead* (1943) and *Atlas Shrugged* (1967), Ayn Rand also wrote four philosophical works: *For the New Intellectual* (1961), *The Virtue of Selfishness* 1964), *Introduction to Objectivist Epistemology* (1979), and *Philosophy, Who Needs It?* (1982).

Ayn Rand's Life

Ayn Rand (1905–1982) was born Alyssa Rosenbaum in St. Petersburg, Russia. Her father was a quiet and austere chemist who had strong convictions. Alyssa respected him, but father and daughter showed little affection for each other. Her educated and extroverted mother was a popular hostess and kept her household socially active. Many lawyers, doctors, and scientists frequented their home. Alyssa considered her mother shallow, and her mother "disapproved of me in every respect except one: she was proud of my intelligence. . . . " Later, she wrote of her mother, "I disliked her quite a lot. We really didn't get along."

At age nine, Alyssa decided to become a writer. That same year, 1914, while vacationing in Switzerland with her family, World War I began and the Rosenbaums had difficulty returning to Russia. In 1917 the Russian revolution ended the world they knew. The new government nationalized her father's business, and the family lost everything. Around her was a communist-ruled world of struggle, pain, and despair. But in the midst of such turmoil, her literary talent allowed her imagination to flow into words. In her mind, she created beautiful worlds peopled with human beings who lived happy, noble, and courageous lives.

When she was sixteen, Rand entered the University of Leningrad (the new name for St. Petersburg). The communist government urged her to become an engineer or mathematician, but she chose to major in history. While in college, she read Aristotle with enthusiasm, detested Plato's idealism, and considered Nietzsche an "intellectual ally." Her philosophy was the concept of man as a heroic being with his happiness the moral purpose of his life, and who held "productive achievement as his noblest activity, and reason as his only absolute."

When she was twenty-one, Rand escaped Russia to come to the United States and live the American dream. In the United States she would be free to be her own person. Her arrival cut her off from her family and her Russian heritage, and she changed her name to Ayn Rand. *Ayn* she adopted from a Finnish writer, and she took *Rand* from her Remington-Rand typewriter. Then she set out to learn English and become an American citizen. Her feeling of communist Russia was one of "complete loathing."

Ayn Rand supported herself in a variety of jobs: one was in Hollywood as an extra in Cecil B. De Mille's story of Jesus, *The King of Kings*. She wrote screenplays, scripts, and short stories but could not get them published. She practiced and rewrote until she could tell a story that publishers wanted. While working on *The King of Kings*, she met Frank O'Connor and married him. This was the period known as the Great Depression, and neither of them had much money. She continued to write, but had only modest success and had to work at other jobs.

In 1934, her play *Penthouse Legend* was a success. The next year she and her husband moved to New York, where the Broadway production of *Penthouse Legend* won favorable reviews. In 1936, *We the Living,* her first novel, sold only 3,000 copies. *Anthem,* her next book, was the story of a struggling hero in a totalitarian state. For the next fifteen years she labored on her two great novels *The Fountainhead* and *Atlas Shrugged.* They became immediate successes. After that, she concentrated on writing philosophy.

Rand called her philosophy "objectivism," and she enjoyed a circle of loyal supporters led by Nathaniel Branden. For eighteen years, he was her companion and "intellectual heir." Rand received honorary degrees from the United States' most prestigious universities, her writings appeared in professional journals, and she started *The Objectivist Newsletter.* But in 1969 a major schism occurred within her circle, and Rand accused Branden of exploitation and excommunicated him from the group. After that, the group and the newsletter both declined. She continued to write and publish the *Ayn Rand Newsletter* until 1975, when she underwent surgery for lung cancer. In 1979, her husband died; three years later, she died at age 77.

Who Is John Galt?

Ayn Rand made famous the question, "Who is John Galt?" In the 60s and 70s the question seemed to be everywhere—on billboards, T-shirts, and posters. The question was asked on radio and television. College students discussed it on campus and at parties. In fact, John Galt is the hero of Rand's book *Atlas Shrugged.* He is Rand's ideal man—a man-become-god—and her answer to Nietzsche's overman. John Galt is the pinnacle of the human species but condemned to work as a greasy laborer in the Taggart tunnels. For Rand, the best examples of the human species are at the bottom in a corrupt society, because they refuse to compromise their ideals and values. Later, however, John Galt becomes society's revered leader, a philosopher and teacher.

> "For twelve years, you have been asking: Who is John Galt? This is John Galt speaking. I am the man who lives his life. I am the man who does not sacrifice his love or his values. I am the man who has deprived you of victims and thus has destroyed your world, and if you wish to know why you are perishing—you who dread knowledge—I am the man who will not tell you."[25]

Pause for Thought   Reflect on John Galt's speech. Why do you think he ends it with "I am the man who will not tell you"?

John Galt's entire speech, which took Ayn Rand more than two years to write, is 35,000 words (fifty-seven pages). Through his speech, Rand presented her own philosophy on individualism and values.

Reason and Emotion

As Ayn Rand read Nietzsche in college, she considered him an "intellectual ally." With Nietzsche, she rejected Kant's view of practical reason and Descartes' view of the mind–body separation. For her, as for Nietzsche, there is no inherent separation between mind and body, no separation between reason and emotion. Rand argued that in the well-integrated person, emotions do not conflict with reason.

> It may be considered strange and denying my own supremacy of reason—that I start with a set of ideas—then want to study in order to support them, and not vice-versa, that is, not study and derive my ideas from that. But these ideas, to a great extent, are the result of a subconscious instinct, which is a form of unrealized reason. All instincts are reason, essentially, . . . *reason is instincts made conscious*. The "unreasonable" instincts are diseased ones. This . . . for the base of the reconciliation of reason and emotions.[26]

Pause for Thought   What do you think Rand meant when she said that unreasonable instincts are diseased instincts? Can an instinct be reasonable?

For Rand, if emotions are to contribute to reasoning, we must hold them under strict control. She also agreed with Nietzsche and rejected religion and the supernatural. We humans, she said, must be free to accept life as an end in itself and to make the most of ourselves. She also rejected priestly authority. Heroes (supermen) must be a law unto themselves both philosophically and socially.

In the end, however, Rand turned away from Nietzsche's influence to create objectivism as her own philosophy. Rejecting Nietzsche's idea that emotion is actually a form of reason, Rand agreed with Aristotle that morality is the conflict between reason and emotion, and thus reason must control the emotions.

Objectivism

Rand believed that the true individualist has the most to contribute to society. But society always alienates the individual, who must struggle continuously to deny and break free of suffering. In her description of the fictional Halley Fourth Concerto in *Atlas Shrugged,* Rand wrote:

> It was a "No" flung at some vast process of torture, a denial of suffering, a denial that held the agony of the struggle to break free. The sounds were

like a voice saying: There is no necessity for pain—why, then, is the worst pain reserved for those who will not accept its necessity?—we who hold the love and the secret of joy, to what punishment have we been sentenced for it, and by whom?[27]

Rand's answer lay in objectivism. If reason is an absolute and good is rational, then evil is irrational and illogical. It contradicts reality and is inherently self-destructive. Left on its own, however, evil would disappear. It is made possible only by the "generous but ill-advised support" and sanction of the good. If good people refused to accept evil, then evil could not exist.

Pause for Thought   Do you agree that if good people declined to accept evil, then evil would eventually cease to exist?

Rand considered altruism the tool of evil. Altruism is a false morality that teaches victims to hate the good in themselves. For each of us, self-esteem is the supreme value. An individual who has no self-worth cannot value anything or anyone. We must value our mind, trust it, love it, nourish it, and treat it with dignity. When we belittle, neglect, and negate it, the mind does not function. When we distrust our mind, we become worthless, we become evil. Only our self-esteem as valuable human beings can create the confidence required for our minds to do their work. We know, said Ayn Rand, that our need of self-esteem is a matter of life and death.

Pause for Thought   If more people had self-esteem, would the crime rate drop?

When others tell us that humans are inherently evil, we hear lies. Rand insisted that human beings are creatures with unlimited capacities for creative accomplishments. We are genetically programmed for joy and happiness, and we are individually free to create our future. If we fail to realize some ultimate end, then our lives will be meaningless and impossible, and we will never experience our inherent potential for joy. The objective of ethics is not simply to maintain our ability to pursue values in life; it is to optimize that ability.

Pause for Thought   Do you agree with Ayn Rand that it is for joy and not sorrow that we are made?

Summary

Kierkegaard, Nietzsche, and Rand asked whether we are living as individuals or conforming to a group. Do we know who we are? What does it mean to be an individual person?

Kierkegaard shifted philosophical thinking from purely rational objectivity to viewing humanity subjectively, that is, as individuals. He wanted to change the philosophical viewpoint from thinking to being. We cannot understand human nature by using science and rational systems of analysis. Humans exist subjectively.

Kierkegaard believed that existence means we have fallen from our essential nature, which is our immortal relationship to God, the infinite. Our existential condition of despair is the result of our alienation from God. Every human has the drive to find his or her essential self, but we cannot bridge the gap between God and ourselves through speculative reason. The only way we can renew our relationship with God is through the "leap of faith." Through faith alone can we find our authentic self. The decision to make the "leap of faith" is an act of will, a commitment.

Nietzsche agreed that we must find our authentic individual self. However, the self is not in God, but in the human being. For Nietzsche, "God is dead" and we have killed him. This news will bring agony to the "herd" but freedom to the true individual. Most human beings are "bungled and botched" and therefore unaware of their true selves. To become true individuals, we must revalue all values. Our so-called goodness is not virtue, and our truths are not truthful. If we don't have the strength to become overmen (supermen), we submit to the crowd—the herd. The herd has a slave morality in which the standard is utility— helping the weak and powerless.

The overman or true individual is of the master morality. He has the courage to revalue all values by creating his own values out of an abundance of inner power. These masters represent ascending life. Those in the slave morality represent inferior or descending life. Overmen consist of a few rare individuals who become masters of themselves, their passions, their powers, and their weaknesses. They are as far beyond the masses in the slave morality as the masses are beyond the monkey. Overman is the human goal.

Ayn Rand agreed with Kierkegaard and Nietzsche that the masses are uninspired, weak-willed followers without originality. Her heroes are individuals who rise out of the masses to overcome group hypocrisy and become their true individual selves. Such heroes are laws unto themselves both philosophically and socially.

Altruism, Rand said, is a tool of evil—a false morality. Self-esteem is the supreme value in an individual.

Connections

Before the nineteenth century, philosophy focused on the human object with questions about what we know and how we know it. Human beings were certainly the objects of philosophy, but we were precisely that—human *objects* instead of human beings. The individual as human "being" was in danger of being lost. The nineteenth century, however, brought a significant change. Philosophers inquired about the psychology and the value of the human being in existence thus, the subjective individual. This inquiry began a revolution concerned with individual values and nobility. Philosophers of individualism delved deeply into the nature of individual persons—our anxieties, guilt, and power—our struggle for freedom, dignity, and personhood.

The enthusiasm of studying human beings as individuals persisted into the twentieth century. William James and Henri Bergson, Edmund Husserl and Martin Heidegger, Jean-Paul Sartre and Simone de Beauvoir—all of them continued the quest to understand the nature of our humanness and the meaning of our existence in the world.

Study Questions

1. What is individualism?

2. How do individualist philosophers differ from systematic philosophers?

3. What was Kierkegaard's personal sacrifice to God?

4. For Kierkegaard, what does it mean to exist?

5. What was Kierkegaard's argument against the value of science and mathematics in our daily lives?

6. Explain what Kierkegaard meant by "truth is subjectivity."

7. What did Kierkegaard mean when he said that humans have fallen from their essential nature?

8. In some detail, explain Kierkegaard's three stages in life.

9. What did Kierkegaard mean by the crowd is untruth?

10. Explain the leap of faith.

11. What did Nietzsche mean when he said "God is dead"?

12. What is nihilism and how does it relate to the death of God?

13. Why was Nietzsche annoyed with Christianity?

14. What is the overman (superman)?

15. Explain, contrast, and evaluate master and slave moralities.

16. Why did Nietzsche say that we must revalue all values?

17. Discuss the significance of the will to power.

18. What is eternal recurrence? What does our reaction to it reveal about ourselves?

19. Why did Nietzsche call woman a "dangerous plaything"?

20. Who is John Galt?

21. What was the difference between Rand's early and later view of the relationship between instinct and reason?

22. Describe Ayn Rand's philosophy of the hero.

23. Explain the role of evil in Rand's philosophy of objectivism.

24. According to Rand, what is our goal in life?

Notes

1. *The Journals of Kierkegaard* (trans. and ed. by Alexander Dru), p. 44. London: Collins, 1958.

2. Ibid., p. 54.

3. W.T. Jones, *A History of Western Philosophy: Kant and the Nineteenth Century*, 2nd ed., p. 213. New York: Harcourt Brace Jovanovich, 1975.

4. *Journals of Kierkegaard*, op. cit., p. 4.

5. *Kierkegaard's Concluding Unscientific Postscript* (trans. by D. F. Swenson; notes and introduction by W. Lowrie), p. 276. Princeton, New Jersey: Princeton University Press, 1941.

6. Ibid., p. 182.

7. Ibid., p. 180.

8. *Either/Or* (trans. by Howard V. Hong and Edna H. Hong), Vol. I, pp. 285–286. Princeton, New Jersey: Princeton University Press, 1983.

9. *Kierkegaard's Postscript*, op. cit., p. 182.

10. Ibid., p. 318.

11. From Søren Kierkegaard, "The Banquet," in *Stages on Life's Way* (trans. by Walter Lowrie). Princeton, New Jersey: Princeton University Press, 1940.

12. Friedrich Nietzsche, *The Gay Science* (trans. by Walter Kaufmann), Book 5, Sec. 344, p. 283. New York: Vintage Books, 1974.

13. Ibid., Book 3, Sec. 125, pp. 181–182.

14. Ibid., Book 5, Sec. 343, p. 280.

15. Walter Kaufmann, *Nietzsche: Philosopher, Psychologist, Antichrist*, 3rd ed., p. 114. New York: Vintage Books, 1968.

16. *Beyond Good and Evil* (trans. by Walter Kaufmann) in *Basic Writings of Nietzsche*, Part 9, Sec. 260, pp. 394–396. New York: Modern Library, 1968.

17. Ibid., p. 397.

18. Ibid., sec. 36, p. 238.

19. *Thus Spoke Zarathustra* (trans. by Walter Kaufmann), in *The Portable Nietzsche,* Part I, pp. 126–127. New York: Vintage Books, 1974.

20. Ibid., p. 125.

21. Ibid., pp. 199–200.

22. *The Gay Science* in *Basic Writings of Nietzsche,* op. cit., Sec. 341, p. 273.

23. *Thus Spoke Zarathustra* in *Basic Writings of Nietzsche,* op. cit., Part 4, pp. 429–430.

24. Friedrich Nietzsche, "Vom Alten und Jungen Weiblein," (Woman as Dangerous Plaything), in *History of Ideas on Woman* (1883), (trans. and ed. by Rosemary Agonito). New York: G. P. Putnam's Sons, 1977. (Originally published in 1883.)

25. Ayn Rand, *Atlas Shrugged* (New York: Random House, 1957), p. 936.

26. Ayn Rand in "Ayn Rand's Unpublished Writings: Philosophic Journal, 1934," *The Objectivist Forum,* Vol. 4, No. 4, 1983.

27. Ayn Rand, *Atlas Shrugged,* in Ronald E. Merrill, *The Ideas of Ayn Rand,* p. 84. Chicago: Open Court, 1991.

CHAPTER THIRTEEN

Pragmatism: Peirce, James, Dewey

In this chapter we shall see that Pragmatism is essentially an American philosophy that developed at the end of the nineteenth century. The movement was begun by Charles S. Peirce and popularized by William James. John Dewey brought Pragmatism to the attention of American education systems. Both Peirce and James wrote extensively to explain their ideas of Pragmatism, although they often gave different meanings to the term itself. Although they were good friends, the differences in their concepts of Pragmatism were so profound that Peirce finally changed the name of his own theory from Pragmatism to *Pragmaticism*. He said that the word *pragmaticism* was "ugly enough to be safe enough from kidnappers." All three philosophers agreed that Pragmatism provided the ground for theoretical thought, but that to be valid all theories must be put into practice. By unifying facts and theories, Pragmatism made it possible to use both science and philosophy in a practical way. Peirce, James, and Dewey were practical men as well as academic men and agreed there should be a close connection between thinking and doing.

These philosophers were contemporaries, and all of them were from New England. But each expressed a different kind of Pragmatism. Peirce was mainly interested in logic and science, James examined psychology and religion, and Dewey concentrated on ethics and social thought. Both James and Dewey acknowledged their debt to Peirce for many of their pragmatic ideas.

Pragmatists view the nature of truth as acceptable "in so far as it works," that is, so long as it is socially useful or fruitful. They hold that we can never have a conception of the whole of reality. Thus, Pragmatism is more a theory of meaning than a theory of truth.

Pragmaticism

As a philosophy, Pragmatism was meant to bridge the widening gulf between scientific Empiricists and traditional Rationalists and Idealists. Based on Darwin's theory of evolution, scientists saw humans as parts of and molded by a mechanical or biological process. According to the biological evolutionists, humans are not creative instruments who can help direct history. However, Rationalists and Idealists such as Descartes, Spinoza, Kant, and Hegel took the opposite standpoint about human nature. James attributed the differences between Rationalists and Empiricists to individual temperament:

> Now the particular difference of temperament that I have in mind in making these remarks is one that has counted in literature, art, government, and manners as well as in philosophy. In manners we find formalists and free-and-easy persons. In government, authoritarians and anarchists. In literature, purists or academicals, and realists. In art, classics and romantics. You recognize these contrasts as familiar; well, in philosophy we have a very similar contrast.
>
> I will write these traits down in two columns. I think you will practically recognize the two types of mental make-up that I mean if I head the columns by the titles "tender-minded" and "tough-minded" respectively.

The Tender-Minded	The Tough-Minded
Rationalistic (going by "principles"),	Empiricist (going by "facts"),
Intellectualistic,	Sensationalistic,
Idealistic,	Materialistic,
Optimistic,	Pessimistic,
Religious,	Irreligious,
Free-willist,	Fatalistic,
Monistic,	Pluralistic,
Dogmatical.	Sceptical.

> The tough think of the tender as sentimentalists and soft-heads. The tender feel the tough to be unrefined, callous, or brutal. . . . Most of us have a hankering for the good things on both sides of the line.[1]

Charles Sanders Peirce

Peirce's Life

Charles Sanders Peirce (pronounced Purse) (1839–1914) was born in Cambridge, Massachusetts, the son of a distinguished Harvard mathematician. From an early age, Charles Peirce was trained in mathematics, science, and philosophy. Like John Stuart Mill, much of his early training took place in the home. He used to claim that he had been brought up in a laboratory. At age sixteen, Charles entered Harvard, in Cambridge, Massachusetts, where his father was a professor. Although a precocious child, he was not an outstanding student and had trouble adapting socially. During his college years, he spent most of his time with his father discussing mathematics.

After graduating from Harvard, Peirce studied chemistry at the Lawrence Scientific School. There he met his first wife, Harriet Melusina Fay. Marriage improved his performance in the academic world, and he graduated from Lawrence *summa cum laude*. After receiving his graduate degree in mathematics and chemistry, he worked for three years at the Harvard astronomical observatory and published his photometric researches. From there, he accepted a position as a scientist for the U.S. Coast and Geodetic Survey, for which he worked for the next thirty years. During this period, Peirce lectured at Harvard on two topics: the history of modern science and logic. He also lectured on logic at Johns Hopkins University in Baltimore and managed to find time to write philosophy.

Peirce's original research in logic contributed to its expansion beyond the Aristotelian syllogism. He also helped form the Metaphysical Club, an informal gathering of friends who discussed philosophical matters. Such thinkers as William James and Oliver Wendell Holmes were regulars at these meetings. Because of his personal eccentricities, however, Peirce was never offered a full-time professorship at a university. His reputation for "loose living" drove his wife to divorce him in 1883. Shortly after the divorce, Peirce married a French woman named Juliette Froisy.

Seven years after his second marriage, Peirce received a small inheritance and retired from his job with the U.S. Coast and Geodetic Survey. He and his wife moved to Pennsylvania, where he lived a reclusive life and wrote philosophy. However, his lack of an academic position brought indifferent responses from publishers, and most of his work remained unpublished during his lifetime. He spent his last years in poverty and failing health. At his death, his wife sold all his papers to Harvard for a mere five hundred dollars.

Although Peirce and James did not always agree philosophically, William James was his loyal friend. Through James, Peirce's Pragmaticism is recognized as one of the major contributions to philosophy in the twentieth century. James wrote:

[Pragmatism] was first introduced into philosophy by Mr. Charles Peirce in 1878. In an article entitled "How to Make Our Ideas Clear" in the *Popular Science Monthly* for January of that year Mr. Peirce, after pointing out that our beliefs are really rules for action, said that, to develop a thought's meaning, we need only determine what conduct it is fitted to produce: that conduct is for us its sole significance.[2]

Pragmatism and Meaning

In the article mentioned above, "How to Make Our Ideas Clear," Peirce explained how words acquire their meaning. The word *pragmatism* came from *pragma,* the Greek word for action. According to Peirce, "The whole function of thought is to produce habits of action." Our ideas are clear and distinct only when we can translate them into some kind of meaningful action. He believed that unless philosophy pays close attention to the question of the meaning of its ideas, its answer to a problem will collapse like a house of cards. Speculative thought cannot be divorced from action. In fact, the function of speculative thought is the production of habits of action. The consequence of a theory is the test of its validity. Only meaning in the concrete reveals truth, which consists of practical experience with concrete things. "Our idea of anything *is* our idea of its sensible effects," he said. For example, the adjectives *hard* and *heavy* have meaning because we can perceive the effects represented by these terms. To say that an object is *hard* means that if we exert pressure on it, the object will not give way as, say, cotton might. Also, not many other substances can scratch a hard object. Thus, the word *hard* tells us the meaning of the concept.

The role of *effects* is critical in the meanings of words because there would be no difference between a hard object and a soft object if they did not test differently. But they do test differently, so we can know the differences between *hard* and *soft*. For words to have meaning, insisted Peirce, we must use the operational formula—if A, then B. This formula implies that if an object has certain qualities, then we can expect certain effects. If a word refers to an object for which we cannot conceive practical effects, then that word has no meaning. A distinct idea "contains nothing which is not clear."

Peirce contrasted *intellectual concepts* with *subjective feelings*. "An intellectual concept is any concept (such as "The concept Hard") upon the structure of which, arguments concerning objective fact may hinge." Subjective feelings produce different types of sensation in us. For example, when I look at the sky, I experience the sensation *blue*. I see the sky as blue. When you look at the sky, you also call it blue. However, these are subjective sensations, and neither of us can know if we are experiencing the same color. You and I agree that a rose is red, but how do I know you are not seeing blue and have learned to call that color red? According to Peirce, the language of subjective feelings has no meaning.

Had the light which, as things are, excites in us the sensation of blue, always excited the sensation of red, and *visa versa,* however great a difference that might have made in our feelings, it could have made none in the force of any argument. In this respect, the qualities of hard and soft strikingly contrast with those of red and blue; because while red and blue name mere subjective feelings only, hard and soft express the factual behaviour of the thing under the pressure of a knife-edge. . . . My pragmatism, having nothing to do with qualities of feeling, permits me to hold that the predication of such a quality is just what it seems, and has nothing to do with anything else. Hence, could two qualities of feeling everywhere be interchanged, nothing but feelings could be affected. Those qualities have no intrinsic significations beyond themselves.[3]

Pause for Thought

Is there any way to test our "subjective feelings"? Can I know with certainty that when you and I agree the lemon is sour we are experiencing the same sensation?

Peirce distinguishes three degrees of clarity in ideas. First, we can recognize a clear idea unmistakably for what it is without the possibility of confusing it with any other. For example, if we can identify a dog from a variety of other animals that are presented to us, then "dog" is clear to us in the first degree. Second, a distinct idea "contains nothing which is not clear." This clarity may come from a verbal definition, such as we might find in and memorize from a dictionary. In the third degree of clarity, we must seek the meaning of an idea in its effects, "which might conceivably have practical bearings." Our conception of the effects is our conception of the object. According to Peirce, the meaning of an idea in its effects or "practical bearings" constitute the conceptual foundation or essence of a given object. For example, if we ask what *hard* means, then we are asking what effects these objects have that we can notice—perhaps that not many other substances can scratch it. There must be a way to test ideas by their effects. Peirce used gravity as another example. He said, "All bodies gravitate," is not about some gravity force that attracts bodies, because it is not possible to verify the existence of such a force. What we actually find is that bodies accelerate in a uniform way, and this is all that "All bodies gravitate" means. In other words, a statement means only what verifies it, nothing more. Thus, any statement (for example, "The absolute exists") that cannot be verified or falsified is meaningless.

If there is no way to test ideas by their effects, then the ideas are meaningless. For Peirce, this meant that meaningful ideas are publicly—never privately or individually—verifiable. Peirce was showing that clarifying what a concept means—*hard,* in this case—is the only real test of an idea, not proving that a particular substance or object is hard or soft.

Doubt, Belief, and Action

For Peirce, doubt, belief, and action are interrelated processes, but each has its specific function. The function of doubt is to stimulate thought. The function of thought is to arrive at belief. When we arrive at the stage of belief, our mental doubts disappear, because belief provides us with rules of action or habits of action.

In nature, habits are "laws." Although such laws constitute part of our human nature, we also acquire beliefs that are more than laws of human nature. "Beliefs are really rules for action, and the whole function of thinking is but one step in the production of habits of action." Belief, then, is a habit, and doubt is the lack of such a habit. Through thought we try to "fix" our beliefs so they will be our guides for action.

Pause for Thought   Does Peirce's formula work for you? Do your doubts stimulate your thoughts, which arrive at a belief that you put into action?

Fixing Belief

Through belief we move from an unsettled, restless, mental state to a settled one. Sometime in the future, our settled mental state may become unsettled with doubt. To fix our beliefs—to make them more stable—Peirce considers four contrasting methods: *tenacity, authority, a priori rationalism,* and *empirical science.*

> If the settlement of opinion is the sole object of inquiry, and if belief is of the nature of a habit, why should we not attain the desired end, by taking as answer to a question any we may fancy, and constantly reiterating it to ourselves, dwelling on all which may conduce to that belief, and learning to turn with contempt and hatred from anything that might disturb it? . . . A man may go through life, systematically keeping out of view all that might cause a change in his opinions, and if he only succeeds. . . . I do not see what can be said against his doing so. . . .
>
> But this method of fixing belief, which may be called the method of tenacity, will be unable to hold its ground in practice. The social impulse is against it. The man who adopts it will find that other men think differently from him, and it will be apt to occur to him, in some saner moment, that their opinions are quite as good as his own, and this will

shake his confidence in his belief. . . . Unless we make ourselves hermits, we shall necessarily influence each other's opinions; so that the problem becomes how to fix belief, not in the individual merely, but in the community.

Let the will of the state act, then, instead of that of the individual. Let an institution be created which shall have for its object to keep correct doctrines before the attention of the people, to reiterate them perpetually, and to teach them to the young; having at the same time power to prevent contrary doctrines from being taught, advocated, or expressed. Let all . . . who reject the established belief be terrified into silence. . . .

In judging this method of fixing belief, which may be called the method of authority, we must, in the first place, allow its immeasurable mental and moral superiority to the method of tenacity. Its success is proportionately greater; and, in fact, it has over and over again worked the most majestic results. . . .

But [even] . . . in the most priest-ridden states some individuals will . . . see that men in other countries and in other ages have held to very different doctrines from those which they themselves have been brought up to believe; and they cannot help seeing that it is the mere accident of their having been taught as they have, and of their having been surrounded with the manners and associations they have, that has caused them to believe as they do and not far differently. . . .

A different new method of settling opinions must be adopted, that shall not only produce an impulse to believe, but shall also decide what proposition it is which is to be believed. Let the action of natural preferences be unimpeded, then, and under their influence let men, conversing together and regarding matters in different lights, gradually develop beliefs in harmony with natural causes. . . . The most perfect example of it is to be found in the history of metaphysical philosophy. Systems of this sort have not usually rested upon any observed facts, at least not in any great degree. They have been chiefly adopted because their fundamental propositions seemed "agreeable to reason." This is an apt expression; it does not mean that which agrees with experience, but that which we find ourselves inclined to believe. . . .

This method is far more intellectual and respectable from the point of view of reason than either of the others which we have noticed. . . . But its failure has been the most manifest. It makes of inquiry something similar to the development of taste.[4]

In the writings above, Peirce has covered three of his four methods. In the method of tenacity, we stick to our beliefs, refusing to entertain any doubts about them or to open our minds to any other arguments or points of view. In the method of authority, we accept as true the statement of persons in authority because they require us to accept certain ideas as true. "Let all who reject the established belief be terrified into silence."

Pause for Thought   Have you ever been afraid to question certain religious doctrines because your priest, minister, rabbi, imam, or guru might be angry? Have you ever refrained from challenging your professor because you are afraid disagreement could affect your grade?

The third method for Peirce, rationalism, is that of the metaphysician or philosopher (such as Plato, Descartes, or Hegel) who develops a vast metaphysical system that is agreeable to reason but not necessarily agreeable to observed facts.

Though these methods play a part in fixing belief, they have no way of preventing these beliefs from becoming unfixed in the future. None of the three is self-corrective. However, empirical science, the fourth method, offers us the opportunity of self-correction and brings us closer to settled beliefs.

> To satisfy our doubts, therefore, it is necessary that a method should be found by which our beliefs may be determined by nothing human, but by effect. . . . The method must be such that the ultimate conclusion of every man shall be the same. Such is the method of science. Its fundamental hypothesis, restated in more familiar language, is this: There are Real things, whose characters are entirely independent of our opinions about them; those Reals affect our senses according to regular laws, and, though our sensations are as different as are our relations to the objects, yet, by taking advantage of the laws of perception, we can ascertain by reasoning how things really and truly are; and any man, if he have sufficient experience and he reason enough about it, will be led to the one True conclusion. The new conception here involved is that of Reality.[5]

The Scientific Method

Only science is pragmatically sound, for it establishes objective beliefs that constitute practical values and true conclusions. Unlike tenacity, authority, and reason, science does not rest on what a person possesses in his or her own mind. Science is not limited to authority, to personal belief, or to reason as an a priori belief. A scientific hypothesis is entirely independent of our opinions. Because "real" things affect our senses, we can make the assumption that they will affect each observer in the same way. In defending his choice of the scientific method for fixing belief, Peirce writes:

> It may be asked how there are any Reals. If this hypothesis is the sole support of my method of inquiry, my method of inquiry must not be used to support my hypothesis. The reply is this: 1. If investigation cannot be

regarded as proving that there are Real things, it at least does not lead to a contrary conclusion; but the method and the conception on which it is based remain ever in harmony. No doubts of the method, therefore, necessarily arise from its practice, as is the case with all the others. 2. The feeling which gives rise to any method of fixing belief is a dissatisfaction at two repugnant propositions. But here already is a vague concession that there is some *one* thing which a proposition should represent. Nobody, therefore, can really doubt that there are Reals, for, if he did, doubt would not be a source of dissatisfaction. The hypothesis, therefore, is one which every mind admits. So that the social impulse does not cause men to doubt it. 3. Everybody uses the scientific method about a great many things, and only ceases to use it when he does not know how to apply it. 4. Experience of the method has not led us to doubt it, but, on the contrary, scientific investigation has had the most wonderful triumphs in the way of settling opinion.[6]

Pause for Thought

Do you agree with Peirce that the scientific method is superior to tenacity, authority, or reason for knowing reality? If not, which method would you choose?

Metaphysics

Peirce's scientific method led him to metaphysics. From Aristotle to Kant, philosophers postulated metaphysics as the most general of the sciences. Kant disagreed when he distinguished between the phenomenal world (things as they appear to us) and the noumenal world (things as they are in themselves). We recall that Kant argued that the human mind is forever limited to knowledge of the phenomenal world. Other philosophers before and after Peirce have gone even farther than Kant by rejecting all metaphysical assertions as meaningless. Peirce disagreed. He thought that if there is an objective reality, then we should be able to know it and explain it through science.

> The common opinion has been that Metaphysics is backward because it is intrinsically beyond the reach of human cognition. But that, I think I can clearly discern, is a complete mistake. Why should metaphysics be so difficult? Because it is abstract? But the abstracter a science is, the easier it is, both as a general rule of experience and as a corollary from logical principles. . . . [Again,] it will be said that metaphysics is inscrutable because its objects are not open to observation. This is doubtless true of some systems of metaphysics, though not to the extent that it is supposed to be true. The things that any science discovers are beyond the reach of direct observation. We cannot see energy, nor the attraction of gravitation, nor the flying mol-

ecules of gases, nor the luminiferous ether, nor the forests of the carbona-
ceous era, nor the explosions in nerve-cells. It is only the premisses of
science, not its conclusions, which are directly observed. . . . The data of
metaphysics are not less open to observation, but immeasurably more so,
than the data, say of the very highly developed science of astronomy. . . .
No, I think we must abandon the idea that metaphysics is backward owing
to any intrinsic difficulty of it.[7]

Peirce regarded the universe as having evolved steadily from chaos and
toward a goal as a consequence of three cosmological forces or principles: (1)
tychism (chance), (2) *agapism* (evolution of love), and (3) *synechism* (principle of
continuity). Tychism accounts for the variety and diversification that is found in
the universe as it evolves in accordance with agapism, the basic principle that
causes all things in the world to be governed by laws. Synechism, "the doctrine
that all that exists is continuous," accounts for the continuity of everything in the
universe and the tendency of things to move toward reason.

The idea of continuity led Peirce to the idea of community.

I can see but one solution. . . . It seems to me that we are driven to this,
that logicality inexorably requires that our interests shall *not* be limited.
They must not stop at our own fate, but must embrace the whole community. This community, again, must not be limited, but must extend to all
races of beings with whom we can come into immediate or mediate intellectual relation. It must reach, however vaguely, beyond this geological
epoch, beyond all bounds. He who would not sacrifice his own soul to save
the whole world, is, as it seems to me, illogical in all his inferences, collec-
tively. Logic is rooted in the social principle.
To be logical men should not be selfish.[8]

A rational person is one whose interests go beyond him- or herself to include
the entire community. From Peirce's notion of fixing beliefs, we can conclude
that individualism is false. That is one reason Peirce rejected the method of
tenacity. The pursuit of truth is the evolution of love toward community—the
community of humankind.

The great bulk of mankind . . . never have leisure to labor for anything
but the necessities of life for themselves and their families. But, without
directly striving for it, far less comprehending it, they perform all that civilization requires, and bring forth another generation to advance history
another step. Their fruit is, therefore, collective; it is the achievement of
the whole people. What is it, then, that the whole people is about, what is
this civilization that is the outcome of history, but is never completed? We
cannot expect to attain a complete conception of it; but we can see that it
is a gradual process . . . whereby man, with all his miserable littleness

becomes gradually more and more imbued with the Spirit of God, in which nature and History are rife. . . . The great principle of logic is self-surrender.

Individual action is a means and not our end. Individual pleasure is not our end; we are all putting our shoulders to the wheel for an end that none of us can catch more than a glimpse at—that which the generations are working out.[9]

Pause for Thought

Do you agree with Peirce that we are evolving from chaos to community as a consequence of cosmological forces? Or do you think the world is the same now as it was in the beginning and the only important goal is individual salvation?

William James

James's Life

Born in New York City to wealthy and highly cultured parents, William James (1842–1910) showed his extraordinary personal and intellectual abilities at an early age. Perhaps because William and then his brother Henry were born within fifteen months of each other, they were always close friends. Their father, Henry, Sr., a Swedenborgian theologian, told them if they were asked their religion, to answer: "Say I'm a philosopher, say I'm a seeker for truth, say I'm a lover of my kind, say I'm an author of books if you like, or best of all, just say I'm a student."

As children, William and Henry experienced unusual schooling. Their primary education took place at home and involved spirited discourses on every topic. Their formal education was irregular, usually in private schools in England, France, Switzerland, and Germany. At home in New England, they met such men as Oliver Wendell Holmes, Sr., and Ralph Waldo Emerson. This type of education especially suited Henry James, who pursued a career in writing to become a famous novelist.

William James tried his hand at many disciplines. He studied art, chemistry, anatomy, and physiology, and he even accompanied renowned naturalist and geologist Louis Agassiz on an expedition to Brazil. He graduated from Harvard in 1869 with a degree in medicine but decided not to go into practice. His uncertainty brought a deep state of depression, and he suffered a severe spiritual crisis, wondering if we live in a deterministic universe with no control over our lives. When he heard French philosopher Charles Renouvier's discussion of free will, his interest soared. Renouvier had said, "My first act of free will shall be to believe in free will." With renewed hope, James moved from medicine to psychology and philosophy.

Three years after his graduation, William James became an instructor of physiology at Harvard. He wrote of it in a letter to his brother Henry.

> The appointment to teach physiology is a perfect god-send to me just now, an external motive to work—dealing with men instead of my own mind, and a diversion from those introspective studies that had bred a sort of philosophical hypochondria in me of late.[10]

From physiology, James moved on to teach psychology and then became a philosophy professor. In 1878, he married Alice Gibbens, a Boston teacher. The marriage spurred his sense of purpose as well as improved his physical health. In 1891, he published his two-volume *Principles of Psychology*. The book won him wide fame and brought a flood of invitations to lecture around the country. From then on, he led an intensely active life, teaching at Harvard, lecturing throughout the United States, and publishing a series of books—*The Will to Believe* (1897), *Human Immortality* (1898), and *Talks to Teachers on Psychology and to Students on Some of Life's Ideals* (1899)—all of which became classics of American philosophy.

James's concern for religion and the "discreditable" attitude of society toward psychical phenomena spurred him to help organize the American Society for Psychical Research in 1884. Two years later, the University of Edinburgh, Scotland, invited him to give the Gifford Lectures on Natural Religion.

In 1898, while vacationing in the Adirondacks, James had a profound mystical experience: "It seemed as if the Gods of all the nature-mythologies were holding an indescribable meeting in my breast with the moral Gods of the inner life. . . . Doubtless in more ways than one, things in the Edinburgh lectures will be traceable to it." Mountain climbing weakened his heart, however, and the next year while climbing in the Adirondacks, he not only lost his way but also his health. The next two years he convalesced. He did not give the Gifford Lectures until 1902, when they were also published in book form as *The Variety of Religious Experience*.

In a series of lectures, James interpreted Charles Peirce's Pragmatism. He also published in a volume titled *Pragmatism* in 1907. His Hibbert lectures at Oxford, England, in 1908 and 1909 were published as *A Pluralistic Universe*. To complete his philosophical views, he began writing *Some Principles of Philosophy* but had to leave it as "an arch built only on one side" because of ill health.

In 1910, he went to Europe for a rest, but too much "sitting up and talking" with friends weakened him even more. He returned to his country home in Chocurua, New Hampshire, but died two days later. He was sixty-eight.

The Pragmatic Method

James reminded us that the term *pragmatism* comes from the Greek *pragma*, meaning action. He interpreted this further by adding that *action* means "practice" or "practical." "Pragmatism is a method only" for resolving disputes that would otherwise remain unsettled, he said. It is an inquiry into the practical meanings of events or issues.

> The pragmatic method is primarily a method of settling metaphysical disputes that otherwise might be interminable. Is the world one or many?—fated or free?—material or spiritual?—here are notions either of which may or may not hold good of the world; and disputes over such notions are unending. The pragmatic method in such cases is to try to interpret each notion by tracing its respective practical consequences. What difference would it practically make to any one if this notion rather than that notion were true? If no practical difference whatever can be traced, then the alternatives mean practically the same thing, and all dispute is idle. Whenever a dispute is serious, we ought to be able to show some practical difference that must follow from one side or the other's being right. . . .
>
> A pragmatist turns his back resolutely and once for all upon a lot of inveterate habits dear to professional philosophers. He turns away from abstraction and insufficiency, from verbal solutions, from bad *a priori* reasons, from fixed principles, closed systems, and pretended absolutes and origins. He turns towards concreteness and adequacy, towards facts, towards action and towards power.[11]

Pragmatism rejects Rationalism as dogmatic, because it gives answers about our world with no application to life. Pragmatism "has no dogmas and no doctrines save its method." Pragmatism looks at results, but it does not look for any *particular* result. If there is a dispute whether God exists, Pragmatism offers no dogmatic answer but asks, does it make a difference to believe God exists? In other words, it asks, "Does it work for you to believe in God?"

Pause for Thought   If it "works for you" to believe in God, is that the same as saying "God exists"?

Pragmatic Theory of Truth

For James, what is meaningful or real must in some way influence our experience, and we must consider anything that has a practical effect meaningful and real. Theories without results are nonsense. Terms such as *God, matter,* and *the absolute* must have "cash-value," that is, they must possess practical worth if they are to be true.

> Pragmatism . . . asks its usual question. "Grant an idea or belief to be true," it says, "what concrete difference will its being true make in any one's

actual life? How will the truth be realized? What experiences will be different from those which would obtain if the belief were false? What, in short, is the truth's cash-value in experiential terms?"

The moment pragmatism asks this question, it sees the answer: *True ideas are those that we can assimilate, validate, corroborate and verify. False ideas are those that we cannot.* That is the practical difference it makes to us to have true ideas; that, therefore, is the meaning of truth, for it is all that truth is known-as. . . .

Our ideas must agree with realities, be such realities concrete or abstract. . . . Primarily, no doubt to agree means to copy. . . . To "agree" in the wisest sense with a reality *can only mean to be guided either straight up to it or into its surroundings, or to be put into such working touch with it as to handle either it or something connected with it better than if we disagreed.* Better either intellectually or practically! . . .

Our account of truth is an account of truths in the plural, of processes of leading, realized *in rebus*, and having only this quality in common, that they *pay.* They pay by guiding us into or towards some part of a system that dips at numerous points into sense-percepts, which we may copy mentally or not, but with which at any rate we are now in the kind of commerce vaguely designated as verification. Truth for us is simply a collective name for verification processes.[12]

Pause for Thought   When James wrote, "Our account of truth is an account of truths in the plural," what did he mean?

James's idea that truth is "agreement with reality" does not indicate any fixed structural relation, such as "copying." He rejected what he called the "copy-view" of truth. The copy-view theory assumes that our ideas are copies of reality; and if our ideas copy reality accurately, then they are true. In opposing this theory, James said truth must be the cash-value of an idea. Something that is true must make a concrete difference in our actual lives.

Pause for Thought   Does James's rejection of the copy-view theory of truth in any way suggest that he did not accept Plato's theory of reality? Why does James disagree with the copy-view theory? Do you agree with him?

James characterized truth as functional harmony in our lives, because it must make a difference in our actual living. He may be considered a humanist because he said that truth is the result of human creativity. Ideas are not from a preordained static truth, they become true. Events make ideas true. Truth happens to ideas.

> Any idea upon which we can ride, so to speak; any idea that will carry us prosperously from any one part of our experience to any other part, linking things satisfactorily, working securely, simplifying, saving labor, is true for just so much, true in so far forth, true instrumentally.[13]

Ideas are true when they help us make connections among our various experiences. Ideas change because we can alter them or replace one idea with another. For example, few people now consider it wrong for men to wear long hair, but that has not always been the case. Today it is acceptable for women to wear jeans in public, but not long ago society considered the wearing of jeans "unlady-like." Social ideas are subject to change just as much as religious ideas. When old religions no longer "work," new religious ideas take their place. Religious councils frequently meet to revise their articles of faith. Today, for example, some religions accept women ministers, same-sex marriages, and abortion rights.

James was astutely aware that society does not easily accept change. People prefer to hold on to ideas that have worked for them in the past. For many people, traditional ideas mean security.

> The individual . . . meets a new experience that puts them to a strain. Somebody contradicts them; or he hears of facts with which they are incompatible; or desires arise in him, which they cease to satisfy. The result is an inward trouble to which his mind till then had been a stranger, and from which he seeks to escape by modifying his previous mass of opinions . . . until at last some new idea comes up which he can graft upon the ancient stock. . . .
>
> This new idea is then adopted as the true one. It preserves the older stock of truths with a minimum of modification, stretching them enough to make them admit the novelty, but conceiving them in ways as familiar as the case leaves possible. . . . We would scratch around industriously till we found something less eccentric. The most violent revolutions in an individual's beliefs leave most of his old order standing.[14]

When we can no longer stand the stress and strain of old ideas, we begin to give birth to new ideas. Seldom do new ideas entirely replace the old ones; instead, they grow from them. Truth must work—and it must work constructively. It must be helpful. If something is "untrue," then it will work destructively. James called truth "one species of the good." He interpreted the good as a plurality of "good fors."

True ideas have practical value, while false ones do not. Pragmatism's only test of truth is what works best in leading us, what fits our life experiences best by combining with the "collectivity of experience's demands, nothing being omitted."

Thus, we create truths the same way we create health and wealth. Just as it pays to stay healthy, it pays to seek the truth. Truth, said James, is a system of verification, a process by which ideas not only become true, but also are made true by events in our experience.

Pause for Thought   Can you think of recent examples of changes taking place in religion, politics, and your own life that would support James's idea that truth happens to ideas?

Consciousness

James's moral philosophy was his answer to Descartes' mind–body problem. As you recall, Descartes discovered two kinds of substance: mind and matter. As extended substance, matter mechanically follows natural laws. Mind, on the other hand, is free. Surprisingly, these two substances interact. When my body feels itself infected with illness, my mind is sluggish. When I will to walk, my body obeys. Descartes' problem was how these two different substances can interact with each other. His solution was that the pineal gland is the base for the connection between mind and matter. This solution, however, was as unsatisfactory for Descartes as for the philosophers who came after him.

Consciousness is the solution to this problem, said James. Dualism arises only if we think that minds are conscious and bodies are unconscious. However, if we look at experience in its purity, we find no such duality. Once the idea that our mind is a distinct entity disappears, then dualism—the opposition between mind and matter—evaporates.

> To deny plumply that "consciousness" exists seems so absurd on the face of it—for undeniably "thoughts" do exist—that I fear some readers will follow me no farther. Let me then immediately explain that I mean only to deny that the word stands for an entity, but to insist most emphatically that it does stand for a function. There is, I mean, no aboriginal stuff or quality of being, contrasted with that of which material objects are made, out of which our thoughts of them are made; but there is a function in experience which thoughts perform, and for the performance of which this quality of being is invoked. That function is *knowing*. "Consciousness" is supposed necessary to explain the fact that things not only are, but get reported, are known. Whoever blots out the notion of consciousness from his list of first principles must still provide in some way for that function's being carried on.

My thesis is that if we start with the supposition that there is only one primal stuff or material in the world, a stuff of which everything is composed, and if we call that stuff "pure experience," then knowing can easily be explained as a particular sort of relation toward one another into which portions of pure experience may enter. The relation itself is a part of pure experience. . . .[15]

Pause for Thought   Can you conceive the primal stuff as "pure experience"? Does James's explanation of pure experience solve the mind–body problem?

James disagreed with the British Empiricists, who stated that we do not experience a connection between things, only discontinuous possibilities or disjunctions. He rejected Hume's idea that the mind is a mere bundle of impressions and ideas because of its failure to see the unity of relationships. Pure experience knows other so-called pieces of experience that are not aspects of ourselves and brings them together in relationship. James did not want to say consciousness is omnipotent in its power to organize our world. The world does have some structure, but the structure is always flexible and subject to change. The world cannot be deterministic, because it allows for a plurality of meanings and values. The world is a world of freedom, and we are responsible for our choices and the quality of our existence.

Freedom

For James, freedom is a process in the powers of consciousness. To say that humans are free means that in the current moment we can control our concentration on feelings, ideas, and objects in the world. James said we all have a "deep spiritual need" to believe that we can control certain aspects of our lives, affect some events, and make a difference in the world.

Pause for Thought   Do you agree with James that a belief in freedom is necessary for our mental and spiritual well-being?

In his essay "The Dilemma of Determinism," James wrote, "I disclaim openly on the threshold all pretension to prove to you that freedom of the will is true. The most I hope is to induce some of you to follow my own example in assuming it true, and acting as if it were true." In opposition to freedom, *determinism* is the belief that everything that happens must, by necessity, happen the way it does. The laws of cause and effect govern all nature and everything in the world.

> What does determinism profess? It professes that those parts of the universe already laid down absolutely appoint and decree what the other parts shall be. The future has no ambiguous possibilities hidden in its womb: the part that we call the present is compatible with only one totality. Any other future complement than the one fixed from eternity is impossible.
>
> Indeterminism, on the contrary, says that the parts have a certain amount of loose play on one another, so that the laying down of one of them does not necessarily determine what the others shall be. It admits that possibilities may be in excess of actualities, and that things not yet revealed to our knowledge may really in themselves be ambiguous. Of two alternative futures which we conceive, both may now be really possible; and the one become impossible only at the very moment when the other excludes it by becoming real itself. Indeterminism thus denies the world to be one unbending unit of fact.[16]

In deterministic thought, the future is already in the present. It will not change. The determinist must define the world as a place where what "could be" is impossible. James considered this not only a chilling thought but also an unacceptable one. If determinism is true, then we face a dilemma: Our sense of moral responsibility becomes nonsense. On the other hand, if determinism does not govern the world, then is everything left to chance?

> To this my answer must be very brief. The belief in free-will is not in the least incompatible with the belief in Providence, provided you do not restrict the Providence to fulminating nothing but *fatal* decrees. If you allow him [God] to provide possibilities as well as actualities to the universe, and to carry on his own thinking in those two categories just as we do ours, chances may be there, uncontrolled even by him, and the course of the universe be really ambiguous; and yet the end of all things may be just what he intended it to be from all eternity.[17]

Pause for Thought   A Hindu aphorism says that at birth we are dealt a hand of cards. We are free to play the hand as we choose. Does this idea fit with the above quote from James?

James argued that although we lack conclusive proof of freedom's existence, the meaning of our lives depends on believing in freedom. We seek for meaning in our lives, and freedom makes that meaning concrete. A strong argument for freedom is that most of us believe everything we think, hope, regret, and act on is of our own free choice. Life presents us with alternatives, and we make judgments of approval or disapproval. We try to persuade others to do or not do certain actions. We reward and punish individuals for their actions. These actions imply choice.

The choices we make and the attitude we use while making them give meaning to our lives. We judge such actions as lying, stealing, and murdering to be wrong. We say people who commit these acts could have done otherwise. James could not conceive of a universe in which murder must happen. He saw this world as a place in which murder can happen but should not. What should we do in such a world? "Be strong and of a good courage," James answered. "Act for the best, hope for the best, and take what comes." To understand what is best, we should live the good life; in this way our efforts can make a difference for ourselves and for the world.

Pause for Thought   Can you imagine your life without believing you have free will? Could such a belief even be possible?

The Moral Life

The profound question that faces moral philosophers is "How do we live the good life?" James reasoned that we must first understand the meaning of "good." Nature, he said, is neither good nor evil. For morality to exist, there must be humanity. "How can one physical fact . . . be better than another? . . . Physical facts simply *are* or are *not*." . . . Nothing can be good or right except so far as some consciousness feels it to be good or thinks it to be right." Ethics, then, looks not to physical nature but to human nature for answers.

James believed that moral philosophers such as Aristotle, Kant, and the Utilitarians had revealed a partial picture of the meaning of "good," but none of those images has been completely satisfactory.

> Various essences of good have been . . . proposed as bases of the ethical system. Thus, to be a mean between two extremes; to be recognized by a special intuitive faculty; to make the agent happy for the moment; to make others as well as him happy in the long run; to add to his perfection or dignity; to harm no one; to follow from reason or flow from universal law; to be in accordance with the will of God; to promote the survival of the human species on this planet,—are so many tests, each of which has been maintained by somebody to constitute the essence of all good things or actions so far as they are good.
>
> No one of the measures that have been actually proposed has, however given general satisfaction. . . . The best, on the whole, of these marks and measures of goodness seems to be the capacity to bring happi-

ness. But in order not to break down fatally, this test must be taken to cover innumerable acts and impulses that never *aim* at happiness; so that, after all, in seeking for a universal principle we inevitably are carried onward to the *most* universal principle,—that *the essence of good is simply to satisfy demand*. The demand may be for anything under the sun. There is really no more ground for supposing that all our demands can be accounted for by one universal underlying kind of motive than there is ground for supposing that all physical phenomena are cases of a single law.[18]

Pause for Thought   Is James saying there is no universal morality? That is, will our moral choices always depend on the situation?

Moral rules do exist, said James, but we should replace these with a critical analysis of facts that fit the situation. His rejection of specific moral rules does not mean he denies moral principles. But there is a difference between specific moral rules such as "Never take a drink" and a general ethical principle such as "Act for the greatest good of the greatest number." The first applies to a specific demand, while the latter requires us to look more deeply into the situation. General moral principles urge us to think carefully about what choices we are going to make.

We should, however, fulfill rather than thwart as many demands as possible. However, we have no way to judge demands before we make them.

> There is hardly a good which we can imagine except as competing for the possession of the same bit of space and time with some other imagined good. Every end of desire that presents itself appears exclusive of some other end of desire. Shall a man drink and smoke, *or* keep his nerves in condition?—he cannot do both. Shall he follow his fancy for Amelia, *or* for Henrietta?—both cannot be the choice of his heart. Shall he have the dear old Republican party, *or* a spirit of unsophistication in public affairs?—he cannot have both, etc. So that the ethical philosopher's demand for the right scale of subordination in ideals is the fruit of an altogether practical need. Some part of the ideal must be butchered, and he needs to know which part. It is a tragic situation, and no mere speculative conundrum, with which he has to deal.[19]

James believed courageous individuals should replace rigid moral rules with more flexible ethical principles.

Although a man always risks much when he breaks away from established rules and strives to realize a larger ideal whole than they permit, yet the philosopher must allow that it is at all times open to any one to make the experiment, provided he fear not to stake his life and character upon the throw. . . .[20]

The job of the moral philosopher, as James defined it, is to clarify the general moral principles that can bring harmony and meaning to our lives. The philosopher will find these principles by reflecting on the relationships between consciousness and value. We need selective consciousness for values to exist, so selecting something as good is a necessary condition for its being good. Demanding is a necessary condition for value to exist, because if we think we should fulfill a certain goal or desire, then that is the reason we fulfill it.

Pause for Thought   James suggested that the best course of action is "to satisfy at all times *as many demands as we can*," and to frustrate as few demands as possible. If you followed his moral guidance, then what changes (if any) would you experience in your life?

Religion

Though there is no absolute proof for God's existence, James argued that people who believe in God have a better chance to discover truth than those who disbelieve in God. Believers don't know if there is truth or whether they can discover it, but they have a will to believe that truth exists. According to James, if we don't leave open the possibility of truth, then we face the risk of losing any chance of discovering it.

Certain truths become possible only when individuals are in the position of receiving them. Suppose you want to know whether a certain person would be your friend. If you decide that person cannot be your friend, then you will never know the truth. But if you will to believe, then you may discover that the same person also wants you as a friend. Belief takes what already is full circle.

In his work *The Will to Believe*, James wrote we have a right to believe in God without absolute proof. Belief in God's existence enriches our lives in a way that disbelief cannot. He did not suggest that our belief in God would create God's existence, but through our will to believe we can experience what actually is already there. His Pragmatism recognized the close relationship between belief and action. "We must judge the religious life by its results exclusively." Religion that enriches our lives fulfills our deepest destiny.

Two Types of Personalities

In his work *Varieties of Religious Experience,* James distinguished between two types of personalities, the *healthy-minded* and the *morbid-minded*. Healthy-minded personalities "look on all things and see that they are good." These individuals are vital, enthusiastic, and joyful.

> In these states, the ordinary contrast of good and ill seems to be swallowed up in a higher denomination, an omnipotent excitement which engulfs the evil, and which the human being welcomes as the crowning experience of his life. This, he says, is truly to live, and I exult in the heroic opportunity and adventure. . . .
>
> The advance of liberalism, so-called, in Christianity, during the past fifty years, may fairly be called a victory of healthy-mindedness. . . .[21]

In contrast, morbid-minded people have the attitude of "old hell-fire theology." They are negative and pessimistic. They base their views "on the persuasion that the evil aspects of our life are of its very essence. . . ."

> But there are others for whom evil is no mere relation of the subject to particular outer things, but something more radical and general, a wrongness or vice in his essential nature, which no alteration of the environment, or any superficial rearrangement of the inner self, can cure, and which requires a supernatural remedy.[22]

Although James was an optimist, he suggested that morbid-minded people recognize a wider range of experience than the healthy-minded and are therefore more realistic.

> The method of averting one's attention from evil, and living simply in the light of good is splendid as long as it will work. . . . But it breaks down impotently as soon as melancholy comes. . . .
>
> The normal process of life contains moments as bad as any of those which insane melancholy is filled with, moments in which radical evil gets its innings and takes its solid turn. The lunatic's visions of horror are all drawn from the material of daily fact. Our civilization is founded on the shambles, and every individual existence goes out in a lonely spasm of helpless agony. If you protest, my friend, wait till you arrive there yourself! . . . The completest religions would therefore seem to be those in which the pessimistic elements are best developed.[23]

Pause for Thought   If James considered morbid-minded people more realistic than the healthy-minded, then why didn't he reverse the labels? Which personality type are you?

James also argued that only out of the realistic morbid-minded soul does profound religious conversion emerge.

Religious Conversion

Conversion, said James, is a profound alteration of consciousness. This change results in a "religious" outlook that brings a decent amount of happiness while acknowledging the presence of evil in the world. Such a spiritual experience is a balance and thus can avoid the extremes of optimism and pessimism.

Not all religious conversions are instantaneous. Some are slower natural processes. Both kinds of conversion are expansions of ordinary consciousness.

> What makes the difference between a sudden and gradual convert is not necessarily the presence of divine miracle in the case of one and of something less divine in that of the other, but rather a simple psychological peculiarity, the fact, namely, that in the recipient of the more instantaneous grace we have one of those subjects who are in possession of a large region in which mental work can go on subliminally, and from which invasive experience, abruptly upsetting the equilibrium of the primary consciousness, may come.[24]

The outcome of conversion leads into two areas: (1) *saintliness* in our conduct, and (2) *mysticism,* or "seeing the truth in a special manner."

Saintliness   In the saint, James found the following attributes: (1) asceticism, (2) strength of soul, (3) purity, and (4) charity. Some saints, he noted, are fanatics, and others are otherworldly and naive. But James's studies show that "fanaticism is found only where the character is masterful and aggressive." And otherworldliness is "a genuinely creative social force."

> If things are ever to move upward, some one must be ready to take the first step, and assume the risk of it. No one who is not willing to try charity, to try non-resistance as the saint is always willing, can tell whether these methods will or will not succeed. When they do succeed, they are far more powerfully successful than force or worldly prudence. Force destroys enemies; and the best that can be said of prudence is that it keeps what we already have in safety. But non-resistance, when successful, turns enemies into friends; and charity regenerates its objects. These saintly methods are, as I said, creative energies; and genuine saints find in the elevated excitement with which their faith endows them an authority and impressiveness which makes them irresistible in situations where men of shallower nature cannot get on at all without the use of worldly prudence. This practical proof that worldly wisdom may be safely transcended is the saint's magic gift to mankind.[25]

Pause for Thought   After reading James's description, do you think a saint would be afraid to pick up a hitchhiker, sleep with unlocked doors, or nurture AIDS patients? Can you think of people in this century who reflect the "saint's magic gift to mankind"?

Mysticism   The mystic, like the saint, has a spiritual gift. For James, there are four "marks" of the mystical state: the (1) inexpressible, (2) the transient, (3) the passive, and (4) "states of insight into depths of truth unplumbed by the discursive intellect." Mystical states are deep inner experiences of the unity of opposites and of the kinship of all life.

> Looking back on my own experiences, they all converge towards a kind of insight to which I cannot help ascribing some metaphysical significance. The keynote of it is invariably a reconciliation. It is as if the opposites of the world, whose contradictoriness and conflict make all our difficulties and troubles, were melted into unity. Not only do they as contrasted species, belong to one and the same genus, but *one of the species,* the nobler and better one, *is itself the genus, and so soaks up and absorbs its opposite into itself.* This is a dark saying, I know, when thus expressed in terms of common logic, but I cannot wholly escape from its authority. I feel as if it must mean something, something like what the Hegelian philosophy means, if one could only lay hold of it more clearly. Those who have ears to hear, let them hear; to me the living sense of its reality only comes in the artificial mystic state of mind.[26]

By "artificial" here, James meant "unnatural" in the sense of unique and short-lived: "Except in rare instances, half an hour, or at most an hour or two, seems to be the limit beyond which they fade in the light of common day."

Religious Experience

Religious experience, not philosophy or theology, should form the foundation of our religious life. Religion, said James, is "mankind's most important function." We find evidence for God's existence in our own inner experiences. These experiences help us realize that the world we perceive is part of a spiritual universe that gives the world value. Our goal should be to unite with that higher spiritual universe through prayer or inner communion with God. In return, the spiritual energy flows in and through us and produces effects in the world. It was James's experience that religious faith gives us a new love of life that results in a higher and richer moral order.

John Dewey

Dewey's Life

John Dewey (1859–1952) was born and grew up in Burlington, Vermont. His father was a successful grocer, and his mother was deeply involved in philanthropic affairs. After graduating from the University of Vermont, Dewey taught classics, algebra, and science for two years at a high school in Pennsylvania. When he returned to Burlington, his former philosophy professor encouraged him to attend graduate school. Heeding his advice, Dewey enrolled in the doctoral program at Johns Hopkins University in Baltimore. One of his teachers there was Charles S. Peirce, although Dewey then was more interested in Hegel's philosophy.

After receiving his Ph.D. in 1884, Dewey became a faculty member of the University of Michigan. While there, he married Alice Chipman, one of his students, and they had five children and adopted a sixth. While teaching at Michigan, Dewey moved from Hegel's idealism to Pragmatism. In 1894, he received a position as chairman of the Department of Philosophy, Psychology, and Pedagogy at the University of Chicago. While there, he set up an experimental school to test his theories of education and teacher training. It was so successful that his view on educational theory, with its emphasis on "learning by doing," spread across the country. In 1904, Dewey moved to Columbia University in New York; for the next twenty-five years, he taught, wrote, and lectured on education in Japan, China, and Russia and the Soviet Union.

Always active in social causes, Dewey was one of the organizers of the American Association of University Professors and of the American Civil Liberties Union. He died at age ninety-two.

Instrumentalism

Charles Peirce concluded that the way to find out what a statement means is to list the operations that verify it. Any statement that cannot be empirically (publicly) verified is literally meaningless. Thus, because a subjective personal statement such as "The absolute exists" cannot be verified, it has no meaning.

William James was less concerned with empirical verification than was Peirce. The pragmatic criterion for James was that an assertion is true if it "works." He did not believe that the conclusions of science were as authoritative as Peirce thought them to be. James believed the important problem of conflict in people was between their religious instincts and their desire to accept scientific facts. Pragmatism meant helping people out of their conflicts: If it is true for me that God exists, then I should act on that feeling. Both science and religion, said James, are based ultimately on commitment more than on verifiable evidence.

Dewey called his version of Pragmatism "Instrumentalism" or "Experimentalism." He built his system on the basis of behavioristic psychology and the pragmatic theory of knowledge. Influenced by Darwin's theory of evolution, Dewey viewed human beings as biological organisms best understood in relation to our natural environment. Based on his ideas of evolution, Dewey had faith in our ability to achieve moral progress and create a more ideal society through improvements in education. He rejected the idea that we could solve ethical problems by returning to the disinterested rationality of the Greeks, and chose instead to follow the method of the natural sciences. He considered his philosophy of "Instrumentialsim" to be a bridge between science and ethics.

Dewey defined Instrumentalism as "an attempt to constitute a precise logical theory of concepts, of judgments and inferences in their various forms, by considering primarily how thought functions in the experimental determinations of future consequences." In *The Quest for Certainty*, he wrote that "the essence of Pragmatic Instrumentalism is to conceive of both knowledge and practice as means of making goods—excellences of all kinds—secure in experienced existence."

Like James, Dewey was interested in "practical problems," but unlike James, he was less interested in inner religious conflicts than with the problems of society. Dewey saw a deep need to reorganize our social and physical environment. He criticized the Empiricists for thinking that our ideas refer to fixed things in nature and that these fixed things have a corresponding reality. For him, theories must be capable of being put into action and yielding desirable or at least predictable consequences. A genuine inquiry, he said, begins with a confused situation. A three-stage process is needed to resolve the confusion and prescribe reasonable solutions. "To see that a situation requires inquiry is the initial step in the inquiry." In other words, being able to articulate the nature of the problem is the first stage. In the second stage we create a hypothesis to resolve the difficulty. In this way we refine the hypothetical solution by clarifying meanings. Both of the first two stages of creating hypotheses and clarifying meanings use concepts as their tools or instruments. Thus follows the third and final stage: testing the reasoned solution. If it is successful, the inquiry will result in "a cleared-up, unified, resolved situation at the close" and we will have a "unified whole."

Pause for Thought   Do you agree with Dewey that a genuine inquiry about anything begins with confusion? If so, do you follow his method to reach clarification?

Human Nature

Impulse   Concerned with practical problems that we humans in society have, Dewey started with psychology. Although he emphasized the social aspect of human nature, he recognized certain inherited patterns as well. All humans have impulses, and the result of an impulse will depend on the way it interweaves with other impulses and with the external environment. No impulse has a definite character in itself; all impulses are "highly flexible."

In the case of the young it is patent that impulses are highly flexible starting points for activities which are diversified according to the ways in which they are used. Any impulse may become organized into almost any disposition according to the way it interacts with surroundings. Fear may become abject cowardice, prudent caution, reverence for superiors or respect for equals; an agency for credulous swallowing of absurd superstitions or for wary scepticism. . . . The actual outcome depends upon how the impulse of fear is interwoven with other impulses. This depends in turn upon the outlets and inhibitions supplied by the social environment.

The traditional psychology of instincts obscures recognition of this fact. It sets up a hard-and-fast preordained class under which specific acts are subsumed, so that their own quality and originality are lost from view. This is why the novelist and dramatist are so much more illuminating as well as more interesting commentators on conduct than the schematizing psychologist . . . .

In the career of any impulse activity there are speaking generally three possibilities. It may find a surging, explosive discharge—blind, unintelligent. It may be sublimated— that is, become a factor coordinated intelligently with others in a continuing course of action. Thus a gust of anger may, because of its dynamic incorporation into disposition, be converted into an abiding conviction of social injustice to be remedied, and furnish the dynamic to carry the conviction into execution. . . . Such an outcome represents the normal or desirable functioning of impulse; in which, to use our previous language, the impulse operates as a pivot, or reorganization of habit. Or again a released impulsive activity may be neither immediately expressed in isolated spasmodic action, nor indirectly employed in an enduring interest. It may be "suppressed."

Suppression is not annihilation. "Psychic" energy is no more capable of being abolished than the forms we recognize as physical. If it is neither exploded nor converted, it is turned inwards, to lead a surreptitious, subterranean life. . . . A suppressed activity is the cause of all kinds of intellectual and moral pathology.[27]

Our natural impulses will differ in various social situations. However, if an impulse reflects itself in the same way time after time, it becomes a *habit*.

Pause for Thought   Do you have any impulses that have become habits?

Habits

We develop habits for dealing with recurring "classes of stimuli, standing predilections and aversions." Habits are not merely mechanical, and Dewey distinguished two types: "intelligent and routine." "The higher the form of life the more complex, sure and flexible" will be the habit. A habit is the function between "organism and environment" that furthers and maintains life. Dewey said we could look at habits as *arts*.

> They [habits] involve skill of sensory and motor organs, cunning or craft, and objective materials. They assimilate objective energies, and eventuate in command of environment.[28]

Habit is only one way of responding to "stimuli, standing predilections and aversions." Dewey found no necessary connection between a particular impulse and a particular response. Thus our responses are learned through interaction between society and our human nature. We can test habits for their usefulness in supporting life and our adaptation to the environment.

The notion of analyzing habits gave Dewey insight into the nature of human and social "evil." For him, evil is the result of the way a culture has shaped and conditioned our impulses. It is, he said, the "inertness of established habit." Intelligence, too, is a habit by which we adjust our relation to the environment.

Intelligence

For Dewey, intelligence is a habit that shows other habits to be insufficient. We are not passive spectators of a neutral world, but organisms plunged into an environment that has its own nature. By developing habits, we make necessary adjustments to the environment, and because adjustments constantly require modification, we need intelligence.

> The function of reflective thought is to transform a situation in which there is experienced obscurity, doubt, conflict, disturbance of some sort, into a situation that is clear, coherent, settled, harmonious. . . .
>
> When a situation arises containing a difficulty or perplexity, the person who finds himself in it may take one of a number of courses. He may dodge it, dropping the activity that brought it about, turning to something else. He may indulge in a flight of fancy, imagining himself powerful or wealthy, or in some other way in possession of the means that would enable him to deal with the difficulty. Or, finally, he may face the situation. In this case, he begins to reflect.
>
> The moment he begins to reflect, he begins of necessity to observe in order to take stock of conditions. . . . Some of the conditions are obstacles and others are aids, resources. No matter whether these conditions come to him by direct perception or by memory, they form the "facts of the case." They are the things that are there, that have to be reckoned with. . . . Until

the habit of thinking is well formed, facing the situation to discover the facts requires an effort. For the mind tends to dislike what is unpleasant and so to sheer off from an adequate notice of that which is especially annoying.

Along with noting the conditions that constitute the facts to be dealt with, suggestions arise of possible courses of action. . . . [These lead] to new observations and recollections and to a reconsideration of observations already made in order to test the worth of the suggested way out. . . . The newly noted facts may (and in any complex situation surely will) cause new suggestions to spring up. . . . This continuous interaction of the facts disclosed by observation and of the suggested proposals of solution and the suggested methods of dealing with conditions goes on till some suggested solution meets all the conditions of the case and does not run counter to any discoverable feature of it. . . . [29]

Although the habit of thinking is learned, much of our thinking is careless and shows little forethought on the part of those who teach. Most of us neither consider that our behavior toward others is a form of teaching nor understand the functional relationships that exist among impulses, habits, and intelligence.

Importance of Education

According to Dewey, nothing is more important in remaking society than education. Unfortunately, educational practices are often based on a misconception of human nature.

Very early in life sets of mind are formed without attentive thought, and these sets persist and control the mature mind. The child learns to avoid the shock of unpleasant disagreement, to find the easy way out, to appear to conform to customs which are wholly mysterious to him in order to get his own way—that is to display some natural impulse without exciting the unfavorable notice of those in authority. Adults distrust the intelligence which a child has while making upon him demands for a kind of conduct that requires a high order of intelligence, if it is to be intelligent at all. The inconsistency is reconciled by instilling in him "moral" habits which have a maximum of emotional empressment and adamantine hold with a minimum of understanding. These habitudes . . . govern conscious later thought. They are usually deepest and most unget-at-able just where critical thought is most needed—in morals, religion and politics. These "infantilisms" account for the mass of irrationalities that prevail among men of otherwise rational tastes. . . . To list them would perhaps oust one from "respectable" society. . . .[30]

Pause for Thought   Recall your own education. Were you taught at an early age to "conform to customs" and avoid critical discussion of "morals, religion, and politics?" Do you agree with Dewey that such conformity is a bad habit?

Dewey thought that school should reflect the community so that when children graduate from school they will be well adjusted to assume their places in society. He believed that a truly democratic society could be more perfectly attained through education that was not afraid to reconstruct and reorganize human life and society. No philosophy is ever fixed, finished, or absolute, and thus all ideas should be tested in the educational laboratory where students can challenge them and evaluate the consequences, reconstructing their ideas when necessary.

Theory of Value

Like James, Dewey believed that we could make the world better through our initiative in bringing about desirable consequences. No one can fully achieve perfect happiness or good, for they are merely steps to higher stages of moral progress. Thus, Dewey rejected any theory of values that said the standard of value—whether moral, social, political, or economic—could be found in the "essences" of things or in some form of transcendent eternal truth. We have no way to grasp "ultimate ends," so we need to put intelligence to work by analyzing the problem of values in its practical context. We must realize, he said, that value must always mean that consequences are satisfactory. However, we cannot decide beforehand what consequences we will call good. Life is too complex and changes too much to make a set list of rules. The problem of values is the problem of intelligent choice, and the importance of philosophy is to study different methods of making intelligent choices.

Dewey distinguished his value theory between the Utilitarian goal of achieving what is desired and his own goal of progressing toward what is most desirable, satisfactory, and enjoyed. An intelligent choice can maintain "a distinction between desire and the desirable" without referring to any transcendental or absolute standards.

> The formal statement may be given concrete content by pointing to the difference between the enjoyed and the enjoyable, the desired and the desirable, the satis*fying* and the satis*factory*. To say that something is enjoyed is to make a statement about a fact, something already in existence; it is not to judge the value of that fact. There is no difference between such a proposition and one which says that something is sweet or sour, red or black. It is just correct or incorrect and that is the end of the matter. . . . The fact that something is desired only raises the *question* of its desirability; it does not settle it. Only a child in the degree of his immaturity thinks to settle the question of desirability by reiterated proclamation: "I want it, I want it, I want it." . . . To say that

something satisfies is to report something as an isolated finality. To assert that it is satis*factory* is to define it in its connections and interactions. The fact that it pleases or is immediately congenial poses a problem to judgement. How shall the satisfaction be rated? Is it value or is it not? Is it something to be prized and cherished, *to be* enjoyed? Not stern moralists alone but everyday experience informs us that finding satisfaction in a thing may be a warning, a summons to be on the lookout for consequences. To declare something satis*factory* is to assert that it meets specifiable conditions. It is, in effect, a judgment that the thing "will do." It involves a prediction; it denotes an attitude *to be* taken, that of striving to perpetuate and to make secure.[31]

Pause for Thought   Does it make good sense to you that our values are based on consequences that are satisfactory, desirable, and enjoyed? Or do you agree with Kant, that moral values are based on duty?

For Dewey, then, the ultimate sources of value are our "prizings, desirings and enjoyings." If we never liked anything, there would be no need for value. However, the things we enjoy are always involved in relation to other things. Some of our enjoyments come only after we sacrifice; thus we have to discover these relations by using our intelligence and scientific method.

For Dewey, science and values are not separated from each other. Situations involving values are the same situations with respect to physical objects. If I stick an oar in the water the oar appears bent. Is it really bent? To find out, I run my hand along it. By using my intelligence, I adapt a scientific method to distinguish between what appears true and what is really true. In similar fashion, science can provide the standard for value judgments. For Dewey, then, desire is the starting point, and then we must engage in intelligent critical inquiry before making a moral choice.

Summary

The word *pragmatism* comes from the Greek *pragma,* meaning action. To emphasize that words derive their meanings from actions of some sort, Charles S. Peirce argued that ideas are clear and have meaning only when we translate them into some mode of action. He found that scientific language was the best instrument for satisfying the pragmatic test for meaning, because meanings are derived by experiment. To have meaning, an idea must be social and public, not individual and private. Because we have no way to test subjective individual ideas, they are meaningless.

For Peirce, belief guides our actions; thus we need to "fix beliefs" by grounding them in real things that can be verified. And it is important that their "fixation" become a public act and not just a private or individual one. Individuals who have fixed belief in science draw similar (public) conclusions.

Peirce believed the universe is evolving from chaos toward the goal of community through three cosmological forces: (1) tychism (chance), (2) agapism (evolutionary love), and (3) synechism (principle of continuity). Evolution, he said, is the pursuit of truth by a community effort (all of humankind) over an indefinitely long period of time.

For William James, action means practicality, a meaningful life experience. Pragmatism is a method of inquiry into the practical meaning of events or issues. Except for its method, Pragmatism has no dogma.

With the Empiricists, James believed we could not know the whole of reality. With the Rationalists and Idealists, he thought that morality and religion are an important part of human experience. James argued that philosophy is not merely theoretical *or* empirical; it is both. Philosophical theories should help us make practical adjustments in ourselves and in the world. For example, if you believe in God, you will act differently than if you do not believe in God. Our beliefs affect our everyday experiences.

Truth for James, must be the "cash-value" of an idea. Ideas are not preordained static truth; they become true. When we no longer can stand the stress and strain of old ideas, new ideas will sprout.

James argued for freedom over determinism. Although we lack proof of freedom's existence, the meaning of our lives depends on believing in freedom. We feel free to make moral choices and to live the good life. We should always be aware of general moral principles, but specific moral situations will be different with different people and sometimes part of the general moral ideal "must be butchered."

In religion, James recognized the close relation between belief and action. "We must judge the religious life by its results exclusively." Religious experience, not philosophy or theology, is the foundation of our religious life.

John Dewey called his version of Pragmatism "instrumentalism" or "experimentalism." He built his system on the basis of behavoristic psychology and the pragmatic theory of knowledge. He viewed human beings as biological organisms evolving to greater knowledge which includes progressing morally and achieving a more ideal society.

Dewey disagreed that our ideas refer to fixed things in nature and that these fixed things have a corresponding reality. For him, all theories must be capable of being put into action and yielding predictable consequences.

Impulses are inherent but highly flexible patterns of human nature. They will differ in various social situations but can become habits under certain circumstances. Habit, said Dewey, is the function that furthers and maintains life. In human beings, intelligence is a habit that shows that other habits are insufficient.

According to Dewey nothing is more important than remaking society through education. Schools should reflect the community so that when children graduate they will be well adjusted to assume their places in society. Adjusted, however, does not mean always conforming to society. It is up to education to reconstruct and reorganize human life and society.

Like James, Dewey believed we could make the world a better place by analyzing the problem of values in proper context. Value always means that the consequences are satisfactory, desirable, and enjoyed.

Connections

Pragmatism is known as the philosophy of America. As we have seen, Peirce, James, and Dewey are the philosophers who brought Pragmatism to the United States, and although they were all Pragmatists, each contributed something different. In contrast with James and Dewey, Peirce took the view that philosophy could not solve vital human problems. He was the pioneer in the development of mathematical logic taught in U.S. universities today. He cultivated the methods of logic and Pragmatism to eliminate ambiguity and vagueness and to build a metaphysical system that explains the universe. By combining philosophy and psychology, James had a strong influence on Henri Bergson (Chapter 14) and the Existentialists (Chapter 17). Dewey had a significant influence on education. In fact, he thought philosophy should be defined as a general theory of education. All of the Pragmatists were radical Empiricists. In the search for truth and meaning, they said, we must look for verification of facts that will unify the way we look at ourselves and the world.

Study Questions

1. What does the word Pragmaticism mean?

2. Why did Charles S. Peirce change the name of his Pragmatic philosophy to Pragmaticism?

3. For Peirce what is a clear idea?

4. Explain Peirce's explanation of the functions of doubt, belief, and action.

5. According to Peirce, what is fixed belief?

6. How does Peirce's theory of evolution differ from Darwin's theory?

7. Compare and contrast the tender-minded with the tough-minded. Which one are you?

8. How did James's mystical experience affect his views on religion?

9. Explain the Pragmatic method. Why does it reject Rationalism?

10. Explain what Pragmatists mean by the "cash-value" of an idea.

11. What is the Pragmatic theory of meaning? Give an example.

12. How does James solve the mind–body problem? Do you agree with his solution?

13. What is the dilemma of determinism? What is James's solution to the dilemma?

14. What place do universal moral principles have in James's Pragmatism?

15. Why does James argue that people who believe in God have a better chance of discovering truth than those who disbelieve in God?

16. Discuss James's notion of the "will to believe."

17. Of the two types of personalities, "healthy-minded" and "morbid-minded," which is the most realistic? Why?

18. What are the similarities and differences between saintliness and mysticism?

19. According to James, what should be the goal of our religious experience?

20. Why was Darwin's theory of evolution significant for Dewey?

21. For Dewey, what are the stages for problem solving?

22. What is Instrumentalism?

23. What did Dewey mean when he said that values must be desirable, satisfactory, and enjoyed?

24. Why did Dewey consider education so important?

25. What, if any, is the connection between impulses and habits?

Notes

1. William James, *Pragmatism* (ed. by Ralph Barton Perry), pp. 22–23. Cleveland, OH: World Publishing, 1964.

2. William James, *Pragmatism: A New Name for Some Old Ways of Thinking, Together with Four Related Essays Selected from the Meaning of Truth*, p. 46. New York: Longmans Green, 1907.

3. Charles Peirce, *Collected Papers of Charles Sanders Peirce* (ed. by Charles Hartshorne and Paul Weiss), Vol. 5, p. 318. Cambridge, MA: Harvard University Press, 1931–35.

4. Ibid., Vol. V, pp. 233–39, 241.

5. Ibid., Vol. V, pp. 240–42.

6. Ibid., Vol. VI, pp. 6–7.

7. Ibid., Vol. VI, pp. 1–2.

8. Ibid., Vol. II, p. 398.

9. Ibid., Vol. V, pp. 258–259.

10. "Biographical Note: William James," in *The Principles of Psychology* (ed. by Robert M. Hutchins), p. v. Chicago: William Benton, 1952.

11. James, *Pragmatism*, op. cit., pp. 126–27.

12. William James, *The Meaning of Truth* (ed. by Ralph Barton Perry), p. 224. Cleveland, OH: World Publishing, 1964.

13. James, *Pragmatism*, op. cit., p. 58.

14. Ibid., pp. 59–64.

15. William James, *Essays in Radical Empiricism* (ed. by Ralph Barton Perry), pp. 4–5. New York: Dutton, 1971.

16. William James, "The Dilemma of Determinism," in *The Moral Philosophy of William James* (ed. by John K. Roth), p. 107. New York: Thomas Y. Crowell, 1969.

17. Ibid., p. 129.

18. William James, "The Moral Philosopher and the Moral Life," in *The Moral Philosophy of William James* (ed. by John K. Roth), pp. 180–181. New York: Thomas Y. Crowell, 1969.

19. Ibid., pp. 202–203.

20. James, *Essays in Radical Empiricism*, op. cit., p. 206.

21. William James, *The Varieties of Religious Experience*, p. 87. New York: Collier, 1961.

22. Ibid., p. 119.

23. Ibid., pp. 140–141.

24. Ibid., p. 194.

25. Ibid., p. 284.

26. Ibid., p. 306.

27. John Dewey, *Human Nature and Conduct*, pp. 95, 155–157. New York: Henry Holt, 1922.

28. Ibid., p. 15.

29. John Dewey, *How We Think*, pp. 100–104. Boston: Heath, 1937.

30. Dewey, *Human Nature and Conduct*, op. cit., pp. 98–99.

31. John Dewey, *The Quest for Certainty*, pp. 10–24. New York: Minton Balch, 1929.

CHAPTER FOURTEEN

Process Philosophy:
Bergson and Whitehead

By the early nineteenth century, a change in worldview had begun. Developments in the physical and biological sciences questioned the validity of Newton's mechanistic world order. New findings in growth formations, reproduction, crystalline designs, chemical action, and electricity appeared to contradict the theory that matter is static.

Charles Darwin's *On the Origin of Species by Means of Natural Selection* was a crucial force in creating the new worldview. As the Copernican revolution of the Renaissance displaced humanity as the center of the universe, so Darwin showed that human beings were subject to the same laws of natural selection as all other life forms. Through random variation, humans have become part of their biological environment—just like other species.

Based on Darwin's evidence, Henri Bergson and Alfred North Whitehead pursued the theory of evolution by natural selection. However, in this chapter, we shall see that Bergson and Whitehead did not believe the changing life process was the result of random variation. There must, said Bergson, be a force or principle directing the course of mutations that result in the process of natural selection. Whitehead's main theme was that "connectedness is the essence of all things." What science had separated in the past, philosophy must learn to see as an organic unity in process. For him, the function of natural philosophy was "to analyze how these various elements of nature are connected."

In the past, science had rejected metaphysics. Both Bergson and Whitehead wanted to show that metaphysics and science could support each other.

Henri Bergson

Bergson's Life

Henri Bergson (1859–1941) was born in Paris. His father was a Polish Jew, musician, composer, and head of the Geneva Conservatory; his mother was English. Bergson thought of himself as French, and the French took pride in him as their representative of literary culture. From childhood, he was bilingual in French and English. Educated at Lycées secondary school in Paris, he was a popular student albeit in frail health. He excelled in mathematics and letters, but eventually opted for the latter. One of his schoolmates described him as charming, innocent, honest, sensitive to the feelings of others, but slightly detached or withdrawn. Henri, he said, was more an observer of the human parade than a participant.

At eighteen, Bergson entered the École Normale Supérieure in Paris in Hellenistic classics. He became student librarian so that he could be in the company of books and spent much of his time in a small, secluded room off the library. He enjoyed studying controversial issues and figuring out the basis of the conflict. His major interests were philosophy, mathematics, and science.

At age twenty-two, he became professor of philosophy at the Angers Lycée for two years, then at Clermont-Ferrand. His students loved him and his lectures. At the age of thirty, he returned to Paris as a professor of philosophy at the College Rollin. At thirty-one, he married Louise Neuberger. They gave birth to a deaf daughter who later became a painter. From 1897 until 1900, he was a professor at the École Normale, then at the Collège de France where he held the chair in Greek philosophy and later in modern philosophy. His lectures attracted academics and nonacademics from all over Paris.

Already known for his works *Time and Free Will* (1889) and *Matter and Memory* (1897), he continued to write and lecture. His books *An Introduction to Metaphysics* (1903) and *Creative Evolution* (1907) won wide attention and stimulated animated discussion. He also wrote a book on laughter, *Le Rire*, which is still quoted today in textbooks on comedy and humor. In 1914, he was elected to the French Academy. He received the prestigious Nobel Prize for Literature in 1921.

In 1914, World War I broke out. Three years later, the League of Nations sent Bergson to the United States to persuade President Woodrow Wilson to enter the war. Suffering from ill health, he retired from public life in 1921 and became honorary professor of the Collège de France. In 1932, he published his last work, *Two Sources of Morality and Religion*. In 1939, as World War II began, France became a member of the Allied forces against Nazi Germany.

When, after the fall of France in 1940, the Vichy government introduced anti-Semitic measures based on the Nazi model, it was proposed, because of

Bergson's international reputation, that he be exempted from them. He refused to be treated differently, resigned his various honors, and, although at that time an enfeebled old man who had to be supported while standing in line, registered with the other Jews. He died a few days later, in January 1941.[1]

Intellect Versus Intuition

The key to understanding Bergson's philosophy is his notion that we have two different ways of knowing something: *intellect* and *intuition*. Intellect "implies that we move around the object." With intuition, however, "we enter into it." It is intuition that gives us direct and immediate access to the nature of reality.

> Philosophers . . . agree in distinguishing two profoundly different ways of knowing a thing. The first implies that we move round the object; the second, that we enter into it. The first depends on the point of view at which we are placed and on the symbols by which we express ourselves. The second neither depends on a point of view nor relies on any symbol. The first kind of knowledge may be said to stop at the *relative*; the second, in those cases where it is possible, to attain the *absolute*.
>
> Consider, for example, the movement of an object in space. My perception of the motion will vary with the point of view, moving or stationary, from which I observe it. My expression of it will vary with the system of axes, or points of reference, to which I relate it; that is, with the symbols by which I translate it. For this double reason I call such motion *relative*: in the one case, as in the other, I am placed outside the object itself. But when I speak of an *absolute* movement, I am attributing to the moving object an interior and, so to speak, states of mind; I also imply that I am in sympathy with those states, and that I insert myself in them by an effort of imagination. . . . I shall no longer grasp the movement from without, remaining where I am, but from where it is, from within, as it is in itself. I shall possess an absolute.[2]

Pause for Thought   Can you find similarities and differences between Bergson's intellect and intuition and Descartes' deduction and intuition?

Like Kierkegaard, Bergson believed that intuitive knowledge is individual and subjective, and not the impersonal objective knowledge of traditional philosophy. Unlike intellectual knowledge, which is limited to analyzing concepts, intuition allows us to understand the true nature of reality and therefore the true nature of ourselves.

When I direct my attention inward to contemplate my own self . . . , I
perceive at first, as a crust solidified on the surface, all the perceptions
which come to it from the material world. These perceptions are clear, distinct, juxtaposed or juxtaposable one with another; they tend to group
themselves into objects. Next, I notice the memories which more or less
adhere to these perceptions and which serve to interpret them. These
memories have been detached, as it were, from the depth of my personality, drawn to the surface by the perceptions which resemble them; they rest
on the surface of my mind without being absolutely myself. Lastly, I feel
the stir of tendencies and motor habits—a crowd of virtual actions, more or
less firmly bound to these perceptions and memories. All these clearly
defined elements appear more distinct from me, the more distinct they are
from each other. . . . But if I draw myself in from the periphery towards
the center, if I search in the depth of my being that which is most uni-
formly, most constantly, and most enduringly myself, I find an altogether
different thing.

There is, beneath these sharply cut crystals and this frozen surface, a
continuous flux which is not comparable to any flux I have ever seen.
There is a succession of states, each of which announces that which follows
and contains that which precedes it. . . . Whilst I was experiencing them
they were so solidly organized, so profoundly animated with a common
life, that I could not have said where any one of them finished or where
another commenced. In reality no one of them begins or ends, but all
extend into each other.[3]

Pause for Thought   David Hume and Henri Bergson discovered many of the same perceptions when searching for self-identity. However, they come to
sharply different conclusions. With which conclusion do you identify?

Evolution

Bergson agreed with Darwin: There is evolution. But he disagreed with Darwin
that it proceeds by random selection. For Bergson, some force or principle is
guiding the course of life that results in the process of natural selection. In his
argument, he used the example of the eye's development.

Let us assume, to begin with, the Darwinian theory of insensible variations,
and suppose the occurrence of small differences due to chance, and continually accumulating. It must not be forgotten that all of the parts of an
organism are necessarily coordinated. Whether the function be the effect of
the organ or its cause, it matters little; one point is certain, the organ will
be of no use and will not give selection a hold unless it functions. However

the minute structure of the retina may develop, and however complicated it may become such progress, instead of favoring vision, will probably hinder it if the visual centers do not develop at the same time, as well as several parts of the visual organ itself. If the variations are accidental how can they ever agree to arise in every part of the organ at the same time, in such a way that the organ will continue to perform its function?[4]

By using the example of the eye, Bergson argued for a directive life force throughout all evolution. This life force, the *élan vital*, is the original impetus to life and represents a directed tendency to change. Therefore, variation in evolution could not be a chance occurrence. Everything is in a constant state of flux. Nothing is permanent with changes from time to time. The impetus of the élan vital is "a current of consciousness" that has penetrated matter, given rise to living bodies, and determined the course of their evolution. Its vital impetus carries life toward a higher and more complex organization.

The earliest living things were physiochemical systems that divided so life could move forward in different directions. Plants took one direction, insects another, and intelligence still another. Functions became perfected through successive stages as well as by an increasing realization of consciousness. The leap from animal to human was sudden, but with the appearance of humans came the "reason to be" of life on Earth.

Bergson likened the vital impetus to steam escaping at high pressure through the cracks in a container. Jets gush out unceasingly, the steam condenses into drops of water, and the drops fall back to the source. Each jet and its drops represent a world of matter animated by life. A small part of the jet remains uncondensed for an instant and makes an effort to raise the drops that are falling. But it only succeeds in slowing their fall. The vital impetus achieves a moment of freedom at its highest point—in humanity.

Time and Duration   Usually, we understand time in moments or unity, and we break these moments into discrete units of hours, minutes, and seconds. Bergson reasoned that this ordinary definition does not accurately represent time as we experience it, as it is in itself. Time, he said, is *duration*—it endures. It is impossible to break time into moments and hours—or past, present, and future—because we cannot determine where one moment ends and another begins. We experience time as indivisible, an ever-present now.

The notion of divisibility of time belongs to the mechanical worldview in a Newtonian universe. Because science focuses on the specific moment and never the interval between moments, its understanding of duration "slips through the cracks." Science "always considers moments, always virtual stopping-places, always, in short, immobilities." As flux, time "escapes the hold of scientific knowledge." By using the scientific method, we see things as separate units, including time. Intellect is the faculty that analyzes and separates these units. Intuition unifies. For example, in a puzzle, intuition sees the whole picture. Intellect extracts each piece and analyzes it and loses sight of the whole. The scientific intellect studies what are merely "snapshots" taken of a constantly changing process.

Intellect can understand the parts, or the snapshots, but it cannot grasp duration. If we are to understand time as we understand reality, then we must understand it intuitively—in duration. Duration is reality.

Pause for Thought   Consider how your intellect works. You analyze problems in math, science, and psychology using the reasoning process. Is it possible for you to set analysis aside and understand intuitively the universality of math, science, and human nature?

The Élan Vital   Bergson's vital and creative life force, the *élan vital*, has duration as its essence. The élan vital drives all organisms toward more complicated and higher patterns of organization. The *élan vital* is itself the essence of all living beings and the creative power that flows in continuity through all things. Though there is one continuous flow of existence (one reality), we understand it in two different ways—intellect and intuition.

Bergson argued that the emergence of intellect and matter occurred together. Our intellect is intended to fit our body to its environment and to make relations of external things among themselves, "to think matter." But, he said, matter does not represent true reality.

The intellect's nature is to separate the process of "becoming" into distinct, static states. It divides and analyzes the constant flow of existence. Limited in its understanding to static states, intellect cannot understand the élan vital—the essence of duration. Because it cannot directly apprehend reality, the intellect superimposes possible fields of action on experience and divides it accordingly. These static snapshots block our ability to understand reality as a continuous flux.

Thus for Bergson, intuition must challenge the falsehood of the static intellect. Intuition can know that reality is continuous and not snapshots of separate parts. Through intuition, we realize that the creative process caused by the élan vital is irreversible. To get a notion of this irreversibility, said Bergson, we must counter the intellect's natural bent. Although this does violence to the intellect, that is the function of philosophy.

With intuition, we consciously participate in duration itself. Where intellect analyzes, divides, and separates, intuition synthesizes, unifies, and enters into the flow of existence. Intuition gives us a unified vision of the field of our experience as it truly is—a continuity of becoming.

Evolution is creative because the future is open. Evolution has no preordained "final" goal; duration constantly endures and creates new events. The creative force, Bergson said, is "of God, if it is not God himself."

For Bergson, then, this vital impetus is "supraconscious," and we can call it God. God is pure activity limited by the material world in which He is struggling to manifest Himself. God is neither omnipotent nor omniscient, and He is constantly changing. God is love and the object of love. Evolution is nothing less than God endeavoring to create creators, so He may have beings worthy of His love.

Pause for Thought   Does Bergson's notion of God differ from your own belief? Can you intuit a God who is always changing? Based on Bergson's view of God, would you feel more or less responsibility for your actions in the world?

Morality and Religion

As all philosophers, Bergson's metaphysical schema provides the basis for his theory of morality and religion. Central to each of his theories of morality and religion is the same concept we find in his epistemology—that human beings have a dual nature. In each of us are two conflicting systems of values that guide our decisions and our activities. These two sources of morality and religion are intellect and intuition. Bergson labeled these two moralities *closed morality* and *open morality*.

Closed Morality   Bergson saw in human beings a basic instinct to form society. This social instinct is necessary to ensure the continued survival and growth of civilization. In nature, bees and ants have instincts to form a hive and the hill and cannot vary from that instinct. Humans have the same instinct, although we also have reason (or intellect) to decide which particular type of society we will form. This social instinct, combined with the rational impulse toward organization, is the foundation of closed morality.

> Social life is thus immanent, like a vague ideal, in instinct as well as in intelligence: this ideal finds its most complete expression in the hive or the ant-hill on the one hand, in human societies on the other. Whether human or animal, a society is an organization; it implies a co-ordination and generally also a subordination of elements; it therefore exhibits, whether merely embodied in life or, in addition, specifically formulated, a collection of rules and laws. . . .

In human society we delve down to the root of the various obligations to reach obligation in general, the more obligation will tend to become necessity, the nearer it will draw, in its peremptory aspect, to instinct.[5]

Pause for Thought   Do you agree with Bergson that human beings have a social instinct? Can you imagine living as an individual without society? Could you furnish everything you need to survive?

Coupled with the rational impulse toward organization, the social instinct is the foundation of closed morality. It is our sense of obligation to conform to the rules of the group. The primary concern of closed morality is the good of the group, so customs, traditions, and laws that grow out of closed morality concentrate on providing social stability. In this context, individuality is of secondary importance and always subordinate to an overriding concern for the stability of society as a whole.

Exclusivity is another characteristic of closed morality. Because it concentrates on the good of the group, closed morality excludes individuals who do not belong. It perceives outsiders as a threat. Customs and traditions that guide social behavior also exclude groups that do not share this common ground. Exclusivity is the obstacle to accepting and understanding persons or groups whom they perceive to be outsiders. Because of its exclusivity, closed morality becomes the source of inequality, persecution, discrimination, nationalism, and patriotism. Individuals may support such values as equality, love, and justice, but they limit these values to their own group. Such attitudes are justifiable when the group sees them as promoting social stability or survival.

Pause for Thought   Can you think of examples in your own life when closed morality gave you a feeling of security and belonging? Do your relationships with your family, race, church, workplace, or nation fit Bergson's notion of closed morality?

If we look closely at ourselves, Bergson said, we will find closed morality as part of our biological heritage. It has provided our continued survival. But we need not limit our understanding of human behavior to closed morality. Much of human history is inconsistent with it. To account for this inconsistency, we must look at the connection between Bergson's epistemology and his ethics.

Any theory of morality depends on the way people understand reality. Closed morality views reality through intellect, whose function it is to divide, analyze, and separate. Closed morality thus perceives reality as fundamentally static, so the ethical system grounded in this perception of reality is incapable of understanding or accepting humanity in any universal sense. There is, however, another morality—open morality—and it has a quite different principle.

Open Morality   As closed morality depends on an intellectual perception of reality, open morality relies on the intuition of unity in nature. Through intuition, we directly experience reality as continuity. The distinctions of intellect dissolve into a direct experience of the process of becoming, a process that is fundamental to reality. Intuition allows us to understand reality and humanity in a universal way. The true experience of reality dictates that no real separation exists between objects and events. Therefore, the ethical system grounded in that experience reflects a universal attitude of acceptance toward humanity as a whole.

As closed morality is exclusive, open morality is inclusive—a morality for all humanity. Because the vision of open morality is a direct experience of the élan vital, it focuses on the individual's creative self-actualization. Open morality manifests itself through our inner aspiration to be true to a higher sense of self. This is borne out by philosophers ever since Socrates and the cry of moral heroes, "To thine own self be true." Bergson looked to such mystics as Jesus, Buddha, and the saints of all of the world's religions as the true moral heroes.

> The great moral figures that have made their mark on history join hands across the centuries, above our human cities; they unite into a divine city, which they bid us enter. We may not hear their voices distinctly, the call has none the less gone forth, and something answers from the depth of our soul. . . . It is these men who draw us towards an ideal society, while we yield to the pressure of the real one.[6]

Conforming to the rules and duties of closed morality brings a sense of self-righteousness that we can use as a yardstick to measure the moral worth of others. But obeying the moral commands of open morality results in an inner aspiration toward self-actualization. It ultimately results in the unconditional acceptance and love of others as members of the grand family of humanity.

Open morality and closed morality are within each of us. This moral duality is the source of our inner moral conflict. Alongside our capacity for racism dwells the capacity for universal love. Alongside our deep sense of national patriotism is our awareness of universal humanity.

Pause for Thought   Is Bergson correct that we find ourselves in both closed and open moralities? If you fail to fulfill the requirements of closed morality, are you ridden with guilt? Do you feel you have betrayed the group? If you fail to strive for the ideal of open morality, do you feel that you have betrayed your true self? Is it possible to fulfill both?

Static and Dynamic Religion   Bergson believed that moral duality also expresses itself in two types of religion: *static* and *dynamic*. Static religion has its roots in closed morality and manifests all of its characteristics.

Static religion's primary focus is ritual and doctrine. Universal spiritual truth is often arranged into a set of dogmas that belong exclusively to a particular religious denomination. In this way, static religion expresses the same attitude of exclusivity that we find in closed morality. Those who do not follow the prescribed set of dogmas and do not conform to ritual and agree with basic doctrine are excluded from the group. The rigidity of structure demands individual conformity.

Dynamic religion, on the other hand, shows little concern with accepting dogma or participating in ritual. Bergson saw dynamic religion best represented in the lives of history's great moral teachers: Socrates, Buddha, Lao Tzu, Jesus, and the saints, all of them examples of the finished products of the evolutionary process. What they signify exists potentially in all of us.

Everyone can reach the stage of enlightenment and moral perfection, Bergson said. First, though, we must reach beyond the narrow confines of rational, analytical existence to a vision of unity. Humanity has a profound destiny, and it is entirely up to us how that destiny will be fulfilled. Whether we choose small measures or great ones, we must make a decision.

> Mankind lies groaning, half crushed beneath the weight of its own progress.
> Men do not sufficiently realize that their future is in their own hands.
> Theirs is the task of determining first of all whether they want to go on
> living or not. Theirs the responsibility, then, for deciding if they want
> merely to live, or intend to make just the extra effort required for fulfilling,
> even on their refractory planet, the essential function of the universe, which
> is a machine for the making of gods.[7]

Alfred North Whitehead

Whitehead's Life

Alfred North Whitehead (1861–1947) was born in Ramsgate, Kent, in southern England. His father, a pastor in the Church of England, educated Whitehead at home. When Alfred was fourteen, his parents sent him to school at Sherborne for a classical education. A precocious student, he received a scholarship to study mathematics at Trinity College, Cambridge. There he became interested in philosophy, and he had memorized much of Kant's *Critique of Pure Reason* by the time he graduated.

While teaching mathematics at Cambridge, Whitehead met and married Evelyn Willoughby Wade, and they had four children.

During his twenty-five-year career at Cambridge, Bertrand Russell enrolled as a student and the two men became lifelong friends. After Whitehead's first book, *A Treatise on Universal Algebra,* he collaborated with Russell on the *Principia Mathematica,* published in 1910. That same year, Whitehead left Cambridge and moved to London. He had no job at first, so he washed bottles until he was soon hired by the University of London as professor of applied mathematics. He later became dean of the faculty of science and president of the university's senate.

In 1924, at the retirement age of sixty-three, Whitehead accepted a position in the philosophy department at Harvard University, where he stayed for thirteen years. Each week, he and his wife, Evelyn, held open house for students, providing hot chocolate and stimulating conversation. During his Harvard period, Whitehead produced his most influential philosophical works, *Science and the Modern World, Adventure of Ideas,* and *Process and Reality,* his major work and the one that is most difficult to understand. In *Process and Reality,* Whitehead emphasized that the "shallow, puny, and imperfect" effort of dogmatic certainty in philosophical discussions was "an exhibition of folly."

Whitehead retired in 1937 and died ten years later at age eighty-seven. His philosophical views reflect the influences of Plato, Aristotle, Spinoza, Leibniz, Kant, and Samuel Alexander, another British philosopher of Whitehead's acquaintance.

The Function of Philosophy

Like Bergson, Whitehead sought to replace the Western philosophy of substance with one of process, and static worldviews with dynamic views. Whitehead held that philosophy's job is to search for the underlying pattern in the universe.

> Philosophy is an attitude of mind towards doctrines "ignorantly entertained." I mean that the full meaning of the doctrine, in respect to the infinitude of circumstances to which it is relevant, is not understood. . . .
>
> The use of philosophy is to maintain an active novelty of fundamental ideas illuminating the social system. It reverses the slow descent of accepted thought towards the inactive commonplace. If you like to phrase it so, philosophy is mystical. For mysticism is direct insight into depths as yet unspoken. But the purpose of philosophy is to rationalize mysticism: not by explaining it away, but by the introduction of novel verbal characterizations, rationally coordinated.

Philosophy is akin to poetry, and both of them seek to express that ultimate good sense which we term civilization. In each case there is reference to form beyond the direct meanings of words. Poetry allies itself to metre, philosophy to mathematic pattern.[8]

According to Whitehead, only a process philosophy can account for the creativity and interdependence of our immediate experience. Above all, it is not the business of philosophy to analyze the world by means of the logic of language. Such analysis divides the world into facts. Philosophy is "akin to poetry" and mysticism, for it probes the depths and then tries to explain its findings in a rational way. For Whitehead, philosophy allies itself to mathematical pattern.

Mathematical Pattern

Because we are finite beings, we can never formulate it completely, said Whitehead, but there is a pattern: the ultimate nature of all things is in harmony. There is no arbitrariness. There is no mystery in the nature of things because we find that basic patterns create a continuity of things. Everything is interconnected, and the universe is ultimately rational. For Whitehead, the pattern is found in mathematics.

> The science of Pure Mathematics, in its modern developments, may claim to be the most original creation of the human spirit. . . . [Its] originality consists in the fact that in mathematical science connections between things are exhibited, which, apart from the agency of human reason, are extremely unobvious . . . .
>
> The point of mathematics is that in it we have always got rid of the particular instance and even of any particular sorts of entities. . . . All you assert is, that reason insists on the admission that, if any entities whatever have any relations which satisfy such-and-such purely abstract conditions, then they must have other relations which satisfy other purely abstract conditions. . . .
>
> Pure mathematics . . . is a resolute attempt to go the whole way in the direction of complete analysis, so as to separate the elements of mere matter of fact from the purely abstract conditions, which they exemplify. . . .
>
> The exercise of logical reason is always concerned with these absolutely general conditions. In its broadest sense, the discovery of mathematics is the discovery that the totality of these general abstract conditions, which are concurrently applicable to the relationships among the entities of any one concrete occasion, are themselves inter-connected in the manner of a pattern with a key to it. . . .[9]

Thus, for Whitehead, mathematics is the philosophical tool for our insights into real connections.

Simple Location

The fallacy of Newtonian physics, according to Whitehead, consisted in its doctrine of "simple location." Whitehead called it the "fallacy of misplaced concreteness." Newton believed, as had Democritus, that the nature of things consists of individual bits of matter (atoms) existing in space.

> One . . . assumption [underlying] the whole philosophy of nature during the modern period . . . is embodied in the conception which is supposed to express the most concrete aspect of nature. The Ionian philosophers asked, What is nature made of? The answer is couched in terms of stuff, or matter, or material—the particular name chosen is indifferent—which as the property of simple location in space and time, or, if you adopt the more modern ideas, in space–time. What I mean by matter, or material, is anything which has this property of *simple location*. . . .
>
> The characteristic common both to space and time is that material can be said to be *here* in time, or *here* in space–time, in a perfectly definite sense which does not require for its explanation any reference to other regions of space–time. Curiously enough this character of simple location holds whether we look on a region of space–time as determined absolutely or relatively. . . .
>
> The fact that the material is indifferent to the division of time leads to the conclusion that the lapse of time is an accident, rather than of the essence, of the material. The material is fully itself in any sub-period however short . . . .
>
> The answer, therefore, which the seventeenth century gave to the ancient question of the Ionian thinkers, "What is the world made of?" was that the world is a succession of instantaneous configurations of matter—or of material, if you wish to include stuff more subtle than ordinary matter, the ether for example.
>
> We cannot wonder that science rested content with this assumption as to the fundamental elements of nature. . . . This is the famous mechanistic theory of nature, which has reigned supreme ever since the seventeenth century. It is the orthodox creed of physical science. Furthermore, the creed justified itself by the pragmatic test. It worked. . . . But the difficulties of this theory of materialistic mechanism very soon became apparent. The history of thought in the eighteenth and nineteenth centuries is governed by the fact that the world had got hold of a general idea which it could neither live with nor live without.[10]

To say that a bit of matter has simple location in space–time means that it is in a definite region of space throughout a definite duration of time apart from any "reference of the relations" it may have to other regions of space or other durations of time. The idea of an isolated atom, said Whitehead, is the product of intellectual abstraction. No element in the world possesses the character of simple location. Mistaking intellectual abstractions for actual entities is what Whitehead meant by his term "fallacy of misplaced concreteness." The concept of bits of concrete matter may be helpful ideas for scientific thought, he said, but when scientists take these concepts as descriptions of ultimate reality, they are mistaken. Such concepts are distortions not only of ultimate reality, but also of concrete reality.

Pause for Thought   In your science classes, have you always been taught that bits of matter or atoms are in a particular region of space and in a definite duration of time, and thus isolated from each other?

Have you studied the notion that all elements in nature are interrelated? With which theory do you agree?

Actual Entities and Actual Occasions

In his writings, Whitehead did not use the word *atom,* because historically the term had meant that the atom's content is hard and lifeless. Whitehead preferred to use the terms *actual entities* or *actual occasions*. Actual entities are bits in the life of nature, always interrelated to the whole field of life, and they are never isolated. In this way, he viewed nature as a living organism. Nothing in the universe lacks the principle of life, even "the most trivial puff of existence." Actual entities or actual occasions, for Whitehead, are "the final real things of which the world is made up." Even God is an actual entity. According to Whitehead, actual entities are evidence that the universe is in constant process.

Pause for Thought   Can you visualize what Whitehead meant when he said that the universe is a "living organism" and thus in constant process and not mechanical in any aspect?

Whitehead claimed that the theory of actual entities or actual occasions freed us from Cartesian dualism and the mind–body problem. For Whitehead, one insubstantial substance undergoes continuous change: What appears, what is given indirect perception, is real. Nothing exists beyond what is present in our direct experience, which exists in relation to its object. As Heraclitus believed, everything is in flux and interconnected. The relations between entities are experienced as a kind of feeling.

Although we often think that we perceive a permanent object "out there" and that we are permanent subjects, both are in a continual process of change.

Every experience we have affects us. But no two experiences are exactly the same: As Heraclitus said, "You cannot step twice into the same river for new waters are ever flowing in upon you." We cannot even think the same way twice, because each experience changes us, therefore we are different after each experience. This is true not only for all human beings but also for all nature.

In contrast to Leibniz's "windowless monads" that followed their predetermined course, Whitehead's actual entities have no permanent identity or preestablished harmony. They are constantly in the process of becoming. The relations between entities are experienced as a kind of feeling. They feel the affects of other actual entities or occasions and absorb them internally. During the process, death and the perishing of actual entities is merely the creativity of the universe moving on to the next birth. Actual occasions come into being, take on a form or character, and perish, and other new actual occasions come into being. In this process, the unique character of the actual occasion continues in the flow of the process. Perishing, said Whitehead, is memory preserved through time.

Prehensions

According to Whitehead, actual entities relate to each other by means of *prehension* (grasping) or *feeling* (sympathizing). Based on these relationships, we see reality as a continual process in which actual entities are always in a process of becoming. Within the process is *creativity*. Creativity, said Whitehead, is the ultimate principle by which the many enter into a complex unity. If we tried to separate each actual entity, the universe would lack unity, but the creative unity of the many constitutes the interrelated universe. Prehension describes how the actual entities relate to each other as well as to other entities. Whitehead labeled prehension and event "categorical" concepts because they explain the whole of nature.

A coming into being of a prehensive unity fits into explanations of quantum physics.

> One of the most hopeful lines of explanation [in quantum physics] is to assume that an electron does not continuously traverse its path in space. The alternative notion as to its mode of existence is that it appears at a series of discrete positions in space, which it occupies for successive durations of time. It is as though an automobile, moving at the average rate of thirty miles an hour along a road, did not traverse the road continuously; but appeared successively at the successive milestones, remaining for two minutes at each milestone. . . .
>
> But now a problem is handed over to the philosophers. This discontinuous existence in space, thus assigned to electrons, is very unlike the continuous existence of material entities, which we habitually assume as obvious. The electron seems to be borrowing the character, which some people have assigned to the Mahatmas of Tibet. . . .

There is no difficulty in explaining the paradox, if we consent to apply to the apparently steady undifferentiated endurance of matter the same principles as those now accepted for sound and light. A steadily sounding note is explained as the outcome of vibrations in the air: a steady colour is explained as the outcome of vibrations in ether. If we explain the steady endurance of matter on the same principle, we shall conceive each primordial element as a vibratory ebb and flow of an underlying energy, or activity. . . . Accordingly there will be a definite period associated with each element; and within that period the stream-system will sway from one stationary maximum to another stationary maximum. . . . This system, forming the primordial element, is nothing at any instant. It requires its whole period in which to manifest itself. . . .[11]

The life of the organism or event has a pattern that comes from the way it prehends into unity all the manifold aspects of nature that it includes. Its enduring pattern through time is the prehension of past patterns with present objects.

For example, a molecule is a pattern exhibited in an event of one minute, and of any second of that minute. It is obvious that such an enduring pattern may be of more, or of less, importance. It may express some slight fact connecting the underlying activities thus individualised; or it may express some very close connection. . . . There is then an enduring object with a certain unity for itself and for the rest of nature. Let us use the term physical endurance to express endurance of this type. Then physical endurance is the process of continuously inheriting a certain identity of character transmitted throughout a historical route of events. This character belongs to the whole route, and to every event of the route. This is the exact property of material. If it has existed for ten minutes, it has existed during every minute of the ten minutes, and during every second of every minute. Only if you take *material* to be fundamental, this property of endurance is an arbitrary fact at the base of the order of nature; but if you take *organism* to be fundamental, this property is the result of evolution. . . .[12]

According to Whitehead, every prehension consists of three factors: (1) the prehending individual or subject, (2) the prehended data or facts, and (3) the subjective form, or the way the individuals or subjects prehend the data. Subjects are the occasions or events, their objects the data, and the relationship between them is prehension. There are, said Whitehead, two kinds of prehensions: (1) *positive prehensions,* which he called feelings; and (2) *negative prehensions,* which negate feeling. The subjective form includes emotions, values, purposes, and consciousness. Even physicists should include the use of feelings in their language because in physical feelings is the idea that energy has been transferred. This is a positive prehension.

Pause for Thought

During the twentieth century physicists disagreed whether electrons were particles or waves in their movements. Could the physicists' feelings have influenced the electrons they were observing?

Eternal Objects

Because everything is in process, nothing can be totally understood because it is always changing. As we have seen, for Whitehead, the mistake people have made throughout history is the fallacy of misplaced concreteness, which means that we mistakenly take intellectual abstractions for actual entities. The only permanence in the world is not in the realm of actuality but in the realm of possibility. Thus, the realm of eternal objects is the realm of possibility; the realm of events is the realm of actuality. Possibilities, then, are eternal objects and similar to Plato's Forms of the Ideal.

Whitehead called the relation between actualities and possibilities *ingression,* meaning that when a possibility has made itself manifest on actuality, it has ingressed or entered and passed through the subject and into the object. The functioning of an eternal object in the self-creation of an actual entity is the ingression of the eternal object in the actual entity. Thus, past actualities or past events achieve "objective immortality," because the actual entities are always involved in the process of actuality, into which eternal objects ingress from universals.

Because events hold unrealized possibilities, a principle of selection is necessary. This is Whitehead's basis for his theory of value.

> The element of value, of being valuable, of having value, of being an end in itself, of being something which is for its own sake, must not be omitted in any account of an event as the most concrete actual something. "Value" is the word I use for the intrinsic reality of an event. . . . But there is no such thing as mere value. Value is the outcome of limitation. The definite finite entity is the selected mode, which is the shaping of attainment; apart from such shaping into individual matter of fact there is no attainment. The mere fusion of all that there is would be the nonentity of indefiniteness. . . . That which endures is limited, obstructive, intolerant, infecting its environment with its own aspects. But it is not self-sufficient. The aspects of all things enter into its very nature. It is only itself as drawing together into its own limitation the larger whole in which it finds itself. Conversely it is only itself by lending its aspects to this same environment in which it finds itself. The problem of evolution is the development of enduring harmonies of enduring shapes of value, which merge into higher attainments of things beyond themselves. Aesthetic attainment is interwoven in the texture of realisation. The endurance of an entity represents the attainment of a limited aesthetic success,

though if we look beyond it to its external effects, it may represent an aesthetic failure.[13]

For Whitehead, an organism is a "unit of emergent value," a real fusion of the characters of eternal objects, arising for fusion's own sake. Looking at the universe as a whole, the electron is as much a unit of emergent value as a great work of art.

Pause for Thought

Do you agree with Whitehead that if we viewed the universe as a whole process, then we would value the electron as much as a great work of art?

God

To call eternal objects *possibilities* required that Whitehead answer how these possibilities exist and how they are relevant to actual occasions. To answer this question, Whitehead said there is one actual entity that is timeless: God. This God, however, is not a creator. God is "not *before* all creation, but *with* all creation."

> We require God as the Principle of Concretion. This position can be substantiated only by the discussion of the general implication of the course of actual occasions—that is to say, of the process of realisation.
>
> We conceive actuality as in essential relation to an unfathomable possibility. Eternal objects inform actual occasions with hierarchic patterns, included and excluded in every variety of discrimination. Another view of the same truth is that every actual occasion is a limitation imposed on possibility, and that by virtue of this limitation the particular value of that shaped togetherness of things emerges. . . .
>
> [Eventually there must be] a ground for limitation . . . for which no reason can be given: for all reason flows from it. God is the ultimate limitation, for just that limitation which it stands in His nature to impose. God is not concrete, but He is the ground for concrete actuality. No reason can be given for the nature of God, because that nature is the ground of rationality. . . .
>
> We have come to the limit of rationality. . . . What further can be known about God must be sought in the region of particular experiences, and therefore rests on an empirical basis. In respect to the interpretation of these experiences mankind have differed profoundly. He has been named respectively, Jehovah, Allah, Brahma, Father in Heaven, Order of Heaven, First Cause, Supreme Being, Chance. Each name corresponds to a system of thought derived from the experiences of those who have used it.[14]

The process of becoming and ceasing to be thus has three formative elements: *potentiality, creativity,* and *God.* Recall that potentiality involves a Platonic conception of the Forms (eternal objects). Creativity is the "principle of novelty" from which actual entities are combined. Through creativity, which is the principle of novelty, God brings into actual existence such novel entities as actual occasions or events. God's nature is consciousness and eternal goodness. The conceptual feelings coming from God's primordial nature are realized through the expression of his role as goodness and conscious activity.

God conceptually grasps all of the possibilities that make up the realm of eternal objects. The creative process is orderly because of eternal objects (possibilities), and these possibilities exist in God as His nature. God mediates between the eternal objects and the actual occasions and chooses the relevant possibilities from the realm of eternal objects.

Thus God has two natures. His *primordial nature* is a timeless entity that eternally values the realm of eternal objects. God's *consequent nature* is "the physical prehension by god of the actualities of the evolving universe." Because God does not impose the eternal objects on actual entities, there is no guarantee that actual entities will choose them. When actual entities *do* select God's possibilities, we have order and harmony. When they reject them, the result is discord and evil. Evil is not the result of God's will, but it exists despite his purpose to abolish it. Humankind will help in this increasingly successful, though still imperfect, process of gaining victory over evil.

Pause for Thought   What do you think Whitehead meant when he said God is not a creator, he is "not *before* all creation, but *with* all creation"?

Summary

Henri Bergson looked to Darwin for evidence of evolution, but he did not believe that the changing life process was a matter of random variation. He saw the changing process as a directive life force that he called *élan vital.* It is a current of consciousness that causes living bodies and determines the course of their evolution.

Bergson argued that we can know the world in two different ways: through intellect and intuition. Intellect "implies that we move around the object." With intuition, "we enter into it." These two ways of knowing are also seen in morality and religion.

The rational impulse (intellect) coupled with social instinct toward organization is the foundation of closed morality. Social instinct is our sense of obligation to conform to the rules of the group. Customs and tradition that grow out of closed morality provide social stability. Closed morality excludes those individuals who do not belong to the group.

As closed morality depends on an intellectual perception of reality, open morality relies on our intuition of unity in nature. Through intuition, we directly experience reality as continuity. Intuition allows us to understand reality and humanity in a universal way. Closed morality is exclusive, but open morality is inclusive and thus a morality for all of humanity. Having a direct experience of the élan vital, open morality focuses on the creative self-actualization of the individual—adherence to the call "To thine own self be true." Like the two types of morality, Bergson posited two types of religion—static and dynamic.

The focus of static religion is on ritual and doctrine, and its dogmas make it exclusive. Dynamic religion has no set of rituals, doctrines, or dogmas. We see it best represented in the lives of great individuals such as Socrates, Buddha, Jesus, and the saints.

Intellectual thinkers give the world organization and security. The future evolution brings with it intuitive individuals who are free to follow truth. We have the responsibility of deciding if we want merely to live in safety or fulfill "the essential function of the universe which is a machine for the making of gods."

Alfred North Whitehead posited an ordered universe that contains within the organic whole ultimately real objects. These objects are actual entities or actual occasions and give evidence to the fact that the universe is in constant process.

The universe develops in time that represents real duration without beginning or end. The entities that make up the universe are always in a state of becoming to fulfill their potentialities. According to Whitehead, only a process philosophy can account for the creativity and interdependence of our immediate experience.

The universe holds harmonious patterns that create the continuity of everything. Thus, everything is interconnected, and the universe is ultimately rational. The patterns, said Whitehead, can be found in mathematics.

Nothing is separate from anything else. Simple location is the fallacy of misplaced concreteness. Whitehead's units of reality differ from the atoms of Democritus and Newton in their context and relations to each other. Instead of the term *atoms*, Whitehead referred to actual entities and actual occasions. As such, they never exist in isolation, but are intimately related to the whole field of life. Actual occasions allow us to view nature as a living organism.

Actual entities relate to each other by means of prehension (grasping) or feeling (sympathizing). They are in a continual process of becoming. Within the process is creativity—the ultimate purpose by which the many enter into complex unity. Prehension describes how the actual entities relate to each other and to other entities and consists of three factors: (1) the prehending individual or subject, (2) the prehended data or facts, and (3) the subjective form. Subjects are the occasions or events, their objects the data, and the relationship between them prehension.

The only permanence in the world is in the realm of possibility. Possibilities are eternal objects that resemble Plato's Forms. In events, there are unrealized possibilities, and this is Whitehead's basis for his theory of value. Value is in everything from the electron to a great work of art.

To call eternal objects "possibilities" left Whitehead to answer how these possibilities exist and how they are relevant to actual occasions. His answer lay in his definition of God. God is not a creator: "God is not *before* all creation, but *with* all creation." God's nature is consciousness and eternal goodness. The creative process is orderly because of eternal objects (possibilities), which exist in God's nature.

Evil is not found in God's nature. Evil in the world is a result of discord. Slowly, humankind is gaining victory over evil.

Connections

The philosophies of Bergson and Whitehead planted seeds for the new climate in quantum physics and alternative views in philosophy. Bergson, as we have seen, denied that any answers to the important "why" questions could be found within the philosophical traditions of Rationalism. Bergson wanted to know why things evolve and change, and he believed the only possible way to reach this deep level was through intuition. As a result, Bergson was rated as a nontraditional metaphysician—even an antirational metaphysician. This attitude conflicted with the Analytic philosophers (Chapter 15) and with the Pragmatists.

Whitehead placed his emphasis on inclusiveness. He wanted his ideas to be relevant to everyday experience as well as to quantum physics. As a metaphysician, he saw the universe in process and philosophical thinking as open-ended. Mathematicians were impressed by the boldness of his categorical scheme, but the Analytic philosophers who followed him were antimetaphysicians: thus, we find the philosophies of both Bergson and Whitehead transferred to the "recycle bin" of philosophy. The word *recycle* is important here, because no matter how many times metaphysics is disavowed by a group of philosophers, it has always been revived.

Study Questions

1. How did Bergson differ from Darwin in his theory of evolution?

2. According to Bergson, what are the two ways of knowing something?

3. How can intuition know reality?

4. What is the élan vital? Give an example of how it works.

5. What does Bergson mean by the term *duration*?

6. What is closed morality? Why does it depend on an intellectual perception of reality?

7. Describe the attitude of exclusivity.

8. What part does intuition play in open morality?

9. Why is open morality inclusive?

10. Compare and contrast the static and dynamic types of religion. Which do you prefer and why?

11. According to Bergson, what is the destiny of humanity?

12. What does Whitehead mean by the term *real objects*?

13. Explain the meaning of *actual entities* or *actual occasions*.

14. Is Whitehead's notion of duration in time the same as Bergson's?

15. Explain what Whitehead means by "everything is interconnected."

16. What are harmonious patterns in the universe?

17. Why did Whitehead say that simple location is the "fallacy of misplaced concreteness"?

18. How do Whitehead's actual entities differ from the atoms of Democritus and Newton?

19. How do actual occasions allow us to view nature as a living organism?

20. What is *prehension*?

21. What did Whitehead mean that the only permanence in the world is in the realm of possibility?

22. Describe Whitehead's view of God.

23. For Whitehead, does evil reside in God's nature?

Notes

1. W. T. Jones, *A History of Western Philosophy*, 2nd ed., Vol. V, p. 17. New York: Harcourt Brace Jovanovich, 1975.

2. Henri Bergson, *An Introduction to Metaphysics* (trans. by T. E. Hulme), 15th ed., pp. 21–22. Indianapolis: Bobbs-Merrill, 1978.

3. Ibid., p. 25.

4. Henri Bergson, *Creative Evolution* (trans. by Arthur Mitchell), p. 72. New York: Random House, 1944.

5. Henri Bergson, *Two Sources of Morality and Religion* (trans. by R. Ashley Auden and Cloudesley Brereton), pp. 27–28. New York: Henry Holt, 1935.

6. Ibid., pp. 59–60.

7. Ibid., p. 317.

8. Alfred North Whitehead, *Modes of Thought*, p. 27. New York: Macmillan, 1925.

9. Alfred North Whitehead, *Science and the Modern World*, pp. 29–34. New York: Macmillan, 1925.

10. Ibid., pp. 71–74.

11. Ibid., pp. 52–53.

12. Ibid., pp. 158–159.

13. Ibid., pp. 136–137.

14. Ibid., pp. 250–257.

CHAPTER FIFTEEN

Analytic Philosophy: Russell, Logical Positivists, and Wittgenstein

So far, the philosophers we have discussed have asked these questions: Who am I? What does it mean to be human? Where does the world come from? What is reality? How much can we know? Their various answers stemmed from their views of metaphysics, epistemology, and ethics. Rather than accept blindly any of these systems of thought, a movement arose in the Western world that came to be known as *Analytic philosophy*. Though Analytic philosophers differ among themselves in many ways, what unifies them is what they consider to be the task of philosophy.

Analytic philosophers rejected the vast systems of thought such as Plato, Aristotle, and Hegel. They considered it nonsense to tell people how they should behave, or, worse, what human nature is. The task of philosophy, they said, is to clarify the meaning of language. In his early work, the *Tractatus Logico-Philosophicus,* Ludwig Wittgenstein wrote, "The object of philosophy is the logical clarification of thoughts," and "The result of philosophy is not a number of philosophical propositions, but to make propositions clear." Bertrand Russell, however, was also interested in the nature of things. For him, analysis was a tool he could use to get at this.

We can trace the analytical tradition back to Hobbes, Locke, and Hume. Like them, Russell, Wittgenstein, and other twentieth-century philosophers refused to speculate on systems of thought about the whole universe. They rejected Kant's noumenal world, Hegel's absolute idealism, Marx's theory of production as history, and Nietzsche's eternal recurrence. These systems, they said, had too many metaphysical and epistemological assumptions. Analytic philosophers believed it was no longer the task of the philosopher to investigate the nature of reality, the universe, or the meaning of life. Such discoveries should be left to the scientist. It was not the philosopher's function to explain the universe or talk about morality and religion. Such concepts are speculative and unclear, and therefore meaningless. Why attempt to explain what is outside of any language?

Most of the Analytic philosophers thought the primary task of philosophy was to unpack complex problems whose origin is found in the imprecise use of language. Scientists stuck to the facts, but even they used misleading and ambiguous terms. The Analytic philosophers hoped to clarify these terms by rigorous linguistic analysis. John Locke was one of the first philosophers to express this attitude:

> It is ambition enough to be employed as an under-labourer in clearing the ground a little, and removing some of the rubbish that lies in the way to knowledge. . . . Vague and insignificant forms of speech, and abuse of language, have . . . long passed for mysteries of science; and hard or misapplied words, with little or no meaning, have mistaken for deep learning. . . . They are but the covers of ignorance, hindrance of true knowledge.[1]

The problem for Analytic philosophers was to find a language simple enough and clear enough to uncover the true meaning of the language we use. In opposition to Pragmatism and Process Philosophy, they saw philosophy as a cognitive rather than therapeutic enterprise. Wittgenstein, however, later moved toward viewing philosophy as a therapeutic enterprise.

Analytic philosophers had no notion of abandoning truth, but they wanted to refine it. Many were realists who saw an objective world that is independent yet accessible to us. For these philosophers, things are what they are. We have only to clear up the language. English Analytic philosopher Bertrand Russell did not want to reject metaphysics in its entirety, but he did want to analyze facts for the purpose of inventing a new theory of language, *logical atomism*. This new theory of language would have the exactness and clarity of mathematics, because it would correspond to the facts.

At the University of Vienna in Austria, another movement was taking place. Between World Wars I and II, a philosophical movement called **Logical Positivism** brought together a group of philosophers who became known as the Vienna Circle. Most members of the Vienna Circle were scientists and mathematicians. With their interests focused on empirical findings, these philosophers rejected everything otherworldly and supernatural. Metaphysical theories had no place in their thinking. In fact, they rejected anything philosophical except the logic of the sciences. The Logical Positivists would agree with David Hume's statement at the end of his *Enquiry:*

When we run over libraries, persuaded of these principles, what havoc must we make? If we take in our hand any volume; of divinity or school meta-physics, for instance; let us ask *Does it contain any abstract reasoning concerning quantity or number?* No. *Does it contain any experimental reasoning concerning matter of fact and existence?* No. Commit it then to the flames: for it can contain nothing but sophistry and illusion.[2]

Empirical in their viewpoint, the Logical Positivists were not skeptics, rela-tivists, or subjectivists. Nor did they wish to justify the sciences on pragmatic grounds. If we use William James's classification of temperaments, we would call the Positivists tough-minded rather than tender-minded.

By using the scientific method, the Logical Positivists sought to produce a system of meaningful and valid knowledge. Among the members of this group were Moritz Schlick, Rudolph Carnap, Herbert Feigl, and Kurt Godel. Ludwig Wittgenstein, a former student of Bertrand Russell, joined in their discussions but was not a member of the group. His early book, *Tractatus Logico-Philosophicus* (1919), expressed exactly the Vienna Circle's philosophical point of view. Wittgenstein said, "Whatever can be said at all can be said clearly," and he con-cluded the book with "Whereof one cannot speak, thereof one must be silent."

Although the Logical Positivists had an enormous impact, it was short-lived. Finding "leaks in their new ship," they continued to patch, to develop an ideal language whose structure would exactly mirror the world. In the end, their ship began to sink, although their no-nonsense, tough-minded point of view was useful to the advancement of knowing what will or will not work philosophically.

The third phase in the history of Analytic philosophy was the work of the later or what philosophers call the "new" Wittgenstein. Between his *Tractatus Logico-Philosophicus* (1919) and his *Philosophical Investigations,* which was published after his death, Wittgenstein had a change of heart. Though both books deal with the nature of language and the nature of meaning, his view of the relation between language and the world changed considerably. In *Investigations*, he moved away from Russell and the Positivists and stepped closer to Nietzsche. The difference in their approaches was apparent, however. Nietzsche was liter-ary, while Wittgenstein's writing was empirical, using a rigorous linguistic analy-sis. But by now, Wittgenstein considered doing philosophy as therapy.

Bertrand Russell

Russell's Life

Bertrand Russell (1872–1970) was born in Wales to a distinguished family, Lord and Lady Amberley. His godfather was John Stuart Mill. When Bertrand was only two years old, his father died; his mother died the following year. He was raised in the house of his paternal grandfather, Lord John Russell, who later became Earl. Lord Russell was twice prime minister and eighty-five-years old when his grandsons came to live with him.

When Bertrand Russell was six, however, his grandfather died. His Scottish grandmother, the dowager countess, disapproved of boarding schools, so she hired governesses and tutors to educate Russell and his brother.

The family was strictly Protestant, and Bertrand spent a rather solitary and lonely childhood. During his teens, he often thought of killing himself but was "restrained by the desire to know more mathematics." Also in his teens he had an intuition that God did not exist, which was a great relief to him.

In the fall of 1890, when he was eighteen, Russell went to Cambridge to study mathematics and philosophy. His undergraduate career was scholastically brilliant and the happiest period of his life. For the first time he had friends with whom he looked to the future.

> The world seemed hopeful and solid; we all felt convinced that nineteenth-century progress would continue, and that we ourselves should be able to contribute something of value. For those who have been young since 1914 it must be difficult to imagine the happiness of those days.[3]

Russell wrote several of his important works in philosophy and mathematics while at Cambridge, first as a student and then as a fellow and lecturer. In 1903, he wrote *Principles of Mathematics,* followed by *Principia Mathematica* (with Alfred North Whitehead, 1910–1913), and *Our Knowledge of the External World* (1914). In 1916, the university dismissed him for his pacifist activities during World War I. While in prison for his pacifism, he finished writing *Introduction to Mathematical Philosophy* (1919), *The Analysis of Mind* (1921), and numerous papers.

As a socialist, Russell was active in politics and championed unpopular causes such as women's suffrage. Parliament debarred him for his lack of religious beliefs. During World War I, he advocated an unpopular negotiated peace to stop the bloodshed. In 1938, he came to the United States to teach at the University of Chicago and then at the University of California at Los Angeles. He declined a permanent appointment to take a position at City College of New York.

Russell was a strong advocate of education. He believed education could allow a person to break out of the prison of prejudices. He and his wife, Dora, founded the Beacon Hill School in 1927. In addition to writing books on education, social, and political philosophy, he wrote a popular book *Marriage and Morals* (1929), which provoked an outcry because of his liberal attitude toward sexual practices (see On Women, p. 415). Russell thought if college students would contract informal trial marriages, it would lessen their obsession with sex and they could study more effectively. The City College of New York dismissed him.

When his brother died in 1931, Russell became the third Earl of Russell. In 1944, Cambridge University asked him to return as a lecturer. With the onset of Nazi aggression and the outbreak of World War II, Russell rejected his pacifism. In 1961, however, he landed in prison again for participating in demonstrations against nuclear weapons, and in 1967 he organized a "war crimes tribunal" directed against American activities in Vietnam.

Russell received many honors in his life. Among them was the Order of Merit, one of Britain's highest honors. And in 1950, he received the Nobel Prize for literature. The prize's citation read: "One of our time's most brilliant spokesmen of rationality, and a fearless champion of free speech and free thought in the West."

Russell wrote, "The secret of happiness is to face the fact that the world is horrible." He spent his adult life trying to make it better. In his autobiography, he wrote that three passions had governed his life: the longing for love, the search for knowledge, and an unbearable pity for the suffering of mankind. Russell died at the age of ninety-eight.

Logical Atomism

Bertrand Russell went through a period when he accepted the philosophies of Hegel and Kant. But later, he rejected Hegel's monism and Kant's transcendental aesthetic. G. E. Moore, his philosophical companion, joined him in revolt.

> Various things caused me to abandon both Kant and Hegel. . . . I thought that all that [Hegel] said about mathematics is muddle-headed nonsense. I came to . . . distrust the logical basis of monism. I disliked the subjectivity of the "Transcendental Aesthetic." . . . Moore took the lead in rebellion, and I followed, with a sense of emancipation. . . . With a sense of escaping from prison, we allowed ourselves to think that grass is green, that the sun and stars would exist if no one was aware of them, and also that there is a pluralistic timeless world of Platonic ideas. . . . Mathematics could be *quite* true, and not merely a stage in dialectic.[4]

As an Analytic philosopher, Russell looked to Locke, Hume, and Mill. As a mathematician, he felt the influence of Pythagoras, Plato, and Descartes. Russell admired mathematics for its certainty: The kind of philosophy that he wished to advocate was what he called Logical Atomism, an outcome of his thinking about the philosophy of mathematics. He was skeptical about concepts of free will, immortality, and God. But he couldn't believe that mathematical principles such as $2 + 2 = 4$ were merely inductive generalizations that come from our experience.

For Russell, logic is the essence of philosophy and the foundation of mathematics. Every philosophical problem, when subjected to analysis and purification, he said, is found to be not philosophical at all, or, "in the sense in which [I am] using the word, logical."

Russell and other new Analytic philosophers thought the power of logic derives from completely abstracting the meaning or semantic content of an assertion. They called it a *formal* logic because the rules governing changes from one symbolic formula to another refer only to the syntactical structures of the formulas, not to the formulas' meaning.

In their *Principia Mathematica,* Russell and Whitehead argued the possibility of constructing a logic in which all mathematics could be derived from a few logical axioms. For example, by letting p and q stand for any two propositions, "If p is true, then p-or-q is true." Based on these findings, Russell reasoned that logic also could form the basis of a language that would accurately express everything that was clearly stated. Thus, the specially constructed logical language would correspond to the world. This language, he said, would be more precise and clear than the language we normally speak. It would be a "logically perfect language" without misleading ambiguity or vagueness.

> In a logically perfect language the words in a proposition would correspond one by one with the components of the corresponding fact, with the exception of such worlds as "or," "not," "if," "then," which have a different function. In a logically perfect language, there will be one word and no more for every simple object, and everything that is not simple will be expressed by a combination of words, by a combination derived, of course, from the words for the simple things that enter in, one word for each simple component. A language of that sort will be completely analytic, and will show at a glance the logical structure of the facts asserted or denied. The language which is set forth in *Principia Mathematica* is intended to be a language of that sort. It is a language which has only syntax and no vocabulary whatever. Barring the omission of a vocabulary, I maintain that it is quite a nice language. It aims at being that sort of a language that, if you add a vocabulary, would be a logically perfect language. Actual languages are not logically perfect in this sense, and they cannot possibly be, if they are to serve the purposes of daily life.[5]

Russell and the language philosophers claimed that ordinary talk "of shoes and ships and sealing wax, of cabbages and kings" leads us away from the logic of philosophical problems. Therefore, to create a new language, Russell set out to analyze the difference between facts and things. He argued that things in the world have various properties and stand in various relations to each other. "That they have these properties and relations are *facts.*" Facts make up the complex relations of things to each other. Because they are complex, facts are subject to analysis. The aim of analysis is to make sure that language statements accurately represent the facts of the world.

For Russell, the words in a proposition in a logically perfect language would "correspond one by one with the components of the corresponding facts." Thus, he proposed a "theory of definite descriptions." A *definite description* is of the form, "the so and so." Sentences with this type of form are paradoxical. Consider the sentence, "The golden mountain does not exist." Although this may appear as a true sentence, Russell asked us to analyze logically. How can it be true that the golden mountain does not exist unless the phrase "the golden mountain" is meaningful? We have to ask, "What does not exist?" That question implies that the "golden mountain" must have some sort of reality or we couldn't say it does not exist. Is it true, then, that "the golden mountain" does not mean anything? How does Russell solve this puzzle?

First, if we translate this sentence as the propositional function "X is golden and a mountain" is false for all values of X, then the meaning of the phrase "the golden mountain" disappears. Russell explained that it is a mistake to think of the phrase "the golden mountain" as a name like "Socrates" or the "Nile River." Logically, we can see that "the golden mountain" is not a definite description or a name, but a disguised predication. Logically, we can say, "There exists no thing which is both golden and a mountain." The clearness of this statement leaves no question in our minds. Russell not only solved the puzzle with the logic of the language, but also used this same application of logic to traditional concepts of metaphysics and epistemology. Thus, although two sentences may look alike grammatically, the theory of descriptions shows that they are different in logical form.

> An important consequence of the theory of descriptions is that it is meaningless to say "A exists" unless "A" is (or stands for) a phrase of the form "the so-and-so." If the so-and-so exists, and *x* is the so-and-so, to say "*x* exists" is nonsense. Existence, in the sense in which it is ascribed to single entities, is thus removed altogether from the list of fundamentals. The ontological argument and most of its refutations are found to depend upon bad grammar.[6]

For Russell, an *atomic* (simple fact) proposition or statement is either true or false. We will call a true proposition *p* and a false proposition *not-p*. *Molecular* propositions consist of two or more atomic propositions. For example, *p* and *q* can be linked together with such logical connectives as *and/or*. A proposition such as (1) *p* symbolizing "the girl has blue eyes," and (2) *q* "the girl is thin" is true only if the propositions *p* and *q* are each true. No atomic fact corresponds to the entire proposition, so we can only determine the truth or falsity of each of its propositions. To say "the girl has blue eyes and is thin" is a truth function of "the girl has blue eyes" and "the girl is thin." By adding more numbers to *p* and *q*, we can state more propositions symbolically. Because the logical forms of language correspond to reality through these logically correct relations of propositions, it is possible to discover the true essence of the world.

Pause for Thought   We can point to a crow and say, "That crow is black." But can we ever account for the truth or falsity of general propositions such as "All crows are black"?

Moral Philosophy

Convinced that our knowledge is limited to science, and "science has nothing to say about values," Russell thought ethics had no place in philosophy. He discusses it only because "[e]thics is traditionally a department of philosophy. . . ."

> When we assert that this or that has "value," we are giving expression to our own emotions, not to a fact which would still be true if our personal feelings were different. To make this clear, we must try to analyze the conception of the Good. . . .
>
> When a man says "this is good in itself," he *seems* to be making a statement, just as much as if he said "this is square" or "this is sweet." I believe this to be a mistake. I think that what the man really means is: "I wish everybody to desire this," or rather "Would that everybody desired this." If what he says is interpreted as a statement, it is merely an affirmation of his own personal wish; if, on the other hand, it is interpreted in a general way, it states nothing, but merely desires something. The wish, as an occurrence, is personal, but what it desires is universal. It is, I think, this curious interlocking of the particular and the universal which has caused so much confusion in ethics. . . .
>
> The consequences of this doctrine are considerable. . . . Our values have been evolved along with the rest of our constitution, and nothing as to any original purpose can be inferred from the fact that they are what they are.[7]

Russell's point of view is one of ethical subjectivism. Our notion of good is nothing more than our personal desire. Social good refers to the collective desires that are common to a given group. Individuals such as Socrates and Kant who attribute universality to good are only trying to universalize their own personal desires. Russell saw human beings as part of nature. Nature has no values, but humans desire to create them, and that is how ethics arise. "In the world of values, Nature in itself is neutral, neither good nor bad, deserving of neither admiration nor censure. It is we who create value and our desires which confer value." Because values are not universal or part of nature, we can see why ethics differs from culture to culture.

> The Aztecs held that it was a duty to sacrifice and eat enemies captured in war, since otherwise the light of the sun would go out. The Book of Leviticus enjoins that when a married man dies without children his

brother shall marry the widow, and the first son born shall count as the dead man's son. The Romans, the Chinese, and many other nations secured a similar result by adoption. This custom originated in ancestor-worship; it was thought that the ghost would make himself a nuisance unless he had descendants (real or putative) to worship him. In India the remarriage of widows is traditionally considered something too horrible to contemplate. Many primitive races feel horror at the thought of marrying anyone belonging to one's own totem, though there may be only the most distant blood-relationship. After studying these various customs it begins at last to occur to the reader that possibly the customs of his own age and nation are not eternal, divine ordinances, but are susceptible of change, and even, in some respects, of improvement. . . .

It is not the province of science to decide on the ends of life. . . . To proclaim the ends of life, and make men conscious of their value, is not the business of science; it is the business of the mystic, the artist and the poet.[8]

Pause for Thought   Do you agree with Russell that our knowledge is limited to science, and moral values are thus merely personal desires? Or was Kant on to something when he said morality has universal maxims based not on desire, but on goodwill and duty?

Russell's liberal attitude toward morals included sexual practices. As mentioned earlier, because of his views on sexual relations, City College of New York canceled his appointment in 1940. Below is a passage about sex from his popular work, *Marriage and Morals* (1929).

If sex is not to be an obsession, it should be regarded by the moralists as food has come to be regarded. . . . Sex is a natural human need like food and drink. It is true that men can survive without it, whereas they cannot survive without food and drink, but from a psychological standpoint the desire for sex is precisely analogous to the desire for food and drink. . . . Healthy, outward-looking men and women are not to be produced by the thwarting of natural impulse, but by the equal and balanced development of all the impulses essential to a happy life.

I am not suggesting that there should be no morality and no self-restraint in regard to sex, any more than in regard to food. In regard to food we have restraints of three kinds, those of law, those of manners, and those of health. We regard it as wrong to steal food, to take more than our share at a common meal, and to eat in ways that are likely to make us ill. Restraints of a similar kind are essential where sex is concerned, but in this case they are much more complex and involve much more self-control. Moreover, since one human being ought not to have property in another, the analogue of stealing is not adultery, but rape, which obviously must be forbidden by law. The questions that arise in regard to health are concerned almost entirely with venereal disease.[9]

Pause for Thought   In the 1930s and 1940s, society considered Russell's views on sex extreme. Would his attitudes on sex shock people today?

Education

Russell was a reformer, not only in the field of moral values, but also in education and politics. Whereas many people look to authority for guidance, Russell thought such a view stifles our creativity.

> Passive acceptance of the teacher's wisdom is easy to most boys and girls. It involves no effort of independent thought, and seems rational because the teacher knows more than his pupils; it is moreover the way to win the favour of the teacher unless he is a very exceptional man. Yet the habit of passive acceptance is a disastrous one in later life. It causes men to seek a leader, and to accept as a leader whoever is established in that position. . . .
>
> It will be said that the joy of mental adventure must be rare, that there are few who can appreciate it, and that ordinary education can take no account of so aristocratic a good. I do not believe this. The joy of mental adventure is far commoner in the young than in grown men and women. Among children it is very common, and grows naturally out of the period of make-believe and fancy. It is rare in later life because everything is done to kill it during education. . . .
>
> The wish to preserve the past rather than the hope of creating the future dominates the minds of those who control the teaching of the young. Education should not aim at passive awareness of dead facts, but at an activity directed towards the world that our efforts are to create.[10]

Pause for Thought   As a youngster, did you have creative ideas only to have your teachers, parents, or peers insist that you "be like the other children"? Do you recall your inner reaction to such criticism?

Religion

Russell abandoned his belief in God at an early age. He believed that nothing in evolution warrants the hypothesis that a divine purpose guides the universe.

And nothing in science suggests the world was created. Though there is no proof for the existence of God, science reveals the "vastness of the universe" and inspires us with "a new form of humility to replace that which atheism has rendered obsolete." Russell had strong, even sublime feelings for the universe, but because evidence was lacking, he could not believe in God. During his old age, he wrote:

> My intellectual journeys have been, in some respects, disappointing. When I was young I hoped to find religious satisfaction in philosophy; even after I had abandoned Hegel the eternal Platonic world gave me something non-human to admire. I thought of mathematics with reverence, and suffered when Wittgenstein led me to regard it as nothing but tautologies. I have always ardently desired to find some justification for the emotions inspired by certain things that seemed to stand outside human life and to deserve feelings of awe. . . . Those who attempt to make a religion of humanism, which recognizes nothing greater than man, do not satisfy my emotions. And yet I am unable to believe that, in the world as known, there is anything that I can value outside human beings, and, to a much lesser extent animals. . . . And so my intellect goes with the humanists, though my emotions violently rebel. In this respect, the "consolations of philosophy" are not for me.[11]

Pause for Thought   Do you ever have religious conflicts between your intellect and your emotions? Do you usually follow your intellect or your emotions in such matters?

On Women

In *Marriage and Morals*, Russell tackled the controversy that surrounded women's liberation. Christian ethics, he said, did a "great deal to degrade the position of women." The moralists were men and woman the temptress. Therefore it was "desirable to curtail her opportunities for leading men into temptation; consequently respectable women were more and more hedged about with restrictions. . . ."

With his famous wit, Russell spoke out about equality between the sexes, including the abandonment of the "double standard."

> Let us, however, pause a moment to consider the logical implications of the demand that women should be the equals of men. Men have from time immemorial been allowed in practice . . . to indulge in illicit sexual relations. It has not been expected of a man that he should be a virgin on entering marriage. . . . And if unmarried men are not going to be conti-

nent, unmarried women on the ground of equal rights, will claim that they also need not be continent. To the moralists this situation is no doubt regrettable . . . he is committed in practice to what is called the double standard, that is to say, the view that sexual virtue is more essential in a woman than in a man. . . .

If . . . the old morality is to be reestablished, certain things are essential. . . . [The] education of girls should be such as to make them stupid and superstitious and ignorant. . . . The next requisite is a very severe censorship upon all books giving information on sex subject. . . . [G]irls must be forbidden to earn their living by work outside the home; they must never be allowed an outing unless accompanied by their mother or an aunt; the regrettable practice of going to dances without a chaperon must be sternly stamped out. It must be illegal for an unmarried woman under fifty to possess a motor-car, and perhaps it would be wise to subject all unmarried women once a month to medical examination by police doctors, and to send to a penitentiary all such as were found to be not virgins. . . . I am inclined to think that moralists would be well advised to advocate that all men should be castrated, with the exception of ministers of religion.

So long as all the moralists content themselves with preaching a return to a system which is as dead as the Dodo, they can do nothing whatever to moralize the new freedom . . . I do not think that the new system any more than the old should involve an unbridled yielding to impulse, but I think the occasions for restraining impulse and the motives for doing so will have to be different from what they have been in the past. In fact, the whole problem of sexual morality needs thinking out afresh.[12]

Logical Positivism

Between World Wars I and II, Moritz Schlick, a professor of philosophy at the University of Vienna, and a group of intellectuals in that city formed the Vienna Circle, which included mathematicians, physicists, sociologists, and economists. They intended to show that metaphysics is impossible by developing a new logic that used an empirical method similar to Hume's; as you recall, Hume posited that our knowledge is limited to experience. They argued that only science could give us reliable information about the world. They called themselves Logical Positivists.

Members of the Vienna Circle related to Bertrand Russell's work in logic and Ludwig Wittgenstein's formulation of language and logic relations in his *Tractatus*. Early on, they eliminated everything metaphysical, which meant everything transcendental, otherworldly, or supernatural. Their grounds for using the scientific method and rejecting metaphysics was found in their famous *verification principle* set forth in Wittgenstein's *Tractatus*.

The Principle of Verification

Science appealed to the Logical Positivists because experiment and controlled observation confirm all scientific facts. But metaphysics, they held, uses meaningless language and propositions that cannot be verified. The verification principle rejects anything that cannot be verified. **Verification** always rests on empirical observation in sense experience. We cannot verify such metaphysical statements as Hegel's "Reason is the substance of the universe" and Plato's "Forms are immaterial essences," so such statements are meaningless. We have no means to verify them.

According to Schlick, the "verifiability criterion of meaning" expresses the foundation of the Logical Positivist's thinking.

It is the peculiar business of philosophy to ascertain and make clear the *meaning* of statements and questions. The chaotic state in which philosophy has found itself during the greater part of its history is due to the unfortunate fact that, in the *first* place, it took certain formulations to be real questions before carefully ascertaining whether they really made any sense, and, in the *second* place, it believed that the answers to the questions could be found by the aid of special philosophical methods, different from those of the special sciences. But we cannot by philosophical analysis decide whether anything is real, but only what it *means* to say that it is real; and whether this is then the case or not can be decided only by the usual methods of daily life and of science, that is, through *experience*. . . .

When, in general, are we sure that the meaning of a question is clear to us? Evidently when and only when we are able to state exactly the conditions under which it is to be answered in the affirmative, or, as the case may be, the conditions under which it is to be answered in the negative. By stating these conditions and by this alone, is the meaning of a question defined.

It is the first step of any philosophizing, and the foundation of all reflection, to see that it is simply impossible to give the meaning of any statement except by describing the fact which must exist if the statement is to be true. If it does not exist then the statement is false. The meaning of a proposition consists, obviously, in this alone, that it expresses a definite state of affairs. And this state of affairs must be pointed out in order to give the meaning of the proposition. One can, of course, say that the proposition itself already gives this state of affairs. This is true, but the proposition indicates the state of affairs only to the person who understands it. But when do I understand a proposition? When I understand the meanings of the words which occur in it? These can be explained by definitions. But in the definitions new words appear whose meanings cannot again be described in propositions, they must be indicated directly: the meaning of a word must in the end be *shown*, it must be *given*. This is done by an act of indication, of pointing; and what is pointed at must be given, otherwise I cannot be referred to it.

Accordingly, in order to find the meaning of a proposition, we must transform it by successive definitions until finally only such words occur in it as can no longer be defined, but whose meanings can only be directly pointed out. The criterion of the truth or falsity of the proposition then lies in the fact that under definite conditions (given in the definition) certain data are present, or not present. If this is determined then everything asserted by the proposition is determined, and I know its meaning. . . .

The content of our insight is indeed quite simple. . . . It says: a proposition has a statable meaning only if it makes a verifiable difference whether it is true or false. A proposition which is such that the world remains the same whether it be true or false simply says nothing about the world; it is empty and communicates nothing; I can give it no meaning. . . .

The results of our discussion may be summarized as follows. . . . The justified unassailable nucleus of the "positivistic" tendency seems to me to be the principle that the meaning of every proposition is completely contained within its verification in the given. . . .

The chief opposition to our view derives from the fact that the distinction between the falsity and the meaninglessness of a proposition is not observed. The proposition "Discourse concerning a metaphysical external world is meaningless" does *not* say: "There is no external world," but something altogether different. The empiricist does not say to the metaphysician "what you say is false" but "what you say asserts nothing at all!" He does not contradict him, but says "I don't understand you."[13]

The meaning of a proposition must coincide with its truth conditions or the proposition is meaningless. If we want to understand a proposition, then we must first know what information is necessary as evidence of its truth. For the Logical Positivist, sense observation is necessary for verification. The method of verifying that "the cat is on the mat" consists in looking at the mat and seeing the cat on it. If you know that this is how to verify the proposition, then you know its meaning; and if you know its meaning, then you know how to verify it.

Logical Positivists agreed that the propositions of mathematics are meaningful, even though such propositions have no empirical content. But Wittgenstein went a step further. He claimed that the propositions of logic and mathematics are *tautologies*, that is, assertions that state nothing factual about the world. They are as empirically void and empty as metaphysical statements because they cannot be verified, even though they are demonstrable. Unlike metaphysics, however, we can say of mathematical and logical propositions that they are valid or invalid, but not true or false in the way that empirical propositions are.

Wittgenstein did say that a metaphysical or mystical idea, though not expressed in words, could be felt or appreciated "without knowing whether it is true." The Logical Positivists disagreed with Wittgenstein's view of mystical or metaphysical propositions. They insisted that these sort of propositions have no meaning. Wittgenstein, however, left the issue open by stating, "What we cannot speak about we must consign to silence." He did not say they have no meaning.

Rudolph Carnap, one member of the Vienna Circle, wanted to get rid of even the name *philosophy* by substituting "Logic of Science." Its task, he said, was to construct an artificial language in which every symbol referred to a concept and was verifiable. He suggested that metaphysicians would do well to construct a similarly precise vehicle for the expression of whatever they want to say.

As it turned out, the verification principle needed verification itself. The Logical Positivists relented slightly on their total rejection of metaphysics. Instead, analysts began to ask what the metaphysicians were really saying. A. J. Ayer described this new viewpoint when he said, "The metaphysician is treated no longer as a criminal but as a patient: there may be good reasons why he says the strange things he does."

In 1936 a mentally disturbed student murdered Schlick for refusing to approve the student's dissertation. In 1938, when the Nazi German *Anschluss* annexed Austria, the Vienna Circle broke up. Some members of the group emigrated to the United States and others to England. Using the verification principle as a solution to the scientific method had landed the Logical Positivists in difficulties, but their contribution to the analysis of language continues to be felt among philosophers today.

Ludwig Wittgenstein

Wittgenstein's Life

Ludwig Wittgenstein (1889–1951) was born in Vienna into a wealthy family, the youngest of eight children. His paternal grandfather, a wool merchant, converted from Judaism to Protestantism. Ludwig's father, Karl Wittgenstein, ran away to the United States when he was seventeen. Two years later he returned to Vienna and became an engineer and industrialist. Ludwig's mother, who was talented in music, was the daughter of a Roman Catholic Viennese banker. Their home was a center for talented musicians. Johannes Brahms was a frequent visitor and close friend of the family when Ludwig was a young boy. One of Ludwig's brothers later became a distinguished pianist. All of the Wittgenstein children showed both artistic and intellectual talent, although some were emotionally unstable and committed suicide. Ludwig himself was to battle mental illness.

Educated at home until he was fourteen, Wittgenstein was an indifferent student who preferred to tinker with machinery than to study. His parents sent him to school in Linz, Austria, to learn mathematics and the physical sciences. After three years in Linz, Wittgenstein decided to study engineering. He went first to Berlin and then to the University of Manchester in England. At

Manchester, he experimented with kites and designed a jet-reaction engine and a propeller.

His interest in engineering led him to pure mathematics and then to mathematics' philosophical foundations. In 1911, he became so intrigued with Bertrand Russell's *Principles of Mathematics* that he gave up engineering to study with Russell at Cambridge. Russell tells a story about Wittgenstein's dilemma of becoming an aeronaut or a philosopher.

> At the end of his first term at Cambridge he came to me and said: "Will you please tell me whether I am a complete idiot or not?" I replied, "My dear fellow, I don't know. Why are you asking me?" He said, "Because, if I am a complete idiot, I shall become an aeronaut; but if not, I shall become a philosopher." I told him to write me something during the vacation on some philosophical subject and I would then tell him whether he was a complete idiot or not. At the beginning of the following term he brought me the fulfillment of this suggestion. After reading only one sentence, I said to him: "No, you must not become an aeronaut."[14]

Under Russell's tutelage, Wittgenstein applied himself intensively to logic. Soon he was doing research that culminated in his *Tractatus*, the work that so strongly influenced the Logical Positivists. During this period, he made friends with David Pinsent, a fellow student to whom he dedicated the *Tractatus*. He and Pinsent did experiments on rhythm in music. Wittgenstein would whistle while Pinsent accompanied him on the piano. Wittgenstein also played the clarinet and had a gift for remembering music as well as sight-reading. His philosophical writings have many allusions to music.

Pinsent affirmed that Wittgenstein often thought of suicide "as a possibility," but studying philosophy with Russell was his salvation. He worked with "fierce energy" at his logical ideas and underwent hypnosis hoping that the hypnotic trance could help him find clear answers to some of the difficulties he confronted in logic. In 1913, he went to Norway, telling Pinsent that he could work better there because there were no distractions. He also said that he had no right to live in a world in which he felt contempt for other people who, in turn, were irritated by his nervous temperament. In Norway, he built a hut near the sea where he lived in complete seclusion, except for the sea gulls that were his close companions.

While in Norway, Wittgenstein corresponded with Russell. The Austrian was full of excitement about his logical discoveries, but he told Russell their ideals were too different for a true friendship. To be friends, he said, both people must be pure, and he harbored "hateful and petty thoughts." How can I, he asked, be a logician before I am a man? "*Before everything else* I must become pure."

In 1914, when World War I broke out, Wittgenstein volunteered in the Austrian army. When time permitted, he worked on his manuscript the *Tractatus*

Logico-Philosophicus. He spent almost a year as a prisoner of war in an Italian war camp, where he completed his manuscript. Through a friend, he sent the manuscript to Russell. Wittgenstein was convinced that his own work in philosophy was over.

Wittgenstein's father had left him a large fortune, and after the war Wittgenstein handed it over to his two sisters and became an elementary school teacher. His days as a teacher did not last long, however. For awhile he worked as a gardener in a monastery, then designed a mansion in Vienna for one of his sisters. In 1929, he returned to Cambridge, received his doctorate in philosophy, and took a position as lecturer. When World War II broke out, Wittgenstein could not sit idly by. He left Cambridge to spend two years as a hospital orderly and another year in a laboratory as a medical assistant.

In 1944, Wittgenstein returned to his Cambridge position but was unhappy with his teaching. Not only did the students not understand his ideas, but also Wittgenstein thought he was having a harmful effect on them. "The only seed I am likely to sow is jargon," he said. He resigned in 1947 with a strong impetus to live in solitude. For some time he had been working on his second major work, the *Philosophical Investigations*, and he wanted to finish it.

He went first to the Irish countryside near Dublin and then to an isolated cottage on the west coast of Ireland. His health was not good, but he worked when he felt strong enough. In the summer of 1949, he left Ireland to spend three months with a friend in the United States. When he returned to England in the fall, he was diagnosed with cancer. He said he had no wish to continue living. He spent time with his family in Vienna, then lived for awhile with a friend in Oxford. Wittgenstein did not want to die in the hospital and was grateful when his physician offered to take him in. He was to spend his last days in the doctor's home.

Realizing that he would soon die, he worked hard on his *Investigations*, and the book would be published two years after his death. On April 27, 1950, Wittgenstein became violently ill. When the doctor told him the end was near, he said, "Good!" When he died two days later, his last words were "Tell them I've had a wonderful life."

The *Tractatus*

Wittgenstein's concern with becoming pure shows in the simple purity of his philosophical work *Tractatus Logico-Philosophicus*, a small book of fewer than one hundred pages. In its preface he wrote:

> The book deals with the problems of philosophy, and shows, I believe, that the reason why these problems are posed is that the logic of our language is misunderstood. The whole sense of the book might be summed up in the following words: what can be said at all can be said clearly, and what we cannot talk about we must pass over in silence.

> Thus the aim of the book is to set a limit to thought, or rather—not to thought, but to the expression of thoughts: for in order to be able to set a limit to thought, we should have to find both sides of the limit thinkable (i.e., we should have to be able to think what cannot be thought).
>
> It will therefore only be in language that the limit can be set, and what lies on the other side of the limit will simply be nonsense.[15]

Using the linguistic approach, Wittgenstein emphasized the need to be clear about the logic of our language. Only then can we understand the limits of language. Kant also had made a distinction between what we can know and what is knowable, arguing that our knowledge begins with experience, but does not arise completely from experience. Knowledge is a product of a priori concepts and principles given by reason. Beyond the phenomenal world (the realm of our experience) is the noumenal world (things-in-themselves). We can think of the noumenal world, but because our knowledge is limited to the phenomenal world, we cannot actually know the noumenal world.

Kant asked, "What can we know?" Wittgenstein asked, "What can be said?" Wittgenstein was more radical than Kant because he set a limit to both knowledge and thinking. He reasoned that Kant's noumenal world is not thinkable. In fact, Wittgenstein called thinking about the noumenal world "nonsense." Trying to talk about what is unsayable is like saying, "It is unsayable, but let's talk about it anyway."

In fewer than eighty pages, Wittgenstein arranged the *Tractatus* in a series of tightly woven numbered propositions stating what can be said about the world.

1. The world is all that is the case.

1.1 The world is the totality of facts, not of things.

1.11 The world is determined by the facts, and by their being *all* the facts.

1.12 For the totality of facts determines what is the case, and also whatever is not the case.

1.13 The facts in logical space are the world.

1.2 The world divides into facts.[16]

For Wittgenstein, the new logic reveals the essence of language; this, in turn, shows us a picture of what the world must be. Because we can say true things about the world, the structure of language must somehow give us a picture of the world.

Picturing   For Wittgenstein, propositions must represent the world. "We picture facts to ourselves," and the picture "must have something in common with what it depicts." What it has in common is its "pictorial form." "A picture agrees with reality or fails to agree; it is correct or incorrect, true or false."

Wittgenstein gave an example of an automobile accident as depicted by lawyers using dolls and toy cars to represent real people and real automobiles involved in the accident. The lawyers' diagram depicts a possible state of affairs, a picture of what might have been the facts. The lawyers probably present conflicting pictures of the accident.

The pictures may correctly or incorrectly represent the facts, but without pictorial form, there would be no representation at all. In any picture there must be a one-to-one correspondence between the picture and the state of affairs it represents. By direct analogy, its logical form shows that a proposition is either true or false. If it lacks logical form, then it would be neither true nor false, or it could not be a proposition, because it would say nothing about the world.

2.1 We picture facts to ourselves.

2.12 A picture is a model of reality.

2.13 In a picture objects have the elements of the picture corresponding to them. . . .

2.14 What constitutes a picture is that its elements are related to one another in a determinate way.

2.141 A picture is a fact.

2.15 The fact that the elements of a picture are related to one another in a determinate way represents that things are related to one another in the same way.

2.151 Pictorial form is the possibility that things are related to one another in the same way as the elements of the picture.

2.161 There must be something identical in a picture and what it depicts, to enable the one to be a picture of the other at all.

2.17 What a picture must have in common with reality, in order to be able to depict it—correctly or incorrectly—in the way it does, is its pictorial form. . . .

2.22 What a picture represents it represents independently of its truth or falsity, by means of its pictorial form.[17]

According to Wittgenstein, even a sentence printed on a page is a picture because of what it represents. Like the sentence, every picture must have something in common with what it represents. This common thing is *pictorial form*. There are different kinds of pictures, but as sentences they must have the same logical form in common with reality before they can picture reality at all.

A picture cannot portray its own form of representation, because it represents its subject from "outside and it can't get outside" itself. A picture, however, may characterize another picture. For example, a picture in sound (as an orchestral score) could portray the representational form of a picture in color if there is something they both have in common (2.161). Wittgenstein suggested the score is also a picture of the grooves in a recording—or today the magnetic tracings on a compact disc. When played, the grooves or magnetic tracings give a picture of the sound. For Wittgenstein, every picture is a logical picture. Pictures may represent reality correctly or incorrectly. Logical pictures can depict the world in the ways the world might be. However, any one picture may not depict the logical form of reality correctly.

> 2.22 What a picture represents it represents independently of its truth or falsity, by means of its pictorial form.
>
> 2.223 In order to tell whether a picture is true or false we must compare it with reality.
>
> 2.224 It is impossible to tell from the picture alone whether it is true or false.
>
> 2.225 There are no pictures that are true *a priori*.[18]

So, no matter how closely you inspect the picture of the accident, you cannot tell if it represents the accident correctly. This is the case with all pictures. True pictures will depict the facts. If a picture were true a priori (independent of experience), then you would not have to "compare it with reality" to tell if it is true. But then how could you know the facts by examining the picture? Wittgenstein said you could not. To tell if a picture is true—that is, if it represents the facts correctly—you have to be sure it fits the facts. Therefore, we can never tell a priori whether a picture is true.

Pause for Thought   How does Wittgenstein's picture theory compare with Descartes' notion from reason that if an idea is "clear and distinct," we can deduce that it is true?

Philosophy   Another feature of the *Tractatus* that the Logical Positivists accepted was Wittgenstein's conception of philosophy:

> 4.003 Most of the propositions and questions to be found in philosophical works are not false but nonsensical. Consequently we cannot give any answer to questions of this kind, but can only establish that they are nonsensical.

6.53 The correct method in philosophy would really be the following: to say nothing except what can be said, i.e., propositions of natural science—i.e., something that has nothing to do with philosophy—and then, whenever someone else wanted to say something metaphysical, to demonstrate to him that he had failed to give a meaning to certain signs in his propositions . . . *this* method would be the only strictly correct one.[19]

Here Wittgenstein expressed the tough-minded position of Logical Positivists, and they looked to his *Tractatus* as useful in their pursuit. Later in his work, however, Wittgenstein's statements disturbed members of the Vienna Circle. They wanted to interpret Wittgenstein's words to mean that metaphysics was meaningless, but his comments bothered them.

6.54 My propositions serve as elucidations in the following way: anyone who understands me eventually recognizes them as nonsensical, when he has used them—as steps—to climb up beyond them. (He must, so to speak, throw away the ladder after he has climbed up it.)

He must transcend these propositions, and then he will see the world aright.[20]

Wittgenstein had admitted that his own propositions were nonsense, albeit a higher type of nonsense. Recall that he wrote, "The whole sense of this book might be summed up in the following words: what can be said at all can be said clearly and what we cannot speak about we must pass over in silence." The Vienna Circle read this with horror. Was Wittgenstein attracted to this metaphysical silence? Did he find something meaningful in it after all?

The Mystic Wittgenstein called "things that cannot be put into words" but which "make themselves manifest" the "mystical." These "things" include our values and religious experiences.

6.41 The sense of the world must lie outside the world. In the world everything is as it is, and everything happens at it does happen: *in* it no value exists—and if it did exist, it would have no value.

6.432 *How* things are in the world is a matter of complete indifference for what is higher. God does not reveal himself *in* the world. . . .

6.44 It is not *how* things are in the world that is mystical, but *that* it exists.

6.4321. . . . The solution to the enigma of life in space and time lies *outside* space and time.[21]

Wittgenstein's mysticism definitely left Russell and the Logical Positivists with a "sense of intellectual discomfort." But Wittgenstein thought he had answered all of the questions in philosophy that one could ask. He remarked that we cannot put an answer into words if we cannot put the question into words; thus, if we can ask a question, it is possible to answer it.

At this point, Wittgenstein dropped out of philosophy. He sought solitude, tried teaching elementary school, and then left for the United States. He returned later to Cambridge in the hope that the university would accept *Tractatus* as his doctoral dissertation.

Gradually, a new Wittgenstein began to appear, one not satisfied with the conclusions of *Tractatus*. During this period, he realized that language might not be as limited as he had thought. With this in mind, he started work on his new ideas, the ones we find in *Philosophical Investigations*.

The New Wittgenstein

Appearing in 1953, Wittgenstein's *Philosophical Investigations* proposed a new view for Analytic philosophy. Analytic philosophers would see the nature of language in a different way—and no longer through the eyes of the Logical Positivists. He saw his work in *Tractatus* as inadequate because he had written that the only function of language was to state facts. And he had assumed that the structure of language is logical and the picture of the world. Now Wittgenstein realized that language has many functions besides picturing. There is no one standard, he said, that is the only meaning of a given word. Language functions in a context, and many contexts and many meanings are possible.

From Socrates and Plato to Wittgenstein, philosophy has been concerned with the problem of meaning. Philosophers have thought that the key to meaning was naming. Wittgenstein, however, saw the error in using naming as a key to meaning in the kind of metaphysical picture presented. Plato, for example, had argued that words were names of Forms, the eternal and unchanging nonmaterial essences in the intelligible (real) world. The physical world was merely the appearance of reality. Aristotle had agreed that words named something unchanging, but he saw the unchanging in the world, namely, substances.

The Empiricists held that words named sense data only. The Pragmatists had argued that words named actions; and Russell, the Logical Positivists, and the early Wittgenstein thought they named atomic facts. While writing *Tractatus*, Wittgenstein had been "held captive" by a "picture" of language that gave names to objects, shapes, colors, pains, moods, and numbers. Naming, he said, is like attaching a label to something. The new Wittgenstein disagreed not only with Russell and the Logical Positivists, but also with his own early writings. In *Philosophical Investigations,* he reasoned that the meaning of a word is its use.

> Think of the tools in a tool-box: there is a hammer, pliers, a saw, a screwdriver, a rule, a glue-pot, glue, nails and screws.—The functions of words

are as diverse as the functions of these objects. (And in both cases there are similarities.)

Of course, what confuses us is the uniform appearance of words when we hear them spoken or meet them in script and print. For their *application* is not presented to us so clearly. Especially not, when we are doing philosophy.

It is like looking into the cabin of a locomotive. We see handles all looking alike. (Naturally, since they are all supposed to be handled.) But one is the handle of a crank which can be moved continuously (it regulates the opening of a valve); another is the handle of a switch, which has only two effective positions, it is either off or on; a third is the handle of a brake-lever, the harder one pulls on it, the harder it brakes; a forth, the handle of a pump: it has an effect only so long as it is moved to and fro.[22]

Like Wittgenstein's tools or locomotive cabin, the meaning of language is in how well it gets the job done. Most of us say, "The sun is coming up" or "The sun is setting," though science has told us the sun does not rise or set and the earth turns on its axis as it revolves around the sun. As we watch the sun rise, we do not say, "The earth is turning on its axis." Such an explanation may be factual, but it is fruitless because it does not get the job done.

Pause for Thought

Let's say a friend of yours brings a saw into your house and starts sawing the coffee table leg. You exclaim, "What are you doing!" Your friend replies, "Saws are for sawing." What would you respond? How would it apply to Wittgenstein's notion of the meaning of language?

The tool can serve many functions. Is it possible, asked Wittgenstein, that language can serve more than the two functions that Logical Positivists suggested?

But how many kinds of sentence are there? Say assertion, question, and command?—There are *countless* different kinds of use of what we call "symbols," "words," "sentences." And this multiplicity is not something fixed, given once for all; but new types of language, new language-games, as we may say, come into existence, and others become obsolete and get forgotten. . . .

Here the term "language-*game*" is meant to bring into prominence the fact that the *speaking* of language is part of any activity, or of a form of life.

Review the multiplicity of language-games in the following examples, and in others:

Giving orders, and obeying them—
Describing the appearance of an object, or giving its measurements—
Constructing an object from a description (a drawing)—
Reporting an event—
Speculating about an event—
Forming and testing a hypothesis—
Presenting the results of an experiment in tables and diagrams—
Making up a story; and reading it—
Play-acting—
Singing catches—
Guessing riddles—
Making a joke; telling it—
Solving a problem in practical arithmetic—
Translating from one language into another—
Asking, thanking, cursing, greeting, praying—

It is interesting to compare the multiplicity of the tools in language and of the ways in which they are used, the multiplicity of kinds of word and sentence, with what logicians have said about the structure of language. (Including the author of the *Tractatus Logico-Philosophicus.*). . . .

"We name things and then we can talk about them: can refer to them in talk."—As if what we did next were given with the mere act of naming. As if there were only one thing called "the talking about a thing." Whereas in fact we do the most various things with our sentences. Think of exclamations alone, with their completely different functions.

Water!
Away!
Ow!
Help!
Fine!
No!

Are you inclined still to call these words "names of object"?. . . .

Naming is so far not a move in the language-game—any more than putting a piece in its place on the board is a move in chess. We may say: *nothing* has so far been done, when a thing has been named. It has not even *got* a name except in the *language-game*.[23]

Language Games   All language does not have the same rules, function, and meanings. But all language is alike in the same way that all games are alike. What do all games have in common? They must have something in common or we would not call them *games*. "Don't think," said Wittgenstein, "but look!" If you look, you will find something that is common to all. All games have rules. In basketball, five players are on the court; in baseball, nine people are out on the field. We don't play baseball with a basketball or a watermelon. We don't play basketball with a bat. As with other games, the language game has lots of different rules—grammatical rules, syntactical rules, semantical rules, and rules of context.

In philosophy, said Wittgenstein, when some of the rules of a language game are broken—"language goes on holiday." The way they are used in certain philosophical theories, words lose their meaning—they have no use in everyday life. We need to "bring words back from their metaphysical to their everyday use." Such an exercise does not use the thinking process of Logical Atomism; it emphasizes the analysis of ordinary language through "common sense."

Pause for Thought

Can you think of metaphysical statements made by philosophers in which "language has taken a holiday"?

Wittgenstein said broken language rules also result in a certain kind of madness. He alluded to *Alice in Wonderland*, one of his favorite books. The White King asks Alice if she sees anyone down the road. "I see nobody on the road," says Alice. The King says, "I only wish I had such eyes to be able to see Nobody! And at that distance too!" Wittgenstein's followers called such language a "category mistake." Because the author miscategorized certain linguistic facts, he drew absurd conclusions.

By recognizing the diversity of the functions of language, Wittgenstein discovered that language analysis should not consist in the definition of language or its meanings, but in a description of its uses. "We must do away with all explanation, and description alone must take its place." We must "stick to the subjects of everyday thinking, and not go astray and imagine that we have to describe extreme subtleties." Confusion only arises when language is not allowed to work, when it is "like an engine idling."

Thus, for Wittgenstein, it was no longer the philosopher's task to reveal the hidden logic behind language; the goal was to reveal the implicit logic of ordinary language. This was the beginning of "ordinary language philosophy." It showed how a failure to grasp that logic might result in "a bewitchment of our intelligence by means of language." And when we tamper with ordinary language, "language goes on holiday." Wittgenstein's aim in philosophy was "to show the fly the way out of the fly-bottle."

The Fly in the Fly-Bottle

Honey is what draws the fly into the fly-bottle. As the fly passes by the bottle, it smells the honey and swerves from its path and through the bottle's narrow neck. The fly buzzes wildly about and slams itself frantically against the sides of the bottle. But once inside the fly cannot find its way out again though the way out is open and clearly visable. This is the problem of metaphysics.

To Wittgenstein, to "show the fly out of the fly-bottle" meant to bring words back from metaphysics to their everyday use—to show those who are lost the way out. His statement is relevant to Augustine's puzzlement: "What is time? If no one asks me, I know: but if I would explain it to someone who asks, I know not." What Augustine needed, according to Wittgenstein, was to refer to something he already knew—the grammar of the word "time."

The Use of Philosophy   "Philosophy," said Wittgenstein, "can in no way interfere with the actual use of language; it can in the end only describe it. Nor can it give it any foundation. It leaves everything just as it is." Philosophy does not provide us with new or more information; it adds clarity by describing the language.

> We must do away with all *explanation*, and description alone must take its place. And this description gets its light, that is to say its purpose—from the philosophical problems. These are, of course, not empirical problems; they are solved, rather, by looking into the workings of our language, and that in such a way as to make us realize these workings: *in despite of* an urge to misunderstand them. The problems are solved, not by giving new information, but by arranging what we have always known. Philosophy is a battle against the bewitchment of our intelligence by means of language.[24]

Philosophy then, does not consist in giving abstract answers to questions. It is a map of the terrain with concrete examples of how language is used in ordinary experience. It is more than just looking at the pieces of a jigsaw puzzle; there must be assembling, selecting, and arranging. Then we have everything we need to solve the problem. Yet, we still "fail to be struck by what, once seen, is *most* striking and most powerful." The most important parts lie hidden "because of their simplicity and familiarity."

Unfortunately, there is no sure way to be struck by the "most striking and most powerful," and therefore we can pass the opening of the fly-bottle without escaping. We have no guarantee of ever satisfying our quest for certainty.

> Where does our investigation get its importance from, since it seems only to destroy everything interesting, that is, all that is great and important? (As it were all the buildings, leaving behind only bits of stone and rubble.) What we are destroying is nothing but houses of cards and we are clearing up the ground of language on which they stand.[25]

Pause for Thought   What does Wittgenstein mean when he says we "fail to be struck by what, once seen, is most striking and most powerful"?

Summary

Analytic philosophers rejected the vast philosophical systems of thought in favor of clarifying the meaning of language. They hoped to clarify terms by rigorous linguistic analysis.

Logical Positivism rejected anything philosophical except for the logic of the sciences. By using the scientific method, the Positivists aimed to produce a system of meaningful and valid knowledge.

Bertrand Russell called his philosophy Logical Atomism. He reasoned that logic could form the basis of a language that would adequately explain everything that was clearly stated. An atomic proposition is either true or false. Logical Atomism would be a "logically perfect language."

For Russell, ethics has no place in philosophy, because our knowledge is limited to science, and "science has nothing to say about values." Our notions of good, he said, are nothing more than our personal desires. His liberal view toward morals included the equality of women and sexual practices. A strong advocate for education, Russell thought looking to authority for answers stifles creativity.

The Logical Positivists wanted to show through their verification principle that metaphysics is impossible. Only science can give reliable information about the world. The verification principle rejects anything that cannot be verified by sense experience.

Moritz Schlick posited the verifiability criteria of meaning as the foundation for Logical Positivism. A proposition's meaning must coincide with its truth-conditions or the proposition is meaningless. Rudoph Carnap wanted to replace the name *philosophy* with the "Logic of Science" by constructing an artificial language in which every symbol referred to a concept and was verifiable.

In *Tractatus* Ludwig Wittgenstein wrote, "what can be said at all, can be said clearly, and what we cannot talk about we must pass over in silence." He reasoned that logic reveals the essence of language, which in turn shows us a picture of the world. To tell if a picture is true, we must be sure it fits the facts.

Later, in his *Philosophical Investigations*, Wittgenstein realized that language has many functions besides picturing. It has many contexts and many meanings. He said the meaning of a word is its use. If a sentence has no meaning, then it is not useful.

Like a game, language has many rules. If the rules are broken, then language "goes on a holiday." Language analysis should not consist in definition, but in description; and description is the role of philosophy.

Connections

The Analytic philosophers found British Empiricism congenial. For them, objects of consciousness are the same as Hume's impressions. But they went a step further and ignored consciousness completely. This point of view was taken up by Russell and supported by the Logical Positivists' verifiability principle. Basically, they said that we could eliminate language about inner states because it had no meaning and replace it with language about bodily states.

In the next chapter, we shall note that the Phenomenologists considered it a terrible mistake and a deliberate blindness to eliminate language about inner states. We can, they thought, be aware of a variety of entities and acts, and they focused their attention on clarifying linguistic muddles and confusions. The Analytic philosophers limited their view to contained simple items, thus missing the importance of consciousness. As the Analytic philosophers looked to Hume, the Phenomenologists looked to Hegel, although they thought they could improve on Hegel's study of consciousness.

The Analytic philosophers argued that each entity in the universe is simple and not complex. Each entity is a collection of "loose and separate" sense data. In contrast, we will see that the phenomenological philosophers believed in the interconnectedness of things.

The Analytic philosophers realized the puzzle between the relation between the world of everyday experiences and the world of physics, but they thought they could solve this puzzle by a rigorous logical analysis of language. Phenomenologists and Existentialists reacted to such limited views of language and thus took a different direction—one that encouraged complex, elaborate, and esoteric language.

Study Questions

1. How does Analytic philosophy differ from the systematic philosophy of Plato, Aristotle, and Hegel?

2. What is the relationship between science and Analytic philosophy?

3. Explain what Russell meant by *logical atomism*.

4. According to Russell, what is the difference between facts and things?

5. Why did Russell say that ethics has no place in philosophy?

6. What are Russell's views on sexual relations?

7. What are Russell's views on the equality of women and men?

8. Why did Russell think people should not look to authority for guidance?

9. What was the purpose of the Vienna Circle?

10. Explain the verification principle.

11. Why did Wittgenstein claim that the propositions of logic and mathematics are tautologies?

12. Why did Rudolph Carnap want to get rid of the name *philosophy*?

13. What did Wittgenstein mean by "language is a picture of the world"?

14. Why is every picture a logical picture?

15. According to Wittgenstein can a picture be a priori? Why or why not?

16. What are Wittgenstein's views on mysticism?

17. Compare and contrast the major points of *Tractatus Logico-Philosophicus* and *Philosophical Investigations*.

18. What did Wittgenstein mean by "language games"?

19. Did Wittgenstein think language analysis should consist of definition or description?

20. How can one "show the fly out of the fly-bottle"?

Notes

1. John Locke, "Epistle to the Reader," in *An Essay Concerning Human Understanding* (ed. by A. C. Fraser). Oxford, UK: Clarendon Press, 1894.

2. David Hume, *An Enquiry Concerning Human Understanding* (ed. by L. A. Selby-Bigge), p. 509. London: Oxford University Press, 1952.

3. Bertrand Russell, "My Mental Development" in *The Philosophy of Bertrand Russell* (ed. by F. Schilpp), p. 9. Chicago: Library of Living Philosophers, 1946.

4. Ibid., pp. 11–12.

5. Bertrand Russell, "Logical Atomism," in Logic and Knowledge, pp. 197–198. London: George Allen & Unwin, 1956.

6. Bertrand Russell, *Portraits from Memory & Other Essays,* p. 54. New York: Simon & Schuster, 1956.

7. Bertrand Russell, *Religion and Science*, pp. 230–231, 235–236, 239–240. London: Thornton Butterworth, 1935.

8. Bertrand Russell, "Styles in Ethics," in *Our Changing Morality: A Symposium* (ed. by Freda Kirchwey), pp. 5–6, 15–16. New York: Boni, 1924.

9. Bertrand Russell, *Marriage and Morals*, pp. 291, 293–294. New York: Liveright, 1929.

10. Bertrand Russell, *Principles of Social Reconstruction*, pp. 163–165, 167. London: Allen & Unwin, 1916.

11. Russell, "My Mental Development," op. cit., pp. 19–20.

12. Bertrand Russell, *Marriage and Morals*, cited in Rosemary Agonito, *History of Ideas on Women,* pp. 290–296. New York: G. P. Putnam's Sons, 1977.

13. M. Schlick, "Positivism and Realism" (trans. by D. Rynin), in *Logical Positivism* (ed. by A. J. Ayer), pp. 86–88, 106–107. New York: Free Press, 1959. Reprinted with permission of David Rynin.

14. Bertrand Russell, "Philosophers and Idiots," in *Portraits from Memory*, op cit., pp. 26–27.

15. Ludwig Wittgenstein, *Tractatus Logico-Philosophicus* (trans. by D. F. Pears and B. F. McGuinness; introduction by Bertrand Russell), p. 3. London: Routledge and Kegan, 1961.

16. Ibid., p. 7.

17. Ibid., p. 17.

18. Ibid., p. 19.

19. Ibid., pp. 37, 151.

20. Ibid., p. 151.

21. Ibid., pp. 145, 147–149.

22. Ludwig Wittgenstein, *Philosophical Investigations* (trans. by G. E. M. Anscombe), Sec. 11–15. New York: Macmillan, 1953.

23. Ibid., Sec. 26–27, 49.

24. Ibid., Sec. 109.

25. Ibid., Sec. 118.

CHAPTER SIXTEEN

Phenomenology: Husserl and Heidegger

In the last chapter we examined the views of the Analytic tradition. In this chapter, we will look at two philosophers who share another set of basic assumptions: Edmund Husserl and Martin Heidegger. We call these philosophers Phenomenologists, and the tradition they represent is Phenomenology (from the Greek *phainomenon* for "appearance"). The use of the word *phenomenon* or *phenomenology* actually began with Kant when he used the word *phenomenon* (meaning "sensible world") as opposed to *noumenon* ("beyond the sensible," or "thing-in-itself"). Hegel also used the word *phenomenology* in his account of the "phenomenology of the mind." For Hegel, phenomenon makes mind knowable. The Phenomenologists agreed with Kant that human experience is limited to phenomena, but they denied that the objects we experience are constructs of the mind or consciousness.

The Analytic philosophers attempted to analyze some whole into its simplest parts, because they believed we could only understand parts. The Phenomenologists, on the other hand, thought we could only understand a part within the context of some whole. They also felt that the Analytic philosophers made a mistake by treating consciousness as merely subjective. They agreed with Whitehead that consciousness is not just subjective, but that all things in life were "interfused" together. They also considered consciousness as the foundation of all philosophy; unlike Descartes and Berkeley, however, they focused on a purely descriptive and nontheoretical account of consciousness.

In general terms, Phenomenology is a philosophy of experience. It attempts to understand how meaning is made in human experience, and it sees our experiences of the world as the foundation of meaning.

Edmund Husserl, the modern founder of Phenomenology, considered the philosophy as essentially a method to see how the world "reveals itself" to consciousness. He focused on careful inspection and description of phenomena or appearances, which can be defined as any object of our conscious experience. He wanted to make philosophy a "rigorous science" by returning it "to the things themselves."

Martin Heidegger, on the other hand, committed himself to the philosophical goal of rethinking the meaning of Being. He wanted to know if it is possible to "get inside" human beings for a firsthand look as to what "Being" might mean. He took this path to inquire into what the human being would reveal about being human. Like Husserl, the method he used was Phenomenology.

Edmund Husserl

Husserl's Life

Edmund Husserl (1859–1938) was born into a Jewish family in the town of Prossnitz, Moravia, now part of the Czech Republic, the same year that Henri Bergson and John Dewey were born. He attended elementary school in Prostejov and high school in Olomouc (both in present-day Czech Republic) and Vienna, Austria, before enrolling at the University of Leipzig in Germany in 1876. He was an excellent student in mathematics, physics, and philosophy. He was particularly intrigued with astronomy and optics. Two years later, he transferred to the Friedrich-Wilhelm University of Berlin to continue his study of mathematics and dabble in philosophy. In 1881, he transferred to the University of Vienna, where he received his Ph.D. in mathematics with a dissertation on the theory of the calculus of variations. He was twenty-four.

While in Vienna, Husserl attended the lectures of Franz Brentano, whose lectures on David Hume and John Stuart Mill and his treatment of problems in ethics, psychology, and logic, inspired Husserl to make philosophy his vocation. He briefly taught at the University of Halle in Germany, where he published his first book, *Philosophy of Arithmetic*. While there, he married Malvine Charlotte Steinscheider, and they were both baptized before their wedding. The couple had three children and remained at Halle until 1901.

In 1901, Husserl joined the faculty at the University of Göttingen, where he taught for the next sixteen years and published many important philosophical works including *Ideas: General Introduction to Pure Phenomenology*.

The First World War disrupted the circle of Husserl's younger colleagues, and his son, Wolfgang, died at Verdun, France. Husserl observed a year of mourning and kept silence professionally during that time.

In 1916, he accepted an invitation to become a full professor at the University of Freiburg, Germany, where he taught until he retired in 1929. While there, he continued to work on various projects, including the manuscripts that would be published after his death as the second and third volumes of *Ideas*. For the rest of his life he remained in Freiburg, but the Nazis barred him from participating in any public academic activities the last five years of his life because he was a Jew. The University of Southern California offered him a professorship, but he chose to stay in Germany. Husserl died of pleurisy in 1938 on Good Friday.

The Crisis of Western Man

According to Husserl, Western man is in crisis, and the cause of that crisis was the gradual decay of belief in rational certainty. Part of the decay, he said, lay in the methods of the natural sciences that over the years had developed the wrong attitude about what the world is like and how to know it. The natural sciences believe that nature is physical and that the realm of spirit, or soul—the realm of knowing, valuing, and judging—is all based on matter. For the natural scientist, the science of the spirit is ignored, even rejected.

> With this the interpretation of the world immediately takes on a predomi-nately dualistic, i.e., psychophysical form. The same causality—only split in two—embraces the one world; the sense of rational explanation is every-where the same, but in such a way that all explanation of spirit, in the only way in which it can be universal, involves the physical. There can be no pure, self-contained search for an explanation of the spiritual, no purely inner-oriented psychology or theory of spirit beginning with the ego in psychical self-experience and extending to the other psyche. The way that must be traveled is the external one, the path of physics and chemistry. . . . This objectivism or this psychophysical interpretation of the world, despite its seeming self-evidence, is a naïve one-sidedness. . . . To speak of the spirit as annex to bodies and having its supposedly spatiotemporal being within nature is an absurdity. . . .[1]

Pause for Thought   Do you, like the natural scientists, tend to look at the world as a duality—matter and spirit? Do you view the physical world as objec-tive and the spirit as subjective?

Husserl sought to save human reason by developing philosophy into a rig-orous science. For him, to say that science is merely physical is naive. This would mean that all psychology is psychophysical and that knowledge and truth are objective and based on a reality beyond the self. He believed such a view by naturalism is a drastic departure from the original philosophical attitude of the ancient Greeks. The only hope for Europe was a return to rationality "in that noble and genuine sense, the original Greek sense."

> There is a sharp cleavage, then, between the universal but mythico-practical attitude and the "theoretical," which by every previous standard is unpractical, the attitude of *thaumazein* [Greek, meaning to wonder], to which the great men of Greek philosophy's first culminating period, Plato and Aristotle, trace the origin of philosophy. Men are gripped by a passion for observing and knowing the world, a passion that turns from all practical interests and in the closed circle of its own knowing activities, in the time devoted to this sort of investigation, accomplishes and wants to accomplish only pure *theoria*. In other words, man becomes the disinterested spectator, overseer of the world, he becomes a philosopher. More than that, from this point forward his life gains a sensitivity for motives which are possible only to this attitude, for novel goals and methods of thought. . . .
>
> With an attitude such as this . . . there arises the distinction between the represented and the real world, and a new question is raised concerning the truth—not everyday truth bound as it is to tradition but a truth that . . . is identical and universally valid, a truth in itself.[2]

Greek philosophy had developed an attitude of a universal critique of life and its goals. It questioned all systems of culture and in so doing aimed to raise humankind through universal reason from ignorance to knowledge. According to Husserl, what the Greeks did was true philosophy, which is actually "nothing but universal science, science of the world as a whole, of the universal unity of all being." This was the beautiful foundation of Western philosophy, but the universal—including the cultural and the physical, ideas and objects—gradually broke into several separate sciences. Eventually, by focusing solely on the physical world, the spirit vanished, and the objective attitude developed. Natural scientists viewed everything as physical or derived from the physical. This was a view similar to Democritus, but one rejected by Socrates, Plato, and Aristotle. For them, the most important aspect of a person was the soul—rational and nonrational.

As the mathematical natural sciences developed, however, a person's spirit was seen as an objective fact founded on the physical, taking on, said Husserl, a dualistic "psychophysical form." Psychologists also have compounded this mistake by treating minds as if they were like bodies.

> It is true that . . . there is psychology, which . . . claims . . . to be the universal fundamental science of the spirit. Still, our hope for real rationality, i.e., for real insight, is disappointed here as elsewhere. The psychologists simply fail to see that they too study neither themselves nor the scientists

who are doing the investigating nor their own vital environing world. They do not see that from the very beginning they necessarily presuppose themselves as a group of men belonging to their own environing world and historical period. By the same token they do not see that in pursuing their aims they are seeking a truth in itself universally valid for everyone. By its objectivism psychology simply cannot make a study of the soul in its properly essential sense, which is to say, the ego that acts and is acted upon. . . . More and more perceptible becomes the overall need for a reform of modern psychology in its entirety. As yet, however, it is not understood that psychology through its objectivism . . . simply fails to get at the proper essence of spirit; that in isolating the soul and making it an object of thought . . . it is being absurd. . . .[3]

Pause for Thought   Do your psychology classes isolate the soul or spirit from the body by focusing on objectively measuring bodily changes that are in some way related to mental states?

Husserl's criticism of experimental psychology was that it copies the natural sciences by trying to be objective like physics. Thus, by following the norms set by scientists, it can only deal with the physical and not the living subject. In contrast, he wanted psychology to observe "norm-setting" from the "inside" as one of the ways in which the ego acts. The only way philosophers can grasp an essential ("inside") nature is if they use the phenomenological method for studying specifically psychic phenomena.

The Phenomenological Method

Husserl thought of Phenomenology as a descriptive analysis of subjective processes or as the intuitive study of essences. Philosophy should describe the data of consciousness without bias or prejudice, ignoring all metaphysical and scientific theories so an accurate description and analysis of the phenomena within consciousness could be intuitively experienced and reported. He wanted to clear away all metaphysical assumptions and unjustifiable presuppositions, and then describe what is given to consciousness. To arrive at this method, Husserl used three techniques: (1) Phenomenological reduction, (2) eidetic reduction or abstraction, and (3) analysis of the "correlation between the phenomenon of cognition and the object of cognition."[4]

In his phenomenological reduction, Husserl excluded anything that is transcendent such as Kant's things-in-themselves because he did not want to make assertions about anything that we do not see ourselves. Also, unlike Descartes, who began by doubting everything, including all phenomena (i.e., the world) except for his thinking self, Husserl brackets all phenomena and all elements of experience. By abstaining from entertaining any opinions or beliefs about experience, he could bracket the whole stream of experienced life, which included objects, other people, and cultural situations. By bracketing phenomena, he was able to view them without judging whether they are realities or appearances and also abstain from giving any opinions, judgments, or valuations about the world. For Husserl, bracketing meant that he could suspend judgment. From the ancient Greek philosophers, he borrowed the term *epoche* (to bracket) to describe his method of "detachment from any point of view regarding the objective world."

> In relation to every thesis and wholly uncoerced we can use this peculiar . . . [epoche], a certain refraining from judgment which is compatible with the unshaken and unshakable because self-evidencing conviction of Truth. . . .
>
> We put out of action the general thesis which belongs to the essence of the natural standpoint, we place in brackets whatever it includes respecting the nature of Being: This entire natural world therefore, which is continually "there for us," "present to our hand," and will ever remain there, is a "fact-world" of which we continue to be conscious, even though it pleases us to put it in brackets.
>
> If I do this, as I am fully free to do, I do *not* then *deny* this "world," as though I were a sophist. *I do not doubt that it is there* as though I were a sceptic; but I use the "phenomenological" . . . [epoche] which completely bars me from using any judgment that concerns spatio-temporal existence (Dasein).[5]

For Husserl, doubt did not mean he refused to believe in certain phenomena, but that he would suspend judgment about it. For example, if I am playing golf and my ball lands on the green, I may wonder whether the ball went in the cup. From where I stand one hundred yards away, I cannot see clearly, thus I may suspend judgment until I get a closer look. When I walk up on the green, I grin happily to find that my ball has gone in the cup. From the natural standpoint, I can see that the ball exists outside of me in space and time and that I am enjoying my psychic state of pleasure. But Descartes had shown that this perception could be mistaken—I could be dreaming that I am standing on the green looking at my ball in the cup. As a result, my knowledge of the ball being in the cup is uncertain. Husserl thus suggested that I suspend judgment not only that I can't get a clear look at the ball, but also whether or not I am actually standing on the green looking at the ball in the cup. He did not say to suspend the experience itself, but to suspend judgment about whether I am actually standing on the green and actually looking at the ball. I could suspend my judgments about the ball by bracketing. This bracketing moves me from a natural to a phenomenological standpoint. According to Husserl, by bracketing, I do not doubt the being of the ball, but I do doubt that the ball has being in "the mode of existence," for it may have being in "the mode of a dream."

Pause for Thought   Can you use Husserl's method of bracketing and detach yourself from judgments about your experiences within the natural world?

If we are able to doubt everything by bracketing both subject and object, what do we have left? For Husserl, the answer is *consciousness*. It would be a consciousness not tainted by prejudgments about where it comes from or what it is about.

> We have learnt to understand the meaning of the phenomenological [*epoche*] but we are still quite in the dark as to its servicability. . . . *For what can remain over when the whole world is bracketed, including ourselves and all our thinking (cogitare)?*
> *Consciousness in itself has a being of its own which in its absolute uniqueness of nature remains unaffected by the phenomenologic disconnexion.* It therefore remains as a "*phenomenological residuum,*" as a region of Being which is in principle unique, and can become in fact the field of a new science—the science of Phenomenology.[6]

Husserl claimed that nothing is lost by bracketing, yet everything is different, because consciousness is neither subjective nor objective, but a meeting of subject and object.

> Let us suppose that we are looking with pleasure in a garden at a blossoming apple-tree, at the fresh young green of the lawn, and so forth. . . . From the natural standpoint the apple-tree is something that exists in the transcendent reality of space, and the perception as well as the pleasure a psychical state which we enjoy as real human beings. Between . . . the real man on the one hand and the real apple-tree on the other, there subsist real relations. . . . Let us now pass over to the phenomenological standpoint. The transcendent world enters its "bracket"; in respect of its real being we use the disconnecting *epoche*. . . . Together with the whole physical and psychical world the real subsistence of the objective relation between perception and perceived is suspended; and yet a relation between perception and perceived (as likewise between the pleasure and that which pleases) is obviously left over, a relation which in its essential nature comes before us in "pure immanence."[7]

When we are wholly disinterested as a result of bracketing, we can observe the essential nature of pure consciousness. Like Bergson, Husserl thought that intuition is the knowing process at work. Intuition is a direct and immediate insight of the given in an act of self-awareness on the part of consciousness. In its primordial form, intuition is a source for knowledge and should be accepted, though it must be accepted within the limits that it presents itself. From this unprejudiced view of his experience, Husserl said he had discovered his true self: He is the pure ego with pure existence. Through the ego, the being of the world—and any being—made sense to him and had validity.

In limiting himself to the realm of experience, Husserl rejected those parts of Descartes' and Kant's philosophies that go beyond the immediate phenomenal realm into the transcendental realm. For Husserl, Kant's distinction between the phenomenal world and the noumenal world of things-in-themselves was unacceptable. Husserl limited his *transcendental* Phenomenology to the realm of experience. By bracketing the realm of experience (remaining untouched if the world is or is not), we are led to the center of reality—the conscious self.

Pause for Thought   Do you find a major difference in Kant's thinking about the noumenal world of things-in-themselves and the role of experience in Husserl's transcendental Phenomenology?

The Phenomenological Ego

Husserl did not want us to confuse the phenomenological ego with the transcendental ego. The former is the psychological or empirical ego that we find in our passing stream of consciousness. The latter is the observer that we find behind that stream of consciousness. The phenomenological is not the same as Descartes' idea of substance; it is closer to the monad of Leibniz. The phenomenological ego is a philosophizing ego—a pure ego. The world is nothing more than the ego's awareness of the world. As an ego, I am the stream of consciousness in which the world acquires meaning and reality. Husserl called the pure ego "the wonder of wonders," and he considered it a mystery that the world had a being that could be aware of its own existence.

According to Husserl, the world makes sense to us only through our ego, and *intentionality* belongs to the ego. We use the word *intention,* for example, when a football player intends to kick a field goal or a horse-show judge intends to choose a winner. Intention means how we direct our consciousness toward an object, that is, we have some object in view that is the center of our attention. According to Husserl, intention is never empty of meaning. "*The essence of consciousness, in which I live as my own self, is the so-called intentionality.* Consciousness is always conscious of something." Thus, the world is neither subjective nor objective, but an example of transcendental subjectivity.

In all of our perceptions, feelings, and thoughts, the ego or unobserved observer resides in a transcendental subjectivity (the phenomenological ego). Through the phenomenological ego, all truth can be found. While everything else is bracketed, the phenomenological ego finds itself the only "apodictically certain being." The world may be transcendent or beyond the limits of experience, but ego also is transcendental and always present in experience. The pure or transcendental ego is prior to the world, and so the individual as a transcendental ego is the only object capable of judgment. To know the world, we must gain knowledge of it through the ego. This is the act of intentionality that is the unique characteristic of our consciousness.

According to Husserl, consciousness constitutes the world because it makes the world exist for *me*. If there were no phenomena, I could never know the world, but in and through phenomena, I know that I am in the world and part of the world. Husserl sometimes referred to this connection between consciousness and the objects whose means are contained within consciousness as "transcendental idealism."

The Life-World

The *life-world (Lebenswelt)* is the world that encompasses our daily experiences and makes up the entirety of our conscious life. It is the world of our perceptions, responses, interpretations, and synthesis or organization of the many aspects of our everyday affairs. This is the world from which scientists must abstract their theories to explain the natural world. Ever since Galileo, science has tried to explain the world objectively.

> The scientist sees himself as overcoming the relativity of our "merely subjective" *pictures* of the world by finding the *objective* world, the world as it really is. Husserl shows that the scientist can just as easily be seen, by a shift in perspective, as a man who himself has a particular sort of *picture* of the world, and that as such both he and his picture belong *within* the "real" world, which Husserl calls the life-world.[8]

But Husserl explained that this objective experience is itself an abstraction from the actually experienced world. Thus the life-world is inaccessible to us when we try to reach it through objective scientific interpretation and can only provide a partial understanding of reality. Husserl called the totality of events of the life-world "our world-experiencing life." Through his notion of the life-world, Husserl wanted to free Phenomenology and its philosophers from the dominating view of the natural sciences. To reach the life-world we must use Phenomenology (the epoche cited earlier) that suspends scientific interpretation and allows us to view directly the life-world and see its structured reality.

Husserl's new look at reality through the phenomenological method was to influence many philosophers in Phenomenology and Existentialism. Martin Heidegger and Jean-Paul Sartre are among those who developed their own philosophies on the strength of Husserl's ideas.

Martin Heidegger

Martin Heidegger was a leader of the phenomenological movement and at one time an assistant to Husserl at the University of Freiburg, where he later taught as Husserl's successor. He adopted the phenomenological method in his approach to problems of the nature of Being, but his interests, unlike those of Husserl, were metaphysical. He wanted to know "What does Being mean?" This question is one that interested Aristotle and most of the Medieval scholastics.

Husserl's phenomenological method had focused on the essences of entities such as trees, but Heidegger focused on Being as such. He thought that Being "gives" itself to the phenomenological seeing that Husserl held so important. Husserl claimed that seeing is pure because what we experience in it is the thing itself. Heidegger agreed, but he applied it to reforming metaphysics rather than natural science. For Heidegger, in transcendentally reduced experience we meet Being itself, not the Being that appeared to metaphysicians, but the very Being they sought. Because their methods were faulty, however, they had failed to find such Being.

The object studied is the major difference between Husserl's and Heidegger's notions of Phenomenology. According to Heidegger, Husserl studied beings, whereas he studied Being. In his masterwork *Being and Time,* Heidegger broadened Phenomenology's focus of analysis from consciousness to *Dasein*, or our "being there"—or "being-in-the-world."

Heidegger's Life

Martin Heidegger (1889–1976) was born at Messkirch, Germany, in the Black Forest. His father was the custodian of the local Catholic Church. Heidegger was raised Catholic and received his early education in the local schools. At an early age, he showed a keen interest in the ancient Greeks and the classics. He attended a Jesuit-run secondary school where he "acquired everything that was to be of lasting value," especially a solid grounding in the classics and Greek culture and language. Here, Heidegger studied Aristotle's notion of Being with deep interest. The interest never faded, and the study of Being became his life's work. He particularly liked the pre-Socratics, Søren Kierkegaard, and Friedrich Nietzsche.

Heidegger became a Jesuit novice, then entered the diocesan seminary at Freiburg. Finding that philosophy was his main interest, however, he left the seminary to enroll at the University of Freiburg and study philosophy. Excused from World War I for health reasons, he completed his studies and was appointed professor at the university. For three years he was Edmund Husserl's assistant and became so immersed in Phenomenology that Husserl later said, "You and I *are* phenomenology."

In 1922, Heidegger was appointed as an associate professor at the University of Marburg, Germany. There he pursued his study of Aristotle, formulated a new interpretation of Phenomenology, and worked on the manuscript that was to be his most famous philosophical work, *Being and Time*. After Husserl's retirement, Heidegger was appointed his successor at the University of Freiburg. When Heidegger published *Being and Time,* he dedicated the book to Husserl. However, years later when he departed from Husserl's method, he withdrew the dedication.

When the Nazis came to power in 1933, the rector of the University of Freiburg was ousted and Heidegger replaced him. At this time he was a strong supporter of the Nazis, but his enthusiasm for the regime declined and a year later he resigned as rector. However, he kept his professorship until the end of the war. Later, based on his record with the Nazis, in 1951 the French occupation forces banned him from teaching for five years. He was allowed to return one year before his retirement.

After his retirement, he visited Greece and France and then withdrew more and more into a secluded life in his hut in the Black Forest. There he wrote several essays and interpretations of the history of philosophy, a two-volume work on Nietzsche, and in 1969 published his last work, *The Matter of Thinking*. Heidegger died at age eighty-six. His *Collected Works* encompass approximately one hundred volumes.

The difficulty of Heidegger's writing is well known. He invented new vocabulary, giving old terms new meaning to express what he wanted to say. Sometimes his words have Greek roots, and other times they are put together in a way that causes translators to disagree on their meaning. One word might be translated in several ways. His objective in creating unique terms was to soar beyond language limitations to help us clarify our understanding of our own being and of Being itself.

To gain some understanding of Being, Heidegger thought we should examine the human being using the phenomenological method, which "unconceals" the data of experience by allowing these data to "show themselves." Using this method to examine the self, we find the self as *Dasein,* or "Being-in-the-world" or "Being there."

The Human Being (Dasein)

One of Heidegger's unique words is *Dasein*, which means "being there" in German. We humans are unique modes of Being. We should not be defined as objects. To be as humans means to wonder about the relation between being and Being—the "ontological difference."

> Dasein is an entity which does not just occur among other entities. Rather it is ontically distinguished by the fact that, in its very Being, that Being is an *issue* for it. But in that case, this is a constitutive state of Dasein's Being, and this implies that Dasein, in its Being, has a relationship towards that Being—a relationship which itself is one of Being. And this means further that there is some way in which Dasein understands itself in its Being, and that to some degree it does so explicitly. It is peculiar to this entity that with and through its Being, this Being is disclosed to it. *Understanding of Being is itself a definite characteristic of Dasein's Being*. Dasein is ontically distinctive in that it *is* ontological. . . .
>
> That kind of Being towards which Dasein can comport itself in one way or another, and always does comport itself somehow, we call "*existence*." And because we cannot define Dasein's essence by citing a "what" of the kind that pertains to a subject-matter, and because its essence lies rather in the fact that in each case it has its Being to be, and has it as its own, we have chosen to designate this entity as "Dasein," a term which is purely an expression of its Being.
>
> Dasein always understands itself in terms of its existence—in terms of a possibility of itself: to be itself or not itself. Dasein has either chosen these possibilities itself, or got itself into them, or grown up in them already. Only the particular Dasein decides its existence, whether it does so by taking hold or by neglecting. The question of existence never gets straightened out except through existing itself. . . .[9]

Here Heidegger gave a distinction between two levels that we can describe as an entity. He called them *ontic* and *ontological*. Ontic is our particularity as individual, historically situated beings. Ontological is the Being that is simultaneously revealed and disguised through our very difference from it. The ontic level is one of ordinary facts. Each Dasein has a certain physical size, lives in a particular culture, experiences moods, uses language and tools, remembers, intends, usually fears death, and often thinks its way of life is the right way. These facts of our awareness are ontic facts. On a deeper, ontological level we can describe Dasein in its way of Being—in the way it is there, present to things, in the world, and related to others. The ontological level of Dasein is what makes the ontic level possible. In other words, for the ontic facts to exist, there must be a basic ontological mode of Being.

Ontically, Dasein is unique among entities because its own Being "is an *issue* for it." According to Heidegger, Dasein is the being that shows concern for its own Being. Dasein is aware of the current moment, its existence within us, the past and what it could become—the future. Thus, Dasein has a priori a certain understanding of Being. At any given point, its own Being is always "disclosed to it." Because Dasein's way of Being involves having an understanding of its own Being, Heidegger called it *ontological*. Ontology is the discipline concerned with Being.

Pause for Thought   Can you describe the difference between ontic facts and the ontological level in your life and Being?

Next, Heidegger searched for a term to designate the way of Being that is characteristic of Dasein. He chose *existence*. Dasein *exists*.

Existence

Our essence as human beings is in our existence, because many possibilities are open for us to choose different kinds of being for ourselves. Thus, we escape the confinement of beings that are not Dasein. For example, dogs never ask, "Why am I a dog and not a hummingbird?" Unlike other creatures, we are uniquely free to develop our existence.

Dasein exists. Furthermore, Dasein is an entity that in each case says, "I am." "Mineness" (I am) belongs to any existent Dasein, and the condition belongs to it to make authenticity and inauthenticity possible. Authentic individuals are those who are true to themselves. They take responsibility for their individual actions and are not dominated by society. Inauthentic individuals are the average people in the masses who live as society expects them to live. Thus, they neither take responsibility for themselves nor are they true to themselves.

But these are both ways in which Dasein's Being takes on a definite character, and they must be seen and understood *a priori* as grounded upon that state of Being which we have called "*Being-in-the-world*." . . .[10]

Being-in-the-World   Unlike Descartes, Heidegger said the human being, the Dasein, is not a thinking substance and the world is not an extended substance. Either hypothesis, he claimed, would portray the world as if it were a container with human beings inside it. For Phenomenologists, picturing humans and the world as objectively separate entities is a false view. Heidegger argued that Descartes' notion of the ego (the thing that thinks) attributes to Dasein a kind of being that belongs simply to an object that he called the *present-at-hand*.

For Heidegger, Being-in-the-world as Dasein is not the same as one object being in another object, as water is in the glass, or the jacket is in the closet. Dasein is in the world not as a separate object, but as "being familiar with." It is not by accident that Heidegger hyphenated "Being-in-the-world." The hyphens tell us that we are dealing with a *unitary phenomenon*. Dasein is not apart from the world, it dwells in the world. To say that Dasein is in the world is not to deny that Dasein is in space, only to describe the structure of existence that makes it possible for Dasein to think meaningfully about the world. According to Heidegger, the world is a characteristic of Dasein itself.

> The compound expression "Being-in-the world" indicates in the very way we have coined it, that it stands for a *unitary* phenomenon. This primary datum must be seen as a whole. But while Being-in-the-world cannot be broken up into contents which may be pieced together, this does not prevent it from having several constitutive items in its structure.[11]

> What is meant by "*Being-in*"? Our proximal reaction is to round out this expression to "Being-in the world," and we are inclined to understand this Being-in as "Being in something." This latter term designates the kind of Being which an entity has when it is "in" another one, as the water is "in" the glass, or the garment is "in" the cupboard. By this "in" we mean the relationship of Being which two entities extended "in" space have to each other with regard to their location in that space. Both water and glass, garment and cupboard, are "in" space and "at" a location, and both in the same way. . . .
>
> All entities whose Being "in" one another can thus be described have the same kind of Being—that of Being-present-at-hand "in" something which is likewise present-at-hand, and Being-present-at-hand-along-with in the sense of a definite location-relationship with something else which has the same kind of Being, are ontological characteristics which we call "*categorical*": they are of such a sort as to belong to entities whose kind of Being is not of the character of Dasein.[12]

Pause for Thought   When you look carefully at your experience, do you see a radical difference between the way human beings are "in" the world and the way that water is "in" a glass or a jacket is "in" the closet?

Concern   Dasein is in-the-world in the same way that you are *in* school or your friend is *in* love. Dasein's Being-in-the-world means involvement with others, engaged *in* projects, or using tools. Dasein dwells in the world; it is not just located there.

> Being-in-the-world has always dispersed itself or even split itself up into definite ways of Being-in. The multiplicity of these is indicated by the following examples: having to do with something, producing something, attending to something and looking after it, making use of something, giving something up and letting it go, undertaking, accomplishing, evincing, interrogating,

considering, discussing, determining. . . . All these ways of Being-in have *concern* as their kind of Being—a kind of Being we have yet to characterize in detail.[13]

For Heidegger, then, Dasein is *concernfully* engaged in the world. There is a way of relating to the things in the world that is fundamental to our nature.

From what we have been saying, it follows that Being-in is not a "property" which Dasein sometimes has and sometimes does not have, and *without* which it could *be* just as well as it could with it. It is not the case that man "is" and then has, by way of an extra, a relationship of-Being towards the "world"—a world with which he provides himself occasionally. Dasein is never "proximally" an entity which is, so to speak, free from Being-in, but which sometimes has the inclination to take up a "relationship" towards the world. Taking up relationships towards the world is possible only *because* Dasein, as Being-in-the-world, is as it is.[14]

Pause for Thought

Do you agree with Heidegger that because Being-in-the-world belongs to Dasein, its Being toward the world is essentially concern? Does every human being care about the world?

Ready-to-Hand   We have seen that Being-in-the-world is the fundamental ontological characteristic of Dasein. Existentially speaking, without Dasein (human beings) there could be no world. We and our world are united. Dasein has two characteristics: (1) the priority of existence over essence, and (2) the fact that Dasein is my existence. Dasein is the "I am" and "you are." Our true essence is in our existence. What Dasein may become depends on personal choices.

Heidegger also described how the world is a characteristic of Dasein in "average everydayness." He wanted to know how Being-in-the-world shows itself in Dasein's everydayness and what form our Being-in takes. He said that in our everyday experience we encounter things as equipment, as utensils.

We shall call those entities which we encounter in concern "*equipment*." In our dealings we come across equipment for writing, sewing, working, transportation, measurement. The kind of Being which equipment possesses must be exhibited. . . .

Equipment—in accordance with its equipmentality—always is *in terms of* its belonging to other equipment: ink-stand, pen, ink, paper, blotting pad, table, lamp, furniture, windows, doors, room. These "Things" never show themselves proximally as they are for themselves, so as to add up to a sum of *realia* and fill up a room. What we encounter as closest to us (though not as something taken as a theme) is the room; and we encounter it not as something "between four walls" in a geometrical spatial sense, but as equipment for residing. Out of this the "arrangement" emerges, and it is in this that any "individual" item of equipment shows itself. *Before* it does so, a totality of equipment has already been discovered. . . .

The peculiarity of what is proximally ready-to-hand is that, in its readiness-to-hand, it must, as it were, withdraw in order to be ready-to-hand quite authentically. That with which our everyday dealings proximally dwell is not the tools themselves. On the contrary, that with which we concern ourselves primarily is the world—that which is to be produced at the time; and this is accordingly ready-to-hand too. The work bears with it that referential totality within which the equipment is encountered.[15]

Consider a hammer. We first encounter the hammer as something to use to accomplish a purpose such as building a shed to provide shelter ("present-at-hand"). The more I use the hammer to pound nails into the boards, the less aware I become of the hammer as an object. When we appear to be one with the hammer, it is "ready-to-hand" (available for its purpose).

We can see the hammer in more than one way—as part of a project filling its purpose (building a shed for shelter) or as an object. Heidegger called the ready-to-hand type of sight "circumspection." In other words, it is not the properties of a thing that determine it as a tool on the one hand and an object on the other; rather it is Dasein's (our own) projection onto that particular item.

Pause for Thought   Can you give examples of projections you make on objects or even on people?

Heidegger then looked further into the way we deal with things ready-to-hand through the notion of work. That we produced a shed or that a cobbler made shoes points beyond the immediate work environment to the larger context of materials. This, in turn, involves the wider environment of animals, people who raise them, and nature. Heidegger gave an example of a cobbler making shoes.

In the work there is also a reference or assignment to "materials": the work is dependent on leather, thread, needles, and the like. Leather, moreover, is produced from hides. These are taken from animals, which someone else has raised. . . . Hammer, tongs, and needle, refer in themselves to steel, iron, metal, mineral, wood, in that they consist of these. In equipment that is used, "Nature" is discovered along with it by that use—the "Nature" we find in natural products.[16]

For Heidegger, nature is part of the world of equipment in which Dasein essentially is. Other entities with the same Being as Dasein are also manifest. The hammer, the board, and the nails to join them did not just happen. Thus, other entities have the same kind of Being (Dasein) as I have. These entities reveal to me that I am not alone in the world. There are others like me. The world shows itself as a public world. Hammers are mass-produced so anyone can use them. Cars are manufactured so that the average person can drive them. There can be different worlds even made of the same things because of the different ways in which individuals project "their" world. We speak of the fashion designer's world, or the artist's world, or the baseball player's world. But each of these worlds is only a part of a larger public world in which Dasein fundamentally dwells. The Being of Dasein is Being-in-*the*-world, and it is a public world that I have in common with others.

Together with the ready-to-hand is the "for-the-sake-of-which." For example, the hammer has its Being as equipment and is ready-to-hand for hammering. As we have seen, the process involved a relationship with nails and boards for the purpose of building a shed. Now, asked Heidegger, is there anything for-the-sake-of-which this set of relations exists? His answer was *yes*. "The totality of involvements

> goes back ultimately to a "towards-which" in which there is no further involvement: this "towards-which" is not an entity with the kind of Being that belongs to what is ready-to-hand within a world; it is rather an entity whose Being is defined as Being-in-the-world, and to whose state of Being, world-hood itself belongs. . . . The primary "toward-which" is a "for-the-sake-of-which." But the "for-the-sake-of-which" always pertains to the Being of *Dasein*, for which in its Being, that very Being is essentially an issue.[17]

Thus for Heidegger, the world is not an entity or a group of entities, it is a structure within which entities have their meaning. The network of in-order-to's, toward-which's, and for-the-sake-of's is the phenomenon of the world. The world is a structure in which entities have their Being.

The "Who" of Dasein

For Heidegger, human existence (Dasein) is where the world takes place. Dasein, we must remember, is not the "I" that we might normally call my "self." The "who" of everyday Dasein has no "self" of its own. Our sense of self, of what we are to do, how we want to live, is for the most part, given from the outside. Heidegger characterizes this as the "they-world," or simply as the "they" (*Das Man*). The "who" of everyday Dasein is Das Man. "Everyone is the other, and no one is himself."

The public character of our world of everyday Dasein . . .

> deprives the particular Dasein of its answerability. The "they" . . . can be answerable for everything most easily, because it is not someone who needs to vouch for anything. It "was" always the "they" who did it, and yet it can be said that it has been "no one.". . .
>
> Thus the particular Dasein in its everydayness is *disburdened* by the "they."[18]

None of us is responsible for the way everyday life goes. We just do it. Dasein conforms to this way of Being. Dasein *falls-in-with-it.*

> The "*they,*" which supplies the answer to the question of the "*who*" of everyday Dasein, is the "*nobody*" to whom every Dasein has already surrendered itself in Being-among-one-another.[19]

Pause for Thought   By saying that we have no "self," Heidegger was saying that we are not subjects (things) separate from other objects, rather we are "in existence." Is it possible to think of yourself as "in existence" and not as a separate "self"?

Modes of Disclosure

According to Heidegger, Dasein has some sort of understanding of its own Being. To find out what sort of understanding it is, Heidegger has us think of a clearing in the midst of a dark forest. The space within the clearing is one in which flowers and trees could appear. The clearing, he said, is Dasein.

> [As] Being-in-the-world it is cleared in itself, not through any other entity, but in such a way that it is itself the clearing. . . . Dasein brings its "there" along with it. If it lacks its "there," it is not factically the entity which is essentially Dasein; indeed, it is not this entity at all. *Dasein is its disclosedness.*[20]

What is the "there" that Dasein brings with it? To answer, Heidegger discusses the "thereness" of *Dasein* under three headings: (1) attunement (mood), (2) understanding, and (3) discourse (speech).

Attunement (Moods)   Attunement addresses the question, "How are you doing?" This expresses the fact that Dasein always finds itself in a situation of some sort. Moods often disclose "how we are." Moods reveal how we are coping with our existence. For Heidegger, the mood penetrates the whole field of Being that we are. In other words, our whole Being (Dasein) is attuned in some way to a mood. We *are* a certain joy, sadness, dread. It permeates our whole existence. Moods color everything.

Pause for Thought

Do you agree with Heidegger that our moods color everything? If you are in a bad mood, is your world radically different from the times when you are in a good mood? Can you think of examples?

Dasein's mood then discloses how Dasein is attuned to its world. This disclosure reveals another aspect of Dasein's Being that Heidegger called "thrownness." Dasein is "thrown" into the world. By this he meant that we suddenly find ourselves within the situation of Being-in-the-world. We are thrown into circumstances not of our own making, such as our body, our parents, our historical moment, and our race. What this situation means depends on how we project ourselves into the possibilities it leaves open, including trying to change it. Given our feeling that we are simply there in the world, the world is not a place we can truly feel at home. We are, as it were, orphans and homeless.

We may feel at home with some things in the world by experiencing them as ready-to-hand (serviceable), but the world as a whole is not ready-to-hand; it is present-at-hand, a hard fact that we have trouble understanding. The question arises, "Why should the world be at all?" Or, "Why should we be at all?"

Dasein understands its own most Being in the sense of a certain "factual Being-present-at-hand." And yet the "factuality" of the fact of one's own Dasein is at bottom quite different ontologically from the factual occurrence of some kind of mineral, for example. Whenever Dasein is, it is a Fact; and the factuality of such a Fact is what we shall call Dasein's "*facticity*." This is a definite way of Being, and it has a complicated structure which cannot even be grasped *as a problem* until Dasein's basic existential states have been worked out. . . . The pure "that it is" shows itself, but the "whence" and the "whither" remain in darkness. . . .

This characteristic of Dasein's Being—that "that it is"—is veiled in its "whence" and "whither," yet disclosed in itself all the more unveiledly; we call it the "thrownness" of this entity into its "there." . . .

Has Dasein as itself ever decided freely whether it wants to come into "Dasein" or not, and will it ever be able to make such a decision? In "itself" it is quite incomprehensible why entities are to be uncovered, why truth and Dasein must be. . . . As something thrown, Dasein has been thrown into existence. It exists as an entity which as to be as it is and as it can be.[21]

As Beings thrown into the world and confronted with forces beyond our understanding, we are bound to experience anxiety. Heidegger discovered that in anxiety this Being-there of our existence arises before us in all its precarious ways. For instance, because we lack understanding of the meaning of human relationships, many of us live inauthentic and anxious lives. We do not make appropriate choices because we do not understand who we are or what we are confronting.

Among moods, said Heidegger, anxiety is the most unique because it has no object. Unlike fear and anger, a person suffering from anxiety cannot point to an object as the cause. There is nothing in the world that is the object of this mood.

> In anxiety what is environmentally ready-to-hand sinks away, and so, in general, do entities within-the-world. The "world" can offer nothing more, and neither can the Dasein-with of Others. Anxiety thus takes away from Dasein the possibility of understanding itself, as it falls, in terms of the "world" and the way things have been publicly interpreted. Anxiety throws Dasein back upon that which it is anxious about—its authentic potentiality-for-Being-in-the-world. Anxiety individualizes Dasein. . . .
>
> Anxiety makes manifest in Dasein its *Being towards* its own most potentiality-for-being—that is, its *Being-free* for the freedom of choosing itself and taking hold of itself.[22]

Not only are we thrown into the world without our knowledge, but also we must become our true self by making appropriate decisions. Thus, said Heidegger, along the way we experience a "fallenness," a loss of our authentic character. To live an authentic existence, we must recognize our own unique self and affirm it with responsibility for our actions. Often we try to escape our authentic character by drifting into an inauthentic existence. In so doing, we seek refuge in a public self, an impersonal one in contrast to the concrete "I."

The inauthentic individual behaves as society expects a person to behave rather than as "I" ought to.

Pause for Thought   Have you ever fallen into inauthenticity by judging music, art, and literature as you were expected to? Have you ever suppressed an urge to be unique and excel because of what your peers would say?

The inauthentic individual is the average person in the masses that Nietzsche called "the bungled and botched." For Heidegger also, the inauthentic individual acts like the average everyman. The inauthentic individual has relinquished responsibility and allows the "one" to take over all decisions. There is no "one" in particular, certainly not the "I" who is answerable for anything. But, as Heidegger said, if an individual continues to avoid responsibility, anxiety is the result. Fallenness then is inauthenticity. It is a mode of Being in which we are lost in, and dominated by, the world. Although we may believe we know everything, we actually understand nothing, especially our own Dasein, from which we have turned away to the world and the "they."

Moods usually tell us something about ourselves, and anxiety is the mood that most clearly reveals the Being of Dasein as "thrown-Being-in-the-world-of-the-One." Anxiety can motivate us to fall back into that world in an inauthentic way.

Understanding

Understanding   As we have seen, Dasein, by the very virtue of Being, has some understanding of its Being. Dasein is always "attuned" to its world, and every attunement or mood has some understanding of that world. For Heidegger, understanding is not abstract or theoretical, but the understanding of Being—the root of our existence. Without such understanding, we could not make propositions or theories that can claim to be true. As such, it lies underneath and at the basis of our ordinary conceptual understanding. We open our eyes in the morning and the world opens before us. We do not reflect enough on what happens in this simple act of seeing—that the world opens around us as we see.

This openness of the world is always given even for those who have no intellectual understanding of the world at all. Without this openness we could not exist, because to exist means to stand beyond ourselves in a world that opens before us.

In Heidegger's terms, understanding exemplifies the character of existence. Understanding is always "ahead of itself," always confronted with "potentiality" and "possibility." All of us are more than a mere collection of facts: We are not something present-at-hand. We are essentially what we can be. We have certain *potentiality-for-Being* and certain *possibilities*.

> As a disclosure, understanding always pertains to the whole basic state of Being-in-the-world. As a potentiality-for-Being, any Being-in is a potentiality-for-Being-in-the-world. Not only is the world, *qua* world, disclosed as possible significance, but when that which is within-the-world is itself freed, this entity is freed for *its own* possibilities. That which is ready-to-hand is discovered as such in its service*ability*, its us*ability*, and its detrimen-*tality*. The totality of involvements is revealed as the categorical whole of a *possible* interconnection of the ready-to-hand. . . .
>
> Dasein is constantly "more" than it factually is, supposing that one might want to make an inventory of it as something-at-hand and list the contents of its Being. . . . But Dasein is never more than it factically is, for to its facticity its potentiality-for-Being belongs essentially.[23]

Pause for Thought   Right now, according to Heidegger, you *are* a certain understanding of your possibilities—the possibility that you will eat a meal after your philosophy class, meet a friend, or go to the gym for a workout. Can you conjure examples of possibilities in your life? Do you need to conceptualize this understanding of yourself?

Heidegger claimed that understanding is a basic part of Dasein and not something added to it because it has the structure of *projection*.

> Projecting has nothing to do with comporting oneself towards a plan that has been thought out, and in accordance with which Dasein arranges its Being. On the contrary, any Dasein has, as Dasein, already projected itself; and as long as it is, it is projecting. As long as it is, Dasein always has understood itself and always will understand itself in terms of possibilities. . . .[24]

Projecting on possibilities is not the same as thinking about possibilities. It is more primordial. To understand a shoe is to be prepared to wear it, not to eat with it. To understand yourself as a philosophy student is to project yourself into potentially understanding Heidegger. Understanding is part of our Being, and to exist in a specific situation is to have some understanding, because it is part of our existence. Possibility is more basic to our Being than even the facts about us, because these possibilities are inside us.

With respect to the potentialities of our Being, understanding is always there, but we can develop it more explicitly. When we do, it takes the form of interpretation, which, said Heidegger, is understanding itself. Consider your computer, something most of you understand pretty well. You use it to type your papers, send and receive e-mail, surf the Internet, and play games. Suppose one day your computer fails to function. Up to this point you had taken the working of your computer for granted, that is, you understood it implicitly. But now you understand it explicitly, as a machine, as a structure. Now it becomes explicit in an interpretation. Interpretation always lays bare "the structure of something as something." Thus, interpretation is always founded on a prior understanding.

> In every case interpretation is grounded in *something we see in advance*—in a *foresight*. . . . In such an interpretation, the way in which the entity we are interpreting is to be conceived can be drawn from the entity itself, or the interpretation can force the entity into concepts to which it is opposed in its manner of Being.[25]

Now we can readily see the differences in the views of understanding between Heidegger and the Analytic philosophers. As you recall, the Analytic philosophers argued that we arrive at understanding when we have analyzed some whole into its simple parts. It is only the parts that we can grasp. Heidegger, on the other hand, claimed that we could only begin to understand a part when we put it into some sort of context of the structured whole. Only when we understand the whole can we understand the parts.

Discourse (Speech)   For Heidegger, dialogue is an example of attunement and of coming to understand. As attunement and understanding, discourse is an essential characteristic of Dasein, because all Daseins talk. Discourse is always expressed in language and is possible only when we perceive those with whom we are communicating as others. Discourse, then, involves Being-with.

> Discoursing or talking is the way in which we articulate "significantly" the intelligibility of Being-in-the-world. Being-with belongs to Being-in-the-world, which in every case maintains itself in some definite way of concernful Being-with-one-another: Such Being-with-one-another is discursive as assenting or refusing, as demanding or warning, as pronouncing, consulting, or interceding, as "making assertions," and as talking in the way of "giving a talk."[26]

Discourse also can be silence like that between good friends. For instance, if two friends are walking together and fall silent, the silence between them is a language that may speak more eloquently than any words. In their mood they are attuned to each other and have reached down into that understanding that lies below the level of articulation. At this point, mood, understanding, and discourse (a discourse that is silence), interweave and are one.

This speaking silence tells us that sounds do not create the essence of language, and silence is not merely a gap in chatter. Silence is the primordial attunement of one existent to another, out of which all language comes. It is only because we are capable of such silence that we are capable of authentic speech. If we cease to be rooted in that silence, then all our talk becomes idle talk or chatter. Or it becomes an attempt to impose opinions on others.

> And because this discoursing has lost its primary relationship-of-Being towards the entity talked about, or else has never achieved such a relationship, it does not communicate in such a way as to let this entity be appropriated in a primordial manner, but communicates rather by following the route of *gossiping* and *passing the word along*. What is said-in-the-talk as such, spreads in wider circles and takes on an authoritative character. Things are so because one says so.
>
> The groundlessness of idle talk is no obstacle to it becoming public; instead it encourages this. Idle talk is the possibility of understanding everything without previously making the thing one's own.[27]

Pause for Thought   When you are with a group of acquaintances, how much of your talk is idle talk or chatter? Do you ever try to force your opinions on others?

Discourse, then, is an existential and essential characteristic of Dasein. But when Dasein falls-in-with others in the world, it also falls-in with this degenerate form of idle chatter. We cannot remove ourselves from it, but we can struggle against it toward genuine understanding. Idle talk is part of our inauthenticity: It is "fallenness." It is that mode of Being in which we are lost in and dominated by the world. Authenticity means living in and with anxiety. When we live an authentic life, we live in freedom by accepting Dasein's mode of Being.

What moves us from the inauthentic life to the authentic one? According to Heidegger, it is the understanding that we are going to die. Our knowledge of death enables us to understand our Being fully as a whole.

Death

Death happens every day in the world. For Heidegger, however, death too often remains a fact outside ourselves. We realize other people die, but we do not come to grips with the truth "I am to die." The authentic meaning of death—"I am to die"—is not as an external and public fact within the world, but the internal possibility of my own Being. It is death that makes Dasein a whole. But the question arises, "What is death?"

Dasein's death is not just its end in a physical or biological sense. As a possibility, death is something that Dasein lives, because it is something that Dasein is bound to realize. Dasein has no choice. "Death is not to be outstripped." We are thrown into this possibility with no chance of escape.

Death is something that stands before us—something impending. . . .

Death is a possibility-of-Being which Dasein itself has to take over in every case. With death, Dasein stands before itself in its ownmost potentiality-for-Being. . . . As potentiality-for-Being, Dasein cannot outstrip the possibility of death. Death is the possibility of the absolute impossibility of Dasein. Thus death reveals itself as that possibility which is one's ownmost, which is non-relational, and which is not to be outstripped. . . .

His ownmost possibility, however, non-relational and not to be outstripped, is not one which Dasein procures for itself subsequently and occasionally in the course of its Being. On the contrary, if Dasein exists, it has already been *thrown* into this possibility. Dasein does not, proximally and for the most part, have any explicit or even any theoretical knowledge of the fact that it has been delivered over to its death, and that death thus belongs to Being-in-the-world. Thrownness into death reveals itself to Dasein in a more primordial and impressive manner in that state-of-mind which we have called "anxiety." Anxiety in the face of death is anxiety "in the face of" that potentiality-for-Being which is one's ownmost, non-relational, and not to be outstripped. That in the face of which one has anxiety is Being-in-the-world itself. That about which one has this anxiety is simply Dasein's potentiality-for-Being. Anxiety in the face of death must not be confused with fear in the face of one's demise. This anxiety is not an accidental or random mood of "weakness" in some individual; but, as a basic state-of-mind of Dasein, it amounts to the disclosedness of the fact that Dasein exists as thrown Being *towards* its end.[28]

The understanding of death means anxiety. To live authentically, we must keep this threat of death constantly before us. We must be vigilant against the tendency to fall back into the security of inauthenticity. We must display the mood in which Dasein comes face-to-face with death and does not flee.

We may now summarize our characterization of authentic Being-towards-death as we have projected it existentially: anticipation reveals to Dasein its lostness in the they-self, and brings it face to face with the possibility of Being itself, primarily unsupported by concernful solicitude, but of being itself, rather in an impassioned freedom towards death—a freedom which has been released from the illusions of the "they" and which is factical, certain of itself, and anxious.[29]

Although terrifying, said Heidegger, taking death into ourselves is also liberating because it frees us from living an inauthentic life. We are then free to be ourselves as a whole.

Pause for Thought   Do you agree with Heidegger that to avoid inauthenticity we must keep the threat of death constantly before us? Or do you prefer to avoid the subject of death?

Summary

In this chapter we examined the views of two major Phenomenologists, Edmund Husserl and Martin Heidegger. As a philosophy, Phenomenology attempts to understand meaning in human experience. For Husserl, Phenomenology is a philosophical method to find out how the world reveals itself to consciousness. By careful inspection of conscious experience, he wanted to make philosophy a rigorous science.

Husserl disagreed with natural scientists that science was merely physical and that minds could be seen as if they were bodies. Instead, he thought philosophy should describe the "data" of consciousness without prejudgment so an accurate description of the phenomena within consciousness could be intuitively experienced and reported. For this endeavor, he used three techniques: (1) phenomenological reduction (bracketing), (2) eidetic reduction, and (3) analysis of the correlation between the phenomenon of cognition and the object of cognition.

Through phenomenological suspension (bracketing) everything in the world is reduced to pure phenomenon. In opposition to Descartes' notion of ego, Husserl's phenomenological ego is a philosophizing ego, a stream of consciousness in which the world acquires meaning and reality. There is no breach between the subjective and objective. The world makes sense to us only through our ego. We cannot reach the world through objective scientific interpretation.

Heidegger wanted to know if it is possible to get inside human beings for a firsthand look at what "Being" could mean. Thus, the major difference between Husserl's and Heidegger's notion of Phenomenology is in the object studied. According to Heidegger, Husserl studied beings, whereas he studied Being. For Heidegger, Being is *Dasein* or "Being-there." Dasein is aware of Being. The kind of Being of which Dasein is aware is called "existence"—"Being-in-the-world."

To be as humans means to wonder about the relations between being and Being, the ontological difference, that is, the difference between our ontic particularity as individual, historically situated beings and the Being that is revealed and disguised through our very difference from it. Being-in-the-world is the ontological character of Dasein.

Heidegger analyzed Dasein as possessing a threefold structure that makes possible the projection of the world: (1) attunement, (2) understanding, and (3) discourse. Attunement or mood is how we encounter our environment. Understanding projects the content of purposes and their interrelationships within which a particular thing derives meaning. Understanding is always ahead of itself because it deals with possibilities. Discourse, our language, is an existential and essential characteristic of Dasein.

He then described existence as thrown into the world. We find ourselves thrown into circumstances that are not of our own making such as our body, parents, historical moment, race, and so on. We define our existence in the world potentialities and possibilities through projection. One important way of being outside ourselves is concern for "Being-with" other people and in how we use tools and address other practical concerns.

Heidegger claimed that anxiety discloses to us our finitude by revealing our existence as transitory, as a Being-toward-death. Orienting our life to consciousness of death will make a difference in the choices we make during life. The understanding of death is that of anxiety. To live authentically, we must keep the threat of death consciously before us. If we don't, we will fall back into inauthenticity. By living authentically, we are free to be ourselves as a whole.

Connections

As Heidegger looked to Husserl for his method in Phenomenology, so Jean-Paul Sartre (Chapter 17) looked to Heidegger for many of his ideas. As Heidegger developed Phenomenology in a direction that Husserl refused to tread, Sartre developed ontology in a way far different from that of Heidegger. Heidegger had wanted to find a means for understanding Being. Sartre, however, reversed Heidegger's position by concentrating exclusively on the existence of the individual. By claiming that existence precedes essence, Sartre laid the foundation for Existentialism. Because of their focus on Phenomenology, a new way of looking at human beings and the world, Husserl and Heidegger strongly affected the Existentialists and the whole of twentieth-century philosophy.

Study Questions

1. Why did the Phenomenologists think the Analytic philosophers made a mistake?

2. Who is the founder of Phenomenology?

3. What did Husserl mean by saying he wanted to make philosophy a rigorous science by returning it "to the things themselves"?

4. What, according to Husserl, is the crisis of Western man?

5. What did Husserl like about Greek philosophy?

6. What was Husserl's criticism of natural science and psychology?

7. What was Husserl's phenomenological method?

8. What did Husserl mean by "bracketing"?

9. Why did Husserl think that suspending judgment was important?

10. For Husserl, why was Kant's noumenal world unacceptable?

11. For Husserl, what is the phenomenological ego?

12. According to Husserl, what is the importance of intentionality?

13. What, for Husserl, is the Life-world?

14. In Heidegger's philosophy, what does the word *Dasein* mean?

15. According to Heidegger, what is the difference between ontic and onto-logical?

16. What is existence to Dasein?

17. Unlike Descartes, Heidegger said the Dasein is not a thinking substance and the world is not an extended substance. What did he mean?

18. How is Dasein concernfully engaged in the world?

19. What did Heidegger mean by the term "ready-to-hand"?

20. If, for Heidegger, the world is not an entity in itself, then what is it?

21. Explain Heidegger's notion of moods.

22. What did Heidegger mean when he said that we are thrown into the world?

23. Why is anxiety so important in Heidegger's philosophy?

24. Explain the difference between Heidegger's notion of authenticity and inauthenticity.

25. What do potentiality and possibility have to do with understanding?

26. In what way does discourse involve Being-with?

27. Explain the importance of keeping the threat of death constantly before us.

Notes

1. Edmund Husserl, "Philosophy and the Crisis of European Man" (trans. by Q. Lauer), in *Phenomenology and the Crisis of Philosophy,* pp. 184–185. New York: Harper & Row, 1965. Reprinted by permission of HarperCollins Publishers, Inc.

2. Ibid., pp. 171, 173.

3. Ibid., pp. 186–188.

4. William S. Sahakian, *History of Philosophy,* pp. 229–230. New York: Barnes & Noble, 1968.

5. Edmund Husserl, *Ideas: General Introduction to Pure Phenomenology* (trans. by W. R. Boyce Gibson),) Sec. 31–32. New York: Macmillan, 1931.

6. Ibid., Sec 33.

7. Ibid., Sec. 88.

8. David Car, "Husserl's Problematic Concept of the Life-World," in *Husserl: Expositions and Appraisals* (ed. by Frederick A. Ellison and Peter McCormick), p. 207. Notre Dame, IN: University of Notre Dame Press, 1977.

9. Martin Heidegger, *Being and Time* (trans. by J. Macquarie and E. Robinson), pp. 59, 61. New York: Harper & Row, 1962. Reprinted by permission of HarperCollins Publishers, Inc.

10. Ibid., p. 78.

11. Ibid., p. 78.

12. Ibid., p. 79.

13. Ibid., p. 83.

14. Ibid., p. 84.
15. Ibid., p. 97.
16. Ibid., p. 100.
17. Ibid., pp. 116–117.
18. Ibid., p. 165.
19. Ibid., pp. 165–166.
20. Ibid., p. 171.
21. Ibid., pp. 82, 174, 271, 321.
22. Ibid., p. 232.
23. Ibid., pp. 184, 185.
24. Ibid., p. 185.
25. Ibid., p. 191.
26. Ibid., p. 204.
27. Ibid., pp. 212–213.
28. Ibid., pp. 293–295.
29. Ibid., p. 311.

CHAPTER SEVENTEEN

Existentialism:
Sartre, de Beauvoir, Camus

Existentialists often call Socrates the first member of their camp, because he focused on the meaning of human nature. Augustine also showed deep insight into the causes of human anxiety and conflict, as did Kierkegaard and Nietzsche, Husserl and Heidegger. But most philosophers had looked at human nature through objective and systematic eyes. As we saw in the chapter on Phenomenology, by the twentieth century interest in individual human qualities lay hidden in the shadow of scientific method and technology. Human qualities had given way to procedures. Persons had become objects instead of subjects. As Samuel Enoch Stumpf points out:

> Existentialism was bound to happen. The individual had over the centuries been pushed into the background by systems of thought, historical events, and technological forces. The major systems of philosophy had rarely paid attention to the uniquely personal concerns of individuals. Although Aristotle, for example, wrote a major treatise on ethics, Montaigne could say that "I can't recognize most of my daily doings when they appear in Aristotle." Nietzsche also wrote that "to our scholars, strangely enough, the most pressing question does not occur: to what end is their world . . . useful?" To be sure, Socrates had focused upon just these matters with his insistence that all thought and activity should be directed toward enhancing the meaning of human existence. St. Augustine also engaged in profound introspective psychological analysis to discover the source of human beings' personal insecurity and anxiety. Still, philosophy for the most part dealt with the technical problems of metaphysics, ethics, and the theory of knowledge

in a general and objective manner, which bypassed the intimate concerns of people about their personal destiny. Historical events, particularly wars, showed a similar disregard for the feelings and aspirations of individuals. And technology, which arose as an aid to humankind, soon gathered a momentum of its own, forcing people to fit their lives into the rhythm of machines. Everywhere men and women were losing their peculiarly human qualities. They were being converted from "persons" into "pronouns," from "subjects" into "objects," from an "I" into an "it."[1]

One predicament that Existentialists find with the technological age is its mechanistic view of humanity. People see each other as objects instead of subjects—as nonbeing rather than being. Because we live with this threat of nonbeing hanging over us, anxiety becomes a way of life. People, as Heidegger recognized, are apprehensive of death, and they fear that freedom is an illusion and that heredity and environment rule our lives. Existentialists wanted to address these problems.

Existential philosophers have no particular system. Their opinions on religion and politics vary. Existentialists can be religious, agnostic, or atheist. Some are liberal, others moderate or conservative. But whatever their viewpoint on religion or politics, all Existentialists agree that traditional philosophy was too remote from life to have any meaning for them. Like the Phenomenologists, they reject systematic philosophy to undertake questions facing each of us, such as questions of choice, individuality, freedom, meaning, self-identity, authenticity, alienation, despair, and mortality.

Opposing the objective scientific approach to human meaning, Existentialists turn their attention to the inner life of an individual. "Who am I?" "What does my life mean?" "Why am I afraid?" "What should I do to become the person I would like to be?" These are personal questions that all individuals ask. Like Husserl and Heidegger, Existentialists insist we cannot answer such questions by using dehumanizing scientific methods. We create our essence through freedom of will and moral responsibility. As human beings, we can decide how we will live.

The first philosopher to express the importance of viewing humanity subjectively and as individuals was Søren Kierkegaard, and he was followed by Friedrich Nietzsche. Existentialism as a philosophy, however, did not bloom until after World War II and perhaps because of it. Jean-Paul Sartre, Simone de Beauvoir, and Albert Camus wrote of the atrocities of the Holocaust, and of turning people into objects.

Existential thought was born in French cafés among young intellectual playwrights, novelists, poets, musicians, and artists far from academia.

As we shall see in this chapter, existential themes fly in the face of twentieth-century Analytic philosophy. The faceless person of the masses and the death of God are not the focus of Analytic philosophy, but themes of life. People suffer, die, and struggle to know who they are. "We cannot," say the Existentialists, "divorce our minds from living."

Though Henri Bergson was not an Existentialist, without his insight into intuition, open and closed morality, and static and dynamic religion, Existentialism would lack its depth and richness. American Analytic philosophers viewed Existentialism as they viewed Bergson: a fad that would soon pass into oblivion. Instead, Existentialism gathered momentum until it became one of the major philosophies of the twentieth century, and contemporary philosophers are taking a new look into Bergson's insights.

Today we can see the basic themes of Existentialism through the writings of Jean-Paul Sartre, Simone de Beauvoir, and Albert Camus.

Jean-Paul Sartre

Sartre's Life

Jean-Paul Sartre (1905–1980) was born in Paris, France. His father was a naval officer, and his mother the first cousin of Albert Schweitzer, the famous jungle doctor and theologian. When Sartre was an infant, his father died. His mother raised Jean-Paul in the home of his grandfather, who taught French and German. As a child, he felt a deep "revulsion" for the mask of nobility his family wore to hide "its real dereliction." A lonely boy, Sartre wrote that until the age of ten he "remained alone between an old man and two women."

Sartre was a precocious child and studied the great works of literature that lined the bookcases of his grandfather's library. Even as a youngster, he was sure he would be a writer. "By writing," he said, "I was existing. . . . I existed only in order to write."

In 1924, Sartre entered the École Normale Supèrieure in Paris. While there, he exhibited his gift for literary expression and became captivated by the philosophy of Henri Bergson. Bergson's ideas left him "bowled over" with the feeling that through philosophy one could learn truth. Following graduation, Sartre entered the German universities of Berlin and Freiburg (1933–1935) for graduate studies. While still a graduate student, he met Simone de Beauvoir, who later played a key role in the early phases of the women's liberation movement, especially with her famous book *The Second Sex* (1948). Their companionship lasted fifty-one years until Sartre's death. Both were brilliant students, committed to their literary work. Both achieved fame as writers. Sartre always had Beauvoir read and criticize his manuscripts before he allowed them to be published. Both Sartre and Beauvoir became two of France's most celebrated writers.

While in Berlin, he worked on his famous novel *Nausea*, which was published in 1938. After graduate school, he taught at several French lycées. Then when World War II broke out in 1939, he was called to active duty and sent to the Maginot Line. Soon after he arrived at the front, the Germans captured him, but he was released from the prisoner-of-war camp and later joined the Resistance. He spent the rest of the war in Paris writing, teaching, and taking part in the Resistance. During this period, he completed *Being and Nothingness*, his major philosophical work. In the postwar years, he wrote the novels and plays that made him world-famous. His brilliant work, *Existentialism Is a Humanism*, was published in 1946.

In 1951, he helped found a new leftist but noncommunist political movement. He also helped found and edit *Les Temps Modernes*, a French journal with a strong leftist orientation. During the 1960s, he actively opposed U.S. intervention in Vietnam. In 1964, the Nobel committee awarded him the Nobel Prize for Literature, but he refused to accept it, saying he did not want to be "transformed into an institution." In the 1970s, his health declined and his eyesight weakened until he was virtually blind. Sartre died April 15, 1980. To honor him, fifty thousand people marched behind his coffin through the streets of Paris.

Sartre's Existentialism

In Berlin, Sartre had studied with Edmund Husserl (1859–1938), one of the founders of Phenomenology, which views consciousness as the basis of reality. The Phenomenologist gives a descriptive analysis of consciousness based on facts and concrete experiences. By avoiding the abstract and theories and relying on descriptive statements, Phenomenology attempts to reveal the essence of human consciousness. Making no conceptual presuppositions, Phenomenologists want to get beyond concepts to consciousness itself. According to Husserl, philosophy should seek its foundation only in man, especially in the essence of his "concrete worldly existence."

Martin Heidegger based his existential philosophy on Husserl's Phenomenology, but he took a direction that Husserl rejected. Husserl's Phenomenology, said Heidegger, yielded only "consciousness and its objectivity," not "the Being [essence] of beings. . . . " Heidegger was mainly interested in Being and with the existence of the person as a way to understand Being. Sartre was impressed with Husserl and Heidegger, but he was more interested in our existence as a way to understand the person than he was with Being. Sartre also disagreed with them on the notion of "being" and our human situation. For Heidegger, our human situation is a moral issue: How do we face the knowledge that we are going to die?

Sartre saw the human situation differently. The most important issue, he said, is our human situation in a world without God. What is such a world? What is a person to do in such a world? Without God, we have no eternal nature to fall back on. It is, then, useless to search for a universal meaning of life. We are condemned to improvise. Like actors dragged onto the stage without knowing their lines and without a script or prompter, we must decide for ourselves how to live.

Pause for Thought   How would you answer Sartre's questions "What is a world without God?" "What is a person to do in such a world?"

Nausea   Through self-conscious writing, Sartre discovered he was "alone, without God." In his novel *Nausea*, his protagonist Roquentin sees life in its nakedness:

> Never until these last few days have I understood the meaning of existence. . . . And then all of a sudden, there it was, clear as day: existence had suddenly unveiled itself. It had lost the harmless look of an abstract category: it was the very paste of things, this root was kneaded into existence. Or rather the root, the park gates, the bench, the spare grass, all that had vanished: the diversity of things, their individuality, were only an appearance, a veneer. This veneer had melted, leaving soft monstrous masses, all in disorder—naked, in a frightful, obscene nakedness. . . .[2]

Roquentin suddenly discovers that being, as it reveals itself in the crisis of consciousness, is pure superfluity, pure excess, and obscene disorder. There is no reason to exist yet we do exist, and we exist in an absurd and meaningless world.

Pause for Thought   If there is no God, said Sartre, then there is no reason to exist. Yet we do exist in an absurd and meaningless world. Do you agree with his perception of the world and our existence? If not, what would you change?

The Absurd

> The word absurdity is coming to life under my pen; a little while ago, in the garden, I couldn't find it, but neither was I looking for it, I didn't need it: I thought without words, *on* things, *with* things. . . . Without formulating anything clearly, I understood that I had found the key to Existence, the key to my Nausea, to my own life. In fact, all that I could grasp beyond that returns to this fundamental absurdity. Absurdity: another word; I struggle against words; down there I touched the thing. . . . The world of explanations and reasons is not the world of existence. A circle is not

absurd, it is clearly explained by the rotation of a straight segment around one of its extremities. But neither does a circle exist. This root, on the other hand, existed in such a way that I could not explain it. . . . This root, with its colour, shape, its congealed movements, was . . . below all explanation.[3]

Only later, upon reflection, does the world become familiar: "The world of explanations and reasons is not the world of existence." The world is without meaning. In such a world, we feel alienated, which creates a sense of despair, boredom, nausea, and absurdity. But we must have such experiences before we can act. In Sartre's play *The Flies*, Orestes says, "Human life begins on the other side of despair." Facing the fact that no God exists, human beings feel abandoned.

Abandonment   Like Nietzsche, Sartre rejected Kierkegaard's subjective leap of faith. First, God is not subject—we are. Second, because God does not exist, we cannot have faith in God as the center of our life. We must make our own center. God is an illusion that clouds our vision of ourselves and our world.

Russian novelist and philosopher Fyodor Dostoevsky wrote, "If God did not exist, everything would be permitted." For Sartre, because there is no God, our psychological condition is one of abandonment. Because there is no God, we cannot look for salvation in Heaven. Without God, no objective system of morality exists. Abandoned in a world in which everything is permitted, we have only ourselves to rely on. Besides our existence, there is nothingness: not Plato's immortal soul, Descartes' *cogito,* or Kierkegaard's subjective self. "Nothingness," said Sartre, "lies coiled in the heart of being, like a worm." In nothingness lies consciousness. We exist in consciousness. It is up to each of us to create our essence.

Existence Precedes Essence   Sartre gave the classic formulation of Existentialism when he stated, "Existence precedes essence." This concept is exactly opposite of that held by Plato, Aristotle, Plotinus, Aquinas, and others that essence precedes existence. For example, Plato and Aristotle believed that the essence of being human was in the rational portion of the soul. The Medieval philosophers believed that humans are created in God's image, therefore, we all possess an essential human nature. Our essence precedes our existence. For Sartre, however, because there is no God, there is no divine reason or inherent essence. There is no human nature common to all humans and no specific essence that defines what it is to be human. Human beings exist. We must produce our own essence. Through our choices, we become who we are. We create our own nature or essence. The future is in our hands.

Sartre also held that when we choose for ourselves, we are choosing for all other people:

If . . . existence precedes essence, and if we grant that we exist and fashion our image at one and the same time, the image is valid for everybody and for our whole age. Thus our responsibility is much greater than we might have supposed, because it involves all mankind. If I . . . choose to join a Christian trade-union rather than be a communist, and if by being a member I want to show that the best thing for man is resignation, . . . I am not only involving my own case—I want to be resigned for everyone. . . . If I want to marry, to have children, even if this marriage depends solely on my own circumstances or passion or wish, I am involving all humanity in monogamy and not merely myself. . . . I am creating a certain image of man of my own choosing. In choosing myself, I choose man.[4]

Pause for Thought

Reflect on the choices you make. Do you agree with Sartre that when you create a certain image of yourself you are creating an image for all humanity?

Being-in-Itself and Being-for-Itself

Because there is no God, we have no destiny. There is no reason that things happen as they do. We exist without any real reason. But our existence is not like the existence of a stone or an insect. Existence does not mean just being alive. Plants and animals are alive, but they do not have to think about what it implies. Conscious of our own existence, we humans have greater dignity. Stones and insects have only *being-in-itself* (*être-en-soi*). A material thing is simply "in itself." But humans have *being-for-itself* (*être-pour-soi*), or consciousness. Humankind is "for itself." The being of humans therefore cannot be the same as the being of things. Unlike stones and insects, humans are self-aware.

For Sartre, we humans are not passive playthings of either unconscious forces or an unconscious mind that determines who and what we are. Sartre denied the existence of an unconscious mind. The mind acts and action is consciousness. He would agree with Descartes' *Cogito ergo sum*—"I think, therefore I exist." Consciousness, said Sartre, is a realm of clear and distinct ideas. But Sartre's protagonist Roquentin also experienced the world of the unconscious: It was only an appearance, a veneer. When the veneer melted, all that was left was disorder of the masses, "a frightful, obscene nakedness." It is the domain of being-in-itself, the realm of nothingness. This realm is the other in ourselves: And the glance of the other, for Sartre, is fearful and petrifying.

All consciousness is consciousness of something. No consciousness can be without affirming the existence of an object that transcends itself. Consciousness is at once consciousness of objects and consciousness of self. With self-consciousness we create who we are now and who we will be in the future.

Neither a stone nor an insect can create its own future. But we are responsible for the existence we have. We create not only our own future but also the future of all human beings.

Our problem, said Sartre, is that the being-for-itself struggles to become the being-in-itself. We try to attain its rocklike and unshakable solidity, but it can never happen so long as we are conscious and alive. We are doomed to the insecurity and contingency of our being. Yet, because we are not merely stones and insects, we can transcend our given situation. This ongoing dialectic between being-in-itself and being-for-itself is our anguish—and also our power and glory.

Responsibility   "In choosing myself—I choose man." This statement sounds like Kant's universal law. Sartre, however, did not agree with Kant that some actions, such as telling the truth, are always right and other actions, such as breaking promises, are always wrong. When we make a certain choice, we are saying, "In creating my own image, I am creating a value for all humankind." However, Sartre did not proclaim a universal law to guide our choices. When we choose an action, we affirm the value of that action and ask ourselves if we would be willing for others to choose the same action.

> The existentialists say at once that man is anguish. What that means is this: the man who involves himself and who realizes that he is not only the person he chooses to be, but also a law-maker who is, at the same time, choosing all mankind as well as himself, cannot help escape the feeling of total and deep responsibility. Of course, there are many people who are not anxious, but we claim that they are hiding their anxiety, that they are fleeing from it. Certainly, many people believe that when they do something, they themselves are the only ones involved, and when someone says to them, "What if everyone acted that way?" they shrug their shoulders and answer, "Everyone doesn't act that way." But really, one should always ask himself, "What would happen if everybody looked at things that way?" There is no escaping this disturbing thought except by a kind of double dealing. A man who lies and makes excuses for himself by saying "not everybody does that," is someone with an uneasy conscience, because the act of lying implies that a universal value is conferred upon the lie.[5]

There are times when we would not want others to act as we do. But, said Sartre, it is *self-deception*—"bad faith"— to say that it is all right for us to act a certain way, because others will not choose to act that way. When we realize we are responsible for others as well as ourselves, we face a deep sense of anguish. Each choice we make helps to create our world. If we deceive ourselves by evading responsibility, we will never be at ease in our conscience.

If Sartre has any universal, it is that all humans are free to make their own choices. We humans are always the same, but our situations vary. Thus, our choices are always choices made in a situation.

Condemned to Be Free If we had an essential nature, said Sartre, we would not be responsible for what we are. But, because there is no God and no divine plan, nothing determines what must happen. "Man is free"—"Man is freedom." In fact, we are "condemned to be free."

> This is the idea I shall try to convey when I say that man is condemned to be free. Condemned, because he did not create himself, yet, in other respects is free; because, once thrown into the world, he is responsible for everything he does. The existentialist does not believe in the power of passion. He will never agree that a sweeping passion is a ravaging torrent which fatally leads a man to certain acts and is therefore an excuse. He thinks that man is responsible for his passion.
>
> The existentialist does not think that man is going to help himself by finding in the world some omen by which to orient himself. Because he thinks that man will interpret that omen to suit himself. Therefore, he thinks that man, with no support and no aid, is condemned every moment to invent man. . . . Whatever a man may be, there is a future to be forged, a virgin future before him. . . . But then we are forlorn.[6]

Pause for Thought

As free individuals, our freedom condemns us to make choices throughout our lives. There are no eternal values we can follow, and that makes our choices even more significant. Are we then responsible for everything we do? Can we avoid such responsibility by following the rules of society?

In a story about one of his students, Sartre gave us an example of the anguish of making a choice. The student's father, a Frenchman, was a Nazi sympathizer. His brother died fighting the Germans and the student wanted to avenge his brother's death. The student lived with his mother, who was depressed because of the death of her son and her husband's betrayal of his country. The student faced the choice of leaving France to fight the Germans or staying in France to give his mother moral support.

> Who could help him choose? Christian doctrine? No. Christian doctrine says, "Be charitable, love your neighbor, take the more rugged path, etc., etc." But which is the more rugged path? Whom should he love as a brother? The fighting man or his mother? Which does the greater good, the vague act of fighting in a group or the concrete one of helping a particular human being to go on living? Who can decide *a priori*? Nobody. No book of ethics can tell him. The Kantian ethic says, "Never treat any person as a means, but as an end." Very well, if I stay with my mother, I'll treat her as

an end and not as a means; but by virtue of this very fact, I'm running the risk of treating the people around me who are fighting, as means; and, conversely, if I go to join those who are fighting, I'll be treating them as an end, and, by doing that, I run the risk of treating my mother as a means.

If values are vague, and if they are always too broad for the concrete and specific case that we are considering, the only thing left is for us to trust our instincts. That's what this young man tried to do. . . .

But how is the value of a feeling determined? What gives his feeling for his mother value? Precisely the fact that he remained with her. I may say that I like so-and-so well enough to sacrifice a certain amount of money for him, but I may say so only if I've done it. I may say "I love my mother well enough to remain with her" if I have remained with her. The only way to determine the value of this affection is, precisely, to perform an act which confirms and defines it. But since I require this affection to justify my act, I am caught in a vicious circle.[7]

According to Sartre, no system of ethics or philosophy could tell the student which choice to make. So he sought Sartre's advice. But, said Sartre, depending on whom we ask for advice, we already know what kind of advice that person will give. "Therefore, in coming to see me, he knew the answer I was going to give: 'You're free, choose, that is, invent.'" In the end, however, the student (faced with anguish) is responsible for his own choice. "Forlornness implies that we ourselves choose our being."

Pause for Thought　　　When you reflect on the choices you make, do you sometimes seek advice from people when you already know the answer they will give? Do we usually seek an answer that will conform to what we want to hear?

Cowards and Heroes　　Of his existential doctrine, Sartre said:

The doctrine I am presenting . . . declares, "There is no reality except in action." Moreover, it goes further, since it adds, "Man is nothing else than his plan; he exists only to the extent that he fulfills himself; he is therefore nothing else than the ensemble of his acts, nothing else than his life."

According to this, we can understand why our doctrine horrifies certain people. Because often the only way they can bear their wretchedness is to think, "Circumstances have been against me. What I've been and done doesn't show my true worth. To be sure, I've had no great love, no great friendship, but that's because I haven't met a man or woman who was worthy. The books I've written haven't been very good because I haven't had the proper leisure. I haven't had children to devote myself to because I didn't find a man with whom I could have spent my life. So there remains within me, unused and quite viable, a host of propensities, inclinations, possibilities, that one wouldn't guess from the mere series of things I've done."[8]

Pause for Thought   Excuses, said Sartre, are ultimately pessimistic. They allow us to blame our genes, our environment, our lack of luck. Do you find yourself blaming your parents or family situation for the way you turned out? Or do you take full responsibility for what you are?

Sartre continued:

To be sure, this may seem a harsh thought to someone whose life hasn't been a success. But on the other hand, it prompts people to understand that reality alone is what counts, that dreams, expectations, and hopes warrant no more than to define a man as a disappointed dream, as miscarried hopes, as vain expectations. In other words, to define him negatively and not positively. . . .

When all is said and done, what we are accused of, at bottom, is not our pessimism, but an optimistic toughness. . . . When the existentialist writes about a coward, he says that this coward is responsible for his cowardice. He's not like that because he has a cowardly heart or lung or brain; he's not like that on account of his physiological make-up; but he's like that because he has made himself a coward by his acts. There is no such thing as a cowardly constitution; there are nervous constitutions; there is poor blood, as the common people say, or strong constitutions. But the man whose blood is poor is not a coward on that account, for what makes cowardice is the act of renouncing or yielding. A constitution is not an act; the coward is defined on the basis of the acts he performs. People feel, in a vague sort of way, that this coward we're talking about is guilty of being a coward, and the thought frightens them. What people would like is that a coward or a hero be born that way. . . .

That's what people really want to think. If you're born cowardly, you may set your mind perfectly at rest; there's nothing you can do about it; you'll be cowardly all your life, whatever you may do. If you're born a hero, you may set your mind just as much at rest; you'll be a hero all your life; you'll drink like a hero and eat like a hero. What the existentialist says is that the coward makes himself cowardly, that the hero makes himself heroic. There's always a possibility for the coward not to be cowardly any more and for the hero to stop being heroic. What counts is total involvement; some one particular action or set of circumstances is not total involvement.[9]

Pause for Thought   Do you consider Sartre's statement about cowards and heroes authentic or absurd? Can we define ourselves by our actions?

Bad Faith   Bad faith (*mauvaise foi*) is trying to flee the anguish of freedom and responsibility. Sartre's conception of bad faith is one of his most well-known ideas. The problem of bad faith is the problem of describing what it is to be a human being. It demonstrates the various ways we escape from what Sartre described as "absolute freedom." Bad faith is present in most or even all of our activities. Bad faith is hiding a truth from ourselves—self-deception. Bad faith is lying to ourselves about ourselves. For Sartre, an example of bad faith is a woman who consents to go out with a man whom she knows to have sexual intentions toward her:

> She knows also that it will be necessary sooner or later for her to make a decision. But she does not want to realize the urgency: she concerns herself only with what is respectful and discreet in the attitude of her companion. She does not apprehend this conduct as an attempt to achieve what we call "the first approach."[10]

The woman interprets whatever her companion says as lacking any sexual suggestion. When he takes her hand, she even divorces herself from it by ignoring that her hand is in his.

> We shall say that this woman is in bad faith. . . . She has disarmed the actions of her companion by reducing them to being only what they are, that is, to existing in the mode of the in-itself.[11]

The woman, said Sartre, is not only deceiving herself about her companion, but also deceiving herself about her own desires. She is deceiving herself about her intentions as well as her own sexual nature. She is pretending that she is not a sexual being and that her companion's advances have nothing to do with her sexually. She is in bad faith for denying the necessity of her own choice in the situation. She has denied the situation in which she must choose to accept or reject her sexuality and her companion's advances.

Pause for Thought   Have you ever found yourself in a situation of bad faith? Have you told yourself that your advances toward someone or your acceptance of another's advances are merely friendly and without sexual intentions?

In Sartre's example, the woman knows the truth on the one hand, but refuses to disclose it to herself on the other. She is lying to herself, which is self-deception. She knows, but is hiding what she knows from herself. Sartre said we do not lie when we are ignorant, duped, or mistaken. We lie when we deceive ourselves. Bad faith is not a conscious act; it is a willful refusal to recognize our freedom. In bad faith, we look at ourselves as a being-in-itself, and not as a being-for-itself. We see ourselves as an object. We should become conscious that we do deceive ourselves and that we are not things.

> That which affects itself with bad faith must be conscious (of) its bad faith since the being of consciousness is the consciousness of its being. It appears then that I must be in good faith at least to the extent that I am conscious of my bad faith.[12]

Although bad faith is "a permanent risk of consciousness," we are not always in bad faith. Bad faith is an ever-present threat, but by being aware of this threat, we can overcome it.

Sartre makes a distinction between "facticity and transcendence." We are *factical* insofar as we are thrown into a world that is not of our making. But we are *transcendent* insofar as we are free (within limits) to remake and reinterpret that world. Bad faith consists either in identifying wholly with our facticity (and thus giving up responsibility) or wholly with our transcendence (and thus denying our limitations).

Simone de Beauvoir

De Beauvoir's Life

Born into a highly respected French family, Simone de Beauvoir (1908–1986) was the older of two daughters. Although her childhood was uneventful, her father experienced financial difficulties that left the family in constant anxiety. At approximately nine years old, Simone decided to be a writer. She expected writing to justify her own existence as well as serve humanity. Later, in her teens when she became an atheist, she expected writing to take the place of God. Later, she admitted that she had expected too much, but she must write anyway.

As a student in the Sorbonne, Simone de Beauvoir discovered philosophy and decided to study it, she said, because it deals with the essentials of existence instead of "an illusory whirlwind of facts." Philosophy gave her a new way of viewing the world and people. While at the Sorbonne's École Normale Supèrieure, she met Jean-Paul Sartre and other young intellectuals who would become well known in twentieth-century French letters and politics. Some of these men and women formed a group they called "The Family." The Family consisted of writers, actors, and activists who found intellectual stimulation and social support together for more than sixty years.

In 1929, she graduated from the Sorbonne second in her class behind only Simone Weil, the Jewish writer and mystic. From the time they met, de Beauvoir and Sartre formed a relationship that lasted a lifetime. The two were an enormous help to each other in their literary work. De Beauvoir achieved such fame as a writer that she moved to first place among women of letters. At the time of Sartre's death, she was France's most celebrated living writer. Her novel *The Mandarins* won the Prix Goncourt, and her book *The Second Sex* gave her recognition as an Existentialist feminist philosopher.

With Sartre, Marxism deeply influenced de Beauvoir's political views. However, she disagreed with the deterministic conclusions of the Marxist perspective. Even though the forces of economic history may influence us, we still are free to "transcend our own immanence" and create who we want to be and thus overcome our cultural conditioning.

Her relationship with Sartre was profound and enduring—and difficult. Sartre said theirs was an "essential" love that would be most important in their lives. However, he added, there would be "contingent" love affairs with other people. In one of her memoirs, de Beauvoir says, "I was vexed with Sartre for having created the situation with Olga." In fact, Sartre's contingent affair with Olga became the theme of de Beauvoir's first novel, *She Came to Stay*. Of her own situation, she said, "From now on we will be a trio instead of a couple." Sartre always insisted that de Beauvoir was his "privileged," but not his only, female companion. His philosophy was "one can always be free." De Beauvoir asked in return, "What is the freedom of the women in a harem?"

Though Sartre developed the reputation of a compulsive womanizer, de Beauvoir claimed that his one-night stands did not bother her at all. She also formed relationships with other men, including Nelson Algren, the American writer. He asked her to marry him, but de Beauvoir declined, saying she refused to put anyone before Sartre.

Growing old tormented de Beauvoir all of her adult life. Society, she said, treated the aged as they did women, giving them the second-class status of the other. After Sartre died, she published *Adieus: A Farewell to Sartre*. The tender documentary details the last ten years of Sartre's life and reveals his many maladies from blindness to incontinence. In the conclusion she writes, "My death will not bring us together again. This is how things are. It is in itself splendid that we were able to live our lives in harmony for so long." After his death, she remained actively involved with writing, traveling, and political work. At age seventy-eight, she died of a respiratory illness, six years after Sartre's death.

Woman as Other   Simone de Beauvoir's Existentialism focused on the cultural forces of oppression. From the beginning, she said, man has viewed himself as Self and woman as Other. In her work *The Second Sex*, she developed the situation of women's essential otherness.

> Now, what peculiarly signalizes the situation of woman is that she—a free and autonomous being like all human creatures—nevertheless finds herself living in a world where men compel her to assume the status of the Other. They propose to stabilize her as object and to doom her to immanence since her transcendence is to be overshadowed and forever transcended by another ego (*conscience*) which is essential and sovereign. The drama of woman lies in this conflict between the fundamental aspirations of every subject (*ego*)—who always regards the self as the essential—and the compulsions of a situation in which she is the inessential. How can a human being in woman's situation attain fulfillment? What roads are open to her? Which are blocked? How can independence be recovered in a state of dependency? What circumstances limit woman's liberty and how can they be overcome? These are the fundamental questions on which I would fain throw some light. This means that I am interested in the fortunes of the individual as defined not in terms of happiness but in terms of liberty.[13]

De Beauvoir concluded that if the other is a threat to the self, then woman is a threat to man. Therefore, if man wishes to remain free, he must subordinate woman to him. To accomplish his superiority, he first exploits her biological functions.

Biology of Women   Woman became other, said de Beauvoir in *The Second Sex,* when men looked upon her as "a womb, an ovary"—as female.

> In the mouth of a man the epithet *female* has the sound of an insult, yet he is not ashamed of his animal nature; on the contrary, he is proud if someone says of him: "He is male!" The term "female" is derogatory not because it emphasizes woman's animality, but because it imprisons her in her sex; and if this sex seems to man to be contemptible and inimical even in harmless dumb animals, it is evidently because of the uneasy hostility stirred up in him by woman.[14]

De Beauvoir argued that biology spews out facts that society interprets to suit its ends. Biology identifies the basic difference between male and female as rooted in the reproductive roles of males and females.

> The fundamental difference between male and female mammals lies in this: the sperm, through which the life of the male is transcended in another, at the same instant becomes a stranger to him and separates from his body, so that the male recovers his individuality intact at the moment when he transcends it. The egg, on the contrary begins to separate from the female body

when, fully matured, it emerges from the follicle and falls into the oviduct; but if fertilized by a gamete from outside, it becomes attached again through implantation in the uterus. First violated, the female is then alienated—she becomes, in part, another than herself.[15]

Because of these reproductive facts, it is harder for a woman to become an independent self, especially if she has a child. However, this does not mean her capacity for self is less than a man's capacity for self. Woman may be physically weaker than man, and she may take a passive role in intercourse, but do these biological facts make her less a person?

The enslavement of the female to the species and the limitations of her various powers are extremely important facts; the body of woman is one of the essential elements in her situation in the world. But that body is not enough to define her as woman; there is no true living reality except as manifested by the conscious individual through activities and in the bosom of a society. Biology is not enough to give an answer to the question that is before us: why is woman the *Other*?[16]

Pause for Thought   Do men still define women as body? Are the names, *chick, cat, bitch, cow* indicative of the way some men view women?

Woman as Being-for-Itself   Using Sartre's concept of consciousness, de Beauvoir insisted that woman is more than a mere body, a being-in-itself, she is also being-for-itself. Like Sartre, she said man and woman have no basic nature to fall back on. We create ourselves. There is no such thing as a basic female nature or male nature. Woman is psychologically conscious.

De Beauvoir found Freud's psychological explanation for the otherness of woman inappropriate. Freud based women's inferior and subservient social status on a castration complex. He said women lack the organ that symbolizes superiority and authority. Women suffer "penis envy." De Beauvoir objected. Women, she said, do not want a penis, they want the privileges that society bestows upon men. "Penis prestige" means power. Thus, women are the other not because they lack penises but because they lack power.

When a little girl climbs trees it is, according to Adler [psychiatrist], just to show her equality with boys; it does not occur to him that she likes to climb trees. For the mother her child is something quite other than an "equivalent of the penis." To paint, to write, to engage in politics—these are not merely "sublimations"; here we have aims that are willed for their own sakes. To deny it is to falsify all human history.[17]

Pause for Thought   Does our culture treat women as the second sex? Does society appropriate certain roles for women to follow? Do these roles keep women
from taking responsibility for their own lives?

Women's Oppression   Finally, de Beauvoir considered Marx's explanation
for why woman is the other nearly as unsatisfactory as Freud's. Marx believed
economic conditions create human history, and throughout history the ruling
class suppressed women. Oppression lies in the social organization through
which one class exploits the labor of others. Until the laborers overthrow capitalism and the proletariat owns production, there will be oppression.

De Beauvoir, however, did not think relations between women and men
will change one iota by moving from capitalism to socialism. Woman will as
likely remain the other in a socialist society as in a capitalistic society. Engels, too,
was mistaken when he traced men's will to power to ownership of private property and women's oppression to capitalism.

> If the original relation between a man and his fellows was exclusively a
> relation of friendship, we could not account for any type of enslavement;
> but no, this phenomenon is a result of the imperialism of the human con-
> sciousness, seeking always to exercise its sovereignty in objective fashion. If
> the human consciousness had not included the original category of the
> Other and an original aspiration to dominate the Other, the invention of
> the bronze tool could not have caused the oppression of woman.[18]

Dissatisfied with the traditional biological, psychological, and economic
explanations of women's oppression, de Beauvoir sought an explanation based
on woman's being. She recognized within woman a self that men defined as
other. When woman asserts herself as subject and free being, the idea of the other
arises because she has become a threat. Men perceive themselves as capable of
risking their lives in combat. They perceive women as capable only of giving life.
Men consider risking life superior to giving life. Because of this difference, men
relegated women to the sphere of otherness—the realm of the body.

Myths About Women   According to de Beauvoir, as civilization developed,
men discovered the way to control women was by creating myths about them.
In these myths, woman fulfills everything that man lacks. She becomes a
chameleon who is as changeable as nature. Characteristic among the myths is
urging the ideal woman to negate or in some way deny herself. De Beauvoir
gave five examples: (1) Woman exists to make her man feel virile; (2) woman
gives up being what she wants to be so her man can be what he wants to be;
(3) woman is the handmaid not only of God, but also of man; (4) woman has

the burden of guilt—if her love is strong enough, she can make or break her man; and (5) woman risks life and limb in a passionate attempt to save her lover from ruin, prison, or death. For de Beauvoir, the ideal woman is problematic because most men and even women think woman has a duty to sacrifice herself for man.

If most women could simply laugh at the image of their ideal, then the situation would be less dangerous for them. Unfortunately, man controls woman and uses her for his purposes. That is the danger. De Beauvoir said Honore de Balzac perfectly summarized man's attitude toward women in his *Physiology of Marriage*:

> Pay no attention to her murmurs, her cries, her pains; *nature has made her for our use* and for bearing everything: children, sorrows, blows and pains inflicted by man. Do not accuse yourself of hardness. In all the codes of so-called civilized nations, man has written the laws that ranged woman's destiny under this bloody epigraph: *Vae victis!* Woe to the weak!"[19]

Pause for Thought   De Beauvoir believed that the most horrible part of the way man defined woman was that many women believed it accurately described her. Do some women still define themselves through men's eyes?

Historically, man has oppressed woman because of his fear and distrust of feminine nature. As creator of life, woman is mystery. She is the awesome mother–goddess. She is also animal-being unable to control her own reproductive processes. Woman is bound to nature, doomed to immanence.

Through history men have argued conveniently that women were mysterious. De Beauvoir ridiculed this idea saying, "If you don't understand what someone else is complaining about, you need not listen sympathetically or try to put yourself in the other person's shoes." Man could not create civilization without freeing himself from feminine mystery. Very handy, said de Beauvoir, but objectifying the mysterious does not make woman inherently inferior.

Woman's Life Today   In a frequently quoted statement, de Beauvoir says, "One is not born, but rather becomes a woman."

> No biological, psychological, or economic fate determines the figure that the human female presents in society; it is civilization as a whole that produces this creature, intermediate between male and eunuch, which is described as feminine. Only the intervention of someone else can establish an individual as an *Other*.[20]

How does society intervene? Speaking from her own experience, de Beauvoir recognized that from the beginning girls are told their bodies are different. Look at the dolls they are given. With puberty, the growth of their breasts, and the beginning of their menstrual flow, girls must accept their "shameful inferior Otherness." From childhood, both family and society teach girls that they are here for marriage and motherhood. First their role as wife, then their role as mother limits their freedom.

Even if a woman chooses a career, the cage of femininity imprisons her. She must always be and act like a woman. As a result, she develops an internal conflict between her professional and feminine interests. Although most women role-play, said de Beauvoir, three kinds of woman play the role of "woman" to the hilt: the prostitute, the narcissist, and the mystic.

The prostitute is a paradigm for woman as other (object). On the one hand, men exploit her; on the other hand, she exploits them. The narcissist is a frustrated woman. Because she is not allowed to define herself and her feminine activities are unfulfilling, she looks for her reality in the immanence of her person and gives herself ultimate importance because no object of importance is accessible to her. She then becomes her one object of fixation (face, body, and clothes). The mystical woman seeks to be the supreme object of a supreme subject. She confuses God with man, man with God. She speaks of men as if they were gods. The mystic wants from God the exaltation of her objecthood. The mystic has but one concern—to love God and to forget self.

Reflecting on her descriptions of the wife, the mother, the career woman, the prostitute, the narcissist, and the mystic, de Beauvoir concluded the tragedy is that these roles are not of woman's making. A society constructed by man has held woman back. Today, however, woman can redefine her role, for she is no more limited to being-in-itself than man is. She is being-for-itself. If woman wants to escape the limits and definitions imposed on her, she has three strategies she can use:

1. Go to work. Like Harriet Taylor, de Beauvoir thought women should share in the job experience.

2. Become intellectual. De Beauvoir encouraged women to study, think, and participate in intellectual matters.

3. Work toward transforming society into one that no longer judges men and women as self–other, subject–object.

Above all, said de Beauvoir, women must help themselves transcend the self–other dichotomy. Alluding to Sartre's concept of bad faith, she said women have bad faith about their own humanity. Women may treat themselves as sexual objects to deny their freedom. She saw the common bad faith of women in an appeal to their "feminine" nature. Woman is a female to the extent that she feels herself a female. Woman is not defined by nature, but by herself. If both men and women could see each other as equals, then it "would bring about an inner metamorphosis."

> The fact that we are human beings is infinitely more important than all the peculiarities that distinguish human beings from one another; it is never the given that confers superiorities: "virtue," as the ancients called it, is defined at the level of "that which depends on us." In both sexes is played out the same drama of the flesh and the spirit, of finitude and transcendence; both are gnawed away by time and laid in wait for by death, they have the same essential need for one another; and they can gain from their liberty the same glory. If they were to taste it, they would no longer be tempted to dispute fallacious privileges, and fraternity between them could then come into existence.[21]

Albert Camus

Camus' Life

Albert Camus (1913–1960) was born in Algeria on the North African coast to a French father and Spanish mother. When Albert was a year old, his father died in battle during World War I. His mother was deaf, illiterate, and suffered a serious speech impediment; she worked as a housemaid to support the family. Albert, his mother, brother, grandmother (who was dying of cancer), and a paralyzed uncle shared a small apartment in a poor section of Algiers.

In a passage of *L'Envers et l'endroit,* Camus writes of the poverty and squalor of their living conditions:

> I think of a child living in a poor district. That neighborhood, that house! There were only two floors, and the stairs were unlit. Even now, long years later, he could go back there on the darkest night. He knows that he could climb the stairs without stumbling once. His very body is impregnated with this house. His legs retain the exact height of the steps; his hand; the instinctive, never-conquered horror of the banister. Because of the cockroaches.[22]

Camus showed no resentment of his childhood poverty. He said it helped him see things clearly. It was his life of poverty among humble people that he felt had shown him the true meaning of life. As a child, he studied the heavens and drank in the "star-filled night and nature's riches." In spite of their poverty, his boundless affection for his mother brought him joy. He remembered her as a silent, uncomplaining, and compassionate woman who worked endlessly. She was to influence him throughout his life.

At the local elementary school, Albert's brilliance caught the attention of a teacher, Louis Germain, who tutored and encouraged him to apply for a scholarship. In 1923, Albert Camus received a scholarship to the local lycée. In 1957, when he won the Nobel Prize for Literature, he dedicated his speech to Louis Germain.

When he was seventeen, Camus nearly died from tuberculosis. At age nineteen, he entered the University of Algiers, where he studied philosophy to become a teacher. His philosophy professor, Jean Grenier, was another strong influence. When Camus read Grenier's *Les Lles*, he wrote, "I think I already wanted to write when I read *Les Lles*; but I really decided to become a writer only after reading this book." Camus acknowledged his philosophy professor by dedicating to him both *L'Enverset l'endroit* (English publications title it either *The Wrong Side and the Right Side* or *Betwext and Between*) and *The Rebel*.

While at the university, Camus joined the communist party, but soon left it. He wrote, acted in, and directed plays. Then, while working on his doctoral studies, his tuberculosis recurred. During the next five years, he spent much of his time in a sanatorium. His bright outlook and love of nature took a dark turn. He became bitter. He protested the cruelties of life and developed an obsession with the absurd. Ill health kept him from completing his dissertation and acquiring his teaching certificate.

In 1939, at the beginning of World War II, Camus went to Paris. Because of the tuberculosis, the military rejected him, so he edited an underground newspaper for the Resistance against the Nazis. The suffering, waste, and death impelled him to ask, "If life is absurd, is there any reason not to commit suicide?" Camus believed this question had to arise when a person stops deceiving him- or herself and begins to see the world as it is.

In 1940, after a short-lived marriage to Simone Hie, he married Francine Faure. While editing the Resistance newspaper, he continued to write, and in 1942 his popular works *The Stranger* and *The Myth of Sisyphus* were published. Overnight, Camus became an international celebrity.

After the war, Camus and Sartre were the most influential writers in France. Both would win the Nobel Prize (although Sartre would reject his). For the first time in his life, Camus was financially independent. With the prize money, he bought a house in the Alps where he could write in privacy. He published *The Plague* in 1947 and *The Fall* in 1956.

Camus was only forty-six when he died in an automobile accident. A rear tire blew out and the car struck a tree. Camus died instantly. In his *Tribute*, Sartre wrote, "For all those who loved him, there is an unbearable absurdity in that death."

The Absurd

Camus is known as an Existentialist, but he disagreed with that label, calling himself the "philosopher of the absurd." He said anyone who does not view the relationship between human beings and the world as absurd lives in self-deception.

For Camus, the *absurd* means living with anxiety, discord, and friction. There is, he said, a "bad fit" between humans and the world.

What is absurd about our relationship to the world? We are born innocent, prepared to love and to live. We long for a good world, but the world is not good. It victimizes and defeats us by the sheer weight of its insanity. We long for justice and honesty, but the world is unjust and humans are dishonest. We look for reason and rationality. We dream dreams. But the unfriendly world is indifferent to reason, rationality, and our dreams. We expect life to be fair. It isn't. The notion of absurdity implies that there is no ultimate reason that things are as they are.

> In a universe suddenly divested of illusions and lights, man feels an alien, a stranger. His exile is without remedy since he is deprived of the memory of a lost home or the hope of a promised land. This divorce between man and his life, the actor and his setting, is properly the feeling of absurdity.[23]

Pause for Thought

Camus saw the world as indifferent to our desires and dreams. We are strangers in a strange land. We dream our dreams, but the world doesn't care. Do you agree with him that life is absurd?

When we realize the absurdity of our condition, we then face how to live and how to die. Camus called this condition the "existential predicament." In the preface to *The Myth of Sisyphus*, he said, "It is legitimate and necessary to wonder whether life has a meaning; therefore it is legitimate to meet the problem of suicide face to face." The shame of traditional science and philosophy is that they have not provided an answer to such an important question.

Pause for Thought

Do you think such traditional philosophers as Socrates and Plato provide an answer to the important question of whether life has meaning or whether we should commit suicide?

> There is but one truly serious philosophical problem, and that is suicide. Judging whether life is or is not worth living amounts to answering the fundamental question of philosophy. All the rest . . . comes afterwards. These are games; one must first answer. And if it is true, as Nietzsche claims, that a philosopher, to deserve respect, must preach by example, you

can appreciate the importance of that reply, for it will precede the definitive act. These are facts the heart can feel; yet they call for careful study before they become clear to the intellect. . . .

If I ask myself how to judge that this question is more urgent than that, I reply that one judges by the actions it entails. I have never seen anyone die for the ontological argument. Galileo, who held a scientific truth of great importance, abjured it with the greatest ease as soon as it endangered his life. In a certain sense he did right. . . . That truth was not worth the stake. Whether the earth or the sun revolves around the other is a matter of profound indifference. To tell the truth, it is a futile question. On the other hand, I see many people die because they judge that life is not worth living. I see others paradoxically getting killed for the ideas and illusions that give them a reason for living (what is called a reason for living is also an excellent reason for dying). I therefore conclude that the meaning of life is the most urgent of questions. . . .

[K]illing yourself amounts to confessing. It is confessing that life is too much for you or that you do not understand it. Let's not go too far in such analogies, however, but rather return to everyday words. It is merely confessing that "it is not worth the trouble."[24]

Pause for Thought   Does it make any sense to go on living if we discover that human life is meaningless?

Although science and philosophy have not come up with answers to the question of committing suicide, Camus did give an answer: "[E]ven if one does not believe in God, suicide is not legitimate." Camus himself was an atheist. Recognizing the absurd, he said, is "a lucid invitation to live and to create, in the very midst of the desert."

Revolt   Accepting the absurdity of everything around us is a necessary experience, because it arouses a revolt within us that can be productive. Revolt, said Camus, is a method, a procedure, one that can help us discover ideas that are capable of restoring meaning to our existence. Revolt affirms the absurd and thus empowers us to continue living without illusion and without suicide.

The revolt gives life its value. Spread out over the whole length of a life, it restores its majesty to that life. To a man devoid of blinders, there is no finer sight than that of the intelligence at grips with a reality that transcends it. The sight of human pride is unequaled. . . . [T]o impoverish that reality whose inhumanity constitutes man's majesty is tantamount to impoverishing him himself. I understand then why the doctrines that explain everything to me also debilitate me at the same time. They relieve me of the weight of my own life, and yet I must carry it alone.[25]

Revolt means abandoning traditional worldviews, the doctrines that define the world and God and humans. It means abandoning the arbitrary do's and don'ts of an immoral world in which we seek a moral life. Revolt means refusing to cooperate with any society that tries to impose its dishonesty on us and with a world that would crush our dreams.

Pause for Thought   Can you give examples of society's dishonesty? Should we abandon traditional worldviews? Would revolt better allow us to create the person we want to be?

For Camus, freedom and innocence are the results of revolt. By revolting against the absurd, we become free. We can do whatever we wish, because we know there is no future and no being superior to us. There are no absolutes or moral laws. All is permitted, for all is equally right and wrong. We become our own masters, free of guilt. We regain our innocence. We are free.

Camus did not mean we should revolt by following blind passions. Revolt is rational and moral. We should resist violence and injustice: "Any mutilation of mankind is irrevocable." We must fight for justice and liberty and against all forms of tyranny: "Let us die resisting," he wrote. Our freedom is to revolt and transcend. However, we must not be under the illusion that we will improve the world, because an absurd world offers no guarantees.

Pause for Thought   Revolt, for Camus, is a moral appeal to transcend passive despair to accept the world's indifference to humanity. Because suicide is not a feasible answer to despair, and no God may exist, do you agree that revolt is the only optimistic decision we can make about life?

The Myth of Sisyphus   In *The Myth of Sisyphus*, Camus gave us an example of the "absurd hero":

The gods had condemned Sisyphus to rolling ceaselessly a rock to the top of a mountain, whence the stone would fall back of its own weight. They had thought with some reason that there is no more dreadful punishment than futile and hopeless labor.[26]

Sisyphus is a king in Greek mythology. He asked for and received Pluto's permission to return to Earth from Hades to chastise his own wife. While on Earth, Sisyphus was so happy that he refused to return to the underworld. The gods threatened him but could not persuade him to return. Zeus then sent Mercury, who snatched Sisyphus from Earth and led him forcibly to Tartarus, the lowest and most awful level of Hades, "where his rock was ready for him." As a punishment for his disobedience, Sisyphus was made immortal and assigned the futile task of rolling a huge boulder up a steep mountain. Each time Sisyphus came close to the mountaintop, the rock rolled back down. The task, which could never be completed, would last forever.

As the hero of the absurd, Sisyphus is conscious that he can never rest, escape the uselessness of his task, or further die. Camus chose Sisyphus as an example of transcending the absurdities in life and yet consciously revolting against the absurd.

You have already grasped that Sisyphus is the absurd hero. He *is* as much through his passions as through his torture. His scorn of the gods, his hatred of death, and his passion for life won him that unspeakable penalty in which the whole being is exerted toward accomplishing nothing. This is the price that must be paid for the passions of this earth. Nothing is told us about Sisyphus in the underworld. Myths are made for the imagination to breathe life into them. As for this myth, one sees merely the whole effort of a body straining to raise the huge stone, to roll it and push it up a slope a hundred times over; one sees the face screwed up, the cheek tight against the stone, the shoulder bracing the clay-covered mass, the foot wedging it, the fresh start with arms outstretched, the wholly human security of two earth-clotted hands. At the very end of his long effort measured by skyless space and time without depth, the purpose is achieved. Then Sisyphus watches the stone rush down in a few moments toward that lower world whence he will have to push it up again toward the summit. He goes back down to the plain.

It is during that return, that pause, that Sisyphus interests me. A face that toils so close to stones is already stone itself! I see that man going back down with a heavy yet measured step toward the torment of which he will never know the end. That hour like a breathing-space which returns as surely as his suffering, that is the hour of consciousness. At each of those moments when he heaves the heights and gradually sinks toward the lairs of the gods, he is superior to his fate. He is stronger than his rock.

If this myth is tragic, that is because its hero is conscious. Where would his torture be, indeed, if at every step the hope of succeeding upheld him? The workman of today works every day in his life at the same tasks, and this fate is no less absurd. But it is tragic only at the rare moments when it becomes conscious. Sisyphus, proletarian of the gods, powerless and rebellious, knows the whole extent of his wretched condition: it is what he thinks of during his descent. The lucidity that was to constitute his torture at the same time crowns his victory. There is no fate that cannot be surmounted by scorn.

If the descent is thus sometimes performed in sorrow, it can also take place in joy. . . . Again I fancy Sisyphus returning toward his rock, and the sorrow was in the beginning. When the images of earth cling too tightly to memory, when the call of happiness becomes too insistent, it happens that melancholy rises in man's heart: this is the rock's victory, this is the rock itself. The boundless grief is too heavy to bear. These are our nights of Gethsemane. But crushing truths perish from being acknowledged. . . .

All Sisyphus' silent joy is contained therein. His fate belongs to him. His rock is his thing. Likewise, the absurd man, when he contemplates his torment, silences all the idols. In the universe suddenly restored to its silence, the myriad wondering little voices of the earth rise up. Unconscious, secret calls, invitations from all the faces, they are the necessary reverse and price of victory. There is no sun without shadow, and it is essential to know the night. The absurd man says yes and his effort will henceforth be unceasing. If there is a personal fate, there is no higher destiny, or at least there is but one which he concludes is inevitable and despicable. For the rest, he knows himself to be the master of his days. At that subtle moment when man glances backward over his life, Sisyphus returning toward his rock, in that slight pivoting he contemplates that series of unrelated actions which becomes his fate, created by him, combined under his memory's eye and soon sealed by his death. Thus, convinced of the wholly human origin of all that is human, a blind man eager to see who knows that the night has no end, he is still on the go. The rock is still rolling.

I leave Sisyphus at the foot of the mountain! One always finds one's burden again. But Sisyphus teaches the higher fidelity that negates the gods and raises rocks. He too concludes that all is well. This universe henceforth without a master seems to him neither sterile nor futile. Each atom of that stone, each mineral flake of that night-filled mountain, in itself forms a world. The struggle itself toward the heights is enough to fill a man's heart. One must imagine Sisyphus happy.[27]

Pause for Thought

Can you relate your life and the workaday world to Sisyphus and his rock? Is your struggle toward the heights enough to fill your heart? Can you imagine Sisyphus happy?

Summary

As a philosophy, Existentialism is a new way of looking at human nature and the lives of individuals. Existential philosophers have no particular system, and they all agree that traditional philosophy was too remote from life to have any meaning for them. As a group, they confront questions of choice, individuality, freedom, meaning, self-identity, authenticity, alienation, despair, and mortality.

Jean-Paul Sartre said human beings exist in an absurd situation facing despair. If we are to find meaning in life, then we must create our own world and its values by making responsible choices. The choices we make for ourselves we make for all humankind. In the face of despair, we can remake the absurd world through these choices and actions. Blaming others for our station in life is senseless. It is we who decide to limit ourselves or act with power. From existential forlornness, anguish, and despair come authentic optimism, a clear vision of who we are. We become cowards or heroes by ourselves alone.

Simone de Beauvoir applied Existentialism to feminism. In the past, woman's inferior physical strength coupled with her status as childbearer allowed her little opportunity to engage in productive work or to think intellectually. Men thus looked upon woman as other. Throughout history man also has oppressed woman, de Beauvoir said, because of his fear and distrust of feminine nature. Accepting Sartre's concept of being-in-itself and being-for-itself, de Beauvoir said that man has portrayed woman as the former. Because human beings are free, and because woman is not born but made (existence precedes essence), de Beauvoir maintained that women should *not* view themselves as other. They are free. With freedom, they need to create themselves anew and overcome the restraints of history.

Albert Camus proposed that none of the traditional belief systems—science, religion, or philosophy—gave adequate answers to what he called the absurdity of the human condition. He thought these traditions were in a state of self-deception about the world and human beings. The conscious individual will experience a sense of absurdity and will ask whether suicide is an adequate response. Camus argued that it is not. Only by continuing to live in the face of absurdity can human beings achieve their full stature.

Living in the face of absurdity includes revolting against human injustice. Because there is no God to rule the world, and the world is indifferent to human hopes and desires for happiness, humans must create and become masters of their own fate. "The struggle itself toward the heights is enough to fill a man's heart." The superiority of the human spirit is its ability to transcend the dread and futility of life in the face of the absurd.

Connections

Although we are at the end of this book, we can never say philosophy has come full circle, for there are always new ways to approach the enduring questions that whet our appetite to understand human nature and the world. The pre-Socratic philosophers expressed their wonder at the unity of the cosmos. Socrates, Plato, and Aristotle probed deeply into the mystery of being and the good life. The Epicureans and Stoics sought wisdom through self-control, and the Medieval philosophers wanted to understand God through faith or reason or both. The modern philosophers and science have awakened inquiries into the problem of knowledge, and Hegel developed a vast metaphysics. The Individualists challenged us to develop greater insight into ourselves; so did the Phenomenologists and Existentialists. The Analytic philosophers emphasized logic and language analysis, and the Process philosophers proposed the interconnectedness of everything in the universe.

The joy and the struggle for truth will never end.

Study Questions

1. What is the main difference between Existentialism and systematic philosophy?

2. What are three of the basic themes of Existentialism?

3. Why did Sartre say it is useless to search for a universal meaning of life?

4. In Sartre's novel *Nausea,* what does his protagonist, Roquentin, discover about the world and the human condition?

5. Why did Sartre say our psychological condition is one of abandonment?

6. What did Sartre mean by his statement "Existence precedes essence"?

7. Explain the importance of knowing the difference between being-in-itself and being-for-itself.

8. Why do we face a deep sense of anguish when we realize our responsibility is for others as well as for ourselves?

9. Explain what Sartre meant when he said we are condemned to be free.

10. Explain Sartre's conception of bad faith.

11. What did de Beauvoir mean by her phrase, "Man has viewed himself as Self and woman as Other"?

12. What did de Beauvoir say about the biological differences between men and women?

13. Explain what de Beauvoir meant when she said there is no such thing as a basic female nature or male nature.

14. Compare and contrast de Beauvoir and Marx in their view of women as other.

15. Why have men created myths about women? What are some of these myths?

16. Why did de Beauvoir say "One is not born, but rather becomes a woman"?

17. For de Beauvoir, what must a woman do to escape the limits imposed on her?

18. According to Camus, why is it important for humans to understand that the world is absurd?

19. Why was the notion of suicide important to Camus?

20. What role does revolt play in Camus' philosophy?

21. Why did Camus consider Sisyphus the absurd hero?

Notes

1. Samuel Enoch Stumpf, *Socrates to Sartre*, 5th. ed., p. 482. New York: McGraw-Hill, 1993.

2. Jean-Paul Sartre, *Nausea* (trans. by L. Alexander), p. 171. New York: New Directions, 1959.

3. Ibid., p. 173.

4. Jean-Paul Sartre, *Troubled Sleep* (trans. by G. Hopkins), pp. 280–287. New York: Bantam Books, 1960.

5. Jean-Paul Sartre, *Existentialism Is a Humanism* (trans. by Bernard Frechtman, 1957), in *The Fabric of Existentialism: Philosophical and Literary Sources* (ed. by Richard Gill and Ernest Sherman), p. 522. Englewood Cliffs, NJ: Prentice-Hall, 1973.

6. Ibid., p. 524.

7. Ibid., pp. 524–525.

8. Ibid., pp. 526–527.

9. Ibid., p. 527.

10. Jean-Paul Sartre, *Being and Nothingness* (trans. by H. E. Barnes), p. 66. New York: Philosophical Library, 1956.

11. Ibid., p. 67.

12. Ibid., p. 59.

13. Simone de Beauvoir, *The Second Sex* (trans. by H. M. Parshley), p. xxxv. New York: Vintage Books, 1989. Copyright 1952 and renewed 1980 by Alfred A. Knopf, Inc. Reprinted by permission of the publisher.

14. Ibid., p. 3.

15. Ibid., p. 22.

16. Ibid., pp. 36–37.

17. Ibid., p. 51.

18. Ibid., pp. 57–58.

19. Ibid., p. 256.

20. Ibid., p. 267.

21. Ibid., p. 728.

22. Albert Camus, "The Wrong Side and the Right Side," in *Lyrical and Critical Essays* (trans. by Ellen Kennedy, ed. by Philip Thody), p. 26. New York: Alfred Knopf, 1968.

23. Albert Camus, *An Absurd Reasoning*, in *The Myth of Sisyphus & Other Essays* (trans. by Justin O'Brien), p. 5. New York: Vintage Books, 1955. Copyright © 1955 by Alfred A. Knopf, Inc. Reprined by permission of the publisher.

24. Ibid., pp. 3–5.

25. Ibid., pp. 40–41.

26. Albert Camus, *The Myth of Sisyphus*, in *The Myth of Sisyphus & Other Essays,* op. cit., p. 89.

27. Ibid., pp. 89–91.

GLOSSARY

Absolute Spirit (Mind, Idea). The ultimate, unconditioned, and uncaused reality in Hegel's philosophy.

Absurd. In opposition to reason and logic. For Existentialists, the absurd lacks any rational explanation.

Aesthetics. The field of philosophy that deals with art and beauty.

Agnostic. An individual who cannot say if the gods or God do or do not exist, because there is no proof either way.

Analytic. A term applied to statements that are necessarily true because the predicate is already contained in the subject. For example, "All bachelors are unmarried men."

Antiquity. Ancient period before the Middle Ages.

Antithesis. An idea set forth in opposition to another, such as the second phase of Hegel's dialectical process. The process of a thesis and antithesis leads to a synthesis.

A posteriori. Knowledge based on sense experience (empirical).

Appearance. The way things present themselves to our senses in contrast with its true reality. The oar in the water appears bent, but it is actually straight.

A priori. Knowledge prior to (or independent of) our sense experience; the opposite of *a posteriori*. For example, "All triangles are three-sided figures" we deem to be true, even though we have not experienced every triangle.

Atomism. From a Greek word meaning "uncuttable," this was the view held by Democritus and others that reality is made up of tiny indivisible atoms and empty space.

Becoming.   Everything in the world of our experience that comes into existence and passes away.

Being.   Ultimate reality. Is neither born nor dies.

Categorical Imperative.   In Kant, the moral law based on duty and goodwill that bids us to act in such a way that the principle of our action would become a universal law.

Categories.   Terms used by Aristotle and Kant to describe the concepts the human mind brings to knowing: substance, quantity, quality, causality, and so on.

Causality.   The relationship between cause and effect, or where one event necessarily follows another.

Cause.   That which has the power to bring about change in another thing; correlates with effect.

Certainty.   The assurance that a theory, proposition, or belief is totally reliable.

Cogito.   Latin for "I think." Descartes used *Cogito ergo sum* ("I think, therefore I exist") to describe his existence as a thinker.

Cognition.   Latin for learning or acquiring knowledge. The act or faculty of knowing.

Concept.   A term that refers to a general idea or universal. Humankind as opposed to a specific individual such as Socrates.

Contingent.   An event that is not necessary; it may be or not exist depending upon other events.

Cosmological argument.   An argument to prove the existence of God as the First Cause of the universe or cosmos. Argument from cause and effect.

Deduction.   Analytic reasoning from general to particular or less general.

Determinism.   The view that every event, including every human action, is necessarily brought about by previous conditions to the exclusion of free will.

Dialectic method or process.   For Socrates, a process of reasoning through questions and answers that leads one from mere opinion to knowledge. For Hegel, a debate over opposites; and for Marx, a clash of material forces and the resulting dynamic change.

Dogmatism.   Making assertions of particular views without proof or evidence.

Dualism.   The view that there are two irreducible substances such as physical and spiritual—in human nature, body and soul.

Eleatic.   School founded by Parmenides.

Empiricism.   The view that all knowledge of facts arises from sense experience. There is no innate knowledge, and humans cannot gain knowledge from reason alone.

Entelechy.   For Aristotle, the end that resides within a thing and guides its development from potentiality to its actuality (end).

Epicureanism.   The philosophy of followers of Epicurus, who believed that personal pleasure is the highest good, but renounced monetary pleasures in favor of more lasting ones.

Epistemology.   Theory of knowledge. The field of philosophy that deals with the nature, conditions, and limits of human knowledge.

Essence.   The chief characteristics or qualities that make a thing uniquely itself.

Ethics.   Moral philosophy. The field of philosophy that studies value judgments of good and evil, obligations and the good life.

Existentialism.   The philosophy that focuses on the individual person, usually stressing choice, freedom, and the problems of existence.

Ex nihilo.   Latin for "out of nothing."

Extension.   In Descartes, the character of physical things as having dimension in space and time.

Forms.   In Plato, Forms are the ideal realities in which particular things of our world are copies and participate, thus deriving their natures. In Aristotle, form is the essential principle in matter that makes an object what it is: "The soul is the form of the body."

Free will.   The doctrine that human beings have free and independent choice that is not determined by divine or physical forces.

Hedonism.   The pursuit of pleasure.

Hypothetical imperative.   An imperative that states what you should do if a certain end is desired.

Idealism.   The philosophy theory that reality consists of ideas, spirit, mind, or thought, as opposed to materialism, which views material things as the basic reality.

Immortality.   The unending existence of a soul or spirit.

Infinite.   Without end. Unlimited or unbounded.

Innate ideas.   Ideas that are inborn and that rational humans are able to know independently of experience.

Instrumentalism.   John Dewey's theory that ideas, judgments, and propositions are not merely true or false, but tools to understand experience and solve problems.

Intrinsic.   That which belongs to a thing by its very nature and not as a means to something else. Not instrumental.

Intuition.   Direct and immediate knowledge. A direct insight into truth that is grasped without any intermediary.

Logic.   The laws of thought. The study of reasoning correctly.

Logical Positivism.   The philosophy of the Vienna Circle, whose members viewed statements as meaningful only if they are verifiable by sense experience. If a statement is not verifiable by such experience, then it is meaningless.

Logos. For Heraclitus and the Stoics, the ordering principle of the world.

Materialism. The theory that all reality is ultimately physical and that mind or spirit are manifestations of the physical reality.

Medieval. From the Latin, meaning "Middle Ages."

Metaphysics. The field of philosophy concerned with the ultimate nature of reality. A study of the nature and fundamental features of being.

Mind–body problem. The puzzle of how the relationship between the nonphysical mind and the physical body takes place in human nature; especially delineated by Descartes.

Mode. The appearance, form, or expression taken by a thing. In Spinoza's philosophy, modes are expressions, forms, or appearances of God's attributes: thought and extension.

Modern philosophy. The philosophies of approximately the fifteenth through the nineteenth centuries.

Monad. From the Greek word meaning "unit." Pythagoras used the word to denote the first number of a series. Gottfried Wilhelm von Leibniz referred to monads as unextended, invisible, autonomous metaphysical entities. Monads are the soul-like basic elements of the universe. Each monad is a single unit.

Monism. The metaphysical view that there is one substance in the universe, usually either spiritual or physical; sometimes referred to as *monistic materialism*.

Mystical experience. A direct intimate union of the soul with God through contemplation or spiritual ecstasy.

Mysticism. Direct or intimate consciousness of divine presence. Union with the divine.

Naive realism. The view that the mind, like a photograph, actually duplicates external reality.

Naturalism. The view that all reality can be understood in terms of what is "natural" as opposed to what is "supernatural." Physical laws are adequate to explain all of reality.

Necessity. That which could not be other than it is.

Nihilism. Nietzsche's belief that the universe has no purpose or meaning.

Noumenal world. The world of reality as opposed to the world of appearance. For Kant, the term for things as they are in themselves independently of how they may appear to us. He said we cannot know the noumenal world.

Nous. Greek word meaning "mind," "spirit," "intelligence."

Objective. Pertaining to the object independently of the person or personal views.

Ontology. The study of being.

Original sin.   According to Christianity, a tendency toward evil inherent in humankind as transmitted by Adam and Eve because of their sin.

Pantheism.   The view that God and the world are identical. God is in the world, and the world is in God.

Phenomenal world.   In Kant, the world of our experience. The world as it appears to us as opposed to the noumenal world of things-in-themselves that is beyond our knowledge.

Phenomenology.   A study of the structures of consciousness and of things as they appear to consciousness. Used by Hegel and later Husserl and Heidegger.

Pluralism.   The view that more than one (monism) or two (dualism) substances make up the world.

Power of thinking.   The understanding.

Power of volition.   The will.

Pragmatism.   A method developed by Peirce, James, and Dewey as a means of clarifying our ideas and emphasizing the practical usefulness of ideas and beliefs as the criteria of their meaning and truth.

Principle of contradiction.   That a proposition and its contradictory cannot *both* be true and one or the other *must* be true.

Principle of identity.   An assertion that two terms refer to the same thing.

Protestant Reformation.   This sixteenth-century movement was born from a common desire to reform the Roman Catholic Church, and it led to the establishment of first one and then many Protestant denominations and churches.

Rationalism.   The view that our knowledge is derived from reason and not from sense experience.

Relativism.   The view that there is no such thing as absolute truth. Truth varies from individual to individual and culture to culture, making it relative to the situation.

Representative realism.   The theory that we perceive objects indirectly by means of representations such as ideas and perceptions of them.

Rhetoric.   The art of persuasive speaking. Taught by the Sophists in ancient Greece.

Scholasticism.   The process of education in Medieval cathedral schools. A combination of theology and philosophy.

Sense–data.   The immediate impressions we receive through our senses.

Skepticism.   The view that knowledge is unobtainable. Skeptics suspend judgment about reality.

Social contract.   For Hobbes, the social contract is drawn up by the absolute sovereign of any commonwealth. The sovereign organizes society and invests it with protection and welfare. "The safety of the people is the supreme law." An agreement among individuals forming an organized society or between the community and the ruler that defines the rights and duties of each.

Solipsism.   The view that the self alone exists as the source of all knowledge. All that is real is one's own mind and its states of consciousness.

Sophists.   Teachers in ancient Greece who specialized in teaching rhetoric and preparing young men for political careers.

Subjective.   Pertaining to the person, the individual; the opposite of objectivism.

Substance.   That which can exist independently, or on its own, and provides the foundation for phenomena. Substance is the essence of a thing.

Synthetic.   For Kant, a synthetic statement does not contain the predicate in the subject but adds something to the subject. "The woman has red hair" is synthetic because not all women have red hair.

Tabula rasa. Latin for "blank tablet," the term is John Locke's metaphor for the condition of the mind before sensory experience is imprinted on it.

Teleology.   The study of purpose or design in human nature or the world.

Transcendent.   That which is higher and beyond the realm of natural experience, as opposed to immanence. For Kant, the transcendent is God and thus naturally unknowable.

Universal.   A general concept (such as human, horse, tree) that is common to several or many particulars.

Utilitarianism.   The view that an action is good or right if it produces the greatest happiness or pleasure for the greatest number of people.

Verification.   Demonstrating something to be true by means of evidence or by formal rules of reasoning. It is also the procedure of finding out whether a sentence (or proposition) is true or false. A certain hypothesis is said to be verified (or confirmed) to a certain degree by a certain amount of evidence.

Vienna Circle.   A group of scientists and philosophers at the University of Vienna in the 1920s and 1930s who were Logical Positivists.

Virtue.   A morally excellent habit or quality of character.

INDEX